JEWS AND CHRISTIANS

JEWS AND CHRISTIANS

The Parting of the Ways
A.D. 70 to 135

edited by

James D. G. Dunn

The Second Durham-Tübingen Research Symposium
on Earliest Christianity and Judaism
(Durham, September, 1989)

WILLIAM B. EERDMANS PUBLISHING COMPANY
GRAND RAPIDS, MICHIGAN / CAMBRIDGE, U.K.

Originally published 1992 by J.C.B. Mohr (Paul Siebeck)
P.O. Box 2040, D-7400 Tübingen, Germany
as volume 66 in the series
Wissenschaftliche Untersuchungen zum Neuen Testament

This edition, with new English translations, published 1999 by
Wm. B. Eerdmans Publishing Company
255 Jefferson Ave. S.E., Grand Rapids, Michigan 49503/
P.O. Box 163, Cambridge CB3 9PU U.K.

03 02 01 00 99   5 4 3 2 1

Library of Congress Cataloging-in-Publication Data

Durham-Tubingen Research Symposium on Earliest Christianity
and Judaism (2nd : 1989 : University of Durham)
Jews and Christians : the parting of the ways, A.D. 70 to 135 : the second
Durham-Tubingen Research Symposium on Earliest Christianity and Judaism (Durham,
September 1989) / edited by James D. G. Dunn.
p.   cm.
Originally published: Tubingen : J.C.B. Mohr (Paul Siebeck), c1992, in series:
Wissenschaftliche Untersuchungen zum Neuen Testament. With new English translations.
Includes bibliographical references and indexes.
ISBN 0-8028-4498-7 (alk. paper)
1. Judaism — Relations — Christianity — Congresses.   2. Christianity and other
religions — Judaism — Congresses.   3. Church history — Primitive and
early church, ca. 30-600 — Congresses.   4. Judaism — History —
Post-exilic period, 586 B.C.-210 A.D. — Congresses.
I. Dunn, James D. G. 1939-   II. Title.
BM535   .D78   1999
261.2'6'09015 — dc21
98-32398
CIP

Contents

Preface

The papers which follow were first delivered at the second Durham-Tübingen Research Symposium on Earliest Christianity and Judaism, which met at the University of Durham in September 1989. The first symposium had met the previous year in Tübingen and focused on an earlier stage of the relationship between earliest Christianity and Judaism, "Paulus, Missionar und Theologe, und das antike Judentum", the papers of which have already been published in the same series[1].

The first symposium commemorated the 50th anniversary of the great Tübingen theologian, Adolf Schlatter, 1852–1938[2]. It was equally fitting that the second should honour the memory of one of the greatest scholars of earliest Christian texts, the Bishop of Durham, Joseph Barber Lightfoot, 1828–89, meeting as it did on the centenary of his death.

It is particularly appropriate that the spirit of Lightfoot should have presided over a joint Durham-Tübingen research symposium and on the subject of why and when earliest Christianity became something different from the Judaism of the same period. For Lightfoot's scholarly work had been very largely dominated by his ongoing debate with F. C. Baur and the Tübingen school[3]. And the main theme of their debate was very close to the theme of the 1989 symposium.

Baur indeed had defined "the ultimate, most important point of the primitive history of Christianity" precisely as the issue of

"how Christianity, instead of remaining a mere form of Judaism ... asserted itself as a separate, independent principle, broke loose from it, and took its stand as a new enfranchised form of religious thought and life, essentially different from all the national peculiarities of Judaism"[4].

And Lightfoot did not disagree:

---

[1] *Paulus und das antike Judentum*, hrsg. M. Hengel & U. Heckel (Tübingen: J. C. B. Mohr, 1991).

[2] See the Vorwort to *Paulus* (n. 1).

[3] See particularly M. Hengel, "Bishop Lightfoot and the Tübingen School on the Gospel of John and the Second Century", *The Lightfoot Centenary Lectures (Durham University Journal*, 1992) 23–51.

[4] F. C. Baur, *Paul, the Apostle of Jesus Christ* (1845; Eng. tr. London: Williams & Norgate, 1873) 3.

"If the primitive Gospel was, as some have represented it, merely one of many phases of Judaism ... then indeed St. Paul's preaching was vain and our faith is vain also"[5].

Nor did Baur und Lightfoot disagree that the overlap between Judaism and Christianity[6] was the crucial area of analysis if this "most important point of the primitive history of Christianity", was to be clarified. It was Baur in fact who drew to historians' attention the importance of the overlap and of the tensions between Jewish Christians and Gentile Christians in the shaping of Christianity. And Lightfoot was not unwilling to recognize the extent of the fractiousness between an expanding Gentile mission and those Christian Jews who continued to consider themselves Jews first and Christians second[7].

Where Baur and Lightfoot disagreed was at three points of significance for the concerns of this volume. (1) Baur was willing to focus "the Christian principle" in an ideal spirituality or religious consciousness, which "looks beyond the outward, the accidental, the particular, and rises to the univesal, the unconditioned, the essential"[8]. He could therefore sum up the relation between Judaism and Christianity as that between Jewish particularism and Christian universalism. Lightfoot, equally concerned lest Christianity be seen simply as "one of many phases of Judaism", could, however, not dissolve away so readily the classic tenets and dogmas of Christian faith regarding the person and work of Christ. Theologically uncritical where Baur was radical, he at least recognized that there is a *christological* particularity in earliest Christianity, as irreducible as the *national* particularity of Judaism. The underlying theological question with which the symposium wrestled was precisely this: how and why the Jewish national particularism and the Christian christological particularism came into ever sharper confrontation until a decisive parting of the ways was unavoidable.

(2) Baur saw a process of development and ongoing struggle between Petrine Christianity and Pauline Christianity which did not come to resolution till the latter part of the second century. Lightfoot did not dispute the aspect of struggle, and thus of development as shaping the character of earliest Christianity. But he took it largely for granted, again rather uncritically, that the essentials of Christian faith were established early on[9], and that the battle for

---

[5] J. B. Lightfoot, *Saint Paul's Epistle to the Galatians* (London: Macmillan, 1865) xi.

[6] We may include in the overlap the Jewish character of Christianity, Christian Jews, Jewish Christians and judaizing Gentile Christians.

[7] "The systematic hatred of St Paul is an important fact, which we are too apt to overlook, but without which the whole history of the Apostolic ages will be misread and misunderstood" (Lightfoot, *Galatians* p. 311).

[8] F. C. Baur, *The Church History of the First Three Centuries* (1853; Eng. tr. Williams & Norgate, 1878–79) 33.

[9] The full quotation cited above in abbreviated form (n. 5) reads: "If the primitive Gospel was, as some have represented it, merely one of many phases of Judaism, if those cherished

the soul of Christianity had been fought by Paul and already won in the first two generations of Christianity[10]. These issues too were at the heart of the symposium's debate: to what extent was the character of Christianity already established within the time of Paul (or even earlier?), and to what extent is the Christianity which emerged in the middle of the second century the product of the tensions experienced during the pulling apart of Christianity and Judaism? To what extent, in other words, was "the parting of the ways" between Christianity and Judaism inevitable and unavoidable from the first, and to what extent was that parting itself a historical accident? And, we may add, to what extent are these mutually incompatible alternatives?

(3) The third decisive difference between Baur and Lightfoot was over method. Baur began with exegetical conclusions drawn from the undisputed Pauline letters, indicating „the opposition between Petrine and Pauline Christianity in the earliest church"[11], but he then extrapolated them to the whole history of Christian beginnings, read through the lenses of an overarching philosophical schema. Lightfoot began, but also continued unbendingly steadfast with rigorous historical analysis of language and context: how these words would have been understood, given the usage of the time; how these arguments or episodes fit into what we know of the history of the period from other sources. There can be no doubt which of the two produced the more convincing and lasting results. If Baur asked legitimate and still pertinent theological questions, Lightfoot provided an essential methodology to answer such questions insofar as they relate to historical texts and events of Christian beginnings.

It is also significant that Lightfoot delivered the *coup de grâce* for Baur's reconstruction of early Christianity by means of his magisterial study of Clement and particularly of Ignatius[12]. For in these volumes he demonstrated beyond reasonable doubt that seven letters are to be attributed to the Ignatius of Antioch who was martyred in about 110, and thus was able to provide a firm historical timescale for the state of affairs which these letters reflect well in advance of Baur's. The same instinct pushed the symposium to focus on the period between the Jewish revolts (70–132), a hunch that the years between apostolic age and post apostolic age, between second Temple Judaism and rabbinic Judaism, between the Jewish Christianity of James and Jerusalem and

---

beliefs which have been the life and light of many generations were afterthoughts, progressive accretions, having no foundation in the Person and Teaching of Christ, then indeed St Paul's preaching was vain and our faith is vain also."

[10] "The great battle with this form of error (Ebionism) seems to have been fought out at an early date, in the lifetime of the Apostles themselves and in the age immediately following" (*Galatians* p. 336).

[11] I refer, of course, to Baur's seminal essay – "Die Christuspartei in der Korinthischen Gemeinde, der Gegensatz des petrinischen und paulinischen Christentums in der älteren Kirche, der Apostel Petrus in Rom", *Tüb. Z. Th.* V: 4 (1831) 61–206.

[12] *The Apostolic Fathers. Part II, S. Ignatius, S. Polycarp* (London: Macmillan, 1885).

the Jewish Christianity of which the Fathers speak, are the hinge on which major issues hung and decisive events turned. It was the urge to shed further light on these obscure but crucial years which was the principal inspiration behind the symposium.

The symposium followed the pattern set at previous symposia mounted by Tübingen, beginning on the Monday evening and lasting till Friday lunchtime. A complete plenary session was devoted to each paper, and social occasions included a reception by the University, a visit to Bishop Auckland to pay our respects to the grave of Bishop Lightfoot, and a tour of the Cathedral and the Lightfoot Exhibition, followed by a reception by the Dean and Chapter. This mix of intensive working sessions (thirteen in all) and opportunity for more casual conversation over coffee, at meals together and on such social occasions, provides a blend which is most conducive to good working relations and which seems to maximise the interchange of ideas and views. The meetings of the Symposium in a room of the old liberary overlooking Palace Green made a most congenial setting in which even strongly held opinions could be critiqued and defendeded without rancour.

As well as the participants who contributed papers, the Symposium included Professor C. K. Barrett, emeritus of Durham, Mr Stephen Barton, who had recently joined the Department of Theology in Durham, and several research students – Ulrich Heckel, Anna Maria Schwemer and Naoto Umemoto (from Tübingen), and John Chow, Ellen Christiansen, Theodore Harman, Herbert Langford, Bruce Longenecker and Nicholas Taylor (from Durham). I am particularly grateful to the latter who provided an indispensable organisation-team to whom the smooth running of the Symposium and its supporting events was largely due. Thanks also to Mateen Elass who has provided the indexes for the volume.

I wish also to express grateful thanks to the British Academy, the University of Tübingen, and the University of Durham's Research Committee and Department of Theology for the financial support which made the Symposium possible. Also to the University of Durham, St Chad's College, SPCK and the Dean and Chapter for their hospitality. Also to J. C. B. Mohr for their readiness to publish both volumes of the two symposia, despite their size. And not least to Martin Hengel, my co-organiser for the two symposia, whose constant concern and counsel made my task in preparing these pages for publication so much easier and the more rewarding.

It should be noted that the working title for the Symposium was the sub-title of the present volume, as is reflected in the many references to "the parting of the ways" in the following pages.

Durham, June 1992   James D. G. Dunn

'The Parting of the Ways' from the Perspective of Rabbinic Judaism

by

PHILIP S. ALEXANDER

A. The Structure of the Problem

"When did Christianity and Judaism part company and go their separate ways?" is one of those deceptively simple questions which should be approached with great care. Though formulated in historical terms it cannot easily be answered within a narrow historicist framework. It raises profound contemporary theological issues and, if not handled sensitively, can quickly become entangled in apologetics and confessionalism. Time spent on clarifying the structure of the question will not, consequently, be wasted.

The standpoint of the question is implicitly modern. In effect what it is asking is how we have reached the present situation in which Christianity and Judaism are manifestly separate religions. Traditionally Christianity has defined itself in opposition to Judaism: a central element of its self-assertion has been that it is *not* Judaism. Two events of the twentieth century have, indeed, strongly challenged this traditional Christian position. The Holocaust has called into question Christian anti-Judaism. And the renaissance of Judaism in modern times, with the establishment of the State of Israel, has cast doubt on Christian triumphalist assumptions that Jews are politically powerless, their culture a fossilized anachronism. There are signs that in some areas of the Church a radical reappraisal of the traditional Christian theology of Judaism is in progress. Nevertheless the belief that Christianity has transcended Judaism, that it stands over against Judaism, remains a pillar of Christian self-definition and self-understanding. Judaism has, perhaps, shown less overt concern to formulate the theology of Christianity. Christianity figures little in traditional Jewish sources. Yet appearances can be deceptive. The very lack of explicit reference can be exploited as an apologetic device to support the view that Judaism is the older faith and so possesses at least *prima facie* a superior claim to legitimacy. In actual fact Judaism has arguably increasingly defined itself in contrast to Christian-

ity. A central element of *its* self-understanding and self-assertion has become
that it is *not* Christianity.

Christianity and Judaism, then, coexist today not only as institutionally and
theologically independent religious systems, but as religions which stake out
their respective territories in a mutually exclusive way. This was not, of course,
always the case, for Christianity originated as a religious movement *within*
Second Temple Judaism. If we picture Judaism and Christianity as circles we
can graphically represent how we reached the present state of affairs as follows.
Today the circles stand side by side essentially in self-contained isolation. If we
move the horizon of time backwards this monadic relationship remains more or
less constant until we come roughly to the fourth century of the current era.
Then an important development takes place: we observe the circles approaching and beginning to overlap. The area of overlap is occupied by a group of
people – the Jewish Christians – who claimed to belong to *both* faith communities, to both Christianity *and* Judaism. If we push the temporal horizon
back still further the overlap steadily increases till we reach a point sometime in
the mid-first century C. E. when the circle of Christianity is entirely contained
with the circle of Judaism. The question to be addressed is how and why did the
circles separate.

A common way of tackling the problem of the parting of the ways is to start
out by establishing a normative definition of Judaism, and then trying to
discover how and when Christianity diverged from that norm. Since there are
clearly radical aspects to early Christianity the tendency has been to see the
parting of the ways as having taken place early, usually in the first or early
second century C. E. Some analyses so stress the radicalism of early Christianity
as to suggest that the parting of the ways occurred almost *ab ovo*. Two main
approaches have been adopted in order to lay down the baseline from which the
divergence of Christianity can be measured. The first involves retrojecting
Rabbinic Judaism into first century Pharisaism and arguing in effect that
Pharisaism is identical with normative Judaism. This approach is broadly
exemplified in the work of Hyam Maccoby and Lawrence Schiffman[1]. The
second approach involves trying to determine the essence of first century
Judaism, the irreducible common denominator of all, or most of, the Jewish
sect or parties. Ed Sanders' "covenantal nomism" represents a brave attempt to
follow this line[2]. Both these approaches are problematic. It is, in fact, extremely
difficult, using strictly historical criteria, to lay down a norm for Judaism in the

---

[1] H. Maccoby, *The Mythmaker: Paul and the Invention of Christianity* (Weidenfeld and
Nicolson: London 1986); L. H. Schiffman, *Who Was a Jew? Rabbinic and Halakhic Perspec-
tives on the Jewish-Christian Schism* (Ktav: Hoboken, New Jersey 1985). In fairness to
Schiffman it must be said that his work is much less obviously polemical and confessional then
Maccoby's (though see note 38 below).

[2] E. P. Sanders, *Paul and Palestinian Judaism* (SCM: London 1977).

first century. The attempt to do so sometimes barely conceals apologetic motives – in the case of Christians a desire to prove the Christianity transcended or transformed Judaism, in the case of Jews a desire to suggest that Christianity was an alien form of Judaism which deviated from the true path.

The following three points will serve to indicate the distinctive standpoint of this paper.

(1) Rabbinic Judaism cannot easily be equated with normative Judaism before the third century C.E., and even then only in Palestine. The reason for this is that it was not until the third century that a majority of the Jews of Palestine accepted the authority of the Rabbinate. Nevertheless Rabbinic Judaism must remain central to discussion of the parting of the ways even when we are talking of the first and second centuries, not because it represented normative Judaism then, but because it was the form of Judaism which ultimately triumphed and *became* normative Judaism. The forward-looking character of the question should always be borne in mind.

(2) It is simplistic to look for a decisive *moment* in the parting of the ways, a crucial doctrine or event that caused the final rupture. There was no sudden break between Christianity and Judaism, but rather an ever-widening rift. The War of 66–74 destroyed whatever existed of a centralized religious authority within Judaism and so removed the institutions which might have speedily and definitively resolved the problem of the status of Christianity. There were radical aspects to the Christian message which aroused opposition not only from the Pharisaic-Rabbinic party, but it was not inevitable that such radicalism should have led to a parting of the ways. History surely can provide examples of radical movements which have sucessfully transformed themselves into the dominant orthodoxy. In the power-vacuum created by the First Revolt the Rabbinic party and the Christians competed for the hearts and minds of Jewry. The Rabbis emerged victorious. It was the gradual rabbinization of Palestinian Jewish society that pushed Christianity and Judaism ever further apart.

(3) Jewish Christianity must be seen as playing a central role in the story of the parting of the ways. Jewish Christianity continued to represent Christianity *within* the Jewish community even after substantial parts of the Church had become Gentile. It blurred the boundaries and retarded the final separation. So long as Jewish Christianity remained a significant presence within the Palestinian Jewish community it is hard to talk of a final rupture. Rabbinic policy towards Christianity was aimed specifically at the Jewish Christians. It attempted successfully to keep them marginalized and to exclude them from *Kelal Yiśra'el*. The story of the parting of the ways is in essence the story of the triumph of Rabbinism and of the failure of Jewish Christianity to convince a majority of Palestinian Jews of the claims of the Gospel.

B. Elements of a Rabbinic Policy Towards the Christians

a) Who was a Jew?

The Rabbinic world-view is expressed first and foremost in the *halakhah*, so it is logical to begin an analysis of Rabbinic policy towards Christianity by consider-ing the question: What was the halakhic status of the Christians?

The *halakhah* defines with reasonable precision who is and who is not a Jew. According to *halakhah* one acquires the status of a Jew either by birth or conversion. Jewishness is acquired by birth if one's *mother* in Jewish; the status of the *father* is immaterial to the status of the child. For conversion to be valid it must be overseen by the appropriate Rabbinic authorities and must follow an established procedure which involves (a) instruction in and acceptance of the Torah, (b) circumcision (for males), (c) ritual immersion (for both males and females), and (d) the offering of a sacrifice[3].

Broadly speaking Jewish status, once acquried, cannot subsequently be lost. This view is obviously logical when applied to the Jew by birth, since the historical facts of one's parentage cannot be retrospectively altered. It is perhaps less obvious in the case of the Jew by conversion, since there is an element of mental assent involved in conversion which can subsequentely be reversed. Rabbinic authorities have tended to be ambivalent about proselytes. According to some traditions a stigma attaches to the proselyte, and proselytes are permitted to marry *mamzerim*, which is forbidden to Israelites. However, the common view appears to be that a valid conversion establishes in irrevers-ible fact just as surely as do the facts of one's birth[4].

It is important to be clear what is implied by saying that Jewish status, once it has been validly acquired, is inalienable. It means that a Jew remains obligated

---

[3] For useful, if late, summaries of the *halakhah* see Massekhet Gerim and Maimonides, *Yad: 'Issurei Bi'ah* XII−XV. Note *'Issurei Bi'ah* XV,4: "The general rule is that the child of a male slave, a male heathen, a bondswoman, or a heathen woman has the status of his mother, the father not being considered." Further discussion in Schiffman, *Who was a Jew?*, pp. 9−49. Much of the "Who was a Jew?" debate fails to mention the fact that "Jew" (*Yehudi*) is not, strictly speaking, a meaningful halakhic category, Mishnah Qiddushin 4:1, which lists the ten genuinely halakhic categories of those who came up from Babylon, does not include "Jew".

[4] Maimonides, *'Issurei Bi'ha* XV,8: "If a proselyte woman marries a proselyte and gives birth to a son, even though both conception and birth have taken place after they had become proselytes, the son is nevertheless permitted to marry a female *mamzer*. And so on down to his great grandson, until his proselyte descent sinks into oblivion, and the fact that he is a descendant of proselytes is no longer known." Cf. *'Issurei Bi'ah* XII,17: "All heathens, without exception, once they become proselytes and accept all the commandments enjoined in the Torah, and all slaves, once they are manumitted, are regarded as Israelites in every respect, as it is said, 'As for the congregation, there shall be one statute both for you and for the stranger (*ger*)' (Nu 15:15)." The traditional view is that the three rites of conversion − circumcision, immersion and sacrifice − replicate the three rites by which Israel entered into the Convenant (*'Issurei Bi'ah* XIII,1−5).

to fulfil the Law, even if he renounces the Law and apostasizes. And if, having apostasized, he desives to return he will be accepted back without conversion. This view came to be classically expressed in the maxime: "Even though he sins he remains an Israelite" (*'af 'al pi še-ḥaṭa' Yiśra'el hu'*)[5] – even if the "sin" involves conversion to, and profession of, another religion. This is not to suggest, however, that apostasy is of little importance. Rabbinic Judaism uses other concepts besides halakhic satus to define the limits of the Community. It has, for example, a strongly developed notion of "heresy" (*minut*). A heretic (*min*), if not strictly outside the Community *de jure,* is certainly outside it *de facto.* He not only loses the blessings of the Convenant in this life, but runs the risk of losing his portion in the world to come. In other words his "Jewishness" in an eschatological perspective may prove to have been of no significance. It is as if he had never bleonged to *Kelal Yiśra'el*[6].

The classic Rabbinic definition of Jewishness is well established by the Amoraic period, and there are signs that it was already current in Tannaitic times. Elements of it have been found even in Second Temple texts. For example, it has been argued that Ezra 10:2–3 already implies that Jewish status is inherited through the mother and not the father[7]. Two point should, however, be made. First, in the absence of clear evidence it would be wrong to retroject the fully articuled *halakhah* regarding who is a Jew back into Second Temple Judaism. Doubtless the *halakhah* grew in fullness and precision over time. Second, the Rabbinic definition of Jewishness was probably not normative within Judaism before Amoraic times at the earliest. It is likely that it was

---

[5] Though the maxim is derived from Bavli Sanhedrin 44a, it has been argued that its *halakhic* use dates only from the Middle Ages. This may be strictly true, but the view which the maxim has been taken to express was surely current in Talmudic times, and, indeed, seems to follow logically from the inalienability of Jewish status. See J. Katz, "*'Af 'al pi še-ḥaṭa' Yiśra'el hu'*", *Tarbiṣ* 27 (1957–58), pp. 203–17. Further, Schiffman, *Who was a Jew?,* p. 97 note 52.

[6] The *locus classicus* is Mishnah Sanhedrin 10:1. Maimonides, in his Commentary *ad loc*, in which he enunciates his famous Thirteen Principles of Judaism, comments thus: "When all these [Thirteen] Principles are held as certain by a man and his faith in them is firm, then he belongs to the Community of Israel (*Kelal Yiśra'el*), and there is an obligation to love him, to have compassion on him, and to perform for him all the acts of love and brotherhood which God has commanded us to perform one for another. Even if he has committed every possible sin because of lust, or because his lower nature got the better of him, though he will surely be punished to the extent of his rebellion, yet he still has a share in the world to come, and is regarded as 'a sinner in Israel'. However, if a man doubts one of these principles he has left the Community, has denied a basic principle, and is called a heretic, an Epicurean, and a 'cutter of plants'. There is an obligation to hate and to destroy him, and of him Scripture says: 'Shall I not hate those who hate you, O Lord' (Ps 139:21)". Cf. also Tosefta Sanhedrin 13:4 quoted in note 12 below.

[7] Mishnah Quiddushin 3:12; Tosefta Qiddushin 4:6; Yerushalmi Yevamot II,6 (4a) ("Your son by a Isralite woman is called your son, but your son by a Gentile woman is not called your son but her son"). Schiffman (*Who was a Jew?* pp. 12–13) argues that the description of Herod as "a half Jew" at Josephus, *Antiquities* XIV 403, relates to the fact that his father was Jewish (though a descendant of a convent), but his mother was non-Jewish.

only one of a number of ways of deciding who was a Jew in the Second Temple and Tannaitic eras[8]. It was not the common law of Israel, but an element of the *halakhah* advocated by the Rabbis, which in the end gained widespread (though by no means universal) acceptance.

Viewed from the perspective of the halakhic definition of who was a Jew, it is clear that for the Rabbis the early Christians fell into two broad groups: (a) there were those who were Israelites by birth and who were halakhically Jewish; and (b) there were those who were non-Jews. Since the latter group had never undergone a valid Rabbinic conversion, they were not in the Convenant and never had been. They were bound by the Noachide commandments, not by the Torah of Moses. Despite their claims to be the "true Israel" and "Abraham's sons through faith", they were halakhically "heathen" (*'ovedei kokhavim*). The former group, however, remained halakhically Jewish and were still obligated to accept the yoke of the Torah. It was with these halakhically Jewish Christians that the Rabbis were most concerned. The Rabbis had at their disposal a variety of terms for those whom they wished to describe as standing outside the Community of Israel: *minim* ("heretics"); *mešummadim* ("apostates"); *ḥiṣonim* ("outsiders"); *Kutiyyim* ("Samaritans"); *'ovedei kokhavim* ("heathens": lit. "star-worshippers")[9]. The Rabbis appear most frequently to categorize the Christians as *minim*. Though they define the detailed relationship between the various types of outsider and the Rabbinic Community in subtly different ways, they broadly treat *all* outsiders alike and often compare one type to another. They advocated a policy of reducing to a minimum contacts between outsiders and Rabbinically observant Jews. Their treatment of the Jewish Christians was in line with this general policy: they tried to exclude them from the synagogues and to persuade other Jews to ostracize them in social and even in commerical life.

b) The Cursing of the Heretics

Bavli Berakhot 28b–29a:

A. "Our Rabbis taught:

B. Shim'on ha-Paqoli arranged the Eighteen Benedictions in order before Rabban Gamliel at Yavneh.

C. Rabban Gamliel said to the Sages: 'Is there no-one who knows how to compose a benediction against the heretics (*minim*)?

D. Shmu'el ha-Qatan stood up and composed it.

E. Another year he forgot it and tried to recall it for two or three hours, yet they did not remove him."

---

[8] For other ways of defining who was a Jew in late antiquity see M. Goodman, *Who was a Jew?* (Oxford Centre for Postgraduate Hebrew Studies: Yarnton, Oxford, 1989).

[9] Mishnah 'Avodah Zarah and Massekhet Kutiyyim are useful texts with which to begin exploring Rabbinic ideas about the limits of the Community.

Birkat ha-Minim (Palestinian Recension)[10]:

A. For apostates (*mešummadim*) may there be no hope,
B. And the arrogant kingdom (*malkhut zadon*) uproot speedily in our days.
C. May the Christians (*noṣerim*) and the heretics (*minim*) perish in an instant.
D. *May they be blotted out of the book of the living,*
   And may they not be written with the righteous (Ps 69:29).
E. Blessed art Thou, O Lord, who humblest the arrogant."

Bavli Berakhot 28a—29b is given as a baraita which claims to report events at Yavneh in the late first century C.E. It should be noted, however, that the baraita is found only in the Bavli. Unit E above, regarding Shmu'el ha-Qatan forgetting the wording of the benediction, is paralleled in Yerushalmi Berakhot V,4 (9c) but not units A to D. Yerushalmi Berakhot IV,3 (8a), in a different tradition, also links the *Birkat ha-Minim* to Yavneh: "If a man says to you that there are seventeen benedicitions, say to him: The Sages set 'Of the Minim' in the prayer at Yavneh." The existence of a *Birkat Minim* can be taced back with some confidence to the first half of the second century C.E. Perhaps the earliest securely dated evidence for its use may be found in Justin's references to the Jews cursing the Christians in synagogue (*Dialogue* xvi, xcvi). But the precise connection of the *Birkat ha-Minim* with Shmu'el ha-Qatan and with an editing of the synagogue liturgy at Yavneh in the time of Gamliel II is attested only in comparatively late strata of Rabbinic literature. This fact should be borne constantly in mind in reconstructing the history of the benediction, and too much weight should not be placed on the uncorroborated testimony of Bavli Berakhot 28b—29b.

The language of Bavli Berakhot 28b—29a seems carefully chosen and precise. The editing of the Eighteen Benedictions to which it refers was "official", since it took place in the presence of the Nasi' ("before Rabban Gamliel"). The editing took the form of arranging in order the benedictions (*hisdir/sidder . . . 'al ha-seder*). Shim'on ha Paqoli produced a *siddur* out of existing material: the implication appears to be that the substance of the benedictions was only minimally affected. In the context of this editing of the benedictions Gamliel asks someone "to compose" (*letaqqen*) a benediction against the *minim*. The implicit contrast between "ordering" and "composing" suggests that the *Birkat ha-Minim* was a new text. However, analysis of the *Birkat ha-Minim* itself throws this in some doubt. Though it is impossible now to reconstruction the original wording of the benediction from the numerous variant texts, it is clear that all the extant versions combine two quite disparate motifs: they pray for the overthrow of the "arrogant kingdom" (which would naturally be taken as a reference to Rome), and they pray for judgement on the *minim*. It is quite clear

---

[10] See S. Schechter, "Geniza Specimens", *Jewish Quarterly Review* o.s. 10 (1896), pp. 656f. Further, J. Mann, "Genizah Fragments of the Palestinian Order of Service", *Hebrew Union College Annual* 2 (1925), pp. 269ff.

from Rabbinic literature that judgement on the *minim* is seen as the focus of the benediction: hence its title "Of the *Minim*". Why then introduce "the arrogant kingdom"? One solution would be to suppose that the reference to the arrogant kingdom is secondary and dates from after the time of Constantine when, to use the language of a late addition to Mishnah Soṭah 9: 15, "the kingdom was turned to *minut*". The *minim* on this view would definitely be the Christians. But this suggestion is not entirely satisfactory. The motif of the arrogant kingdom actually forms the framework of the benediction: note how the concluding formula, which normally draws out the central point, refers to "humbling the arrogant" and makes no mention of the *minim*. It is more likely that the *Birkat ha-Minim* is a restatement of an erlier benediction calling for the overthrow of Israel's oppressors. The question remains: why insert a condemnation of the *minim* specifically into a benediction directed against the political oppressors of Israel? It has been suggested that the benediction as it now stands is a prayer for divine judgement and envisages that judgement as beginning first with the wicked of Israel and then extending to the nations[11]. This is speculative and perhaps a little oversubtle. The point may simply be to condemn the *minim* by association, by lumping them together with the enemies and oppressors of Israel.

Who were the *minim* against whom the benediction was directed? Patristic evidence makes it clear that the *Birkat ha-Minim* was undoubtedly applied to Christians, and, indeed, the Palestinian recension quoted above specifically mentions "the Christians" (*noṣerim*), in what may be, in effect, an explanatory gloss on *minim*. However, the term *minim* in Rabbinic literature is not confined to Christians, but applies to "heretics" in general. Other pejorative terms are found in the various versions of the benediction: "wicked" (*reša'im*), "sinners" (*poše'im*), "slanderers" (*malšinim*), "informers" (*moserim*), "apostates" (*mešummadim*), "renegades" (*perušim*)[12]. But it should be noted that these terms are general and uncontentious in a way that *minim* is not. There would

---

[11] W. Horbury, "The Benediction of the *Minim* and Early Jewish-Christian Controversy", *Journal of Thoelogical Studies* 33 (1982), p. 42.

[12] *Perušim* can, of course, mean "Pharisees" (see e. g. Mishnah Yadayim 4:4–6), but there was surely never a Benediction against the Pharisees! It is normally assumed (e. g. Jastrow, *Dictionary* 1222a) that *paruš* was used in two opposed senses: (1) "seceder", "renegade", and (2) "abstemious", "saintly" = "Pharisee". However, it is possible that the Benediction against the *Perušim* was aimed not at seceders like the Samaritans, or even like the Qumran sect, but at over-scrupulous people, too holy to worship or socialize with the rest of the Community. Note Hillel's dictum in Mishnah Pirqei 'Avot 2:4; "Do not separate yourself from the Community" (*'al tifroš min ha-ṣibbur*), and Tosefta Sanhedrin 13:5 (cf. Bavli Rosh ha-Shanah 14a): "But as for the *minim*, and the apostates (*mešummadim*), and the betrayers (*mesorot*), and the *'epiqorsin*, and those who have denied the Torah, and those who have departed from the ways of the community (*porešin mi-darkhei ha-ṣibbur*), and those who have denied the resurrection of the dead, and anyone who has sinned and caused the congregation (*ha-rabbim*) to sin, and those 'who have set their fear in the land of the living' (Ezek. 32:24), and those who have stretched out their hand against Zebul [= the Temple], Gehinnom is closed in their faces

doubless have been a consensus within a congregation that "apostates" and "sinners" should be damned: they had self-evidently put themselves beyond the pale. The term *min*, however, was much sharper, in that it discriminated among those who continued to worship with the Community and to proclaim their loyalty to Israel. It is as important to note the term *min* itself as it is to identify the specific group or groups to whom is refered. The term marks a significant attempt to draw a distinction between orthodoxy and heresy. In Rabbinic terms a *min* was basically a Jew who did not accept the authority of the Rabbis and who rejected Rabbinic halakhah. Hence insofar as it applies to Christians, it must refer primarily to *Jewish* Christians. In condemning the *minim* the Rabbis were in effect condemning all who were not of their party: they were setting themselves up as the custodians of orthodoxy. The original benediction against the arrogant kingdom may have contained also references to the "wicked" and other general types of miscreant. The Rabbinic reformulation, which almost certainly used the term *minim*, turned the benediction into a pointed attack on the Rabbis' opponents. This growing consciousness of orthodoxy shows a turning away from the more pluralistic attitudes of Second Temple times. Indeed, it is possible that the use of the term *min* in the sense of "heretic", rather than "member of a sect" (in a broadly neutral sense), was a distinctively Rabbinic usage[13].

What was the purpose of introducing the *Birkat ha-Minim*? If our earlier line of reasoning is correct, then the answer must be: To establish Rabbinism as orthodoxy within the synagogue. The power of cursing was taken seriously in antiquity: no-one would lightly curse himself or his associates, or put himself voluntarily in the way of a curse. A Christian, or any other type of *min*, could not act as precentor if the *Birkat ha-Minim* were included in the Eighteen Benedictions, for by reciting it he would be publicly cursing himself, and the congregation would say, Amen!. Nor could a *min*, even as a member of the congregation, easily say Amen! on hearing the benediction[14]. Thus the *minim*

and they are judged there for ever and ever". Note also the negative list of the seven types of *paruš* in Yerushalmi Berakhot 9:7 (14b).

[13] It is curious that the etymologies of the terms *min*, *mešummad* and *mumar* (which often interchanges with *mešummad* in the manuscripts) are *all* problematic. They *all* appear to be distinctively Rabbinic, in the sense that they are unattested outside Rabbinic texts. The definition of a *mešummad* in Bavli Horayot 11a as "one who ate animals not ritually slaugh-tered..." must surely represent an intensification and Rabbinization of the term. The defini-tion of *mešummadim* in Sifra Va-yiqra 2:3 (ed. Weiss 4b) as those who "do not accept the Convenant" is more likely to correspond to common usage.

[14] Tanḥuma Vayyiqra 3 (ed. Buber 2a): "He who goes before the ark and makes a mistake – in the case of all other benedictions he is not made to repeat, but in the case of the *Birkat ha-Minim* he is made to repeat whether he likes it or not, for we take into consideration that he may be a *min*. He is made to repeat so that if he should have a heretical tendency he would be cursing himself and the congregation would answer, Amen!" The argument of R. Kimelman ("*Birkat ha-Minim* and the Lack of Evidence for an Anti-Christian Jewish Prayer", in: E. P. Sanders (ed.), *Jewish and Christian Self-Definition* [Fortress Press: Philadelphia 1981], p.227)

would effectively be excluded from public worship. There are other examples of ritual cursing being used in ancient Jewish liturgies as a way of publicly marking the boundaries of a group. The most pertinent example is the recitation of the negative form of the Priestly Blessing to curse "the men of the lot of Satan" during the festival of the renewal of the covenant at Qumran (1Qs II).

According to Bavli Berakhot 28b–29a the *Birkat ha-Minim* was formulated at Yavneh. But it would be wrong to imagine the Yavneh was in any position to force it upon the synagogues of Palestine, let alone of the Diaspora. The synagogue was not a Rabbinic institution and there was no mechanism by which the Rabbis could have imposed their will directly on it. How then was the *Birkat ha-Minim* introduced into the synagogue? A Rabbi, or a follower of the Rabbinic party, if asked to act as precentor in the synagogue, would have recited the Rabbinic form of the Eighteen Benedictions. Since the text of the prayers was still fluid, such innovation in itself would probably have caused little surprise. It is also possible that Rabbinic Jews would have interrupted the service from the body of the congregation and insisted on the Rabbinic *Birkat ha-Minim* being recited. Mishnah Megillah 4:9 alludes to the practice of rebuking a *meturgeman* publicly during the service if he delivers one of the forbidden Targumim[15]. A similar strategy could have been used to impose the *Birkat ha-Minim* on the synagogues. Bavli Berakhot 29a states: "If a reader errs in any other benediction, he is not dismissed, but if he errs in that of the *minim*, he is dismissed, for he himself may be a *min*" (cf. Yerushalmi Berakhot V,4 [9c]). In this way the Rabbinic *Birkat ha-Minim* may have been introduced into the synagogue service. In the end it was accepted as standard, but this acceptance undoubtedly would have taken some time.

and S. T. Katz ("Issues in the Separation of Judaism and Christianity after 70 C.E.: A Reconsideration", *Journal of Biblical Literature* 103 [1984], pp. 74f.) that the benediction against the *minim* would not be specific enough to cause problems for the Jewish Christians (since the Christian could always say to himself, "I am not a heretic; the benediction must apply to someone else") has some force. Magical praxis in the ancient world certainly tried to name the object of an incantation as precisely as possible. However, it should be borne in mind that the *Birkat ha-Minim* was a *Rabbinic* benediction (indeed, *min* = "heretic" may be a Rabbinic coinage: see note 13 above). So anyone opposed to the Rabbis would have felt threatened.

[15] Mishnah Megillah 4:9: "If a man says in his prayer, 'Good men shall bless you!' this is the way of heresy (*minut*); if he says, 'Even to a bird's nest do your mercies extend', or 'May your name be remembered for the good you have done!' or 'We give thanks, we give thanks!' they silence him. He who paraphrases the laws regarding the forbidden degrees (Lev 18:6–18), they silence him. He who says, 'And you shall not give any of your seed to make them pass through [the fire] to Molech' (Lev 18:21) means 'And you shall not give of your seed to make it pass to heathendom', they silence him with a rebuke." Cf. Mishnah Berakhot 5:3. This tradition of interrupting the service to insist that a particular order should be followed, or particular forms of prayer used, should, perhaps, be set in the context of the long established tradition of "zeal for the Law", whereby private individuals had a right and a duty to enforce the Law, even to the extent of resorting to violence. See M. Hengel, *The Zealots* (T. & T. Clark: Edinburgh 1989), pp. 146–228.

It should be noted that the *Birkat ha-Minim* would not have been the only benediction of the Eighteen Benedictions that could have created problems for Jewish Christians in synagogue. The Eighteen Benedictions pray for the coming of the Messiah, and for the restoration of statehood and of the Temple service. This nationalism contrasts sharply with the more generalized language of the Paternoster, the distinctive early Christian prayer. The Palestinian recension of the Eighteen Benedictions from the Cairo Genizah is less specifically nationalistic than the Babylonian recensions. It is possible, therefore, that with careful exegesis Jewish Christians could have said Amen! in good faith to some forms of the Eighteen Benedictions (though not, of course, to the *Birkat ha-Minim*)[16].

There is evidence to suggest that some synagogue authorities hostile to Christianity used a formula for cursing Jesus as a test of membership. This practice is alluded to by Justin (*Dialogue* xlvii, cxxxvii; cf. *I Apology* xxxi), and may lie behind 1 Cor 12:3 (cf. Acts 26:11). But it does not seem to have been advocated by the Rabbis. The Rabbis adopted a more subtle ploy: they appear to have set out first and foremost to establish Rabbinism as orthodoxy, knowing that once that happened the exclusion of the Christians from the synagogue would inevitably follow.

c) The Books of the Heretics

Tosefta Yadayim 2:13:

A "The Gospels (*gilyonim*) and the books of the heretics (*sifrei minim*) do not defile the hands.

B. The Book(s) of Ben Sira, and all books that were written from then on, do not defile the hands."

Tosefta Shabbat 13(14):5:

A. "The Gospels (*gilyonim*) and books of heretics are not saved but are left where they are to burn, they and their sacred names.

B. Rabbi Yose ha-Gelili says: On a weekday one cuts out their sacred names and hides them away (*gonez*) and burns the rest.

C. Rabbi Tarfon said: May I bury my sons! If they were to come into my hand I would burn them along with their sacred names. For if a pursuer were pursuing after me, I would enter a house of idolatry rather than enter their

---

[16] It is, perhaps, not impossible that Jewish Christians would have recited the Paternoster in synagogue. The synagogue service in Talmudic times gave scope for individual prayer (see J. Heinemann and J. J. Petuchowski, *The Literature of the Synagogue* [Behrman House: New York 1975], pp. 47–51), and there is nothing in the words of the Paternoster which could have given offence or been contentious. Matthew envisages the Paternoster being prayed in the privacy of one's room (Matt 6:6), but this idea is absent from Luke (Lk 11:1–4).

houses, because the idolators do not acknowledge him and then deny him, but *they* do acknowledge him and then deny him. Of them Scripture says: 'Behind the door and the doorpost (*mezuzah*) you have set up your symbol (*zikkaron*)' (Is 57:8)[17].

D. Rabbi Ishmael said: If to bring peace between a husband and his wife, the Omnipresent has said that a scroll (*sefer*) which has been written in holiness may be erased by means of water, how much more should books of heretics, which cause enmity, jealousy and strife between Israel and their Father in heaven, be erased, they and their sacred names. With regard to them scripture says: 'Do I not hate them, O Lord, who hate You? Do I not strive with those who rise up agianst You? I hate them with utmost hatred; I count them as my enemies' (Psalm 139:20−21).

E. Just as they are not saved from fire, so they are not saved from a cave-in, nor from water, nor form anything which would destroy them."

Bavli Giṭṭin 45b:

A. "R. Naḥman said: We have a tradition that a Scroll of the Law (*Sefer Torah*) which was written by a *min* should be burned.

B. One written by heathen ('*oved kokhavim*) should be withdrawn.

C. One that is found in the possession of a *min* should be withdrawn.

D. One that is found in the possession of a heathen, according to some should be withdrawn, but according to others may be read."

The meaning of the expression "defile the hands" in Tosefta Yadayim 2:13 has been much discussed. The idea is on the face of it paradoxical since only *holy* texts "defile the hands". That is to say, only *holy* texts are impure in the first degree and convey second degree impurity which is removed by washing the hands (*neṭilat yadayim*). Why it was decided that holy texts defile the hands is obscure. The Rabbis themselves appear to be a little uncertain of the reason. It is possible that declaring that certain texts imparted impurity was an effective, if curious, way of differentiating them from ordinary texts and of increasing the reverence with which they were handled (cf. Mishnah Yadayim 4:6; Tosefta Yadayim 2:19). Whatever its origin, the significance of the expression for the Rabbis is reasonably clear – clearer and more consistent than is often supposed[18]. The text which first and foremost defiles the hands is a Sefer Torah that

---

[17] The quotation from Is. 57:8 is very suggestive. Does it imply that Jewish Christian houses would have been indistinguishable from the houses of other Jews, even to the extent of having *mezuzot* on the doorposts, and that only when one entred the house would one find evidence of Christian symbolism?

[18] M. Goodman, "Sacred Scriptures and Defiling the Hands", *Journal of Theological Studies* 41 (1990), pp. 99−107, in line with other recent analysis, stresses the paradoxes and anomalies of the Rabbinic position. He does not, however, make a sharp enough distinction between the origins of the concept and its use. It is the former which is unclear; the latter is

has been written out properly for liturgical purposes. To say that a work like Song of Songs defiles the hands is to say that it has the status of a Sefer Torah and is inspired. The link between divine inspiration and "defiling the hands" is clearly made at Tosefta Yadayim 2:14: "Rabbi Shim'on ben Menasya says: The Song of Songs renders the hands unclean because it was composed under divine inspiration (*mi-penei še-ne'emarah be-ruaḥ ha-qodeš*). Qohelet does not render the hands unclean because it is [merely] the wisdom of Solomon." The same link is implied at Tosefta Yadayim 2:13B, which alludes to the Rabbinic doctrine of the cessation of prophecy. The Rabbis accepted the view, widespread from late Second Temple times, that prophecy had come to an end some time in the past (in the time of Ezra, or of Haggai, Zechariah and Malachi, or in the time of Alexander the Great)[19]. And they applied it as one of their criteria for determining the canon of Scripture. Any text written after a certain period cannot *ipso facto* be inspired. Ben Sira, for all that it was admired and quoted by the Rabbis, is too late, and so cannot qualify as Holy Scripture. Of course, *we* have reason to believe that some texts (e. g. Daniel), which are as late as Ben Sira, have been included in the Rabbinic canon. But the Rabbis did not know this. They accepted books such as Daniel at their face value, and as a matter of principle did not include any text which they thought was written after their cut-off date for the cessation of prophecy.

To say that a given text "defiled the hands" may, however, have had a further implication. Only a liturgical copy of the Torah, i. e., one written in "Assyrian" characters in its orginal Hebrew and Aramaic on a parchment scroll in ink, defiles the hands: a translation of the Torah, or even a text in the original, written, for example, on papyrus in the form of a codex, does not defile the hands (Mishnah Yadayim 4:5). So the question whether or not a given text defiles the hands envisages that text being written out like a liturgical copy of the Torah. "Defiling the hands" is a complex concept which seeks to establish an analogy between a given text and a Sefer Torah: it implies (a) that the text is inspired, and (b) that, if prepared like a liturgical copy of the Torah, it is fit to be read in public worship.

Gilyonim in Tosefta Yadayim 2:13A and Tosefta Shabbat 13(14):5A probably refers to the Gospels: cf. the Rabbinic deformation of εὐαγγέλιον as *'aven gilayon* (Bavli Shabbat 116a). The expression *sifrei minim* has two possible meanings. Either it could refer to other Christian writings, besides the Gospels, which were claimed to be Holy Scripture. Or it could refer to Christian Torah

---

reasonably clear and consistent. For a careful discussion of the Rabbinic references see S. Z. Leiman, *The Canonization of Hebrew Scripture: The Talmudic and Midrashic Evidence*, Transactions of the Connecticut Academy of Arts and Sciences 47 (Archon Books: Hamden, Connecticut 1976), pp. 102–119.

[19] Tosefta Soṭah 13:2; Bavli Soṭah 48b; Bavli Yoma 9b; Bavli Sanhedrin 11a; Seder 'Olam Rabba 30. See further, E. E. Urbach, "*Matai paseqah ha-nevu'ah*", *Tarbiṣ* 17 (1945–46), pp. 1–11.

Scrolls. The former sense is perhaps more likely at Tosefta Yadayim 2:13 in view of the mention of Ben Sira. The latter sense is clear at Bavli Giṭṭin 45b. For present purposes there is no need to decide between these two possible meanings, since it is beyond any doubt that the Rabbis would have denied the validity of Christian Torah Scrolls *and* the inspiration of the Christian Scriptures[20].

Torah Scrolls written by Christian scribes were declared unfit (*pasul*) for public worship presumably on the grounds that their origin puts them under suspicion. The implications of this ruling are far reaching. It could have put Christian Torah scribes out of business, and made it impossible for a congregation obeying this ruling to make use of their services. Significantly "heretical" Torah scrolls are seen as more suspect than "heathen" Torah scrolls (Bavli Giṭṭin 45b). The idea that the *minim* are worse than the heathen (*'ovedei kokhavim*) comes out again at Tosefta Shabbat 13(14):5C, and elsewhere in polemical contexts. Since a *sefer minim* was unfit for public worship, to hear the Torah read from such a scroll would presumably not have been a valid hearing of the Law. These rulings would have strongly discouraged Rabbinic Jews from attending synagogues where there was a Christian presence or influence. *A fortiori* they would heave been discouraged from attending more distinctively Christian conventicles where Christian Gospels and other "heretical" books might have been read publicly as Scripture. There is some indirect evidence that already in the first century the Christians in their conventicles may have used Gospels as *hafṭarot* to readings from the Tora[21]. The point of the Rabbinic legislation is clear: it is aimed at extending Rabbinic supervision over the synagogue service and at forcing a separation in public worship between Rabbinic and non-Rabbinic Jews.

Tosefta Shabbat 13(14):5 makes a distinction between Gospels and *sifrei minim* on the one hand and proper Torah Scrolls on the other not by using the concept of "defiling the hands" but by using the concept of "carrying on Shabbat". Basically the argument appears to be that if a Torah Scroll is in a

---

[20] Would the Rabbis have said that a Christian Torah scroll was not "inspired"? The probable answer is, Yes. The Rabbis saw inspiration as inhering in a very concrete way in the graphic form of the text. Strictly speaking only that which can be seen in a properly written Torah Scroll is word of God. The inspiration of a defective Torah Scroll is, therefore, in some doubt. See A. Goldberg, "The Rabbinic View of Scripture", in: P. R. Davies and R. T. White (eds.), *A Tribute to Geza Vermes* (Sheffield Academic Press: Sheffield 1990), pp. 153–66. The early Church in general favoured the codex over the scroll, but there is no reason to exclude the possibility that Jewish Christians would have used scrolls not only for their copies of the Torah, but also for their sectarian Gospels and writings.

[21] See M. D. Goulder, *Midrash and Lection in the Gospel of Matthew* (SPCK: London 1974); Goulder, *The Evangelists' Calendar* (SPCK: London 1978). For a lucid evaluation of the problem see J. L. Houlden, "Lectionary Interpretation (New Testament)", in: R. J. Coggins and J. L. Houlden (eds.), *A Dictionary of Biblical Interpretation* (SCM: London 1990), pp. 388–90. On the possibility of specifically Jewish Christian Gospels in Hebrew, see P. A. Pritz, *Nazarene Jewish Christianity* (Magnes Press: Jerusalem; E. J. Brill: Leiden 1988), pp. 83–94.

building which catches fire on Shabbat, or which collapses, or which is flooded, it is permitted to rescue the Scroll and carry it outside, even though in doing so one may be violating the laws of Shabbat by carrying from one domain (the inside of the building) to an other (the street). The sanctity of the Torah Scroll overides the sanctity of Shabbat. One may not, however, behave in the same way towards *sifrei minim* or towards the Gospels: one leaves them to burn, or to be buried, or to be washed clean – sacred names and all! *Sifrei minim* and Gospels do not have the sanctity or status of genuine Torah Scrolls.

d) Social Contact and Commensality

Tosefta Ḥullin 2:20–21:

A. "If meat is found in the hand of a gentile, it is permitted to derive benefit from it, but if it is found in the hand of a *min*, it is forbidden to derive benefit from it.

B. That which comes out from the house of a *min* [reading *mi-bet ha-min* for *mi-bet 'avodah zarah* of the Vienna ms] is indeed meat of sacrifices to the dead.

C. For they said: The slaughtering of a *min* is idolatry; their bread is the bread of a Samaritan; their wine is the wine of libation; their fruits are untithed; their books are the books of diviners, and their children are *mamzerim*.

D. We do not sell to them, nor do we buy form them. We do not take from them, nor do we give to them. We do not teach their sons a craft. We are not healed by them, neither healing of property of healing of life."

This text clearly illustrates a major social weapon deployed by the Rabbis against the Jewish Christians – ostracism. Rabbinic Jews are forbidden to eat with Jewish Christians. They are forbidden to have any kind of commercial or business dealings with them, even to the extent of taking on their sons as apprentices[22]. They are forbidden to read their books, which are classified as "witchcraft". "Magic" was universally condemned in antiquity, so to designate one's opponents activities as magic is a common ploy for holding them up to public disapproval. The prohibition may also reflect the Rabbinic tradition that Jesus was a magician. Rabbinic Jews are forbidden to be healed by *minim*, presumably on the grounds that there would be a suspicion that they would be healed by magic, or in the name of Jesus. The children of the *minim* are brought under the general classification of *mamzerim*, presumably because there was doubt as to how strictly they observed the laws regarding the forbidden degrees. This would have had the effect of restricting their options for marriage with other Jews. The text of Tosefta Ḥullin continues with the Story of Rabbi

---

[22] The question of apprenticeships was an issue in dealing with "outsiders": cf. Massekhet Kutiyyim 1:10, "An Israelite may give his son in charge of a Samaritan to teach him a trade".

Eleazar ben Damah and the Jewish Christian healer, Jacob of Kefar Sama (Tosefta Ḥullin 2:22–23). This is then followed by the long tale of how Rabbi Eliezer ben Hyrcanus was arrested on a charge of *minut* (Tosefta Ḥullin 2:24). There has been fierce discussion of the historicity of the stories, but much of it is beside the point[23]. They are introduced as exempla (*ma'asim*) to illustrate the rulings given earlier. Their message is clear: all normal social contact with the *minim* is forbidden. It is better to die than be healed by a *min* in the name of Jesus (so the tale of Eleazar ben Damah), and one should not talk with a *min* in the street, lest one brings on oneself the suspicion of *minut*, and gets arrested and brought before the Roman court (so the tale of Rabbi Eliezer).

The rulings of Tosefta Ḥullin 2:20–21 are tantamount to imposing a ban on the Jewish Christians. There is no evidence that the Rabbinical authorities promulgated a formal *ḥerem* against the Jewish Christians. Until the third century at the earliest they did not possess the sort of centralized authority that would have made such a general ban possible. But they did not need to issue a general ban. The rulings of Tosefta Ḥullin 2:20–21, even if advocated piecemeal, would in the end have had the same effect. Rabbinic *halakhah* in all its fulness did not represent the common law of the Palestinian Jewish community. It was sectarian in origin and in a number of areas probably represented the intensification of commonly accepted practice. It was divisive: not only did it divide Jew from gentile, but it divided Jew from Jew. For example, a Jew following strictly the Rabbinic laws of *kashrut* would have found it difficult, if not impossible, to eat at the home of a non-Rabbinic Jew. The Rabbis tirelessly advocated acceptance of their *halakhah* as a way of rabbinizing Jewish society. It had the effect of setting up a closed circle of "observant" Jews and ostracizing the rest. It must initially have split Jewish towns such as Sepphoris, Tiberias, Capernaum and Nazareth – all of which, in their time, probably contained Jewish Christians. As acceptance of Rabbinic *halakhah* grew the Jewish Christians of such towns would have come under growing pressure, and found themselves increasingly "ghettoized".

e) Propaganda and Polemics

Babylonian Talmud, Sanhedrin 107a–107b (// Soṭah 47a):
A. "Our Rabbis taught: Always let the left hand thrust away and the right hand draw near.
B. Not like Elisha who thrust away Gehazi with both hands, nor like Rabbi Joshua ben Peraḥiah who thrust away Yeshu ha-Noṣri with both hands.
C. What was the case of Elisha? ... [Story of Elisha and Gehazi]

---

[23] For a recent, balanced assessment see R. J. Bauckham, *Jude and the Relatives of Jesus in the Early Church* (T. & T. Clark: Edinburgh 1990), pp. 106–121.

D. What was the case of Rabbi Joshua ben Peraḥiah?

E. When King Yannai put the Rabbis to death, [Shim'on ben Shetaḥ was hidden by his sister and] Rabbi Joshua ben Peraḥiah and Yeshu fled to Alexandria in Egypt.

F. When there was peace, Shim'on ben Shetaḥ sent [a letter] to him: 'From me, the Holy City (Jerusalem) to you Alexandria in Egypt, my sister. My husband dwells in your midst while I sit desolate!'

G. Rabbi Joshua arose to go back and chanced upon a certain inn.

H. They showed him great honour, and he said: 'How beautiful is this *'akhsanya* (= inn *and* innkeeper)!' Yeshu said to him: 'Rabbi, her eyes are narrow!' He replied, 'Wretch, is this how you employ yourself?'

I. He sent out four hundred horns and excommunicated him.

J. Yeshu came before him on many occasions, saying: 'Receive me back!' But he took no notice of him.

K. One day, while Rabbi Joshua was reciting the *Shema'*, Yeshu came before him. His intention was to receive him back, and he made a sign to him with his hand, but Yeshu thought he was repelling him. He went away, set up a brick and worshipped it.

L. Rabbi Joshua said to him: 'Return!', but he replied: 'Thus have I received from you, that everyone who sins and who causes the congregation (*harabbim*) to sin is deprived of the ability to repent.'

M. Mar said: 'Yeshu ha-Noṣri practised magic and deceived and led Israel astray.'"

The tradition-history of this passage can be traced with a tolerable degree of certainty. The Yeshu ha-Noṣri material (D–M) is secondary: it has been added to the Gehazi material (C) in order to provide a further illustration of the dictum, "Always let the left hand thrust away and the right hand draw near". The parallel section of the Yerushalmi (Sanhedrin X,2 [29b]) has only the story of Gehazi. The story of Yeshu ha-Noṣri is broadly modelled on the story of Gehazi, but it also draws inspiration from the story of Judah ben Tabbai's flight to Egypt recorded at Yerushalmi Ḥagigah II,2 (77d) (cf. Yerushalmi Sanhedrin VI,9 [23c]). The concluding saying (M) is found also independently at Bavli Sanhedrin 43a[24].

Though the sources of the passage are reasonably clear, its message is curiously enigmatic and ambivalent. The note of self-criticism is rather striking. Though Jesus is excommunicated (I) and charged with the grave crimes of magic and "deceiving Israel" (M), at the same time his sins are seen as in some part the fault of Joshua ben Peraḥiah. Jesus comes across as a rather simple-

---

[24] For a detailed discussion of the tradition-history see J. Maier, *Jesus von Nazareth in der talmudischen Überlieferung* (Wissenschaftliche Buchgesellschaft: Darmstadt 1978), pp. 104–129.

minded student who is dealt with by his teacher in a harsh and thoughtless manner, in contravention of the maxim to repel with the left hand and draw near with the right. As a result of his banishment the pupil goes seriously astray, damns himself and leads Israel into sin. One wonders at the historical situation envisaged by the story. It appears to be admonishing the Rabbinical authorities not to be too severe on Jewish Christians, not to ostracize them so totally that they are denied all possibility of repentance and of returning to the fold.

The story of Jesus and Joshua ben Peraḥiah comes from the late Amoraic period but it contains old polemical elements that were already current in New Testament times. Two charges are levelled agains Jesus. First, he practised magic. This comes out explicitly only at M, but may be implicit elsewhere in the story. Joshua ben Peraḥiah, Jesus, teacher, is well-known in Jewish magical tradition as an exorcist.[25] It is probably for this reason that he, and not Judah ben Tabbai, was chosen as the Rabbinic protagonist of the tale. The choice of Alexandria as the place to which Joshua ben Peraḥiah and Jesus flee is also suggestive: Egypt is closely associated in Rabbinic literature with sorcery. Second, Jesus is charged with "deceiving and leading Israel astray". This charge often relates specifically to idolatry. This would chime in with the curious reference at K to Jesus worshipping a brick. It is possible, however, that the sense is more general: note the parallel at L: "sins and causes Israel to sin". Both these charges are echoed in the New Testament in contexts of conflict between the early Church and its opponents. In Matt 27:63–4 the Pharisees describe Jesus as a "deceiver", his message as a "deception". In Mark 3:22, Matt 9:34, 12:24 and Luke 11:15 Jesus is accused of casting out demons by the power of Beelzebul. The early Christians warned that anyone asserting this was guilty of an unforgivable blasphemy (Mark 3:28; Matt 12:31). It is interesting to note that the Rabbinic text has its own version of the sin against the Holy Ghost: whoever not only sins but leads Israel into sin has put himself beyond the power of repentance (L)[26].

The general tone of Rabbinic anti-Christian polemic in the period of the

---

[25] The link between Joshua and magic appears to be found only in Babylonian Jewish sources: see J. Neusner, *History of the Jews in Babylonia*, vol. V (E. J. Brill: Leiden 1970), pp. 218–43; P. S. Alexander, "Incantations and Books of Magic", in: E. Schürer, *The History of the Jewish People in the Age of Jesus Christ*, vol. III,1, rev. G. Vermes, F. Millar and M. Goodman (T. & T. Clark: Edinburgh 1986), pp. 354f.

[26] The arch-heretic Elisha ben Avuyah ("Aḥer") is also said to have commited the unforgivable sin. In Yerushalmi Ḥagigah II,1 (77b) this is defined, rather vaguely, as "knowing God's power yet rebelling against him". In Bavli Ḥagigah 15a (cf. 3 Enoch 16:1–5) it is defined as mistaking the angel Meṭaṭron for a Second Power. In both texts a *bat qol* goes forth inviting erring Israelites in the words of Jer 3:22 to return in repentance, but specifically excepting Elisha. Tosefta Sanhedrin 13:5 (quoted in note 12 above) comes close to the concept of the unforgivable sin. There the various miscreants listed are said to be damned eternally. The idea may be that Gehinnom will not be a place of purgatory from which they will ultimately escape. Rather they will suffer there eternal torment.

Talmud can hardly be described as high. Bavli Sanhedrin 107b is typical, though it does not descend to the scurrility of some parts of the *Toledot Yeshu* traditions. There are possible examples in Rabbinic literature of a more serious engagement with Christian ideas. For example, it has been suggested that Genesis Rabba constitutes an elaborate defence of the election of Israel in response to the Christianization of the Roman Empire in the fourth century. And some have seen in the Rabbinic doctrine of the Aqedah a response to the Christian doctrine of the atonement[27]. But I am not fully persuaded. In general the Rabbis' direct contacts with Christianity were slight, and their knowledge of the finer points of Christian doctrine slighter still. There was no real meeting of minds till the Middle Ages[28]. Most anti-Christian polemic in the Talmudic period was rather crude propaganda – though probably none the less effective for that.

C. The Widening Rift

Having surveyed the main elements of early Rabbinic policy towards the Christians, I shall conclude by offering some notes, from a Rabbinic perspective, towards the history of the Jewish-Christian schism.

1. It is abundantly clear from the New Testament itself that Christianity before 70 not only attracted support but also encountered strong and widespread opposition within the Jewish community. That opposition ranged from the central authorities in Jerusalem (the High Priest and the Sanhedrin) to the leaders of the local synagogues. It extended from Palestine (both Galilee and Jerusalem) to the Diaspora (e. g. Asia Minor and Achaea). It began in the time of Jesus himself and continued unabated in the period after the crucifixion. The reasons for the opposition were manifold and diverse. Jesus' triumphal entry into Jerusalem and his attack on the money-changers in the Temple doubtless fostered the view among some of the pre-70 authorities that he was a dangerous revolutionary who had to be stopped. Some Jews, zealous for the Law, were outraged by the antinomianism of certain Christian teachings, and the failure of some Christians to observe the laws and customs of Isarel. Other, as Paul recognized, found the idea of a crucified Messiah simply too paradoxical to swallow (I Cor 1:23). High Christology would also have been a problem. There can now be no question that early Judaism did know of powerful semi-divine mediator figures, so the high Christology of some of the early Christian writings

---

[27] See J. Neusner, *Genesis and Judaism: The Perspective of Genesis Rabbah* (Scholars Press: Atlanta 1986); P. R. Davies and B. D. Chilton, "The Aqedah: A Revised Tradition History", *Catholic Biblica Quarterly* 40 (1978), pp. 514–46.

[28] Perhaps the earliest Jewish writer to make a serious effort to understand Christianity is Judah Halevi in the *Kuzari*.

can actually be given a *Jewish* context[29]. But such notions may well have been confined to small groups of Jewish intellectuals interested in esoteric doctrines. Acts 7:54–60 probably describes accurately the attitude of the majority of Jews to such outlandish ideas. The precise reasons for the opposition to the Gospel need not detain us here. Suffice to say that the extent and intensity of the opposition points clearly to one conclusion. Christianity emerged at the margins of Jewish society and was widely seen as being a radical movement. It had, therefore, a daunting hill to climb before it could Christianize Jewish society.

2. Whether or not the tradition of the flight of the Jerusalem Church to Pella is accurate, the First War against Rome (66–74 C.E.) must have been a time of tribulation for the Jewish Christians of Palestine. They could hardly have felt comfortable with the upsurge of Jewish nationalism during the War, especially when in some quarters it assumed a messianic tinge. However, the debacle of the War opened for them a window of opportunity. It swept away the authorities who had shown themselves so hostile to emergent Christianity, and it removed for the foreseeable future the danger of Christianity being excommunicated from Israel by decree form Jerusalem. The destruction of the Temple also handed the Christians a propaganda coup, for it gave them the chance to argue that the catastrophe was a divine judgement on Israel for the rejection of Jesus. The War of 66–74 opened a window of opportunity also for another first century Jewish religious party – the Pharisees. In the period before 70 it is unlikely (*pace* Josephus, *Antiquities* XVIII, 14–15,17), that the Pharisees represented the real rulers of the state. They were only one of a number of religious parties, and probably by no means the most influential politically. However, they made a determined bid to fill the power-vacuum created by the War. If tradition is to be believed, the *Bet Din* at Yavneh attempted to assert its authority to determine the calendar with some success (cf. Mishnah Rosh ha-Shanah 2:8–9). But there can be no question of a sudden Rabbinic accession to power. The Rabbis remained a sect within Judaism down to the third century C.E. This is suggested by a number of considerations. The conflict with the *'ammei ha-'areṣ* which echoes through Tannaitic literature points to the existence of socially powerful elements who resisted Rabbinic claims to authority. Significantly disputes with the *'ammei ha-'areṣ* die away in the third century Rabbinic sources[30]. The development of Rabbinic ordination points to a steady centralization of power as the Rabbis became increasingly involved in the administraiton of justice. According to Yerushalmi Sanhedrin 1:2 the Sages originally ordained their own pupils; later the approval of a *bet din* was required; finally ordination could only take place with the approval of the

---

[29] See L. W. Hurtado, *One Lord: Early Christian Devotion and Ancient Jewish Monotheism* (Fortress Press: Philadelphia 1988).

[30] See A. Oppenheimer, *The 'Am Ha-'Aretz: A Study in the Social History of the Jewish People* (E. J. Brill: Leiden 1977).

Nasi'. In Tannaitic sources there is little evidence of the Rabbis actually judging concrete cases. In Amoraic sources, however, they are regularly depicted as functioning within a well-regulated system of Jewish courts supervised by the Nasi' (cf. Yerushalmi Yevamot 12:6; Yerushalmi Hagigah 1:7)[31].

3. The Patriarchate of Judah ha-Nasi' probably marks a decisive upswing in the fortunes of the Rabbinic party within Judaism. Judah ha-Nasi' was a man of considerable wealth and social standing who appears to have had the backing of the Roman autorities. But at the same time he was a supporter of Rabbinic Judaism and a promoter of Rabbinic *halakhah*. Only in the third century can one begin to talk of a "triumph of Rabbinism", and even then only in carefully considered terms. The triumph was initially only in Palestine. From there Rabbinism was transplanted to the Diaspora, notably to Babylonia. Its spread was gradual. The outlying Jewish community of Spain probably did not become rabbinized till after the eighth century when the Muslim conquest led to an influx of Rabbinic Jews from North Africa and the Middle East, and linked the Spanish Jews to the great Rabbinic academies of Iraq within the same broad cultural framework. The Rhineland communities may also not have been rabbinized till the early Middle Ages, possibly not till the Kalonymide migration from Italy (9th century). The Rabbis have remained down to the present day essentially a scholarly élite within Judaism, who have by no means always had things their own way, even within the communities which in principle have recognized their authority. Rabbinic Judaism triumphed and survived partly because Rabbinic *halakhah* proved to be a flexible instrument, capable of responding to changing historical circumstances, partly because Rabbinism successfully transformed itself from a sect into (if the term may be excused) a "broad Church" which was able to accomodate mystical and philosophical movements and ideas, some of which were potentially inimical to it.

4. The triumph of Rabbinism did not result, as Sir John Seeley said of the British Empire, from "a fit of absence of mind", but from a concerted bid for power[32]. Implicit in the Rabbinic position was a claim to legislate for *all* Israel in

---

[31] The view that the Pharisees were a sect before 70 and their sucessors the Rabbis remained a sect within Palestinian Judaism down at least till the third century C. E. runs counter to much received wisdom. The new "Schürer", if it does not bluntly assert that Pharisaism was normative Judaism, comes close to it: "No peculiarity emerges from the characterization of Pharisaism which might distinguish it from Judaism in general during the period of the Second Temple. Regarded as a spiritual orientation, it was simply identical with the trend adopted by the main body and the classical representatives of post-exilic Jewry." "Schürer" goes on, indeed, to state that "the Pharisees formed a party within the nation", but immediately describes that party as an *ecclesiola in ecclesia*, thus suggesting that it possessed legitimacy as against other parties (E. Schürer, *The History of the Jewish People in the Age of Jesus Christ*, Vol. II, rev. G. Vermes and F. Millar [T. &T. Clark: Edinburgh 1979], pp.395f.). It is hard to see how, if this view is maintained, one can avoid de-legitimizing Christianity *ab ovo*.

[32] Sir John Seely, *The Expansion of England* (1883), Lecture I: "We [English] seem, as it were, to have conquered and peopled half the world in a fit of absence of mind." Katz has

all aspects of life. The Rabbis claimed to have the authoritative interpretation of the Law of Moses, which had been passed down through their schools by a secure line of tradents from Moses himself. The Mishnah is a manifesto, and there is every reason to believe that the Rabbis did their best to implement that manifesto in the wider community. The Rabbinic power-base lay within the Rabbinic schools. The battle for hearts and minds was fought out in the synagogues, in the Jewish courts, in the market-places, in the homes, and, perhaps even at times, in the Roman tribunals. In all these areas the Rabbis steadily pressed for the aceptance of Rabbinic *halakhah* as the legitimate law of Israel. In the end they managed to marginalize all opposition groups, including the Christians, and to again acceptance by the majority of Jews as the leaders of the community.

5. Why did Rabbinism and not Christianity triumph within in Palestinian Jewish communities? The thrust of our analysis has been to show that there is no simple answer to this question. There was no decisive moment of victory and defeat, only a long drawn out series of skirmishes in which the Rabbis steadily rolled back the opposition and gained control of the communitiy. However, two major, inter-related causes of the failure of Jewish Christianity can be identified.

First, Jewish Christianity would have found it hard to cope with Jewish nationalism, and nationalist sentiments were strong among the Jews of Palestine in the first two centuries of the current era. It should be remembered that in this period the Palestinian Jews fought two disastrous wars of liberation against Rome (not to mention a number of abortive uprisings in the Diaspora). We have already referred to the First War as a time of trouble for the Jewish Christians. The Second War was probably equally disastrous for them, and their failure to support Bar Kokhba may have cost them dear[33]. Nationalism was bound up with traditionalism (zeal for the Law) and attachment to the Land of Israel, and it easily took on messianic overtones. Christians proclaimed that

---

argued that "there was no official anti-Christian policy at Yavneh or elsewhere before the Bar Kochba revolt and no total separation between Jews and Christians before (if immediately after?) the Bar Kochba revolt" ("Issues in the Separation of Judaism and Christianity after 70 C.E.", p. 76). But this conclusion is comprehensively denied by the evidence which he himself so fully presents. Note, e.g. is unconvincing attempt to argue that the Rabbis did not try to impose some sort of ban on Jewish Christians (pp. 48–53, especially p. 53 note 40).

[33] Justin, *I Apology* xxxi: "In the Jewish war which raged lately, Barcochebas, the leader of the revolt of the Jews, gave orders that Christians alone should be led to cruel punishments, unless they would deny Jesus Christ and utter blasphemy". (Ethiopic) Apocalypse of Peter 2: "But this deceiver is not the Christ. And when they reject him, he will kill with the sword and there shall be many martyrs." See further: P. Schäfer, *Der Bar Kokhba-Aufstand* (Mohr-Siebeck: Tübingen 1981), pp. 59–62; R. J. Bauckham, "The Two Fig Tree Parables in the Apocalypse of Peter", *Journal of Biblical Literature* 104 (1985), pp. 269–87; D. D. Buchholz, *Your Eyes Will be Opened: A Study of the Greek (Ethiopic) Apocalypse of Peter* (Scholars Press: Atlanta 1988), pp. 408–12.

the Messiah had come, but Jesus had clearly failed to deliver the kingdom in the form in which most had anticipated it. This problem may have been ameliorated so long as the Second Coming was seen as imminent, but the longer the *Parousia* was delayed the more acute it became. Christians stressed the spiritual nature of the kingdom and de-emphasized "the territorial dimension of Judaism"[34]. Such radicalism was out of joint with the spirit of the times. By way of contrast the Rabbis, though they too were in many ways innovators, were not nearly as radical as the Christians, and they always took care to stress their zeal for the Law and to articulate their views in the language of loyalty to the tradition.

Second, the Gentile mission of the Church, perhaps initially provoked by frustration over a lack of success among the Jews (cf. Acts 13:46), must surely have created problems for the Jewish Christians who carried on with the mission to Israel[35]. The success of the Gentile mission created a Church which was increasingly Gentile in membership. Moreover, though the Church proclaimed itself as the true Israel, Gentile converts were not expected to live as Jews. Given the nationalism, even xenophobia, of the Palestinian Jewish community in the first and second centuries of the current era, Christianity must have found it increasingly difficult to establish itself in the eyes of Jews as a *Jewish* movement. The Jewish Christians would have had what in today's political jargon would be called "an image problem".

That image problem reflected a deep crisis of identity within the early Church. What was to be done with the Gentile converts? Should they be expected to take upon themselves the yoke of the Law? Acts 15 and 21 propose a compromise: Jewish Christians were to continue to follow "their way of life", observing the food laws, circumcising and keeping Sabbath; Gentile Christians were not to be obliged to adopt Jewish customs, but were to be subject only to general "Noachide" laws[36]. This compromise, however reasonable it may seem, was in practice unworkable, since it presupposed that the Jewish and

[34] It is W. D. Davies who has raised most acutely the important question of how early Christianity responded to the "Land-centredness" of Palestinian Judaism: see his *The Gospel and the Land: Early Christianity and Jewish Territorial Doctrine* (University of California Press: Berkeley, Los Angeles, London 1974); and *The Territorial Dimension of Judaism* (University of California Press: Berkeley, Los Angeles, London 1982). For further discussion see: K. E. Wolff, *"Geh in das Land, das ich Dir zeigen werde..." Das Land Israel in der frühen rabbinischen Tradition und im Neuen Testament* (Peter Lang: Frankfurt a. M. 1989).

[35] Pritz, *Nazarene Jewish Christianity*, p. 110 reasonably cites the *Rabbinic* evidence as proof that the Jewish Christians never abandoned their mission to Israel. He refers appositely to the Nazarene commentary on Is 31:6−9 where the original "Return to him from whom you have deeply revolted, O Sons of Israel" is paraphrased as "O Sons of Israel, who deny the Son of God with base counsel, return to him and to his apostles" (quoted by Jerome, *Commentary on Isaiah* [*Corpus Christianorum* 73, 404]). The generally *pešer* style of Nazarene Bible-commentary is stirking.

[36] The definitive Rabbinic list of the Seven Commandments to the Sons of Noah was probably formulated later (Tosefta 'Avodah Zarah 8(9),4−6; Bavli Sanhedrin 56a), but it

Gentile groups could be kept segregated. But what would happen in mixed Churches? If Jewish Christians were to continue to observe some form of *kashrut*, socializing with their Gentile brethren would have become problematic. Commensality, that most basic expression of community, would have been jeopardized. Moreover, there would always be those who wanted to cross over to the other camp – Gentiles who wanted to Judaize because they thought Jewish Christianity was more authentic; Jews who wanted to abandon their ancestral customs and live like the Gentiles. This crossing over would have ensured that the Churches were kept in a perpetual ferment of controversy. Paul, who witnessed the problem at first hand, adopted a position that was at total variance with the Jerusalem compromise. He had no doubt that the formula that in Christ there was "neither Jew nor Greek" meant not only that Gentile Christians did not have to keep to Law, but also that the Jewish Christians did not have to keep it either. Paul seems to have despaired of Israel: his view that Israel had been "blinded" till the fullness of the Gentiles came in (Rom 11:25) virtually writes off the Jewish mission at least for the immediate future.

The parting of the ways between Judaism and Christianity only takes on an air of finality with the triumph of Rabbinism within the Palestinian Jewish community and the virtual disappearance of Jewish Christianity. Till that happened there was always the possibility that the Jewish Christians would succeed in Christianizing Israel. Jewish Christianity found itself caught between Scylla and Charybdis: the closer it moved to the Gentile Churches the less credible it would have become within the Jewish community; the more it emphasized its Jewishness the more difficult would have become its relations with the Gentile Churches, the more it would have been viewed with suspicion by the Gentiles. Jewish Christianity was finally destroyed between the upper and nether millstone of triumphant Gentile Christianity and triumphant Rabbinism. Drawing on Pauline theology the Gentile Church became increasingly anti-Judaic in its stance: it defined itself ever more sharply over against Judaism. The existence of a Jewish Christianity blurred the sharp edges of Christian self-definition. From the standpoint of the Gentile Church it was expedient that the Jewish Church should fade away[37]. Suppose the Jewish Christians, and not

---

represents a discussion which goes back at least to Jubilees (7:20). The discussion forms the historical context of Acts 15:29 und 21:25.

[37] The fourth century Church Fathers treat Nazarene Christianity as a heresy. See, e. g. Jerome, *Epist.* 112,13: "Until today a heresy is to be found among the Jews throughout all the synagogues of the east, which is called 'of the Minaeans [= *minim*]', and is cursed by the Pharisees up till now. Usually they are called Nazaraeans. They believe in Christ, the Son of God born of the Virgin Mary, and they say about him that he suffered and rose again under Pontius Pilate, in whom we also believe. But since they want to be both Jews and Christians, they are neither Jews nor Christians." The drawing apart of Rabbinism and Gentile Christianity, leaving Jewish Christianity exposed and vulnerable between the two camps, may be

the Rabbis, had won the battle for the hearts and minds of Israel? The result would not necessarily have meant the end of the Jewish people and their absorption into the Gentile Church[38]. It is just as possible that two forms of Christianity would have emerged, possibly even two religions. The contradiction which the Jerusalem compromise tried to cover over would have played itself out with a vengeance.

---

illustrated by the fate of the Ḥaninah ben Dosa traditions within Rabbinic Judaism. G. Vermes shrewdly explains the fact that traditions about the Galilean *ḥasid* are more numerous paradoxically in Babylonian Rabbinic sources than in Palestinian as follows: "It seems that the transmitters of the Ḥanina traditions may have felt embarrassed by the similarities between his charismatic activites and those attributed to Jesus and his Jewish followers, among whom a certain Jacob from the Galilean locality of Kefar Sekhaniah (or Sama), an acquaintance of Eliezer ben Hyrcanus, achieved definite notoriety in rabbinic circles. Fear of blurring the distinction between Judaism and Judeo-Christianity was probably the main contributing factor, in third century Galilee, to the dissolution of the legend surrounding the figure of Ḥanina ben Dosa" (*Post-Biblical Jewish Studies* [E. J. Brill: Leiden 1975], p.213). To avoid blurring the boundaries Rabbinic Judaism was prepared to play down part of its own tradition. Gentile Christianity would also doubtless, have rejected any parallelism between Jesus and Ḥaninah (had it known the Ḥaninah traditions), as Petrus Alphonsi was to do later (see Vermes, p.214). Jewish Christianity, however, continued to follow the charismatic healing tradition of Galilean ḥasidism.

[38] *Pace* Schiffmann, *Who was a Jew?* p.77: "Had the rabbis relaxed these standards, accepting either the semi-proselytes or the earliest Gentile Christians into the Jewish people, Christians would quickly have become the majority within the expanded community of 'Israel'. Judaism as we know it would have ceased to exist even before reaching codification in the Mishnah and the other great compilations of the tannaitic tradition. Christianity would have been the sole heir of the traditions of biblical antiquity, and observance of the commandments of the Torah would have disappeared within just a few centuries. In short, it was the *halakhah* and its definition of Jewish identity which saved the Jewish people and its heritage from extinction as a result of the newly emerging Christian ideology". Is it unfair to see a certain tendentiousness here? Is there the implication that just as Rabbinic *halakhah* saved the Jewish people from cultural and religious extinction in the past, so it can do so again today – against inroads not only from Christianity, but from secularism and, perhaps, even Reform?

Diaspora Reactions to the Destruction of the Temple

by

MARTIN GOODMAN

How much did Jews in the diaspora care about the catastrophic defeat of their brothers in Judaea in A. D. 70? It is noticeable that in A. D. 66 – as Agrippa II is said by Josephus (perhaps with hindsight) to have warned would be the case (*B. J.* 2.345–404) – the considerable aid that these Jews could have provided to the rebels was not forth-coming: Jews in the cities around Palestine, as also in Antioch and in Alexandria by Egypt, were dragged into the conflict by the attacks of their gentile neighbours, but they singularly failed to flood to the rescue of Jerusalem as optimistic Judaeans might have hoped[1].

The cause of such inactivity was not, I suspect, indifference so much as over-confidence. Until the very last months of the war, from the spring of A. D. 70, the risk of the fall of Jerusalem, let alone the destruction of the Temple, must have seemed minimal. After all, no Roman forces came near to the walls of the city for more than three years after the resounding defeat of Cestius Gallus in October A. D. 66. The rapid siege and capture of Jerusalem may have been brought about almost entirely by the need of the new emperor Vespasian to justify to the Roman people his seizure of the purple by military force despite his humble origins; victory over foreign enemies was the surest route to prestige in Roman society. Only the pressing need for such a propaganda coup can explain the extraordinary waste of life among his own soldiers considered acceptable by Titus in subjecting the city to a direct assault on its formidable walls rather than allowing the starvation induced by his circumvallation to bring the enemy to surrender more slowly but at far less cost[2].

There is, then, every reason to suppose that the rasing of the Temple horrified diaspora Jews as much as their Judaean compatriots. Jews outside Palestine seem to have presumed the central importance of the Temple in Jewish worship despite the physical obstacles to their frequent attendance at the cult. Thus Ps. Aristeas, who wrote probably in Alexandria and probably in

---

[1] On the reactions of diaspora Jews to the outbreak of revolt, see Jos. *B. J.* 2.457–98.

[2] For these arguments in greater detail, see further M. Goodman, *The Ruling Class of Judaea: the origins of the Jewish revolt against Rome, A. D. 66–70* (Cambridge, 1987), pp. 176–97.

the second century B.C., assumed that it was from Jerusalem and the priest-hood based there that authoritative religious knowledge came. Philo, in Alexandria in the mid first century A.D., made the same assumption that Jerusalem is the mother-city of all Jews (*Flacc.* 46). By his time emphasis on the Jerusalem Temple by Jews in Egypt is particularly striking, for the rival temple of Onias in Leontopolis had been in existence for about two centuries without displacing Jerusalem from its primacy even among local Jews[3]. For at least one diaspora Jew, the historian Josephus living in Rome in the nineties A.D., Judaism without the Temple seems to have been unthinkable: in his summary of the Law in *Contra Apionem* he included the Temple cult as the first item in his list of the essentials of Jewish worship (*C. Ap.* 2.193–8)[4].

It is then a fair assumption that even those diaspora Jews within the Roman empire who had not themselves suffered in the war of A.D. 66–70 were profoundly affected by its consequences. Finding out more about their precise reactions is not, however, altogether easy, for direct evidence is hard to find. The rabbinic texts which refer to this period were all compiled either in Palestine or in Mesopotamia at least a century after the destruction of Jerusalem, and in most cases at a much later date. Their interests lay in the development of rabbinic halakhah and (to a much lesser extent) the biographies of individual Palestinian rabbis; it is not reasonable to expect in them any useful information on the state of the diaspora. It is true that certain rabbis are said to have gone on journeys to Syria and other are said to have travelled to Rome, but what they did on arrival is unknown[5]. By the fourth century A.D. the rabbinic patriarch in Galilee had established semi-formal control over many, eventually perhaps all, Jewish communities in the diaspora ruled by Rome, and the patriarch's *apostoloi* collected contributions on his behalf which by the 390s A.D., if not before, enjoyed the official sanction of the Roman government[6]. But it is highly implausible that any such system was in operation, even in embryonic form, between A.D. 70 and 132: in A.D. 70 the rabbinic sages, who to a large extent continued the traditions of the Pharisees, were presumably still competing for influence among thinking Jews in Palestine with other Jewish

---

[3] On the Leontopolis temple and its relationship to the Jerusalem cult, see E. Schürer, *The History of the Jewish People in the Age of Jesus Christ*, rev. and ed. G. Vermes, F. Millar, M. Black and M. Goodman, 3 vols. (Edinburgh, 1973–86), 3:145–7.

[4] On Josephus' summary of the Law, see G. Vermes, 'A summary of the law by Flavius Josephus', *Novum Testamentum* 24 (1982), 289–303.

[5] On the visits by Rabban Gamaliel to Syria (*m. Eduyoth* 7:7), and by him and others to Rome (*m. Maaser Sheni* 5:9 and parr.), see my comments in M. Goodman, *State and Society in Roman Galilee, A.D. 132–212* (Totowa, 1983), pp. 113, 240–1.

[6] On the power of the patriarch in the diaspora in the late fourth century, see S. J. D. Cohen, 'Pagan and Christian evidence on the ancient synagogue', in L. I. Levine, ed., *The Synagogue in Late Antiquity* (New York, 1987), pp. 172–5; M. Goodman, 'The Roman State and the Jewish Patriarch in the third century', in L. I. Levine, ed., *Galilee in Late Antiquity* (New York, 1992), pp. 127–39, with refs.

philosophies (described by Josephus as Essenism and Sadducaism, whose existence he still took entirely for granted in the nineties A.D. (*A. J.* 18.12–22))[7]. *A fortiori* in the diaspora, where only two Pharisees are attested from any period (St. Paul and Josephus), it is implausible that the successors of the Pharisees will have won immediate authority. It is entirely possible that the rabbis lacked any say in the Greek-speaking diaspora until well into the third century A.D. or even later.

Possible – but hard to prove, for the supply of literary evidence from the Greek-speaking diaspora itself begins to dry up towards the end of the first-century A.D. Of Jewish literature composed in Greek after A.D. 70, only the writings of Josephus survive in any quantity. Some of the Jewish forgeries inserted by some devious means now forgotten into the corpus of Sibylline oracles were composed probably under Domitian and Hadrian, but the complex psychology of the author of such oracles, whose success depended on his (or her?) ability to achieve the tone of a pagan prophetess, precludes use of such material as reliable evidence of Jewish self-perception in this period[8]. The romantic and mysterious novel called *Joseph and Asenath* may have been written by a Jew in this period; but its composition, which is firmly dated only by the *terminus ante quem* of the sixth-century translation of the work into Syriac, may also have been either much later or much earlier. A date before A.D. 117 is suggested only by the eirenic attitudes expressed towards gentiles, which may be regarded as unlikely in any work written in Egypt soon after that date[9]. Similar arguments apply to the *Testament of Job*, possibly to be attributed to an author in Egypt because of the reference to Job as king of all Egypt (28.8), but, though possibly composed in this period, firmly dated only to before the Coptic versions partially preserved in the fifth-century Papyrus Cologne 3221[10].

This dearth of extant Jewish literature in Greek is not accidental. It relates directly to, indeed was caused by, the phenomenon which is the subject of this book, namely, the "Parting of the Ways". Almost all the surviving Judaeo-Greek writings were preserved by the Christian rather than the Jewish tradition. Thus Philo's treatises were kept by the Church as edifying tracts; Philo, like Josephus, was treated by some early Christian fathers as an honorary Christian. But after c. A.D. 100 it became decreasingly likely that any work composed by a Jew would be viewed by Christians as relevant to them. If such works were written, then, they were mostly ignored by later generations and lost to posterity: *Joseph and Asenath* and the *Testament of Job* will have been exceptions.

---

7 Goodman, *State and Society*, pp. 93–118.
8 On the Sibyllines, see Schürer, *History* 3:618–54. On the date of Books iv and v, see *ibid*, pp. 641–5.
9 Schürer, *History* 3:546–52.
10 Schürer, *History* 3:553–4.

Not that evidence for Jewish life in the Mediterranean diaspora in this period is therefore entirely lacking. As will become apparent in the pages which follow, something can be surmised from the fragmentary testimony of inscriptions (particularly in North Africa), from papyri (mostly in Egypt), from occasional hints out of archaeological sites, and from passing references to Jews in the quite full narrative histories of much of this period which record the political and military adventures of the Roman state and its rulers. For the immediate reaction after A.D. 70 much more detailed evidence is available from Josephus. Refugees from the war in Judaea – Josephus calls them *'sicarii'* – fomented disturbances in Alexandria and Cyrene which were only suppressed after heavy loss of life (*B. J.* 7.409–42). Josephus was at pains to insist that only lower-class Jews were led into such disaffection and that men of means attempted to impose moderation, but his veracity in this regard may reasonably be doubted since he himself was apparently accused by some of his compatriots of complicity in the uprisings (*Vita* 424). Doubt about Josephus' depiction of these disturbances, like the Judaean revolt itself, as a class struggle should not, however, extend to his insistence that Judaean rather than diaspora Jews were responsible: the historian held no special brief for diaspora Jewry, and no source suggests any anti-Roman move by those other diaspora communities which were too far removed from Judaea to act as hosts for more than a few refugees, such as the large settlements of Jews in Asia Minor.

The pacific inclinations of such Jews, however, did not prevent them too suffering in the backlash after the revolt. On the one hand the gentile inhabitants of the great city of Antioch in North Syria, where there was a sizeable Jewish minority, took advantage of the presumed anti-Jewish prejudice of the Romans immediately after the war to institute a systematic persecution aimed at the extinction of Jewish religious practices: all who failed to sacrifice to pagan deities were to be punished, cessation from work on the sabbath was forbidden, Jewish privileges were withdrawn. All this was much too extreme for the governor of Syria who, presumably with the approval of Titus, who was resident in the south of his province at the time, restored the Jews of Antioch to their former rights (*B. J.* 7.100–11).

On the other hand the instinct of the Antiochenes, that the Roman state might look not unfavourably on such persecution, was not very wide of the mark. The Flavians trumpeted their victory throughout the empire: coins proclaimed *Judaea Capta*, and the restoration of the *Pax Deorum* was symbolised by the dedication of the Temple of Peace on the Capitol in A.D. 76. No apology, therefore, for the destruction of the Temple, despite Josephus' optimistic assertion (cf. *B. J.* 6.241) that it had all been a terrible mistake[11]. On

---

[11] For the coins, see H. Mattingly and R. A. G. Carson, eds., *Coins of the Roman Empire in the British Museum*, 9 vols. (London, 1923–75) 2:115–18 and passim. On the temple of Pax,

the contrary the inoffensive sanctuary at Leontopolis, which had never yet served as rallying point for hostility to Rome of any kind, was arbitarily closed down for ever (*B. J.* 7.420−36).

At the root of this behaviour by the Romans, and the subsequent sufferings of diaspora Jews, was the ambiguity inherent in the Latin name *Iudaeus*, Greek *ioudaios*. The Flavian victory had been won over the inhabitants of Judaea, whom Romans naturally termed "Judaeans", but the identical term was used to refer to Jews wherever they lived, however little contact they maintained with the national homeland. Roman reprisals for the rebellion of Jerusalem thus fell on all Jews within the empire, symbolically expressed through the vigorous exaction of a special poll tax imposed on all Jews, the *fiscus Judaicus*[12].

The collection of the *fiscus Judaicus* in the years immediately following the revolt can be traced in some detail from papyrus records and ostraca in Egypt (*CPJ* nos. 160−229). It appears that every Jew, male or female from the ages of three to sixty, was required to pay two denarii a year; the original destination of the funds was the rebuilding of the destroyed temple of Jupiter Capitolinus in Rome, but the tax continued long after that project was complete. In Egypt at least arrears from the last year of the war (A. D. 69) were added to the first demands made from Jews in A. D. 71. For poorer Jews with large families the sum required was a considerable burden; for others, it signified ignominy – and strong identification with the defeated nation in Judaea[13].

Is is evident that this treatment of diaspora Jews by Rome presupposed that the *Iudaei* were an ethnic group all of whom subscribed to a particular religious cult. In practice matters were more complex. Some people who were born to Jewish parents might apostatize from Judaism, as had Tiberius Iulius Alexander[14]. Some gentiles might become Jews by conversion to Jewish religious practices, a process explicitly formulated in the mid first century by Philo (*Virt.* 108) but perhaps not always so clear-cut in particular cases (cf. Jos. *A. J.* 14.403)[15]: it is striking that no gentile writer before the end of the first century A. D. seems to have been aware of the Jewish concept of proselytism, desite the fact that such converts left their ancestral pagan cults and thus might become in

---

see Jos. *B. J.* 7.158−62. On Titus' destruction of the Jerusalem Temple as deliberate, see Goodman, *Ruling Class*, pp. 237−8.

[12] On the term *ioudaios*, see *TDNT* s.v.; Ross S. Kraemer, 'On the meaning of the term "Jew" in Graeco-Roman inscriptions', *HTR* 82 (1989), 35−53. For some of the arguments which follow, see now in greater detail M. Goodman, 'Nerva, the *fiscus Judaicus* and Jewish identity', *JRS* 79 (1989), 40−4.

[13] On the *fiscus Judaicus* in general, see V. A. Tcherikover and A. Fuks, *Corpus Papyrorum Judaicarum*, vol. 1 (Cambridge, Mass., 1957), pp. 80−2; vol. 2 (Cambridge, Mass., 1960), pp. 111−16.

[14] Tacitus at *Ann.* 15.28.3 did not mention his Jewish origin. On his career, see V. A. Burr, *Tiberius Iulius Alexander* (Bonn, 1955).

[15] S. J. D. Cohen, 'Crossing the boundary and becoming a Jew', *HTR* 82 (1989), 13−33; M. Goodman, 'Identity and authority in ancient Judaism', *Judaism* 39 (1990), 192−201.

gentile eyes objectionable atheists. Other gentiles were attracted to Jewish customs such as the sabbath, without necessarily being thought of by other Jews as proselytes; of these a large number in Antioch had, according to Josephus, been made by the resident Jews "in some way a part of themselves" (*B. J.* 7.45). Which, if any, of these anomalous characters were to pay the Jewish tax?

It is likely enough that Vespasian and Titus gave no thought to such problems. But some idea of the people who in practice were compelled to pay may be culled from the report of Suetonius, *Domitian* 12.2, that in Rome the incidence of the tax was tightened up under their successor Domitian, who ruled A.D. 81–96. Domitian was not said to have changed the policy over who should pay. He was simply alleged to have exacted the tax *acerbissime*, a charge which Suetonius went on to elucidate by explaining that people who had previously got away without payment were now compelled to pay up. Who were these people? According to Suetonius, they were those who *vel inprofessi iudaicam viverent vitam vel dissimulata origine imposita genti tributa non pependissent*, that is, those who either followed Jewish customs without admitting to their Jewishness and/or those who disguised their (ethnic) origin as Jews. It seems that under the Flavians only those of Jewish ethnic origin were compelled to pay. Gentiles who had picked up Jewish customs mostly went scot free; those who did not were subjected not to taxation but to prosecution as atheists (Cassius Dio 67.14.1–2). Conversely, claiming not to be Jewish because one had left the faith was evidently ineffective since the tax had been placed on the *gens* regardless of religious loyalties. Presumably even a respectable Roman citizen like Tiberius Iulius Alexander was compelled to pay despite the ignominy. Suetonius records that in his youth he saw, presumably in Rome, a man ninety years old being stripped naked before a procurator and a crowded *consilium* to see whether he was circumcised (*Dom.* 12.2)[16].

What reaction to Domitian's increased rigour would one expect there to be from diaspora Jews? Perhaps not very much among the bulk of ethnic Jews, most of whom probably clung to their ancestral customs[17]. The hostility to Rome, and solidarity with Jews elsewhere, which had been engendered by the original imposition of the tax would not be much affected by its extension to apostates. But for the apostates themselves Domitian's rigour was much more likely to produce great resentment. Many of the numerous Jews who lived in the city of Rome in the late first century A.D. were descended from slaves who had been brought to Rome by Pompey in 63 B.C. and had then been freed and granted Roman citizenship[18]. By the time of Domitian such people could think

---

[16] See L. A. Thompson, 'Domitian and the Jewish tax', *Historia* 31 (1982), 329–42; Goodman, 'Nerva and the *fiscus Judaicus*', pp. 40–1.

[17] Josephus, *C. Apionem* 2.225–35, boasted that Jews stayed loyal to their ancestral rites more than any other people.

[18] Schürer, *History* 3:73–81.

of themselves as fourth, fifth or sixth generation Romans. It was shocking enough for such people to be penalised for the revolt of the Jews far away in Judaea when they continued to practice Judaism. Those in Rome whose connection with the rebellious nation was purely by accident of birth must have felt the insult to their Roman identity even more strongly.

It therefore seems to be no accident (although the connection cannot be proved) that one of the highly publicised acts of Domitian's successor, the emperor Nerva, was to reform the collection of the Jewish tax. Nerva had probably connived in Domitian's murder and thus had a strong interest in winning popular support in Rome by countermanding his predecessor's unpopular actions. His coins proclaim FISCI IUDAICI CALUMNIA SUBLATA. The precise translation of this phrase is uncertain, but its most likely meaning is "the malicious accusation with regard to the Jewish tax has been removed". It is reasonable to surmise that from now on those who wished to deny their Jewishness could do so. For the third century historian Cassius Dio (66.7.2), the tax was to be paid only by those who followed their ancestral customs.

All sorts of consequences may have resulted from this reform by Nerva. On the one hand it seems likely that the Roman state, and Romans in general, for the first time came properly to appreciate that people of non-Jewish origin could become Jews[19]. It is striking that, in contrast to the silence on the subject of proselytism in gentile texts before A.D. 96, there survives a series of comments, mostly very unfavourable, about such conversions in texts written in the early second century A.D. (Epictetus, ap. Arrian *Diss.* 2.9.20; Juvenal, *Sat.* 14.96–104; Tacitus, *Hist.* 5.5.2.). On the other hand the definition of apostasy became startlingly clear for Jews. Before A.D. 96 someone who, like Herod the Great, occasionally attended pagan sacrifices (Jos. *A.J.* 14.388) might nonetheless proclaim himself to be a religious Jew (even if some other Jews thought of him as sinful). It is difficult to establish precisely what behaviour was so totally unacceptable within the wide spectrum of Jewish practice in the first-century A.D. that all Jews would count it as apostasy. Perhaps the only clear-cut case would be a symbolic denial of the covenant by epispasm, an operation apparently undergone by some Jews during the revolt of the Maccabees. But after A.D. 96 any ethnic Jew who publicly refused to pay the annual levy to the *fiscus Judaicus* on the grounds that he was no longer religiously Jewish thereby put his apostasy beyond doubt.

It seems to me no accident that a clear distinction between Jews and Christians begins regularly to appear in pagan Roman texts after A.D. 96. The distinction is first evident in the letters of the younger Pliny (*Epp.* 10.96): Christians, if they did not pay the tax, were clearly not Jews. The psychological

---

[19] For this and the following remarks, see further Goodman, 'Nerva and the *fiscus Judaicus*', p. 43.

condition of Jews who believed in Christ ("Jewish Christians") must have been particularly tormented. Non-payment signified apostasy from Judaism but, then, payment might be reckoned a great sin in itself, since the funds raised went (at least in theory) to the upkeep of the temple of Jupiter Capitolinus in Rome (Jos. *B. J.* 7.218); but perhaps this theory had by now been forgotten.

After A. D. 96, then, the definition of a Jew by the Roman state was, for the purpose of the tax, a religious one. For Romans, Jews were those who worshipped the divinity whose temple had been destroyed in Jerusalem and who refused worship to the other gods. I suspect that this innovation had a profound effect on the self-perception of Jews in the diaspora.

The Jews of Cyprus, Cyrene and Egypt, who had remained (as far as is known) entirely pacific since the early seventies A. D., erupted in A. D. 115 into a massive rebellion[20]. The causes, much debated because unspecific in the scanty narrative sources which survive, cannot be discussed properly here. Arguments have been put forward for viewing the rebellion as a concerted attack on the rearguard of Trajan's forces, motivated by the opportunity for mayhem or possibly coordinated by Mesopotamian Jews determined to thwart the emperor's Parthian campaigns; or as a series of unconnected local disturbances caused by friction between local Greeks and Jews regardless of the suzerain power; or as an eschatological crusade, perhaps with messianic leaders (Andreas or Lukuas in Cyrene, Artemion in Cyprus), perhaps espousing a scorched earth policy as the insurgents uprooted themselves and moved towards the land of Israel, where trouble was probably threatened (an extra legion was probably moved to Legio at this time) but was not given an opportunity to materialise[21]. But the aspect of the revolt which I want to emphasise here, while it may or may not have been a fundamental cause of the uprising, may, it seems to me, represent a novel attitude by diaspora Jews, in which case it deserves rather more attention than it customarily receives.

During the revolt a number of pagan temples in the city of Cyrene, including those of Apollo, Zeus, Demeter, Artemis and Isis, were destroyed or damaged. The archaeological evidence for destruction under Trajan is extensive, and a number of inscriptions refer to the destruction of shrines during the *tumultus Iudaicus*[22]. It should be clearly stated that no evidence survives to link such destruction explicitly to *deliberate* action by Jews against paganism, and that the destruction of some sites in this period is surmised only from reconstructed versions of fragmentary inscriptions or from rebuilding at a date later in the

---

[20] Schürer, *History* 1:529–34; M. Pucci, *La rivolta ebraica al tempo di Traiano* (Pisa, 1981).

[21] For an analysis of possible causes, see Pucci, *Rivolta ebraica*; S. Applebaum, *Jews and Greeks in Ancient Cyrene* (Leiden, 1979), pp. 201–344; T. D. Barnes, 'Trajan and the Jews', *JJS* 40 (1989), 145–62.

[22] For the archaeological evidence, see Applebaum, *Jews and Greeks*, pp. 269–85; for the inscriptions, see G. Lüderitz, *Corpus jüdischer Zeugnisse aus der Cyrenaika* (Tübingen, 1983), nos. 17–25.

second century. It should also be admitted that there is little evidence of attacks on temples elsewhere in the regions affected by the revolt, and that the weight of information from Cyrene may simply reflect the extent of general destruction in the city, but the same phenomenon may also be accounted for by the intensity of archaeological investigation in Cyrene compared to that in the rest of the region. Nonetheless, with all such *caveats* accepted, it seems likely that the obvious explanation is the best: that the Jewish rebels deliberately destroyed the shrines of paganism.

If this is correct, it reveals a new attitude by these diaspora Jews. Both Josephus (*A. J.* 4.207) and Philo (*De Spec. Leg.* 1.53) wrote quite explicitly that it was in their view in order for gentiles to worship pagan gods[23]. Their attitude reflects the assumption of the Septuagint translators, and therefore, presumably, of most Greek-speaking Jews, that the Hebrew of Exodus 22:27 (Heb.) should be read to mean "You shall not revile their gods" (cf. Jos. *C. Ap.* 2.236−7). Paganism was to be attacked in the land of Israel, where it polluted the holy soil and brought Jews into dangerous temptation, but the idea that gentiles should be forbidden idolatry wherever they lived was a new notion. It was, of course, rapidly to become widespread, for it is a constant element in the formulations of the Noachide Laws found, in varying guises, in rabbinic texts from the mid third century A. D. onwards (*tAb. Zar.* 8:4)[24]. But not universal, for there is every likelihood that some of the gentile godfearers honoured in the Jewish synagogues in Aphrodisias in Asia Minor in the early third century continued to participate in pagan worship – those who held the rank of city councillor had little option in the matter[25].

The suppression of the revolt was exceptionally bloody. Curiously enough the only surviving Jewish document likely to have been written in the region in the aftermath of the war, *Sibylline Oracles* 5.1−50 (to be ascribed to a Jewish author in Egypt before A. D. 130 if verse 51 was a later addition composed under M. Aurelius), alludes in optimistic and friendly terms to Hadrian[26]. But Hadrian (before the Bar Kochba revolt) may have been seen as friendly compared to Trajan – he had, after all, withdrawn Roman troops from Mesopotamia, presumably to the great relief of the Jewish communities there. It seems likely enough that the outbreak of the Bar Kochba war in A. D. 132 was in part caused by the horror of Palestinian Jews at the fate of their diaspora compatriots, but no text attests the link: rabbinic sources which refer to the latter revolt

---

[23] See G. Delling, 'Josephus und die heidnischen Religionen', *Klio* 43−45 (1965), 263−9.

[24] D. Novak, *The Image of the Non-Jew in Judaism* (Toronto, 1983). See also R. Goldenberg, 'The place of other religions in ancient Jewish thought, with particular reference to early rabbinic Judaism', in M. E. Marty and F. E. Greenspahn, ed., *Pushing the Faith* (New York, 1988), pp. 27−40; M. Goodman, 'Proselytising in rabbinic Judaism', *JJS* 40 (1989), 175−85.

[25] J. Reynolds and R. Tannenbaum, *Jews and God-Fearers at Aphrodisias* (Cambridge Philological Society, suppl. vol. 12) (Cambridge, 1987).

[26] On the date, see Schürer, *History* 3:644−5.

are almost totally silent about the former, and the evidence which is sometimes adduced for long-term preparations by the rebels in Palestine during the decades of the 120s is rather tenuous[27].

Where Jewish communities survived – and that included huge numbers in Northern Syria, Asia Minor and Greece, and the city of Rome itself – life appears to have continued remarkably unaffected by the revolts under Trajan and Hadrian. In his description of the Jew Trypho in Asia Minor after A. D. 135 (*Dial. c. Tryph.*, passim), Justin Martyr gives the impression that the freedom of this Jew at least to practise his religion had been quite unaffected by any religious persecution that may have been inflicted on Jews in Judaea after Bar Kochba's defeat. It may be that the prohibition of religious practice recorded by the tannaitic texts as a feature of a "time of danger" which, if it is to be situated in any particular time, should probably be located in this period (cf. *mErub* 10:1; *mM.Sh* 4:11; *tErub* 5(8):24; *tMeg* 2:4) was confined to Judaea, and that the ban on Jews living near Jerusalem, as recorded by Justin (*Dial. c. Tryph.* 16), was enforced not by wholesale forcible removal of the peasantry but by forbidding the existing population to continue with their religious customs, which were seen as responsible for the outbreak of the war. In that case diaspora Jews were not touched by such hostile actions. But one cannot tell from the magnificence of the huge synagogue erected in the very centre of Sardis in the mid third century A. D. or some time after whether the Jews there enjoyed peaceful and harmonious relations with their neighbours or, like the Jews whose synagogue at Alexandria had been one of the wonders of the world before its destruction in A. D. 117 (*tSukk* 4:6), whether they may have displayed their wealth and power in an attempt to claim rights and prestige from generally hostile fellow citizens[28].

At any rate it seems likely that in the eyes of the Roman state they, like all Jews, continued to be identified as Jews primarily by their religious customs. This preference for a religious more than ethnic definition of Jewishness may have had considerable consequences. When the Roman emperor finally felt a need for a single Jewish leader with whom the state could negotiate on behalf of the Jews, it was to a religious leader, the rabbinic patriarch, that he turned. Such formal recognition may not have come about until well into the fourth

---

[27] On the causes of the Bar-Kochba war, see the various works quoted in the survey by B. Isaac and A. Oppenheimer, 'The revolt of Bar-Kokhba, scholarship and ideology', *JJS* 36 (1985), 33–60; for alleged evidence of long-term preparations, see S. Applebaum, *Prolegomena to the Study of the Second Judaism Revolt* (British Archaeological Reports, supp. series 7) (Oxford, 1976); A. Kloner and Y. Tepper, *The Hiding Complexes in the Judean Shephelah* (Tel-Aviv, 1987) (in Hebrew).

[28] On the synagogue in Sardis, see A. R. Seager and A. T. Kraabel, 'The synagogue and the Jewish community', in G. M. A. Hanfmann, ed., *Sardis from Prehistoric to Roman Times* (Cambridge, Mass. 1983), chapter 9. see also A. T. Kraabel, 'The Roman diaspora: six questionable assumptions', *JJS* 33 (1982), 445–64.

century, by which time the emperors were Christian. It is impossible to calculate how important was such recognition by Rome of the institutions of the Palestinian patriarch, and the grant to him of the right to raise taxes for the rabbinic academies, in the eventual (and undated) rise of rabbinic Judaism to the status of a normative religion, espoused in one form or another by Jews throughout the diaspora as much as in the land of Israel[29].

Bibliography

Applebaum, S., *Prolegomena to the Study of the Second Jewish Revolt* (British Archaeological Reports, supp. series 7) (Oxford, 1976).
– *Jews and Greeks in Ancient Cyrene* (Leiden, 1979).
Barnes, T. D., 'Trajan and the Jews', *JJS* 40 (1989), 145–62.
Burr, V. A., *Tiberius Iulius Alexander* (Bonn, 1955).
Cohen, S. J. D., 'Pagan and Christian evidence on the ancient synagogue', in L. I. Levine, ed., *The Synagogue in Late Antiquity* (New York, 1987), pp. 159–81.
– 'Crossing the boundary and becoming a Jew', *HTR* 82 (1989), 13–33.
Delling, G., 'Josephus und die heidnischen Religionen', *Kilo* 43–45 (1965), 263–9.
Goldenberg, R., 'The place of other religions in ancient Jewish thought, with particular reference to early rabbinic Judaism', in M. E. Marty and F. E. Greenspahn, ed., *Pushing the Faith* (New York, 1988), pp. 27–40.
Goodman, M., *State and Society in Roman Galilee, A. D. 132–212* (Totowa, 1983).
– *The Ruling Class of Judaea: the origins of the Jewish Revolt against Rome, A. D. 66–70* (Cambridge, 1987).
– 'Proselytising in rabbinic Judaism', *JJS* 40 (1989), 175–85.
– 'Nerva, the *fiscus Judaicus* and Jewish identity', *JRS* 79 (1989), 40–4.
– 'Identity and authority in ancient Judaism', *Judaism* 39 (1990), 192–201.
– 'The Roman State and the Jewish Patriarch in the third century', in L. I. Levine, ed., *Galilee in Late Antiquity* (New York, 1992), pp. 127–39.
Isaac, B. and Oppenheimer, A., 'The revolt of Bar Kokhba, scholarship and ideology', *JJS* 36 (1985), 33–60.
Kloner, A. and Tepper, Y., *The Hiding Complexes in the Judean Shephelah* (Tel Aviv, 1987) (in Hebrew).
Kraabel, A. T., 'The Roman diaspora: six questionable assumptions', *JJS* 33 (1982), 445–64.
Kraemer, R. S., 'On the meaning of the term "Jew" in Greco-Roman inscriptions', *HTR* 82 (1989), 35–53.
Lüderitz, G., *Corpus jüdischer Zeugnisse aus der Cyrenaika* (Tübingen, 1983).
Marty, M. E. and F. E. Greenspahn, ed., *Pushing the Faith: Proselytism and civility in a pluralistic world* (New York, 1988).

---

[29] On formal recognition of the Patriarch by the Roman state, see *Cod. Theod.* 16.8.13 and *passim*. See also Goodman, 'Jewish Patriarch', for the argument in greater detail.

Mattingly, H. and Carson, R. A. G., eds., *Coins of the Roman Empire in the British Museum*, 9 vols. (London, 1923–75).

Novak, D., *The Image of the Non-Jew in Judaism* (Toronto, 1983).

Pucci, M., *La rivolta ebraica al tempo di Traiano* (Pisa, 1981).

Reynolds, J. and Tannenbaum, R., *Jews and God-Fearers at Aphrodisias* (Cambridge Philological Society, suppl. vol. 12) (Cambridge, 1987).

Seager, A. R. and Kraabel, A. T., 'The synagogue and the Jewish community', in G. M. A. Hanfmann, ed., *Sardis from Prehistoric to Roman Times* (Cambridge, Mass., 1983), chapter 9.

Tcherikover, V. A., Fuks, A. and Stern, M., *Corpus Papyrorum Judaicarum*, 3 vols. (Cambridge, Mass., 1957–64).

Thompson, L. A., 'Domitian and the Jewish tax', *Historia* 31 (1982), 329–42.

Vermes, G., 'A summary of the Law by Flavius Josephus', *Novum Testamentum* 24 (1982), 289–203.

The Septuagint as a Collection
of Writings Claimed by Christians:
Justin and the Church Fathers before Origen

by

MARTIN HENGEL

1. The Translation Legend in Judaism
and the Number of Translators

Despite its Jewish origin, what we today call the "Septuagint," at least as regards its designation, transmission, and use, is first of all a *Christian* collection of writings. We do indeed know from the legend of the epistle of Pseudo-Aristeas[1] and from Josephus (himself dependent on Pseudo-Aristeas)[2] that the law of Moses allegedly was translated from Hebrew to Greek under Ptolemy II Philadelphus (282-246 B.C.E.) by seventy-two Jewish elders (six from each tribe) sent to Alexandria by the high priest of Jerusalem. In Jewish-Hellenistic sources, however, we never encounter what among Christian authors later became the frequent, indeed typical designation οἱ ἑβδομήκοντα as a reference to the translators themselves. The actual translation of the Pentateuch into Greek during the time of the second Ptolemy in Alexandria is probably historically accurate, since its earliest witness, the Jewish chronographer Demetrius, was still using that translation in his own exegetical work toward the end of the third cen-

---

[1] *Ep. Arist.* 50, 273; the translation took seventy-two days (307).
[2] *Ant.* 12.11-118.

This study is dedicated to Peter Stuhlmacher at his sixtieth birthday (January 1, 1992).

When I came to Tübingen in 1964 from the business world, he was an assistant to Professor Käsemann. We completed our *Habilitationsschriften* almost concurrently at the beginning of 1967, and received positions together at Erlangen in 1968, then at Tübingen in 1972. I view our friendship and professional relationship — extending over more than twenty-five years — as a very special gift.

Thanks to Marietta Hämmerle for copying the difficult manuscript, and to Anna Maria Schwemer, Dr. Christoph Markschies, and Friedemann Steck for careful proofing and sundry suggestions.

tury B.C.E. during the time of Ptolemy IV Philopator. The number seventy-two, however, is legendary, and was probably derived in analogy to Num. 11:24ff. and 26ff. (70 + 2).

In his own account of the translation, Philo does not mention the number of participants at all, making do instead with the assertion that the high priest "selected the most respectable of the Hebrews whom he had about him, who in addition to their knowledge of their national scriptures, had also been well instructed in Greek literature."[3] Although Josephus, with the carelessness typical of his writing, speaks about "the names of the *seventy* elders," "it does not seem to me to be necessary to set down the names," a few lines before he had recounted that *six* elders from each of the *twelve* tribes came, and that the work was completed in seventy-two days.[4]

Although this carelessness may, as Pelletier suspects, derive from the fact that "the Seventy" had already become a fixed expression in Greek-speaking Judaism for the translation of the law used in worship services, we still have no concrete witnesses to this. Nor do any New Testament authors or the apostolic fathers provide any witness for the designation of the translators of the Pentateuch or even of the Greek Old Testament in general as "the Seventy," or even any reference to the "seventy elders" or "translators" and their work. Their references instead were, as in Judaism, to "scripture" or "scriptures," to "writings," to the "law and prophets,"[5] or simply to "the prophets." The overall scope of these collection(s) of writings remains vague, since we have no witnesses for any pre-Christian "Alexandrian Septuagint *canon*."[6] At most, one might deduce from the unusual number of seventy-two dispatched disciples in Luke 10:1 (secondary *varia lectio:* seventy) that Luke or his source was familiar with the number of translators. Just as they translated the Torah for the entire world, so also were the disciples to spread the message of God's kingdom. But all this remains conjecture. It is only in later rabbinic traditions, themselves obviously in part presupposing the Christian version of the legend, that reference is made *expressis verbis* in *Jewish* sources to the seventy-two (or seventy).[7] Here, refer-

---

[3] *Vit. Mos.* 2.32; see p. 73 below.

[4] *Ant.* 12.57, cf. 56, 99 (12 x 6), 107; cf. A. Pelletier, *Flavius Josèphe adapteur de la Lettre d'Aristée* (Études et commentaires XLV; Paris, 1962) 125-27, 199.

[5] Concerning this designation, see J. Barton, "'The Law and the Prophets': Who Are the Prophets?" *OTS* 23 (1984) 1-18. Concerning the formulation, see already the prologue to Sirach: ὁ νόμος καὶ αἱ προφητεῖαι καὶ τὰ λοιπὰ τῶν βιβλίων; see in this regard H. P. Rüger, in J.-D. Kaestli and O. Wermelinger, eds., *Le Canon de l'Ancien Testament* (Geneva, 1984) 59, 66-69; also D. Barthélemy, in op. cit., 13.

[6] See the fundamental critique of the hypothesis of an Alexandrian canon in A. C. Sundberg, *The Old Testament in the Early Church* (Cambridge/London, 1964); cf. M. Harl, G. Dorival, and O. Munnich, *La Bible Grecque des Septante* (Paris, 1988) 112-19.

[7] *b. Meg.* 9a, Billerbeck 3.322; Sof. 1.7; see in this regard G. Veltri, "Die Tora des Königs Ptolemäus. Untersuchungen zum Übersetzungsverständnis des hellenistischen und palästinischen

ence could in isolated cases also be made to the "Seventy."[8] At the same time, however, direct reference was also made to only five elders,[9] a number recalling Jesus' five disciples in *b. Sanh.* 43a, especially since the number five was associated with a brusque devaluation of the translation: "This day was as fateful for Israel as the day on which the golden calf was erected, for the Torah would not be adequately translated."[10]

2. Justin

Against this background, one cannot fail to notice that the expression οἱ ἑβδομήκοντα as a designation for a "holy text" in the Greek language (or, in reality, for the translators of this text) is first used in a stereotypical fashion only by *Christian* authors, the first instance of which occurs where an author adequately trained in rhetoric and philosophy squares off apologetically against a Jewish dialogue partner, namely, in Justin's *Dialogue with Trypho*.

2.1. The Legend in Justin's Apology

Justin speaks twice in what one would have to call a rather striking fashion about the "seventy elders at the court of Ptolemy," the king of Egypt (or of the Egyptians),[11] once in an abbreviated fashion about "your elders at the court of Ptolemy, the king of the Egyptians,"[12] and five times simply about "the Seventy," associating formulaically the verb ἐξηγεῖσθαι (once also ἐξήγησις) with the Seventy.[13] In the process, Justin uses his favorite word ἐξηγεῖσθαι without distinction in the sense of both "interpret" and "translate" while avoiding the more unequivocal ἑρμηνεύειν.[14] Beyond this, he mentions the Egyptian king

---

Judentums" (diss., Berlin, 1991), to appear in Texte und Studien zum antiken Judentum. Cf. also G. Doreval, in M. Harl et al. (note 6), 120-25, and Karlheinz Müller, "Die rabbinischen Nachrichten über die Anfänge der Septuaginta," in *Wort, Lied und Götterspruch. Beiträge zur Septuaginta. Festschrift Joseph Ziegler*, ed. J. Schreiner and J. Schnackenburg (Würzburg, 1972) 72-93. Concerning the number seventy or seventy one/two in connection with the elders of Num. 11:16, 24ff., see *b. Sanh.* 16b par., Billerbeck 2.166: Moses, too, chooses six from each tribe, but marked only seventy notes with "elders," leaving two blank (Num. 11:26).

[8] Sepher Torah 1.6; Al-Qirqisani, Kitab al-riyad 1.4.16; see in this regard Veltri, op. cit. (note 7), 74ff., 88ff.

[9] Sof. 1.7; ARN Rec. B §37 et passim; see Veltri, op. cit. (note 7), 76.

[10] Sof. 1.7; Veltri, op. cit. (note 7), 70ff. This is followed by the positive estimation of *b. Meg.* 9a; Veltri, 66f. Cf. n. 75 below. Perhaps the "Pentateuch" is also behind the number five.

[11] *Dial.* 68.7; 71.1.

[12] 84.3.

[13] 120.4: οὕτως ἐξηγήσαντο οἱ ἑβδομήκοντα; 131.1: ὅτι οἱ ἑβδομήκοντα ἐξηγήσαντο; 137.3 (bis): ὡς ἐξηγήσαντο οἱ ἑβδομήκοντα; cf. 124.3: ἐν τῇ τῶν ἑβδομηκόντα ἐξηγήσει εἴρηται.

[14] See E. J. Goodspeed, *Index Apologeticus* . . . (1912) 106f.: ca. 45 times; ἐξήγησις 15 times. See also n. 58 below.

Ptolemy five times in connection with the venerable translation of the seventy elders, including once in the earlier first *Apology*.[15]

There he also deals more in depth with the translation legend itself, albeit in a highly peculiar form deviating both from the *Epistle of Aristeas* (or Josephus) and from Philo, and showing that he was familiar neither with the *Epistle of Aristeas* nor with Philo's account, and that he had only a relatively superficial acquaintance with the resulting legend.[16] On the other hand, he presupposes that both his fictitious dialogue partners in the *Dialogue* and his (probably over-whelmingly Christian) readers[17] are already familiar with the story of the seventy elders and their translation work, and that he no longer need recount the story as he did for the (not least also) gentile readers of the apology. He is in all likelihood referring back here (as is often the case in the *Dialogue*) to older sources. It may, as Prigent suspected, involve his *Treatise Against All Heresies That Have Arisen* already mentioned in *Apol.* i.26.8. The frequent references to the Seventy in the *Dialogue* might also be echoing the dialogue between the Jewish Christian Jason and the Jew Papiscus composed shortly after the Bar-Cochba revolt (132-135 C.E.), presumably from the hand of the otherwise little-known Jewish Christian Aristo of Pella; this dialogue, like that with Trypho, discusses the fulfillment of Old Testament prophecies in Jesus Christ.[18] It seems likely to me that this apologetic writing was already appealing to the authority

---

[15] *Apol.* i.31.2; *Dial.* 68.7; 71.1, 2; 84.3.

[16] *Apol.* i.31.1-5. See pp. 45f., 71ff., 79f. below.

[17] Concerning the probable readership of the *Dialogue,* see C. H. Cosgrove, "Justin Martyr and the Emerging Christian Canon," *VigChr* 36 (1982) 209-32 (esp. 211ff.). The discussion revolved around whether the intended readers were Jews or gentiles; Justin could hardly have convinced Jews with this argument, and gentiles would have found the whole thing almost unreadable. The readers were more likely educated Christians positioned at the double front between Marcion (or gnostics) on the one hand and "hellenistic" Judaism (as strong as ever) on the other; or they were educated (gentile or Jewish) sympathizers of the new faith. The *Dialogue's* ponderous argumentation made it ill-suited for use as a "missionary writing."

[18] P. Prigent, *Justin et l'Ancien Testament* (EtB; Paris, 1964); P. Nautin, in *École des Hautes Études* (1967/68) 162-67, first drew attention to the connection with Aristo of Pella. Concerning this problem, see recently the splendid work of O. Skarsaune, *The Proof from Prophecy: A Study in Justin Martyr's Proof-Text Tradition* (1987) 3ff., 22ff. Concerning Justin's *Syntagma,* cf. also Eusebius, *HE* 4.11.10, who adduces *Apol.* i.26.8, but then cites Irenaeus in 4.18.9; Irenaeus in *Haer.* 4.6.2 quotes from a *Syntagma contra Marcion* (cf. *Apol.* i.58.1). The reference is presumably to the same earlier work. Concerning Aristo of Pella, see op. cit., 234f., note 13; text fragments can be found in C. T. von Otto, *CorpApol* IX (1872; repr. 1969) 356ff. The dialogue appears for the first time in Celsus, i.e., not all that long after Justin; see Origen, *Cels.* 4.52: ἐν ᾧ ἀναγέγραπται Χριστιανὸς Ἰουδαίῳ διαλεγόμενος ἀπὸ τῶν ἰουδαϊκῶν γραφῶν καὶ δεικνὺς τὰς περὶ τοῦ Χριστοῦ προφητείας ἐφαρμόζειν τῷ Ἰησοῦ. John of Scythopolis is the first to mention Aristo as an author (see in this regard H. Urs von Balthasar, *Scholastik* 15 [1940] 16-38; reference from C. Markschies). See further A. von Harnack, *Geschichte der altchristlichen Literatur* (1893) 1.1.92ff. For more recent bibliography, see V. Zangara, in *Dictionnaire Encyclopédique du Christianisme Ancien* (1990) 1.228, and B. Altaner and A. Stuiber, *Patrologie* (⁹1978) 62; H. Schreckenberg, *Die christlichen Adversus-Judaeos-Texte und ihr literarisches und historisches Umfeld* (Frankfurt/Berlin, 1982) 604f.

of the Seventy as allies of the Christians over against Jewish dialogue partners, and that this might also explain Justin's self-confidence in the matter.

In the *Apology*, Justin's treatment of the translation legend is associated with his proof of Christ's divine sonship on the basis of the witness of "God's prophets" among the Jews, whose prophecies (προφητεῖαι) the prophets themselves committed to written form in scrolls in their mother tongue, Hebrew, and which the kings at the time acquired and carefully preserved. When King Ptolemy was collecting the writings of every nation for his library and heard of these prophecies, he allegedly sent to Herod (!), the king of the Jews at that time, and requested that these prophetic writings be sent to him. Herod did so, and because the Egyptians could not read them, Ptolemy sent anew to Herod "and asked for some persons to translate them into the Greek tongue" (τοὺς μεταβαλοῦντας αὐτὰς εἰς τὴν ἑλλάδα φωνὴν ἀνθρώπους ἀποστεῖλαι). "After this was accomplished, the books remained in the possession of the Egyptians from that day to this, as they are also in the possession of every Jew, wherever he be. But these Jews, though they read the books, fail to grasp their meaning."[19]

In contradistinction to the *Dialogue*, this earlier narrative (ca. 152-155 C.E.) does not mention the *seventy elders;* in other ways, too, its deviation from the traditional translation legend is considerable. The telling discrepancy, however, the one revealing that this already represents a typical *Christian* version, is that Justin no longer speaks about the translation of the Mosaic law, that is, of the Pentateuch; instead, he speaks of all the *"prophetic writings"* that were preserved for the sake of their prophecies (προφητεῖαι) and translated into the language of the Greek world at the initiative of the Egyptian king. That is, the "law" or the Pentateuch is now being subsumed under these "prophetic writings." Both Judaism and even New Testament authors of early Christianity (e.g., Paul and John) could still refer to all the Holy Scriptures as "Torah" (νόμος), since according to the Jewish view the "prophets" and "writings" basically merely interpret the Torah. Justin and later Christian authors, however, view all the books of the Bible as "prophetic writings" because their decisive content actually consists of prophecies foretelling Christ and his eschatological salvific community.[20]

---

[19] *Apol.* 31.1-5. Concerning the lack of understanding on the part of the Jews, see p. 46, n. 28; p. 61, n. 88; and p. 66, n. 107 below.

[20] Concerning the entirety of scripture as "Torah" in Judaism and Christianity, see Billerbeck, 2.542f. (on John 10:42; cf. also 12.34; 15.25), 3.159 on Rom. 3:19, and 3.462 on 1 Cor. 14:21. Concerning the early Christian interpretation of the scriptures as prophecies, see already Rom. 1:2; Heb. 1:1; 1 Pet. 1:10; etc. In both Judaism and Christianity, the notion of *pars pro toto* applied, though with different centers of gravity. Judaism considered the law to be determinative and the prophets its interpreters; Christianity considered the messianic prophecies to be determinative, while ritual law was under certain circumstances viewed as a later concession to the Jews' "hardness of heart" (cf. Mark 10:5; *Dial.* 18.2; 45.3; 46.7). The scriptures were read from the perspective of their fulfillment in the eschatologically determined present: 1 Cor. 10:11; Rom. 4:23f. This represents a hermeneutic at least partially prefigured in Qumran; see 1QpHab 2:8f.; 7:4f.; CD 6:10f.; and in this regard O. Betz, *Offenbarung und Schriftforschung in der Qumransekte* (WUNT 6; 1960) 62ff., 73ff.

Shortly after recounting his own version of the translation legend, Justin calls Moses "the *first of the prophets*"; he is then able to use this reference to Moses as a prophet almost stereotypically in the *Apology*.[21] To gentile readers, this effectively introduces Moses, the familiar lawgiver of the Jews, as a prophet who foretold Christ. That is, for the Christians the prophet displaces the Jewish lawgiver, and the real lawgiver now becomes Christ, the bringer of the New Law, himself identical with God's word and law.[22] By contrast, the designation of Moses as a "prophet" appears nowhere in the *Dialogue,* presumably out of consideration for Justin's Jewish dialogue partners, with whom the simple name "Moses" now suffices (ca. twenty-five times).

That Justin's account of the translation in the *Apology* is more likely addressing gentile readers also emerges from his reference, one not found in the *Epistle of Aristeas,* to a double initiative on the part of the (gentile) king Ptolemy, who requests first the prophetic writings and only then the translators.[23] The seventy Jewish elders are not mentioned at all. One key element here is the assertion that these writings can be found "until this day" in Egypt, that is, in the world-famous library in Alexandria, and furthermore also "everywhere among the Jews." That is to say, not only the royal library itself but also the Jews dispersed throughout the kingdom have faithfully preserved the Greek translation of the ancient Hebrew prophecies that have now been fulfilled for Christians. Justin's account serves thus as an introduction to the scriptural quotations used in the *Apology*. Skarsaune believes that the mention of the translation here is con-

---

[21] *Apol.* 32.1: πρῶτος τῶν προφητῶν γενόμενος, cf. 32.2; 33.6; 44.1; 60.8; and p. 48 below. The prophetic Spirit speaks through Moses: 54.5, 7; 62.2; 63.16; 44.8. Plato was dependent on the prophet Moses. Concerning Moses as a prophet, see Deut. 18:15; 34:10; Sir. 46:1; further J. Jeremias, *TDNT* 4.849ff.; cf. *Ass. Mos.* 11.16 and A. Rosmarin, *Mose im Lichte der Aggada* (1932) 19f. See already Deut. 18:15-20 and 4QTestim 5ff. Compared with Moses' other designations, this one is not found all that frequently in Judaism, though it is unequivocal given Deut. 34:10. There, too, later midrashim refer to him as the first of all prophets (Rosmarin, loc. cit., n. 28); indeed, "he is the father of prophecy itself" (19f., n. 32). In *Barn.* 6.8, Moses is introduced as ὁ ἄλλος προφήτης Μωϋσῆς after "prophet citations" from the Psalms and Isaiah, he being the only one mentioned by name. *Barnabas* otherwise normally uses the nameless προφήτης as an introduction to scriptural citations (26 times).

[22] Cf. *Dial.* 14.3; 18.3, 12: Christ as καινὸς νομοθέτης. By contrast, Moses is merely the lawgiver of the Jews, *Dial.* 1.3; cf. 112.3; 127.2. According to 11.4, Christ is the "new law and the new covenant"; cf. 12.1; 122.5; cf. also Melito, *Passahomile* 45f.; *Barn.* 2.6; *Herm. Sim.* 8.3.2 (69.2); *Ker Petri* 1 (*NTApo* [5th ed.] 2.38: Clement of Alexandria, *Strom.* 1.29.182; 2.15.68).

[23] *Apol.* i.31.2-4; cf. by contrast *Ep. Arist.* 35–51, the single piece of correspondence between Ptolemy and the high priest Eleazar requesting translators along with the law. Only in the utterly deviating and fantastically embellished version of Epiphanius does the king again write two letters to "the teachers in Jerusalem." In answer to the first, he receives the writings themselves; only after the second do the translators come (see *De mens et pond* 10ff., ed. E. Moutsoulas [Athens, 1971] 153ff., and in the complete Syriac text, ed. J. E. Dean, *Epiphanius' Treatise on Weights and Measures: The Syriac Version* [Oriental Institute of the University of Chicago Studies in Ancient Oriental Civilization 11; Chicago, 1935]; see n. 143 below).

nected with the mission to the gentiles, while the attendant "text-critical" problems arise only in connection with the dispute with Jews in the *Dialogue*.[24]

The completely anachronistic introduction of King Herod as sender derives from Justin's utter lack of familiarity with postexilic Jewish history; on the basis of the Gospels (and Acts), Herod was for Justin the name of the Jewish king during the Hellenistic-Roman period. Historical training was not his strength. Furthermore, mention of Herod drew the translation closer to the period of the fulfillment (Matt. 2:3ff.; Luke 1:5). Justin commits other historical errors as well in connection with the Jewish "King Herod";[25] he apparently possessed neither interest in nor knowledge of history. He mentions no Jewish high priest by name, nor does he really follow the synchronism of Luke's Gospel (3:1f.), a work he otherwise highly values.[26] Things are much different in Irenaeus and Tertullian (see §§4.3, 4.4 below). This historical ignorance on the part of the first Christian "philosopher" stands in peculiar contrast to his otherwise extremely attentive dealing with the "scriptures" and their text (see §2.6 below).

2.2. Justin's "Old Testament Library"

Justin does not further identify the prophetic writings that King Ptolemy had translated. We may assume that he is including the overwhelming majority of those

---

[24] *Op. cit.* (note 18), 45f. Skarsaune suspects that this narrative already constitutes "an introduction to the scriptural quotations in the testimony source(s)" Justin used. He is overestimating, however, the dependence on the *Epistle of Aristeas*, with which Justin was doubtless not familiar. Although in *Ep. Arist.* 9, Demetrius of Phaleron commands πρὸς τὸ συναγαγεῖν . . . ἅπαντα τὰ κατὰ τὴν οἰκουμένην βιβλία, while in *Apol.* i.31.2 we read that the king tried τὰ πάντων ἀνθρώπων συγγράμματα συνάγειν, this still does not suggest literary dependency.

[25] Although a medieval Samaritan chronicle mentions that Ptolemy had a commander in Palestine by the name of Herod, this does not permit one to assume the presence of a Samaritan tradition in Justin; so P. R. Weis, "Some Samaritanisms of Justin Martyr," *JTS* 45 (1944) 199-205, and W. Schmid, "Ein rätselhafter Anachronismus bei Justinus," *HJ* 77 (1957/58) 358-61; cf. by contrast Skarsaune (note 18), 46, n. 62. Justin often refers to a Jewish "King Herod": *Apol.* 40.6; *Dial.* 52.3; 77.4; 78.2; 102.3; 103.3, 4, emphasizing his lawless behavior. In connection with Isa. 8:4, he is thus called the King of the Assyrians (77.4). In *Dial.* 103 he distinguishes between the Herod associated with the infanticide, on the one hand, and his successor with the same name, on the other. The direct successor of the first Herod, Archelaus (Matt. 2:22), allegedly died young (!), and the second Herod became king of the Jews in his stead. It is to this Herod that Luke 23:7 is referring, as predicted in Hos. 10:6. Cf., e.g., also the naive identification of the Roman inscription concerning the god of oaths and treaties, Semo Sancus, with Simon Magus in *Apol.* i.26.2. And Justin was writing in Rome! He was utterly unfamiliar with Josephus.

[26] *Apol.* i.13.3 might refer to this. In *Apol.* i.35.9, Justin "invents" the *Acts of Pontius Pilate* in which one can allegedly read about the events surrounding Jesus' trial; cf. 48.3. That is, he is assuming that Pilate's official records in Rome are naturally still accessible; cf. Tertullian, *Apol.* 21.18, 24. See in this regard also L. Abramowski, in P. Stuhlmacher, ed., *Das Evangelium und die Evangelien* (WUNT 28; Tübingen, 1983) 351f., n. 37; concerning apocryphal material associated with Pilate, see recently W. Speyer, "Neue Pilatusapokryphen," *VigChr* 32 (1978) 53-59 = *Frühes Christentum im antiken Strahlungsfeld* (WUNT 50; Tübingen, 1989) 228-34.

particular "holy scriptures" also found in the developing Jewish canon itself, including the historical books up to Chronicles and Ezra, whose use is, admittedly, already somewhat questionable.[27] He cites only two passages from Job,[28] and none at all (excepting a possible allusion) from Qoheleth (Ecclesiastes), the last writing of the LXX to be translated. References to Canticles and Esther are entirely absent. Even in Judaism itself, these last three writings were yet the objects of dispute during the first half of the second century.[29] Hence we cannot determine exactly what Justin included in these "prophecies," nor what in his view King Ptolemy actually had translated into Greek. For example, he cites Lamentations only once (*Apol.* i.55.5) as a prophetic oracle in what is already an altered Christian form and as proof that the nose has the form of the cross.[30]

Hence the "Old Testament library" to which Justin had direct access may have included not only the Psalter but also the prophetic books (including Daniel), the Pentateuch, and perhaps also Proverbs, Job, and the historical books. It is difficult to decide in each individual instance whether he did not also excerpt texts from older or even his own testimonial collections or from earlier apologetic works. The presence of more extensive Christian alterations in the texts suggests the involvement of such collections, though these alterations were admittedly incorporated into the Christian LXX manuscripts as well. In any event, there was as yet no "canon" that was as clearly defined as the Jewish canon with

---

[27] In *Apol.* i.41.1-4, Justin presents 1 Chron. 16:23-31 as the preferred text form of a Davidic prophecy, one largely identical with Ps. 95(LXX 96):1, 2, 4-10. The Christian addendum at the end shows that the text derives from a testimonial collection; cf. in this regard O. Skarsaune (note 18), 35-42: "The text in 1. Apol 41,1-4 looks like a carefully composed harmony between the two LXX texts with 1. Chron 16 as the basic text" (p. 35). Whereas in 1 Chron. 16 the psalm of Asaph and his kin is sung, Ps. 95 is a psalm of David, and in *Dial.* 73.1, Justin expressly accuses the Jews of having omitted the decisive statement ἀπὸ τοῦ ξύλου in "David's ninety-fifth psalm"; see pp. 57ff. below. Concerning the other two references to Chronicles, see *op. cit.*, 38, n. 43. Although Justin does twice mention the name Ezra as that of a biblical prophet (72.1; 120.5), the text he cites concerning the Passover as a *typos* for Christ is not found in the LXX manuscripts and probably derives from a Christian testimonial collection; see P. Prigent (note 18), 174f., and O. Skarsaune (note 18), 42. See in this regard pp. 56f. below. The form in which Justin was familiar with "Ezra" (Esdras, 1 or 2 Esdras, Esdras-Apocalypse) thus remains a completely open question.

[28] Job 1:6 and 2:1 in *Dial.* 79.4.

[29] Cf. Eccl. 12:7 with *Dial.* 6.2, though there the issue involves considerations within the framework of generally obtaining ancient or stoic (ζωτικὸν πνεῦμα) doctrines of the soul. Concerning Qoheleth and Canticles and the Jewish canon, see D. Barthélemy, in J.-D. Kaestli and O. Wermelinger, eds., *Le Canon de l'Ancien Testament* (Geneva, 1984) 20f., 26-30; cf. also G. Dorival in M. Harl, G. Dorival, and O. Munnich, *La Bible Greque des Septante* (Paris, 1988) 92f., 97, 111, 105ff., 114.

[30] Lam. 4:20: πνεῦμα προσώπου ἡμῶν χριστὸς κυρίου (conjecture by Rahlfs instead of χριστὸς κύριος mss; Ziegler follows him; cf. Ps. Sol. 17:32). Justin, *Apol.* i.55.5 reads: πνεῦμα προσώπου ἡμῶν χριστὸς κύριος. This is the first witness for this *emendatio christiana,* an emendation that, with the exception of the Ethiopic and Arabic translations, succeeded in completely displacing the original. See Ziegler in loc. cit. O. Skarsaune (note 18), 162, suspects that this derives from a testimonial collection, and refers to its use in Irenaeus and Tertullian.

its twenty-two writings in Josephus[31] and the twenty-four among the rabbis following the "council of Jamnia."[32] In all likelihood, this canon was essentially identical with the writings used in the Roman worship service and in catechetical instruction, something suggested by the extensive concurrence between the biblical books cited by Justin and by Clement of Rome.[33] The first writer known to us to address the problem of the canonical "writings of the Old Covenant" (τὰ τῆς παλαιᾶς διαθήκης βιβλία) was Melito of Sardis, approximately one or two decades after Justin; he brought home from a pilgrimage to the Holy Land an exact list of these "writings of the Old Covenant." From these writings he assembled excerpts (ἐκλογαί) in six books "on the Redeemer and our entire faith"; that is, he composed an extensive testimonial collection of his own, doubtless also providing a commentary.[34] The interest of the addressee, Onesimus, in such testimonials and in the "number" and "sequence of the old books" shows that the "canon" had not yet been fixed unequivocally and that the

---

[31] *Ap.* i.38-46; see in this regard D. Barthélemy in Kaestli and Wermelinger (note 4), 29f.; R. Beckwith, *The Old Testament Canon of the New Testament Church and Its Background in Early Judaism* (London, 1985) 72ff., 79f., 118f., 371ff., 451.

[32] Concerning the twenty-two or twenty-four books, see R. Beckwith, op. cit., 235-73, and M. Harl et al. (note 6), 116f. The twenty-two corresponding letters of the Hebrew alphabet then become determinative for the church. Concerning the rabbinic canon, see D. Barthélemy (note 5), 9-46. Cf. also H. P. Rüger (note 5), 55-60. This, too, was still discussed with regard to its "peripheries" in the second millennium.

[33] See the passages printed in bold in the index of A. Jaubert, *Clément de Rome. Épître aux Corinthiens* (SC 167; 1971) 212ff.: Pentateuch, 1 Samuel, Psalms, Proverbs, Job, Habakkuk, Malachi, Isaiah, Jeremiah, Ezekiel, Daniel. 1 Clement also mentions Judith and Esther (55.5f.) and contains several apocryphal citations. The actual number of biblical books cited by Justin is correspondingly larger given the greater scope of his writings. Although he doubtless was also familiar with "apocrypha," he mentions almost none; see n. 38 below on *1 Enoch*. Conflicts arise involving addenda deriving from testimonial collections; see in this regard already G. Archambault, *Justin Dialogue avec Tryphon* (Paris, 1909) 1.344f., note with reference to *1 Clement; Barnabas;* (Pseudo) Cyprian on *Dial.* 71.2.

[34] Eusebius, *HE* 4.26.12-14. It contains the books of the Hebrew canon excepting Esther and Lamentations, the latter of which he (as probably also Justin; see n. 30 above) ascribed to Jeremiah. See in this regard R. Beckwith, op. cit. (note 31), 183-85, 389f. Cf. also the *Eclogae Propheticae* of Clement of Alexandria; on Clement, see also A. Méhat, "Hypothèse des 'Testimonia' à l'épreuve des Stromates. Remarques sur les citations de l'Ancien Testament chez Clément d'Alexandrie," in André Benoit and Pierre Prigent, eds., *La Bible et les Pères* (Paris, 1971) 229-42. Concerning the Old Testament florilegia in general, see H. Chadwick, "Florilegien," *RAC* 7.1146ff. (with reference to Justin as well). By their very nature, such collections were extremely variable and by no means, as J. Rendell Harris suspected (*Testimonies* [Cambridge, 1916; ²1920]), traceable back to a single, original Pauline source document identical with Matthew's collection of logia according to Papias (ii.58-70; cf. ii.108: "we may be sure that the average Christian man and woman had a slender Biblical collection, and depended for the most part on the hand book, which was published under the name and authority of St. Matthew." Here Harris transfers Reformational notions of the cathechism onto the early church. Testimony collections were also of interest primarily for the educated and were continually reissued and varied. One example can be found in Papyrus Michigan 3718; see A. Henrichs and E. M. Husselman, eds., "Christian Allegorizations (Pap. Mich. Inv. 3718)," *Zeitschrift für Papyrologie und Epigraphik (Bonn)* 3 (1968) 175-89.

testimonial tradition itself was still quite fluid. Of course, "the fact that the scope of neither the Christian nor the Jewish canon was completely fixed . . . did nothing to undermine its authority."[35]

One must admittedly supplement Campenhausen's assertion here by pointing out that, during the second century, the Christians lagged considerably behind the Jews in this process of fixing the canon, and, as the example of Melito demonstrates, from case to case took their orientation *nolens volens* from the more clearly delineated Hebrew canon itself. At least in the East, this particular tendency continued during the third and fourth centuries, constituting in the process one of the disruptive factors militating against the formulation of a clearly delineated Christian "Septuagint canon." In contrast to the Latin Bible in the West, such a canon never completely emerged in the East.

In his *Dialogue with Trypho* (as already in the *Apology*), Justin, too, limits his own use of "prophecies" to writings and quotations of recognized biblical authors, albeit ascribing to them in the process several texts that do not appear as such in our own LXX editions, something possibly attributable in part to his use of the rather fluid testimonial collections.[36] These are thus not independent "apocrypha" in the real sense. Accordingly, Moses remains "the first prophet" (see p. 44 above); this excludes any reference to the book of *Enoch*[37] or to any writings of the patriarchal collections. References to apocryphal apocalypses or wisdom works are similarly absent. This is all the more striking insofar as Justin, like *Barnabas* before him, was probably familiar with the book of *Enoch*.[38] Although he does mention the legend according to which Isaiah was martyred through being sawn asunder, this does not necessarily derive from a written source; it could just as easily have come from oral tradition or — even more likely — again from a testimonial collection.[39]

The later apocrypha of the LXX are also entirely absent.[40] In the *Dialogue*,

---

[35] H. von Campenhausen, *Die Entstehung der christlichen Bibel* (BHT 39; Tübingen, 1968) 79.

[36] So, e.g., a text of Ezra; see n. 27 above and p. 56 below.

[37] Even though *Enoch* is mentioned six times (*Dial.* 19.3; 23.1; 43.2; 45.2, 4; 92.2). He is above all a model for Christians, who like him live in spiritual rather than physical circumcision. A certain contradiction arises through his mention in *Apol.* i.31.7 of prophecies allegedly spoken 5,000, 3,000, 2,000, 1,000, and 800 years earlier. Still, according to him, the older prophecies since Adam apparently were mediated only through the "first prophet Moses." This would make Moses the first "written prophet." There has been prophecy since the Fall (Gen. 3:14 = *Dial.* 91.4).

[38] See in this regard R. H. Charles, *The Book of Henoch or 1. Enoch* (Oxford, 1912) LXXXIf., and *Apol.* ii.5.3; cf. i.5.2 with *1 Enoch* 7:1ff.; 9:8f., 15ff., 19ff., as well as *Apol.* ii.7.5. See also pp. 80f. below. *Barn.* 16.5 already cites as a γραφή an unknown apocryphon related to *1 Enoch* 89:56, 58, 66-88; see also 4.3. He is possibly using a testimonial witness here that condensed the *Enoch* text.

[39] *Dial.* 120.5; cf. *Asc. Isa.* 5 = *NTApo* (5th ed.) 2.553; *Vit. Proph.* 1.1; cf. Heb. 11:37; rabbinic references can be found in Billerbeck, 3.747 in loc., also *Tg. Isa.* 66:1; *Pes. Rab.* 4:3. See in this regard pp. 61f., n. 89 below.

[40] In *Dial.* 136.2 and 137.3, he is citing not Wis. 2:12 but Isa. 3:9f. Nor is Sirach referenced.

Justin is apparently limiting himself to those particular writings of the Jewish canon recognized by his Jewish dialogue partners. As he tells Trypho himself, he intends to discuss only "those textual passages recognized among your people."[41] Elsewhere, he accordingly states that he is trying to conduct his christological proof (τὴν ἀπόδειξιν τὴν περὶ Χριστοῦ) "not from the perspective of authors you do not recognize, but of those whom you still recognize even today."[42] One must point out that the references cited refer not really to entire books of scripture, but to individual textual *passages* being discussed. Even here, where the situation is much more complicated, Justin is taking his dialogue partners into consideration (apart from the one, bitterly contested exception, Isa. 7:14).

The Septuagint text, albeit limited to those particular books recognized by the Jews, apparently still represented the basis of dialogue on both sides of the Jewish-Christian debate. We find no evidence in Justin that his Jewish opponents were referring to any completely new recension of the Greek text such as that of Aquila, which presumably was introduced in Palestine as a Greek "targum" for translating the Hebrew scripture reading and only gradually asserted itself in the Diaspora as well.[43] Only Irenaeus first speaks about the translations of Theodotion and Aquila, while Symmachus is not attested until the third century.[44] Precisely in the case of Justin, however, the problem of the LXX text becomes even more complicated insofar as anonymous, earlier Palestinian recensions existed even before the great retranslations of the LXX oriented toward the original Hebrew text and associated with the names of the translators. Justin seems to have used such recension texts especially for quotations from the minor prophets in his *Dialogue,* while in the *Apology* he drew primarily from Christian versions of testimonial collections on the basis of the older LXX text.[45] This suggests that he was already becoming increasingly conscious of what we may call a "text-critical" problem.

Justin has no familiarity whatever with the books of the Maccabees, otherwise he could not have brought Ptolemy and Herod together.

[41] *Dial.* 7.12; ἐπὶ τὰς ἐκ τῶν ὁμολογουμένων ἔτι παρ' ὑμῖν τὰς ζητήσεις ποιεῖν ἔρχομαι. Cf. the end of 73.6. See pp. 60f. below.

[42] *Dial.* 120.5; ἀπὸ τῶν ὁμολογουμένων μέχρι νῦν ὑφ' ὑμῶν. Cf. in this regard O. Skarsaune (note 18), 34: in the case of Isa. 7:14 (see pp. 50ff. below) — "and in this case only — he refuses to argue from the text recognized by the Jews."

[43] See in this regard G. Veltri (note 7), 282-89, 316ff.

[44] *Haer.* 3.21.1 = Eusebius *HE* 5.8.10. According to him, both were proselytes. He first mentions Theodotion from Ephesus, and only then Aquila, who allegedly came from Pontus; see in this regard nn. 54 and 75 below. Origen was the first to use Symmachus; see n. 54 below.

[45] See in this regard the foundational study by O. Skarsaune (note 18), 17-23, 424ff. (esp. 426), based on the earlier investigations of W. Bousset, H. Köster, and P. Prigent (note 18). This interdependence between recension texts emerged through a comparison of Justin's own quotations from the minor prophets (esp. Mic. 4:3-7) and the Scroll of the Greek Minor Prophets from Naḥal Ḥever, written around the turn of the millennium. See D. Barthélemy, *Les devanciers d'Aquila* (SVT 10; Leiden, 1963) 203-12; Emmanuel Tov, *The Greek Minor Prophets Scroll from Naḥal Ḥever (8Ḥev*

In addition to the consistent christological hermeneutic of following in a concentrated fashion the various Old Testament–early Christian lines of tradition leading to Christ,[46] Justin's conscious self-limitation to those particular books and textual forms recognized by his Jewish partner shows that he is dealing in a carefully considered fashion with the "prophetic writings." If we are genuinely to do justice to him, however, we must admittedly not limit our own search merely to pre-Justinian sources from which he may have drawn, and must consider instead that in the *Dialogue* he is already drawing on two or three decades as a Christian teacher himself, decades in which in both Ephesus and Rome he had ample opportunity to accumulate experience in discussions with Jewish teachers (see §2.6 below). This consideration also includes what is for us his especially interesting reference to the history of translation of the LXX and the strikingly frequent references to the seventy elders under King Ptolemy. Not only is he the first Christian known to us to use this legend for apologetic ends (see p. 43 above); at the same time he does so in an obviously excessive fashion with missionary-apologetic intentions. He is the first in a long series of Christian witnesses extending well into the Byzantine age.[47] This confirms Campenhausen's conclusion that "Justin is the first orthodox theologian who possesses something akin to a 'doctrine of Holy Scripture.'"[48] The repeated references to the seventy translators are to be viewed within the framework of this "doctrine of Scripture."

2.3. The Dispute concerning the Translation of Isa. 7:14

The point of departure for their introduction within the *Dialogue* is the dispute concerning the LXX wording of Isa. 7:14, the only fully articulated controversy between Justin and Trypho concerning a concrete translation question. In *Dial.* 43.5, 6, the apologete had already quoted the entire text of Isa. 7:10-17 (including 8:4 in the middle of 7:16),[49] concluding that from among Abraham's descen-

---

XIIgr) (DJD VIII; Oxford, 1990), see esp. 158 concerning Justin's text of the prophets. See also A. Sundberg, *The Old Testament of the Early Church* (HTS 20; Cambridge, Mass., 1964) 91ff., 159; M. Harl et al. (note 6), 140ff., 160 (cf. also the index s.v. Justin).

[46] See in this regard O. Skarsaune (note 18), passim and the summary on 428ff.

[47] See the (incomplete) list of testimonies in P. Wendland, ed., *Aristeae ad Philocratem Epistula* (Leipzig, 1900) 121-66; R. Tramontano, *La lettera di Aristea a Filocrate* (Naples, 1931); A. Pelletier, *Lettre d'Aristée à Philocrate* (SC 89; Paris, 1962) 78-89; G. Dorival, in M. Harl et al. (note 6), 47ff. (with bibliography).

[48] Op. cit. (note 35), 106.

[49] This insertion is repeated in 66.2, 3; furthermore, 7:16 also plays an important role in connection with 8:4 in the argumentation in 77.2f., where the dispute involves whether Isa. 7:14 could be referring to Hezekiah; cf. 7:9. This prompts Skarsaune (note 18), 32f., cf. 201ff., to suspect that Justin is drawing from a Christian "anti-Hezekiah" source rather than directly from the LXX text. Tertullian allegedly confirms this suspicion, *Adv. Marc.* 3.12.1 and *Adv. Jud.* 9.1f., where Isa. 7:14 and 8:4 are similarly combined (239ff.). The question is only whether this of necessity implies a

dants "none would ever be born of a virgin (ἀπὸ παρθένου) . . . except this our Christ." The Jewish teachers, however, dared to assert that "Isaiah's prophecy does not say: Behold, a virgin will become pregnant ('Ιδοὺ ἡ παρθένος ἐν γαστρὶ ἕξει), but that a young woman will conceive and bear a son ('Ιδοὺ ἡ νεᾶνις ἐν γαστρὶ λήψεται . . .)," and that this prophecy refers to their former king Hezekiah; hence Justin must try to prove the contrary.[50] But he takes his time, and it is Trypho whose own numerous interposed questions repeatedly raise, among other things, the contentious question of the virgin birth (50.7; 57.3; 63.1). It is only in 66.1-3, at the end of his complicated christological proof, that he goes about fulfilling his promise, repeating the same text (interpolated with Isa. 8:4) of Isa. 7:10-14 already cited in 43.5-6, including the ensuing confession concerning the singularity of Christ's virgin birth (43.7 = 66.4).[51] The extent to which in the *Dialogue* the entire argument is concentrating on *scriptural proof* emerges from the fact that Justin mentions the birth "by the virgin" at least twenty times, while only twice in connection with the virgin birth does he men-

---

complete older written source, or whether the accumulation of Jewish objections Skarsaune observes might rather derive at least in part from an oral doctrinal tradition specific to Rome and Asia Minor, or from Justin's own personal experiences. On the other hand, Skarsaune's suggestion that the dialogue of Aristo of Pella might have been the primary influence seems plausible (242), though the extent of that influence can no longer be determined. One should not underestimate Justin's own contribution, since he was himself a successful teacher (*Mart. Just.*, rec. A and B 4.7; cf. rec. B 5.1; see pp. 64f. below). Justin may also have used his own notes!

[50] Isa. 7:14 is already introduced in *Apol.* 33.1ff. after the story of the translation during the time of King Ptolemy and the reference to the first prophet Moses as the second prophecy of the ἄλλος προφήτης Isaiah (preceded only by the quotation of Isa. 11:1); the purpose is to create a bridge to the "reminiscences of the apostles" (cf. Luke 1:31f.; Matt. 1:21). The reading ἐν γαστρὶ ἕξει in *Dial.* 43.8 is dependent on Matt. 1:23, cf. already *Apol.* 33.1, and may betray the presence of a Christian source; see Skarsaune (note 18), 32f., 101. Justin repeatedly returns to the Jewish interpretation (one he rejects) of prophetic texts as referring to King Hezekiah (*Dial.* 67.1; 68.7; 71.3; 77.1f. [Isa. 7:14]; 33.1; 83.1 [Ps. 110:1]; 85.1 [Ps. 24:7]).

[51] This is not the place to explicate the dogmatic significance of the virgin birth in Justin's thinking, a significance that can hardly be overestimated. As early as the *Apology,* he already addresses the issue at least seven times: i.22.5; 31.7; 32.14; 33.1, 4ff. (= Isa. 7:14); 46.5; 54.8; 63.16. At the same time, he already rejects the charge that this involves merely a motif of pagan mythology by arguing that this similarity derives only from imitation of the demons (cf. 23.3; 22.5; 54.8). In the dispute with Trypho, Justin bitterly opposes the assertion that Jesus is merely a man like any other; rather, the Son of God was born of the virgin Mary according to God's will (23.3; 43.1; 63.1, 3). The apologete is inclined to associate formulaically preexistence and virgin birth (45.4; 48.2; 84.2; 85.2; cf. in this regard Trypho's own objection in 50.1; 100.4). It is necessary in order through just this οἰκονομίαν τὴν διὰ τῆς παρθένου Μαρίας (120.1; cf. 45.4) to eliminate from the world the misfortune begotten by the serpent with the aid of the "virgin" Eve, which in its own turn gave birth to death (*Dial.* 100.4f.). This miracle of divine οἰκονομία (a word occurring at least ten times in Justin and six in his pupil Tatian) represents a fundamental constituent part of the divine salvific work, one through which "the fathers of the virgin," such as the psalmist David (101:1), are also delivered. This is why it appears several times in confession-like enumerations (*Dial.* 63.1; 85.2; cf. *Apol.* i.31.7; 46.5; 61), just as it does later in the Roman baptism symbol. See in this regard F. Kattenbusch, *Das Apostolische Symbol II* (Leipzig, 1900; repr. Hildesheim, 1962) 279ff. (286, 294), 620.

tion the name of Mary (113.4; 120.1), and for all practical purposes does not really address at all the particular role the Spirit plays in the incarnation.[52] *That
the virgin birth occurred is decisive, not how it occurred.*

Whereas in 43.8 Justin himself was yet drawing attention to other translations of Jewish teachers, in the ensuing discussion it is Trypho who articulates
their objection: According to scripture (ἡ γραφὴ οὐκ ἔχει . . . ἀλλ' . . .), the reading is not παρθένος, and the prophecy refers to Hezekiah in any case. For the
rest, the story of the virgin birth recalls pagan "Greek mythology," and Christians "should be ashamed" to tell such stories and should instead "acknowledge
this Jesus to be a man of mere human origin. But do not dare to speak of miracles, lest you be accused of talking nonsense, like the Greeks."[53] Shortly before,
Justin himself had admitted that at least some Jewish Christians "acknowledge
that Jesus is the Christ, but claim that he has a merely human origin" (48.4). We
hear later from Irenaeus[54] of the Jewish Christian Ebionites' assertion that Jesus
was "begotten of Joseph," prompting them to follow the translation νεᾶνις in
Theodotion and Aquila. In this particular point, then, Justin is not only debating
with Jewish scholars but also contesting "heterodox" views in the church itself:
"I naturally disagree with such persons, nor would I agree with them even if the
majority of those who share my opinions were to say so. For we have been told
by Christ himself not to follow the teachings of men, but only those which have
been announced by the holy prophets and taught by himself."[55] The incarnation
of the preexistent Logos in connection with the virgin birth is a major stumbling
block for the Jewish partner in the dialogue, one toward which everything else

---

[52] See F. Kattenbusch, op. cit., II, 294.

[53] 48.1f. In *Apol.* 1.22, Justin himself had used in a positive sense the example of the birth of
Perseus from Danaë and Zeus used in turn by Trypho; cf. by contrast Aristides, *Apol.* 9.7, and
Athenagoras, *Supplication* 21.4.

[54] *Haer.* 3.21.1 = Eusebius, *HE* 5.8.10. See in this regard pp. 74, 77f. below. Accordingly, the
translation νεᾶνις is found not only in the proselytes Theodotion and Aquila (see n. 44 above) but
also in Symmachus, whom Irenaeus does not yet mention, and who, according to Eusebius, *HE* 6.17,
was allegedly a Jewish Christian; see O. Munnich, in M. Harl et al. (note 6), 148-50. He appears first
in connection with Origen's Hexapla, *HE* 6.16.1. Concerning the Ebionite rejection of the virgin
birth, see H. J. Schoeps, *Theologie und Geschichte des Judenchristentums* (1949) 73f. Despite the
scholarly investigation of A. Salvesen, Eusebius's account seems to me to be dependable (*Symmachus in the Pentateuch* [JSS MonSer; Manchester, 1991]. In their own way, the Ebionites were at
the same time also Jews; nor was there any need for another "orthodox"-Jewish translation in addition to Aquila and Theodotion.

[55] *Dial.* 48.4. This rejection of the virgin birth is found not only among the Ebionites but according to Irenaeus, *Haer.* 1.26.1, in Cerinth as well; see Hippolytus, *Haer.* 7.33.1f., cf. 10.22: τὰ δὲ
[περὶ τὸν] Χριστὸν ὁμοίως Κερίνθῳ. See in this regard Skarsaune (note 18), 407-9, who finds in *Dial.*
118.2 an allusion "to the existence of crude chiliasm of the type attributed to Cerinth" (409). Perhaps
Justin is also thinking of him along with others in 48.4. Concerning Cerinth, see also M. Hengel, *The
Johannine Question* (London/Philadelphia, 1989) 59ff., 182ff., notes 38-41. It is certainly conceivable that Cerinth might have associated a realistic notion of chiliasm with the human being Jesus.
Concerning the virgin birth among the gnostics, see n. 60 below.

moves. Trypho, who has hitherto insisted unwaveringly that the messiah is to be an ἄνθρωπος ἐξ ἀνθρώπων,[56] accuses Justin of having asserted "something incredible and practically impossible" (68.1), and that rather, commensurate with Nathan's prophecy, the messiah was to be a descendant of David.[57] Justin then cites for the fourth time the prophecy of the virgin birth, even though he is well aware of the objections of the Jews and even though Trypho himself has already rejected Justin's translation and interpretation as incorrect. In this one point, the apologete cannot yield even an inch. This text is a pillar of his own system of prophetic-christological scriptural proofs:

If, then, I establish the fact that this prophecy of Isaiah speaks of our Christ and not Hezekiah, as you claim, will you not be obliged to doubt your teachers who dare to assert that *the translation made by your seventy elders at the court of the Egyptian King Ptolemy is inaccurate in some places?* For whenever there arises in the scriptures an evident contradiction of their silly and conceited doctrine, your teachers boldly affirm that it was not so written in the original text.[58]

Just as the previous discussion found (see p. 49 above), Justin is here presupposing that his Jewish dialogue partners, even if they come from Palestine like Trypho and his companions (1.3), on the whole already acknowledge the text of the LXX and are not, for example, appealing to the authority of a new translation or recension. This also applies to the pseudo-Justinian *Exhortation to the Greeks* (written presumably at the beginning of the third century; see n. 131 below). In the *Apology* (see n. 24 above), he had, after all, already emphasized that the translation of the Seventy could be found among all Jews, that is, in their synagogues. He is also aware, however, that in several points (ἔν τισιν) Jewish scholars allegedly have found errors in the traditional Greek translation; for Justin, this is the translation of the seventy elders of King Ptolemy, who according to the Christian view translated not the Law of Moses, but all inspired "prophetic" writings. Peculiarly, Justin deals rather reservedly with just this problem despite the considerable deviations of the LXX from the Hebrew text, deviations even affecting the scope of various writings of the prophets and hagiographers. Of course, one might counter that Justin was not yet the kind of "scholarly mind" that Julius Africanus, Origen, or Jerome was; neither was he completely uneducated, however, and he was as a matter of fact all too familiar

---

[56] 49.1; 67.2; cf. 50.1.

[57] 68.5; cf. 2 Sam. 7:12-16 and Ps. 131:11.

[58] *Dial.* 68.6-8; the fulcral passage reads: οἵτινες τολμῶσι λέγειν τὴν ἐξήγησιν ἣν ἐξηγήσαντο οἱ ἑβδομήκοντα ὑμῶν πρεσβύτεροι παρὰ Πτολεμαίῳ τῷ τῶν Αἰγυπτίων βασιλεῖ γενόμενοι, μὴ εἶναι ἐν τισιν ἀληθῆ; (7). In *y. Pe'a* 2:6 §17a, lines 43ff., R. Yehuda b. Pazzi (early fourth century) is alleged to have said that oral teaching was to be preferred to written tradition because it alone separated Israel from the other nations, since they, too, like Israel, appealed to the authority of the written word; see in this regard G. A. Wewers, *Pea, Üs. d. Talmud Yer. I.2* (1986) 61, n. 109 (par.). See also Billerbeck 4.339ff., and n. 118 below.

with certain of the disputed textual variants. The problem was presumably not as urgent then as in the third and fourth centuries, when it led to Origen's monumental philological work and to Jerome's reworking of the Latin Bible. First, until approximately the mid-second century there was apparently a kind of basic Jewish-Christian consensus concerning the LXX as the basis of scholarly argumentation. Second, the apologete might not have wanted to grasp this hot iron too forcefully. Even though he had to have been aware that the "proto-Theodotion" recension as corrected according to the Hebrew text deviated from the traditional LXX (he does, after all, use such a text in the *Dialogue*), he passes over this entire complex in silence and offers variant readings in only a few instances (see §2.5 below), and then primarily concerning the text that is fulcral to his own argument, namely, Isa. 7:14. At the same time, he raises in a general fashion the charge of textual falsification against the Jewish scholars, falsification putting them at odds with their own famous seventy predecessors who rendered the inspired writings of the prophets into Greek for King Ptolemy. *Like the prophets themselves, the Seventy, too, thus become witnesses against their own colleagues in the present for the Christian truth advocated by Justin.*

It is no accident that this conflict flares up precisely in the case of Isa. 7:14. The begetting of Jesus through the Holy Spirit and his birth by the virgin Mary are indeed recounted in the two prehistories of Luke and Matthew; the first proof-text in the first Gospel (Matt. 1:23) adduces Isa. 7:14, whereas the carefully composed narrative of Luke 1:26-44 presupposes this text as its basis. Nowhere else in the New Testament, however, is it mentioned again, a situation applying equally to the "apostolic fathers" with the exception of Ignatius, who does admittedly attach particular significance to it.[59] This may suggest that even toward the end of the first and during the first half of the second century, the notion of the virgin birth was by no means a settled matter. Certain circles, such as the Pauline school or the Johannine community, apparently were not particularly interested in it in the first place, and so had nothing to say about it, and it was roundly rejected not only by Jewish Christians but in part also by certain gnostics.[60]

On the other hand, the virgin birth is mentioned with surprising frequency in

---

[59] *Smyrn.* 1.1; cf. *Eph.* 7.2; 18.2; *Trall.* 9.1. Elsewhere, too, he uses the Gospel of Matthew; see W. D. Köhler, *Die Rezeption des Matthäusevangeliums in der Zeit vor Irenäus* (WUNT 2/24; Tübingen, 1987) 77ff., concerning *Smyrn.* 1.1 = Matt. 3:15. Concerning Justin, see n. 50 above.

[60] Concerning the Jewish Christians, see n. 54 above; concerning the gnostics, see W. Bauer, *Das Leben Jesu im Zeitalter der neutestamentlichen Apokryphen* (1909) 31f.: Besides Cerinth (see n. 55 above), Irenaeus mentions (*Haer.* 1.25.1) the Carpocratians, and in his enumeration of gnostic doctrines of christology (3.11.3) he mentions that *alii rursum Jesum quidem ex Joseph et Maria natum dicunt, et in hunc descendisse Christum qui de superioribus sit, sine carne et impassibilem existentem;* this might be referring to Cerinth and Carpocrates. In Hippolytus, *Haer.* 5.26.29, the gnostic Baruch mentions Jesus the son of Joseph and Mary, who as a twelve-year-old shepherd receives the revelation of Elohim. Marcion denied that Christ had any birth at all, believing instead

the "orthodox" apocryphal literature.[61] That is to say, Justin and his possible predecessors had to contest this point on several fronts: against Jews, Jewish-Christians, and gnostics. Even someone like Marcion (and in part also other gnostics) could go along with this doubting of the LXX text's reliability because they wholly rejected the prophetic christological scriptural proof anyway. The *Apology* shows that Justin considered Marcion to be the most dangerous heretic,[62] and Justin expressly emphasizes that Marcion did not recognize Christ as the Son of the Creator foretold by the prophets. In the *Dialogue,* he mentions heretics who blaspheme the Creator and Christ, whose advent was foretold by the prophets, and the first among these are the Marcionites.[63] Skarsaune has pointed out that the portrayal of the theophany of the thornbush (Exod. 3:2ff.) in *Apol.* 1.63 contains, among other things, arguments against Marcion. In the reworking of the material in the *Dialogue,* "he may still be writing with an eye to Marcion and his disciples."[64] Along with the rejection by the Jews and "heretical" Jewish Christians, this may represent one additional reason why Justin becomes increasingly interested in the virgin birth and Isa. 7:14. He cites the Isaiah text altogether nine times, and simultaneously four times the version he rejected, namely the Jewish-Christian version with νεᾶνις. In the *Apology* and the *Dialogue,* he addresses the matter at least forty times (see n. 51 above). For the much more voluminous work of Irenaeus, the *Biblia Patristica* notes only twenty-five citations and allusions to this passage from Isaiah, with eleven occurring in *Haer.* 3.21.1-6 alone, the section on the translation of the LXX and the Immanuel-prophecy, with which we will deal later (see §4.3 below). Twenty occurrences are found in Tertullian, none at all (peculiarly) in Clement, and only sixteen in Origen. The unique, new, and sheer number of fronts against which the apologete must struggle — involving Jews, Jewish Christians, Marcion, and other gnostics — explains why Justin refers with increasing frequency to the Immanuel-prophecies in Isaiah and why in the *Dialogue* he insists with such persistence (six times) on the authority of the seventy elders and translators. The same situation applies in a tempered form in Irenaeus.

---

that Christ appeared in the fifteenth year of Tiberius with an apparent body (see A. von Harnack, *Marcion* [TU 45; ²1924 (1960)] 124ff., 183ff.; W. Bauer, op. cit., 34f.); by contrast, Marcion's pupil Apelles ascribed to Christ a special body while denying his birth (Hippolytus, *Haer.* 7.36.3, cf. 10.20.2; W. Bauer, op. cit., 37). The docetists, too, such as Satornil, Basilides, and the Valentinians, were able to deny the virgin birth. Their emphasis in Ignatius has anti-docetic significance; see n. 59 above, and cf. p. 51 above. See also Justin's anti-heretical syntagma, n. 18 above.

[61] See the proto-gospel of James; *Asc. Isa.* 11.2f.; *Epistula apostolorum* 3 (14); *Acts Pet.* 8 (24) with a citation from Isa. 7:14; *Sib. Or.* 8.456ff.; *T. Jos.* 19.3 (Christian addendum).

[62] *Apol.* i.26.5; 58.1.

[63] *Dial.* 35.5f.; cf. *Apol.* i.58.1.

[64] Op. cit. (note 18), 409-24 (citation on 424). P. Prigent (note 18) had already suspected that one of the "main sources" in the *Dialogue* might have been his earlier syntagma contra Marcion.

2.4. Appeal to the Authority of the Seventy and the Charge of Scriptural Falsification

The apologete first sets out to refute the charge that this notion merely constitutes an imitation of pagan myths by the Christians. It is rather the demons who, with the aid of such myths to seduce human beings, have actually imitated the predictions of the prophets. Even the assertion that "Perseus was born of a virgin" is merely "another forgery of that treacherous serpent" (70.4). At the same time, he intensifies the charge of scriptural falsification: "I certainly do not trust your teachers when they refuse to admit that the translation of the Scriptures made by the seventy elders at the court of King Ptolemy of Egypt is a correct one, and attempt to make their own translation."[65] Although this last sentence might suggest that Justin may well already have known about complete new recensions of the Greek Bible by Jewish scholars, he seems (as in 69.7) to be thinking of their having tampered with individual passages. The defense of the Seventy is now transformed into the direct charge of scriptural falsification: "You should also know that they have deleted entire passages from the version composed by those elders at the court of Ptolemy, in which it is clearly indicated that the Crucified One was foretold as God and man, and as about to suffer death on the cross" (71.2).[66]

Apparently this involves especially *addenda within the Christian testimonial collections* about which Justin, drawing on his own experience, could not dispute with the Jews since they — quite justifiably — rejected them. As was the case previously, he thus would like to "limit the controversy to those passages which you admit as genuine" (ἐπὶ τὰς ἐκ τῶν ὁμολογουμένων ἔτι παρ' ὑμῖν τὰς ζητήσεις ποιεῖν ἔρχομαι). This is why they recognized the authenticity of the previous (carefully chosen) passages, with the exception of the translation of παρθένος in Isa. 7:14, the real stumbling block (71.3).

Trypho, however, wants more concrete examples of this serious charge that scriptural passages have been deleted. Justin does present four examples, but precisely these examples show that his charges really have no objective basis at all.

He presents first "expositions of Esdras concerning the law of the Passover" that occur neither in the biblical manuscripts of the Esdras books themselves nor in any apocryphal works and that presumably refer to Christ as the Passover

---

65 71.1: Ἀλλ' οὐχὶ τοῖς διδασκάλοις ὑμῶν πείθομαι, μὴ συντεθειμένοις καλῶς ἐξηγεῖσθαι τὰ ὑπὸ τῶν παρὰ Πτολεμαίῳ τῷ Αἰγυπτίων γενομένῳ βασιλεῖ ἑβδομήκοντα πρεσβυτέρων, ἀλλ' αὐτοὶ πειρῶνται.

66 Καὶ ὅτι πολλὰς γραφὰς τέλεον περιεῖλον ἀπὸ τῶν ἐξηγήσεων, τῶν γεγενημένων ὑπὸ τῶν παρὰ Πτολεμαίῳ γεγενημένων πρεσβυτέρων, ἐξ ὧν διαρρήδην οὗτος αὐτὸς ὁ σταυρωθεὶς ὅτι θεὸς καὶ ἄνθρωπος καὶ σταυρούμενος καὶ ἀποθνήσκων κεκηρυγμένος ἀποδείκνυται, εἰδέναι ὑμᾶς βούλομαι.

lamb (cf. 1 Cor. 5:7). Presumably either they come from a now-lost Christian redaction of the Esdras-apocryphon or they represent a Christian addendum to a text of 1 or 2 Esdras in connection with the Passover celebration.[67]

The second text (72.2), apart from a few deviations, is identical with the LXX text of Jer. 11:19 and is contained in all manuscripts.[68] Justin admittedly adds that this section "is still found in some copies of scripture in the Jewish synagogues, for it was deleted only a short time ago."[69] All the same, this information, though based on what to our knowledge is an incorrect assumption, does make it clear that Justin discussed just such "proof-texts" with Jewish dialogue partners and received from them information about their own texts; indeed, on occasion he may even have been able to examine Jewish LXX manuscripts.

The third text tells of a κατάβασις of Israel's Lord and God to the dead. Although it, too, derives allegedly from Jeremiah, it is found neither in any manuscript of the prophet's book nor in any apocryphon, and like the Esdras text almost certainly has a Christian origin, perhaps from a Jeremiah-apocalypse. Irenaeus cites the passage six times in slightly modified form, ascribing it once to Isaiah and twice to Jeremiah.[70]

The fourth text is the most interesting. Here Justin accuses the Jews of hav-

---

[67] 72.1, cf. 1 Esdras 1:1ff.; 7:10ff.; 2 Esdras 6:19ff. See in this regard O. Skarsaune (note 18), 40, 42. Lactantius mentions a Latin version, *Inst. div.* iv.18.22 (CSEL 19, 355f., ed. S. Brandt). Concerning their possible Christian origin, see also C. T. Otto, *Justini . . . Opera* (Corpus apologetarum I.1; [3]1876) 258 in loc., and A. Resch, *Agrapha* (TU NF 15ff. 3/4; [2]1906; Darmstadt, 1967) 304f.

[68] See in this regard O. Skarsaune (note 18), 40, 42, 178, 301, 452. It is also attested in numerous testimonial series of the early church; see P. Prigent (note 18), 173ff., 178ff., 181, 190ff. Also A. Lukyn Williams, *Adversus Judaeos: A Bird's Eye View of Christian Apologiae until the Renaissance* (Cambridge, 1935) 287, n. 1.

[69] O. Skarsaune (note 18), 42: "One can hardly escape the impression that Justin has a feeling that he is on feeble ground, when he includes Jer. 11:19 in his list." Nor are the deviations from Aquila and Symmachus so considerable that a completely altered meaning emerges; see Field and Ziegler in loc. Of course, one cannot exclude the possibility that this particular text was indeed absent at that time in some LXX manuscripts. Justin probably did not have the luxury of examining numerous manuscripts and was not yet working as a focused philologist of the sort represented by Origen.

[70] Isaiah: *Haer.* 3.20.4; Jeremiah: 4.22.1; epideixis: 78; anonymous: 4:33.1; others: 4.33.12; prophets: 5.31.1. See in this regard A. Resch (note 67), 320ff. The editors A. Rousseau and L. Doutreleau, *Sources chrétiennes,* 210, 354, in the commentary in loc. suspect the presence of scribal error. The text touches on the (proto-)Theodotion rendering of Dan. 12:1: τῶν καθευδόντων ἐν γῆς χώματι; *Dial.* 72.4: τῶν κεκοιμημένων εἰς γῆν χώματος. See also C. Wolff, *Jeremia im Frühjudentum und Urchristentum* (TU 118; 1976) 181f. In *Apol.* i.51.8f., Justin was already appealing to the authority of an apocalyptic-sounding passage allegedly from Jeremiah, one pointing back to Dan. 7:13 in connection with Matt. 25:31b and similarly of Christian origin. C. Wolff (op. cit., 179) suspects a memory lapse here. The complete citation of Dan. 7:9-28 in *Dial.* 31.1 deviates in v. 13 from the LXX and the (Proto-)Theodotion text in a similar fashion, suggesting the presence of direct Christian influence, possibly again by way of a testimonial source. See Skarsaune (note 18), 88f. Concerning the motif of *katabasis,* see M. Hengel, "'Setze dich zu meiner Rechten,'" in M. Philonenko, ed., *Le Trône du Dieu,* forthcoming in WUNT.

ing deleted the last three words ἀπὸ τοῦ ξύλου from Ps. 95:10 after ὁ κύριος ἐβασίλευσεν, words which according to Justin prove that the Lord and Creator of the world is identical with the crucified Jesus.[71] In reality, this is merely an early Christian addendum found only in a few LXX witnesses, one Greek manuscript (1093), the Sahidic, Bohairic, and old Latin translations. It is also mentioned by Tertullian and Pseudo-Cyprian and in a somewhat altered version in *Barn.* 8:5.[72] Justin himself had already cited Ps. 95:1-10 in *Apol.* i.41.4, albeit in a somewhat abbreviated form strongly adapted to the parallel text in 1 Chron. 16:23-31; his version probably derives in its own turn from a Christian testimonial collection, and he concludes it quite effectively with the ὁ κύριος ἐβασίλευσεν ἀπὸ τοῦ ξύλου.[73] In *Dial.* 73, following this charge of a deletion of David's prophecy concerning Jesus' crucifixion and exaltation, Justin once again cites the same psalm, and does so in full, though this time in a "cleansed" version corresponding to the traditional LXX text without the addendum ἀπὸ τοῦ ξύλου rejected by the Jews. Skarsaune departs from the opinion of previous editors in observing (probably correctly) that Justin is citing here from a LXX manuscript which, because it lacks the words ἀπὸ τοῦ ξύλου, he considers to have been falsified by Jewish scholars.[74] In spite of this, Justin is confident enough to debate with his dialogue partners even on the basis of this abbreviated "Jewish" text. Even if such a corruption of the text of the Seventy is "more dreadful than the erecting of the golden calf,[75] and more re-

---

[71] *Dial.* 73.1f.

[72] Concerning witnesses, see A. Rahlfs, *Psalmi cum Odis. Göttinger Septuaginta* ([2]1967) 31 and 247 in loc. See already H. B. Swete, *An Introduction to the Old Testament in Greek* ([2]1914; repr. New York, 1968) 423f.; O. Skarsaune (note 18), 35-42; Tertullian, *Adv. Marc.* 3.19.1; *Adv. Jud.* 10.11f.; cf. 13.11; Pseudo-Cyprian, *De mont Sina et Sion,* 9 (CSEL 3.3, 113). J. Briktine's attempt, *BZ* N.F. 10 (1966) 105-7, to construe an original Hebrew form מֵעֵץ, "in contrast (to the idol) of wood," is unpersuasive. This addendum derives from Christian exegesis. See also A. Lukyn Williams (note 68), 287, n. 2. This formula also appears in the fourth strophe of the familiar hymn *In honore sancti crucis* of Venantius Fortunatus (*Carm. Lib.* II.6; MGH AA 4.1, 34): "Inpleta sunt quae concinit/David fideli carmine/dicendo nationibus/regnavit a ligno deus."

[73] Concerning the interpretation of these words, words David allegedly spoke fifteen hundred years before the crucifixion of Christ, see *Apol.* i.42: Only "our Jesus Christ, after his crucifixion and death, arose from the dead and, after ascending into heaven, became king (ἐβασίλευσεν)" (cf. *Dial.* 73.2). Concerning the textual problem here, see n. 27 above, and O. Skarsaune (note 18), 35-41.

[74] See in this regard O. Skarsaune (note 18), 38f.: The only normative Justin manuscript, namely, Cod. Paris Graec. 450, does not contain the addendum in 73.4. Earlier editions, e.g., that of Otto, *Corp. Ap.* II *Justini . . . Opera* I.2 ([3]1877) 262 (cf. 263, n. 10), add the words ἀπὸ τοῦ ξύλου as having been omitted through scribal error; see by contrast already Goodspeed, 183, who refers to the addendum only in his apparatus. Concerning the earlier position, see A. Rahlfs, *Septuagintastudien* II (1907) 205f. ([2]1965, 309f.).

[75] Rabbinic teachers will later claim that the day on which the Torah was translated into Greek was as fateful for Israel as the day on which the golden calf was erected (Sefer Torah 1.8, cf. Tr. Sopherim 1.7); see pp. 40f. above. In rabbinic thinking, the sin of the golden calf was the worst in Israel's history. The rabbinic haggadah repeatedly confronts the problem of how, despite this sin, an

volting than the sacrifice of their children to demons or the slaughter of the prophets," still the previously cited Septuagint text (the text to be cited in the future and the text "recognized" by his opponents) more than suffices to prove the points at issue.[76] That is, quite apart from the difference concerning the wording of Isa. 7:14, Justin can also debate solely on the basis of the texts accepted by the Jews, particularly since Trypho assures Justin that such a charge of falsification on the part of the leaders of his people seems incredible in any case, and that he thus prefers to leave the matter to God (73.5); furthermore, Justin does indeed consider it an acceptable excuse that his dialogue partner knows nothing about the allegedly deleted texts. Unfortunately, his interpretation of the "cleansed" Jewish text of Ps. 95 breaks off in 74.3 as a result of a larger lacuna in the *Dialogue*. The discussion of the first day concludes in that lacuna.

Beginning with the second day, new Jewish dialogue partners enter who are hostile to Christians.[77] It is only in ch. 84, after long detours, that Justin concludes his as yet outstanding demonstration that the child promised in Isa. 7:14 could never be Hezekiah,[78] and is to be understood rather as Christ, the "firstborn of all creatures," who "took flesh and truly became a human being by means of a virgin's womb." God would not have spoken of a "miraculous sign" (σημεῖον) in the case of a mere natural birth. This miracle can be compared only with the creation of all living things by the word of God in the beginning (84.2).

In what has become the almost stereotypical form, the charge of scriptural falsification is again raised in connection with reference to *the translation made by the elders at the court of King Ptolemy:*

---

intact relationship is still possible between God and Israel; ever new variations are found: Memory of the golden calf is extinguished (WaR 27.3, ed. Margulies, 625-27; PesK Shor o kesev, ed. Buber, 75b-76a et passim); where such memory is absent, precisely that absence is a sign that God regards this sin as nothing (WaR 27.8, ed. Margulies, 640f.; 77b). Anything that might recall the golden calf may not be used in any atonement ritual (*y. Yoma* 7.3, 44b, 47-51; *y. Roš Haš.* 3.2, 58d, 15-22), or is for precisely that reason perfectly suited for atonement (SifDev 1, on Deut. 1:1, ed. Finkelstein, 6; PesK Para, ed. Buber, 40b; MHG Devarim on Deut. 1:1, ed. Fisch, 8). References from Friedrich Avemarie.

[76] *Dial.* 73.6, μετὰ τῶν . . . παρ' ὑμῖν παραπεφυλαγμένων; cf. 71.2, τῶν ὁμολογουμένων ἔτι παρ' ὑμῖν; see p. 49 above and 120.5, οὐδὲ ἀπὸ τῶν μὴ ὁμολογουμένων μέχρι νῦν ὑφ' ὑμῶν.

[77] *Dial.* 85.6; 94.4; 122.4. The text begins again on the second day in the middle of a citation from Deut. 32:16. Apparently, the *Dialogue* originally consisted of two parts; see the citation from the *Sacra Parallela* of John of Damascus, ed. K. Holl, *Fragmente vornicänischer Kirchenväter aus den Sacra Parallela* (TU NF V/2; Leipzig, 1899) 34, concerning a fragment from *Dial.* 82: ἐκ τοῦ πρὸς Τρύφωνα β λόγου. Thus we do not know how Justin concluded his discussion of Ps. 96(LXX 95):10. Concerning the content of the lacuna, O. Skarsaune (note 18), 213f., suggests that Justin possibly understood Ps. 96:10, which he last cites without the Christian addendum "from the cross," as referring to Christ's dominion in the thousand-year kingdom; cf. *Dial.* 80/81.

[78] *Dial.* 77; 78. Concerning the course of the argumentation, see O. Skarsaune (note 18), 202f. Here a decisive role is played by Matt. 2:1-12 and the verse inserted into Justin's text of Isa. 7:16, namely, Isa. 8:4; see op. cit., 200ff. Cf. n. 49 above.

But here, too, you dare to distort the translation of this passage made by your elders at the court of Ptolemy, the Egyptian king, asserting that the real meaning of the scriptures is not as they translated it, but should read "behold, a young woman shall conceive,"[79] as though something of extraordinary importance was signified by a woman conceiving after sexual intercourse, as all young women (νεάνιδες), except the barren, can do.

Yet if he so wills it, God can grant children even to these, as shown by the examples of the mothers of Samuel and John the Baptist. Justin's dialogue partners must acknowledge "that nothing is impossible for God to do if he wills it." Above all, however — and this is the most important argument — they should not venture to mutilate[80] or misinterpret[81] the prophecies.

2.5. The "Generous" Treatment of Lesser Variants

Toward the end of the dialogue, the apologete refers three more times to the translation of the Seventy in adducing additional textual variations, though in these cases he admittedly is able to be more generous than was the case with Isa. 7:14, where the truth of the Christian faith was at stake.

In *Dial.* 120.3, he cites Gen. 49:10, from the blessing of Jacob: "A ruler shall not be missing from Judah . . . until he comes to whom it [the royal office] belongs (ἕως ἂν ἔλθῃ ᾧ ἀπόκειται), and he shall be the expectation of the Gentiles." This promise is referring to the parousia of Jesus, just as foretold in Dan. 7:13 as well. He then adds: "Now, gentlemen, I could argue with you about the passage which you claim should be written, 'until the things laid up for him come' (Ἕως ἂν ἔλθῃ τὰ ἀποκείμενα), for the Seventy did not translate as you do, but Ἕως ἂν ἔλθῃ ᾧ ἀπόκειται" (120.4). In reality, this involves an old LXX variant in which both textual forms derive from a possible interpretation of the disputed Hebrew text.[82] Admittedly, the version cited by Justin as a Jewish variant, that is, the one allegedly not corresponding to the opinion of the Seventy, is actually better attested than the other, appearing in all the great

---

[79] The form influenced by Matt. 1:23, ἐν γαστρὶ ἕξει (so here in 84.3) and the LXX version, ἐν γαστρὶ λήψεται (so in 84.1), are peculiarly intertwined; see 43:5: παρθένος . . . λήψεται; 43.8: παρθένος . . . ἕξει and νεᾶνις λήψεται; 67.1: παρθένος and νεᾶνις λήψεται, similarly in 71.3; 66.2; and 68.6: παρθένος λήψεται, with the more frequent λήψεται corresponding to the LXX text. Justin hardly pays any attention to such details. Contra the edition of Ziegler, who incorporates ἕξει into the text, the LXX itself in all probability read λήψεται; ἕξει already represents an *interpretatio Christiana* even in Matthew.

[80] 82.4: μὴ παραγράφειν (cf. 71.4; 73.5; and 84.3).

[81] μὴ παρεξηγεῖσθαι (cf. 82.4, which speaks of blaspheming Christ and misinterpreting the scriptures). Concerning the charge of falsification, see also terms such as περικόπτειν in 72.2, 4; 73.6 conj., or ἐκκόπτειν in 72.3; and ἀφανῆ ποιεῖν in 120.5.

[82] See in this regard the detailed discussion of A. Posnanski, *Schiloh. Ein Beitrag zur Geschichte der Messiaslehre, 1. Teil: Die Auslegung von Gen 49,10 im Altertum* (Leipzig, 1904) 49-51 et passim; O. Skarsaune (note 18), 26f.; M. Harl, in *La Bible d'Alexandrie. La Genèse* (Paris, 1986) 308f. concerning Justin, Irenaeus, and the twofold interpretation in Origen.

uncials.[83] Justin's reading derives presumably from a secondary Palestinian recension related to the messianic interpretation of the Targum Onqelos. The only peculiar feature here is that although Justin adduces twice in the *Apology* what in his opinion is the genuine translation of the Seventy,[84] he adduces the "Jewish version" in *Dial.* 52.2 with no further comment.[85] Although he apparently was familiar with several different textual forms, and even compared them, he did not always take them all that literally, which is why he is now rather generous in contrast to his attitude toward Isa. 7:14. Even though he considers the more strongly messianic-sounding version to be more original, he is able to dispense with quibbling about a philological triviality (λεξείδιον) because the context, namely, the salvific expectation of the gentiles, secures the messianic interpretation in any case. He repeats the old asseveration of proving his own teaching about Christ only on the basis of texts recognized by his opponents,[86] adducing once again the messianic texts of Jeremiah, Esdras, and David which were allegedly deleted from the scriptures, texts he mentions only as examples of Jewish scriptural falsification but has not adduced in support of his argumentation.[87] That Justin is able to adduce so many messianic proof-texts from the Septuagint, which, even though the Jews still recognize it, in reality is allegedly already falsified and abbreviated in part, proves for him that the Jewish scholars did not understand these texts at all. He concludes with malicious irony: "for if your teachers had understood them *they would most assuredly have expunged them from the text.*"[88]

As an additional example of such expunging, Justin now adduces the *Martyrdom of Isaiah,* who allegedly was sawed in half with a wooden saw. Since this would be the only time Justin would be adducing *expressis verbis* a legend from a Jewish apocryphon outside the "canonical" Jewish texts, it again seems more likely that, as with the apocryphal texts of Jeremiah and Esdras, he owes his familiarity with this particular tradition to a testimonial collection containing this biographical item about the prophet's violent death.[89]

---

[83] See the Genesis edition of the Göttinger LXX by J. W. Wevers, p. 460 in loc., and the overview in Skarsaune (note 18), 26. The translation of Aquila omits the problematical שׁילה entirely.

[84] I.32.1; 54.5; cf. 32.2: ἕως ἂν ἔλθη ᾧ ἀπόκειται τὸ βασίλειον.

[85] The Parisian manuscript as well as one copy attests in the margin: ᾧ ἀπόκειται; concerning this variant, see Wevers, *Genesis,* loc. cit., 460.

[86] See *Dial.* 71.2; 73.6; and in this regard p. 49, n. 41 above.

[87] 84.5; cf. *Dial.* 71; 73.

[88] ἀφανῆ ἐπεποιήκεισαν; cf. n. 19 above.

[89] *Dial.* 120.5. Cf. n. 39 above. The formulation πρίονι ξυλίνῳ corresponds to *Asc. Isa.* 5.1: "wood saw" (so Tisserant) or "tree saw" (so C. Detlef and G. Müller, *NTApo* [3rd ed.], 2.553), suggesting that Justin might have been acquainted with the *Ascension of Isaiah* and viewed it as an inspired writing. The *Vit. Proph.* 1.1 contains a reference to the "wood saw" only secondarily at the periphery of the rather circuitous tradition (e.g., the so-called Hesianic recension [= PG 93.1348] and Syr. See T. Schermann, *Prophetarum vitae fabulosae* [Leipzig, 1907] 8.104). On the other hand, Justin's interpretation of the legend as a reference to the division of the people recalls the wording of

Even in this peculiar account, Justin sees a μυστήριον . . . τοῦ Χριστοῦ. Isaiah's having been sawn in half foretells that Christ "is going to cut your nation in two," a polemical statement then additionally supported by Matt. 8:11ff.

A few paragraphs later, he debates whether Christians embody the true people of God, namely, Israel, and initially cites Ps. 81:1-8 (MT 82) "*as translated by you yourselves* (ὡς μὲν ὑμεῖς ἐξηγεῖσθε)."[90] There then follows the citation of Ps. 81:6f. (MT 82), which is almost completely identical with the LXX text.[91] A deviation Justin considers worthy of mention occurs only in v. 7, where the "Jewish" text allegedly reads ὑμεῖς δὲ ὡς ἄνθρωπος[92] ἀποθνήσκετε, while "*the translation of the Seventy*" (ἐν τῇ τῶν ἑβδομήκοντα ἐξηγήσει εἴρηται) reads Ἰδοὺ δὴ ὡς ἄνθρωποι ἀποθνήσκετε. Justin wants to apply this to the case of the first human couple and the resulting fate of all human beings. The textual evidence before us today is somewhat peculiar. In view of the introduction ὑμεῖς δὲ, which was meaningless for Justin himself, most textual witnesses show the "Jewish" text to be right, while in concurrence with Justin they have ἄνθρωποι according to Rahlfs: ὑμεῖς δὲ ὡς ἄνθρωποι.[93] The singular might stem from an all too literal translation of the collective *k^e'adam t^emûtûn*[94] of the MT in a manuscript recension. In this case, Justin has the real LXX text on his side. Since the apologete has cited the psalm (incorrectly ascribed to David) because of its unequivocal anthropological statement and not because of the "Jewish text" that deviates from the Seventy, he can again be generous: "Hold whatever translation of the psalm you please!"[95] That is to say, he refers to this particular

---

the primary tradition of the *Vit. Proph.*: πρισθεὶς εἰς δύο (for the text of the recension, see Schermann, op. cit., 8, 41, 60, 68). The LXX manuscript of the book of Isaiah does not contain the legend of his death; only the Marchalianus (sixth century) positions the *Vit. Proph.* before the prophetic corpus as a whole. It is not until the Targum that (only a few) manuscripts again insert the legend of Isaiah's death at Isa. 66:1. Concerning the textual form in the prophetic targum, see P. Grelot, "Deux tosephtas targoumiques inédités sur Isaie LXVI," *RB* 79 (1972) 511-43; concerning the *Ascension of Isaiah,* see M. Pesce, "L'utilizzazione storica dell' AI," in *idem,* ed., *Isaia, il diletto e la chiesa. Testi e ricerche die Scienze religiose* 20 (1983) 13-76 (40). References from Anna Maria Schwemer.

[90] *Dial.* 124.2; cf. 122-24. Justin ascribes the psalm to David, whereas according to the LXX it comes from Asaph.

[91] *Dial.* 124.3f. See in this regard O. Skarsaune (note 18), 34f.

[92] Thus the text as emended by the editors, while the Parisian manuscript follows the LXX in using the plural, completely contradicting Justin's own explication of the text.

[93] See A. Rahlfs, *Psalmi c. Odis,* 224, and *idem, Septuaginta-Studien II* (1907) 205 (²1965, 309). Swete in loc. refers to the reading ἄνθρωπος in the Psalterium Veronense (R).

[94] The psalm targum correctly reads *hyk bny nš'.* Concerning this matter, see also O. Skarsaune (note 18), 34f.

[95] ἐχέτω καὶ ἡ ἑρμενεία τοῦ ψαλμοῦ ὡς βούλεσθε· (124.4). By way of exception, he uses a word here with a root he otherwise seldom uses, namely, ἑρμην-; cf. also 103.5, where the syllable -νας (cf. *naḥaš* in Gen. 3:1ff.) is reinterpreted into Satanas as a translation of serpent, while Σαταν in the language of the Jews and Syrians allegedly means ἀποστάτης. The question arises whether, despite his origin in Flavia Neapolis in the territory of Samaria, Justin knew Aramaic. Although in *Dial.* 120.6 he does mention the Samaritans as his people, whom he warned against the magician Simon,

translation variant only in order to demonstrate his own familiarity with the various textual versions and, commensurately, his own superior position in the current debate. *The Seventy are always on his side,* even though as a rule he does not even need their help.

Justin cites four times the command to persecute the righteous from Isa. 3:10. Twice, at the beginning and toward the end of the two-day debate, he does this within the framework of a longer quotation from the LXX version that has come down to us: *Δήσωμεν τὸν δίκαιον, ὅτι δύσχρηστος ἡμῖν ἐστι.*[96] But then, just after the second quotation, he suddenly alters the text following a highpoint of his own polemic: "And the height of your iniquity is this, that you hate the righteous one whom you put to death, as well as those who through his grace are pious, just, and charitable." Thus does the cry of woe in Isa. 3:9f. apply to the Jews: "because they have said: *Ἄρωμεν τὸν δίκαιον, ὅτι δύσχρηστος ἡμῖν ἐστιν.*" The expression "let us bind the righteous one" is replaced here by the more incisive "let us take away the righteous one" (an expression simultaneously recalling Christ's passion). Shortly after this polemical climax of the dialogue, Justin adds a surprising justification for this textual change:[97] "My friends, I will now quote scripture *according to the translation of the Seventy.* For when I cited those passages as you read them,[98] I was trying to ascertain your frame of mind. In quoting the passage, 'woe to them, because they have taken evil counsel against themselves, saying,' I added the words *from the translation of the Seventy,* 'let us take away the righteous one, for he is distasteful to us.' Yet at the beginning of our discussion I cited it *according to your version,* 'let us bind the righteous one, for he is distasteful to us.' At the time you seemed to have been preoccupied, and to have heard my words without due attention" (137.3, 4). With this ironic charge intended to demonstrate that he is more familiar from memory with even the details of the LXX text than are his opponents, Justin concludes the highpoint of his two-day discussion with Trypho and the latter's friends. Because "the day is now almost at an end and the sun is ready to set," he will now merely add some concluding thoughts on matters he has already addressed (137.4; cf. 138-41).

---

immediately thereafter he speaks about "their nation." The name of his father is Latin, that of his grandfather Greek, and he may be a descendant of the veterans whom Vespasian settled there.

[96] *Dial.* 17.2 in a citation from Isa. 3:9-11; 133.2 from Isa. 3:9b-15.

[97] *Dial.* 136.2; 137.3. Concerning the text, see I. Ziegler, *Isaias. Göttinger Septuaginta* (²1967) 132 in loc., and the Introduction, 20; R. Gryson, *Esaias* VL 12,2 (1987) 119f. The reading ἄρωμεν appears in no manuscript but only in a few of the early church fathers, as in a citation from Hegesippus's account of the martyrdom of James, Eusebius, *HE* 2.23.15; cf. also *Apoc. Jac.* 2, NHC V.4.61.16f., ed. C. W. Hendrick, in D. M. Parrot (chief ed.), *NHS* XI (Leiden, 1979) 142; Clement of Alexandria, *Strom.* 5.108.2, who associates this with Plato, *Pol.* 362a, and Tertullian, *Adv. Marc.* 3.22.5: *venite auferamus iustum, quia inutilis est nobis.* Concerning Justin's various texts, see O. Skarsaune (note 18), 30-32.

[98] *Dial.* 17.2; 133.2 with the reading δήσωμεν.

Yet even with this final reference to the christologically concurring version of the Seventy, Justin is historically incorrect. The reading δήσομεν is assuredly the original one. The term ἄρωμεν may have found its way into some manuscript as a scribal error[99] and then been incorporated into Christian testimonials, especially since the cries αἶρε or ἆρον ἆρον[100] occur in the Passion narrative and since this more precisely represents the death of the righteous one.

2.6. Justin's Appeal to the Authority of the Seventy in His Discussion with Jews in Rome

On the one hand, Justin is firmly convinced that he is rendering the true opinion of the venerable seventy translators of King Ptolemy in his own "Christian" text, which itself may well have been assembled largely from testimonial collections. He presumably appropriated the texts he uses in the *Apology* from christologically reworked collections of proof-texts; apart from the Christian addenda and alterations, these texts as a rule genuinely do correspond to the old, uncensored version of the LXX, and this may account for his confidence. Although he may have extracted these in part from collections that were already extant, he may also have assembled such a collection himself during his almost thirty years of teaching. That is, we should not underestimate the considerable significance of ongoing oral teaching traditions during the first and second centuries, particularly as this influenced the recasting of scriptural quotations. In addition to the *Treatise Against All Heresies,* especially against Marcion (see p. 42, n. 18 above), the lost writing Ψάλτης, for example, the Psalm Singer, may have contained a collection of prophetic reference texts from the psalms and from other Old Testament poetic writings (possibly even with accompanying "commentary").[101] Justin no doubt acquired some of this facility in his debates with the Jews, and acquired his in part remarkable familiarity with Judaism less through literary than through oral means. He preferred a discussion with Jews to a public debate with the philosopher Crescens, about which he himself reports.[102] As the *Dialogue* shows, he was able

---

[99] Unclear handwriting can certainly cause the word ΔΗΣΩΜΕΝ to be misread as ΑΙΡΩΜΕΝ.

[100] Luke 23:18; John 19:15; but cf. also Mark 15:1 (Matt. 22:13; John 18:12): δήσαντες τὸν Ἰησοῦν. Wis. 2:12 (ἐνεδρεύσωμεν τὸν δίκαιον) has conceivably also exerted some influence here; itself dependent on Isa. 3:10 LXX, it portrays the persecution of the righteous to the point of shameful death. Concerning the influence of all three versions on the tradition of the Latin fathers, see W. Thiele, *Sapientia Latina* (VL 11/1; Freiburg, 1980) 273f. Ambrosius, for example, uses *tollamus* in several instances. On the other hand, early witnesses such as *Barn.* 6.7 and Melito, *Passahomilie,* 532f. (Perler = 516f. Hall) attest δήσωμεν.

[101] Concerning Justin as a teacher, see recently U. Neymeyr, "Die christlichen Lehrer im zweiten Jahrhundert," *VigChr* Sup. 4 (1989) 16-35. Unfortunately, the significance of scriptural exegesis in Justin's teaching overly recedes in his presentation. Concerning Justin's writings, see Eusebius, *HE* 4.18.4ff.

[102] *Apol.* ii.3.1-6; cf. Tatian *Or.* 19.1, and in this regard Neymeyr (note 101), 25f.

to gain access to Jewish Septuagint-texts, and (as a comparison with the Minor Prophetic Scroll of Naḥal Ḥever [8 Ḥev XIIgr] reveals) even to Septuagint-texts in part revised according to the original text; this situation represents a distinctively new, almost "scholarly" feature in the history of early Christianity. Justin inaugurates here a new development that then culminates in Origen and Jerome. This suggests, as does his emphasis on basing his argumentation only on texts recognized by the other side, that he had (in my opinion considerable) experience with Jewish (and Jewish-Christian) dialogue partners in Rome, which at that time had a large Jewish community with close ties to Palestine. During Justin's time, Rome even had a rabbinic school led by Mattiah ben Ḥeresh, who (like Trypho) emigrated from Palestine either during or shortly before the Bar-Cochba revolt.[103]

After the destruction of the Jewish community in Egypt in the revolt of 115-117 C.E., the Jewish community in Rome became the most important outside Palestine. So it was precisely during the Antonine period in Rome that there would have been ample opportunity to debate with Jews, and Justin seems to have used this opportunity.

By appealing to the authority of the Seventy and by using Jewish recensions of texts, Justin sought first of all to demonstrate his own sovereignty in argumentation. Significantly, it is only in the second half of the increasingly vehement debate that he adduces the Seventy, when discussion of the translation of Isa. 7:14 creates an impasse at which Justin can no longer allow the "Jewish" text to be used, and where (by way of exception) he genuinely has the "Seventy" on his side. In contrast to his later, adjusted use of the term, here he is still genuinely using οἱ ἑβδομήκοντα to refer to the seventy translators as Jewish authorities during the time just preceding Christ, and not merely just as texts. This is why he initially adds πρεσβύτεροι (ὑμῶν) and the reference to King Ptolemy.[104] Only toward the end, after the reference is clear, does he make do with a mere appeal to "the Seventy."[105] The high frequency with which Justin makes this reference is, as far as I can see, unique in early Christian literature, and probably derives from an argument Justin repeatedly used in his debates with Jewish (and Jewish-Christian) opponents (whether justifiably or not is another question entirely), namely this: We have the seventy elders on our side, that is, those who translated the prophetic writings (i.e., the entire inspired Holy Scriptures; see p. 43 above) at the court of King Ptolemy. By contrast, your own present scriptural scholars fell away from these writings after the advent of the Christ variously foretold in these very writings, and have not only falsified and abbreviated

---

103 See in this regard H. J. Leon, *The Jews of Ancient Rome* (1960) passim and pp. 38, 246; Billerbeck, 3.24; W. Bacher, *Die Aggada der Tannaiten* (Strassburg, ²1903) 1.380-85. Yet another legendary authority of this period is Theudas, "the man from Rome" (Billerbeck, 1.23).

104 68.7; 71.1; 84.3 (without the seventy).

105 120.4; 124.3; 131.1; 137.3 (bis). See also pp. 41ff. above!

the prophetic writings in the translation of the Seventy,[106] but have not even understood them in the first place.[107]

This charge of having falsified scripture, first appearing in such concentrated form in Justin's writings and in connection with the translation of the Seventy, would go on to become a common topos of later dialogues and of the *adversus Judaeos* literature in general.[108]

On the other hand, precisely Justin's self-limitation to writings and textual forms recognized by his opponents betrays a degree of uncertainty that cannot be eclipsed by the Christian teacher's confident demeanor in his self-portrayal. Not only did the Jews already have an (almost unequivocally) completed "canon" (see pp. 46ff. above); they also had at their disposal the original text and a translation revised according to that text. It is precisely the demonstrable incorrectness of Justin's own accusations that reveals his fundamentally weaker position, and for precisely that reason the translation legend acquires significance for him in its form altered according to Christian interests and in its association with the entirety of Holy Scripture as a collection of prophetic statements. *This legend must provide help in wresting away from the Jews the translation of the Seventy and in turning it into a Christian writing.* The translation was still being used by the Jews; Aquila was still far from having established himself among the Jews of the Diaspora by the middle of the second century, which is why it is only an entire generation later that Irenaeus first mentions him. The text of the Greek Bible, however, was still lacking in unity as a result of recension activity extending back even into the pre-Christian period, and this disunity had been amplified even more on the Christian side through the influence of the testimonials. Despite the apologete's considerable naivete and presumption toward his fictitious Jewish dialogue partners, a particular embarrassment already becomes visible that would flare up revealingly two generations later in the letter of Julius Africanus to Origen regarding the book of Susanna[109] and in the latter's response, a discomfiture prompting the greatest theologian and philologist of the ancient church to produce the monumental synopsis of the Hexapla, itself probably a singular accomplishment in antiquity.[110]

Finally, the unadorned form of the "translation legend" Justin uses is also

---

[106] See pp. 56-60 above.

[107] *Apol.* i.31.5: οἳ καὶ ἀναγιγνώσκοντες οὐ συνιᾶσι τὰ εἰρημένα, cf. 36; 54; *Dial.* 9.1; 12.3; 14.2; 78.10; 123f.; 126.2; 134f. Cf. M. Simon, *Verus Israel* (Paris, 21964) 177ff., 189ff.

[108] See in this regard H. Schreckenberg (note 18), 186, 197 (Justin), 234 (Origen), et passim; A. Lukyn Williams, *Adversus Judaeos* (note 68), 33ff., 205, 402; M. Simon (note 107), 169ff., 177ff., 194f.; N. de Lange, *Origen and the Jews* (Cambridge, 1976; repr. 1978).

[109] Ed. N. de Lange (SC 302; 1983) 469-589, see §§4f. (517), and the response in §§5ff. (524ff.).

[110] See in this regard recently B. Neuschäfer, *Origenes als Philologe* (SBA 18.1/2; Basel, 1987) 86ff. See also p. 70, note 123 below.

rather striking. He is familiar neither with the *Epistle of Aristeas* nor with the Philonic version of the translators' prophetic inspiration, a motif he could well have employed and which shortly thereafter would be used by Irenaeus, by Clement, and then in a concluding, intensified form by the pseudo-Justinian *Exhortation to the Greeks*.[111] The former "Platonist" Justin, despite occasional resonances, is relatively far removed from Philo and from Alexandrian religious philosophy.[112] Clement was the first to rediscover Philo for the larger church; Justin was more inclined to view as his opponents the Alexandrian gnostics following in Philo's tracks such as Basilides and Valentinus, the latter of whom picked up on Philo's tradition in Rome during Justin's time.[113]

3. The "Seventy" in Later Dialogues

As far as I can see, the unique feature here is the *intensity* with which Justin appeals to the authority of the Seventy; he does this much more frequently than is the case in the later, more schematic dialogues between Jews and Christians for which Justin's own *Dialogue* became the model. This motif recedes even in the *Adversus Judaeos* writings, though textual questions and philological details admittedly have hardly any role at all to play there. The later texts are polemic pure and simple, showing that Justin still stood relatively close to the original dialogue situation in which, among other things, such questions must indeed have been at issue.

The fifth- or sixth-century *Dialogus christiani et Judaei* between the Christian Timothy and the Jew Aquila (this name being no accident) represents a certain exception.[114] Here the dialogue begins by mentioning the scope of the canon, about which Christians and Hebrews agree and which the Hebrew translators as well as Aquila, Symmachus, and Theodotion translated.[115] To the Jews'

---

[111] See pp. 71-74 below.

[112] See in this regard P. Heinisch, *Der Einfluss Philos auf die älteste christliche Exegese* (ATA 1 and 2; Munich, 1908) 36ff., 195-211, 391f.; W. A. Shotwell, *The Biblical Exegesis of Justin Martyr* (London, 1965) 93-115; O. Skarsaune (note 18), 409-24, esp. 423f.

[113] *Dial.* 35.6, concerning polemic contra the Marcionites, Basilidians, Valentinians, and Saturnilus (Satornilus). Concerning Valentinus and Philo, see C. Markschies, *Valentinus Gnosticus?* (WUNT 65; Tübingen, 1992).

[114] Ed. F. C. Conybeare, *The Dialogues of Athanasius and Zacchaeus and of Timothy and Aquila* (Anec. Ox. Class. Ser. VII; Oxford, 1898) 66-104. The second is probably dependent on the first. Conybeare tries unpersuasively to establish a connection between these dialogues and that between Papiscus and Jason by Aristo of Pella. See in this regard M. Simon (note 107), 185; H. Schreckenberg (note 18), 391f.

[115] Fol 77 r./v. (Conybeare, 66). Admittedly, Judith is then still mentioned as the twenty-first book before Esther among the canonical books. The seventy-two translators allegedly reckoned Tobias, Wisdom, and Sirach among the apocrypha. This clearly reveals how much confusion in part still obtained in the fifth or sixth centuries concerning the Old Testament canon; it was precisely in

charge that the Christians falsify scripture by adducing texts found only in the Greek Bible and not in the Hebrew, the Christian issues the countercharge that the translator Aquila concealed the witnesses to Christ by distorting scripture in his own turn so that the Christians would not receive the (unadulterated) text of the seventy-two translators from the court of Ptolemy. Here the narrator makes the transition to an embellished and circuitous account of the translation of the seventy-two elders and of the life of Aquila, an account quite similar to that found in Epiphanius's *De mensuris et ponderibus*.[116] Here, as in Justin, Ptolemy must write two letters. Aquila is made into the party bearing primary responsibility for having falsified scripture; that is, both the original Hebrew text and the translation of the Seventy-two,[117] who were inspired by the Holy Spirit, allegedly rendered the original text without error. This shows that, at this late date, Aquila's translation had displaced the LXX in the synagogue, whereas Justin does not yet mention him at all, ascribing guilt instead in a general fashion to the Jewish elders during the period following Christ. It also shows clearly how the Christian version of the translation hypothesis had developed further. In the interim, the LXX had long become an exclusively Christian writing, something not yet the case for Justin though he did campaign vehemently for it.

The same situation — namely, one resulting in the Jews' rejection of the Greek Bible — appears in the later disputation between the bishop Gregentius of Tafra in Yemen and the Jew Herban.[118] The Jew admits at the beginning of the discussion: "It was wrong for our fathers to translate the [holy] books of Israel voluntarily into Greek, that you might then take possession of those books and silence us."[119] To this, Schreckenberg remarks that "the Christian reception of the Septuagint and its use as an anti-Jewish apologetic weapon alienated it from the Jews themselves. . . . Judaism [withdrew] . . . both theologically and religiously into its own Hebrew linguistic sphere, and Christianity took possession of both the tradition and intellectual property of the Greek Bible, just as it

---

the Greek East that such concurrence with the "Hebrews" and their alleged canon of twenty-two books was still valued.

[116] Fol. 115-18, Conybeare, 89-91, cf. XXVIff., and see n. 23 above and pp. 73f. below.

[117] Fol. 119 (Conybeare, 92f.).

[118] MPG 86.1.622-783; see in this regard A. Labate, *Dictionnaire encyclopédique du christianisme ancien*, vol. 1 (1990) 1099. The disputation allegedly took place in 535. The legendary account comes from a Gregentius-Vita and is considerably later. See also H. Schreckenberg (note 18), 397-400, 632. There are some interesting rabbinic parallels to this: NuR 14:10 suggests that the oral Torah was not given in written form so that the "Ishmaelites" could not falsify it as they did the written version, asserting then that they were (the true) Israel; similarly also PesiqtaR 5, 15b, which asserts that God gave Moses the Mishnah only in oral form after seeing that the nations would later "translate the Torah and read it in Greek (לתרגם את התורה ולהיות קוראים בה יוונית), saying then that the others [the Israelites] were not [the true] Israel." See Billerbeck 1.219f.; cf. also 4.439ff., §d; see also n. 58 above.

[119] Op. cit., 624; see H. Schreckenberg (note 18), 399; concerning the rabbinic texts, see pp. 40f. and 58f. above.

did the Jewish authors who wrote in Greek, namely, Philo and Flavius Josephus."[120] This development, one that not even Aquila could thwart, was introduced in what was already an unequivocally forceful manner by Justin's own appeal to the Seventy.

4. The Translation Legend among the Early Fathers after Justin

4.1. The Enduring Impasse

Several motifs are attested in Justin: the expansion of the work of the Seventy to include all the writings of the Hebrew Bible considered to be inspired; the splendid quality of the translation itself, completely free of errors, a motif which as early as Irenaeus could be amplified according to the model of Philo's account into an assertion of miraculous inspiration on the part of the translators; the (substantively unjustified) charge that the Jews falsified the holy text; and the temporal relation[121] between the translation work itself and the advent of Christ and its universal applicability. All these motifs became determinative for the further understanding of the LXX as a collection of writings claimed by the Christians as their own.

This fundamentally exclusive claim to the work of the Seventy for the church, however, invariably led to new conflicts. One could not escape the fact that the model of the translation was the *Hebrew* Bible, and that, in one form or another, this Bible (not least along with its canon) had to remain that model.

The Jews, who gradually lost possession of the earliest translation of the Old Testament books into Greek through this (what must be called aggressive) claim, responded first with the great revisions of the second century mentioned earlier, revisions going far beyond the older revision activity. This applied especially to the work of Aquila, which presumably was conceived from the very outset as a Greek Targum of the accepted Hebrew text and had also gradually asserted its position alongside that text in the worship of diaspora synagogues. That toward the end of the second century the Jewish Christian Symmachus produced his own recension, one which, like that of Aquila, came close to being a translation itself, shows that even Jewish Christians loyal to the law (whom since Irenaeus were viewed as "Ebionites" and as heretics) considered the shortcomings of the old LXX and the growing textual confusion to be unacceptable.[122] Not only were the

---

[120] Loc. cit.

[121] The line of argumentation could vary on this point. The later fathers, for example, were inclined to emphasize the temporal distance between the two in order to underscore the utter independence of the seventy from later salvific events.

[122] Irenaeus, *Haer.* 1.26.2; 3.11.7; 3.21.1; 4.33.4; 5.1.3. Concerning the denial of the virgin birth, see also n. 55 above. See in this regard A. F. J. Klijn and G. Reinink, *Patristic Evidence for*

translations of the individual books done over a period of at least three hundred years, but a whole series of books also attested competing textual forms; furthermore, beginning in the first century before Christ, there were numerous corrections of older translations against the Hebrew text. One must also consider that, as Qumran has made quite clear, the original Hebrew texts themselves were in part anything but uniform. The Masoretic "unified text" is a construction of postbiblical Judaism. The charge of textual falsification, which since Justin had been raised against the Jews and which the Jews in their own turn raised against the Christians, derives at least in part from this chaotic textual tradition.

In order to organize this chaos and to provide an overview of it, Origen undertook what in antiquity represents the unique, almost superhuman task of creating the gargantuan work of his Hexapla, even presenting for the psalms six different Greek textual forms.[123] In spite of this, he held fast to the ecclesiastical significance and recognition of the LXX, which had come about through God's own "providence."[124] In his commentary on Canticles, he expressly emphasizes with regard to a reading contradicting his own *spiritualis interpretatio: tamen nos LXX interpretum scripta per omnium custodimus.*[125] This did not, however, prevent him from using a corrected text in his own homilies, and under certain circumstances even from following a reading approaching that of Aquila, since he was familiar with the quality of that translation and was uninterested in charges of falsification.[126] And though he was doubtless only too familiar with the story of the seventy translators, he never appealed to the authority of a translation or inspiration legend such as that of Philo and his Christian imitators after Justin and Irenaeus. Although the "seventy translators" represent for him a fixed, oft-used formula, he never relates any apologetic stories about them, though this does not exclude the possibility that he defended their reading as the better one since it was the one pointing toward the Christians.[127] He more fre-

---

Jewish-Christian Sects (Leiden, 1973) 19ff., 104ff. Justin distinguished more precisely here between Jewish Christians who themselves kept the law while not forcing gentile Christians to do so, and those who asserted that salvation depended on obedience to the law. Full church fellowship is possible with the former; see *Dial.* 47.1-6. Concerning Symmachus, see n. 54 above.

[123] Eusebius, *HE* 6.16; P. Nautin, *Origène. Sa vie et son oeuvre* (1977) 303-61: "in a church that had canonized a Greek version of the Bible, Origen affirmed the prevalence of Hebrew." G. Sgherri, "Sulla valutazione origeniana dei LXX," *Biblica* 58 (1977) 1-28; B. Neuschäfer (note 110), 1.86ff., 2.370ff.; C. P. Bammel, "Die Hexapla des Origenes. Die Hebraica Veritas im Streit der Meinungen," *Augustinianum* 28 (1988) 125-49.

[124] C. P. Bammel (note 123), 126, with reference to *Ep. ad Afric.* 8, ed. N. de Lange (SC 302; 1983) 532; cf. also P. Nautin (note 123), 345.

[125] Cited after A. von Harnack, *Der kirchengeschichtliche Ertrag der exegetischen Arbeiten des Origenes. II. Teil* (TU 42/4; Leipzig, 1919). *Comm. Cant I* (GCS VIII) 100f.; see also C. P. Bammel (note 123), 131, note 24. Cf. *Ep. ad Afric.* 9 (SC 302) 534: μετὰ τοῦ ποσῶς μᾶλλον ἀσκεῖν τὴν ἑρμηνείαν τῶν ἑβδομήκοντα, ἵνα μή τι παραχαράττειν δοκοίημεν ταῖς ὑπὸ οὐρανὸν ἐκκλησίαις.

[126] P. Nautin (note 123), 345.f.; C. P. Bammel (note 123), 130ff.

[127] See, e.g., *Hom. in Lev.* 12.5 (SC 287; ed. M. Borret, II; 1981) 188.61ff.

quently ascribes mistakes and deviations to the scribes than to the translators themselves.[128]

In addition to the general helplessness in the face of corrupted texts and their variants, one also finds a measure of uncertainty over against Jewish dialogue partners, partners who (quite differently than Christian dialogues with Jews portray the situation) mocked the Christians' ignorance and gullibility, an experience that, as the letter of Africanus to Origen shows, was indeed able to impress precisely the genuinely educated. The Seventy had, after all, translated the *original Hebrew text,* that is, from the very language in which the men of God of the Old Covenant had received their revelations through inspiration.[129] On the other hand, the "Old Testament" in Greek contained long passages lacking any parallel Hebrew textual basis at all; by contrast, the original Hebrew text contained material not found in the Greek. Furthermore, the Jews even denied the existence of any original text for entire books, for example, the story of Susanna. Intellectually discriminating Christians could not entirely escape these Jewish arguments. The path taken by Origen, however, a path that Jerome also took after him (again, in a different and simultaneously more radical fashion), remained the exception.

4.2. The Pseudo-Justinian Exhortation

Faced with these impasses, the majority of Christians appealed all the more emphatically to the translation legend, which now came to be used in ever new variations as an argument against the Jewish use of scripture. In the apparatus to his edition of the *Epistle of Aristeas,* Wendland enumerates nearly seventy witnesses of different authors.[130]

Thus is that legend also used in the *Exhortation to the Greeks (Cohortatio ad Graecos),* a writing incorrectly attributed to Justin and dating probably from the second half of the third century. On the one hand, the scope of the unknown author's education considerably surpasses that of Justin; on the other, his arguments are more superficial.[131]

In the second section of his work, he demonstrates that true knowledge of God can be based only on revelation through God's own Spirit, which allegedly uses holy men like musical instruments in order "to reveal to us divine and ce-

---

[128] C. P. Bammel (note 123), 129ff. See esp. *Comm. in Mt* XV,14 (GCS 40) 387f. concerning the situation surrounding the LXX-text tradition and his mode of working within the Hexapla.

[129] *Ep. ad Afric.* §5 (SC 302) 516: Ἐξ Ἑβραίων δὲ τοῖς Ἕλλησι μετεβλήθη πάνθ' ὅσα τῆς παλλαιᾶς διαθήκης φέρεται παρὰ Ἰουδαίοις.

[130] P. Wendland, ed., *Aristeae und Philocratem epistula cum ceteris de origine versionis LXX interpretum testimoniis* (Leipzig, 1900) 87-166, 228f.

[131] *Pseudo-Justinus. Cohortatio ad Graecos,* ed. M. Marcovich (PTS 32; 1900) 1-78; see pp. 4ff. concerning the dating and characterization of the unknown author. Marcovich arrives at a more positive estimation than did earlier scholars.

lestial truths."[132] Like Justin, this author views Moses as the first and earliest prophet, earlier than all other barbarian and Greek authors — a favorite theme of Jewish and early Christian apologetics.[133] To answer the objection that the work of "Moses and the other prophets" was not written in Greek and with Greek letters,[134] this author tells his own relatively thorough version of the translation legend, which picks up on either the *Epistle of Aristeas* or Josephus and Philo. He amplifies their account in a revealing fashion, however, by insisting that Ptolemy housed the seventy Jewish sages from Jerusalem, who were to translate "the Mosaic and *other prophetic writings*" into Greek, in seventy separate rooms on the island of Pharos. Separated from the others by attendants, each translator was to translate alone, so that the king might ascertain the accuracy of their work by the uniformity of the translations. When it became apparent that their work "not only conveyed the same meaning, but had done so with the same words,[135] and had not contradicted one another in a single instance, but had described the same things in the same way, he was so astonished that he concluded that the translation had been made by divine power."[136] In support of his contention that this is not a matter of mere legend (μύθος) or of fictitious stories (πεπλασμένας ἰσοτρίας), the erudite author relates that he himself has seen the remains of the little rooms on the island of Pharos and has heard these traditions from the Alexandrians themselves. The work of the Seventy had in the meantime become a tourist attraction. As further witnesses, he adduces the accounts of famous authors such as Philo, Josephus,[137] and many others. Reference to the miraculous, complete concurrence of the translations and the divine power the pagan king finds attested there corresponds more closely to the secondary account of Philo than to that of the *Epistle of Aristeas* or to that of Josephus (which is dependent on the latter), who do not yet associate any miracle with the translation. According to Aristeas, the translators worked together in a single house, comparing their work daily to insure uniformity,[138] whereupon it was then copied by Demetrius. Josephus, *Ant.* 12.104, remarks merely that they worked "with great zeal and great pains" in making their translation as accurate as possible. The *Epistle of Aristeas* cautiously suggests divine participation in the fact that the translation was concluded after exactly seventy-two

---

[132] 8.2 (ed. Marcovich, p. 33).

[133] P. Pilhofer, *Presbyteron Kreitton* (WUNT 2, R. 39; 1990) passim.

[134] The letters having been brought to the Greeks by Cadmus from Phoenicia (12.2f.; ed. Marcovich, pp. 38f.). By contrast, Moses, inspired by God's Spirit, wrote in Hebrew letters.

[135] 13.3 (ed. Marcovich, pp. 40f.): Ἐπεὶ δὲ ἔγνω τοὺς ἑβδομήκοντα ἄνδρας μὴ μόνον τῇ αὐτῇ διανοίᾳ, ἀλλὰ καὶ ταῖς αὐταῖς λέξεσι χρησαμένους, καὶ μηδὲ ἄχρι μιᾶς λέξεως τῆς πρὸς ἀλλήλους συμφωνίας διημαρτηκότας.

[136] Θείᾳ δυνάμει τὴν ἑρμηνείαν γεγράφθαι.

[137] He mentions these two Jewish authors several times; cf. 9.2 (34.21ff.); 10.1 (6.9f.). With regard to Josephus, he is familiar with, among other things, the title of the *Antiquities*.

[138] *Ep. Arist.* 302: Οἱ δὲ ἐπετέλουν ἕκαστα σύμφωνα ποιοῦντες πρὸς ἑαυτοὺς ταῖς ἀντιβολαῖς.

days, that is, as if the whole thing "occurred according to a specific design (οἰονεὶ κατὰ πρόθεσίν τινα)."[139]

By contrast, Philo puts considerably more emphasis on the miraculous, supranatural character of the translation. The "most respectable of the Hebrews" (*Vit. Mos.* 2.32) "like men inspired, prophesied (καθάπερ ἐνθουσιῶντες προεφήτευον), not one saying one thing and one another, but every one of them employed the self-same nouns and verbs, as if some unseen prompter had suggested all their language to them." This is why these men should be called "not mere translators, but hierophants and prophets to whom it had been granted through their honest and guileless minds to go along with the most pure spirit of Moses."[140]

Philo's emphasis on the divine inspiration of the translators finds its counterpart in Pseudo-Justin's reference to the divine, miraculous power at work in the translation and attested by the king himself. To the objection that these books are meant not for the Christians but for the Jews, the author emphasizes that "their doctrinal content belongs to us [Christians], and not to the Jews," a claim quite similar to the one Justin had made earlier.[141] Furthermore, "the fact that these books containing our religious doctrines (τῇ ἡμετέρᾳ θεοσεβείᾳ) are preserved among the Jews even to this day is but the work of divine providence (θείας προνοίας ἔργον) on our behalf," for the Christians can adduce proofs for their claim from within the "very books [of the LXX] still preserved among them [the Jews]" rather than from their own books, which might be subject to the charge of having been falsified from the very outset. This is commensurate with a remark made by the editor Marcovich, namely, that "the author is careful not to quote the New Testament, only the Old Testament."[142]

Here in Pseudo-Justin, the translation legend in its Christian form reaches its highpoint. Only in Epiphanius does it acquire a new, novelistic form, with (as with Justin) the king sending two letters to Jerusalem. Instead of the seventy small rooms, he needed only thirty-six in which to house the scholars, two in each room.[143] While Origen tactfully circumvented any mention of the legend at all, Jerome, the friend and contemporary of Epiphanius, vehemently rejected it

---

[139] *Ep. Arist.* 307. The πρόθεσις might also, however, suggest some agreement reached among the translators themselves.

[140] *Vit. Mos.* 2.37, 40.

[141] 13.5 (Marcovich 41.35): ὅτι οὐκ αὐτοῖς, ἀλλ᾽ ἡμῖν ἡ ἐκ τούτων διαφέρει διδασκαλία; cf. Justin, *Dial.* 29.2: μᾶλλον δὲ οὐχ ὑμετέροις ἀλλ᾽ ἡμετέροις. Cf. *Barn.* 4.6ff: The διαθήκη of Sinai belongs to the Christians.

[142] Op. cit. (note 131), 12.

[143] *De mens et pond* 5.6, ed. E. Moutsoulas (Athens, 1971); see also the complete Syriac Text, ed. J. E. Dean, *Epiphanius' Treatise on Weights and Measures: The Syriac Version* (Oriental Institute of the University of Chicago Studies in Ancient Oriental Civilization 11; Chicago, 1935) §3 fol. 48 b/c/d Eng. trans., 18; see also P. Wendland (note 47), 139ff., and pp. 67f. above (dialogue between Timothy and Aquila).

as a lie: "Nor do I know which author first invented the seventy small rooms through his lies, since neither Aristeas the bodyguard of the same Ptolemy nor, much later, Josephus recount anything of the sort. They write rather that those assembled in the hall compared their work and did not prophesy. It is one thing to be a prophet, and something entirely different to be a translator (*sed in una basilica congregatos contulisse scribant, non prophetasse. Aliud enim est vatem, aliud esse interpretem*). I neither condemn nor accuse the Seventy, but to all of them I in full confidence prefer the apostles."[144] Jerome's protest, however, remained a lone voice.

4.3. Irenaeus

Irenaeus and, dependent on him, Clement of Alexandria and Tertullian occupy the space between Justin and the anonymous *Exhortation to the Greeks* in the presentation of the translation legend. One might say that these three represent the continuing "normal form" of the legend in the church. In contrast to Justin's looser, rather poorly planned manner of presentation, Irenaeus wrote the first relatively well-organized "systematic theology" in the early church with a biblical and salvific-historical orientation. Everything has its specific place here. The point of departure for his introduction to the LXX problem is his discussion of the incarnation, and here again especially of the virgin birth. The "τὸ τῆς παρθένου σημεῖον" foretold by the prophet in Isa. 7:14 guarantees the reality of the incarnation, and this is why one should reject the translation νεᾶνις = *adulescentula* of Theodotion from Ephesus and of Aquila from the Pontus; the Jewish-Christian Ebionites, who follow these two, in their own turn believe that Jesus was begotten of Joseph. All of them together "destroy thus the divine salvific plan (*dispositio* = οἰκονομία),[145] destroying and eliminating in the process the witness of the prophets which God himself brought about."[146] Irenaeus has at his disposal more extensive scholarly training and a broader knowledge of history than does Justin. He knows that this prophecy comes from the time predating the Babylonian exile and the time of the Medes and Persians; similarly, the disputed "translation into Greek was completed by the Jews themselves long before the time of the advent of our Lord." This eliminates any suspicion that the Jews wanted thereby to do the Christians a favor, as it were. Quite the contrary, if they had known about the future existence of Christians, and that these same Christians would be using the prophetic writings from scripture, they would surely have burned all these writings, writings which prophesy to all the

---

[144] *Praef. in Pent.*, see *Biblia Sacra iuxta Vulgatem versionem* (Stuttgart, ²1975) 1.3f. = *Apologia adv. Rufinum* 2.25, ed. P. Lardet, CCSL 79, 3, 1, 62f.

[145] This term already appears with this meaning in Justin's own writings precisely in connection with the virgin birth; see n. 51 above.

[146] *Haer.* 3.21.1.

other nations that they would participate in eternal life while they, the Jews who "boast of being the house of Jacob and the people of Israel, would be disinherited of God's grace."[147]

There then follows this historically knowledgeable account, which I cite in full:

Before the Romans had established their power, and the Macedonians still ruled Asia, Ptolemaeus, the son of Lagus, wanting to add to his library in Alexandria the significant writings of all peoples, sent to the Jerusalemites, telling them of his wish to possess their writings in the Greek language. They sent to Ptolemaeus seventy elders, those among them who were especially experienced in the two languages, to fulfill his wish.[148] But because Ptolemy feared they might veil the true content of the writings on the basis of some arrangement, he decided to test each of them, and separated them from one another, commanding them to translate the same work; and he did this with regard to all the books.[149] And when they came together before Ptolemy and compared their translations, God was glorified, and the writings shown to be genuinely divine. For all had rendered the same texts with the same words and the same meanings . . . so that even the gentiles who were present saw that the books had been translated through divine inspiration (κατ' ἐπιπνοίαν τοῦ θεοῦ = *per aspirationem Dei*).[150]

In contradistinction to the *Epistle of Aristeas,* Philo, and Josephus, Irenaeus credits the founder of the dynasty, Ptolemy I Soter (died 282), with having provided the initiative for the translation. Although this is historically inaccurate, it may derive from the fact that Demetrius of Phaleron, who plays a decisive role in the *Epistle of Aristeas,* was a counsel of the first rather than the second Ptolemy.[151] The strict separation of the translators and the concurrence between their translations — *a motif appearing here for the first time,* then elaborated by the *Exhortation to the Greeks* and Epiphanius with a considerable element of fantasy — combine to demonstrate unequivocally the inspired

---

[147] *Haer.* 3.21.1: Exheredatos ostendunt a gratia Dei; cf. a similar but weakened argument in Justin, *Dial.* 120.5; see p. 61 above. The verb *exheredare* appears only here in the Latin translation; cf. however also 4.8.1 contra the "Marcionites": *exheredes sunt.* The equivalent might be ἀπόκληρος or ἀποκληρόνομος in connection with a verb such as δείκνυμι; see G. W. H. Lampe, *A Greek Patristic Lexicon* (Oxford, 1968), 196.

[148] In his own quotation from Irenaeus, Eusebius, *HE* 5.8.12, has ποιήσαντος τοῦ θεοῦ ὅσπερ ἠβούλετο instead of *facturos hoc quod ipse uoluisset.* This involves a characteristic, secondary theological interpretation, reflecting perhaps the influence of Clement of Alexandria, *Strom.* 1.149.2: θεοῦ γὰρ ἦν βούλημα.

[149] Here, too, Eusebius (5.8.13) attests an interpretive alteration. Instead of *iussit omnes eandem interpretari Scripturam,* he reads ἐκέλευσε τοὺς πάντας τὴν αὐτὴν ἑρμηνείαν γράφειν. The demand for the same translation model becomes that for a uniform translation.

[150] *Haer.* 3.21.2 = Eusebius, *HE* 5.8.11-14.

[151] Concerning Demetrius, see *KP* 1.1468f.; P. M. Frazer, *Ptolemaic Alexandria* (Oxford, 1972) 3.28f., index s.v. Demetrius was never head of the library; he merely advised the first Ptolemy concerning its founding and was then banished at the accession of the second Ptolemy. The *Epistle of Aristeas* is already reporting historical contradictions here; see op. cit., 1.689f.

condition of the translators, a motif already attested in Philo. The complete uniformity of these renderings can only be a result of God's own miracle, and this concurrence, encompassing every word and every expression, makes the entire work sacrosanct and excludes any and all criticism of its original text, that is, of the text not yet corrupted by its scribes. This basically makes the LXX superior to the Hebrew original, since it contains the divinely legitimated interpretation of what in the original Hebrew text were yet obscure passages; and even where the LXX text obviously deviates from the original Hebrew, this, too — for whatever reasons — is willed by God. The fixed form of the translation legend following Irenaeus was apparently able to provide Christian exegetes with firm footing. The translation was extended to include all the genuine Holy Scriptures, though Irenaeus, presumably for good reasons, chose not to provide any more specific details concerning the scope of those writings. One may assume that, as was the case with Justin, apocryphal writings did not play any significant role in his work.[152]

Irenaeus additionally refers to a second, even earlier "miracle of inspiration":

And it is by no means surprising that God made this happen, since even when his people were in captivity under Nebuchadnezzar and the writings were lost, and the Jews returned to their land after seventy years, during the time of the Persian king Artaxerxes he inspired the priest Ezra . . . to write down all the words of the earlier prophets and to reproduce for the people the law given to them by Moses.[153]

Here Irenaeus is appealing to the Jewish legend of Ezra as found in similar form at the end of 4 Esdras (Eng. 2 Esdras; Latin Esdras), according to which Ezra, after the law had been burned,[154] was inspired by God and dictated for forty days to five scribes. Of the ninety-four books resulting from this dictation, the twenty-four of the Jewish canon were to be made public, while the other seventy were concealed "in order to give them to the wise among your people."[155]

---

[152] Irenaeus references the Wisdom of Solomon in a lost writing (Eusebius, *HE* 5.26) and cites at the end of *Adversus Haereses* 4.38.3 Wisdom 6:19 without adducing the source. Of course, Irenaeus recognizes the additions to Daniel, thus also Susanna (*Haer.* 4.26.3, cf. 3.25.6; *Bel.* 4.5.2). All are part of his book of Daniel. Twice he cites the book of Baruch (*Haer.* 5.35.1 = Bar. 3:29–5:9; *Epideixis* 97 [SC 62, 166f.] = Bar. 3:29–4:1) as words of the prophet Jeremiah. Jeremiah and Baruch constituted a unity in his codex of prophets; cf. Tertullian, *Scorpiace* 8.5. His reserve with regard to apocryphal texts may derive in part from the fact that the heretics excessively adduced such texts (*Haer.* 1.20.1).

[153] 3.21.2 = Eusebius, *HE* 5.8.15.

[154] 4 Esdras 14:21; cf. 4:23. This legend might be based on Ezra 7:14.

[155] 4 Esdras 14:37-46. Irenaeus must not necessarily have been familiar with 4 Esdras itself, and might be drawing merely from the oral legend. Clement of Alexandria, himself dependent here on Irenaeus, adopts this in *Strom.* 1.149.3. Cf. similarly Tertullian, *De cultu feminarum* 1.3.2; Pseudo-Tertullian, *Adv. Marcionitas* 280f. Origen, too, is familiar with the tradition of Ezra as the one who "reproduced the Holy Scriptures from Jewish tradition," A. von Harnack (note 125), 11f.; cf. N. de Lange, *Origen and the Jews* (Cambridge, 1976; repr. 1978) 55. See also E. Schürer, *The History of*

Here Irenaeus is drawing on a legend that was widespread during his time among both Jews and Christians. His point is that the miracle of inspiration among the Seventy is not unique in salvific history; in fact, an even greater miracle occurred with Ezra, the last inspired prophet and first scriptural scholar.

In this miraculous way, God himself preserved the truth of those prophetic writings through which he "prepared and preformed" *(praeparavit et praeformavit)* the Christian faith, and did so in Egypt, where first the family of Jacob and later the infant Jesus found refuge. While Justin mentions King Herod to underscore the proximity to the advent of Christ, Irenaeus emphasizes the temporal distance. "Ptolemy, under whom these writings were translated," was much older than Augustus, in whose forty-first year the Lord was born. This alone demonstrates the shamelessness of those who "want to make other translations when we convert them on the basis of the scriptures and push them to believe in the advent of the Son of God." The Christian faith is "not invented and is alone true" because it possesses its "open proof from those scriptures which were translated in the way we mentioned earlier; also the proclamation of the church is free of falsification" *(sine interpolatione)*. The apostles are older than those new translators Theodotion and Aquila, and they and their successors "proclaim the words of the prophets as contained in the translation of the elders *(quemadmodum seniorum interpretatio continet)."*[156] It is thus the same Spirit of God who spoke through the prophets about the advent of the Lord, and "who correctly translated through the elders what was correctly foretold *(in senioribus autem interpretatus est bene quae bene prophetata fuerant),* and who through the apostles has proclaimed the fulfillment of the promises."

It is only after this long "hermeneutical preparation" that Irenaeus can now direct his attention toward his real goal, namely, the birth of Jesus from the virgin Mary; he refers first to the New Testament witnesses Matt. 1:18, Luke 1:35, and the fulfillment quotation Matt. 1:23 from Isa. 7:14, followed by the complete quotation from Isa. 7:10-16. After interpreting this text and supplementing it with Ps. 131:11 and Luke 1:27 and 41f., he turns anew against those "who alter what we find in Isaiah: behold, a young woman *(adulescentula)* will conceive and will claim (the child) is a son of Joseph: They did not understand (the text), otherwise they would not have dared to change it."[157]

---

the Jewish People in the Age of Jesus Christ, ed. G. Vermes, F. Millar, and M. Goodman, vol. 3.1 (London, 1986) 301; L. Ginzberg, *Legends of the Jews* (Philadelphia, 1928; 1959) 6.445f., n. 50. Resistance against this legend may have prompted the assertion ascribed to Rav Hananel (ca. 260), namely, that "even if someone knows the Torah as well as Ezra, he may still not recite it from memory, but must read it aloud, as we read in Baruch . . . (Jer. 36:18)," *y. Meg.* 50f.; cf. *Gen. R.* 36:8. Concerning this legend, see the thorough discussion in J.-D. Kaestli, "Le récit de IV Esdras 14 et sa valeur pour l'histoire du Canon de l'Ancien Testament," in J.-D. Kaestli and O. Wermelinger (note 5), 71-102, with references to additional texts of later church fathers.

156 *Haer.* 3.21.3.
157 3.21.5; cf. 3.21.9: the doctrine of the *mali doctores.*

In contrast to Justin's ever new approaches in his *Dialogue* to the hot topic of Isa. 7:14, approaches that seem more to circle the topic than genuinely to address it, the approach of the "systematic" biblical theologian Irenaeus lends to his whole undertaking more the character of a genuine disputation. Irenaeus proceeds straight toward his goal, creating through a demonstration of the inspiration of the translation of the Seventy a basis from which he can then easily present his proof of the virgin birth. The scholarly explications of Jerome in his own commentary to Isaiah, replete with a not inconsiderable number of lexical references, shows that without this (questionable) basis it is philologically difficult if not completely hopeless to justify the translation of ʿalmâ in Isa. 7:14 with παρθένος.[158]

Jerome's sincere philological efforts, however, remained the exception. Irenaeus's impressive grounding of the inspiration of the LXX, understandable when viewed from his position and yet at the same time highly questionable, had provided an (apparently) firm foundation.

4.4. Clement and Tertullian

Irenaeus's explications concerning the translation of the Seventy sounded so convincing that Clement of Alexandria incorporated them in a somewhat altered form into his *Stromata*, even though he cites Philo's *De Vita Mosis* several times and was doubtless also familiar with Josephus and the other Jewish-Hellenistic writers.[159]

After a chronological discussion at the end of which he mentions Josephus, Clement places his report before his account of Moses' lifework.[160] With better training in history than Irenaeus, he leaves open the question whether the translation was undertaken under the first or second Ptolemy. As did Irenaeus and many other ancient church authors of a later period, he emphasizes the Spirit-

---

[158] *Comm. in Es.* (CCSL 73.I.2, ed. M. Adriaen; 1963) 102-5. Cf. H. Wildberger, *Isaiah 1–12* (Minneapolis, 1991) 308: "What is the meaning of עלמה? The translation of the word with παρθένος (virgin), which has caused the passage to be interpreted as the account of the virgin birth, is not impossible from the outset. . . . Only in Prov. 30:19 could the term be understood to include the idea that this is a married woman." The interpretation "virgin" is to be given up merely because it "is not forthcoming." See also O. Betz, *Was wissen wir von Jesus* (Wuppertal/Zurich, 1991) 128f. Concerning Isa. 7:14 among the Latin (and Greek) fathers, see R. Gryson, *Esaias* (VL 12/2; 1987) 119f. Concerning the later translation παρθένος, see H. Gese, "Natus ex Virgine," in *Vom Sinai zum Zion* (Munich, 1974) 145: "The Septuagint could understand παρθένος in an archaizing fashion as in early Greek as 'young girl/young woman,'" with reference to G. Delling, *TDNT* 5.832f.; cf. also 131f. One thing is certain, namely, that the translation νεᾶνις in Aquila, Theodotion, and Symmachus represents a conscious protest against the Christian interpretation of Isa. 7:14 as a reference to the birth of the Son of God; see pp. 52f. above.

[159] Although Clement does not cite the *Epistle of Aristeas,* he was probably familiar with it. He refers to *De Vita Mosis* around thirty times, and mentions Josephus in *Strom.* 1.147.24.

[160] *Strom.* 1.148f.; concerning Moses, see 180-82.

induced concurrence "in sense and wording" of the separately undertaken translations revealed upon comparison,[161] adding "for God's will was aimed at reaching the ears of the Greeks." Clement, as the first really learned, that is, well-versed Christian theologian in the ancient church, and as an enthusiastic Greek, found this translation to be, as it were, a divinely inspired prophecy in the Greek language (οἱονεὶ Ἑλληνικὴν προφητείαν). A reference to Ezra's prophetic-inspired renewal of the Holy Scriptures concludes his account.

Tertullian, who had read both Justin and Irenaeus, was the first Christian writer to appeal to the *Epistle of Aristeas*.[162] In his masterfully composed *Apologeticum,* he begins in chap. 17 with the *demonstratio religionis nostrae* (16.14).

In this piece, one train of thought leads with inner necessity to the next. After the model of philosophy, Tertullian demonstrates the existence of God first on the basis of the order of the cosmos itself, and then on the basis of the inner conviction of human beings. He supports the proof with documentation, namely, from the Holy Scriptures. Since their authority must be secured, he recounts first the story of their translation into Greek, and then proceeds to secure their credibility in a twofold fashion: First, through a demonstration on the basis of their age; second, on the basis of present events which confirm the prophecies of the Bible.[163]

In his work directed at gentiles, the sober, rational African jurist with a distinct sense for measure and form held the witness of the "Greek" Aristeas to be more persuasive than the Jewish-Christian legend of the translation miracle. The result is that the Greek participants occupy a more prominent position in his presentation than do the Jews. First he praises King Philadelphus, *Ptolemaeorum eruditissimus . . . et omnis litteraturae sagacissimus,* who by founding his library was trying to outdo his rival, a certain Pisistratus. At the behest of Demetrius, he sent for the books of the Jews, who simultaneously sent him the seventy-two translators. In contrast to the *Epistle of Aristeas,* however, Tertullian does not speak here about the Jewish law, but about the fact that "the prophets had always spoken to the Jews" because the latter were God's chosen people. To this cautious *interpretatio christiana* he adds a second that can be interpreted in a twofold fashion. He mentions the philosopher Menedemus of Eretria as a witness to these events. Menedemus admired the seventy-two translators "as a defender of belief in providence because of their agreement with his views" *(quos Menedemus quoque philosophus, providentiae vindex, de sententiae communione suspexit).* This refers to the table conversations at the royal banquet in the *Epistle of Aristeas* (or in Josephus), where the philosopher agrees

---

[161] 149.2: συνέπνευσαν αἱ πᾶσαι ἑρμηνεῖαι συναντιβληθεῖσαι καὶ τὰς διανοίας καὶ τὰς λέξεις.

[162] *Apol.* 18.5-9: *affirmavit haec vobis etiam Aristaeus.*

[163] Carl Becker, *Tertullians Apologeticum* (1954) 244.

to the answer one of the elders gives to the question about providence, and praises their religious views.[164]

Tertullian formulates his praise of their "common sentiment" such that one might understand the expression *de sententiae communione suspexit* also as praise of the concurring translations.[165] So in addition to the second Ptolemy and Aristeas, Menedemus counts as the third gentile witness for this work. To these is then added the possibility of examining these works in the present: "Even today, the libraries of Ptolemy with the Hebrew writings are still in the Serapeum" (in these writings Tertullian is probably also including the translation). They are also read in the synagogues. "Whoever listens to them will find God; and whoever goes beyond even this and tries to recognize him will be forced to believe."

It is peculiar that the Latin West could be more generous toward the translation legend than were the Greek fathers. Because the dispute with the Jews was neither as intensive nor as urgent, one was less dependent on the auxiliary construction of divine inspiration. On the other hand, this greater measure of freedom facilitated the fixing of the writings of the Old Testament in use in the church at the time, including those transcending the Hebrew canon, at the Third Council of Carthage in 397 C.E.[166]

Although Tertullian is indeed familiar with the legend of Ezra that both Irenaeus and Clement associate with the miraculous translation, he mentions it in a different context, one revealing his as yet rather open "understanding of the canon." The discussion concerns *1 Enoch,* which he and many of his contemporaries counted among the inspired biblical writings.[167] In *Apol.* 22.3, he men-

---

[164] *Ep. Arist.* 199-201: "'But your counsels, Your Majesty, are all good, and are carried out by God to your advantage.' . . . And the philosopher Menedemus of Eretria said, 'True, Your Majesty, for inasmuch as all things are governed by providence, and these men [the Jewish elders] are right in holding that man is a creature of God, it follows that all power and beauty of discourse have their starting point from God.'" Concerning the philosopher Menedemus, see K. von Frizt, *PW* 15.1 (1931) 788f. He died after 278 B.C.E. at the court of Antigonus Gonatas, the adversary of the second Ptolemy.

[165] See in this regard C. Becker, ed., *Tertullian Apologeticum. Lateinisch und deutsch* (Munich, 21961) 303. The author must have done a very precise reading of the *Epistle of Aristeas* or of its rendering in Josephus, *Ant.* 12.11-118, if his mention of this particular philosopher as a defender of divine providence is any indication, a philosopher appearing only once in the work, and then only on the periphery (*Ep. Arist.* 201: πρόνοιᾳ . . . τῶν ὅλων διοικουμένων; cf. Josephus, *Ant.* 12.101: προνοίᾳ διοικεῖσθαι πάντα). Concerning the motif of divine providence in the translation, see pp. 43f., 71ff. above. Tertullian mentions Josephus in *Apol.* 19.6: *Judaeus Josephus antiquitatum Judaicarum vernaculus vindex;* see in this regard R. Heinze, *Tertullianus Apologeticum* (BVS GW 62.10; Leipzig, 1910) 379, who suspects that Tertullian did know Josephus; also H. Schreckenberg, *Die Flavius-Josephus-Tradition in Antike und Mittelalter* (ALGHJ 5; Leiden, 1972) 71.

[166] See in this regard E. Preuschen, *Analecta II. Teil: Zur Kanonsgeschichte* (SQS 8/2; Tübingen, 21910) 72f., and J. D. Kaestli and O. Wermelinger (note 5), 86-89, 170-74, and index s.v. 391. Concerning the later Latin witnesses to the translation, see P. Wendland (note 47), 160ff.

[167] See in this regard J. H. Waszink and J. C. M. Van Winden, *Tertullianus. De Idololatria. Criti-*

tions those particular *litterae sanctae* that recount the fall of the angels, the origin of demons, and God's punishment of them, all of which apparently refers primarily to the book of *Enoch*.[168] In *De idol.* 15.6, he relates how through the "oldest prophet Enoch" the Holy Spirit foretold the Greco-Roman door cult, a cult mediated by the demons.[169] He repeats this in a more general statement in *De idol.* 4.2.[170] In *De cultu feminarum* 1.3, he defends the book of *Enoch* against his Christian contemporaries who reject it "because it was not received into the Jewish Torah shrine."[171] To this is added the historical argument that this work could not have survived the Flood. Tertullian counters that Noah, the prophet's great-grandson, could have received the Enoch-prophecy either through oral family tradition *(domestica et hereditaria traditione)* by way of Enoch's son Methuselah, or, if Enoch's writing had been destroyed "through the violence of the Flood," could have reproduced it just as after the Babylonians' destruction of Jerusalem Ezra reproduced all the works of the Jewish canon.[172] In this way, Tertullian could very well have supported the miracle of inspiration in his account of the seventy-two translators. That he did not do so in the *Apologeticum*, but at most merely alluded to it, may derive from his consideration of the educated among his gentile readers. Apparently, he felt it better to present to them the "gentile" and "objective" report of the *Epistle of Aristeas,* along with three non-Christian "witnesses," than a Jewish-Christian miracle legend.

Finally, the christological witnesses militate for this writing. "Enoch also spoke [there] about the Lord" — that is, 2 Tim. 3:16 also applies to this writing. This may indicate that the version of *Enoch* available to Tertullian contained the similitudes.[173] In a reverse fashion, he asserts that precisely this would have given the Jews ample reason to reject it, "as is the case with everything else dealing with Christ." The final reason is the witness of the apostle Judas for Enoch's writing (Jude 14f.). There can be little doubt that Tertullian also counted *Enoch* among the writings of the seventy-two translators and viewed it as "canonical." That this book was rejected during the fourth century in church decisions despite its wide-

---

cal Text, Translation and Commentary (VigChr Sup. 1; 1987) 113f., and J. T. Milik, *The Books of Enoch. Aramaic Fragments of Qumran Cave 4* (Oxford, 1976) 78-80.

[168] Cf. *1 Enoch* 6–20. Concerning the punishment of the angels, cf. also *De cultu feminarum* 2.10.3 with *1 Enoch* 7:1f., and *De idol.* 9.1f. with *1 Enoch* 6:1ff. Concerning Justin, see n. 38 above.

[169] *Haec igitur ab initio praevidens spiritus sanctus etiam ostia in superstitionem ventura pracecinit per antiquissimum propheten Enoch.* See in this regard *1 Enoch* 19 and p. 44, n. 21 above concerning Moses as the first prophet in Justin's thinking.

[170] *Antecesserat Enoch praedicens omnia elementa, omnem mundi censum . . . in idolatrian versuros daemonas . . . , ut pro deo adversus deum consecrarentur.*

[171] 1.3.1: *Scio scripturam Enoch . . . non recipi a quibusdam, quia nec in armañum Iudaicum admittitur.* Concerning the book cabinet of the Christian and Jewish congregational libraries, see M. Hengel, *Die Evangelienüberschriften* (SAH.PH; 1984) 37ff.

[172] 1.3.2: *Omne instrumentum Iudaicae litteraturae per Esdram constat restauratum.* See in this regard pp. 76f., n. 155 above.

[173] *De cultu fem.* 1.3.3: *Sed cum Enoch eadem scriptura etiam de domino praedicarit.*

spread popularity in churches during the third century derives from its popularity among heretics such as the Manichaeans and Priscillian and his adherents, though it also had to do with the "pressure" of the Jewish canon itself; ultimately, one could not afford an older written prophet than Moses.[174]

5. Findings

The Christianized legend of the translation of the "Seventy" appears first in Justin; its form is not yet fully developed, and yet it already functions as an important means of argumentation. In Irenaeus, the *Exhortation to the Greeks,* and Clement of Alexandria it then manifests its fully developed form. In all these cases, it constitutes a kind of *hermeneutical prologue* for the Christian use of the Greek Old Testament. This made it possible to transfer the already familiar notion of the prophetic inspiration of Holy Scripture to its Greek translation as well, and to ascribe to that translation the same, indeed, under certain circumstances an even higher dignity than to the Hebrew original. The inspired translators on the one hand, and the Spirit-filled apostles who used the LXX on the other, mutually confirm one another. At the same time, they provided the foundation for the charge of scriptural falsification toward Jewish dialogue partners. This act of violence was, however, historically understandable, and in a certain sense even necessary; because a return to the original Hebrew text was (at least initially) impossible, the alternative would have been a complete rejection of the Old Testament writings, as was indeed the case with Marcion and many gnostics. The basic requirements needed for a discovery of the *Hebraitas* were not yet present. Nonetheless, a degree of uncertainty remained concerning the correct textual form and the true scope of the "canon" of the Holy Scriptures. Against this background, the theological-philological accomplishments of those such as Origen and Jerome — quite in contradiction to widespread ecclesiastical misunderstanding or even outright rejection — cannot be appraised highly enough.

That this legend, one so significant and yet so dangerous for Christians, really could constitute something like a (doubtless questionable) "hermeneutical prologue" for the Old Testament "prophetic" writings can be seen in its remarkable history of influence extending even to the advent of the historical-critical method in the seventeenth century, and simultaneously in the simple fact that practically all of the over twenty manuscripts of the *Epistle of Aristeas* introduce a catena to the octoteuch (Genesis-Ruth).[175]

---

[174] Concerning the book of *Enoch* in the ancient church, see R. H. Charles, *The Book of Enoch* (Oxford, 1912) LXXXI-XCV, and E. Schürer (note 155), 3.1.351ff. Cf. already *Barn.* 4.3; 16.2; Irenaeus, *Haer.* 4.16.2. The work is frequently adduced without mention of Enoch.

[175] P. Wendland (note 47), VIIf.; A. Pelletier (note 4), 9f.

This oldest account, one which an unknown Hellenistic Jew had a Greek sympathizer write and which the Christian fathers then not only secured but also surpassed, constituted for the ancient church the objective proof that the translation into a new world language was willed by God and from the very outset universally recognized, and that with the work of the Seventy the Christians possessed the prophecies of the Old Covenant as inspired by God's Spirit, prophecies that had been fulfilled for them in Jesus Christ.

Syncretistic Features in Jewish
and Jewish-Christian Baptism Movements

by

HERMANN LICHTENBERGER

For Hans L. Merkle in Gratitude, At His 80th Birthday

I. The Problem

Insoluble problems plague any attempt to write a history of the Jewish, Jewish-Christian, and Christian groups that existed alongside developing rabbinic Judaism, on the one hand, and that competed with the emerging church, on the other. The sources available for such a history already impede the undertaking insofar as all the portrayals of such movements from the outside invariably reflect an anti-heretical, polemical tone. To this is added the sheer number and the complicated nature of traditions dealing with such groups, groups mentioned, for example, by the likes of Irenaeus, Hippolytus, and Epiphanius.[1] I will thus delimit the material in two ways: first, substantively by examining only a selection of baptism movements; second, as regards sources, by choosing only those that are attested by primary as well as by polemical documents. These include the Qumran-Essenes, early Christianity, the Ebionites, the Elkesaites, and the Mandaeans. We also possess ancient accounts regarding John the Baptist and his adherents,[2] while sometimes more, sometimes less extensive accounts of baptism groups can be found in Josephus,[3] in the Jewish *Sibylline Oracles*,[4] in

---

[1] For an introduction and texts, see A. F. J. Klijn and G. J. Reinink, *Patristic Evidence for Jewish-Christian Sects* (Leiden, 1963).

[2] See in this regard (with bibliography) H. Lichtenberger, "Täufergemeinden und frühchristliche Täuferpolemik im letzten Drittel des 1. Jahrhunderts," *ZTK* 84 (1987) 36-57.

[3] The figure of Banus, in Josephus, *Vita* 11.

[4] Lichtenberger, op. cit., 38-40 (*Sib. Or.* iv.161-69).

Thanks to K. Lehnardt and E. Reimann for copying the manuscript, and to J. Kalms for proofing.

the *Vita Adae et Evae*,[5] in the *Pseudo-Clementine* literature,[6] and in rabbinic tradition.[7]

II. Presuppositions

1. Jewish Presuppositions

(a) The bases of all Jewish notions of purity are the Old Testament ordinances concerning purity, impurity, and the possibility of attaining cultic purity.[8] The water rite for reestablishing ritual purity after defilement (contact with the dead, sexually related impurity) was the common property of ancient Judaism in all its manifestations.[9]

(b) The Qumran community (1QS 2.25ff.) associates purity and atonement with the water rite, yet does so such that repentance constitutes the presupposition for the cleansing water's efficacy.[10]

(c) John the Baptist preached and practiced a "baptism of repentance for the forgiveness of sins" (Mark 1:4), a one-time, unrepeatable, symbolic-sacramental and prophetic act as a baptism of deliverance from final judgment. The typical characteristic for John is the epithet "the Baptist" (so also Josephus), one identifying this baptism as something unmistakably personal. Although in his account of the Baptist (*Ant.* 18.116-19)[11] Josephus denies that baptism possesses the sacramental capacity to forgive sins, and allows only that it can indeed purify the body, still precisely his negation of the atoning effects of baptism shows that Josephus was well aware of the special understanding of the kind of baptism associated with John and is seeking merely to classify it according to the commonly accepted Jewish understanding of purity.

---

[5] *Vita Ad.* 6-11.

[6] See §IV.3 below.

[7] *t. Yad.* 2.2; *y. Ber.* 3.5.6d; *b. Ber.* 22a.

[8] Basic studies include R. Wolf, *Aqua religiosa. Die religiöse Verwendung von Wasser im frühen Christentum und in seiner Umwelt* (diss.; Leipzig, 1956); J. Neusner, *A History of the Mishnaic Law of Purities*, 22 vols. (SJLA 6/1-22; Leiden, 1974-1977), esp. vol. 22; idem, *A History of the Mishnaic Law of Holy Things*, 6 vols. (SJLA 30/1-6; Leiden, 1979).

[9] J. Neusner, *The Idea of Purity in Ancient Judaism* (Leiden, 1973); idem, "Geschichte und rituelle Reinheit im Judentum des 1. Jahrhunderts n. Chr.," in *idem, Das pharisäische und talmudische Judentum* (ed. H. Lichtenberger; Tübingen, 1984) 74-92.

[10] See H. Lichtenberger, *Studien zum Menschenbild in Texten der Qumrangemeinde* (Göttingen, 1980) 118-22.

[11] See Lichtenberger, "Täufergemeinden," 43-47; idem, *The Dead Sea Scrolls and John the Baptist: Reflections on Josephus' Account of John the Baptist* (Congress Volume 1987; Jerusalem, forthcoming).

2. Christian Presuppositions

One of the most secure accounts concerning primitive Christian history is that Jesus was baptized by John the Baptist. Jesus probably spent time among those who, like himself, were baptized by John, and the Gospel of John relates that several of his disciples came from the circle around the Baptist.[12] Jesus and his first followers acknowledged John's baptism as fully valid, and although the early community did also adopt the act of baptism and the understanding of a baptism of repentance with regard to the forgiveness of sins, it performed such baptisms in the name of Jesus Christ. The Baptist himself was no longer the integrative figure; through baptism, the believer is dedicated to Christ. Both historically and substantively, Christian baptism has its origin in and is based upon John's baptism of Jesus.

These two aspects of water rites constitute basic presuppositions for the later history of both Jewish and Jewish-Christian baptism movements: (1) a repeatable rite for attaining cultic purity (with the Qumran variation), and (2) one-time baptism by baptists for the forgiveness of sins. Between the two, we find proselyte baptism,[13] representing an initial baptism for the attainment of cultic purity, upon which additional ones follow depending on cultic need.

III. Individual Accounts of Water Rites

1. Baptists (Justin, Dial. 80.4), Hemerobaptists, Masbothei (Hegesippus in Eusebius, HE iv.22)

Information on some of these groups and other related groups is so sparse that often only the name itself suggests that baptism groups are involved at all. It is only about the hermerobaptists that Epiphanius (*Haer.* 17.1-5) provides more precise information. In both summer and winter, they immerse themselves daily in water. "The hermerobaptists are no different from the Jews except that they claim there is no eternal life for a man unless he is washed daily with water" (Epiphanius, *Anac.* 17). The *Apostolic Constitutions* (vi.3) follow Mark 7:3f. in portraying them commensurate with a Pharisaic ideal of purity.

They are usually associated with the שַׁחֲרִית טוֹבְלֵי, the "early bathers," who according to *t. Yad.* ii.20 (Zuckermandel, 684.6f.) criticize the Pharisees "because you utter the Name without having taken an immersion bath." The Pharisees respond by "charging you early bathers with uttering the Name from a body

---

[12] John 1:37; see in this regard C. K. Barrett, *The Gospel According to St. John* (London, ²1978) 180.

[13] Concerning proselyte baptism, see K. G. Kuhn and H. Stegemann, "Proselyten," *Pauly-WSup* 9 (1962) 1248-83, esp. 1274-76.

tainted with impurity." The Pharisees are apparently denying the efficacy of baths taken to cleanse oneself from nocturnal impurities if such are taken every morning, that is, even without any new defilement having taken place.[14]

The available accounts are not at all unequivocal, and the sources themselves are often characterized by misunderstanding. Tertullian, for example, thought that all Jews were obligated to take a daily immersion bath (*De bapt.* 15). The Samaritan Dositheans allegedly took part in frequent water rites,[15] though it is unclear whether they are to be associated with the Samaritan Sebuaeans mentioned by Epiphanius (*Haer.* 10).

2. Isolated Accounts of Baptist Activity

(a) According to Josephus, *Vita* 11, a certain Banus "bathed himself in cold water frequently, both by night and by day, in order to preserve his purity."

(b) *4 Sib. Or.* 161-69: Immersion in running water in connection with the request for forgiveness and with praise will deliver a person from divine wrath.

(c) To attain forgiveness and mercy after their expulsion from paradise, Adam intends to spend forty days in the Jordan, Eve thirty-seven in the Tigris in neck-deep water (*Vita Adae et Evae* 6-11).

(d) Epictetus, *Diss.* ii.9.21, betrays familiarity with Jewish baptismal rites.

(e) Finally, reference should be made to the spread of John the Baptist's adherents (at Ephesus: Acts 19:1-7; Rome as well?).

On balance, at the turn from the first to the second century we find a great variety of baptism movements with Jewish influences dispersed over a wide geographical area. In various ways and with varying emphasis, they all adopt the two fundamental aspects of baptism: (1) attainment of cultic purity, and (2) the forgiveness of sins through water rites. We will examine the Ebionites as our first detailed example.

IV. The Ebionites

The appropriate point of departure for understanding the Ebionites includes the Gospel of the Ebionites along with Irenaeus's account, the latter of whom seems indeed to have been familiar with a Gospel of the Ebionites. Let us consider Irenaeus's account first.

---

[14] Cf. in this regard also *y. Ber.* iii.5.6d; *b. Ber.* 22a.

[15] K. Rudolph, *Antike Baptisten. Zu den Überlieferungen über frühjüdische und -christliche Taufsekten* (Sitzungsberichte der Sächsischen Akademie der Wissenschaften zu Leipzig. Philosophisch-Historische Klasse 121.4; Berlin, 1981) 9f.

1. Irenaeus, Adversus haereses

*Solo autem eo, quod est secundum Matthaeum, evangelio utuntur et apostolum
Paulum recusant, apostatam eum legis dicentes. Quae autem sunt prophetica,
curiosius exponere nituntur; et circumciduntur ac perseverant in his
consuetudinibus, quae sunt secundum legem, et iudaico charactere vitae, uti et
Hierosolymam adorent, quasi domus sit Dei (Haer. 1.26.2).*[16]

Elements of significance for our investigation include:

(1) The Ebionites keep Jewish law, practice circumcision, and face Jerusalem
in prayer. In connection with their keeping of the law, they reject Paul
apostatam eum legis dicentes.

(2) Although reference to water rites is made only in connection with the
eucharist (water instead of wine, v.1.3), still the general expression "they have
maintained circumcision and the other customs according to the law as well as
the Jewish life forms" doubtless also includes the purification rites known especially from Epiphanius's account. Origen confirms Irenaeus,[17] maintaining that
the Ebionites practice circumcision, live according to the Jewish dietary laws,
and accuse others of transgressing against the law.

Epiphanius describes the thoroughgoing Jewish character of the Ebionites
right at the beginning of his extensive presentation in *Haer.* 30, in connection
with his introduction of the alleged founder of the Ebionites, Ebion. After discussing his christology (Christ as having been born from sexual intercourse and
from the seed of a man, namely, Joseph) and his agreement with others,
Epiphanius delineates the differences: "He agreed with the others in everything,
with this one difference, his attachment to Judaism's Law of the Sabbath, circumcision, and all other Jewish and Samaritan observances.

(3) But like the Samaritans he goes still further than the Jews. He added the
rule about care in touching a gentile,

(4) and that a man must immerse himself in water every day he has been with
a woman, after he leaves her — any water he can find, the sea or other.

(5) Moreover, if he meets anyone while returning from his plunge and immersion in the water, he runs back again for another immersion, often with his
clothes on too" (*Haer.* 30.2.2-5). Here the basic Jewish character becomes clear
that is also influencing the Ebionites' christology. In the following discussion,
however, our attention will focus primarily on questions of baptism; concerning

---

[16] "They use only the Gospel according to Matthew and reject the Apostle Paul, saying that he is
an apostate from the law. The Prophetical Writings, however, they strive to interpret in a rather curious manner. They circumcise themselves and continue in the practices which are prescribed by the
law and by the Judaic standard of living, so that they worship Jerusalem as the house of God."
Translation according to Dominic J. Unger, *St. Irenaeus of Lyons Against the Heresies,* vol. 1 (New
York: Paulist Press, 1992) 90.

[17] S. Klijn and Reinink, op. cit., 124-35.

the Jewish character of the Ebionites, see also Eusebius, *HE* iii.27.5: "Like the former they used to observe the sabbath and the rest of the Jewish ceremonial, but on Sundays celebrated rites like ours in commemoration of the Savior's resurrection."

2. The Gospel of the Ebionites

The Gospel of the Ebionites, attested only in Epiphanius (*Haer.* 30.13), which according to Epiphanius was actually a distorted Gospel of Matthew, began with the appearance of the Baptist and with Jesus' baptism. The Gospel of the Ebionites combines the baptism accounts of the synoptic gospels such that the heavenly voice issues a threefold proclamation: "'And then,' it says, 'John fell down before him and said, I pray thee, Lord, do thou baptize me. But he forbade him, saying, Suffer (me), for thus it is meet that all be fulfilled."[18] The Jewish-Christian character also emerges clearly in the presentation of John the Baptist and his food: "'And his meat,' it says, 'was wild honey, whose taste was the taste of manna, as a cake in oil.' This, if you please, to turn the speech of the truth into falsehood, and substitute 'a cake in honey' for 'locusts'" (*Haer.* 30.13.4f.). John was thus a vegetarian like the Ebionites themselves (cf. *Haer.* 30.22.4). The rejection of the temple cult is doubtless also to be viewed in this connection: "I came to abolish the sacrifices, and if ye cease not from sacrifice, wrath will not cease from you" (*Haer.* 30.16.4).

In *Haer.* 30.15.1, Epiphanius also mentions an Ebionite work with the title *Periodoi Petrou;* he recounts the Ebionites' assertion that Peter, like them, washed daily for the sake of cleansing (*Haer.* 30.15.3); he, too, commensurate with Ebionite custom, is alleged to have been a vegetarian.

According to Epiphanius (*Haer.* 30.16.1), the Ebionites practice *baptisma* in addition to daily washings. He summarizes their customs in *Anac.* 30.2-4: "Although they are Jews, they use gospels. They loathe meat, yet hold water to be divine. In his appearance in the flesh, Christ put on the form of a man, as I said. They bathe incessantly, summer and winter, apparently for cleansing *(hagnismos)*, like the Samaritans."

3. The Pseudo-Clementines[19]

The Pseudo-Clementine literature amplifies these features. We encounter a high regard for baptism on the one hand and purification rites after sexual intercourse on the other.

---

[18] Translation according to Frank Williams, *The Panarion of Epiphanius of Salamis. Book I (Sects 1-46)* (Leiden/New York: E. J. Brill, 1987) 130.

[19] G. Strecker, "Judenchristentum," *TRE* 17.310-25 (bibliography 323-25).

Concerning baptism, *Ps.-Clem. Hom.* xi.27.1 recounts: "But just come, whether you are righteous or unrighteous. For if you are righteous, for salvation you need but be baptized; an unrighteous person, however, should not only be baptized for forgiveness of sins committed unknowingly, but should also do good commensurate with his godlessness, just as is necessary for baptism. (2) So make haste, whether you are righteous or unrighteous, that you are soon born to God, the Father, who begets you from water."

Concerning purification in water following menstruation or sexual intercourse: "Because one must observe the monthly purification and must wash after sexual intercourse, nor can one reject such a purification when practiced by those living in error" (*Ps.-Clem. Hom.* xi.33.4; see further vii.8.2; xi.30.1).

4. External Influences

Epiphanius also suggests that external influences had an effect on the Ebionites: "When one of them falls ill or is bitten by a snake, he gets into water and invokes the names in Elxai — heaven and earth, salt and water, winds and 'angels of righteousness' as they say, bread and oil — and begins to say 'Help me, and rid me of my pain!'" (*Haer.* 30.17.4). Here water functions therapeutically only on a superficial level, the basis of the praxis actually being the high regard for water as holy.

Finally, the fundamentally Jewish character of the Ebionites also emerges clearly in their attitude toward circumcision. According to Epiphanius (*Haer.* 30.26.1-2), they justified their own circumcision by pointing out that Christ was himself circumcised: "It is enough for the disciple that he be as his master; Christ was circumcised, you be circumcised too!" Sanctification of the sabbath is also a Jewish feature: "He [Ebion] attached himself to Judaism's Law of the Sabbath, circumcision, and all other Jewish and Samaritan observances" (*Haer.* 30.1.2.2). One clear indication of their Jewish self-understanding is their designation of their assembly places as synagogues (*Haer.* 30.18.2).

Scholars have quite rightly pointed out that Epiphanius's presentation of the Ebionites starts with the assumption that everything Jewish-Christian is also "Ebionite" — that is, derives from this one heresy founded by a certain Ebion. Even long after they had disappeared, the main charge against the Ebionites was their christology (Jesus' natural conception and birth) and their adherence to Jewish law.

As far as Elkesai's influence on the Ebionites is concerned, it is probably true that these groups, with their water rites, shared a great many features from the very outset, features deriving from the time around the turn of the first/second century. Both probably acquired the custom of baptism and purification rites from a common environment east of the Jordan.

V. Elkesai and the Elkesaites[20]

The clearest example of syncretistic doctrine is found in connection with a movement normally associated with the "Elkesaites," the implication being that this was actually one unified group, and that the sources (Hippolytus, *Haer.* ix.13-17; x.29; Epiphanius, *Haer.* 19 and 30; Origen in Eusebius, *HE* vi.38) all refer in a harmonizing fashion with regard to both geography and time frame to a single "sect." In fact, however, one must distinguish between the book of revelation given to Elkesai through divine revelation (Hippolytus: as the revelation of an enormous angel; Origen: as revelation fallen from heaven), on the one hand, and the preaching of Alcibiades on the other, who while referring to the revelation at the time of Trajan in Mesopotamia was himself actually active in Rome about a century later. Hippolytus's text thus contains parts of that book of revelation as well as of Alcibiades's preaching.

Hippolytus (*Haer.* ix.13.3-4) writes: "He utters the following sentence: that there was preached unto men a new remission of sins in the third year of Trajan's reign [100/101]. And [Elkesai] determines the nature of baptism, and even this I shall explain. He alleges, as regards those who have been involved in every description of lasciviousness, and filthiness, and in acts of wickedness, if only any of them be a believer, that he determines that such a one, on being converted, and obeying the book, and believing its contents, should by baptism receive remission of sins."[21]

The possibility for a (second) baptism in the case of grievous sins is asserted even more clearly and more radically: "If, thereby, my children, one shall have intercourse with any sort of animal whatsoever, or a male, or a sister, or a daughter, or has committed adultery, or been guilty of fornication, and is desirous of obtaining remission of sins, from the moment that he hearkens to this book let him be baptized a second time in the name of the Great and Most High God, and in the name of his Son, the mighty king. And by baptism let him be purified and cleansed, and let him adjure for himself those seven witnesses that have been described in this book — the heaven, and the water, and the holy spirits, and the angels that are objects of prayer, and the oil, and the salt, and the earth" (Hippolytus, *Haer.* ix.15.1-2). And further: "Again I say, O adulterers and adulteresses, and false prophets, if you are desirous of being converted, that your

---

[20] Basic information can be found in W. Brandt, *Elchasai. Ein Religionsstifter und sein Werk* (Leipzig, 1912); on the history of scholarship, see G. P. Luttikhuizen, *The Revelation of Elchasai* (Tübingen, 1985) 1-37. His summary appropriately describes the status of scholarship: "The foregoing review of past research shows that there is divergence of opinion on almost all the important points" (p. 34). Quite rightly, the author considers the most urgent task to be an analysis of Hippolytus, *Haer.* ix.13-17, precisely in view of its polemical character (p. 36).

[21] Translation according to J. H. Macmahon, *The Refutation of All Heresies by Hippolytus* (Edinburgh: T. & T. Clark, 1813) 345-51.

sins may be forgiven you, as soon as ever you hearken unto this book, and be baptized a second time along with your garments, shall peace be yours, and your portion with the just" (Hippolytus, *Haer.* ix.15.3).

In addition to this second baptism, certain other water rites can be practiced at any time or place: "If a dog rabid and furious and in whom inheres a spirit of destruction, bite any man, or woman, or youth, or girl, or may worry or touch them, in the same hour let such a one run with all their wearing apparel, and go down to a river or to a fountain wherever there is a deep spot. And here let him or her be dipped with all their wearing apparel, and offer supplication to the Great and Most High God in faith of heart, and then let him thus adjure the seven witnesses described in this book: 'Behold, I call to witness the heaven and the water, and the holy spirits, and the angels who are objects of prayer, and the oil, and the salt, and the earth. I testify by these seven witnesses that no more shall I sin, nor commit adultery, nor steal, nor be guilty of injustice, nor be covetous, nor be actuated by hatred, nor be scornful, nor shall I take pleasure in any wicked deeds.' Having uttered, therefore, these words, let such a one be baptized with the entire of his wearing apparel in the name of the Mighty and Most High God. . . . also those afflicted with consumption should be dipped in cold water forty times during seven days; and similar treatment for those possessed of devils" (Hippolytus, *Haer.* ix.15.4-16). Here the reference is clearly to a repeated and repeatable immersion bath without any officiating baptist, that is, to self-immersion that delivers a person from defilement and sin and is also therapeutic.

These comprehensive water rites appear later in the Cologne Mani-Codex, but now with a critical turn; Mani says: "But that, too, makes no sense, namely to baptize yourselves every day in water. Why do you baptize yourselves each day anew even though you have already been baptized and cleansed once? This, too, shows that you find yourselves disgusting every day, and because of that disgust you baptize yourselves without being able to cleanse yourselves" (82.23–83.13). This already presupposes Mani's break with the Elkesaites.

The rejection of sacrifice and priests adduced by Epiphanius is probably also connected with such magical-sacramental baptism praxis: "He bans burnt offerings and sacrifices, as something foreign to God and never offered to him on the authority of the fathers and Law . . . and yet he makes the claim that water is fortunate while fire is inimical" (Epiphanius, *Haer.* 19.3.6).

The composition of the book Alcibiades brought to Rome can be precisely dated: In *Haer.* 9.13.4, Hippolytus announces that a cosmic war will occur at the end of three years after Trajan's submission of the Parthians.[22] The revelation

---

[22] "Since when three years of the reign of the emperor Trajan are again completed from the time that he subjected the Parthians to his own sway, war rages between the impious angels of the northern constellations; and on this account all kingdoms of impiety are in a state of confusion."

must have been composed before the end of the war in 117.[23] "Apparently, the author of the book expected that after the completion of another period of three years of Roman occupation a new war would rage, a war of much larger dimensions, in which the impious angels of the North would be involved and which would cause apocalyptic troubles in Trajan's empire and in all godless kingdoms."[24] The book continued to be used even though the announced catastrophe did not in fact occur, and a century later Alcibiades brought it to Rome in a Greek version based in all probability on an Aramaic original.[25]

This book exhibits all the features of Jewish apocalypse, beginning with the vision of the two gigantic heavenly figures and extending to the expectation of coming judgment (see also the Aramaic riddle: "I am a witness over you on the day of the great judgment"). According to Luttikhuizen's understanding, the political-eschatological character of the announcement of judgment in the Aramaic original became in Alcibiades' Greek version a presentation of how to attain forgiveness of sins and redemption. Its author, an unknown Jewish apocalyptist in northern Mesopotamia during the time of Trajan, composed the book in the year 116.

Pagan-syncretistic features include astrological speculations and horary (Hippolytus, *Haer.* ix.16.2-4); the rather lax delimiting from paganism emerges in the possibility of a *reservatio mentalis:* "He claims that even though one should happen to worship idols at a time when persecution threatens, it is not a sin — just so long as he does not worship them in his conscience" (Epiphanius, *Haer.* 19.1.8-9).

Even if one cannot ascribe all these features to the "Elkesaites" as a whole,[26] one can with great certainty characterize the preaching of Alcibiades in Rome ca. 220 C.E. as syncretistic. It does share several points of contact with the Helkesaites around 245 C.E. as portrayed by Origen (in Eusebius, *HE* vi.38). One of the most important shared features is the proclamation of a new forgiveness of sins with reference to a book of revelation, the basic substance being Jewish-Christian and suggesting provenance in western Syria. "The combination of circumcision, a life in conformity with the Law, and the rejection of the Apostle Paul[27] suggests that the Judeo-Christianity of the religious propagandists was related to that of the Ebionites. But Alcibiades and/or Origen's

---

[23] Luttikhuizen, op. cit., 190; Luttikhuizen quite rightly associates the Parthian War with the Jewish revolt in Cyrenaica (115-117). See in this regard M. Hengel, "Messianische Hoffnung und politischer 'Radikalismus' in der 'jüdisch-hellenistischen Diaspora,'" in D. Hellholm, ed., *Apocalypticism* (Tübingen, ²1989) 655-86.

[24] Luttikhuizen, op. cit., 192.

[25] See the Aramaic sentence in Epiphanius, *Haer.* 19.4.3; see in this regard Irmscher, op. cit., 623; Luttikhuizen, op. cit., 193.

[26] The pioneering work of G. P. Luttikhuizen, *The Revelation of Elchasai* (Tübingen, 1985), has shown this to be impossible.

[27] According to Origen (Eusebius, *HE* vi.38).

Helkesaites had also features in common with the 'ps.-Clementine' Judeo-Christians: christological speculations, selective use of the Old Testament, rejection of the Apostle Paul, and the baptism of initiation."[28]

Alcibiades' doctrine, however, also exhibits pagan elements, including astrology, Pythagorean teaching, and magic. His origin in Apamea may suggest that he brought with him a connection with Jewish, Jewish-Christian, and pagan traditions from Syria. This would also suggest that such doctrines were extant (cf. Origen's account) in Syria-Palestine, albeit for only a short time (Origen: "they died out even as they arose").

VI. The Mandaeans[29]

The Mandaeans offer yet another model of a syncretistic baptism sect, one with a rich, albeit young tradition and yet whose actual origins derive from the same baptist-sectarian milieu as those of the Ebionites, Elkesaites, and other baptism groups of Palestine and especially of the area east of the Jordan.

Each Sunday the Mandaeans engaged in self-immersion three times in running water ("Jordan"), followed by a threefold marking of the forehead with water accompanied by the baptismal formula "the name of life and the name of the Manda da Hayyê has been spoken over you" and three drinks of water. This is followed by a whole series of additional acts in water and on the shore, along with an apotropaic sealing against evil powers. "This baptism is also performed in a slightly altered form on children and the dying. In the case of ritual transgressions, it is performed multiple times (up to 360)."[30] In addition to this more complex baptism ceremony on Sundays, each member also practiced daily (morning) self-immersion as a form of cleansing, and there was also a sacramental act at death, the heavenly baptism of the soul.

In the early period, the water rites of the Mandaeans, a sect still practicing even today, underwent strong ritualization and formative development (Nestorian influence); their origin, however, can be discerned among the heretical Jewish and Jewish-Christian baptism sects of the first two centuries on the eastern periphery of Syria-Palestine.[31]

---

[28] Luttikhuizen, op. cit., 213.

[29] Basic information can be found in K. Rudolph, *Die Mandäer I + II* (Göttingen, 1960; 1961). For a brief summary, see *idem, Antike Baptisten,* 17-19.

[30] Rudolph, *Antike Baptisten,* 18.

[31] See Rudolph, *Antike Baptisten,* 18: "Even if the Mandaean religion underwent a development resulting in a stringent rejection of both Judaism and Christianity, it is still a good example of how an originally heretical-Jewish baptism sect ultimately developed into an extremely original religion."

VII. Conclusions

The Jewish-Christian baptism movements maintain the same two possibilities for using and understanding water rites as developed in the Jewish and Christian traditions: (1) the Old Testament-Jewish praxis of self-immersion for the attainment of cultic purity after ritual defilement; (2) the understanding of one-time baptism by a baptist as a "baptism of penitence for the forgiveness of sins," an understanding similarly deriving from Judaism and then mediated to early Christianity by John the Baptist.

Both the Ebionites and the "Elkesaites" practiced this double form of water rite: the one-time baptism of initiation (the "Elkesaites" also embracing the possibility of a second baptism for the forgiveness of sins) and the repeated cultic-ritual washings after defilement. The "Elkesaites" entertained pagan-magical (therapeutic) notions as well.

The tenacity of such water rites thus provided a bridge between Jewish-Christian groups and Judaism even beyond "the parting of the ways." The syncretistic character and accompanying adaptability provided, on the one hand, the basis for the quick success of these movements, and on the other — given their lack of clarity — one reason for the historic demise of almost all "heretical" baptism groups.

Selected Bibliography

W. Brandt. *Elchasai. Ein Religionsstifter und sein Werk* (Leipzig, 1912; repr. Amsterdam, 1971).

―――. *Die jüdischen Baptismen* (Giessen, 1910).

J. Daniélou. *Théologie du Judéo-Christianisme* (Tournai, 1958).

A. Hilgenfeld. *Judentum und Judenchristentum* (Leipzig, 1886; repr. Hildesheim, 1966).

A. F. J. Klijn and G. J. Reinink. *Patristic Evidence for Jewish-Christian Sects* (Leiden, 1973).

H. Lichtenberger. "Täufergemeinden und frühchristliche Täuferpolemik im letzten Drittel des 1. Jahrhunderts," *ZTK* 84 (1987) 36-57.

J. B. Lightfoot. "The Essenes," in *Saint Paul's Epistles to the Colossians and to Philemon* (London, 1892) 346-417.

G. P. Luttikhuizen. *The Revelation of Elchasai* (Tübingen, 1985).

J. Neusner. *The Idea of Purity in Ancient Judaism* (SJLA 1; Leiden, 1973).

―――. *A History of the Mishnaic Law of Purities,* vol. 22 (SJLA 6/22; Leiden, 1977).

―――. *Das pharisäische und talmudische Judentum* (ed. H. Lichtenberger; Tübingen, 1984).

K. Rudolph. *Die Mandäer,* vols. 1-2 (Göttingen, 1960-1961).

―――. *Antike Baptisten. Zu den Überlieferungen über frühjüdische und -christliche Taufsekten* (Sitzungsberichte der Sächsischen Akademie der Wissenschaften zu Leipzig. Philosophisch-Historische Klasse 121.4; Berlin, 1981).

W. Schneemelcher. *Neutestamentliche Apokryphen,* vols. 1 and 2 (5th ed.; Tübingen, 1987, 1989).

H. J. Schoeps. *Theologie und Geschichte des Judenchristentums* (Tübingen, 1949).

M. Simon. *Recherches d'histoire Judéo-Chrétienne* (Paris, 1962).

E. Stommel. "Christliche Taufriten und antike Badesitten," *Jahrbuch für Antike und Christentum* 2 (1959) 5-14.

G. Strecker. "Judenchristentum," *TRE* 17.310-25.

J. Thomas. *Le mouvement baptiste en Palestine et Syrie* (Gembloux, 1935).

R. Wolf. *Aqua religiosa. Die religiöse Verwendung von Wasser im frühen Christentum und seiner Umwelt* (diss., Leipzig, 1956).

Matthew's Christology and the Parting of the Ways

by

GRAHAM N. STANTON

Matthew has written his gospel to a cluster of Christian communities which have recently parted company painfully with Judaism. Several of the gospel's most distinctive features are related to the 'parting of the ways': the strengthening of anti-Jewish polemic; the greater prominence given to apocalyptic themes; the evangelist's claim that the church is the true heir and interpreter of Scripture; the care with which a Gentile mission is defended. Matthew's call for a 'greater righteousness' and concern over internal dissent, as well as his warnings to his readers to be prepared for the parousia promote group cohesion; this cohesion is necessitated both by the perceived threat from Judaism and by the new communities' need for self-definition and legitimation[1].

Are Matthew's rich and varied Christological themes related in any way to this social setting? At first sight, in sharp contrast to John's gospel, Matthew's Christology seems to have little to do with 'the parting of the ways'. In Matthew, as in John, there is a strong emphasis on Jesus as the Son (of God); in both gospels Jesus repeatedly refers to God as his Father. In John 5–10 the claim that Jesus is the Son of God and the relationship of the Son to the Father are at the heart of the disputes between Jesus and the Jewish leaders, disputes which are usually taken to reflect a community at odds with the local synagogue.

In Matthew, however, matters seem to be different. The claim that Jesus is the Son of God is one of the most important and impressive features of Matthew's Christology, but it is rarely opposed by the Jewish leaders[2]. With the exception of Matt 11.27 (Q), there is hardly any discussion of the precise

---

[1] I have discussed the origin, purpose, and social setting of Matthew in *A Gospel for a New People: Studies in Matthew*, Edinburgh 1992. See also J. Andrew Overman, *Matthew's Gospel and Formative Judaism: the Social World of the Matthean Community*, Minneapolis 1990.

[2] Matt 27.39–44 is an interesting exception. On Matthew's Son of God Christology, see, for example, J. D. Kingsbury, *Matthew: Structure, Christology, Kingdom*, London 1975, 42–83. Kingsbury has shown that 'Son of God' is the most prominent Christological title in Matthew, but his further claim that other Christological themes are subsumed under this title is not convincing. See also D. Verseput's important article, 'The Role and Meaning of the "Son of God" Title in Matthew's Gospel', *NTS* 33 (1987) 532–56.

relationship between Jesus and the Father. Most of the Christological claims which are made by Jesus himself, by his disciples, and by would-be disciples, go unchallenged by the Pharisees and the other religious leaders who are so prominent in Matthew's story.

First appearances are, however, often deceptive. In this paper I want to argue that closer inspection of a number of passages indicates that hostile accusations levelled against Jesus are being carefully countered: we are in touch with the claims and counter-claims of Jews and Christians in the evangelist's day. Matthew was well aware that his rivals saw Jesus as a magician and a deceiver of Israel. And as we shall see, in four redactional passages acknowledgement of Jesus as the 'Son of David' by participants in Matthew's story provokes hostility from the Jewish leaders. Since no other major Christological theme in Matthew provokes such sustained opposition from the Jewish leaders, our suspicions are roused: are the 'Son of David' passages intended by the evangelist to be a response to some of his critics? Although the Christological disputes are neither as intense nor as sustained as they are in John's gospel, they are an important feature of Matthew.

Most of Matthew's Christological emphases should be seen primarily as an extension (which is sometimes considerable) of themes which were already prominent in the sources on which the evangelist drew. However since some of those themes are set by Matthew himself in the context of disputes with Jewish leaders, they are related to the conflicts and apologetic of the evangelist's own day. The text of the gospel itself points clearly in this direction: Matthew claims that the allegation that the disciples stole the body of Jesus from the tomb 'has been spread among Jews to this day' (28.15), and takes pains to refute the charge.

First, some brief comments on method. Scholarly study of Matthew is in some disarray at present. Scholars who have pioneered social scientific or literary critical methods have often ignored one another's work and have turned their backs on redaction criticism which has been so fruitful in the last four decades[3]. Most scholars who are still wedded to redaction criticism have failed to do more than nod in the direction of the newer methods.

---

[3] See, for example, B. J. Malina and J. H. Neyrey, *Calling Jesus Names: the Social Value of Labels in Matthew*, Sonoma, Calif. 1988. This stimulating book draws on insights from cultural anthropology in its dicussion of 'name-calling' in Matthew. Although the authors claim that they have used 'social science models closely in conjunction with the findings of the historical critical method' (p. 137), they make hardly any use of redaction criticism. The accusations against Jesus which they assign to 'early Matthean tradition' (by which they mean Q) have been sharpened and extended considerably by the evangelist Matthew himself. For two examples of very different literary critical studies of Matthew which largely ignore redaction criticism, see J. D. Kingsbury, *Matthew as Story*, Philadelphia 2nd ed. 1988, and D. Patte, *The Gospel According to Matthew: a Structural Commentary on Matthew's Faith*, Philadelphia 1987. On the latter, see my review in *Interpretation* 43 (1989) 184–6.

I am still convinced that redaction criticism is the basic tool for serious study of Matthew. I have no doubts at all about Marcan priority, and not many about Q! Of course Matthew accepted the traditions he has incorporated into his gospel, so it is undoubtedly helpful to study the whole gospel as it now stands. On the other hand, if we want to appreciate fully the evangelist's distinctive emphases, we do well to pay close attention to the changes he has made to his sources. Since Matthew is a 'conservative redactor'[4], more often than not the changes he makes are significant. Although I am an unrepentant redaction critic, I am convinced that results garnered from this method of gospel critisicm will be more compelling when they are supplemented by insights drawn from the social sciences and from narrative criticism[5].

Jesus is a Magician and a Deceiver

In Matthew two hostile comments from the opponents of Jesus are of particular interest[6]. The first is the three-fold accusation that the exorcisms of Jesus have been carried out 'by the prince of demons': 9.34; 10.25; 12.24,27; as we shall see, the first and the last of these are responses to acknowledgement of Jesus as 'Son of David'. In the second hostile comment Jesus is referred to as 'that deceiver' (ἐκεῖνος ὁ πλάνος) and his life is summed up as 'deception' (πλάνη, 27.63—4).

These two criticisms are closely related to the double accusation against Jesus which is found in a wide range of early Christian and Jewish writings: Jesus is a magician and a deceiver. I have shown elsewhere that the accusation that Jesus was a deceiver was a stock jibe which is found in some Jewish traditions (which are admittedly difficult to date) and in a remarkably wide range of early Christian writings[7]. In many of these writings (most notably Justin *Dialogue* 69, b.Sanh 43a and b.Sanh 107) it is linked with a second critical comment: Jesus is a magician (μάγος).

---

[4] This is U. Luz's description of the evangelist; see volume I of his commentary, 56—9.

[5] For a fuller discussion, see chapters 1—3 of my *A Gospel for a New People*.

[6] Most of the other critical questions and comments on the lips of opponents fall into one or more of the following categories: they are neutral (e.g. 12.38, 'Teacher, we wish to see a sign from you'); they concern the law rather than the person of Jesus (e.g. 15.2); they are taken from the evangelist's sources without emphasis or development (e.g. 9.3, 'This man is blaspheming'; 9.11 'Why does your teacher eat with tax collectors and sinners'; 9.14, 'Why do your disciples not fast?'). There are of course several passages in Matthew which may well be a response to hostile allegations: e.g. 1.18—25; 5.17—20.

[7] See G. N. Stanton, 'Early Christian-Jewish Polemic and Apologetic', *NTS* 31 (1985) 377—92, now reprinted as chapter 10 in *A Gospel for a New People*. In that article I referred to Matt 27.63, but I was then unaware of the possible relevance of the three-fold accusation in Matthew that Jesus was in league with the prince of demons.

It is not at all far-fetched to associate the sharp criticisms of Jesus as exorcist which are so prominent in Matthew with the charge that Jesus was a magician or sorcerer. Exorcism is unquestionably the best-attested form of magic among the Jews before Bar Kokhba[8]. In Acts 19.11−20 Luke almost equates exorcism and magic. According to Josephus, Solomon 'composed incantations by which illnesses are relieved, and left behind forms of exorcisms with which those possessed by demons drive them out, never to return'. He then recalls that he himself witnessed an exorcism carried out with magical rites and incantations by a fellow Jew called Eleazer in the presence of Vespasian (*Ant.* VIII.45−9). Justin Martyr refers to Jewish exorcists, who, like the heathen, use fumigations and magic knots (*Dialogue* 85.3).

Jewish and pagan opponents of Christianity in the late first century and in the second century readily claimed that the exorcisms (and miracles) of Jesus (and of his later followers) were the result of magical powers. One of the central planks in the attack made on Jesus by Celsus's Jew is that the healings and exorcisms of sorcerers are the result of possession by an evil demon (Origen *Contra Celsum* I.68); 'the actions of Jesus were those of one hated by God and of a wicked sorcerer' (I.71). The pagan philosopher Celsus agrees with the Jew whom he quotes: 'it was by magic that Jesus was able to do the miracles which he appeared to have done' (Origen *Contra Celsum* I.6). While it is true that not all exorcisms involved magical practices (and vice versa)[9], critics of Jesus (and of his later followers) naturally wrote off his exorcisms as deeds of a magician or sorcerer.

Matthew seems to have known that his readers might well be confronted by their Jewish rivals with this stock criticism of Jesus. Since this is, I think, a fresh suggestion as far as Matthew's gospel is concerned, we must now look at the evidence on which it is based.

'He casts out demons by the prince of demons'

The first two of Matthew's three references to this accusation, 9.34 and 10.25, come from the hand of the evangelist himself. The third, 12.24,27, is taken from Mark 3.22 and from Q (= Luke 11.19), but as we shall see, Matthew has redacted his traditions considerably at this point. Whereas Mark includes this jibe against Jesus once (3.22), and Luke twice (in the same passage, 11.15,18), it is found no less than four times (in three different passages) in Matthew. So

---

[8] So P. S. Alexander, 'Incantations and Books of Magic' in E. Schürer, *The History of the Jewish People in the Age of Jesus Christ* III.1, eds. G. Vermes, F. Millar, and M. Goodman, Edinburgh 1986, § 32.VII, 342−79, here 342.

[9] H. C. Kee, *Medicine, Miracle and Magic in New Testament Times* Cambridge 1986, 114, criticizes J. M. Hull's assumption that in the Hellenistic period all exorcisms were magical. Kee notes that belief in angels and demons was operative in Judaism (especially apocalypticism) and in early Christianity in contexts where magic was not present or not a significant factor.

there are strong grounds for concluding that the evangelist had a special interest in this criticism of Jesus.

(a) Matthew 9.34

Matthew's first reference to the charge that Jesus performed his exorcisms by the prince of demons comes at the climax of the cycle of miracle stories in chapters 8 and 9. It is followed by the second of Matthew's important summary accounts of the teaching, preaching and healing ministry of Jesus (4.23 and 9.35). Immediately before this summary, which marks a major structural division in the gospel, the evangelist includes the first versions of two stories he will repeat later (cf. 9.27−31 and 20.29−34; 9.32−4 and 12.22−3). Commentators usually note that both pericopae are included here in order to prepare for the list of miracles recorded in 11.5, but most fail to observe the important role 9.34 plays in Matthew's overall presentation of the story of Jesus.

The reaction of the crowds to the healing of the two blind men and the exorcism of the demon from the dumb man is almost ecstatic: 'Never was anything like this seen in Israel' (9.33). It is balanced antithetically in good Matthean fashion by the sharp comment of the Pharisees: 'He casts out demons by the prince of demons' (9.34). Here, as also in the 'second edition' of this tradition (12.24), the evangelist changes 'the scribes who came down from Jerusalem' (Mark 3.22) to 'the Pharisees'. As in two other pericopae in this cycle of miracle stories, Matthew has singled out redactionally the Pharisees as the arch-opponents of Jesus[10]. The hostile reaction of the Pharisees to Jesus in 9.34 comes as the first climax in Matthew's careful presentation of the developing conflict between Jesus and the Pharisees[11]. Not until 12.14 is the reader informed of the Pharisees' conspiracy to destroy Jesus[12]. 9.32−4 function as a literary foreshadowing of the conflict which will dominate chapter 12[13].

Many recent writers have simply accepted without discussion the decision of the editors of the 26th edition of the Nestle-Aland text to include Matt 9.34. But the absence of the whole verse in a handful of manuscripts is striking and should not pass without comment[14]. Although 9.34 is omitted in the New English Bible

---

[10] Compare Matt 9.11 and 9.14 with Mark 2.16 and 2.18.

[11] See J. D. Kingsbury, 'The Developing Conflict between Jesus and the Jewish Leaders in Matthew's Gospel: A Literary-Critical Study', *CBQ* 49 (1987) 57−83.

[12] In Mark matters are different. The first reference to a plot against the life of Jesus comes much earlier in the story at 3.6 where the Pharisees are joined by 'the Herodians'.

[13] See B. J. Malina and J. H. Neyrey, *Calling Jesus Names: the Social Value of Labels in Matthew,* Sonoma, Calif. 1988, 59.

[14] U. Luz is an exception. In his commentary (II, 1990, 62 n. 2) he includes this brief comment: 'Er ist nicht nur gut bezeugt, sondern auch kompositionell als Fortsetzung von 9, 1b−17 und als Vorbereitung auf 10,25 unentbehrlich.' Similarly, B. M. Metzger (*A Textual Commentary of the Greek New Testament,* London & New York 1971) suggests that 9.34 seems to be needed to prepare the reader for 10.25. This line of argument is plausible, but it

(1970)[15] and in the Revised English Bible (1989), I am convinced that the cumulative arguments for its inclusion as the first part of a carefully constructed three-fold criticism of Jesus (and corresponding set of responses) are strong.

(i) According to the apparatus of the Nestle-Aland text, with the exception of Codex Bezae, two Old Latin manuscripts (a and k), the Sinaitic Syriac palimpsest, and Hilary of Poitiers, the verse is found in all the ancient witnesses to the text[16]. (ii) The NEB and the REB seem to have omitted it on the basis of a misguided preference for the shorter reading and a lingering commitment (here, and in other passages) to Westcott and Hort's theory of 'western non-interpolations'. However several textual critics have recently argued that the *lectio brevior potior* rule of thumb is misleading[17]. (iii) The wording of 9.34 differs from the parallel passages within Matthew (10.25 and 12.24,27) and from Mark 3.22, the only parallel passage in Mark. Hence 9.34 is unlikely to have originated as an addition by a 'harmonising' scribe. (iv) If 9.34 is accepted as part of the original text, why is it omitted in some witnesses? In this case it is not difficult to account for later abbreviation of the text: a few scribes were reluctant to allow the Pharisees to have the last word about Jesus at the climax of this section of the gospel; they preferred to conclude the pericope (and the preceding cycle of miracle traditions) with the positive response of the crowds: 'Never was anything like this seen in Israel' (9.33b). Surely it is most unlikely that a later scribe would have added a hostile criticism of Jesus on the lips of the Pharisees as the climax of the cycle of miracle traditions in chapters 8 and 9. Taken cumulatively, then, there are good reasons for accepting 9.34 as part of the original text; the longer reading is more difficult than the shorter reading and should be retained.

---

can be reversed: an early scribe may have felt that 10.25 was so enigmatic that an explanation at an appropriate earlier point in the gospel was necessary. Neither Luz nor Metzger attempts to account for the omission of the verse in some witnesses.

[15] The first edition of the New English Bible (1961) contains a curious error. 9.33b and 34 are translated as follows: Filled with amazement the onlookers said, 'Nothing like this has ever been seen in Israel. He casts out demons by the prince of devils.' Both the positive and the negative assessments of Jesus are placed on the lips of the crowds! This translation is not supported by a single manuscript and seems to be an error which mysteriously escaped detection until the second edition of the NEB was published in 1970. Prior to the Passion narrative the crowds in Matthew never respond negatively to Jesus.

[16] Rather surprisingly, the Huck-Greeven *Synopse*, Tübingen 1981, fails to note the absence of 9.34 in some witnesses, though the Huck-Lietzmann *Synopse* which it replaces had noted the absence of the whole verse in D sy[s] Hil.

[17] See, for example, P. M. Head, 'Observations on Early Papyri of the Synoptic Gospels, especially on the "Scribal Habits"', *Biblica* 71 (1990) 240−7. Head refers to a thesis by J. M. Royse (which I have not seen) which shows that six important papyri (45, 46, 66, 72, 75) all demonstrate a tendency to shorten the text. See also J. K. Elliott, 'Why the International Greek New Testament Project is Necessary', *Restoration Quarterly* 30 (1988) 203.

(b) Matthew 10.25

The next reference to this jibe against Jesus is part of the 'missionary discourse' in chapter 10. In 10.25 Jesus states that his opponents have called him Βεεζεβούλ. This enigmatic accusation is not explained in the immediate context. Presumably Matthew's readers knew who Βεεζεβούλ was, since Matthew does not explain that he was 'the ruler of the demons' until 12.24. In 10.25 Jesus warns his disciples to expect the same reaction to their own preaching and healing ministry as he himself has received: εἰ τὸν οἰκοδεσπότην Βεεζεβοὺλ ἐπεκάλεσαν, πόσῳ μᾶλλον τοὺς οἰκιακοὺς αὐτοῦ. This sentence rounds off a set of carefully structured statements in which Matthew has expanded considerably a Q logion (cf. 10.24–5 and Luke 6.40). The context leaves the reader in no doubt that Jesus is referring to himself as ὁ διδάσκαλος, ὁ κύριος, and ὁ οἰκοδεσπότης. Disciples of Jesus form a household of which he is the master[18].

For our present purposes two points are of special interest. First, even though Christological titles are not used, the whole passage contains a rich Christology which stems from the evangelist himself. And secondly, the accusation that Jesus is *himself* Βεεζεβούλ is an intensification in a highly compressed logion of the charge in 9.34 and 12.24 that he is in league with the prince of demons. The jibe in 10.25 points back to 9.34; the disciples are warned that the bitter abuse hurled at Jesus will also be thrown at them. Since the sayings in the second part of Matthew 10 refer so clearly to the post-Easter period[19], 10.25 implies that the persecution of Christians in the evangelist's own day will include this form of abuse (cf. 10.16–23 and also 5.11). In other words, the accusation that Jesus and his followers are in league with the prince of demons is not a matter of past history; for Matthew and his readers it is a present experience.

(c) Matthew 12.24,27

The third reference to this hostile assessment of Jesus is in two verses in the Beelzebul controversy, 12.22–30. The first, v. 24, is taken from Mark 3.22; the second, v. 27 from Q (cf. Luke 11.19). As in 9.34, Matthew makes two important redactional changes: Mark's 'scribes who came down from Jerusalem' become 'the Pharisees', and their reaction is contrasted with the

---

[18] R. H. Gundry (commentary ad loc.) and Michael H. Crosby, *House of Disciples*, Maryknoll 1988, 66–7, both claim that there is a play on words in 10.25: Βεεζεβούλ = 'master of the house'. Even if this is the correct interpretation of rather complicated linguistic evidence, Matthew has failed to unravel the word play for his readers, few of whom are likely to have known Hebrew or Aramaic.

[19] See U. Luz, 'The Disciples in the Gospel according to Matthew', in ed. G. N. Stanton, *The Interpretation of Matthew*, London 1983, 98–128, especially 100.

favourable comments of the crowds: 'Perhaps this is the Son of David' (12.23)[20].

Only in this passage is there a reply to the three-fold accusation that the exorcisms of Jesus are the result of collusion with the prince of demons. Matthew insists that it is not ἐν Βεεζεβούλ that Jesus casts out demons, but ἐν πνεύματι θεοῦ (12.28). This exact antithesis is the result of Matthean redaction of the Q logion (Luke 11.20) which referred to the finger of God[21].

Matthew includes further references to the Spirit of God immediately before and immediately after this pericope. In the preceding verses the evangelist has claimed that God's promise given through Isaiah the prophet (Isa 42.1) has been fulfilled in Jesus: God has placed his Spirit upon his servant Jesus (12.17−21); the healing ministry of Jesus is the result of the gift of the Spirit (cf. vv. 15b and 18c). Immediately after the Beelzebul pericope Matthew combines Mark 3.10 and the Q saying behind Luke 11.10. The end result in 12.31−2 is a most solemn double warning that blasphemy against the Spirit will never be forgiven. The διὰ τοῦτο λέγω ὑμῖν of v. 31 leaves no room for doubt: in Matthew's view the Pharisees' claim that Jesus is in league with the prince of demons is blasphemy against the Spirit of God.

The anti-Pharisaic polemic is sustained in the pericopae which follow. The Pharisees are 'a brood of vipers' (12.34; cf. 3.7 and 23.33); they are 'evil' (12.34f.). The polemic continues in 12.38−45, where Matthew has reversed the order of Q traditions in order to sharpen his counter-accusation. The scribes and Pharisees are part of an adulterous and evil generation which seeks a sign (12.38−9), a generation which is possessed by seven evil spirits (12.43−5). The latter point, which is the climax of the sustained polemic which becomes ever more intense throughout chapter 12, is made by the evangelist's own addition to the Q parable (cf. Luke 11.24−6): 'So shall it be also with this evil generation.' The Pharisees and the scribes are demon possessed, not Jesus.

In Matthew, then, there is a three-fold accusation that the exorcisms of Jesus have been carried out by dint of collusion with Beelzebul, the prince of demons (9.34; 10.25; 12.24,27). But there is also a three-fold insistence that Jesus acts ἐν πνεύματι θεοῦ (12.18,28,31−2). Whey are the charge and the response so prominent in passages in which the evangelist's own hand is evident? The most obvious reason is that the significance of Jesus is still being bitterly contested in Matthew's own day. This conclusion is strongly implied by 10.25b: disciples (i.e. readers of the gospel) who belong to the 'household' whose master has been so savagely maligned in the past, must expect that 'all kinds of evil will be spoken against them falsely on account of their commitment to Jesus' (cf. ἕνεκεν ἐμοῦ, 5.11).

---

[20] See the further discussion of this verse on pp. 110−11.

[21] If 'Spirit of God' was the original wording of the Q logion, Luke's special interest in the Spirit would have discouraged him from making a change to 'finger of God'.

'That deceiver'

The final words attributed to the Jewish leaders in Matthew include a second important critical judgement on Jesus. In 27.63–4 he is referred to as 'that deceiver' (ἐκεῖνος ὁ πλάνος) and his life is summed up as 'deception' (πλάνη). Once again the Pharisees are singled out as the arch-opponents. They have been conspicuously absent from Matthew's story-line since the end of chapter 23, but in 27.62–6 they join the chief priests (whose presence is demanded by the preceding narratives) in petitioning Pilate. The whole pericope is thoroughly Matthean, so here we have further evidence of the evangelist's own special interest in a hostile assessment of Jesus[22].

This time Matthew does not reply directly to the polemic. He takes great pains to convince the reader that the resurrection of Jesus from the tomb in which he was buried was not the 'final deception', but he simply lets the Jewish leaders' critical comments stand. Presumably he is convinced that readers of his gospel will readily agree that the claim of the Jewish leaders that Jesus is a 'deceiver' is monstrous; perhaps the closing verses of the gospel (28.18–20) were intended to prove the point. Matthew stresses that the chief priests and Pharisees are without excuse: they themselves 'remember' that Jesus had told them that he would rise from the dead (v. 63). In a final poignant note the evangelist notes that the tale of the bribing of the soldiers who had guarded the tomb of Jesus 'has been spread among Jews' to this day (28.15). This comment underlines once again the yawning gulf between the Christian communities to whom the evangelist is writing and local synagogues.

Matthew, then, was well aware of the double accusation regularly levelled against Jesus by Jewish opponents: he was a magician and a deceiver. The evangelist does not respond directly to the second taunt, but the first is taken very seriously indeed. As we have seen, in Matthew 12 the evangelist himself insists that the Pharisees' assessment of Jesus is wrong-headed: Jesus does not act ἐν Βεεζεβούλ, but ἐν πνεύματι θεοῦ. The three-fold accusation that Jesus is demon-possessed is matched by the three-fold reference to the Spirit of God. The Pharisees' accusations against Jesus are hurled back: *they* are possessed by evil spirits, not Jesus.

Matthew's emphasis on the Spirit's relationship to Jesus is a neglected aspect of his Christology. This is one of the first notes he sounds in his presentation of the story and significance of Jesus. In 1.18–25, where once again his own hand is clearly evident in the vocabulary and style, he stresses twice that Jesus was conceived 'of the Holy Spirit'. As has often been noted,

---

[22] For details of Matthean vocabulary and style in this pericope, see R. H. Gundry's commentary ad loc.

Matthew's insistence on the role of the Spirit in the conception of Jesus may be (in part) a response to Jewish claims that Jesus was born as the result of an illegitimate union.

Hostility to Jesus the Son of David

There is a further set of passages in Matthew which seem to be related to disputes with Jewish opponents in the evangelist's day concerning the significance of Jesus. Matthew expands Mark's three references to the title 'Son of David' to nine: 1.1; 9.27; 12.23; 15.22; 20.30,31 (= Mark 10.47,48); 21.9,15; 22.42 (= Mark 12.35), where the title Son of David is implied. Why does Matthew open his gospel with a reference to Jesus as 'Son of David' and then proceed to add five further references in contexts which are broadly Marcan (9.27; 12.23; 15.22; 21.9,15)? As several writers have noted, Matthew connects the 'Son of David' title with the healing minstry of Jesus, but that observation hardly accounts for the evangelist's strong emphasis on this particular Christological theme[23].

While four of the six redactional passages are connected with the healing ministry of Jesus, most scholars have overlooked the fact that another motif is equally prominent in the 'Son of David' passages which come from the evangelist's own hand. In four such passages acknowledgement of Jesus as the 'Son of David' by participants in Matthew's story provokes hostility from the Jewish leaders[24]. These four passages come at critical points in the evangelist's presentation of one of his major themes: the conflict between Jesus and the Jewish leaders[25]. From these general observations we may conclude that Matthew insists vigorously that Jesus is the Son of David, even though he is aware that some of his readers will soon learn that this claim is unacceptable to their Jewish rivals.

Before I suggest a more specific setting for these disputes, we must consider the four redactional passages in which the claim that Jesus is Son of David is disputed.

---

[23] So, for example, C. Burger, *Jesus als Davidssohn*, Göttingen 1970, 72−106; J. M. Gibbs, 'Purpose and Pattern in Matthew's Use of the Title "Son of David"', *NTS* 10 (1963−4) 446−464; J. D. Kingsbury, 'The Title "Son of David" in Matthew's Gospel', *JBL* 95 (1976) 591−602; D. C. Duling, 'The Therapeutic Son of David: An Element in Matthew's Christological Apologetic', *NTS* 24 (1978) 392−409; U. Luz, 'Eine thetische Skizze der matthäischen Christologie' in *Anfänge der Christologie* (FS F. Hahn), eds. C. Breytenbach and H. Paulsen, Göttingen 1991, 223−6.

[24] A notable exception is D. Verseput, 'The Role and Meaning of the "Son of God" Title in Matthew's Gospel', *NTS* 33 (1987) 533−7. Verseput does not discuss the reasons for this link.

[25] See J. D. Kingsbury, 'The Developing Conflict between Jesus and the Jewish Leaders in Matthew's Gospel', *CBQ* 49 (1987) 57−73. Kingsbury fails to note that confession of Jesus as 'Son of David' provokes hostility from the Jewish leaders.

(a) Herod the king was troubled (2.3)

Narrative critics have reminded us of the crucial importance of the openings of writings. Matthew's gospel is no exception. 'Son of David' is the very first Christological title used by the evangelist in his opening line which functions as a heading (1.1). The genealogy sets out carefully the Davidic origin of Jesus. At the end of its first section the reader is reminded that David was king over Israel (1.6).

In the account of the birth of Jesus Joseph is addressed by an angel of the Lord as 'son of David' (1.20) and great pains are taken to show how Jesus was adopted into the kingly line of David even though Joseph was not his physical father. The first reaction to the birth of Jesus, king of the Jews, is positive: the magi (who are clearly Gentiles) search out the place of his birth in order to worship him.

But their arrival in Jerusalem causes consternation. At the news of the birth of the Davidic king, who is explicitly identified in the narrative as the Messiah (2.4), Herod is terrified (ἐταράχθη) and *all* Jerusalem (πᾶσα – a good Matthean word) with him (2.3). An even stronger verb is added by Matthew to Mark's narrative to describe the reaction caused by the 'triumphal' entry of Jesus into Jerusalem: all Jerusalem is deeply stirred (ἐσείσθη πᾶσα ἡ πόλις) (21.10). This is only one of a number of themes from chapters 1 and 2 which recur later in Matthew's story.

At this point Matthew associates the chief priests and the scribes with Herod: as the story develops they take over his role as the arch-opponents of Jesus. Before the plot against Jesus unfolds, a strongly ironical note is introduced: the Jewish religious leaders are well aware of the Scriptural prophecy concerning the birth of the promised king of Israel (2.5–6). The same ironical note recurs at the very end of Matthew's story: the Pharisees know that Jesus had predicted that he would rise again from the dead; they are able to quote the words of 'that impostor' to Pilate (27.63)[26].

The implacable hostility of Herod (and, by implication) of the Jewish religious leaders is contrasted sharply with the determination of the magi to find the Davidic Messiah and to worship him. Later in the gospel various individuals will seek out Jesus with equal determination (and in some cases faith) and worship him.

Why are Herod and the religious leaders so hostile to the birth of the promised Messiah? The obvious answer is surely the correct one: they perceive the Davidic King to be a threat. Matthew hints (but does not explain fully) that their understanding of Messiahship is faulty. Their hostility is certainly ridiculed: Jesus is but a child! The evangelist does not refer to Jesus as 'king of the Jews' beyond 2.2, but he repeatedly uses the phrase 'the child and his

---

[26] Cf. John 5.39.

mother'. Later in the gospel Matthew's portrait of Jesus as the harmless and humble Davidic Messiah becomes one of its most distinctive features.

(b) 'Have mercy on us, Son of David ... Lord' (9.27—8)

Matthew rounds off his presentation of Jesus as 'Messiah of Deed' in chapters 8 and 9 with two pericopae in which his own hand is evident. The evangelist includes two accounts of the healing of two blind men. The second (20.29—34) is modelled closely on Mark 10.46—52. The first account (9.27—31) is a careful rewriting of the same Marcan tradition. The two blind men cry out to Jesus, 'Have mercy on us, Son of David' and later address Jesus as 'Lord' (κύριε) (9.27—8). These Matthean phrases express the believing response of the blind men.

The final pericope in this chapter is also the first part of a reduplication of another Marcan tradition (Mark 3.22 = Matt 9.32—4 and 12.22—4). This time Matthew has incorporated some Q material (Luke 11.14). The two incidents are carefully linked together by Matthew: the dumb demoniac approaches Jesus as the two men who have received their sight are going their way (9.32). So the contrasting responses of the crowds and of the Pharisees are in effect responses to both incidents.

Once this is observed, it is clear that the hostile comment of the Pharisees in 9.34, 'He casts out demons by the prince of demons', is a reaction to the confession of Jesus as 'Son of David' in 9.27. Their critical accusation occurs as the climax of an important section in the gospel. This is the final pericope in the cycle of traditions in chapters 8 and 9; it is followed immediately by the evangelist's summary of the teaching, preaching and healing ministry of Jesus and his introduction to the mission of the disciples (9.35—8).

(c) The crowds said, 'Perhaps this is the Son of David' (12.23)

A similar pattern is found in Matthew's second account of the healing of the dumb demoniac. The crowds respond hesitantly, but positively: μήτι οὗτός ἐστιν ὁ υἱὸς Δαυίδ, which we may translate as 'Perhaps this is the Son of David'. Since the crowd's reaction is contrasted with the negative reaction of the Pharisees in the verse which follows, μήτι can hardly have its more usual sense as an introduction to a question which expects a negative response, i.e. 'Surely this can't be the Son of David'[27]? Once again reference to Jesus as 'Son

---

[27] Other examples of μήτι with a hesitant or positive sense are noted in Blass-Debrunner-Funk's *Grammar*, § 427 (2). See especially John 4.29 and 7.26.

of David' draws an exceedingly hostile response from the Pharisees: 'It is only by Beelzebul, the prince of demons, that this man casts out demons.'

(d) 'Hosanna to the Son of David' (21.9,15)

By introducing a direct reference to Jesus as 'Son of David' Matthew makes a major change to Mark's account of the acclamation of the crowds as Jesus enters Jerusalem (21.9). Immediately after his account of the cleansing of the temple, Matthew notes that Jesus healed the blind and the lame and that children in the temple repeated the acclamation of the crowds at the 'triumphal' entry (21.9,15). Once again reference to Jesus as 'Son of David' draws an angry response from Jewish religious leaders (here, the chief priests and the scribes): 'they were indignant' (21.14–15).

This clash is followed immediately by the cursing of the fig tree (21.18–22), the challenge from the same opponents, "Who gave you this authority?" (21.23–27) and the important trilogy of polemical and very 'Matthean' parables (21.28–22.14). At this point in the gospel the gulf between Jesus and the Jewish religious leaders becomes steadily wider. The double confession of Jesus as 'Son of David' by the crowds at the 'triumphal entry' and by the children in the temple sparks off the bitter disputes between Jesus and his opponents which follow.

We have now noted four redactional passages in which acknowledgement of Jesus as 'Son of David' is vigorously opposed by the Jewish religious leaders. This is the very first conflict in the gospel (2.1–6); two passages are found at important turning points in the evangelist's story (9.34; 21.9,15); the fourth passage (12.23) is an integral part of the important set of claims and counter-claims in chapter 12 which we discussed above.

Why does the evangelist stress so strongly that Jesus is the Son of David? Why is acknowledgement of Jesus as 'Son of David' so vigorously opposed by the Jewish religious leaders? And why does Matthew set out so carefully this four-fold pattern of positive response by some and rejection by the Jewish leaders?

Once again we are in contact with claims and counter-claims being made at the time Matthew wrote. The evangelist is well aware that his communities will face fierce opposition to their claims that Jesus was indeed the Davidic Messiah. Matthew insists that this claim is part of the very essence of Christian convictions about the significance of Jesus. But at the same time in several redactional passages he sets out a portrait of the Davidic Messiah which differs from many current expectations. The one born 'king of the Jews' is the child Jesus, the Davidic Messiah (2.2–6); in accordance with prophecy Jesus heals every disease and infirmity (8.17); Jesus is the one who is 'meek and lowly in heart'

(11.29), the chosen Servant of God (12.17–21), 'the humble king' (21.5). All these passages bear the stamp of the evangelist himself. They convey a quite distinctive portrait of Jesus[28]. What lies behind it?

An early form of the 'two parousias' schema

I now wish to build on the above observations concerning Matthew's presentation of the Davidic Messiahship of Jesus and to suggest that in Matthew we have an early form of the 'two parousias' schema which became a prominent feature of later Christian disputes with Jewish opponents[29].

In the middle of the third century Origen noted that critics of Christianity who based their case on the interpretation of Scripture 'failed to notice that the prophecies speak of two advents of Christ. In the first he is subject to human passions and deeper humiliation ... in the second he is coming in glory and in divinity alone, without any human passions bound up with his divine nature.' (*Contra Celsum* I.56) The schema of two contrasting advents is found nearly a century earlier in Justin, who insists that some of the words spoken by the prophets refer 'to the first coming of Christ, in which he has been proclaimed as about to appear both without form and mortal, but others have been spoken with reference to his second coming, when he will be present in glory and upon the clouds ...' (*Dialogue* 14.8; cf. 40.4; 52.1; 110.1–5). Similarly, and perhaps from about the same time as Justin, the Anabathmoi Iakabou source of the Pseudo-Clementines: 'He (Moses) therefore intimated that he (Christ) should come, humble indeed in his first coming, but glorious in his second ...' (*Recognitions* I.49)[30].

This schema became both popular and widespread in the later Christian tradition. For our present purposes it is important to note that it seems to have arisen as a response to Jewish claims that the 'unsuccessful' life of Jesus did not correspond at all to the prophecies of Scripture concerning the coming triumphant Messiah. Origen quotes the objection raised by Celsus's Jew (c. 177–180): 'The prophets say that the one who will come will be a great prince, lord of the whole earth and of all nations and armies, but they did not proclaim a pestilent fellow like him (Jesus).' (*Contra Celsum* II.29) But Origen treats the criticism with disdain by appealing to the 'two advents' schema he had expounded earlier.

Justin's Jewish opponent Trypho also raised the same objection: '... pas-

---

[28] See the discussion of these passages by G. Barth in G. Bornkamm, G. Barth, and H. J. Held, *Tradition and Interpretation in Matthew*, E. Tr. London 1963, 125–31.

[29] H. Conzelmann noted that it is quite justifiable to speak of 'two advents' in Luke, even though the actual terminology is not found. *The Theology of Luke*, E. Tr. London 1961, 17 n. 1. Conzelmann did not relate this observation to later Christian apologetic.

[30] I owe this reference to O. Skarsaune, *The Proof from Prophecy*, Leiden 1987, 285.

sages of Scripture compel us to await One who is great and glorious, and takes over the everlasting kingdom from the Ancient of Days as Son of Man. But this your so-called Christ is without honour and glory . . .' (*Dialogue* 32.1; cf. 39.7; 89.1–2; 90.1; 110.1–5) Justin, like Origen, insists that the Scriptures had prophesied two contrasting advents of Christ.

As far as I know, explicit evidence either for the Jewish objection that the life of the Christian Messiah did not fulfil scriptural prophecies, or for the Christian response in terms of the 'two advents' schema, appears for the first time in the middle of the second century. But the roots of this dispute may well be much deeper. Early in the post-Easter period Christians began to claim that their convictions about Jesus were 'in accordance with the Scriptures'. It would not have been difficult for opponents to refute such claims on the basis of Scripture. In particular, in Jewish circles where there were lively expectations concerning the triumphant Davidic Messiah, it would have been natural to insist that Christian claims concerning the Messiah did not correspond to Scripture[31]. And a Christian counter-claim in terms of the 'two advents' of the Messiah, both foretold in Scripture, may also have been formulated long before Justin's day.

An early form of the 'two advents' schema as a Christian response to Jewish objections is found, I suggest, in Matthew. This proposal is based on a set of cumulative arguments. (i) As noted above (p. 108), Matthew repeatedly reminds his readers that in his earthly life Jesus was the Son of David. In this emphasis (as in so many others) Matthew developed a theme found in earlier Christian traditions. Matthew seems to concede that such a claim flew in the face of some Jewish expectations concerning the Davidic Messiah[32], for in four redactional passages acknowledgement of Jesus as 'Son of David' is vigorously opposed by the Jewish religious leaders. (ii) In Matthew's day, as in Justin's, Christians and Jews could agree that certain passages in the prophets referred to the *future* coming of the Messiah, but agreement concerning the 'first coming' was another matter. The burden of proof clearly lay with Christians, for they were making the novel claims. In these circumstances it is no surprise to find that nine out of ten of Matthew's formula quotations claim that the 'coming', teaching and actions of Jesus are in fulfilment of Scripture[33].

(iii) In a series of redactional passages Matthew emphasizes more strongly than the other evangelists the humility of the earthly life of Jesus the Son of

---

[31] Luke refers repeatedly to Paul's disputes over Scripture with Jews, but tells us little about the issues: Acts 17.2; 18.4; 19.8; 28.23–8.

[32] Jewish messianic expectations were very varied, but there is no doubt that in some circles there were lively hopes for a future triumphant Davidic Messiah. See *Judaisms and their Messiahs at the Turn of Christian Era*, eds. J.Neusner, W. S. Green, E. Frerichs, Cambridge 1987, and also E. Schürer, *The History of the Jewish People in the Age of Jesus Christ* II, eds. G. Vermes, F. Millar and M. Black, Edinburgh 1979, § 29 'Messianism', 488–549.

[33] See G. N. Stanton, *A Gospel for a New People*, chapter 15; B. Lindars, *Jesus Son of Man*, London 1983, 115–83.

David, the glory of his future coming as Son of Man and judge, and the contrast between the two 'comings'. The main features of Matthew's distinctive portrait of Jesus as the humble servant have been sketched above (p. 111); although this is not the only way in which Matthew interprets the life of Jesus, this is a prominent and striking feature of his redaction of his sources.

Matthew's extension of the apocalyptic themes found in his sources is well-known. He repeatedly emphasizes redactionally the future glorious coming of Jesus as Son of Man[34]; he is the only evangelist to use the word παρουσία of the future coming (24.3,27,37,39).

Although Matthew does not refer to the life of Jesus as his παρουσία, he does contrast sharply the humble life of the Davidic Messiah with his future coming in glory in ways which are reminiscent of the later 'two parousias' schema. The Jesus who must go to Jerusalem and suffer many things (16.21–3) is contrasted much more sharply than in Mark with the Son of Man who will come in the glory of his Father and then reward each person for what he has done (16.27–8). The 'humble king' who enters Jerusalem (21.5) will come in glory, sit on his throne, and as king he will judge the nations (25.31–46). At the hearing before the sanhedrin Jesus is asked by the high priest, 'Are you the Christ, the Son of God?' The reply of Jesus is either evasive or hesitant. By adding to Mark 14.62 a strongly adversative πλήν and ἀπ' ἄρτι, Matthew contrasts the present role of Jesus with his future role as Son of Man and judge (27.64).

Matthew's redactional juxtaposition of the present humility of Jesus and his future coming in glory is not related to the incarnational pattern found in other New Testament writings in which the one who was with God humbled himself among men (even to death) and was exalted by God (e. g. Phil 2.6–11; 2. Cor 8.9). Nor is it related to the pattern of reversal found in Acts: in raising Jesus God reversed the actions of those who put Jesus to death (e. g. Acts 2.23–4; 3.13–15). Matthew simply sets the two contrasting 'comings' side by side, just as Justin and Origen were to do much later.

The development of the 'two parousias' schema in the second and third centuries may have been partly influenced by Matthew's gospel, but there are no signs of direct literary dependence. In Matthew, Justin, the so-called AJII source behind the Pseudo-Clementines, and in Origen, the 'two advents' scheme is a response to the sharp criticisms of Jewish opponents who insisted that Christian claims about the Davidic Messiahship of Jesus were not in accordance with the prophets.

---

[34] See G. N. Stanton, *A Gospel for a New People*, chapter 6.

Conclusions

What is the relationship of Matthew's Christology to the 'parting of the ways'? Most of Matthew's major Christological emphases are a development or modification of themes which were already prominent in the sources on which the evangelist drew, and hence are not directly related to the 'parting of the ways'. Some of Matthew's Christological themes are related indirectly to the parting. For example, Matthew's strong insistence in redactional passages on the presence of Jesus with his people (1.23; 18.20; 28.20) and his claim that 'something greater than the temple is here' (12.6) is undoubtedly set out as a counterpoise to Jewish views about God's presence.

In this paper I have concentrated on themes and passages which may be related more directly to disputes between Christians and Jews, and hence to the 'parting of the ways'. At the very end of his gospel Matthew refers explicitly to the rival explanations of the empty tomb held by Christians and Jews in his own day (28.1–15). This passage strongly suggests that other passages in Matthew's gospel may reflect rival assessments of the significance of Jesus.

I have argued that two accusations levelled against Jesus, that he was a magician and a deceiver, are related to stock anti-Christian polemic. It is no coincidence that these hostile accusations of Jewish leaders occur in Matthean passages which are clearly redactional: they almost certainly reflect the claims and counter-claims of Christians and Jews in the evangelist's day – though the roots of the polemic may be even deeper.

Matthew's repeated insistence that in his earthly life Jesus was Son of David may well have been a response to known Jewish objections. The four redactional references to the hostility evoked among the opponents of Jesus by this assessment of Jesus strongly suggests that this was the case.

In the final part of this paper I have taken a further step. In Matthew we have an early form (perhaps the earliest) of the 'two parousias' schema which was one of the ways Christians countered Jewish claims that the life of Jesus did not correspond to the prophecies concerning the future coming of the Messiah.

Matthew contrasts the humility and meekness of the life of Jesus the Son of David with the glory of his future coming as Son of Man and judge. This Christological patterns reflects (in part) the self-understanding of the communities for which Matthew wrote his gospel: Christology and ecclesiology are inter-related. Matthew's Christian readers are encouraged to live by the conviction that the Risen and Exalted Lord is with them (28.20); they are urged to be ready for the parousia of the Son of Man. But since their Lord who was sent by God (10.40; 21.37) is also the humble servant of God who was confronted at every turn by his opponents, they themselves must reflect that role. Their message and ministry are the same as that of Jesus himself (10.7–8). They are 'the little ones' (10.42; 18.6,10,14; 25.40) who must face fierce opposition

(5.10–12; 10.11–42; 23.34), but their cause will be vindicated at the future coming of the Son of Man himself (25.31–46).

A note on the textual evidence for the omission of Matthew 9.34

by

J. NEVILLE BIRDSALL

At Professor Stanton's personal request, I made some observations on the problem of the omission of Matthew ch.9 verse 34, to which he alludes in his contribution (pages 103–104). The chairman curtailed my presentation of the interpretation of the data on grounds of exigency of time. The note as now presented is therefore somewhat expanded by comparison with the verbal contribution, yet the data deserve a full treatment. Textual criticism is, at the present time, a most despised cinderella amongst the varied disciplines which one must apply to the text if one's exegesis is to be sound; I hope that this note will do something to show its true beauty and claim to preferment. The remarks are mainly factual and methodological, and need to be taken into account, whether one supports Stanton's conclusion or an opposing one.

The witnesses to the absence of the verse known to Professor Stanton are given as D a k "the Sinaitic Syriac palimpsest" and Hilary of Poitiers. Some additions can be made to this, which I will rehearse with comment on the significance which the respective parts of the attestation possess, taking the additional evidence into account.

To the Latin evidence there may be added the poet Juvencus, who composed a Vergilian paraphrase of the gospels, Evangeliorum libri quattuor[1]. Book II, lines 417 to 424, follows the order of Matthew 9.32 to 36, but omits any words dependent upon verses 34 and 35[2]. In the technique of the genre of this paraphrase, repetitions were to be eliminated[3]. This would explain the absence of a link with verse 35, since this repeats the thought of chapter 4 verse 23 in almost identical words. Verse 34 however has not been anticipated. It would

---

[1] Gai Vetti Aqvilini Ivvenci evangeliorum libri quattvor recensuit ... Iohannes Huemer (C.S.E.L. XXXIV) Vindobonae. MDCCCLXXXXI. pg. 60.

[2] Tischendorf noted the omission of the verse in Juvencus. A concordance of the gospel passages used by Juvencus is given in Nils Hansson. Textkritisches zu Juvencus, Lund 1950, pg. 18. A concordance compiled by Manfred Wacht, Hildesheim, 1990, has been published.

[3] Cp. Michael Roberts. Biblical Epic and Rhetorical Paraphrase in Late Antiquity. (Liverpool 1985) pp. 108–123.

seem likely that the gospel text followed by Juvencus did not contain the verse. He lived in Spain roundabout AD 330; he is then, like Hilary, a writer of the pre-Vulgate period. We perceive then that these two patristic witnesses, together with the Old Latin manuscripts *a* and *k*, make a compact group of testimony. Links between *a* and *k* have been documented by Adolphine Bakker as long ago as 1933[4]. She did not allude to this common omission in the first part of her study (the only part published), but the "Full Collation"[5] of *k*, which appeared at the same time as that study, lists the omission, with the supporting attestation. That includes all the data alluded to here, except the paraphrase of Juvencus.

It is common ground to students of the Old Latin version that *k* (Codex Bobbiensis) presents the gospel text known in Africa about AD 230. The other evidence shows that the absence of Matthew 9.34 in that text was passed on into strata of the European branch of the Old Latin. It represents a coherent yet developing strand of the greatest antiquity within the Old Latin version.

The Sinaitic Syriac palimpsest too has some further support in the absence of Matthew 9.34 from its text. The Arabic Diatessaron, chapter 12, section 39 gives Matthew 9.33 and section 40 gives 9.35 but there is no trace of verse 34[6]. The text of this harmony was translated from Syriac into Arabic: the Syriac form had already suffered correction to the standard of the Peshitta before translation, but the original affinity with the Old Syriac is shown by a number of close textual agreements in all four gospels. The presence of the Matthaean text without 9.34 in this source, then, shows that the reading of the Sinaitic Syriac is not a result of the whim or error of its scribe, but is part of the Old Syriac tradition of the separated gospels. Whether it was also the text of an early form of the Diatessaron is uncertain, since the earliest access which we have to that, in the Commentary of Ephraem the Syrian upon the Concordant Gospel[7], shows that in the text lying before that father, there was one incident alone for the two "Beelzebul" episodes in chapter 9 and 12 of the canonical gospel. The presence of the equivalent of the demonstrative pronoun οὗτος in two of the three references suggests, however, that the text of Matthew 12.24 was dominant in the composition of this section, since there is no evidence for the pronoun in chapter 9.

It may be added that, in preparing this note, all references were checked in the

---

[4] Adolphine Bakker. A Study of Codex Evang. Bobbiensis (k). (Proefschrift, Free University of Amsterdam) N. V. Noord-Hollandsche Uitgeversmaatschappij, Amsterdam, 1933. Pp. 68–71.

[5] Adolphine Bakker. A Full Collation of Codex Evang. Bobbiensis (k). No date or publisher's details are given, but the colour of the cover and typeface of the title are uniform with the "Study" (fn. 4).

[6] A.-S. Marmardji O. P. Diatessaron de Tatien. Beyrouth. 1935. pp. 116f.

[7] Saint Ephrèm. Commentaire de l'évangile concordant. Texte syriaque ... édité et traduit par Dom Louis Leloir, O.S.B. (Chester Beatty Monographs no. 8) Dublin. 1963. Ch.X,7a (pp. 42f.) cp. Louis Leloir. Le Témoignage d'Ephrèm sur le Diatessaron (C.S.C.O. vol. 227) Louvain 1962 pp. 142 & 233.

first three volumes of Biblia Patristica[8], that is covering the fathers up to, and including, Origen. There are few explicit quotations before Origen, and both these, and those which may be traced in Origen's works, are more easily identified with Matthew 12,24 through the presence of οὗτος or its equivalent or by the inverted construction with οὐχ . . . εἰ μή. The manuscript tradition does not record variants of 9.34 through the intrusion of these elements.

To return to the testimony of the ancient versions, we should note that the absence of Matthew 9.34 is known from two groupings of coherent witness, each clearly identifiable within the history of the versions in question. There can be no treatment of the variant as a chance emendation of the text, ventured on by a few isolated scribes, as the lecturer suggests. If the variants arose by excision of words from the original text, this act will have taken place at the roots of these two traditions, to be dated in the case of the Latin in the third century, and in the case of the Syriac, certainly before the fifth century.

The witness is not numerous, and Stanton appears dismissive of it on those grounds. He may here be indirectly dependent upon B. M. Metzger, whose discussion in the Textual Commentary of the Greek New Testament he mentions in a footnote. Metzger terms the attestation meagre. It is sad to see a scholar to whom non-specialists turn for guidance in textual matters writing in this way; although he has written at great length, and often valuably, about the versions, he seems in this comment to have quite deserted any attempt to bring a historical vision to the interpretation of the evidence. It is no surprize then to see the non-specialist lured into curt dismissal of the versional evidence, however much it is to be lamented. The inherent logic of such dismissal is to accept the text with the greatest number of witnesses counted by heads, and would lead to the acceptance of the longer version of the Lord's Prayer in Luke, the addition of the doxology to that Prayer in Matthew, the originality of the last twelve verses of Mark, and the admission of the Pericope Adulterae as part of the original text of John, to mention some well-known and striking instances of longer texts supported by a majority. The opinion of the community of scholars about these textual cruces, which one presumes both Metzger and Stanton share, is based on a sophisticated understanding of the individual witnesses involved and a reconstruction of the history of the text to which such understanding leads.

We must attempt such an understanding of the evidence for the absence of Matthew 9.34 in the witnesses here adduced. When a few witnesses in outlying borders of the early church concur against the rest in any kind of variant, we must entertain the possibility that here early readings are preserved, even perhaps original forms of text. We know that in the Greek area, and in the areas

---

[8] Biblia patristica. Index des citations et allusions bibliques dans la littérature patristique. Tomes 1–3 Paris 1975, 1977, 1980.

served by these versions, revising and regularizing movements took place. The variants left upon the fringe untouched by later uniformity are like flotsam of earlier episodes in its history, left behind by the ebbing sea, or *Leitfossilien* of species now disappeared, noted here and there in an ancient geological stratum. They are signs that once, earlier than the witnesses which attest them, there existed, in East and West, texts of Matthew fairly widely known, which lacked the words which we conventionally term verse 34 of chapter 9. The Latin evidence dates to the third century and persisted at least in Spain into the fourth century. The Syriac evidence derives from the creation of the Old Syriac from the congress of the Diatessaron with Greek separated gospels. This had taken place before the work of Ephraem.

Does the Codex Bezae, the one Greek manuscript to attest the absence of 9.34, show us a form of such a Greek text as the Latin and Syriac presuppose? The author of this note believes that the origin of Codex Bezae lies in the East (as many other scholars do), and in a personal view, thinks that it may plausibly be considered to represent a text intended for lection in a pilgrim centre of Greek liturgical practice, where a Latin gloss was needed for Western pilgrims, say, such a centre as Jerusalem[9]. Nonetheless, he admits as do all workers on the manuscript, that the two columns, Greek and Latin, in which the text is found in it, have exercized a mutual interaction in the course of their underlying evolution as a bilingual. The absence of the Old Latin ms. *d* from the attestation is the result of a judgement that the Greek side of Codex Bezae has influenced its Latin side; yet Bakker showed some affinities of *d* to *k* in the monograph already mentioned[10]. If, however, the Greek side of the manuscript is dominant in its history, we might link the absence of the Matthaean verse in question from its text, with the silence of the patristic early evidence about that verse. But this must remain uncertain and any argument hypothetical.

The three groups of related evidence which witness to an early absence of Matthew 9.34 in copies of the gospel known in both East and West, and in the Greek-speaking centre of the early Christian world, are the three which constituted the data behind the notion of a "Western Text". This term was a misnomer from the beginning, but refers to an entity which any perusal of the data of variation in second century material must reveal. The concept has recently been called in question by Kurt Aland, sometimes with a ferocity which suggests personal antagonism to the Cambridge scholars of a century ago, Westcott and Hort, in whose reconstruction of the history of the text it played a central part. We cannot analyze the psychology of this, but would draw atten-

[9] Studien zum Text und zur Ethik des Neuen Testaments. Festschrift zum 80. Geburtstag von Heinrich Greeven. hrsg. von Wolfgang Schrage (BZNW 47) Berlin 1986. pp. 102–114. "The geographical and cultural origin of the Codex Bezae Cantabrigiensis" by J. Neville Birdsall.

[10] Op. cit. (fn. 4 supra) pp. 41–52.

tion to the strengths and weaknesses inherent in any criticism. Westcott and Hort treated the text of Codex Bezae as if it were a second century text, although they dated the manuscript as late as the sixth century. Their successors, especially Rendel Harris, established that this was too simple an analysis of the text of the manuscript. Nevertheless, as I have demonstrated in a symposium paper published in 1989[11], "in the second century, textual forms existed which were not characteristic of the Alexandrian tradition". In that demonstration there could be utilized early Greek material, both in gospels on papyrus, and in the remains of the Greek Irenaeus, and Latin material. Syriac material was not directly used, since the Old Syriac gospels – as the consensus of scholars appears to agree, – are a secondary stage in the transmission of the gospel text in Syriac, and are probably greatly influenced by the text of Tatian's Diatessaron. While this probably does not rule their evidence out of court, it demands a lengthy examination to demonstrate their admissibility, and within the remit of the symposium only absolutely certain evidence could be admitted.

Westcott and Hort thought that generally the Western Text, although early, was corrupt, arising from careless treatment at a time when the scriptural status of the gospel writings was not clearly perceived. This corruption showed itself often in addition to the text. Yet in the Gospel of Luke, and once in that of Matthew, the longer text showed itself in the witnesses which they called "Neutral". These nine passages were the Western "non-interpolations"[12] which Stanton brings into his argument. Matthew 9.34 was never amongst them. The omission there attested was one of "an intermediate class of Western omissions that may be non-interpolations", about which the "internal evidence, intrinsic and transcriptional" was "open to some doubt"[13]. It is too easy to speak rather superciliously, about "a lingering commitment to Westcott and Hort's theory", as Stanton does. It was carefully thought out within a coherent framework of explanation. But it is not immediately relevant here.

More important is the question of the "shorter reading", for which the NEB and REB are accused of having "a misguided commitment". In support of this summary judgement, he mentions "several textual critics" as having recently called it in question. One of these, J. M. Royse, I have not seen. P. M. Head dismisses the principle on the basis of a survey of papyri of the gospels, in the collation of which he concentrates on singular readings. For *p 4*, to take an example, he can find six omissions over parts of chapters 1–6 of Luke. Five are of one word, one of two words. The tale is the same throughout the population, except for two homoioteleuta, acknowledged as accidental. On the basis of this

---

[11] *Gospel Traditions in the Second Century*. William L. Petersen. Editor. Notre Dame and London. 1989. pp. 3–17 "The Western Text in the Second Century" J. Neville Birdsall.

[12] *The New Testament in the Original Greek*. Introduction. Appendix. (1896) Paragraphs 240 (pg. 175) & 383 (pp. 294f.).

[13] Ibid. Paragraphs 240 (pg. 176) & 384 (pp. 295f.).

sort of evidence, he solemnly counsels us to prefer the longer reading. J. K. Elliott, as referred to by Stanton, would prefer the longer reading, since to add to a text demanded a conscious mental effort, whereas omission will be accidental. This possibly points to the importance of examining variants before making judgement, which many of us still do, as did Westcott and Hort. It is precisely because the added words of the "non-interpolations" do appear to be thoughtful additions, drawing upon "stray relics from the apostolic or subapostolic age" (to use Hort's phrase)[14], that addition is the likely transcriptional option. The other instances from the "intermediate class of Western omissions" are "open to some doubt". If the words *were* omitted, it will not be accident or caprice which lay behind that, but either a literary or a theological judgement. If the words in question here are an addition, then a climax to the miracle series in a hostile criticism of Jesus by his adversaries, does not seem to me at all unlikely, while it does to Professor Stanton. Another possibility is that some early lectionary system used a pericope ending at 9.33, and the words of 9.34 were formed to round off the lection. There is in the Georgian tradition of the Jerusalem lectionary[15] the most meagre hint that this might have been so, but not enough firm evidence to justify another paragraph here.

My comments have been mainly factual and methodological, and with Hort, I remain with an open mind about the resolution of this crux of the text. I would argue nevertheless that whatever the conclusion we may reach about it, or any other textual crux of moment, we should have dealt with it against a background of full knowledge of the data, and of the ramifications of any theories which we need to invoke. The problem in point, whether omission or addition in relation to the original of the gospel, has very ancient evidence on both sides, and the evolution of the text, and the preservation or creation of the texts as we have them, did not come about by accident, and need to be studied with great care and due seriousness.

---

[14] Ibid. Paragraph 384 (pg. 296).

[15] Le grand lectionnaire de l'église de Jérusalem. Tome II édité par M. Tarchnischvili. (C.S.C.O. vol. 204: scriptores iberici T. 13) pg. 15 Lection 1025 *inc.* Matt. 9.35; Tome II traduit par Michel Tarchnischvili. (C.S.C.O. vol. 205: scriptores iberici T. 14) *similiter.* (Louvain 1960).

"In Him was Life"

by

JOHN MCHUGH

In the Synoptic Gospels Jesus is presented as preaching to Jewish audiences the Good News of the kingdom of God, and part of his purpose must have been either to correct or to refine contemporary Jewish ideas of that kingdom. The editorial work of later Christians has, of course, set in relief the differences between the kingdom as preached by Jesus and as expected by Judaism, to such an extent that it is now difficult to discern how far these differences were perceptible to Jesus' hearers, and how far the gospels represent the interpretations of the early church. Most people, however, would admit that on this topic there is some authentic connection between the teaching of Jesus and that of the early church.

It is a commonplace to say that where the Synoptic Gospels speak of the kingdom, the Fourth Gospel, with the sole exception of Jn 3:3,5, speaks instead about life. My purpose is to inquire whether, as in the Synoptic presentation of the kingdom, there is a discernible continuity between the teaching of Jesus and the concept of life presented in the Fourth Gospel, in the hope that this quest may throw some light on the theme of the parting of the ways.

We may begin by comparing the Synoptic teaching concerning the kingdom with the teaching of John concerning life. The kingdom of God is said to have approached, or to have come close, and even to have already arrived (ἤγγικεν, Mk 1:15; Mt 4:17; 10:7 etc., ἔφθασεν, Mt 12:28 = Lk 11:20). Though already present during the ministry of Jesus, it is capable of further growth (Mk 4:26–32); indeed, it will not reach its final consummation until the end of history (Mk 4:29; Mt 13:30,41–43). Thus it has both a present and a future aspect. It is also, of course, essentially a collective noun, denoting the society of those individuals who accept it or enter it, by acknowledging here on earth God's sovereignty.

Certain points of comparison with the concept of life in John are immediately evident. Life is already offered during the ministry of Jesus (Jn 4:14; 11:26), and this life is capable of growth (10:10b); it has both a present and a future aspect on this earth, and leads to the world of the resurrection (5:29; 6:53–54,59). On the other hand, the idea of life is, by contrast with the notion of the kingdom,

individual rather than collective, more personal than social, and the stress falls
not on a final consummation at the end of history, but on the victory of life over
death for the individual. It is easy to see that entering into eternal life and
entering the kingdom of God may quite reasonably be regarded as two sides of
the same coin.

Of the 16 occurrences of the word ζωή in the Synoptics, two refer to life on
this earth (Lk 12:15; 16:25), and may for our purposes be discounted. Of the
other 14, six are without any adjective, but clearly refer to a state of blessed
existence after death, which one may enter by keeping the commandments (Mt
7:14; Mk 9:43,45 = Mt 18:8.9; plus Mt 19:17). The other eight all speak of ζωὴ
αἰώνιος, and six of them occur in the story of the rich young man or in the
discussion which follows it (Mk 10:17,30 = Mt 19:16,29 = Lk 18:18,30); the
seventh (Lk 10:25) looks as if it is inspired by that tradition, and the remaining
instance (Mt 25:46) refers to the happy estate of the righteous at the end of
world history. Thus in the Synoptics "life" as a religious concept always refers to
"eternal life", a state of beatitude after death[1].

Such preaching could only have commended Jesus to all who believed in a life
after death, and however displeasing it might have been to the Sadducees, there
was nothing offensive to mainstream Judaism in the affirmation that God would
reward the righteous either by bodily resurrection (Dan 12:2; 2 Macc
7:14.22−23) or by a blessed immortality of the soul (Wis 3:1−9; 5:1−8.15−16).

Everything was altered when the early Christians began to preach that the
eschatological kingdom of God had been inaugurated by the public ministry of
Jesus of Nazareth, and had been definitively established by his rising from the
tomb. For then it was quite consistent for these Christians to add that "eternal
life" was already being proffered to all who entered this kingdom during their
sojourn on this earth (cf. Acts 2:28; 3:15; 5:20; 11:18; 13:36.48). For these early
Christians, there was no doubt that the kingdom of God had already arrived.

Most Jews, on the other hand, were equally certain that it had not. They had
not observed any great change in the balance of power, and could see no
evidence that Jesus had established on earth the kingdom foretold by the
prophets, or anything like it; on the contrary, the world and its wickedness were
going on just as before, and there was nothing new under the sun. For them, Job
and Ecclesiastes were a wiser and more practical guide than the novel so-called
"messianic" teachings of the followers of the Nazarene.

The scene was therefore set for dissent and eventual confrontation between

---

[1] Whether Jesus ever spoke of "inheriting" eternal life is problematical: the verb occurs on
the lips of the rich young man in Mk 10:17 = Lk 18:18 (and of the lawyer in Lk 10:25) but
(significantly?) not in Matthew's version of the young man's question (Mt 19:16, τί ἀγαθὸν
ποιήσω ἵνα σχῶ ζωὴν αἰώνιον;). On the other hand, Matthew alone has Jesus speaking of that
eternal life which will be the disciples' "inheritance" (Mt 19:29, ζωὴν αἰώνιον κληρονομήσει,
by contrast with Mk 10:30 and Lk 18:30, but in alignment with Mt 25:34). If Jesus' teaching
centred on the fatherhood of God, it was logical to speak of inheritance also.

the Christian church and the Jewish synagogue. What began as a profound disagreement about the nature of the kingdom of God and of the kingdom of the Messiah inevitably evolved into a more fundamental confrontation. From disagreement about the nature of the eschatological kingdom promised by the prophets, it became a all-embracing dispute about the religious concept of "life". Where and when do we come to "have life"? During our earthly existence or only after death? How does one attain to it? By following the Torah or (only?) by following Jesus?

I. Towards a Reinterpretation of the Gospel Tradition contained in the Synoptics (Jn 1—2)

The Johannine account of the Baptist's ministry differs strikingly from those in the Synoptics. Though John's ministry of baptizing is presupposed (Jn 1:25—26,31,33), its purpose is neither defined nor described, and of his stern prophetical rebuke to Pharisees and Sadducees, there is not one word. The Fourth Gospel is completely silent about John's baptism of Jesus; there is no hint that it ever took place. We read only that the Baptist, seeing the Spirit descending upon Jesus, and remaining upon him, knew thereby that Jesus was to baptize in the Holy Spirit, and was indeed the Son of God (contrast Mk 1:9—11 = Mt 3:13—17 = Lk 3:21—22 with Jn 1:29—34).

In the Fourth Gospel, John the Baptist ist seen solely as a witness to Jesus (Jn 1:6—8, cf. 1:19—28). The public ministry begins when John points to Jesus as the Servant of the Lord, the Lamb that takes away the sin of the world, the Chosen One of God[2]; within days a small group had recognized Jesus as the Messiah (1:41), the prophet foretold in Deut 18:18 (1:45), the Son of God and the king of Israel (1:49). Jesus' response to these seven titles was to speak about the heavens opening, and the angels ascending and descending on the Son of Man (1:51).

Then, "on the third day" (2:1), the seventh day from the beginning of John's testimony in 1:19—28[3], "he manifested his glory" by commanding that six

---

[2] Following J. Jeremias, and taking ὁ ἀμνὸς τοῦ θεοῦ as reflecting an Aramaic original *talya' delaha'*, *talya'* being a homonym which can mean either "a boy or servant" or "a lamb". The rendering "Behold the Servant of God who takes away the sin of the world" would produce a clear reference to Isa 53, but at the price of sacrificing the equally apposite translation "lamb" (cf. Isa 53:7), so important in John's Passion chronology. See TWNT I 342-5, and V 698—713, the latter article (παῖς θεοῦ) being reprinted in a revised form in *Abba: Studien zur neutestamentlichen Theologie und Zeitgeschichte* (Göttingen 1966), 191—216. The references for Jn 1:29.36 are in TWNT V 700 = *Abba* 194-5. If one accepts Jeremias' preference for "servant" as the primary meaning of *talya'*, there is a strong case for accepting also, in Jn 1:34, because of Isa 42:1, the variant reading ὁ ἐκλεκτὸς τοῦ θεοῦ: see J. Jeremias, *New Testament Theology* I (London 1971), 53—54.

[3] That is, assuming that in Jn 1:41 the preferable reading is not πρῶτον, but πρωΐ.

water-jars, intended for Jewish ritual purification, should be filled with water which, once tasted, proved to be not water, but the finest wine. The symbolism is inescapable: "on the third day", the seventh day of the week, Jesus makes the cleansing water of the Old Covenant taste like the best of wine. That is, the ancient traditions of Israel acquire through him a new and exhilarating interpretation[4]. The triumphant account of the first week of the public life of Jesus with which the Fourth Gospel opens (1:19–2:11) could hardly be more different from the comminations of the Baptist in the Synoptics.

The following episode, the Cleansing of the Temple (Jn 2:14–11), is therefore instructive. It comes at the beginning of the Gospel-story, and marks the formal opening of the public ministry, because the author is eager to elaborate the theology of the Temple. The harsh phrase from Jeremiah 7:11 ("den of robbers"), common to all three Synoptics, is replaced by "a house of commerce" (2:16), "the chief priests and scribes and elders" are not mentioned, and the challenge to Jesus is not worded as "By what authority?" Instead we read that "the Jews" said "What sign do you show us for doing these things?" and that Jesus at once offered them a sign: if they were to destroy "this temple", he would raise it up in three days (2:18–22). The Johannine version is completely formal, provokes no controversy (not even in 2:23–25), and speaks only hypothetically of the destruction of "this temple" (2:19). There is not one word of criticism of any Jewish institution, of any person in authority, or of any Jewish doctrine (not even in 2:23–25).

II. The Presentation of the New Order (Jn 3–4)

Chapter 3 and 4 fall naturally into four sections. In the first three sections, the evangelist calls into question the sufficiency of mainstream Judaism, of John's baptism, and of Samaritan worship; in the fourth, he admonishes God-fearing Gentiles who frequent the synagogue not to wait for signs and wonders before beginning to believe (4:48). In three of the four sections, the person representing the group responds positively (in 3:30, the Baptist, in 4:29, the Samaritan woman; in 4:50, the official); only Nicodemus, personifying the sympathetic stream of Judaism (3:2), remains at this stage puzzled (3:7,9–10). For the development of the argument, it is essential that the response of Judaism to Jesus' first pronouncement should be at this stage non-committal.

---

[4] E.g. Augustine, *Tract. in Ioannem* IX,5: "Quomodo autem fecit de aqua vinum? Cum aperuit eis sensum, et exposuit eis Scripturas." Augustine's use of the Emmaus story ("on the third day") to expound the meaning of Cana symbolically is a sermon of genius. "Intellexerunt Christum in his Libris in quibus eum non noverant. Mutavit ergo aquam in vinum Dominus noster Iesus Christus, et sapit quod non sapiebat, inebriat quod non inebriebat."

a) The Evangelist's Testimony to the Jews

Jn 3:1−22 is a presentation of the main theme of the Fourth Gospel, namely, that in the cross alone is victory over all that is evil achieved. These verses outline the central conviction of those who had been converted from mainstream Judaism to Christianity, and their message, though ostensibly addressed to Nicodemus in private, is manifestly directed to all adherents of Pharisaic Judaism. It originated, I suggest, as follows.

Suppose that the Baptist's message was "I baptize you with water, but there is one coming, greater than I, who will baptize you with fire", *i. e.*, with the fire of judgment. The Synoptics gloss over the contrast between the Baptist's predictions of doom and the reality of Jesus' ministry of mercy either by suppressing any mention of fire and substituting a reference to a holy spirit (Mk 1:15), or by adding a reference to a holy spirit (Mt 3:11 = Lk 3:16). John, like Mark, has no reference to fire, and writes only (1:33): "This is he who baptizes in a holy spirit[5]." If John was written after A.D. 70, why did the evangelist not leave the Baptist's original doom-laden words unaltered?

The question becomes particularly acute when we consider the destruction of Jerusalem and the burning of the Temple in A.D. 70. Jew and Christian alike might with equal sincerity have acknowledged that these terrible events were a manifestation of the absolute sovereignty of God over history[6], and it was not the first time that the faith of Israel had been so severely tested. Jeremiah, Ezekiel and Daniel had all seen in the destruction of Jerusalem and of its Temple an exercise of the sovereignty and power of the God of Israel; and all had spoken with confidence of the restoration of the city and of its worship. One text supremely applicable to the desolation in Jerusalem and Judaea after A.D. 70 is Ezekiel 36:1−7; but the remainder of this chapter confidently assures the people of their deliverance, telling them of their cleansing by water and of the gift of a new spirit (36:24−27), and so leads into a description of the resurrection both of Israel and of Judah (37), and on to the prophecy of the building of a new Temple (Ezek 40−48). In similar vein, the evangelist is concerned to dwell not on past punishment, but on the positive gifts which Jesus brings for the future. Like Ezekiel, he focusses attention on the gift of the Spirit, and on the new Temple. That is why in 1:33 the Baptist speaks of Jesus' baptizing with a holy spirit, and not with fire.

But how could a Christian explain all this to a Jew? The evangelist introduces here the figure of Nicodemus, an upright and honourable Pharisee, who approaches Jesus very respectfully ("Rabbi") and speaks for a group (οἴδαμεν) which acknowledges that Jesus is a teacher sent from God (Jn 3:1−2). To

---

[5] This interpretation is cogently presented in T. W. Manson, *The Sayings of Jesus* (repr. London 1957), 39−41 and 66−71 *passim*.

[6] Though not of course a messianic or eschatological manifestation.

Nicodemus, then, as a well-disposed representative of mainstream Judaism, the evangelist addresses his first message.

Before Nicodemus puts any question, John places on the lips of Jesus a statement, not unthinkable in the context of the public ministry, which yet addresses primarily the agony and the bewilderment of devout Jews around 80–90. In Mt 18:3, underlying the Greek στραφῆτε there may be an Aramaic verb *(tûb, hᵃzar* or *hᵃdar)*, which would give the interpretation "Unless you turn back again and become like children ..."[7]. John has transposed this saying into Ἀμὴν ἀμὴν λέγω σοι, ἐὰν μή τις γεννηθῇ ἄνωθεν, οὐ δύναται ἰδεῖν τὴν βασιλείαν τοῦ θεοῦ. Of course it is not a matter of re-entering one's mother's womb; that would, as Nicodemus says, be absurd. But the evangelist contends that it is possible, indeed necessary, to start a new life by rebirth "from on high", by being reborn "of the Spirit"; and that such rebirth "from the Spirit" will enable a person ἰδεῖν τὴν βασιλείαν, that is, "to see" all around, even in the ruins of Jerusalem and in the destruction of the Temple, the presence of "God's sovereign rule and reign". So it had been for Jeremiah, and Ezekiel, and Daniel, and so it was to be always: only someone who is reborn of the Spirit can either perceive God's kingship or enter into that domain where God reigns.

Later, either the evangelist or an editor inserted in 3:5 the words "of water and ...", to specify that Christian baptism is the soure of that cleansing water and of the lifegiving Spirit foretold in Ezek 36:24–27 which leads to the resurrection of Israel. This (3:5) is the last mention of "the kingdom of God" in the Fourth Gospel, and it is probable that John avoids the term thereafter because he does not wish to engage in needlessly distracting discourses confirming that Jesus was not a political or military messiah. The only other occurrence of the noun ἡ βασιλεία is when Jesus reminds Pilate, "My kingship is not of this world" (18:36–37), confirming that his followers too do not seek to usurp the rights of the civil authority. The Fourth Gospel sees the resurrection of Israel foretold in Ezek 37 as something that will be achieved not by a political restoration, but in a spiritual manner, through the Christian Church.

Jn 3:6–8 dwell therefore on the genuineness of the new life given by birth from the Spirit, a life that is as real in its effects as the air we breathe, affirmations which prompt Nicodemus to ask "But how can this be?" Jesus in reply asks how one who is a recognized teacher in Israel can fail to perceive the possibility of such a new beginning, in which a society bound together by purely spiritual ties might in God's providence replace an earthly group held together by political authority (compare Jer 29). Indeed, on this matter the Christian community can speak out of its own knowledge and experience (3:9–11). The οἴδαμεν in 3:11, spoken by Jesus on behalf of the Christian community, makes a

---

[7] For the list of linguistic parallels in support of this rendering, see J. Jeremias, *New Testament Theology* I, 155: "These verbs are often used alongside another verb to express our 'again'".

neat *inclusio* with the οἴδαμεν in 3:2, uttered by Nicodemus on behalf of his favourably-disposed colleagues, and the scene closes in 3:12 with the statement that unless these good people first accept the need for rebirth here on earth (τὰ ἐπίγεια), they will hardly find it possible to share the Christian experience of life in the spirit (τὰ ἐπουράνια).

Deut 30:12 has regularly been cited to throw light on Jn 3:13, but its relevance is much enhanced if we compare the felicitous renderings in the Palestinian Targums. In the *editio princeps* of Neophyti 1, the English translation of this verse reads: "The law is not in the heavens, that one should say: Would that we had one like Moses the prophet who would go up to heaven and fetch it for us ..."[8], and Michael L. Klein, translating a Fragment Targum, gives: "If only we had someone like the prophet Moses, who would go up to the heaven and bring it to us"[9]. With these renderings in mind, I like to think of Jn 3:13 as the Christian answer to this yearning, and to paraphrase it as "No-one has gone up into heaven, but there is one who came down from heaven, the Son of man"[10].

Jn 3:14–15, about the bronze serpent, then follow smoothly as a second statement by the Christian community addressed specifically to Judaism. Just as the Israelites in the desert were saved from death by gazing on the image of the poisonous serpent (Num 21:8; and cf. Wis 16:7,12), so it was divinely ordained that the Son of man should be raised on high (οὕτως ὑψωθῆναι δεῖ τὸν υἱὸν τοῦ ἀνθρώπου), in order that humankind might perceive, in the death-dealing instrument of the cross, God's chosen instrument of eternal life. Since G. Kittel's article in 1936[11], many have seen behind the Johannine ὑψόω the Aramic verb *zkf*, the use of which is well attested for impaling, hanging or crucifying, but for the evangelist, the advantage of the Greek verb (here used for the first time) is that it carries the triple meaning of being raised high on the cross, being raised high into glory, and being raised high into heaven (3:14; 8:28; 12:32.34)[12].

So we come to Jn 3:16–21, verses analogous to a Greek chorus, in which the Christian community sings its creed and affirms its faith, and invites Judaism to recognize that God so loved the world that he gave his only-begotten Son (cf.

---

[8] A. Diez Macho, *Neophyti 1: Targum Palestinense MS de la Biblioteca Vaticana, Edición Principe, Introducción y Versión Castellana: Tomo V: Deuteronomio* ... English translation by Martin McNamara and Michael Maher (Madrid 1978), 554.

[9] M. L. Klein, *The Fragment-Targums of the Pentateuch according to their Extant Sources*, Volume 2: Translation (Rome 1980), 84, cf. 181.

[10] The variant at the end of the verse which adds ὁ ὢν ἐν τῷ οὐρανῷ would support the interpretation given in the paraphrase above, since it appears to deem it necessary to stress that the Son of man is now in heaven.

[11] ZNTW 35 (1936) 282-5.

[12] A slight variation from G. Bertram's "bewußt doppelsinnig gebraucht" in TWNT VIII 608, but with a similar meaning. For John, not only the resurrection and ascension, but the acceptance of crucifixion also, because of the perfect obedience there displayed, was an exaltation into glory.

Gen 22:16 and Rom 8:32), that the world might be saved through him, by learning to believe in his name. Note that in this hymn, the message of Jesus' relationship to the Father is light to the world, and that all who believe, and practise the truth, will come to the light. Such is the evangelist's first plea, addressed to Jews in the last part of the first century.

b) The Evangelist's Testimony to Followers of John the Baptist

From the *Clementine Recognitions* (I 54.60:III 61), we know that groups of disciples of the Baptist who did not belong to the Christian Church existed well into the second century, if not later. These the evangelist now addresses, affirming that the necessary rebirth through water and the Spirit is not to be found in John's baptism, as the Baptist himself had well understood (3:27–30: cf. 1:33).

It seems that the evangelist (or his source) has here taken the generally applicable parable about guests not fasting while the bridegroom is present (Mk 2:18–20), and applied it to Jesus specifically, even to the extent of referring to him as the bridegroom, a divine title if ever there was one. In the context of the Fourth Gospel, the clause ὁ ἔχων τὴν νύμφην νυμφίος ἐστίν (3.29) can bear no other meaning. In the light of this, the Baptist's protestation of his own relative lowliness (Mk 1:7; Jn 1:27 etc.) naturally evokes the conclusion: "He must increase, and I must decrease" (3:25–30).

Aenon, some 9 kilometres north of Salim, on the wadi el-Farah, lies on the edge of Samaria. The further implication is that those who came there for John's baptism were perhaps not pure-blooded Jews at all, and that the Baptist, in his lifetime, had accepted them just as they were, without insisting on a rigorous observance of halakhic law. Now, long after his death, the evangelist presents him as instructing all his remaining disciples to follow Jesus ("He must increase, and I must decrease", 3:30), and to seek the Christian baptism mentioned in 3:22 and 26.

Jn 3:31–36 is then yet another Christian hymn about him who came from above (31), to whom the Baptist had borne witness (32–34). Whoever does not believe (ἀπειθῶν) shall not "see" life, a phrase which immediately recalls 3:3, about "seeing the kingdom of God" (35–36). This section too ends, with a "choral profession of faith" affirming that the believer already possesses eternal life (compare 3:36 with 3:16–18).

c) The Evangelist's Testimony to the Samaritans

The references to Samaria in Lk 9:52 and 17:11 (cf. 17:16 and Mt 10:5) indicate that on at least one occasion Jesus passed through Samaritan territory. Acts 8:1–25 implies that there was a thriving community of disciples in Samaria from quite early days, and the words "fields white for the harvest" (Jn 4:35) suggest than Jn 4:1–42 may have been written to help Christians of Samaritan origin to evangelize their fellow-countrymen.

There is no obvious Synoptic source for this narrative, but the main themes are easily seen. We may begin by recalling first that the episode of the bronze serpent in Num 21:8–9, which forms the basis of Jn 3:14–15, was followed almost immediately by the digging of a famous well (Num 21:10–17); and by recalling secondly, that John the Baptist has just referred to Jesus as the bridegroom (Jn 3:29). Given these clues, one may reasonably inquire whether Jn 4 should be interpreted as the story of a bridegroom seeking a bride at a well, in a context which will speak to Samaria[13].

The location is at Jacob's well, near Sychar (Jn 4:5), the successor to Shechem, where Abraham built his first altar in the geographical centre of the Promised Land (Gen 12:6–7)[14], and where true worship began. The scene is closely parallel to that in Gen 24, where Abraham's servant meets Rebecca, and to that in Gen 29, where Jacob finds Rachel, at the village well. Gen 24 has frequent references to the requesting and giving of a drink of water (14,17,18,43–45), and both Rebecca and Rachel are presented as beautiful young maidens (24:16; 29:17). Samaria, by contrast, the kingdom of Ahab and Jezebel, had, in the eyes of orthodox Judaism, been further corrupted by the transportation of "people from Babylon, Cuthah, Avva, Hamath and Sephar-vaim" (2. Kgs 17:24), five cities with five patronal gods.

Yet Hosea's great promise ("I will betroth you to me for ever", 2:19), and Ezekiel's ("Samaria and her daughters shall return to their former estate", 16:36) still stood firm, and so Jesus comes to Jacob's well. He comes not like a young man seeking out a spotless virgin bride, but as her former bridegroom, bringing pardon and reconciliation, in fulfilment of the words of Hosea. The Samaritan woman had had five men, five *be'alim*. The uncharacteristic refer-ence to Jesus' exhaustion in Jn 4:6 intimates that there is no limit to the distance the Son of God is prepared to travel to meet the sinner (cf. Hosea): *quaerens me sedisti lassus*.

In Jesus's words of reassurance to the woman (Jn 4:10), four points should be noted. (1) The phrase τὴν δωρεὰν τοῦ θεοῦ occurs in the story of Simon Magus (Acts 8:20), which is also set in Samaria, where it refers explicitly to the giving of a holy spirit by the laying on of hands (8:17); and the word δωρεά, with reference to the Spirit, recurs in Acts 2:38; 10:45; 11; 15 and Heb 6:4. This word

---

[13] Much of what follows is inspired by F.-M. Braun, *Jean le Théologien III: Sa Théologie* (Etudes bibliques: Paris 1966), 90–95, and by G. Bienaimé, *Moïse et le don de l'eau dans la tradition juive ancienne: targum et midrash* (Analecta Biblica 98: Rome 1984), especially 154–99 *passim* and 278–81.

[14] No one has made this point more eloquently than George Adam Smith, in *The Historical Geography of the Holy Land*, 115–121 in the 25th ed. (London 1931): "The View from Mount Ebal." (The pages are almost the same in other editions).

(as distinct from δῶρον, δώρημα etc.) emphasizes the greatness of the gift and the absolute freedom of the giver (such as a king); *munificentia* would render it well. Fr. Büchsel mentions that in the papyri it is used also for a wedding gift to a spouse (*Brautgeschenk*)[15]. The meaning is therefore "if only you had known the bountiful goodness of God . . ." (2) If only she knew the identity of the man who asked for "one little drink" of water (this must be meaning of the aorist πεῖν), then she would have known that he was seeking not to receive, but to confer, a favour: *ille qui bibere quaerebat, fidem ipsius mulieris sitiebat*[16]. (3) σὺ ἂν ἤτησας αὐτόν. In the protasis, the personal pronoun is not expressed (εἰ ἤδεις); σύ in the apodosis is therefore emphatic[17]. Likewise, in the words σὺ ἂν ἤτησας, "the unusual position of ἂν calls strong attention to the hypothesis"[18], stressing that "you would most certainly have asked", by contrast with the more normal order in the following clause (καὶ ἔδωκεν ἄν σοι). (4) καὶ ἔδωκεν ἄν σοι ὕδωρ ζῶν. Ὕδωρ ζῶν provides the first climax, specifying the object of God's munificence.

Will the woman who personifies all Samaria be willing to accept "living water" from a Jew? She temporizes with the words: "Are you greater than our father Jacob?" Only one person in the five books of the Torah could answer this description, the one who having "nothing to draw with" gave Israel "living water" at Rephidim (Exod 17:1−7) and Meribah (Num 20:1−18), where "water came forth abundantly, and the congregation drank, and their cattle" (v. 11: cf. Jn 4:12). There is some evidence that the many stories about the patriarchs and their wells were, in New Testament times, being steadily interpreted in terms of the one great well which provided the water of life in inexhaustible profusion, namely, the Torah. The *Damascus Rule,* for example, reads "they dug a well rich in water" (CD III 16) and gives, as a comment on Num 21:18, "the Well is the Law" (VI 4,4−10)[19]. So when the evangelist has the Samaritan woman asking "Are you greater than our father Jacob?", she is implicitly inquiring, "Are you the prophet like Moses?" (Deut 18:15.18−19), and the evangelist is hinting that Jesus is about to offer a gift superior to anything which Moses had offered, water that will quench thirst for ever, and will become within the one who drinks it "a spring of water welling up to eternal life". The scene can therefore end quite naturally with the woman of Samaria asking Jesus to give her once for all (δός, not δίδου) *this* water (τοῦτο τὸ ὕδωρ)[20], that she may never again thirst nor *keep coming through* here (διέρχωμαι ἐνθάδε) *to go on continually drawing water* (ἀντλεῖν, not, as in 4:7, αντλῆσαι), without prospect of release.

---

[15] TWNT II (1935) 169.

[16] *Tract. in Ioannem* 15, 11.

[17] E. A. Abbott, *Johannine Grammar* (London 1906) 296 n. 2400.

[18] Abbott, *op. cit.* 409, n. 2553 a.

[19] See G. Vermes, *The Dead Sea Scrolls in English* (Harmondsworth 1962, revised 1965), 100 and 102.

[20] Note the position of τοῦτο. In John, this word, when used as a pronominal adjective, seems to carry a certain emphasis if it precedes the noun: cf. οὗτος in Jn 9:24; 11:47; 12:34; 21:23.

When Jesus, before consenting to her request, asks her to summon her husband, she admits she has five "masters" – five *be'alim* (4:16–18: see above). If we recall the Baptist's designation of Jesus as the bridegroom, it is not fanciful to see here an echo of Hosea's words: "I will remove the names of the Ba'als from her mouth, . . . And I will betroth you to me for ever . . . and you shall know the Lord" (cf. Hos 2:14–17.19–20).

Finally, the woman asks Jesus to adjudicate on the central point of dispute between Samaritan and Jew: on this mountain, or in Jerusalem? Would Samaria have to abandon worship on Gerizim, or would this very unconventional Jew be prepared to abandon the principle of worship in Jerusalem? The reply placed on Jesus' lips by the evangelist is that the question is no longer relevant: "Woman, believe me, the hour is coming when neither on this mountain nor in Jerusalem will you worship the Father" (4:21). The essential truth is that God is in future to be adored as *Father*. The words "You worship what you do not know" are then a sympathetic, even "ecumenical", approach to the Samaritans: they are in reality already worshipping their Father. They are not to be required positively to renounce worship on their holy mountain, any more than Jews are required to renounce worship in the Temple at Jerusalem. The place of worship is irrelevant. Both Jew and Samaritan must acknowledge that God, since he is Father of all, accepts true worship wherever it is offered. So on the very spot where Abraham first offered sacrifice in the centre of the Promised Land, Jesus extend the lawful place of worship (cf. Deuteronomy) to encompass all the earth (cf. Ps 24:1). The evangelist can therefore say in the name of all Christians: "We worship what we know, for salvation is from the Jews. But the hour is coming, and now is, when the true worshippers will worship the Father in spirit and truth, for such the Father seeks to worship him. God is spirit, and those who worship him must worship in spirit and truth" (4:21–24).

From this we may conclude that in the last years of the first century, the gospel-writer felt the need to assert that "salvation is from the Jews", and to affirm it strongly, perhaps to Christian converts among the Samaritans, but certainly to his readers. Disputes between Samaritans and Jews he regards as belonging, doctrinally, to the past, but perhaps there was still tension between Christian converts of Samaritan origin and those of pure Jewish race, or between Christians of Jewish or Samaritan origin, and those of Greek blood. It is all too possible, but in the words "the hour is come when true worshippers will worship the Father in spirit and truth", the evangelist unambiguously declares that people disputing about these issues cannot really claim to be "true worshippers" of the Father.

Andrew, the first disciple to follow Jesus, had spoken of him as Messiah (1:41); but in the Fourth Gospel, it is to a Samaritan woman that Jesus first identifies himself as such (4:25–26). No Samaritan would be in any danger of interpreting the term "Messiah" as applying primarily to a nationalist, Davidic, military leader, and therefore Jesus can here identify himself as Messiah, using the language of later Christians, to designate himself as the Lord's Anointed. It is a significant *inclusio*. from 1:41 to 4:25−26.

d) The Evangelist's Testimony to the God-fearing among the Gentiles

In the fourth episode of this section, the healing of the ruler's son, many see a Johannine rewriting of the Synoptic narrative about the centurion's servant (Mt 8:5−13 = Lk 7:1−10), where the centurion is presented as the model *par excellence* of the Gentile believer. In that case, why did John alter the term "centurion" to βασιλικός, denoting an official in the employment of King Herod Antipas?

I suggest it was because he did not wish to present the father in the story as Gentile, a risk all the greater when the Synoptic story had for years been preached as the paradigm example of Gentile faith, because he did not wish to introduce at this stage a message for the Gentile as such. By so doing, he could postpone their entrance to 12:20−26, where their arrival signals the start of the Passion story (12:23); more importantly, this means that in this gospel, the first and only time that Jesus converses with a Gentile is at his trial before Pilate, the servant and envoy of God face to face with the servant and envoy of Caesar.

Βασιλικός, by contrast, is an ethnically neutral term: the official is not represented as being either of Jewish or of Gentile stock, though one can hardly fail to remember that in Luke, the centurion was one "who loves our nation and himself had our synagogue built for us" (Lk 7:5). Luke's centurion appears to have been one of those "God-fearing" Gentiles who attended the synagogue and kept the moral precepts of the Mosaic Law, like the centurion Cornelius in Acts 10:1−2. To this group of sympathetic Gentiles, *i.e.* to the devout and God-fearing, the evangelist now addresses himself. Just as Nicodemus stands for mainstream Judaism, in particular the party of the Pharisees,and for all who are learned, influential, and well-to-do (cf. Jn 3:1; 8:50−52; 19:39), and just as the Samaritan woman stands for all Samaria, and in particular for all who are outcast because of their irregular life, so the king's official here represents all who are neither leaders of the people nor the poorest of the poor, but who are trying to serve God with a sincere heart, perhaps, if my suggestion is right, being Gentiles living on the edge of Judaism. The words in 4:48 "You [plural] will never begin to believer", must be addressed to the bystanders in general, rather than to the God-fearing father whose son was ill. When Jesus's said to him: ὁ υἱός σου ζῇ, the father without more ado took this to mean "Your son is going to live" (the only sensible rendering). The further statement that the father believed, and all his household (4:53) implies that the whole household came to eternal life.

Thus chapters 3–5 affirm that no one can begin life afresh except by being reborn of water and the spirit; not out of water alone, as was the case of those who in repentance followed the Baptist, but only out of that water which signifies the Spirit (cf. Ezek 36:25–28). The people of Judah expected that, on the day of the Lord, life-bringing water would flow from the Temple into Jerusalem and then through all the land as far as En-gedi (Ezek 47:1–10; cf. Zech 13:1; 14:8); the evangelist, when addressing the Samaritans, adroitly bypasses the Jerusalem motif, and chooses a different paradigm wholly acceptable to the Samaritans. This enables him to emphasize that the water he has in mind is something greater than the life-giving well-spring of the Torah, and that the one who gives it must therefore be not merely equal to (cf. Deut 18:18), but greater than, Moses himself, for it is water that will well up continually to life eternal.

The Christian reader of the Gospel (though not the disciples) has already been told that the body of the risen Lord will be a new Temple (Jn 2:21), but even this Christian reader would perhaps not have perceived without prompting that one of the first consequences of this piece of theologizing in Jn 2:19–22 must be that the ground of the schism between Jerusalem and Samaria will cease to exist. Much is still veiled in futurity, but the faith of many Samaritans (4:39), like the faith of the civil servant and all his household (4:50.53), is a harbinger of what is yet to come. The Jews have yet to decide, and so far, Jesus has not presented his case to them.

III. Jesus Reveals to the Jews the Fatherhood of God, the Source of Life Eternal (Jn 5–11)

Every commentator remarks on the absence from the Passion narrative of a formal trial of Jesus by the Sanhedrin, but if the words in Jn 18:20 ("I taught always in a synagogue or in the Temple") are taken as a cross-reference back to the teaching in chapters 5–10, then it is permissible to see these chapters as embodying the Johannine version of the Jewish legal process in which the actions and teaching of Jesus are examined according to Jewish law. This then becomes the major section of the Gospel as far as Judaism is concerned.

From a literary standpoint, these chapters are genuinely creative. I am working on the theory that in the pericope about the healing at the pool of Bethzatha (Jn 5:1–18) we have a conflation of (a) the healing of the paralysed man at Capernaum (cf. "Take up your bed" and "Your sins are forgiven" in Jn 5:8.12, cf. 14 and Mark 2:9)[21]; and (b) the healing on the sabbath in Mark

---

[21] The phrase αἴρειν τὸν κράββατον occurs three times in the Markan story (vv. 9.11.12) and four times in John (vv. 8.9.10.11), and nowhere else in the NT; add Mk 2:4, and the two

3:1−6 (cf. John 5:19), with the story thus rewritten transferred to a location in Jerusalem in order to stage there the grand debate that follows. If the suggestion made in the preceding paragraph about the Jewish trial is admitted, such a change of location would be, if not essential, at least highly advantageous for the achieving of dramatic credibility.

On this theory, what is in Mark veiled, but certainly implied, becomes explicit in John. For instance, after Mark's account of the baptism of Jesus, the reader known that Jesus is in some sense God's Son (Mk 1:11), and this gives the reader (though not the bystanders in the pericope) an insight into the irony of Mark 2:7, "Who is able to forgive sins except the one God"? and into the true implications of the gospel-story thereafter. With that background in mind, we can see that John has here condensed into one short narrative the essence of all the controversies about the sabbath and the forgiveness of sins and the claims of Jesus which are recounted in the Synoptic Gospels. With everything condensed into one story, he can devote all his skill to composing one comprehensive answer to the one great Synoptic question, "By what authority?", and to interpreting the deepest meaning of the Synoptic traditions. Jesus'claim is unequivocally formulated in John 5:17, and made utterly explicit by the evangelist in verse 18: "he called God his own father, making himself equal with God". Jesus' monologue in 5:19−46 is a defence of the words in 5:17, in the sense in which they are interpreted in 5:18.

"My Father is working still, and I am working" (Jn 5:17). Though the work of creation is said to have been completed on the sixth day (Gen 2:2), this does not mean that God ceases from activity (cf. Ps 121:4), only that he ceases from producing new kinds of creatures. Billerbeck cites Philo: "For God never leaves off making, but even as it is the property of fire to burn and of snow to chill, so it is the property of God to make . . . nay more so by far, inasmuch as He is to all besides the source of action[22]", and adds a long series of rabbinical texts to the same effect[23]. 5:19−47 is a commentary on the words in 5:17.

Jesus begins his self-defence with an aphorism analogous to the Synoptic logion in Matt 11:27 = Lk 10:22 about the mutual knowledge of a father and a son. C. H. Dodd and others have argued that we have in John a parable about a father instructing his son in his hereditary craft: the son watches his father, and imitates his actions (5:19−20a)[24]. In Jn 5, Jesus, having stated this general

---

passages supply eight out of the eleven occurrences of κράβαττος in the NT, the other three being Mk 6:55; Acts 5:15 and 9:33.

[22] *Legum Allegoria* I,5, cited in the translation by G. H. Whitaker, in the Loeb Library, vol. 1 (London 1926), 149−51.

[23] Strack-Billerbeck, *Kommentar zum Neuen Testament II*, (Munich, repr. of 1965) 461−2. Compare, in the same sense, a modern rabbinical commentary by Rabbi Meir Zlotovitz, *Bereishis: Genesis, A New Translation with a commentary anthologized from Talmudic, Midrashic and Rabbinic Sources* (Mesorah Publications: Brooklyn, New York 1977), 82−84.

[24] C. H. Dodd. "A Hidden Parable in the Fourth Gospel", in *More New Testament Studies*

principle, applies it to the immediate context where he is accused of having offended first against the sabbath law by restoring a sick man to health, and then against the law of blasphemy by calling God his own Father. In 5:21 he repudiates the two charges together, with one answer, arguing that as it is the Father who raises the dead and brings them to life, so anyone who brings life to whomsoever he wills must be in some sense the Father's Son, and equal to him. The logical consequence is that "as the Father raises the dead and gives them life, so the Son too gives life to whom he will" (5:21).

In 5:25 he goes even further, asserting that the hour is coming (and now is, adds the evangelist or editor) when the dead shall "listen to" the voice of the Son of God, and those who listen shall live. These words refer almost certainly to those who are spiritually dead, asserting that if they "listen to the voice of the Son of God", they will *begin to* live (translating ζήσουσιν as an inceptive future). This first comment would then refer to a spiritual resurrection in this life. But what of the dead who are in their tombs (5:28)? Here the evangelist (or his editor) has added a second comment, about the bodily resurrection, stating a truth which follows logically from the statement in 5:21.

So, far from moderating his claims in the face of opposition, the Johannine Jesus has amplified them to a point where they cannot be disregarded, much less ignored. The evangelist formulates for the Christian reader the full implications of Jesus' claims, so that he may then display over the following chapters the full array of arguments supporting those claims.

First then, can Jesus call upon two witnesses to support his claims in a Jewish court? The Baptist had been on his side, and had been accepted as a worthy witness even by those who were now challenging Jesus (5:33–35), but Jesus has someone greater to bear witness on his behalf, his own Father, witnessing by his works, and by his words in Holy Scripture (5:36–40). Indeed, if they would only search the scriptures, they would find a second witness, Moses himself, standing up to speak for Jesus, and accusing them (5:45–47). The following chapters provide the proof from Scripture for the assertion in 5:46, "If you were accustomed to believing Moses, you would now be believing me".

a) At Passover: Jesus Gives Bread that will bring Eternal Life

"The Passover of the Jews was near at hand" (Jn 6:4): one may surmise that the writer intends not merely to indicate the season of the year, but to interpret the next event in terms of the Exodus. The evangelist compares the sign of the loaves with the equally astounding gift of manna, and makes this the starting-

---

(Manchester 1968), 30–40; the idea was proposed also, apparently independently, by P. Gächter, "Zur Form von Joh. 5:19–30", in *Neutestamentliche Aufsätze: Festschrift für J. Schmid*, ed. by J. Blinzler, O. Küss and F. Mussner (Regensburg 1969), 65–68. Many have followed them.

point of his argument. He reminds the reader that it was not Moses who gave the Israelites bread from heaven[25], and boldly asserts that the one whom Jesus calls, uncompromisingly, *"my* Father" is at present giving to those who are being addressed (δίδωσιν ὑμῖν) "bread which is the true bread from heaven" (6:32). *"My* Father": apart from 2:16, this term (as distinct from *the* Father) was first used in 5:17 to place on record Jesus's claim, and in 5:43 ("I have come *in the name of my* Father") to confirm it. This is the first example of the evangelist's "searching the Scriptures" to give a midrashic exposition of his faith in Jesus as the Christ, and the Son of God.

The Feeding of the Five Thousand, close to the feast of Passover (6:4: cf. Mk 6:69 "green grass") provided an appropriate occasion to present Jesus as the bread of life (6:35). The implicit identification of Jesus with the word of God (cf. Deut 8:3; Amos 8:11−12; Isa 55:1−2) and with the wisdom of God (Prov 9:1−6; Sir 15:3; 24:19−22; Wis 16:26), makes excellent theological sense; the word and wisdom of God had been embodied in the Torah, the prophets and the holy writings. Now, the evangelist affirms, Jesus is the embodiment of God's word and God's wisdom, his teaching the bread of life, by which the world can live (cf. Deut 8:3).

The more audacious claim, that Jesus himself will, at the last day, raise to life those who believe in him needs more careful thought, for it is beyond all question a claim to be able to do what only the Creator can do. The foundation for the idea is clear enough in 6:40: everyone who recognizes Jesus as the Son of God, and reflects upon it, must infer that God is an all-merciful Father, which leads to the conclusion that such a Father will not permit his creature to perish eternally. Thus the word of God proceeding from the mouth of Jesus, proclaiming his divine Sonship (as in 5:17−18), becomes the seed of eternal life[26]. In this sense, Jesus, *qua* Son, is truly "the bread of life" in a manner and to a degree transcending even the holy word and wisdom of God embodied in the Law, the Prophets and the Writings. Such is the message of what we may call the first homily on the text "He [God] gave them bread from heaven to eat" (Jn 6:32−40.47−50): "my Father is at this moment giving you the true bread from heaven" (6:32).

A second homily, on living bread (Jn 6:51−59), develops this concept in a new direction: to eat and drink the eucharistic bread and wine is also source of life in the present world and of unending life in the world to come. When Jesus says (6:53), "Amen, amen, I say to you, unless you eat the flesh of the Son of man and drink his blood, you have no life in you", the time-reference is clearly to the present world: the present tense οὐκ ἔχετε ζωὴν ἐν ἑαυτοῖς must refer to life here on earth. Self-evidently, it does not refer to biological existence on the

---

[25] Reading οὐ Μωϋσῆς δέδωκεν, in preference to ἔδωκεν.
[26] Note the variant readings in 6:47.

planet, for in this sense the addresses are most certainly alive; it must denote some other kind of life, different even from the psychological activity of a thinking human being. The next verse explains: "whoever eats my flesh and drinks my blood has eternal life, and I will raise him up at the last day" (6:54). Ζωὴ αἰώνιος must refer to a life which extends beyond the boundaries, temporal and spatial, in which the natural life of humankind is passed: yet it must be present here also, in earthly time and space, for in 6:54, the verb ἔχει denotes the present time in the strict sense. Ἔχει cannot be, for example, a *futurum instans*, because its coordinate verb, ἀναστήσω, is, both by grammatical form and by contrast ("on the last day"), so indubitably future.

Given these facts, we may look afresh at the two phrases in vv. 51 (ἐάν τις φάγῃ ἐκ τούτου τοῦ ἄρτου ζήσει εἰς τὸν αἰῶνα), and 58 (ὁ τρώγων τοῦτον τὸν ἄρτον ζήσει εἰς τὸν αἰῶνα), the *Incipit* and the *Explicit* of what we have called this second, "eucharistic" homily. To translate these two verses as affirming that whoever eats the eucharistic bread, "*will live* for ever", is to make the promise into a simple statement about the future. This is the normal rendering, but it is open to serious criticism. V. 54 affirms that whoever eats Christ's flesh and drinks his blood already has eternal life, here and now. Given that such a person already has eternal life here and now (54), and *is going to live* for ever (51,57 and 58), it is surely reasonable to translate the word ζήσει, in vv. 51,57 and 58, as an inceptive future, with the meaning "will here and now *begin to* live for ever". The giving of this "living bread" (the Eucharist), is, however, at this point in the ministry, still in the future (δώσω), whereas the teaching of Jesus, who offers himself as the bread of life, can be apprehended by faith even during his Galilean ministry (6:35, in the so-called first homily).

Thus, in accordance with the promise in 6:39, the evangelist gives a new turn to the text "He gave them bread from heaven to eat", by referring it first to Jesus as teacher (6:32−50), and then to the sacramental eating of Jesus' body and blood (6:51−58). In either case, the message is that everyone who accepts Jesus' teaching and partakes of his body and blood *begins*, here on earth, to live with a life that is of its nature eternal.

Naturally enough, some of the Jews, knowing his parentage, could not accept that Jesus was in any special way God's Son (6:41−43). Less surprisingly, there was a profound dispute *among the Jews* about the very possibility of "eating his flesh" (6:52), a verse which can hardly refer to a dispute in Galilee in A.D. 29. The most plausible explanation is that it is evidence of a controversy among Jewish-Christians about the eucharistic teaching of the early church. The main message of chapter 6, however, is that many Jews in Galilee were unconvinced by Jesus' claims (6:60), and that many of his erstwhile disciples "walked no more with him" (6:66). So the evangelist takes the unresolved dispute back to Jerusalem.

The Johannine narrative depicts a repudiation stronger than the rebuff in Mk

6:2–6; Mt 13:54–58, where there is at least open acknowledgement of his wisdom and power (cf. also Lk 4:22). John's rewriting of that story discloses the consequences of not accepting Jesus. The people of Galilee believed they were rejecting propositions concerning Jesus. From the evangelist's standpoint, they were rejecting teaching about the nature of God. This is the import of Simon Peter's profession of faith in Jn 6:68–69.

b) At Tabernacles: Jesus Promises Water that will bring Eternal Life

The location of the drama is transferred from the backwaters of Cana and Samaria and Capernaum, and as in Luke, once Jesus has begun the journey to Jerusalem, there is no turning back. Most significantly, in the Fourth Gospel he travels to Jerusalem apparently unaccompanied by any disciples (cf. 7:10, ὡς ἐν κρυπτῷ): in Jn 7–10, no-one from Galilee ever intervenes on behalf of the Master (only Nicodemus, 8:50–52). Jesus had earlier begun his apologia in the Temple (cf. 5:14), and it was to the Temple that he now returned, "and began to teach" (ἐδίδασκεν: 7:14).

A slight, but important, difference from chapter 5 is that in chapter 7 the evangelist inserts two additional points which flow from the teaching in chapter 6. First, he affirms that for the one who truly seeks to do God's will, the divine origin of Jesus' teaching is self-authenticating (7:17: cf. 6:37–40 and 45b). Secondly, in 7:38 Jesus for the first time pleads with people in Jerusalem to "believe in him" (πιστεύειν εἰς with the accusative): all previous uses of this phrase are either the comment of the evangelist (1:12; 2:11,23; 3:16,18*bis*,36; 4:39; 7:5,31), or addressed to the people in Galilee (6:29,35,41). Now the crowds in Jerusalem are challenged to make a judgment about the nature of God, and it is no accident that Jesus' first discourse ends with the words: "Stop judging by outward appearances, and start making the right judgment instead!" (7:24)[27].

The crowd proves to be uncertain and divided (7:25–31), so the High Priests and the Pharisees sent officials to arrest him (7:32). This is the first hostile move by officialdom. "Jesus *therefore* said" (note the οὖν): "Only for a little time am I with you, and I am on my way to him who sent me. *You will seek me, and you will not find me* . . ." The misunderstanding about his departing for the Diaspora justifies him in repeating the saying, as if the evangelist, not content to give the cross-reference, wants to write out in large letters, "See Proverbs 1:28, and the whole context".

---

[27] This is an attempt to catch the full force of the present imperatives in μὴ κρίνετε κατ'ὄψιν, ἀλλὰ τὴν δικαίαν κρίσιν κρίνετε. In Nestle-Aland NT[26] the evidence for κρίνατε in the second clause is strong ("make the right judgment"), but even if the *lectio difficilior* be accepted (as above), it makes good exegetical sense as saying "from now on, make the right judgment".

On the last day of the feast Jesus proclaimed, "If anyone thirsts, let him come to me and drink" (7:37). Time and place are deliberately chosen. The feast of Sukkoth or Tabernacles, the principal feast of the year, coincided with the anniversary of the dedication of Solomon's Temple (1 Kgs 8:2). Our interest, however, is in the two liturgical ceremonies which, though not mentioned in the Old Testament or in Josephus[28], characterized the feast in New Testament times, as may be seen from the relevant treatise in the Mishnah. The first was the ceremony of pouring water drawn from the spring Gihon (*cf.* perhaps Isa 12:3?) into a bowl beside the Altar of Holocausts, to be used for a daily libation at the Altar, whence it would it would flow away, thus symbolizing the day of the Lord when the promise of Ezek 47:1−12 would be fulfilled (cf. Zech 13:1; 14:8). The second custom also lasted throughout the week: the Court of the Women was kept ablaze with light throughout the night, to symbolize that the day of the Lord, when it came, would be a day without night (cf. Zech 14:7, and especially Isa 60:19−20)[29].

"On the last day, the great day of the feast, Jesus stood up and proclaimed, 'If any one thirst, let him come to me and drink. He who believes in me, as the scripture has said, 'Out of his heart shall flow rivers of living water'" (7:37−8). The reader is inevitably reminded of the words about "a spring of water welling up to eternal life" (4:14). Jesus had promised the Samaritan something greater than the life-giving well-spring of the Torah, and the evangelist now reveals to the reader what that was to be. "Now this he said about the Spirit, which those who believed in him were to receive" (7:39).

So, in public, in Jerusalem, Jesus offers to *all* who hear him rivers of life-giving water, flowing from the Temple, divinely promised for the end-time, the Day of the Lord. The words of Ps 36:9−10 come to mind:

> "They shall drink their fill of the abundance of thy house,
>   and thou shalt let them drink of the river of thy delight,
> for with thee is the fountain-head of life,
>   and in thy light shall we see light."

The crowd remained divided, as did the High Priests and Pharisees, with Nicodemus contending that it was illegal to condemn anyone unheard, and so provoking the retort: "Search the Scriptures and see that no prophet arises out of Galilee" (7:51−52).

"Again Jesus spoke to them, saying, 'I am the light of the world; he who follows me will not walk in darkness, but will have the light of life'" (8:12). The

---

[28] For the detail on the feast in Old Testament times, see R. de Vaux, *Ancient Israel: Its Life and Institutions* (London 1961), 495−500. Josephus describes the feast in *Ant.* III x 4 = X 244−47, but without saying anything about either custom, perhaps because he is there relating what was laid down as law by Moses.

[29] See Danby, *The Mishnah* (Oxford 1933) 179−80, *Sukkah* 4.8 for the ceremony of libation, and 5.2−3 for the ceremony of lights.

evangelist replies to the challenge by sending the reader direct to the one and only prophetical text which mentions Galilee ("the people that walked in darkness ... upon whom light has shined") and which also celebrates the birth of an heir to David's throne (Isa 9:2−7). Just as the water-ceremony in the Temple foreshadowed the life-giving water of the Spirit, so the lighting in the Temple courts was a symbol of the light streaming outward from the new Temple to the entire world.

But what Jesus says is: "I am the light *of the world*." If the phrase about not "walking in darkness" points directly to the text which describes the joy attendant upon the birth of the child Immanuel (Isa 9:2; cf. 7:14), the most obvious allusion of the words "light of the world" is to the other great figure of the Isaian corpus, the Servant of the Lord. In Isa 42:6, we read "I have appointed you for a covenant with the people, and for a light to the Gentiles", and in 49:6, "I will make you a light for the Gentiles, that my salvation may reach to the ends of the earth." Jn 8:12 means that a prophet from Galilee is destined to be the light of the entire world.

On another occasion (πάλιν) a dispute began when Jesus told some Jews that they could not follow him because they "belonged to this world", and would die in their sin (8:21−25). The context shows Jesus explaining that it is a matter of following him into another world "above", from which he comes and to which he will return; his hearers belong to "this world" below (v. 23), and the question is whether they are willing to leave it. 8:24 may be rendered as "unless you come to believe what I am, you will die in your sins"; 8:28 would then make excellent sense if γνώσεσθε is taken as an inceptive future, "When you lift up the Son of Man, then you will *begin to know* what I am." The passage concludes that "while he was speaking thus, many believed in him" (8:30), and to the Jews who had come to believe in him, Jesus said: "if you hold fast by my word, you are truly disciples of mine, and you will come to know the truth, and the truth will set you free" (8:32).

Though the reader knows well what is "the truth that will set them free" (faith in the divine Sonship of Jesus), the Jews of the time did not, not even those who had come to "believe him" (πρὸς τοὺς πεπιστευκότας αὐτῷ Ἰουδαίους, 8:31), for he finds it necessary to say Ἐὰν ὑμεῖς μείνητε ἐν τῷ λόγῳ τῷ ἐμῷ, ἀληθῶς μαθηταί μού ἐστε. The debate is moving forward to the question whether (as Jesus, and his disciples later on, maintained) it is necessary to believe in the teaching of Jesus about God as Father in order to be free, or whether by the mere fact of belonging to the race of Abraham, the Jews are already free.

c) *Jesus, greater than Abraham, is the life-bringing Son of God*

Jn 8:30–59 has long been a problem text, not least because of the words in 8:31: "Jesus said to the Jews who had believed in him [RSV *sic*]". Professor Lindars speaks for many when he writes: "though these words are found in all MSS., it is best to follow Dodd and Brown and to excise them completely[30]." Yet it seems neither necessary nor beneficial to resort to textual surgery, if a satisfactory meaning can be found without doing so.

"To the Jews who had come to believe him, Jesus said ..." (Jn 8:31). I suggest that the entire passage from 8:31 to 8:59 is an apologetic, even a polemic, directed not against Jews but against Jewish converts to Christianity who were unwilling to accept the full Johannine doctrine about Jesus Christ.

Boismard writes that the first section (8:31–36), plus 37, "offre un vocabulaire et un style incontestablement johanniques. Il s'y rencontre cependant une accumulation de termes qui ne se lisent nulle part ailleurs chez Jn mais qui ont une saveur paulinienne indéniable, fréquents surtout dans les épîtres aux Galates et aux Romains ... En fait, *tous* les termes non johanniques de Jn 8:31–37 se lisent, souvent à plusieurs reprises, dans les chapîtres 3 et 4 de l'épître aux Galates[31]."

One must therefore be alert to the themes of freedom versus slavery, of sonship and of inheritance. Jesus, reminding his disciples that as long as they commit sin (for ὁ ποιῶν τὴν ἁμαρτίαν cf. also 1. Jn 3:8), they remain slaves of sin (compare Rom 7), also affirms that they are not yet in reality (ὄντως) free (8:33–36). The fate of Ishmael (cf. Gal 4:30 = Gen 21:10 LXX) proves that physical descent from Abraham is no guarantee that one will inherit his blessings.

In the second section (8:37–47) this critique becomes more open. The evangelist places on the lips of Jesus an argument against Jewish Christians of his own day who did not accept what the Johannine community held to be essential doctrine. The Johannine Jesus is speaking to this later generation from a prestigious plaform, from the Herodian Temple that was as yet undestroyed.

"He said to them: I know that you are Abraham's offspring, but you are about to seek to kill me, because my word is making no headway among you (οὐ χωρεί ἐν ὑμῖν). I am speaking of what I have seen beside the Father (παρὰ τῷ πατρί) and you therefore should do what you have heard from the Father

---

[30] B. Lindars, *The Gospel of John* (New Century Bible: London 1972), 323. The fullest account of C. H. Dodd's view is given in *More New Testament Studies*, chapter 4, "Behind a Johannine Dialogue", 41–57. The interpretation of R. E. Brown, *The Gospel according to John* I (The Archor Bible: London 1971) 354–5, 362–3, is rather more complex than the summary statement in the text above might imply.

[31] M. E. Boismard and A. Lamouille, *Synopse de Quatre Evangiles en français: III L'Evangile de Jean* (Paris 1977), § 261, 241. Where there is a hiatus above after "aux Romains", their text continues: "Dressons-en l'inventaire matériel." and gives the list.

(παρὰ τοῦ πατρός)." Though πατήρ has no possessive (pronominal) adjective, the intended reference is clear enough, but the wording ambiguous enough to permit misinterpretation.

"They answered and said to him, "Abraham is our father." Jesus said to them, "Suppose that you are children of Abraham – then you would be performing the works that Abraham did, whereas in fact you are going to seek (ζητεῖτε) to kill me, a man who has spoken to you the truth which I heard from God; this Abraham did not do." "Performing the works that Abraham did" can only be, as in Rom 4, believing in God; "seeking to kill a man who speaks the truth from God" is the very opposite of this. Hence Jesus, by the words "You are performing the works that your father did" (8:41), intimates that they are not spiritually the children of Abraham, but of another father, and the rest of the discourse follows logically. The proof that they are not children of God is that they do not recognize the sinless Son of God when he speaks the truth to them (8:45–46): διὰ τοῦτο ὑμεῖς οὐκ ἀκούετε, ὅτι ἐκ τοῦ θεοῦ οὐκ ἐστέ (8:47).

"The Jews answered him, "Are we not right in saying that you are a Samaritan and have a demon?" (8:48). If Jn 8:30–36 are addressed to Jewish Christians, then the obvious temptation is to make a break somewhere, perhaps before v. 37, and to take the exceedingly harsh words in vv. 37–47 as addressed to Judaism in general, but not to Jewish Christians. In that case, the Jews mentioned in v. 48 would be any Jews who had not come to believe in Jesus Christ. However, I prefer to think that the writer has in mind not Jews in general, but certain Jewish Christians; and that he is confronting them with the kind of stark alternative presented by Paul in Gal 4:30, except that now the alternatives concern not the Law, but the true nature of Jesus. He is asking them whether they wish to be Jews *or* Christians, convinced that the time is past when one could be both. For the question now is whether the man called Jesus of Nazareth was, antecedently to his earthly life, and indeed before the creation of the world, the co-eternal Son of God.

To orthodox Judaism, the very suggestion is diabolic, and the debate now becomes an exchange of mutual accusations. Each party claims to be the true offspring of Abraham (compare 8:37 with 8:33,39 and 53), and indeed of God (for the Jews, see 8:41,42; for Jesus, 8:36,38,40,42,54,55). The other party is, by contrast, "the offspring of the devil" (compare 8:44 with 8:48 and 52). The point in dispute in 5:18 is more sharply focussed than ever, and Jesus' consistent answer to the charge of blasphemy is that he is talking about the nature of God. "Jesus answered, 'I do not have a demon; but I am bringing honour to my Father, while you are refusing to honour me. Yet I am not seeking my own glory; there is One who seeks it and he will be the judge'" (8:49–50).

The evangelist is mow asking which of the disputing parties best describes the nature of God, traditional Judaism as taught in the synagogue, or those Christian communities whose faith is expressed in the words of the Johannine Jesus.

The only people disconcerted by this dilemma were, of course, Jewish followers of Jesus who did not recognize him as fully divine (for example, the Ebionites). We know the answer the evangelist will give; but the proof he offers them is astounding in its novelty. He affirms that the genuine followers of Jesus will not die.

"Amen, amen, I say to you, if any one keeps my word, he will never see death (θάνατον οὐ μὴ θεωρήσῃ εἰς τὸν αἰῶνα). The Jews said to him 'Now we know that you have a demon. Abraham died, and the prophets; and you say, 'If any one keeps my word, he will never taste death (ἐάν τις τὸν λόγον μου τηρήσῃ, οὐ μὴ γεύσηται θανάτου εἰς τὸν αἰῶνα).' Surely you are not greater than our father Abraham, who died? And the prophets died! Who are you making yourself out to be?'" (8:51—4).

Since there is no evidence to justify the drawing of a real distinction between the two terms θάνατον θεωρήσαι and γεύσασθαι θανάτου[32], the interpretation must be sought elsewhere, and the key lies, I suggest, in *The Testament of Abraham*, the date and provenance of which are so imprecise. Suffice it to say that it is certainly of Jewish origin, and that its story was almost certainly current at the time the Fourth Gospel was taking shape[33]. When the time came for Abraham to depart, God sent the archangel Michael to instruct him to prepare for his departure, assuring him of a superlative welcome, and trusting that he would voluntarily surrender his soul to Michael, and follow the archangel back to heaven. Abraham, however was most reluctant to leave his home in Mamre. So God sent Michael a second time, saying: "Go to my friend Abraham one more time and say to him ... 'Tell me why you are resisting me? Do you not know that all who (spring) from Adam and Eve die? And not one of the prophets escaped death ... Not one of the forefathes has escaped the mystery of death. All have died, all have departed into Hades, all have been gathered by

---

[32] The *Greek-English Lexicon* of Liddell-Scott-Jones cites no example of either phrase from classical literature. Further, θάνατον θεωρήσαι is a hapaxlegomenon in the NT, and neither the solitary reference in the Old Testament to "not seeing death" (οὐκ ὄψεται θάνατον: Ps 88:49 in the LXX), nor the two NT instances of μὴ ἰδεῖν θάνατον (Lk 2:26 and Heb 11:5) are of any help in determining a more precise connotation. Likewise, the phrase "to taste death" is nowhere found in the Old Testament, Greek or Hebrew, and where it occurs in the NT (Mt 16:28 = Mk 9:1 = Lk 9:27; Jn 8:52; Heb 2:9), it is generally taken to be a linguistically insignificant semitism which was soon to become, if it was not already, common in Aramaic, and in later rabbinical Hebrew. The most one can say is that the latter term may place some stress upon the bitterness of death, for the nearest cognate phrases are in 1 Sam 15:32, where Agag says to Samuel "Surely the bitterness of death is past", Sir 41:1 "O death, how bitter is the reminder of you", and 1. Cor 15:56. See M. J. Lagrange, *Evangile selon Saint Jean* (Etudes bibliques: Paris 1925), 252: "-'goûter' la mort est une autre métaphore que voir la mort, avec une nuance légèrement plus accusée, comme si l'on pouvait échapper à cette amertume."

[33] See *The Testament of Abraham*, translated and edited by E. P. Sanders in *The Old Testament Pseudepigrapha* edited by J. H. Charlesworth, I, 869—902. Sanders writes: "It seems best to assume a date for the original of c. A. D. 100, plus or minus twenty-five years" (875).

the sickle of Death. But to you I did not send Death . . . I did not ever want any evil to come upon you . . . I have done these things not wanting to grieve you. And so why did you say to my Commander-in-chief, 'I will not by any means follow you?' . . . Do you not know that if I give permission to Death, and he should come to you, then I should see whether you would come or not come[34]?" In the end, Abraham, for all his unwillingness, has to go.

If we allow that this story of Abraham's pleading to put off his death was current around the years 70–100, the Johannine text takes on heightened contours. "Abraham died, and the prophets; and you say, 'If any one keeps word, he will never taste death at all! Surely you are not greater than our father Abraham, who died? And the prophets died! Who are you making yourself out to be?'" (8:51–54). The story about Abraham is set outside time, in a world where (as in the Book of Job) the Jewish listener is invited to eavesdrop on God's conversations and plans. The Christian reader is now invited to listen to the words of the Johannine Jesus with that story in mind.

Jesus has been charged with glorifying himself to the extent of setting himself up as equal to God (Jn 5:18). His constant reply has been that he has been talking not about himself, but about God. They do not know God, because they do not recognize his fatherhood. "I know him and I keep his word", and hence whoever keeps Jesus' word, about the fatherhood of God, will not, like Abraham in the story, strive by every means to escape the ending of earthly life, as if this departure inevitably entailed a terrifying death and a most severe judgment. Θάνατον οὐ μὴ θεωρήσεται εἰς τὸν αἰῶνα. The reader who reflects on God's dealings with Abraham, can truly say that father "Abraham rejoiced that he was to see my day; he saw it and was glad."

The Jews then said to him, "You are not fifty years old, and have you seen Abraham?" Jesus has made no such claim (it is Abraham who has seen him), but once the matter is raised, he replies quite frankly, "Before Abraham came into being, I am." This is the evangelist's ultimate reply to those Christians of Jewish origin who could not accept that Jesus was, in anything more than an adoptive sense, Son of God; for if he was in truth only an adopted Son, then he was not unique, not the one and only saviour, and God was only in a metaphorical sense, Father (cf. 1. Jn 2:22–25). If that is so, how can anyone be sure that he will not, when this earthly life is over, "die for ever"?

---

[34] In Sanders' translation of the Long Recension (A, by others called 1) of *The Testament of Abraham*, 8, nn. 4–12, the passage referred to is on 886.

d) *"He opened my eyes"*

All three Synoptics relate, as the last miracle of healing in the public ministry, the healing at Jericho of a blind beggar (Mk 10:46–52; Lk 18:35–43), or of two blind men (Mt 20:29–34). Mark and Luke speak of the blind man's "seeing again" (ἀναβλέπω, Mk 10:51,52; Lk 18:41,42,43); only Matthew writes of the request that "their eyes might be opened (Mt 20:33)[35]. John too places his one and only story about the healing of a blind man at the end of Jesus' public ministry.

The use of saliva in Jn 9:6 leads some to suggest that the author may be rewriting the story about the blind man of Bethsaida in Mark 8:21–26[36], but the other details do not support this view, for Mark's description of the healing step by step, using βλέπω (23–24), ἀναβλέπω (24) διαβλέπω and ἐμβλέπω (25), has no suggestion of any washing, a factor which in the Fourth Gospel is central to the cure. Besides, the Holy City has, sad to say, always had too many blind beggars.

The scene-setting in Jerusalem may be intended to illustrate the theme that "the eyes of the blind shall be opened" when God comes to Zion (Isa 35:4–5). But why is washing in Siloam needed in addition to the anointing? The only OT reference to Siloam (Isa 8:6) is a rebuke to the people for refusing to trust the gently-flowing waters which are proof and symbol of the divine protection of Zion. Hence "he orders him to hasten to what is at least a symbol of holy baptism, the washing in Siloam," as the evangelist implies[37]. Washing in the waters of Siloam, then, is affirming before the Jews one's faith and trust in the God of Zion, and one's faith in Jesus. From our point of interest, however, the main thrust of the story lies in 9:5: "As long as I am in the world, I am the light of the world", recalling not merely the ceremonial lights of Tabernacles, but also 8:12, and above all the programmatic statement in the Prologue: "There was the true light, enlightening every one, coming into the world" (1:9).

The parallels between this passage and the story of the paralyzed man in Jn 5 are quite striking. Both healings take place at a Pool in Jerusalem (5:2 and 9:7). In the case of the cripple, seven times we read that he was made "healthy" (ὑγιής: 5:4,6,9,11,14,15; 7:23),seven being the number representing totality,

---

[35] In the Synoptics, the only other occurrence of this phrase is at Mt 9:30, in the only other detailed narrative of the restoration of sight to two blind men, which may well be a doublet of the story in 20:29–34. Mark and Luke seem almost deliberately to avoid the phrase: compare Mk 8:24–25 (βλέπω, ἀναβλέπω, διαβλέπω and ἐμβλέπω), and Lk 4:18; 7:21–22; 18:35.

[36] Perhaps incorporating also a memory of Mk 7:33, though the use of saliva on eyes is attested elsewhere (notably in the story of Vespasian at Alexandria: Tacitus, *Historiae* IV 81; Suetonius, *Vespasian* 7; Dio Cassius 65,8).

[37] εἰς εἰκόνα γεμὴν τοῦ ἁγίου βαπτίσματος τὸ ἐν τῷ Σιλωὰμ ἀπονίπτεσθαι δραμόντα κελεύει κτλ. Cyrilli Archiepiscopi Alexandrini In D. Ioannis Evangelium edidit P. E. Pusey, Lib. VI, Cap. 1, vol. 2 (Oxford 1872), 172, lines 20–21. I have paraphrased, to avoid the textual problems in the second half of the sentence.

and on the seventh occurrence: ἐμοὶ χολᾶτε ὅτι ὅλον ἄνθρωπον ὑγιῆ ἐποίησα ἐν σαββάτῳ ...[38]. In the case of the man born blind, we read seven times the phrase about his eyes being opened (9:10,14,17,21,26,30,32), and when the climax comes with the charge that he was "born in sins, wholly so" (ἐν ἁμαρτίαις σὺ ἐγεννήθης ὅλος, 9:34), Jesus leads him to complete faith in the Son of Man[39].

Note that the words "opening the eyes of the blind" occur nowhere in the first account of the healing. In Jn 9:2–3 Jesus assures his disciples that the man's blindness is not the result of anyone's sin, but has been divinely ordained "in order that the works of God may be made manifest in him"; 9:6–7 state merely that Jesus "smeared the mud on his eyes" and that "he went away and washed and came back seeing". At this stage, the evangelist says nothing of the man's reaction, implying that the gift of physical sight does not, apparently, lead automatically to faith. Lagrange comments: "Il faut convenir que le miraculé lui-même ne montre pas beaucoup d'empressement envers son bienfaiteur[40]."

From this point onwards, the dialogue in chapter 9 is structured on several levels. The evangelist refutes first the suggestion of mistaken identity (8–12), then the charge that someone who does not observe the sabbath cannot be from God (13–17), then the argument that the healed man could not possibly have been truly blind (18–24). Each of these arguments takes the story forward: it is the same man, he was healed as described, and he was in fact born blind.

Secondly, the man when questioned by his neighbours and acquaintances, relates without comment what had happened, and attributes his healing only to "the man called Jesus" (9:8–12). But when the Pharisees question him, some affirming that his benefactor cannot be from God because he does not observe the sabbath, he takes a step forward and asserts that Jesus is a (NB) prophet (9:13–17). Finally, when some other Jews declare that Jesus must be a sinner (9:24), he is aroused to full confrontation, and thus eventually comes to a profession of faith. It will be observed that among the common people there is no hostility (9:8–12), that among the Pharisees there is a division between those with insuperable theological objections and those still puzzled and in doubt (9:16), and that the real hostility is found among those Jews who have the authority and the power to exclude people from the synagogue (9:22).

Thirdly, the phrase "he opened my eyes" does not occur in the narrative of the healing (9:6–7), and neither is it used by the man born blind in his first account of the cure (9:11): its first appearance is on the lips of the neigbours in 9:10. Its second occurrence comes in a statement of the evangelist (9:14), but it does not appear in the beneficiary's second account of his cure (9:15). The third occurrence is when some of the Pharisees ask what he has to say about Jesus

---

[38] See Boismard and Lamouille, *Synopse III, Introduction* 7m (61) and § 148 IV B 6 a (162).

[39] *Ibid.* § 262 III C 5 a (260).

[40] *Evangile selon Saint Jean*, 263, on 9:12.

"because he opened your eyes", and it is at this point that he says, for the first time, "He is a prophet!" (9:17).

The fourth instance of the phrase is placed on the lips of the man's parents, who (like all the previous speakers) equate it with the gift of physical eyesight: "How he now sees we do not know, nor do we know who opened his eyes" (9:21). And it is at this point in the narrative that we learn that the reason the man's parents refused to take a stand was "because they feared the Jews, for the Jews had already agreed that if any one should confess him to be Christ, he was to be put out of the synagogue" (9:22).

With the fifth use of the term, we reach the turning point of the story. The man himself, questioned by the Jews who had interrogated his parents and who now declare that "we know that this man is a sinner" (9:24), replies quite calmly, "Whether he is a sinner, I know not; but one thing I do know, that whereas I was blind, now I see" The first sentence is, given the Johannine background, breathtaking in its boldness, but it has the advantage of concentrating all attention on the question of fact: τυφλὸς ὢν ἄρτι βλέπω (9:25). The man himself has so far spoken only of "seeing" (βλέπειν), and has not yet spoken of "his eyes being opened". And it is the Jews who force the issue, equating two different phrases, when they ask: "What did he do to you? How did he open your eyes?"

When he insists that they have already heard his story, and asks (ironically) whether they too wish to become disciples, their reply is that they are, and intend to remain, disciples of Moses, "to whom we know God has spoken; but as for this man, we do not know where he comes from" (9:29). The principal texts affirming that God spoke to Moses are Exod 33:11 ("Thus the Lord used to speak to Moses face to face, as a man speaks to his friend"); Num 12:2–8, which ends with the commination: „Why then were you not afraid to speak against my servant Moses?" and the conclusion of Deuteronomy: "There has not arisen a prophet since in Israel like Moses, whom the Lord knew face to face ..." (34:10–12).

"We know that God has spoken to Moses; but as for this man, we do not know where he comes from" (9:29). These words finally "open the eyes" of the man born blind, and for the first time in the story, at 9:30, the phrase is used to denote not merely physical seeing, but true spiritual insight. "To have one's eyes opened" is in Hebrew a regular term for intellectual or spiritual perception[41]. "Surely, the marvel is in this, that you do not know where he comes from, even though he opened my eyes ...[42]" (9:30–33). In the context of the

---

[41] See Brown-Driver-Briggs, *A Hebrew and English Lexicon of the Old Testament*, (Oxford 1906), 774a עַיִן 1 j and F. Zorrell, *Lexicon Hebraicum Veteris Testamenti quod aliis collaborantibus edidit* (Rome 1940–84), 591, under עַיִן i 3, "oculi videntes ponuntur pro mente quae cognoscit, intellegit", with references to Gen 3:5,7 onwards.

[42] The sixth occurrence of the phrase in chapter 9.

objection that God's certainly spoke to Moses, the import of the former blind man's answer is that his own healing is equally certain proof that Jesus must be *the* prophet like Moses, predicted in Deut 18:18: "Never since the world began has it been heard that any one opened the eyes of a man born blind", the seventh and final instance of the phrase.

"They cast him out" (9:34). With this sad remark, one part of the story ends, but the evangelist picks up the theme by affirming that Jesus "found him". This touch makes a fine *inclusio* with 5:14; just as Jesus "found" the former paralytic in the Temple, so at the close of this section he "found" the man born blind, outside the Temple and synagogue, debarred from both. Jesus said "Do you believe in the Son of Man?", and to the simple query of the now excommunicate Jew, "Who is he, Lord, that I may believe in him?" responded with the revelation of himself in the words ἑώρακας αὐτόν (9:35–38). The verb ἑώρακα gives, by way of a second *inclusio*, an even longer overarching span; so far, only John the Baptist had "seen" who Jesus was (1:34).

Chapter 9 is therefore a discussion in which the gradual opening of the eyes of the blind man is contrasted with the continuing, and increasing, blindness of so many of the Jews, and it is this episode, more than any other in the Fourth Gospel, which portrays the parting of the ways between Judaism and early Christianity. What began in chapter 5 as a presentation of defence of Jesus in terms of an appeal to Moses ends here in chapter 9, with a third well-planned *inclusio*, in the counter-charge that the synagogue of the late first century cannot recognize the prophet like Moses, who was destined to come (Deut 18:18).

e) *The Risen Lord's Address to the Early Church*

The evidence has been presented, and the Jews in Jerusalem are divided between those accept, those who reject, and those who are still unsure about Jesus's claims. Jesus now makes a final speech before the Jews, a speech in which the evangelist, reflecting on the past, addresses the problems of the closing years of the first century of the Christian era, and seeks to uphold the morale of Jewish and Gentile Christians alike.

"Jesus said, "For judgment I came into this world, that those who do not see may see, and that those who see may become blind" (9:39). This is the only occurrence of κρίμα in John, the word denoting an act of decision, a verdict. A Samaritan, a civil servant of Herod, and various Jews of lowly social standing have come to believe, whereas the leaders of the people have shut their eyes to the evidence.

So Jesus addresses a parable to some unsympathetic Pharisees: "whoever enters through the door is a shepherd of the sheep" (10:2). He himself had come as an observant Jew, to whom the doorkeepers of Israel, the custodians of its traditions, ought to have opened when he came to call "his own sheep" in that fold (10:1–6). Alternatively, one could say that he himself was the door, by contrast with his opponents who are all (as in 10:2) thieves and robbers (10:7–10). In the context of the Feast of Tabernacles, at which the Hallel was sung[43], the reference can only be to Ps 118:19–20, "the door of righteousness, the door of Yahweh", by which alone the Israelite enters into the true Temple and dwelling-place of God on earth (cf. Jn 1:14 and 14:6).

Or one can call him "the good shepherd who lays down his life for the sheep". There are few more powerful images of Jesus as fulfilling the role both of Yahweh himself, and of the new Davidic king, at the end of time, by assembling both Israel and all the Gentiles into one sheepfold, with one shepherd (Jn 10:16; cf. Ezek 34:11–16,23–24). In the vision of the evangelist, it is the divine will (δεῖ) that Jesus should become the leader of those other sheep also, who "will listen to his voice". The phrase ἀκούω τῆς φωνῆς occurs once only more in the Gospel, when Jesus tells Pilate, representing the Roman Empire and all future civil authorities, that everyone who is on the side of truth "listens to his voice" (18:37). In short, the evangelist is declaring to the Pharisees, the leaders of late first-century Judaism, that it is God's will that Jew and Gentiles should be united, under a new David, in an everlasting covenant of peace, with his sanctuary in the midst of them for evermore (Ezek 37:24–28).

"That is why the Father loves me, because I am about to lay down my life, that I may again take it up" (Jn 10:17). All the awkward pseudo-theological problems about the placating of an angry God by the shedding of blood that have been occasioned by this sentence disappear once it is regarded as a word of the Johannine Christ to the Church at the end of the first century. Διὰ τοῦτο: because Jesus had been prepared to lay down his life, even though he could at any stage have stopped the proceedings against him, the Father loves him: this was the most perfect act of unselfish generosity. But he laid his life down only "in order that he might again take it up", i.e. as Risen Lord, over whom death has no more dominion, now gathering his sheep, generation by generation, into the new Temple of the New Covenant. Such was the plan and the command of the Father (10:18).

Sadly, the immediate result was yet another schism among the Jews (10:19), the strength of which is illustrated by the episode at the Feast of the Dedication, in which Jesus once again insists that those who believe in his doctrine of the Fatherhood of God, not merely have their eyes opened, but have life eternal, because no one can snatch them out of God's hand – or out of his – for "I and the Father are one" (10:28–30). "The Jews", however (*i.e.* the Jewish doctors of the late first century) would still not acknowledge that the funda-

---

[43] Danby, *The Mishnah*, Sukkoth 3:9; 4:8, 117,179.

mental point at issue concerned the nature of God, even though Ps 82:6 implies that there is a sense in which humankind shares in the nature of God (10:31–39).

f) The Revelation of Life Eternal

This section ends with the raising of Lazarus. To understand this narrative, it is essential to recognize that John is here using the term "resurrection" in the way contemporary Pharisees used it, in line with Dan 12:2. They thought of a human being as a psycho-somatic unity, not as a composite of body and soul; even texts which speak of a "soul" do not regard that soul as a spiritual being, capable of an immortal existence when separated from the body, but only as a life-giving principle quickening the body, which ceases to function at death. It is almost exactly the opposite of the Platonic concept of the immortal soul, as reflected, for example, in the book of Wisdom. The Pharisees did, however, most firmly believe that "at the time of the end" (Dan 12:9), "at the end of days" (Dan 12:13), "at the last day" (Jn 11:24) the dead would reawaken to consciousness, and return to a fully integrated life, both of body and mind[44]. This much is fundamental for understanding the story about the raising of Lazarus.

Chapter 11 opens with Jesus stating, for the second time, that the ultimate purpose of a particular illness is to contribute to the glory of God (compare 11:9 with 9:3–5). This time, however, Jesus is portrayed as healing the whole person, saving humanity, not from partial physical incapacity (contrast 5:3 and 9:1), but from the power of death itself. The raising of Lazarus is from every angle the climax of this section of the Gospel.

Consequently, the care taken in chapter 9 to assure the reader that there was no question of any mistake about the man's identity, or about the reality of the cure, is in chapter 11 matched, indeed surpassed, by a scrupulous concern to establish the facts of Lazarus' death. When Jesus first hears that Lazarus is sick, he does nothing, but merely waits two days until he can assure the disciples that his friend is in fact dead (11:7,11–14). The purpose of this delay becomes apparent later, when both Martha (11:21) and Mary (11:32) assert in almost identical words that if Jesus had been present, their brother would not have died: clearly, they are convinced that if only he had been present, he would have been able to prevent Lazarus from dying (cf. 4:48–54), and equally clearly, Lazarus has died. The fact is indisputable. When Jesus arrives, we are told that Lazarus is already four days dead, the point at which Jews believed that the soul finally abandoned the body and decomposition set in (11:39). Perhaps it is no accident that, because of the two day delay in starting, the

---

[44] For Jewish beliefs on resurrection, see E. Schürer, *The History of the Jewish People in the Age of Jesus Christ*, revised edition by G. Vermes, F. Millar and M. Black, vol. II (Edinburgh 1979), 391–2, 494–5, 500–01, 540–3.

raising of Lazarus takes place on the seventh day after Jesus has been told of his sickness.

We are about to read of Jesus' last and greatest "sign". The use of the term "sign" is informative. The first two signs took place at Cana (2:11; 4:54); the healing of the paralyzed man in chapter 5 must be included among the "signs" envisaged by the evangelist or his editor at 6:2, and the Feeding of the Five Thousand is termed a "sign" in 6:14, making, thus far, four signs. The walking on the water (6:22–25) is nowhere referred to as a sign, so the healing of the man born blind should be counted as the fifth sign (cf. 9:16 and 10:41, "John performed no sign . . ."). The raising of Lazarus is therefore the sixth sign narrated in the Gospel (cf. 11:47 and especially 12:17–18). As the sixth sign, one naturally suspects that it may be the penultimate event in the series, and therefore of particular significance. In 12:17, note the double affirmation that "he had called Lazarus out of the tomb, and raised him from the dead", and in 12:18, note the emphatic position of τοῦτο, separated from its noun by the verb: ὅτι ἤκουσαν τοῦτο αὐτὸν πεποιηκέναι τὸ σημεῖον – "because he had done *this* sign". The text continues: "The Pharisees then said to one another, "You see that you can do nothing; look, the world has gone after him" (12:19), a virtual repetition of 11:48, "What are we to do, for this man is doing many signs?"

It is significant that the Fourth Gospel, with one exception[45], never uses any word which could be translated "miracle"[46]. Its preferred word is ἔργον (5:20,36; 7:3,21; 9:3–4; 10:25,32–38), for those "works" of Jesus which are also termed "signs". The presentation of the raising of Lazarus as a sixth sign points unerringly to the seventh event that will complete the series, the event foretold when Jesus was first asked, "What sign do you show us for doing these things?" (2:18).

In the narrative of the sixth and penultimate sign, Martha is the central figure, and she plays a role analogous to that of the mother of Jesus in the first sign. At Cana, the mother of Jesus is shown as having believed in her Son before he has worked and sign: contrast 2:5 ("Do whatever he tells you!") with 2:11 (about the disciples). At Bethany, Martha supplies an *inclusio* to that first Cana story by making her great profession of faith (11:27) solely in response to Jesus's word in 11:25–26, before any action has started. Thus the first half of the Gospel, the Book of Signs, begins and ends with two exemplars of faith, two women supremely qualified for that beatitude with which the Gospel ends (20:29).

When Jesus assures Martha that her brother will rise, she naturally under-

---

[45] τέρας, in 4:48, in the phrase (a cliché?) "signs and wonders" (cf. any Greek concordance *sub voce*, and note its regularity in Acts).

[46] Neither δύναμις (so frequent in the Synoptics, but never once found in the Fourth Gospel), nor θαῦμα (never found in this sense in the Bible), nor θαυμάσιον (Mt 21:15 only), nor παράδοξον (Lk 5:26 only), nor ἀρετή (1 Pet 2:9 only).

stands this as referring to the general resurrection at the last day. This supplies Jesus with the cue for the great affirmation, "I am [the] Resurrection and [the] Life" (the text makes better sense if one suppresses, in English, the definite article): "whoever believes in me, even though he should die, shall continue-to-live, and everyone alive who believes in me shall not die for ever" (11:23–26). Here what Jesus is positively *excluding* is the "Pharisaic" concept of a temporary cessation of real life, as if the person slept devoid of consciousness until the last day. Here he affirms that for those who believe in him, there is no interruption in life.

The reader, of course, understands why: it is because the Omnipotent and Eternal is "embodied" in the man from Nazareth. Anyone who believes that this is possible, and is indeed realized, is aware that Martha is here face to face with the origin and source of all resurrection and of all life. The evangelist expresses it perfectly when Martha says, "Yes, Lord! I have believed [note the perfect] that you are the Christ, the Son of God, come into the world" (11:27).

Yet even Martha is so little conscious of the extent of Jesus' power that she warns against opening the tomb (11:39). Even she had not appreciated the implications of her statement in 11:22: "Even now I know that whatever you ask from God, God will give you." That is why Jesus, for the very first time in the Fourth Gospel, addresses his Father in prayer. "They raised the stone, and Jesus raised his eyes upwards, and said, "Father, I thank thee that thou hast heard me. I knew that thou hearest me always." This is also the first time in the Fourth Gospel that Jesus uses the vocative πάτερ, in words that clearly echo Martha's words in 11:22: *God always hears him.* And it is because Jesus desires that all shall come to share Martha's great faith, that he continues: "I have said this on account of the crowd standing around, that they may believe that thou didst send me." "That they may believe that thou didst send me" reflects Martha's wholehearted profession of faith in 11:27, "You are the Christ, the Son of God, come into the world" (11:27).

The emergence of the dead man from the tomb is the ultimate and irrefutable proof that the onlookers were face to face with someone who was the source of resurrection, and therefore of life. They were confronted not with a man blasphemously claiming to be equal with God, as alleged in 5:18, but with a God humbling himself to live on a level of equality with a creature. Once again, the Gospel is rounding off a section (in this case 5–11) with a returning *inclusio*, to remind us that Jesus had already proclaimed, in Jerusalem, at the beginning of this section, that "whoever hears my word has passed from death to life" (5:24), and that "the hour is coming . . . when the dead will hear the voice of the Son of God, and having heard it, will live" (5:25–29). The offer to the (spiritually) dead in Jerusalem was unconditional, and the raising of Lazarus proves the veracity of Jesus' promise.

Is there a more profound meaning? The description of the apparition is unusual. The dead man was bound hand and foot, with a sudarium around his face. Boismard comments: "Une telle manière d'ensevelir les morts était inconnue du monde juif: on est donc en droit d'en conclure que le thème des pieds et des mains liés pourrait avoir une valeur symbolique[47]." He suggests that the description is intended to describe a man held prisoner by bonds of death, as in the Psalms. In Ps 116:3 we read of "the snares of death encompassing" someone, whose "bonds" are later "loosed" by God (v. 16), with similar phrases in Ps 18:4,5,19; and one cannot overlook Ps 118:16–19. Indeed, verse 21 of this Psalm in the LXX version (Ps 117:21), ἐξομολογήσομαί σοι, ὅτι ἐπήκουσάς μου, matches Jesus's words in Jn 11:41, Πάτερ, εὐχαριστῶ σοι ὅτι ἤκουσάς μου. All the promises in these psalms are made to those whom God loves.

Sadly, the Lazarus story closes on a note not of rejoicing but of division: while many of the Jews believed in Jesus, some went to tell the Pharisees what Jesus had done (11:45–46). But many do believe. If the words "and Martha" in 11:1 are redactional ("Bethany was the village of Mary *and Martha*") to start the narrative, is it fortuitous that the name of Martha, this paragon of faith, is mentioned exactly seven times in the story (11:5,19,20,21,24.30.39)[48]? With this, Jesus's self-defence "according to John" is complete, and it is now time for the verdict and judgment.

Psalm 118 (LXX 117):21 has just been quoted; it continues in v. 22 with the words so prominent in early Christian preaching (cf. Mt. 21–42; Mk 12:10; Lk 20:17; Acts 4:11; 1 Pet 2:7; also Barn 6:4): "The stone which the builders rejected has become the chief cornerstone."

"So the chief priests and the Pharisees assembled a council" (11:47): this is the one and only mention of the word συνέδριον in John, a fact which would corroborate the theory that chapters 5–11 are a Johannine variation on the theme of a trial before the Jewish authorities. Their problem was what to do: "What are we to do? For this man is performing many signs. If we let him go on like this, every one will begin to believe in him, and the Romans will come and do away with both our Place and our nation" (Jn 11:47–48)[49]. The "Place" is clearly the Temple; the "nation" calls for comment. In Jn 11:49–50 we read: "Caiaphas, who was high priest that year, said to them, "You know nothing at all; you do not understand that it is expedient for you that one man should die for the people (λαός), and that the whole nation (ἔθνος) should not perish." The LXX sense of λαός denoting the people as a religious group is carried over in Luke, who also employs the term to denote also Christians of Jewish origin and even Gentiles who have chosen to join the (Christian) Church (Acts 15:14).

---

[47] *Synopse III*, 293. III 6a.

[48] Boismard, *Synopse III*, 290 under III C 2a.

[49] The upper case P intentional, to be as literal as possible; note the use of the same word in 4:20, and compare 14:3.

I suggest that Jn 11:50 carries, with a quite deadly irony, the same connotations: it was expedient that Jesus should die on behalf of the (spiritual) People of God, and that the entire nation should not perish (spiritually). "Many believed" (11:45;12:11). The *double-entendre* in Caiaphas's words is evident, and the evangelist comments: "He did not say this unprompted, but being high priest that year prophesied that Jesus should die on behalf of the nation, and not on behalf of the nation alone, but that he might also assemble into one the children of God that are dispersed far and wide" (11:51–52).

VI. The Parting of the Ways (Jn 11:55–12:50)

As in Matthew (26:1–13) and Mark (14:3–9), so in John (12:1–8), the decision to arrest Jesus is followed by the account of the anointing at Bethany, but with three significant differences. Whereas the two Synoptic Gospels place the anointing two days before their Passover (i.e. on the Tuesday), John places it six days before his Passover (i.e. on the Saturday evening); he is thus able to conclude the great and final week of Jesus' life on earth with the scene of his exaltation on the seventh day, John's Passover Feast.

More significant is the manner of the anointing. Mary anoints not Jesus' head, but his feet: the former action would have been a mark of honour to a guest (cf. Ps 23:5), but in the Johannine setting, Mary is here matching the faith of her sister Martha (11:27) with a profound act of humility towards One who is truly the Anointed of God. If Mary's anointing is seen in this light, then Judas' protest is appalling, and the evangelist means that Judas has already lost all faith (cf. 13:2). The extravagant anointing, and Judas' protest, start the week of the Passion, as the outcome of Judas' treachery and the even more extravagant and solemn anointing by Joseph and Nicodemus (19:38–42) will close it.

From this point onwards, the story proceeds at speed, always with a double interpretation. Outwardly, it is the story of Jesus' final suffering and public execution; for the initiated Christian reader, well aware that every single step is taken when, and only when, Jesus wills it, it is the record of the victory of God's love for mankind over human refusal to obey God.

The first episode describes Jesus' triumphal entry into Jerusalem, with John alone of the evangelists saying that the crowd carried psalm-braches (12:13), for the Greeks a symbol of victory (cf 1 Macc 13:51; 2 Macc 10:7). The next episode peculiar to John shows some Greeks who had come for the Passover (perhaps God-fearers, but certainly sympathetic Gentiles) approaching Philip with the request, "Sir, *we want to see Jesus*". The climax of Part One of the Gospel is reached. Jesus answered: "The hour has come for the Son of man to be glorified." He then stresses that it is only through suffering and death that he can prove the greatness of the Father's love, just as his disciples will have to prove their love for the Father by following in his footsteps (12:23–26). At the human level his triumph will not be painless: the prayer of the agony is repeated in Jn 12:27–33, but in John it ends with the assurance of victory. "Now is the judgment of this world, now shall the ruler of this world be cast out; and I, when I am lifted up from the earth, will draw all men to myself. He said this to show by what death he was to die." This is the first occasion on which this Gospel speaks of Jesus' "dying", the first occasion on which the dark side of the verb ὑψόω is unveiled.

The crowd then puts two questions: (a) what do you mean when you say the Son of Man must be raised on high, when we have always been taught that according to the Law, the Messiah will remain for ever? (b) who is this Son of Man? Chapter 12, and Part One of the Gospel, ends with two citations from the Book of Isaiah, the first recalling the opening words of the Fourth Servant Song (answering the first question), the second recalling the fruitlessness of Isaiah's preaching (hinting at the answer to the second).

V. Conclusion

In the Fourth Gospel, "the Jews" are for the most part spoken of, and addressed, without any reference to their diversity. Nowhere is there any mention of the Sadducees; the nearest approach is a reference to the high priests, but they again are mentioned only twice, in 7:32 and 45, until the action of the Passion opens. From this point onwards (11:47), they naturally play a part, but it is a purely political part, and does not involve any Sadducean doctrine. In chapter 7–9, the debating opponents in Jerusalem are often Pharisees, but one cannot overlook the fact that Nicodemus (7:50) was ready and able to speak up in favour of Jesus. No other Jewish group is mentioned. From this it would seem that by the time the gospel was published, the Johannine community at least had put behind it debates with the Judaism of long ago, and, insofar is it was engaged in debate or dialogue with the synagogue, was interested only in the surviving form, Pharisaism. Nicodemus (3:1–9; 7:50; 19:39) is undoubtedly meant to represent those Pharisees who came to believe.

Consequently, when we come to the Passion narrative proper, in John 18–19, we find not a kerygma directed to Jew or Gentile or honest inquirer from outside, with some measure of apologetic motif, but a finely wrought treatise of Christian didache, in which the author gives a profound interpretation of the great events. In the nature of the case, this can only be given *post factum*, and this is why the evangelist places on Jesus' lips so many promises that the disciples' view of the cross will be transformed "when the Paraclete comes" (14:26; 15:26; 16:7). 16:13 is escpecially significant:

ὁδηγήσει ὑμᾶς ἐν τῇ ἀληθείᾳ πάσῃ. The word ὁδηγήσει, and the use of the dative with ἐν rather than the accusative with εἰς, imply that it will be a long ongoing process.

If we put all these ideas together, then I do not think the Fourth Gospel can be called polemically anti-Jewish. There is certainly a powerful and deep stream of apologetic directed towards those of the Jewish faith who might wish to understand how the new Christians looked at Jesus, but hostility in principle seems too strong a word. Even in chapters 7–11, where the debate is at its most heated, the evangelist continually reminds the reader that during the preaching of Jesus, the Jews of the day were divided, and many believed in him (7:11 – 12,25–31,40–44,45–52; 8:30–36; 10:19–21,41–42; 11:45–46). In these chapters, too, the Jewish actors are stylized rather than personalized, set up to speak their parts in the drama, a drama that was for the evangelist more poignant than any Greek tragedy. Perhaps that is why there is no formal religious trial before the Sanhedrin, only a civil trial before Pilate. For the ultimate point at issue between Jesus and the religious leaders of the Jewish people concerned the very nature of God, since Jesus was teaching humankind about a spiritual recognition of the Father that is conditional upon the gift of the Father (Jn 6:44,65; cf. 6:37,39; 10:29; 17:2,5–9.12,24; 18:9), and the evangelist quite evidently judged this matter to be outside the competence of any human court established to deal with purely human affairs. Nevertheless he was willing to have Jesus' case presented before a human jury. It is when the Greeks arrive that we hear the words, "Now is the judgment of this world, now shall the ruler of this world be cast out; and I, when I am lifted up from the earth, will draw all men to myself" (12:31–32). As the last voices of the apostolic generation passed away, they were content to leave the final judgment on Jesus' teaching to the verdict of history.

The Understanding of Christ in the Pauline School: A Sketch

by

PETER STUHLMACHER

For Oswald Bayer at His 50th Birthday

I

In a programmatic essay on "Paul and Wisdom," Hans Conzelmann suggested that various pieces of tradition in the Pauline corpus indicate that Paul "consciously organized a school, a kind of 'Pauline School' . . . where theology was engaged as schooling in wisdom."[1] Conzelmann amplified this thesis in a brief essay on "The Pauline School" in the *Festschrift* for Erich Dinkler.[2]

Indeed, the accounts from Acts 11:26, 18:1-11, and 19:8-10 do suggest that Paul was conducting such a mission school (at the latest) ever since his Antiochene period. The numerous doctrinal traditions adduced in the Pauline letters and the technical terminology variously appearing there in reference to the adoption and transmission of doctrinal traditions (διδάσκειν, παραλαμβάνειν, παραδιδόναι) confirm this (cf. merely 1 Thess. 4:1; 1 Cor. 4:17; 11:23; 15:1-3). Rather than the apostle's fellow workers (to whom we owe the Deutero-Pauline epistles), it was Paul himself who, long before, founded and ran the Pauline "school." The early Jewish "wisdom schools" described by Martin Hengel[3] and Helge Stadelmann[4] show *per analogiam* just how this mission school must have appeared. As an apostle of Christ, Paul was also a teacher of the faith, not only preaching in a missionary setting and engaging in exegetical

---

[1] Hans Conzelmann, *Theologie als Schriftauslegung. Aufsätze zum Neuen Testament* (BEvT 65; Munich: C. Kaiser, 1974) 177-90, here 179.

[2] *Theologia crucis — Signum crucis,* ed. C. Andresen and G. Klein (Tübingen: J. C. B. Mohr/Paul Siebeck, 1979) 85-96.

[3] Martin Hengel, *Judentum und Hellenismus* (WUNT 10; Tübingen: J. C. B. Mohr/Paul Siebeck, ³1988) 143-52.

[4] Helge Stadelmann, *Ben Sira als Schriftgelehrter* (WUNT II/6; Tübingen: J. C. B. Mohr/Paul Siebeck, 1980) 293ff.

debates in synagogues, but also giving ongoing instruction in "his" mission school.

II

The traditions available to us in the Pauline letters suggest that the themes Paul addressed in instruction included not only the interpretation of the "Holy Scriptures" and the doctrines of faith but also and especially christology, which itself included the acquisition and transmission of Jesus traditions (cf. 1 Cor. 11:23ff.). One can come to an appropriate historical evaluation of the apostle's reception and transmission of Christ and Jesus traditions only by maintaining clarity regarding at least the following four issues:

(1) According to Acts 22:3, Paul acquired all of his own "schooling," not in Tarsus or elsewhere in the Diaspora, but in Jerusalem. When in Phil. 3:5 the apostle calls himself a Ἑβραῖος ἐξ Ἑβραίων, κατὰ νόμον Φαρισαῖος, we must see in him a Jerusalem (or Diaspora) Pharisee knowledgeable in Aramaic and Hebrew as well as Greek. Insofar as Martin Hengel's suspicions concerning Gal. 5:11 are correct (presented at the Tübingen symposium on "Paul, Missionary and Theologian and Ancient Judaism," September 1988), Paul, in his role as such a bilingual Pharisee prior to his own conversion, gave Torah-instruction to Jewish pilgrims coming to Jerusalem from the Diaspora.[5] The activity of this pre-Christian "Saul" coincides temporally with the final activities of Jesus in Jerusalem, his condemnation and execution on the cross on Golgotha, and with the founding of the original Christian community in Jerusalem.

2. Paul's persecution of the circle around Stephen also begins in Jerusalem and only then spreads to the Diaspora. The occasion for this persecution seems to have been the criticism (briefly described in Acts 6:13-14) raised by the "Hellenists" against the (sacrificial cult in the) temple and the Torah, criticism grounded in its own turn in their confession of Christ.

This is evident from the following nexus of tradition. In a paper on "Jewish-Christian Relations in Barnabas and Justin Martyr,"[6] William Horbury draws attention to the parallelism between Acts 26:11 and Justin, *Apol.* i.31.6. "Justin says in his First Apology (xxxi) that the Jewish leader [Bar Cocheba] punished

---

[5] M. Hengel, "Der vorchristliche Paulus," *Paul und das antike Judentum,* ed. M. Hengel and U. Heckel (WUNT 58; Tübingen: J. C. B. Mohr/Paul Siebeck, 1991) 177-291, here 261f. Hengel's thorough presentation deals in a larger sense with Paul's pre-Christian identity and his subsequent conversion. Early Jewish ossuary inscriptions document the existence of bilingual (Pharisaic) διδάσκαλοι in Jerusalem during the time of earliest Christianity; cf. in this regard Alfred F. Zimmermann, *Die urchristlichen Lehrer* (WUNT II/12; Tübingen: J. C. B. Mohr/Paul Siebeck, ²1988) 69ff.

[6] Page 339 in the present volume.

Christians, if they would not deny Christ and 'blaspheme' [him]." Acts 26:11 attests that these measures involved a traditional Jewish tactic against the Χριστιανοί. Luke uses the same terminology as Justin in recounting that "by punishing them often in all the synagogues," Paul "tried to force them [the members of the congregation] to blaspheme [Christ]." These punishments refer probably to the public scourging with "forty-minus-one" (lashes) commensurate with Deut. 25:3, something Paul himself suffered five times in various synagogues after his own calling to be an apostle (cf. 2 Cor. 11:24). Such scourging could be life-threatening. In view of Gal. 1:13, 1 Cor. 15:9, and 2 Cor. 5:16, this Lukan account of Paul's persecution of Christians does not in principle elicit any historical mistrust. Reference to the "blaspheming" (of Christ) forced upon Christians documents rather that one fundamental reason why the circle around Stephen and its adherents were persecuted was precisely the "Hellenists'" confession of Christ, a confession from which they drew conclusions concerning both the temple and the validity of the Sinaitic Torah that were unacceptable for the Jewish side (see §V.3 below).

3. With his calling to be an apostle of Jesus Christ at Damascus, Paul became a messenger for precisely the same Christian faith he had previously persecuted. Paul's words in 2 Cor. 4:5-6 and 5:16 suggest what this conversion meant for him. As an apostle, he now also became acquainted from the inside with the Jesus tradition and the tradition of faith preserved and practiced in the Christian communities founded both before and independently of him in Damascus, Jerusalem, and Antioch. Over the course of his (Christian) life, Paul maintained contact with these communities and their leading representatives — James the brother of Jesus, the apostles Peter and John — and with Barnabas, Silas/ Silvanus, and so on. Following the arrangements at the apostolic council, Paul conducted his mission to the Gentiles "from Jerusalem" (Rom. 15:19), and in carrying out the collection for "the poor among the saints at Jerusalem" (Rom. 15:26) he lost both his freedom and, ultimately, his life (cf. Acts 21:15–28:31). In view of these facts, it is inconceivable from the perspective of tradition history that the apostle could have had no acquaintance or could have claimed to have no acquaintance with the Jesus and Christ traditions of Jerusalem (Damascus) and Antioch.

4. Nor does Paul appear anywhere in his letters as an opponent in principle of the Christian doctrines of Jerusalem or Antioch; quite the contrary, he incorporates considerable materials of tradition from these communities into his own proclamation, instruction, and letters (cf. merely 1 Cor. 15:1-11 and 11:23-25). Following the emergence of two communities in Jerusalem, the so-called "Hebrews" and "Hellenists," and the development of their missionary activities, these traditions were transmitted not only in Aramaic and Hebrew but also in Greek. In order to introduce Christ as "Lord and Messiah" (Acts 2:36) to Jews from the Palestinian homeland and the Diaspora, and to God-fearers and gen-

tiles, one had to have access to the essential Christian traditions in both Semitic and Greek versions.

Given these circumstances, one must be extremely cautious with the customary distinctions and delimitations applied to early Christian tradition. What is known as "Hellenistic Jewish-Christianity" did not emerge first only in Antioch but already in Damascus and Jerusalem, and its thinking by no means differed in all aspects and in principle from the faith of the "Hebraists" remaining in Jerusalem until 62 c.e. During his entire life, James tried to keep Jewish and gentile Christians together, and in this sense he functioned as the head of the original Jerusalem community as the mother community of all Christians.

The numerous citations and allusions to Jesus and Christ traditions permeating the Pauline letters reflect both his acquaintance with and his high estimation of all the παραδόσεις preserved in missionary Christianity from Jerusalem to Damascus and on to Antioch, παραδόσεις which Paul adopted and which he and his co-workers then passed on.

III

In all likelihood, the reception and transmission of traditions of faith and Jesus traditions in the Pauline school were not carried out according to any modern standards. Doctrinal traditions did not represent merely extant materials from which one selected certain features according to one's own discretion and which teachers and pupils then critically (re-)interpreted. As was customary in ancient pedagogy, Paul and his pupils believed, reflected on, and argued with the traditions they received and passed on. In any event, nowhere in his letters does the apostle cite Jesus traditions or confessions of Christ in order then to criticize and alter them; rather, he repeats them and then argues with them in favor of the gospel revealed to him at Damascus. He does this so unaffectedly that he often dispenses entirely with citational formulae, expecting instead that his readers will readily recognize the traditions to which he is referring (cf., e.g., Rom. 1:3f.; 3:21-26; 10:9f.). The "specifically Pauline" features are thus not to be found just in the texts framing the citations from and allusions to tradition within the Pauline letters themselves, but already in the simple fact that he has picked up and passed on these traditions in the first place. The παραδόσεις are essential parts of the doctrine of the gospel, which Paul has independently developed in light of his own conversion experience, but which he in part has also received and transmitted further. The understanding of Christ in the Pauline school thus emerges simultaneously both from the tradition materials Paul himself has picked up and from the textual passages framing these materials, and the distinction between pre-Pauline and Pauline traditions — a useful traditio-historical distinction — is not immediately to be associated with the modern notion that only the second group is original and thus determinative.

One additional problem involves Paul's overall doctrine, and especially his relationship to the (synoptic) Jesus tradition. Because all of Paul's letters, including that to the Romans, are what is known as "occasional writings," they always offer only a quite specific, partial aspect of the overall Pauline views. In the mission school he ran both in Antioch and in Corinth and Ephesus over a long period, the apostle most certainly presented far more (and different) material than seemed worthy of mention in any given letter.

As self-evident as this observation may well be, it becomes even more significant when viewed against the background of Paul's relationship with the (synoptic) Jesus tradition, including the Passion narrative(s). The easily verified observation extending even to the letter to the Romans, namely, that the apostle rarely cites sayings of Jesus or Jesus traditions, has recently even led some to conclude incorrectly that the apostle had no real acquaintance with the traditions preserved in the gospels (works redacted in their final form only after his death).[7] Since not a single (!) apostolic letter in the New Testament contains any genuinely extensive citation from the Jesus tradition (not even the Johannine letters), one must assume that the apostolic letter was neither the customary locus nor the medium of communication through which (complete) Jesus traditions were transmitted. Paul in his own turn demonstrably assumes that the communities he himself has founded are acquainted with (essential) parts of the Jesus and Passion traditions, and in 1 Cor. 11:23 he even expressly points out that he "received from the Lord what I also handed on to you" (i.e., the eucharist-παράδοσις). This sort of reception and transmission can only have taken place in the mission instruction he himself had experienced and then conducted. It thus seems more advisable to me to locate the *Sitz im Leben* of the (synoptic) Jesus tradition and the Passion narrative(s) not simply in the early Christian "proclamation" but rather, more specifically, in the early Christian mission instruction.[8] This is suggested, for example, by the tradition terms used in Luke 1:1-4 and Matt. 28:19-20. If this view is correct, then the numerous and much-discussed allusions in the Pauline letters (indeed, in the apostolic letters at large) to the sayings of Jesus and to gospel traditions might derive from the apostle(s) reminding his (their) addressees of logia and stories already familiar to them (or which they should remember) from mission instruction. Only additional re-

---

[7] Nor is this view changed by the studies of Frans Neirynck, "Paul and the Sayings of Jesus," in *L'Apôtre Paul,* ed. A. Vanhoye (BETL LXXIII; Leuven University Press, 1986) 265-321, or Nikolaus Walter, "Paulus und die urchristliche Jesustradition," *NTS* 31 (1985) 498-522.

[8] Cf. in this regard also the authors mentioned by A. F. Zimmermann, *Die urchristlichen Lehrer* (see note 5 above), 28ff., 62ff.: B. Gerhardsson, H. Greeven, A. Polag, H. Riesenfeld, R. Riesner, H. Schürmann, et al.

search into the early Christian (mission) schools will provide greater clarity with regard to this important question.

The scope of the Jesus tradition influencing the understanding of Christ in the Pauline school is disputed. I find at least four noteworthy elements in this context. (1) The remarkable coincidence between 1 Thess. 2:14-16; 4:15-17; 5:1-11 and passages from Matt. 23:31-36; 24:30-31, 36, 43; 25:1-13, and others suggests that Paul had specific knowledge of these (pre-)Matthean traditions. (2) Gal. 4:6 and Rom. 8:15 also suggest that the apostle was familiar with the cry (one going back to Jesus) ἀββᾶ (and thus probably also with the [pre-] Markan Gethsemane-tradition in Mark 14:36). (3) According to 1 Cor. 10:16-17, 21 and 11:23-26, the apostle was familiar with both the (pre-)Lukan and the (pre-)Markan tradition of the Lord's Supper. (4) Extremely interesting links emerge even beyond this between Paul and the Jesus and community traditions collected by Luke. One notices first of all that the Pauline account of the Lord's Supper in 1 Cor. 11:23-26 is closely related to Luke 22:19f.; this obviously involves an excerpt from the (pre-)Lukan Passion story that has been recast into a "cult etiology." It is no less striking that in his allusion to Jesus' Passion in 1 Cor. 2:6ff. the apostle is following precisely the presentational schema and terminology found in Acts 3:17 and 13:27f. (cf. with Luke 23:13, 35; 24:20). No other New Testament textual complex can better illustrate the doctrinal traditions of 1 Cor. 15:3ff. today than can Luke 24 and the introductory chapters of Acts. Rom. 1:3f. recounts in a formulaic fashion an abbreviated version of the Christ story and emphasizes exactly, as does Luke in Acts 13:23ff. and 32ff., that Jesus' entire life, from his birth to his exaltation as the "Son of God," stood under the premonitory sign of God's messianic promises (2 Sam. 7:12, 14; Isa. 55:3). The wording of Rom. 12:14 strongly recalls especially Luke 6:27f. and parallels. If in Rom. 13:1-7 Paul is thinking at all of one of the synoptic versions of Jesus' saying regarding the emperor's tax, it can only be the Lukan text (Luke 20:20-26) with the catchword φόρος (cf. Luke 20:22 with Rom. 13:7). Rom. 14:20 conspicuously recalls Luke 11:41, and so on. All these allusions leave the impression that Paul wrote his letters with a sound knowledge of the Jesus tradition used in mission instruction in Antioch, a tradition of the sort evidenced for us today especially in the Lukan writings. The apostle is not, of course, fixated on the Lukan material alone.

These observations mean that the Pauline school's understanding of Christ cannot be evaluated apart from and certainly not as an alternative to the narrative portrayal of Christ in the synoptic tradition; rather, the two belong together. Or put differently: The apostle's school presupposes the teaching and story of Jesus, and its understanding of Christ can be grasped only with reference to this teaching and story.

IV

This insight has considerable consequences for the christological evaluation of individual traditions Paul cites in his letters. Five examples can illustrate this.

1. In 1 Cor. 15:11, Paul himself alleges that the παράδοσις he cites in vv. 3b-5 (continuing in vv. 6-8) is determinative not only for his own kerygma but also for that of the apostles called before him. One may thus assume that the formulaic summary of the "gospel" (15:1f.) involves older, apostolically recognized material from (the Jerusalem) tradition. Both in Jerusalem and in Pauline mission instruction, vv. 3b-5 summarize in four sentences the essential facts of Jesus' (Passion) story: Christ, the Messiah, died a representative sacrificial death on the cross commensurate with Isa. 53:11f.; his burial (commensurate with Isa. 53:9?) makes it clear that this was not merely an apparent death, and that Jesus' resurrection involves the death of death itself (cf. Isa. 53:9 MT and LXX); God resurrected Christ according to Hos. 6:2 on the third day, making him thus the victor over death. The appearance of the Resurrected Christ to Peter, the "Rock" (cf. Matt. 16:18 with Isa. 51:1), and then to the Twelve (i.e., to the future regents of the eschatological people of the twelve tribes, cf. Luke 22:29/Matt. 19:28), resulted in the founding of the original community in Jerusalem and set into motion the apostolic proclamation of the gospel. Just like that of the apostles called before him, so also does Paul's own proclamation of the gospel and his mission instruction begin with these basic christological facts.

2. The παράδοσις of the Lord's Supper (1 Cor. 11:23-26 [+ 10:16f.]) Paul traces back to Jesus is best understood from the perspective of the ἀνάμνησις of Jesus' Passion, an anamnesis corresponding to the Israelite Passover anamnesis (cf. Exod. 12:14; 13:3-10; Deut. 16:3; *Jub.* 49:15): Just as according to *m. Pesaḥ.* 10.5 every Jewish participant in the Passover meal "must so regard himself as if he came forth himself out of Egypt," so also should all members of the congregation at the "table of the Lord" (1 Cor. 10:21) regard themselves as represented in the Twelve who were actually Jesus' table guests "on the night when he was betrayed" and when he assured them a part in his own atoning death. The παράδοσις teaches us to regard Jesus' death as the representative atoning death of the messianic Son of God who opens up to those who believe in him the forgiveness of sins and participation in God's "new covenant" (commensurate with Jer. 31:31ff.). Insofar as the Lord's death is proclaimed publicly in the eucharistic celebrations (in Corinth), and indeed is proclaimed "until he comes" (1 Cor. 11:26), Jesus' representation of existence on the cross appears as the quintessential salvific event pointing forward in promise to the consummation of the ἀπολύτρωσις in the parousia of the Κύριος.

3. Paul speaks of the parousia not only in 1 Thess. 4:15ff. (see p. 164 above)

but also in 1 Cor. 11:26. The Christians in Corinth pray for this parousia with a cry going back to the Aramaic-speaking original community: μαρὰν ἀθά = מָרַן אֲתָא = "our Lord, come!" (1 Cor. 16:22; cf. Rev. 22:20; *Did.* 10:6). This cry documents that Paul adopted the address to the exalted Christ as "Lord" (מַר or κύριος) from Jerusalem, and that he must also have spoken in his own mission instruction about Jesus' eschatological coming (ἔρχεσθαι, as the Son of Man–Messiah).

4. The Christ formulation in Rom. 4:25, construed from the (Hebrew) text of Isa. 53:11f., evokes the real issue raised for believers by Jesus' death and resurrection: God handed over his Son (as the messianic Servant of God) for the trespasses of sinners; Jesus is thus the guilt offering of Isa. 53:10 (אָשָׁם) in person, an offering selected and presented by God himself. His resurrection by God happened for the justification (announced in Isa. 53:11) of the πολλοί, a justification which itself is both a present and a future event affecting the πιστεύοντες. It assures them of the intercession of the Servant of God at the final judgment, a Servant exalted by God (commensurate with Isa. 52:13; 53:11f.; cf. Rom. 8:34 with Isa. 53:12), and opens up to them a portion in his future exercise of the reign of God over the world (cf. Rom. 5:17 with 1 Cor. 6:2 and Dan. 7:14, 27). Here Paul is appropriating not only Jesus' own interpretation of his sacrifice (from the perspective of Isa. 53; cf. Mark 10:45 par.; 14:24 par.)[9] but also essential elements of the doctrine of the Son of Man, a doctrine similarly going back to the earthly Jesus (cf. merely Luke 12:8f.; 12:32; 22:28-30).

5. Since Mark 10:45 (Matt. 20:28) and the παράδοσις of the Lord's Supper can be traced back to the earthly Jesus, we find that Paul's own understanding of Christ stands in continuity with the view of Jesus' messianic sending as founded by Jesus himself. Just like the community of Jerusalem and that of Antioch (founded independently of Paul), so also does the Pauline school teach that Jesus of Nazareth is to be understood as the Χριστός, the Κύριος, the Servant of God, and the Son of Man–Messiah. Even the basic christological premise of the apostle's doctrine of justification is provided by Jesus' own behavior (cf. merely Luke 15:2), Jesus' teaching (cf. Luke 18:9-14), and the interpretation of Jesus' death on the cross and resurrection from the perspective of Isa. 53:11f.

---

[9] Cf. my essay "Jesus von Nazareth und die neutestamentliche Christologie im Lichte der heiligen Schrift," in *Mitte der Schrift? Ein jüdisch-christliches Gespräch. Texte des Berner Symposions vom 6.-12. Januar 1985,* ed. M. Klopfenstein, U. Luz, S. Talmon, and E. Tov (Judaica et Christiana 11; Bern/Frankfurt a.M.: Peter Lang, 1987) 81-95, here 93ff.

V

A concrete illustration of this can be found in three pieces of tradition which Paul appropriated from Hellenistic Jewish Christianity: Rom. 1:3-4; 3:25-26; and Phil. 2:6-11.

1. The Christ formula Paul incorporates into the prescript of his letter to the Christians in Rome (Rom. 1:3f.) has long prompted readers to assume the presence of a basic model for an early Jewish-Christian christology of adoption. It was (only) at Easter (commensurate with Ps. 110:1) that God first appointed the man Jesus of Nazareth, from the line of David, as the "Son of God." Eduard Schweizer speaks in an exemplary fashion of a christology in which "in a distinctive way, the two titles which were identical in the Old Testament, i.e., 'Son of David' and 'Son of God,' now succeed one another as two stages."[10] It was allegedly only the later Hellenistic community that expanded this two-stage christology with the dimension of preexistence — more exactly, in light of the late Old Testament, early Jewish wisdom tradition (cf. Prov. 8:22-31; Wis. 9:1-2, 9-10). This familiar interpretive schema (one with considerable christological consequences) in Rom. 1:3f. is, however, inconsistent in a threefold fashion: It fails to consider adequately that, according to the Old Testament and early Jewish tradition, the messiah is animated by the wisdom of God (cf. Isa. 11:2f.; *1 Enoch* 49:1-4). Nor does it take into consideration that, according to Mic. 5:1, the messiah's origin actually resides in God's own prehistory. If one follows J. H. Charlesworth,[11] M. Hengel,[12] and others[13] in dating the similitudes of *1 Enoch* to the end of the first century before Christ (or slightly later), this view can be made even more precise. According to *1 Enoch* 48:3, 6, not only was the name of the Son of Man–messiah, chosen by God, uttered before the creation of the world before God, but he himself was already "chosen and hidden before God before the world was created" (cf. similarly *1 Enoch* 62:7). This is clearly referring to the preexistence of the messiah. Finally, the usual interpretation of Rom. 1:3f. fails to consider that the earthly Jesus had already claimed to be the messianic Son of Man, and that according to Mark 14:61f. and parallels he was condemned and crucified (by the Romans) because of this claim (cf. Mark 15:26).[14] If this early Jewish tradition of the messiah and the Son

---

[10] E. Schweizer, "υἱός κτλ," *TDNT* 8.367; a similar view is taken by J. D. G. Dunn, *Christology in the Making* (London: SCM Press Ltd., ²1989) 35, 139, 209ff.

[11] J. H. Charlesworth, "The SNTS Pseudepigrapha Seminars at Tübingen and Paris on the Book of Enoch," *NTS* 25 (1978/79) 315-23; idem, *The Pseudepigrapha and Modern Research* (SBL-Septuagint and Cognate Studies Series 7S; Chico, Calif.: Scholars Press, ²1981) 98.

[12] M. Hengel, *Judentum und Hellenismus* (see note 3 above), 321.

[13] Cf., e.g., C. L. Mearns, "Dating the Similitudes of Enoch," *NTS* 25 (1978/79) 360-69, and E. Isaac, in *Old Testament Pseudepigrapha,* ed. J. H. Charlesworth, vol. 1 (London: Darton, Longman & Todd Ltd., 1983) 6f.

[14] Cf. in this regard my book *Jesus von Nazareth — Christus des Glaubens* (Stuttgart: Calwer, 1988) 34, 55.

of Man was transferred onto Jesus' life[15] and then christologically appropriated after Easter, then from the very outset the (Son-of-Man) christology deriving from this tradition was three- or even four-dimensional: It speaks of the preexistence, the earthly appearance, the cross, and the exaltation of the Son of Man–messiah Jesus Christ. Under these circumstances, the adoptionist two-stage christology derived from Rom. 1:3f. has no traditio-historical *Sitz im Leben,* neither in Jerusalem nor in Damascus or Antioch. In my opinion, it is an artificial construct of liberal critical scholarship. As O. Betz already pointed out years ago, the background to the Jewish-Christian formulation of Rom. 1:3f. is the Nathan prophecy from 2 Sam. 7:12-14.[16] The formula describes Jesus' path from the perspective of this text (and its subsequent early Jewish interpretation): According to the promise, God had his Son descend "from the seed of David" (and this Son traveled his earthly path in obedience and humility). At Easter, God then "raised him up" (from the dead; cf. 2 Sam. 7:12) and (commensurate with Ps. 110:1) appointed him to the position of honor as the messianic Son of God, a position designated for him from prehistory and yet denied him by his earthly opponents. Paul picks up the formula in precisely this sense,[17] and then refers back to it once more in Rom. 15:8f.

2. According to the instructive analysis presented by Otfried Hofius,[18] the Philippians hymn is actually a Christ hymn which Paul has appropriated in its entirety, a hymn revealing most ably the fourfold dimension of Hellenistic-Jewish-Christian christology. On the basis of the tradition in Isa. 52:13–53:12, this hymn celebrates "the revelation of the eschatological reign of God in the exaltation of the crucified Christ,"[19] describing in the process Christ's life under the four aspects of preexistence, incarnation, death on the cross, and exaltation. The issue dominating the second part of the Christ hymn — namely, the bestowing of the divine name Κύριος on the exalted Christ — has functional meaning: The Son of God, appointed from the ignominy of death on the cross, obediently endured, to

---

[15] See F. Lang, "Erwägungen zur eschatologischen Verkündigung Johannes des Täufers," in *Jesus Christus in Historie und Theologie. Festschrift H. Conzelmann,* ed. G. Strecker (Tübingen: J. C. B. Mohr/Paul Siebeck, 1975) 459-73, here 470f.; as Lang has shown, the Baptist confronted Jesus with the announcement of the "stronger one" to come after John, and his experience of the Spirit at baptism taught him to identify himself with this ἐρχόμενος (cf. my essay "Jesus von Nazareth und die neutestamentliche Christologie im Lichte der heiligen Schrift" [see note 9 above], 87ff., and my book *Jesus von Nazareth — Christus des Glaubens* [see previous note], 27f.).

[16] O. Betz, *Was wissen wir von Jesus?* (Stuttgart: Kreuz, 1965) 65ff.

[17] Cf. R. Pesch, "Das Evangelium Gottes über seinen Sohn. Zur Auslegung der Tradition in Röm 1,1-4," in *Christus bezeugen. Festschrift W. Trilling,* ed. K. Kertelge, T. Holtz, and C.-P. März (Leipzig: St. Benno, 1989) 208-17.

[18] O. Hofius, *Der Christushymnus Philipper 2,6-11* (WUNT 17; Tübingen: J. C. B. Mohr/Paul Siebeck, ²1991). In the new edition of his study (which originally appeared in 1976), Hofius also addresses the highly problematical thesis of J. D. G. Dunn, *Christology in the Making* (see note 10 above), 114ff., which asserts that Phil. 2:6-11 is "through and through an expression of Adam christology" (119).

[19] Hofius, *Der Christushymnus Philipper 2,6-11* (see note 18), 65 (italicized in the original).

the highest heavenly honor, is to implement God's rule over all creatures in heaven, on earth, and in the underworld, and will do so εἰς δόξαν θεοῦ πατρός. Paul neither deletes from nor adds to this hymnic confession of Christ,[20] adopting it instead in its entirety as the basis of his paraclesis. But this means that even with his theology of the cross and the eschatological perspective of his christology, Paul is not standing alone in early Christianity; rather, he represents this together with (Antiochene) Jewish Christianity, whence the hymn in all likelihood derives. The new name applied to the Jewish Christians in Antioch according to Acts 11:26, namely, Χριστιανοί = "people of Christ," makes it clear yet again that the decisive feature of the mission community that distinguished them from both Jews and gentiles was (this) their confession of Christ.

3. The Jewish-Christian formula in Rom. 3:25f. that Paul integrates into the central section of his letter to the Romans (Rom. 3:21-26) points in the same direction. The center of this παράδοσις is the daring assertion that God himself publicly appointed his Christ on Golgotha as the ἱλαστήριον = כַּפֹּרֶת, that is, as the locus of God's indwelling (cf. Exod. 25:22) and of the atonement of the world God sets into motion (cf. Lev. 16:12-15). The ultimate means of atonement is the blood of Christ containing the life of the Son of God (cf. Lev. 17:11). Christ on Golgotha is God indwelling his own community, and in one and the same person is the sin-offering presented by God on behalf of sinners; Good Friday becomes the great day of atonement for the Christian community. This assertion implies a fundamental criticism of the Jerusalem temple as the locus of the cult of atonement. As I have tried to show elsewhere,[21] our pre-Pauline text from tradition allows us to discern the content of the critique presented by Stephen (Acts 6:13f.; with reference to Jesus): κατὰ τοῦ τόπου τοῦ ἁγίου τούτου καὶ τοῦ νόμου, that is, against the temple and the Torah. It brought stoning upon Stephen and provoked Paul to persecute the "Hellenists." The christology of atonement, emphasizing Christ's once-for-all sacrifice on Golgotha, along with its consequences for one's estimation of the temple and Torah were probably the decisive factors provoking the outrage against Stephen, on the one hand, and Paul's ensuing persecutions of the Hellenistic-Jewish community of Christians, on the other, persecutions in which, as we saw (see p. 161 above), he tried to force the Christians into blaspheming Christ (cf. Gal. 1:13; 1 Cor. 15:9; and 2 Cor. 5:16 with Acts 8:1; 9:1f.; 22:4f.; and 26:10f.). After Paul adopted this un-

---

[20] Hofius, *Der Christushymnus Philipper 2,6-11*, 9ff., 63f., has shown persuasively that the three words θανάτου δὲ σταυροῦ, words concluding v. 8 and repeatedly judged to be a Pauline addendum, actually belonged to the original hymn. R. P. Martin, *Carmen Christi* (Grand Rapids: Wm. B. Eerdmans Publishing Co., ²1983), xvi, 221f., rejects Hofius's view without addressing the latter's arguments.

[21] See my essay "Zur neueren Exegese von Röm 3,24-26," in P. Stuhlmacher, *Versöhnung, Gesetz und Gerechtigkeit* (Göttingen: Vandenhoeck & Ruprecht, 1981) 117-35; cf. also my commentary on Romans, *Der Brief an die Römer* (NTD 6; Göttingen: Vandenhoeck & Ruprecht, 1989) 55-58.

derstanding of Christ, he was himself quite logically persecuted by the enraged Jews (cf. 2 Cor. 11:24f.; Acts 9:29; 21:30f.; 23:12). This confirms the view we have been following: The falling out between Jews and Christians already discernible in Jerusalem had its roots in the confession of the πιστεύοντες. The insight and conviction that God made Jesus of Nazareth into the Κύριος καὶ Χριστός (Acts 2:36) — the same Jesus whom the Romans had crucified at the behest of the Sanhedrin — and on Golgotha presented a once-for-all atonement for the people of God (Rom. 3:25-26) brought about a separation between those who followed this confession and those who considered it erroneous or even blasphemous.

VI

Paul not only positioned the tradition of Rom. 3:25f. at the center of his doctrine of justification; he also subjected to fundamental rethinking the critique of the ἔθη ἃ παρέδωκεν ἡμῖν Μωϋσῆς, critique already raised by the circle around Stephen (Acts 6:14). The apostle anchors his dialectical criticism of the law of Moses in his christology because at his conversion at Damascus he was enlightened by the realization that God's splendor on the countenance of the crucified and resurrected Christ eschatologically eclipsed the glory of the Sinaitic Torah (cf. 2 Cor. 3:7-11; 4:6).

The following statements exemplify Paul's christologically based critique of the law. In Gal. 3:13, the apostle puts a soteriological slant on the fact that Jesus died the cursed death of the cross at Golgotha commensurate with Deut. 21:23: Christ, righteous and innocent, bore the curse of the law representatively "for us"; through this representation, he "redeemed" sinners from servitude under the law and opened up to them the υἱοθεσία promised to the people of God in the promise of Abraham (Gal. 4:4f.). As much as the law does indeed mark and condemn sinners in the name and commission of God, just as little can this condemnation hand those who believe in Jesus as atoner and Lord over to the judgment of death. Sin and law no longer have power over them; Christ is their redeemer and master.

Paul also emphasizes in the letter to the Romans that God sent his own beloved Son, surrendering him as a sin offering in order to free those Jews and gentiles caught in servitude under the law. The goal of this act of deliverance was not only to break the power of sin over sinners but also by the power of the Holy Spirit to place them into the fulfillment of God's will (Rom. 8:3f.). Those who by virtue of Jesus' sacrificial death have been freed from servitude to the law are not, according to Paul, ἄνομοι, but rather are those who do the will of God as Jesus taught in "his" Torah (cf. Rom. 8:2, 3 with Gal. 6:2 and 1 Cor. 9:21). Martin Hengel is probably correct in suspecting that in speaking about the νόμος χριστοῦ Paul is actually picking up and developing further an idea already entertained in the circle around Stephen.[22]

The apostle emphasizes more concisely and consistently than all the Christian witness preceding him that in view of the justification brought about by God in Jesus' death and resurrection, "works of the law" can contribute neither to justification by baptism nor to any final justification (cf. Gal. 2:16; Rom. 3:20).[23] In presenting this view, the apostle appeals to the authority of the spiritual saying of Holy Scripture in Ps. 143:2. Yet this had already become evident to him earlier at his own conversion: His militant zeal for the Sinaitic Torah and its exposition in the πατρικαὶ παραδόσεις (Gal. 1:14) was able to contribute not the least to his office and ministry as an apostle of Jesus Christ; and precisely as a former persecutor of the Christian community who now was called to be an ἀπόστολος, Paul remains even to the final judgment completely dependent on God's justifying grace (1 Cor. 9:16).

The Pauline critique of the Mosaic law in favor of the crucified and resurrected Christ culminates in 2 Cor. 3 and Rom. 10. In 2 Cor. 3, Paul juxtaposes his service to the gospel, service bestowed upon him under the "new covenant" (of Jer. 31:31ff.) set up by God in Christ, with the service of Moses under the "old covenant" (of Exod. 24). Expressed as provocation: Just as Moses did in the old covenant, so also does Paul function in the new covenant, proclaiming the εὐαγγέλιον that now eclipses the Mosaic Torah. In Rom. 10:3f., the apostle then offers the brief and pregnant assertion that Christ is "the end of the law so that there may be righteousness for everyone who believes." In view of the appearance of Jesus Christ, the Torah can no longer lead to eternal life.

Rom. 8:3f. shows with sufficient clarity that Paul is not asserting with this theological principle of justification that the crucified and resurrected Christ also did away with the will of God revealed in the Mosaic law. All the same, the critique of the law contained in Paul's christology and proclamation of the gospel was offensive enough to his Jewish counterparts, on the one hand, and to many within the Jewish Christianity emanating from Jerusalem and Antioch, on the other, to prompt considerable countermissionary measures against the apostle to be taken in all the larger Pauline communities. James the brother of Jesus

---

[22] Martin Hengel, *Between Jesus and Paul* (London: SCM Press, 1983) 151.

[23] The expression ἔργα (τοῦ) νόμου is not just a Pauline coinage; rather, it occurs already in 4QFlor 1:7 and 4QMMT 21:3. In both cases, מעשׂי (ה)תורה refer to deeds that fulfill individual stipulations within the Torah. 4QMMT 21:7 articulates the hope that God will credit such deeds to a person for justification. *2 Bar.* 57.2 speaks in the same sense of "works of the commandments." Hence in both Gal. 2:16 and Rom. 3:20, Paul is referring to incidents of fulfilling the law which God, at the final judgment, will credit to a person for justification, and he declares precisely this expectation — one common to early Judaism, as the examples show — to be illusory: No sinful person can hope to attain justification before God at the final judgment through works of the law.

supported the countermissionaries in substance (cf. Jas. 2:14-26) without, however, definitively breaking with Paul.[24]

As far as the question of a parting of the ways between Jews and Christians in the first and second centuries is concerned, this means that the christologically grounded critique of the law presented by Paul and his school deepened and rendered completely irreversible the disputes between Jews and Christians which since the martyrdom of Stephen could not be overlooked.

VII

The Pauline doctrine of reconciliation the apostle presents in 2 Cor. 5:14-21 and Rom. 5:1-11 represents a special theological accomplishment. It finds its most comprehensive christological expression in the Colossians hymn (Col. 1:15-20).

The association of motifs and traditions concerning release, atonement, justification, and redemption is already discernible in Deutero-Isaiah (cf. Isa. 43:3-5, 19; 45:6-8; 52:3; 52:13–53:12). It is found in the Qumran texts as well (cf. 1QS 11:13ff.; 1QH 3:19ff.; 4:29-37; 7:26ff.) and came by way of the Jesus tradition (cf. Mark 8:36f.; 10:45; 14:22-25) into the early Christian doctrinal tradition, and from there to Paul and his school. In 2 Cor. 5:14-21 and Rom. 5:1-11, the Greek word groups καταλλαγή/καταλλάσσεσθαι and δικαιοῦσθαι (ἐν τῷ αἵματι [τοῦ Χριστοῦ]) or ἱλάσκεσθαι (cf. Rom. 3:25) are used together, constituting in the process a word- and motif-complex of considerable biblical-theological scope and integrative power.[25] Through it, the apostle is able to assert that in the sacrificial surrender of his beloved Son, God has reconciled the world with himself, and that precisely this act of reconciliation already opens up to those who believe in Jesus Christ the εἰρήνη πρὸς τὸν θεόν as well as certain hope of deliverance in the coming judgment of wrath. Both justification and reconciliation are grounded in the eschatological event of atonement on Golgotha, which God himself set into motion; justification is inconceivable without this divine deed, and reconciliation designates the status attained by those who have been justified before God through the atoning effects of Christ's blood. God's act of reconciliation as a salvific event is announced and made accessible for all to hear in the gospel the λόγος τῆς καταλλαγῆς entrusted to Paul.

The hymn in Col. 1:15-20, a hymn characteristic of the understanding of Christ in the Pauline school, shows how great is the integrative power of this doctrine. In my opinion, not a word should be altered in this hymn, and interpretations go astray when they embrace the notion (one well entrenched in the his-

---

[24] Cf. in this regard my commentary on Romans (see note 21 above), 9-12.

[25] Cf. my essay, "Sühne oder Versöhnung?" in *Die Mitte des Neuen Testaments. Festschrift E. Schweizer,* ed. U. Luz and H. Weder (Göttingen: Vandenhoeck & Ruprecht, 1983) 291-316.

tory of scholarship) that hymnic tradition and Pauline insertions can be distinguished especially in Col. 1:18-20.[26] Rather, the hymn as a whole is a perfect example of the kind of wisdom christology that emerged in early Christianity from the late strata of the Old Testament, on the one hand, and the Jesus tradition, on the other.[27] It is subjected to comprehensive exposition in Col. 1:15-20 and grounded in atonement theology: The indwelling of the divine fullness in the Christ of God, and his God-willed sacrifice, bring peace, reconciliation, and new being before God to a world that has fallen into hostility against God. This event reveals that the creation of the All through Christ (along with the angelic powers that maintain the cosmic order) was aiming at God's creative act of reconciliation in and through Christ. Creation and new creation of the world through Christ belong together. This insight allows those who believe in Jesus Christ to confess that the All subsists in Christ, the mediator of creation and the atoning reconciler, and that it is he who presides as head over the congregation. The ἐκκλησία that confesses Christ appears thus as the body of Christ, that is, as the portion of the All that is at peace, the portion in which even before the day of Christ's final revelation (Col. 3:4) it will become clear that God does not allow his creation to fall, but will both redeem and renew it. It is no accident that the Colossians hymn develops all these assertions in the style of Hellenistic-Jewish hymns, that is, the kind of praise found in worship. During its worship service, the congregation singing Col. 1:15-20 joins with its spirit-filled praise (Col. 3:16) the heavenly praise due to the slaughtered and resurrected Christ-Lamb according to Rev. 5:9-10, 12 as the πρωτότοκος ἐκ τῶν νεκρῶν (cf. Col. 1:18 with Rev. 1:5).

The Colossians hymn was probably developed in the Pauline "school." The exposition of the tradition of reconciliation corresponding to it in Eph. 2:11-22 documents that the Christians fused together into a salvific community through the power of the knowledge of Christ in Col. 1:15-20 constitute the new people of God composed of Jews and gentiles in juxtaposition to Israel and to gentile religious groupings. Expressed in words reflecting the theme of the present symposium, "the parting of the ways," the Christian congregation that sings Col. 1:15-20 and also confesses, in Eph. 2:14, Christ as the messianic peacemaker constitutes a new, third community over against those Jews and gentiles who do not believe in Jesus Christ.

---

[26] Cf., e.g., E. Schweizer, *The Letter to the Colossians* (Minneapolis: Augsburg, 1972) 55-88; also P. Pokorný, *Der Brief des Paulus an die Kolosser* (THKNT 10/1; Berlin: Evangelische Verlagsanstalt, 1987) 47-76.

[27] Cf. H. Gese, "Die Weisheit, der Menschensohn und die Ursprünge der Christologie als konsequente Entfaltung der biblischen Theologie," *SEÅ* 44 (1979) 77-114, here 108.

VIII

The Pastoral Epistles, composed a considerable period of time after Paul's martyrdom, present an understanding of Christ closely oriented to the Pauline tradition, on the one hand, and that of the gospels, on the other. The Pastorals find in Paul's own teachings the doctrinal traditions that sustain faith. His letters are the παραθήκη to which one must hold fast in the struggle against nascent (Christian) gnosticism.[28]

According to 1 Tim. 2:5-6, the one God who created the world wants to lead all human beings — that is, both gentiles and Jews — to deliverance and recognition of the truth through the one mediator sent by him, namely, the (Son of) man Christ Jesus. In these two verses, the Jesus saying from Mark 10:45 (Matt. 20:28) finds its way into the Christian confession, a confession whose framework and basic assertions are already given by Paul (cf. 1 Cor. 8:6). The following verse in 1 Tim. 2:7 shows how the confession as a whole is to be understood: The apostolic witness to the gospel grounded by God through Jesus' sacrifice is entrusted to Paul. He and his school are charged with transmitting it faithfully. What the apostle teaches as gospel is the doctrinal norm for the "church of the living God" as such (1 Tim. 3:15).

This can also be seen in 1 Tim. 3:16. This brief Christ hymn, composed from the perspective of the Greek text of Isa. 53:11f.,[29] brings to expression the truth that the church as God's own people on earth is to keep and preserve, a truth embodied by the Christ who was crucified and then justified to heavenly honor and exalted by God over his earthly opponents. He alone is the Lord and Savior of the world. A church with this self-understanding, and one that confesses this Christ, has already undergone the separation between (unbelieving) Jews and (believing) Christians and is able to differentiate itself with equal clarity from all gentile/pagan cult associations.

In retrospect, a clear line emerges. The christology derived from Jesus' own consciousness of his messianic sending and grounded in his Passion and resurrection is the real driving force behind the separation of Jews ([and Gentiles] who do not believe in Jesus as Lord and Messiah) on the one hand and Christians on the other. The traditions preserved in the school founded by Paul show with particular clarity how this christology came about and what it is saying. Paul and his pupils elevated it into the determinative doctrinal norm for the en-

---

[28] Cf. J. Roloff, *Der erste Brief an Timotheus* (EKKNT XV; Zurich/Neukirchen: Benziger/ Neukirchener Verlag, 1988) 377.

[29] In the LXX, unlike in the MT, Isa. 53:10f. is understood with an eye not on the "justification" the Servant of God provides for the "many" through his sacrifice but on the Servant of God himself, whom after suffering and ignominy God exalts and places at his right hand: βούλεται Κύριος . . . δικαιῶσαι δίκαιον εὖ δουλεύοντα πολλοῖς.

tire church, and the path they took can be reversed only at the cost of the gospel and the Christian faith itself.

The Question of Anti-semitism in the New Testament Writings of the Period

by

JAMES D. G. DUNN

1. Introduction

The Holocaust made it impossible to deny or explain away the shameful history of anti-semitism within Christianity. Ever since, Christians and Christian scholarship have been attempting to come to terms with that frightening heritage[1]. Initially the prospects looked bright. Anti-semitism, it was widely argued, while part of Christianity's history, was not, strictly speaking, part of Christianity. For example, Jules Isaac, the French historian, and himself a Jew who lost much of his family in the Holocaust, showed how much anti-Jewish polemic drew on the NT[2], but he could nevertheless maintain that "Christianity in its essence excludes anti-semitism"[3]. Gregory Baum, while acknowledging the polemical edge of NT writings against the religion of Israel, could nevertheless argue that the anti-Jewish trends in Christianity were peripheral and accidental, not grounded in the NT itself[4]. In the same relatively up-beat mood, the Second Vatican Council sought to close the door on the embarrassments of the past by directing that,

---

[1] For a brief review of most of the key literature see W. Klassen, "Anti-Judaism in Early Christianity: The State of the Question", *Anti-Judaism Vol. 1* (n. 16) 1–19. And for recent, more broad ranging discussions see F. Mussner, *Tractate on the Jews. The Significance of Judaism for Christian Faith* (Philadelphia: Fortress/London: SPCK, 1984); P. von der Osten-Sacken, *Christian-Jewish Dialogue. Theological Foundations* (Philadelphia: Fortress, 1986); M. R. Wilson, *Our Father Abraham. Jewish Roots of the Chrisitan Faith* (Grand Rapids: Eerdmans, 1989).

[2] J. Isaac, *Jesus et Israel* (1984, [2]1959; Eng. tr. New York: Holt, 1971).

[3] J. Isaac, *L'Antisémitisme a-t-il des racines chrétiennes?* (Paris: Fasquelle, 1960) 21; cited by A. T. Davies, ed., *Anti-Semitism and the Foundations of Christianity* (New York: Paulist, 1979) xiv.

[4] In Introduction to R. R. Ruether, *Faith and Fratricide. The Theological Roots of Anti-Semitism* (New York: Seabury, 1974) 3, referring to his earlier study, *The Jews and the Gospel* (New York: Newman, 1961), revised as *Is the New Testament Anti-Semitic?* (New York: Paulist, 1965).

"Although the Church is the new people of God, the Jews should not be presented as repudiated or cursed by God, as if such views followed from the holy Scriptures ... The Church repudiates all persecutions against any man ... she deplores the hatred, persecution, and display of anti-Semitism directed against the Jews at any time and from any source[5]."

And the early attempt to argue that the division between Western Church and Synagogue was a tragic schism within God's people[6], has borne fruit in recent years in the increasing recognition by the World Council of Churches that the most important schism is not that between Catholic and Protestant, or between Eastern and Western Christianity, but between Jew and Christian, "that the relation of Church and Jewish people is an essential aspect of the apostolic faith"[7].

In the past fifteen years, however, a darker note has emerged, as the issue has been analysed in greater depth. Rosemary Ruether in particular has challenged the earlier view as an attempt to heal the deep hurt too lightly. It is not simply a case of anti-Jewish attitudes going back to the beginnings of Christianity; rather, such attitudes are endemic to Christianity, an inevitable corollary to the Church's proclamation of Jesus as Messiah. She poses the question starkly: "Is it possible to say 'Jesus is Messiah' without, implicitly or explicitly, saying at the same time 'and the Jews be dammed'[8]?" Baum, in turn, persuaded by Ruether that his older apologetic must be abandoned, asks "It it possible to purify the Christian message of its anti-Jewish ideology without invalidating the Christian claims altogether[9]?" And Samuel Sandmel, who has contributed greatly to Jewish scholarship on Christian beginnings, takes up Ruether's question and adds, "It does not seem to me that she exaggerates the extent to which Judaism appears in Christian theology as that which needs negation and rejection[10]." Even blunter is Robert Wilken, "Christian anti-Semitism grew out of the

---

[5] *Declaration on the Relationship of the Church to Non-Christian Religions (Nostra Aetate)* 4, though the last sentence was weakened by dropping the phrase "and condemns" from the earlier draft (W. M. Abbott, *The Documents of Vatican II* (America Press, 1966) 666–7 and notes).

[6] Baum, in Ruether (n. 4) 9, refers to P. Démann, "Israel et l'Unité de l'Eglise", *Cahiers Sionens* 7.1 (March 1953) 1–24; K. Thieme, *Biblische Religion Heute* (Heidelberg: Schneider, 1960).

[7] "The Apostolic Faith in the Scriptures and in the Early Church", *Rome Report 1983*, in H.-G. Link ed., *Apostolic Faith Today* (Geneva: WCC, 1985) 259–60, 265.

[8] Ruether (n. 4) 246.

[9] Baum in Ruether (n. 4) 8.

[10] S. Sandmel, *Anti-Semitism in the New Testament* (Philadelphia: Fortress, 1978) 163. Cf. D. Flusser in his Foreword to C. Thoma, *A Christian Theology of Judaism* (New York: Paulist, 1980): "If a Christian were to find anywhere such inimical statements about Christianity, would he not call them anti-Christian? I even dare to say that many Christians would not hesitate to state openly this more or less pronounced anti-Jewishness if such passages were found anywhere else but in the New Testament. Do not tell me that such statements and ideas are merely inner-Jewish polemic scoldings" (17).

Christian Bible, that is the New Testament ... Christians have been anti-Semitic because they have been Christians[11]."

The challenge thus posed to Christian NT scholars in particular cannot therefore be ducked. The depth and uncomfortable sharpness of the issue can be readily demonstrated by noting simply two NT texts which probably more than any others over the centuries have provided foundation and fuel for much of the most virulent Christian anti-Jewish polemic. I have in mind Matt 27:25 – "All the people answered, 'His blood be on us and on our children'" – the scriptural warrant for countless denunciations of Jews of later centuries as "Christ-killers"[12]. And John 8:44 – "You are of your father the devil, and your will is to do your father's desires" – sufficient excuse for many to identify Jews with the power of evil and to seek their destruction. The influence of these passages is well illustrated already in early centuries in the tirade of Gregory of Nyssa against the Jews – "Murderers of the Lord ... They are confederates of the devil ..." (*PG* 46.685). And in the savage invective of John Chrysostom – those who killed Christ, whose synagogue is "a resort of demons, the devil's citadel" (*PG* 48.915)[13]. The question we must face, then, is whether such attitudes are already inseparable from the scriptures on which they were based. Is anti-semitism integral to the Christianity of the NT, the denunciation of Judaism essential to the affirmation of Christianity's own identity from the beginning? Or, in terms of the present inquiry, Does the attitude to Jews in the post-70 NT documents indicate that the final breach, the decisive parting of the ways between Christianity and (rabbinic) Judaism, has already happened?

2. The problem of definition

2.1. It is important, first of all, to clarify our terms. Is "antisemitism" the best or most appropriate term to use? After all, not only Jews are Semites. And the term itself seems to have emerged only in the late 19th century, to describe the powerful blending of ideas of race and of nationalism which reached their nadir in Nazism[14]. We need not pursue the question as to whether there were racial elements in older hostile attitudes to Jews[15]. There is sufficient consensus that

---

[11] R. L. Wilken, *The Myth of Christian Beginnings* (New York: Doubleday/London: SCM, 1979) 197.

[12] Sandmel (n. 10) 155 gives examples from his childhood.

[13] Both cited by M. Simon, *Versus Israel* (1964; Eng. tr. Oxford University, 1986) 216, 219. See further R. Kampling, *Das Blut Christi und die Juden. Mt 27:25 bei den lateinisch-sprachigen christlichen Autoren bis zu Leo dem Grossen* (Münster: Aschendorff, 1984).

[14] Sandmel (n. 10) xix–xx.

[15] Simon (n. 13) e.g. argues that "the basic cause of Greco-Roman anti-Semitism lay in Jewish separatism ... Any racist element was entirely lacking" (202). Nor will we have need or time to take up the question of whether Christianity introduced anti-semitism to or inherited it

the primary motive up until the 19th century was religious and not racial; as is
indicated by the fact that in earlier centuries Jews could escape persecution
from Christians by converting to Christianity. But should we confine "anti-
semitism" to cases where the denigration of Jews is racially motivated and
directed against the race as such?

Such considerations have encouraged most recent discussions in this area to
use the alternative terms "anti-Judaism", or "anti-Jewish"[16]. The problem with
the latter is that it may not be specific enough. Does "Jewish" here denote
people, or customs, or religion, or what? If it could be restricted to the sense
"prejudice and hostility against all things Jewish", that would help – a specific
case of an unthinking bias against the foreign or strange, whether cultural,
religious, or racial in motivation. But it becomes less helpful when the issue is
whether unfair or unjustifiable objection is being made to (only) some characteristically Jewish beliefs or practices. For example, is Paul the Jew "anti-
Jewish" because he objects to the characteristic attitudes towards the law
maintained by most (but by no means all) of his fellow Jews?

There is a similar problem with the term "anti-Judaism". It has the advantage
of focusing the issue on religion – "a prejudicial denial of the validity of the
Jewish religion". The problem here, however, is that it implies that "Judaism"
is a clear-cut entity, whose content and outline is fully agreed by its practition-
ers, and which is being opposed from "outside". Here again the question can be
fairly asked as to whether Paul's letters provide examples of "anti-Judaism".

In recognition of the problem Douglas Hare has suggested greater refine-
ment. He distinguishes three kinds of "anti-Judaism". (1) Prophetic anti-
Judaism – typified by prophetic and sectarian critique of the religious practices
of the time. (2) Jewish-Christian anti-Judaism – criticism by Jews who have
come to believe in Jesus as Messiah of their fellow Jews who have failed so to
believe. (3) Gentilizing anti-Judaism – emphasizing the Gentile character of
the new movement and claiming God's rejection of the "old" Israel[17]. This
distinction is helpful, at least to the extent that it highlights the danger of
lumping very different things under the one label. But it does not resolve the
problem satisfactorily. How can prophetic critique of priest or people be

---

from the wider Greco-Roman world of antiquity; see particularly J. G. Gager, *The Origins of
Anti-Semitism. Attitudes towards Judaism in Pagan and Christian Antiquity* (New York:
Oxford, 1985).

[16] E. g. *Anti-Judaism in Early Christianity. Vol. 1. Paul and the Gospels,* ed. P. Richardson;
Vol. 2 Separation and Polemic, ed. S. G. Wilson (Waterloo, Ontario: Wilfrid Laurier Univer-
sity, 1986); N. A. Beck, *Mature Christianity. The Recognition and Repudiation of the Anti-
Jewish Polemic of the New Testament* (London/Toronto: Associated University Presses,
1985). See also E. H. Flannery, "Anti-Judaism and Anti-Semitism: A Necessary Distinction",
Journal of Ecumenical Studies 10 (1973).

[17] D. R. A. Hare, "The Rejection of the Jews in the Synoptics and Acts", in Davies (n. 3)
27–47, here 28–32.

described as an example of "anti-Judaism"? And while a *Gentile* dismissal of Jewish religion, as in the case of Barnabas, can certainly be regarded as an example of "anti-Judaism", the term still remains question-begging when levelled in criticism against Jews claiming to be faithful to their religious or ancestral heritage.

2.2. The problem underlying all this is that the key categories are themselves not fixed. "Who is a Jew?" is a question still unresolved within the state of modern Israel. Does "Jew" denote ethnic or religious identity? And if the latter, the problem simply shifts to the definition of "Judaism". "What is Judaism?" is a central question for scholars of the second temple period and beginnings of Christianity. Jacob Neusner now speaks regularly of "varieties of Judaism" or of "Judaisms" (plural) for our period[18]. Is "anti-Judaism" then an appropriate term to describe the polemic of the Psalms of Solomon or of the Qumran covenanters against the other forms of Judaism of their day? – other forms which would seem to have greater claim at the time to the title "normative Judaism"[19]. John Gager accepts Hare's three kinds of anti-Judaism, with the single qualification that "prophetic anti-Judaism" would be better described as "intra-Jewish polemic"[20]. But should not Hare's second category, "Jewish-Christian anti-Judaism", also be described as a form of "intra-Jewish" debate?

This underlying issue is one of no little importance for our present study. If it is the case that "Judaism" was a word or concept whose reference was in some dispute, whose range was shifting, whose identity was developing, what meaning can we give to the term "anti-Judaism", how appropriate is its use when the usage in question falls within that disputed, shifting, developing territory[21]? Likewise with the term "anti-Jewish". Where "Jew" is a form of religious identity, can those caught up within the debate about that identity, or claimants to that identity be classified as "anti-Jewish"? By raising this issue I do not mean to duck or diminish the still sharp problem of NT texts which at least seem to

---

[18] J. Neusner, "Varieties of Judaism in the Formative Age", *Formative Judaism. Second Series* (BJS 41; Chico: Scholars, 1983) 59–89; J. Neusner, et al. ed., *Judaisms and their Messiahs at the Turn of the Christian Era* (Cambridge: Cambridge University, 1987).

[19] It is usually inferred that the Psalms of Solomon were attacking the Sadducean priesthood, while Qumran was fiercely critical of both the Jerusalem temple authorities and also the Pharisees.

[20] Gager (n. 15) 9.

[21] Although E. P. Sanders, *Paul and Palestinian Judaism* (London: SCM, 1977), has done more than most to alert us to the presence in much NT exegesis of an unhistorically justified denigration of "Palestinian Judaism", his attempt to clarify the historical realities by means of "a comparison of patterns of religion" seems to give credence to the idea of a clearly defined "Judaism" to which Paul in particular opposed "Christianity". "This is what Paul finds wrong in Judaism: it is not Christianity" (552). Contrast also J. Neusner, *Jews and Christians. The Myth of a Common Tradition* (London: SCM/Philadelphia: TPI, 1991): "From the very beginnings the Judaic and Christian religious worlds scarcely intersected"; "Judaism and Christianity are completely different religions, not different versions of one religion" (x, 1); though with various qualifications in the following pages.

denigrate Judaism from outside, or to express hostility to Jews as such. The question of anti-Judaism or anti-Jewishness, or even of anti-semitism, within the NT cannot be resolved by semantic sleight-of-hand – certainly not when texts like Matt 27:25 and John 8:44, already quoted (§ 1), have to be accounted for. Nevertheless, the warnings are clear that failure to take account of the currents and eddies within the broad stream of first century Jewish religion, from which both Christianity and rabbinic Judaism emerged, may result in judgments which are anachronistic and unfair.

2.3. Bearing all this in mind we turn to the problem raised by texts like Matt 27:25 and John 8:44 in the NT, whatever the term we use to describe the attitudes they express. Given the time-span under review, AD 70–135, we will focus particularly on the three NT documents which are usually dated to this period, and which bring the issue to sharpest focus within the NT – Acts, John and Matthew. But first we will consider an issue which stretches across more than one of these documents, the significance of the phrase οἱ ’Ιουδαῖοι as used by John and Acts in particular.

3. Who were "the Jews"?

3.1. Discussions on this topic have given particular attention to the use of the phrase οἱ ’Ιουδαῖοι in John and Acts. For two reasons. The first is statistical. The frequency with which ’Ιουδαῖος occurs in these documents far exceeds its usage elsewhere in the NT.

Mt	Mk	Lk	Jn	Ac	Paul	Rom	1Co	Total
5	6	5	71	79	26	11	8	194

In other words, John and Acts account for more than 75% of total NT usage, and mostly in the plural form, "the Jews"[22]. The word, then, provides an important indicator to attitudes to "the Jews" on the part of the authors of John and Acts.

Second, and more important is the *negative* portrayal of "the Jews" which is a regular feature of both John and Acts, paralleled elsewhere in the NT only by 1. Thes 2:14[23]. In John the opponents·of Jesus are regularly described simply as "the Jews" – as in 5:16, "the Jews persecuted Jesus", and 5:18, "the Jews sought all the more to kill him" (see also 7:1; 8:48,52; 9:22; 10:31,33; 11:8; 19:7). And in Acts the trouble-makers who pursue and harry Paul during his missionary journeys are consistently referred to in blanket terms as "the Jews" (9:23;

---

[22] 12 of the 16 references in the Synoptic Gospels are parallel occurrences of the phrase "king of the Jews" in reference to Jesus.

[23] In Rev 2:9 and 3:9 note that Jewish identity and the appropriateness of the designation "Jew" is what is in question. In each case the opponents are a synagogue; but are they "Jews"?!

13:45,50; 17:5; 18:12,14; 20:3; 21:12), with Paul himself regularly designating his opponents and accusers as "the Jews" (20:19; 25:10; 26:2,21; 28:19).

The first problem posed by such passages is the apparently blanket character of the charges made. "The Jews" as a whole seem to be portrayed as consistently hostile to Jesus and to the mission of Paul. Whether the context in Acts is the diaspora or Jerusalem, it is the all-embracing nature of the description which catches the eye. Whether in John the reference should generally be taken as to "the Judeans" (7:1 and 11:7 being the clearest examples)[24], or more consistently to the authorities in Jerusalem (note particularly 7:13, 9:22, 19:38 and 20:19 where Jews fear "the Jews")[25], it is the sweeping nature of the charge which impresses most deeply by its constant refrain. Such an indiscriminating condemnation of "the Jews" seems to warrant the equally indiscriminating charge of "anti-Judaism" or "anti-Jews" as such. The issues raised by both Acts and John cannot, of course, be reduced to the occurrences of οἱ Ἰουδαῖοι, as we shall see. But these references to "the Jews" are an important part of the overall issue and it is necessary, therefore, to put them in perspective before we press more deeply into the questions raised by them.

3.2. The fact is that Ἰουδαῖος, like most words, has a range of meaning. In its basic and most traditional sense it was the name used by foreigners for a person belonging to Judea. But in the Hellenistic period Judea functioned politically as a temple state, so that Ἰουδαῖος included a religious as well as geographical and ethnic reference. Following the expansion of Judea's political authority under the Hasmoneans and the increasing experience of diaspora, it could be used of those who ethnically derived from Judea or the expanded temple state, and whose religious world of meaning focused on the temple in Jerusalem[26].

Οἱ Ἰουδαῖοι therefore would normally denote a group identified by ethnic origin and religious practice, and as such distinct from others around. The precise reference of the group would depend on who the others were from whom the group was being distinguished – the Jews distinct from the Samaritans, or as opposed to the Syrian overlords of the Maccabean period, or as a distinct entity within a diaspora city; the customs of the Jews, which disting-

---

[24] As argued particularly by M. Lowe, "Who were the Ἰουδαῖοι?", *NovT* 18 (1976) 101–30.

[25] As argued particularly by U. C. von Wahlde, "The Johannine 'Jews': A Critical Survey", *NTS* 28 (1982) 33–60.

[26] W. A. Meeks, "'Am I a Jew?' Johannine Christianity and Judaism", *Christianity, Judaism and Other Greco-Romans Cults*, M. Smith Festschrift, ed. J. Neusner, Vol. 1 (Leiden: Brill, 1975) 163–86: "Ancient authors in the age of syncretism tend to identify a cultic community either by its principal deity ... or by its place of origin ... When pagan authors speak of *Ioudaioi*, as they usually do when referring to the people we call Jews, the term denotes the visible, recognizable group with their more or less well-known customs, who have their origin in Judea but preserve what we would call their 'ethnic identity' in the diaspora" (182).

uished them from those with different customs, and so on. This covers the great preponderance of usage in the documents of the time, not least Philo and Josephus. For example, Philo speaks regularly of "the nation of the Jews" or of Moses as "the lawgiver of the Jews". But in *In Flaccum* and *de Legatione ad Gaium* he can often use οἱ 'Ιουδαῖοι to denote Jews who are more specifically defined by their context, as Jews of a particular region or city. Josephus in *The Jewish War* speaks typically of "the Jews" in opposition to such as Antiochus, Pompey, Herod and Pilate, and in the build-up to the revolt against Rome, but he can also speak with equal meaningfulness of "the Jews" of specific cities such as Alexandria or Damascus, or switch from specific to general reference (as in *J W* 2.532) without confusion.

This helps explain the usage in Acts, at least in some measure. Luke's pattern of usage, in fact, is very similar to that of Josephus. He will often identify "the Jews" in question more precisely, as from Antioch, or Thessalonica, or Asia (Acts 14:19; 17:13; 21:27; 24:18); but when the context makes more precise definition unnecessary, he can refer simply to "the Jews" (as in the examples given in § 3.1). Wherever an incident involves Jews in a city where there are different ethnic groups, it is sufficient to refer to "the Jews" as those involved in the incident. "The Jews", in other words, function in these cases at least in part as an ethnic identification, distinguishing them from other groups in the city as much as from the Christian missionaries.

So too Paul's apparent readiness to distinguish himself from "the Jews" in the latter stages of Acts should not be given exaggerated significance as though he thereby distanced himself from and disowned his own Jewishness. Josephus also can speak of Alexander and Alexandra as over against "the Jews" (*JW* 1.107), or of himself as apparently distinct from "the Jews" (*JW* 3.130, 136, 142; *Life* 113, 416). And John's use of "Jews" both in reference (apparently) to Judeans and in speaking (apparently) of the Galilean crowd (John 6:41,62) is paralleled in Josephus by a similar readiness to talk of Galilee as "the territory of the Jews" and of the residents of Galilee as "Jews" (*JW* 1.21; 2.232). In all these cases the usage is hardly exceptional and would hardly cause confusion[27].

3.3. There is a further factor, however, and one of no little importance: the fact that religion and specific religious assertions were so fundamental to Jewish identity. For these religious assertions were a matter of some dispute, so that the description of some as 'Ιουδαῖοι was a way of making a religious claim to

---

[27] A modern parallel would be a Scot attending a football match in England or elsewhere in Europe, along with many of his fellow countrymen. In a case where there was some crowd trouble, the Scot, whether involved or not, would quite naturally speak of those Scots who were involved in the trouble as "the Scots" when speaking of the incident itself. Thereby he neither would be indicting *all* Scots who attended the match (or Scots as a nation), nor would he necessarily be denying his own part in the episode or distancing himself from his fellow Scots (as through by describing others as "the Scots" he was somehow denying that he himself was a Scot).

that epithet over against others, including other claimants to the epithet. John Ashton notes two cases in Josephus[28]: in *Ant.* 11.173 Josephus observes that οἱ Ἰουδαῖοι was "the name by which they (the returnees from Babylon) have been called from the time when they went up from Babylon". This reflects a claim that "the Jews" properly speaking were not those who had remained in Judea (a *geographical* designation), but those who had remained faithful in Babylon and returned to the land of promise at the earliest opportunity to become the basis of the renewed and revitalized people in the post-exilic period (a *religious* designation). From the same period comes Josephus' account of the Samaritans who were prepared to identify themselves as Ἰουδαῖοι when it seemed propitious to do so, but whom Josephus regarded as "apostates from the Jewish nation" (*Ant.* 11.340–4). Hence also Josephus' attitude to Herod the Great, designated a 'half-Jew' (ἡμιουδαῖος) because he was an Idumean (*Ant.* 14.403), and his unwillingness to use the term 'Jew' of the apostate Tiberius Alexander (cf. *Ant.* 20.100). At the same time there are indications that the term Ἰουδαῖος could be used irrespective of nationality, that is, in a "purely" religious way[29].

A related factor of some significance is the emergence of Ἰουδαϊσμός during the Maccabean period as a way of designating the religion of the Jews in its self-conscious distinctiveness and fierce loyalty to the law and the traditional customs (initially in 2. Macc 2:21; 8:1; 14:38) – "Judaism" by definition distinct and different from and defined by opposition to the hellenizing policies and influences of the Syrians and the apostate Jews who sided with them. The same sense of distinctiveness and fierce loyalty is present in Paul's use of the word in Gal 1:13–14, in his description of his way of life as a Pharisee. And it was precisely the tightness of his old definition which his new faith called in question, as Rom 2:17–29 clearly indicates[30].

If the emergence of post-exilic Judaism, and the Maccabean crisis provided two of the main crises for Jewish identity, the third most serious single crisis of the second temple period was the destruction of the temple in AD 70 and its aftermath. Since both Acts and John were almost certainly written in that period, we would expect the use of Ἰουδαῖος in these documents, and any question regarding the propriety of any claim to it as a self-designation, to reflect something of the larger context. In particular, as we shall see, this may provide an important part of the explanation for John's varied use of οἱ Ἰουδαῖοι, with "the Jews" denoting the claim of a particular leading group

---

[28] J. Ashton, "The Identity and Function of the Ἰουδαῖοι in the Fourth Gospel", *NovT* 27 (1985) 40–75, here 51–2, 73.

[29] See W. Gutbrod, *TDNT* 3.370–71; R. S. Kraemer, "On the Meaning of the Term 'Jew' in Greco-Roman Inscriptions", *HTR* 82 (1989) 35–53.

[30] See my contribution to the previous Symposium, "What was the Issue between Paul and 'Those of the Circumcision'?", *Paulus und das antike Judentum*, hrsg. M. Hengel & U. Heckel (WUNT 58; Tübingen: Mohr, 1991) 295–317.

among the ethnic Jews of John's day to religious authority, to be the authoritative representatives of Judaism, to be, if you like, "the Jews" (§ 5.2).

3.4. A further factor of relevance is that Ἰουδαῖος was not the only name by
which a Jew might identify himself. Indeed, Ἰουδαῖος was not the most natural
self-designation for many Jews. K. G. Kuhn notes that in the post-biblical
("intertestamental") period Ἰσραήλ was the people's preferred name for itself
(cf. e. g. Sir 17:17; Jub 33:20; PssSol 14:5), whereas Ἰουδαῖος was the name by
which they were known to others[31]. In other words, "Jew" was a designation by
which Jews were distinguished from other ethnic and religious groups. But
"Israel/Israelite" denoted a self-understanding in terms of election and covenant promise. "Jew", we might say, always had something of an outsider's
perspective (hence the regularity of its use by Philo, in *Flacc.* and *Legat.*, and by
Josephus); whereas "Israel(ite)" was much more an *intra muros* designation.
Most striking here is the usage of CD, where 'Israel' is clearly the preferred self-
designation (e. g. 3:19 – 'a sure house of Israel'), and the sect sees itself as those
who 'have gone out from the land of Judah' and who will 'no more consort with
the house of Judah' (4:2−3,11)[32].

It would be possible, then, for an early Jewish believer in Jesus Messiah to
cede the use of the name "Jew" to others within the broad spectrum of late
second temple Judaism, while clinging to the title "Israel(ite)". In other words,
Ἰουδαῖος would not necessarily be regarded as catching the essence of Jewish
identity, but rather as lending itself to too superficial (external) an identification; whereas Ἰσραηλ(ίτης) was much the more worthy of retention, as reaching to the true heart of Jewish identity. This certainly seems to be the case with
Paul. In Rom 2−3 Ἰουδαῖος is used, since the talk is of "Jew" in his distinction
from "Greek"; whereas in Rom 9−11 Ἰσραηλ(ίτης) dominates, where Paul
speaks much more as an insider (9:1−3; 11:1). Both designations and their
proper reference are still in dispute (Rom 2:28−9; 9:6), but whereas Paul
addresses his imaginary interlocutor as Ἰουδαῖος (Rom 2:17), he identifies
himself as Ἰσραηλ(ίτης) (11:1).

Something equivalent is true also of the Fourth Gospel: to the outsider Jesus
is "king of the Jews" (John 18:33,39; 19:3,19,21); but to the insider, the true
Israelite Nathanael (1:47), Jesus is "king of Israel" (1:49), and in the most
positive of all John's treatments of the "crowd" (12:12−19), they too make the

---

[31] K. G. Kuhn, *TDNT* 3.359−65.

[32] Something similar may be reflected in the second century BCE inscription from the island
of Delos from a community describing themselves as "Israelites of Delos, who offer first fruits
at sacred Har Garizim" (P. Bruneau, "'Les Israélites de Délos' et la Juiverie délienne",
Bulletin de Correspondance Hellénistique 106 [1982] 465−504; cited by W. A. Meeks, "Breaking Away: Three New Testament Pictures of Christianity's Separation from the Jewish
Communities", *"To See Ourselves as Others See Us". Christians, Jews, "Others" in Late
Antiquity,* ed. J. Neusner & E. S. Frerichs [Chico: Scholars, 1985] 93−115, here 100).

same confession (12:13)[33]. Acts, on the other hand, does not manifest the same concern to treat the alternative designations differently: Paul is shown as laying claim to the title Ἰουδαῖος (Acts 21:39; 22:3 – "I am a Jew"); whereas Ἰσραηλίτης appears to be equally appropriate on the lips of Paul as on the lips of his opponents (13:16; 21:18). At the same time "Israel" remains a distinctly more positive concept and symbol of hope for Luke (Acts 5:31; 9:15; 10:36; 13:17,23; 28:20)[34].

3.5. In short, the identification of certain groups as "the Jews" in Acts and John should not be treated as a description of Jews as a whole, nor as a distancing on the part of the speaker from Jews as a whole. Moreover, the usage itself may reflect some debate as to who is a Jew, where the appropriateness of the designation is only part of a larger debate over Jewish identity and heritage. However, the reference and function of οἱ Ἰουδαῖοι in Acts and John is only part of the larger question as to anti-semitic or anti-Jewish tendencies or attitudes in these documents. And we must turn now to this larger question.

We start with Acts. Of the three documents to be considered it is the one most likely to have been written by a Gentile, and so is most likely to betray the perspective of an "outsider". And to many the charge (of anti-semitism or anti-Judaism) appears particularly appropriate in the case of Acts. Although the accusation is levelled at both of Luke's volumes, the main weight of the charge undoubtedly hangs on the evidence of Acts.

4. Is Acts "anti-semitic"?

4.1. The indictment of Acts has recently been pressed with greatest vigour by J. T. Sanders[35]. In his preface he notes that the charges are hardly new. Overbeck had accused Acts of "national anti-Judaism", while Harnack had called Acts "the first stage of developing early Christian anti-semitism"[36]. Following Gager's definition of anti-semitism as "a fundamental and systematic hostility towards Jews", Sanders has no hesitation in describing Acts as "antisemitic"[37]. Similarly Sandmel, who finds in Luke "a frequent subtle, genteel anti-Semit-

---

[33] In the light of the present discussion, it is perhaps significant that Pilate is represented as declining the request that the title over the cross be altered to read "This man said, 'I am king of the Jews'" (19:21). Even in mockery that would not be the appropriate self-designation for Jesus.

[34] Cf. H. Conzelmann, *The Theology of St Luke* (London: Faber, 1960): "We can say that the Jews are now called to make good their claim to be 'Israel'. If they fail to do this, then they become 'the Jews'" – 145). A justifiable way of putting the point, though not actually borne out by Luke's use of the concept "Israel" itself.

[35] J. T. Sanders, *The Jews in Luke-Acts* (Philadelphia: Fortrtess, 1987).

[36] Cited by Sanders (n. 35) xvi.

[37] Sanders (n. 35) xvi–xvii.

ism", whereas in Acts "anti-Semitism becomes overt and direct"; "in Acts, "the Jews" are villains and their villainy could not be worse"[38]. And in the judgment of Beck, Acts is the most anti-Jewish document in the NT[39]. But the most thoroughgoing treatment is that of Sanders; discussion of the topic will therefore proceed primarily in dialogue with him.

It is impossible within the scope of this essay to do anything like complete justice to Sanders' monograph (394 pages!). It will have to suffice to focus attention on the main line of investigation on which his conclusion, quoted above, is based, and to deal more briefly with the other strands of his indictment.

4.2. The main weight of Sanders' argument rests on his examination of a motif on which we have already commented to some extent (§ 3) – "the Jewish people"[40]. In brief, Sanders distinguishes Luke's treatment of "the Jews" in (1) the speeches from his treatment of them in (2) the narrative of Luke-Acts. (1) "The witness of the speeches in Acts is ... that the Jews generally are irredeemably resistant to God's will and his offer of salvation, and that they are the murderers of Jesus." He describes this perspective as of the "blanket condemnation" variety, "according to which Jews are by nature and congenitally obstreperous and opposed to the will and purpose of God"[41]. The evidence for this conclusion is particularly Acts 2:36, 4:10, 5:30, 10:39 and 18:6 (Jews guilty of the death of Jesus), and 20:19, 22:5 and 28:19,26 (Jewish hostility to the Christian mission). (2) In his analysis of the narratives of Acts he takes account of the more mixed evidence, including the various positive references to Jews who believed (as particularly 21:20), but finds the solution in a carefully constructed progression intended to put "the Jews" increasingly in a bad light – "a picture of increasing Jewish hostility and opposition to the gospel"[42]. It reaches its climax in "the Pauline passion narrative" (21:11,30,36; 22:22,30; 23:12; 25:24; 26:2,21). In the end the opposition is simply "the Jews". "Jewish opposition to Christianity is now universal and endemic[43]." Whatever has gone before, the final climax (28:26–28) shows that "Luke has written the Jews off"[44].

Sanders builds up a strong case, but it is very much open to question whether

---

[38] Sandmel (n. 10) 73, 100.

[39] Beck (n. 16) 270.

[40] Sanders (n. 35) chap. 3.

[41] *Ibid.* 54, 49; similarly 63.

[42] *Ibid.* 77.

[43] *Ibid.* 80.

[44] A phrase which Sanders quotes regularly from E. Haenchen, "The Book of Acts as Source Material for the History of Early Christianity", *Studies in Luke-Acts.* ed. L. E. Keck & J. L. Martyn (Philadelphia: Fortress/London: SPCK, 1966) 258–78, here 278. See also L. Gaston, "Anti-Judaism and the Passion Narrative in Luke and Acts", *Anti-Judaism Vol. 1* (n. 16) 127–53, here 137–9, 151.

the evidence can bear the weight he wants to put on it. We have already given some preliminary consideration to much of that evidence above (§ 3.2), but since this argument is at the heart of Sander's indictment of Luke it requires a somewhat fuller treatment.

(a) We should note first of all that Luke intersperses what we might call "neutral" references to Jews along with the more negative ones – "the synagogue(s) of the Jews" (13:5; 14:1; 17:1,10; cf. 17:17; 18:19), "Jews and Greeks" (14:1; 18:4; 19:10,17; 20:21), "the principal men of the Jews" (25:2), "the law of the Jews" (25:8), "the customs of the Jews" (26:3), "the local leaders of the Jews" in Rome (28:17). These are wholly "natural" references, parallel, for example, to the fragmentary inscription at Corinth – συναγωγὴ ῾Εβραίων; or to Paul's regular usage – "Jew and Greek" (Rom 1:16; 2:9–10; 3:9; etc.); or to Josephus' regular reference to "the patriarchal customs" or "the customs of the Jews" (as in *Ant.* 15.268). What is noteworthy here is that such usage is interspersed among the more "negative" references.

(b) There are also the positive references to Jews – particularly Jews who believe and respond positively to Paul's message (13:43; 14:1; 21:20[45]; 28:24), Jews who speak well of such as Cornelius (10:22 – "the whole nation of the Jews") and Ananias (22:12 – "all the Jews living there"), and, of course, the repeated self-affirmation of Paul himself (21:39 and 22:3 – "I am a Jew"; cf. 16:20; 18:2,24). One who so speaks of Jews is certainly not intent to make a "blanket condemnation" of the Jews as a whole. And since such references continue up into and through "the Pauline passion narrative" it suggests that other references which are being read as "blanket condemnations" are being mis-read[46]. With these positive references to Jews, of course, has to be grouped the motif in Acts familiar to scholarship since Schneckenburger and the

---

[45] M. J. Cook (below n. 60) argues that "the myriads in Acts 21 only summarize conversions accomplished before chap. 7" (121). But πόσαι μυριάδες must mean many more than is indicated in the figures given in Acts 1–7 (2:41; 4:4; 5:14; 6:7): where μυριάς has a specific value it = 10,000; and in Josephus, *Ant.* 7.318 the same phrase (πόσαι μυριάδες) denotes the whole people of Israel. If Luke intended to imply that all expansion of the Jerusalem church stopped after 6:7 (Sanders, cited by Cook 121) he has gone about it in a very odd way. The obvious implication of 21:20 is that "the Jewish mission" in Judea has continued to have marked success up till that point.

[46] Cf. particularly J. Jervell, *Luke and the People of God. A New Look at Luke-Acts* (Minneapolis: Augsburg, 1972), who in his chapter, "The Divided People of God" (41–74), argues that Luke intends to show the Jewish people divided in their response to the gospel: some are convinced and believe; others remain unbelieving. Sanders (n. 35) documents those who follow or agree with Jervell (46); to whom now add M. Salmon, "Insider or Outsider? Luke's Relationship with Judaism", *Luke-Acts and the Jewish People*, ed. J. B. Tyson (London: SCM, 1988) 76–82, who can even argue that Luke speaks of Judaism as an insider rather than, as is normally assumed, as an outsider. For critique of Jervell's further argument that the way to the Gentiles is through Israel's acceptance rather than rejection of the gospel, see also S. G. Wilson, *The Gentiles and the Gentile Mission in Luke-Acts* (SNTSMS 23; Cambridge University, 1977) 226–33.

Tübingen school: that is, in particular, the re-judaizing of Paul, who accepts the apostolic decree, circumcises Timothy, makes a vow at Cenchreae, takes part in temple purificatory ritual, and appeals to "the promises made by God to our fathers, to which our twelve tribes hope to attain . . ." (16:3–4; 18:18; 21:26; 26:6–7). Sanders deals with these passages by arguing in effect that Luke distinguishes Jewish Christians and Jewish customs from his theology of the Jews, and that by stressing the continuity between Judaism and Christianity Luke indicates how baseless is Jewish hostility to Paul[47]. But in the last case the repetion of the first person plural, "our fathers" and "our twelve tribes", reads much more naturally as a continuing affirmation by Paul of his identification with his people. In the same way, in 15:16–17, the quotation by James of Amos 9:11–12 reads most naturally as an affirmation both of Israel's reconstitution and of the Gentiles incorporation therein[48], a typically Jewish hope[49], reworked by Paul in Rom 11; whereas Sanders sees in it a further indication that for Luke the primary divine purpose is now centred in Gentile Christianity[50].

(c) Regarding the negative references to "the Jews", it needs to be asked whether Sanders has allowed sufficiently for the variety of factors which may have influenced Luke's usage.

(1) We have already mentioned the *"neutral"* references, where "the Jews" denote simply the bulk of the Jews in a place already indicated by the context, or "the Jews" actually involved in the incident narrated (13:45,50 – "the Jews" of Antioch; 14:4 – "the Jews" of Iconium; 17:5 – "the Jews" of Thessalonica; 18:12,14 – "the Jews" of Corinth; 18:28 – "the Jews" of Ephesus; 24:9 and 26:2 – "the Jews" bringing the indictment against Paul).

(2) Linked into this may be a *religious* factor (already referred to in § 3.3). That is to say, where an attitude was being expressed by the bulk of the Jews in any place or region, and where that attitude consisted of a strong affirmation of what had usually been recognized as characteristically and distinctively Jewish, those who maintained that attitude with some force had a prior claim to the designation "Jews". Hence the characteristically "Jewish" nature of the opposition to Paul (particularly 21:20ff. – including Jewish Christians).

(3) We should also allow for some *rhetorical* considerations in the heightening of emotional impact – particularly in the accusations levelled against the Jerusalem audiences for their part in the death of Jesus (2:23,36; 3:15; 4:10;

---

[47] Sanders (n. 35) 269–70, 295–6. See also Tyson (n. 53 below).

[48] Cf. particularly Jervell (n. 46) 51–3; G. Lohfink, *Jesus and Community* (London: SPCK, 1985) 139–40.

[49] See e.g. E. P. Sanders, *Jesus and Judaism* (London: SCM, 1985) Part One.

[50] Sanders (n. 35) 268–9 rejects Jervell's view on the ground that it is out of harmony with the rest of Luke-Acts, despite the fact that the evidence marshalled by Jervell demonstrates precisely such harmony.

5:30), in the prophet-style denunciation of 7:51−53[51], and in the flourish of 18:6 ("Your blood be upon your heads!")[52].

(4) Also of some relevance is the fact that Luke can vary his reference from a quite specific description (14:2 − "the unbelieving Jews" of Iconium; 14:19 − Jews from Antioch and Iconium; 16:3 − the Jews in these places; 17:13 − the Jews from Thessalonica; 21:11 − the Jews in Jerusalem; 2:27 and 24:18 − the Jews from Asia; 22:12 − the Jews who lived there; 25:7 − the Jews who have come down from Jerusalem), to the less immediately specified "the Jews" (references already given), to the anarthrous usage ("Jews") which seems to increase towards the end of Acts (21:21; 24:18; 25:10; 26:2−4,7,21). Much at least of this must be a matter of simply *stylistic variation*; but the evidence certainly weakens the case for seeing a climactic build-up of outright hostility to "the Jews" (6 of the last 10 references are anarthrous). These considerations are probably also a major factor in the weight to be given to 23:12 − the plot of "the Jews" to kill Paul. If Luke really did wish thereby to indict "the Jews" in some blanket condemnation, his further identification of them as "more than forty who made this conspiracy" is something of a *reductio ad absurdum*.

In the light of such considerations, the question needs to be asked whether in all this Luke is any more tendentious and motivated by anti-Jewish malice than, say Suetonius in his much quoted "Iudaeos impulsore Chresto assidue tumultuantis Roma expulit" (*Claudius* 25.4), or Paul in his own description of his hardships − ὑπὸ Ἰουδαίων πεντάκις τεσσεράκοντα παρὰ μίαν ἔλαβον (2. Cor 11:24)?

(*d*) Sanders' case depends most of all on the weight given to the final paragraph of Acts − 28:17−30[53]. For him it is the climax of Luke's anti-semitism: it was because "the Jews" objected that Paul has come to Rome; the final quotation, from Isa 6:9−10, "must refer not only to Jews in Rome, but to all Jews"; and the final word, the Lukan interpretation of the passage (28:28), shows that for Luke salvation is for the Gentiles and was never intended for the Jews, the cycle of rejection and further mission ends with rejection. "Luke has written the Jews off[54]."

But here again Sanders has surely overstated his case. (1) Luke does not go out of his way to blacken the character of "the Jews": Paul is still speaking

[51] See below n. 64 and § 7.2.

[52] Beck (n. 16) shows himself quite insensitive to such considerations (213, 221, 230). In contrast, S. G. Wilson, "The Jews and the Death of Jesus in Acts", *Anti-Judaism Vol. 1* (n. 16) 155−64, notes that "Luke is careful to include a number of mitigating factors" (163).

[53] The crucial nature of this final passage for the present debate is also indicated by the volume edited by J. B. Tyson (n. 46). See particularly the essay by Tyson, "The Probelm of Jewish Rejection in Acts" (124−37), particularly 124−7 and nn. 3−5. See also n. 45 above.

[54] Sanders (n. 35) 80−3, 297−9. In v. 25 "Paul turns viciously on his auditors" (80)! For those who agree with Sanders see Tyson (n. 53) 159 n. 5.

positively of the ancestral customs (v. 17)[55], of "my nation" (v. 19), of "the hope of Israel" (v. 20); the part played by "the Jews" is hardly a point of emphasis or indeed of exaggeration (v. 19); and the Jews of Rome are depicted as remarkably open, with nothing having been said against Paul or his message by other Jews from elsewhere (vv. 21–2)[56]. (2) Paul succeeds in "convincing" (ἐπείθοντο) some, which was what he was trying to do (vv. 23–4), and which could mean a full acceptance of Paul's message (if 17:4 and 19:26 are anything to go by)[57]; or, if we give weight to the imperfect tense (cf. 13:43; 18:4), the implication would presumably be that many of the Roman Jews were on the verge of accepting the message – at any rate, hardly a negative portrayal[58].

(3) The portrayal of the Jews (of Rome) as divided between those persuaded by and those unbelieving in Paul's message is a regular feature of Acts (13:43–5; 14:1–2; 17:4–5,10–14; 18:4–8); what is noticeable here, though, is that Luke depicts them as continuing to be divided as they departed, *after* Paul's final statement. (v. 25 – ἀσύμφωνοι δὲ ὄντες πρὸς ἀλλήλους ἀπελύοντο εἰπόντος τοῦ Παύλου ῥῆμα ἕν); the implication being that whatever the force of that final statement it does *not* refer to the Jews *en masse*[59]. (4) This raises the further possibility that this final turning of Paul to the Gentiles is no more final than the earlier turnings (13:46–8; 18:6; 22:21; 26:17–18), no more final indeed than the words of Isa 6:9–10 were for Isaiah's mission to his people (to be noted is the fact that Luke follows the LXX almost verbatim, that is, without tendentious modification). Certainly the implication of 28:30–1, that Paul continued to preach openly to "all who came to him", must be that the "all" included Jews as well as Gentiles, at the very least those Jews already (being) "persuaded" by Paul. And Luke has made no attempt to exclude that most natural inference[60].

---

[55] Tyson (n. 52) 129 however thinks there is a contrast between "the ancestral customs" (v. 17 – τοῖς ἔθεσι τοῖς πατρῴοις; *not* "our fathers") and "your fathers" (v. 25 – τοὺς πατέρας ὑμῶν).

[56] The Roman Jews' description of the movement represented by Paul as a αἵρεσις has, of course, no note of rejection in it; Josephus uses the same word to describe the "sects" within Judaism (as in *Ant.* 13.171 – Pharisees, Saduccees and Essenes); and Luke is well aware of this usage (Acts 5:17; 15:5; 26:5; so also 24:5,14).

[57] Sanders (n. 35) denies that ἐπείθοντο can mean "converted" here (298) on the surprising ground that ἔπειθον αὐτούς (those Jews and proselytes who followed Paul from the synagogue in Antioch) προσμένειν τῇ χάριτι τοῦ θεοῦ (13:43) must mean that Paul persuaded them to "stay good Jews" (261–2), despite Luke's consistent use of "the grace of God" in reference to believers (11:23; 14:26; 15:40; 20:24).

[58] So also particularly R. C. Tannehill, "Rejection by Jews and Turning to Gentiles: the Pattern of Paul's Mission in Acts", in Tyson, ed. (n. 46) 83–101, here 97.

[59] Cf. particularly Jervell (n. 46) 49 and n. 21, and 63.

[60] See also Tannehill (n. 58) who recognizes the importance of vv. 30–1 (particularly 99–101), although the contributors to the Tyson volume (n. 46) are almost equally divided on the point. D. L. Tiede, "'Glory to thy people Israel': Luke-Acts and the Jews", in Tyson ed. (n. 46) 21–34, sees Luke 2:32 as programmatic for Luke-Acts; "the ending of the narrative in

In short, Sanders has oversimplified the evidence of Acts on "the Jews" by reading it resolutely through and in conformity with one sequence of references, a sequences which at the very least may be better explained by reference to other factors and considerations. There is clearly something wrong when, for example, despite Paul's repeated self-identification, "I am a Jew" (21:39; 22:3), Sanders can still conclude that for Luke "all Jews are equally, in principle at least, perverse"[61].

4.3. Sanders' other arguments are of relatively less importance in terms of the weight they bear for his thesis. In ch. 1 he develops the assertion that "the Jewish religious leaders in Luke-Acts are enemies of Jesus and the church". In the event this boils down to the recognition that Luke places the responsibility for Jesus' crucifixion squarely on the "chief priests and rulers". That Luke does indeed emphasize the responsibility of the temple authorities for Jesus' death, and probably over-emphasize it, is clear (Luke 23:25−6 and 24:20 are particularly noticeable)[62]. But it is also noticeable that Luke exempts the Pharisees, who would represent the principal Jewish leaders at the time he wrote. And most students of the period would agree that the temple authorities (as distinct from the Pharisees) were active in seeking to remove Jesus from the scence[63]. In other words, Luke's portrayal is more an exaggeration of historical reality than a polemical fiction. And it is questionable whether hostility shown against one faction within Judaism should be described as anti-semitism rather than, say, factional polemic. Otherwise the denunciation of national cult by biblical prophet, by the Psalms of Solomon or by Qumran covenanters[64] would have to be regarded equally as anti-semitic[65].

Acts 28 is, therefore, not the end of the story, but it is a resumption of the themes sounded in Simeon's oracles" (29). And D. P. Moessner, "The Ironic Fulfilment of Israel's Glory", in Tyson ed. (n. 46) 35−50, sees Acts 28:26−8 as modelled on the Deuteronomic pattern, spelling out disaster following rejection, but also implying hope if Israel repents. But his conclusion is overstated: "Far from sounding certain and ultimate doom from Israel as a whole, Paul in Acts 28:26−8 declares unflinchingly that the promises of God surely shall prevail" (49−50). Contrast M. J. Cook, "The Mission to the Jews in Acts: Unravelling Luke's 'Myth of the "Myriads"'", in Tyson ed. (n. 46) 102−23, a critique of Tannehill's contribution (n. 58); J. T. Sanders, "The Jewish People in Luke-Acts", in Tyson ed. (n. 46) 51−75, a slightly revised version of chap. 3 of his book (n. 35); and Tyson (n. 53), who concludes: "Two facts seem clear: for Luke the mission to the Jewish people has failed, and it has been terminated" (137). D. Juel, *Luke-Acts* (London: SCM, 1984) 111, agrees with Jervell (n. 46) 63−4, that "with the ending of Acts an era is over. The restoration of Israel . . . has now been completed . . . The future of Israel lies with the Gentiles: they will listen". But, like Sanders, he ignores vv. 30−1.

[61] Sanders (n. 35) 317.

[62] The point is also noted by Beck (n. 16) 177, 179.

[63] See e. g. E. P. Sanders (n. 49) 309−17; E. Rivkin, *What Crucified Jesus? The Political Execution of a Charismatic* (Nashville: Abingdon, 1984).

[64] The point is recognized with regard to Acts 7:52, e. g. by Ruether (n. 4) 74, 77 and Hare (n. 17) 35 ("prophetic anti-Judaism"). See also below § 7.2.

[65] The same would apply to H. Maccoby, *The Mythmaker. Paul and the Invention of*

Ch. 2 finds Luke's portrayal of Jerusalem as "characterized primarily by enmity towards God . . .", "the uniformly evil portrait of the city . . . the place quintessentially opposed to God and his will", "Satan's capital"[66]! The case here too is much overstated. The more negative data of Luke-Acts regarding Jerusalem is explained more or less completely by the two facts, that Jerusalem was where Jesus was put to death, and that it became one pole of the broadening movement. Sanders can only achieve such a lop-sided reading by ignoring the positive role which Luke otherwise gives to Jerusalem and temple: not simply by his framing his Gospel with positive references to the temple (Luke 1:8 and 24:50–3 – neither of which Sanders even mentions); but also after the Stephen episode, with his portrayal of the apostles as alone remaining in Jerusalem (Acts 8:1) and supervising the expanding mission from there (8:14ff.; 11:22ff.), and with his account of the temple still as a place of divine revelation and offering in 22:17ff. and 24:17–18[67]. Of course, Luke wishes to describe some shift in the centre of gravity ("how the good news was brought from Jerusalem to Rome"), but the salvation-history significance of Jerusalem is still clear in his two volumes as a whole[68].

Ch. 4 wrestles with one of the most intractable elements in Luke-Acts so far as Sanders' thesis is concerned – Luke's presentation of the Pharisees. The problem is that Luke portrays so many non-Christian Pharisees in a positive light (Luke 7:36; 11:37; 13:31; 14:1; Acts 5:34–9; 23:9); and also reports that a number of Pharisees became Christians, though these he portrays in a negative light (Acts 15:5; like the Pharisees of Luke 6:2,7; 11:39–53; 12:1; 15:2; 18:10–11). Sanders' solution is that Luke uses the positive portrayals to indicate that "Christianity is the true and authentic Judaism"; whereas, the negative portrayals indicate Luke's opinion of Jewish-Christians, who may escape the epithet "hypocrites" only if they deny the validity of their own traditional religion[69]. The process by which this conclusion is reached is rather tortuous, and if that was indeed Luke's intention he has hardly made it clear and has succeeded in confusing almost all his readers ever since. The more striking point is surely that Luke, writing at a time when the rabbinic successors of the Pharisees were fast becoming the only main alternative claimants to the herit-

---

Christianity (London: Weidenfeld & Nicolson, 1986), who does not hesitate to use such ill-flavoured and hostile descriptions of the high priests as "quisling" and "Gauleiter" (78, 168).

[66] Sanders (n. 35) 32, 30.

[67] Sanders (n. 35) notes that in Acts 21:30 "the whole city" turns on Paul, as though this is an expression of Luke's hostility to the city as a whole (27). But even a quick glance at a concordance should be sufficient to reveal that Luke loves to use ὅλος in a characteristically stylistic hyperbole (Luke 1:65; 4:14; 7:17; 8:39; 23:5; Acts 2:47; etc.); we might mention also Acts 21:20 – "how many thousands among the Jews have believed".

[68] Contrast Cook (n. 60) who in arguing a similar thesis (that Luke has driven a wedge between "Judaism" and "Jews") points to the *positive* references to Jewish institutions (109–17).

[69] Sanders (n. 35) 97, 128.

age of second temple Judaism, takes such pains to portray so many of them so positively. Moreover, Paul the great hero of the Gentile mission in Luke's portrayal, is shown as going out of his way to announce not only that he had been a Pharisee, but that he still was one (23:6; 26:5; just as twice he had professed, "I am a Jew" – 21:39 and 22:3). This surely betokens a greater openness on Luke's part to continuing dialogue between synagogue and church, albeit marked by blunt talking on both sides, rather than a complete closing of the door on his part.

4.4. To sum up, Sanders must be judged to have greatly overstated his case. He has been selective in his choice of evidence and tendentious in his evaluation of it. He has not given enough weight to the positive elements in Luke's presentation of Jews and Judaism. Even the most negative of Luke's statement regarding the Jews may be best explained by a combination of historical fact (including the destruction of Jerusalem), rhetorical effect, stylistic variation, and awareness of current tensions between the different groups claiming the heritage of second temple Judaism. Luke certainly does intend to demonstrate how Christianity took on an increasingly Gentile face, and "the Jews" of various cities and regions are often foil to that purpose; like others he remained puzzled by the fact that the bulk of Jews continued to reject their Messiah. But the continuity between (second temple) Judaism and Christianity is a much more living reality for Luke than Sanders allows, and Luke portrays a Gentile Christianity in the person of its great apostle as much more positive about its Jewish heritage and as more effective among and open to Jews to the last, than Sanders allows. In short, Luke's anti-semitism is much more in Sanders' reading of the text than in the text itself[70].

5. Is John "anti-semitic"?

5.1. With John the issue is more serious, the evidence apparently more damning. Urban von Wahlde, for example, counts about 40 instances of οἱ Ἰουδαῖοι being used in a hostile sense[71], that is, a more consistent and unremitting hostility when compared with Acts. R. H. Fuller attributes three critical developments to the Fourth Evangelist.

---

[70] Contrast the reading of J. Jervell, "The Church of Jews and Godfearers", in Tyson ed. (n. 46) 11–20, who can only maintain that Luke thinks of the church as consisting of Jews and God-fearing Gentiles by reading Ἕλληνες in 11:20–21, (19:10?) and 20:21, and ἔθνη in 28:28, in the sense of "God-fearing Greeks/Gentiles" – also tendentious, but somewhat more securely rooted in the text than Sanders' thesis.

[71] Von Wahlde (n. 25), collating the results of ten earlier studies.

1. He altered the designation of Jesus' opponents in many places to "the Jews" and introduced this new designation into his own composition.

2. He reinterpreted the issues between Jesus and his opponents in explicitly christological terms.

3. He gave the hostility between Jesus and his opponents a previously unparalleled bitterness[72].

More serious is the way in which "the Jews" seem to have become representatives of unbelief and of the hostile unbelieving "world" in general[73], and not just of the world, but of the devil (John 8:44, cited at the beginning). By thus "mythologizing" Jewish opposition "John gives the ultimate theological form to that diabolizing of 'the Jews' which is the root of anti-Semitism in the Christian tradition"[74]. Here too Ruether's claim that anti-Judaism is the inevitable consequence of christology reaches its sharpest point within the NT in the response of "the Jews" to Pilate: "We have a law, and by that law he ought to die, beause he has made himself the Son of God" (19:7). Not altogether surprising, then, is Sandmel's finding that "John is widely regarded as either the most anti-Semitic or at least the most overtly anti-Semitic of the Gospels[75]."

5.2. However, even here there is a danger of exaggerating the case against John, particularly by focussing too narrowly on particular texts and by taking them too much out of the context of the Gospel as a whole, and of its historical context.

a) As in Acts, so in John there are both neutral or national references to "the Jews" and also positive references. In the former category would certainly fall the regular references to Jewish customs and feasts (2:6,13; 4:9b; 5:1; 6:4; 7:2; 11:55; 19:40,42) as well as such phrases as "ruler/land/king/chief priests of the Jews" (3:1,22; 18:33,39; 19:3,19,21), to which should probably also be added 3:25 and 18:35[76]. Von Wahlde in focusing on the hostile references falls into the trap of designating only them (the hostile references) as "the Johannine use" =

---

[72] R. H. Fuller, "The 'Jews' in the Fourth Gospel", *Dialog* 16 (1977) 31–37, here 35; cited by R. H. Culpepper, "The Gospel of John and the Jews", *RevExp* 84 (1987) 273–88, here 284–5.

[73] R. Bultmann, *The Gospel of John* (Oxford: Blackwell, 1971) 86; N. A. Dahl, "The Johannine Church and History", *Current Issues in New Testament Interpretation*, ed. W. Klassen & G. F. Snyder (New York: Harper & Row, 1962) 129, 133–5, 139; A. Grässer, "Die antijüdische Polemik im Johannesevangelium", *NTS* 11 (1964–65) 74–90; Ruether (n. 4) 113–5; others in J. T. Townsend, "The Gospel of John and the Jews: The Story of a Religious Divorce", *Anti-Semitism* (n. 3) 72–97, here 92 n. 50.

[74] Ruether (n. 4) 116.

[75] Sandmel (n. 10) 101. See also particularly E. J. Epp, "Anti-Semitism and the Popularity of the Fourth Gospel in Christianity", *Central Conference of American Rabbis* 22 (1975) 33–57, cited by Beck (n. 16) 248.

[76] These do not indicate the standpoint of an "outsider"; the Bar Kochba letters speak in similar terms of the "citron festival of the Jews" – noted by Meeks (n. 26) 181 and n. 67.

the characteristic Johannine use or typical Johannine usage[77]. The choice of terms is understandable (given the weight of the hostile references), but nevertheless very misleading. When the neutral/national usage is as consistent and widespread as the above references indicate, it is simply wrong to exclude them from "the (typical/characteristic) Johannine use". They may be different from the other usage, they may be the result of John incorporating earlier tradition, but that does not make them any the less "Johannine". And any attempt to characterize John's perception of or attitude to "the Jews" must also take them into account. John is not so uniformly or unremittingly hostile to "the Jews" as a more selective choice of texts might seem to imply.

The point has even more force when we consider the more positive references. These are few in number when only the use of Ἰουδαῖος is considered, but they are nonetheless significant. Apart from Jews who believe in Jesus (to whom we shall return), there are the two references in ch. 4 – 4:9 (Jesus designated as "a Jew") and 4:22 (Jesus affirms, "Salvation is from the Jews")[78]. Again these should not be discounted as though the fact that John has (perhaps) taken them over from earlier tradition or an earlier version somehow makes them less "Johannine"[79]. An out-and-out anti-semite would hardly leave such references in his final version. So too the attitude to Jewish festivals and institutions (e. g. 7:10,37−8; 19:36) and to the law (as in 1:17,45; 5:45−7; 7:19,51; 15:25) is hardly hostile (in the case of law, far less than Paul). Of course there is the contrast between preparation and fulfilment (between water and wine, between temple and body of Christ, between water from Jacob's well and the living water of Christ, and so on), but that is more a claim from *within* Judaism (analogous to that of the Qumran covenanters) than a case of anti-Judaism. This too is part of the complete Johannine attitude to Jews and Judaism.

b) Von Wahlde focuses his discussion on the dispute as to whether the hostile references denote only and consistently "the Jewish authorities" or sometimes and occasionally "the Jewish/common people". His conclusion is that with the exception of 6:41 and 52, the hostile references to "the Jews" refer only to the authorities[80]. This result, however, follows directly from the methodological decision to distinguish the hostile references from the rest. In consequence of which, for example, 8:31 can be dismissed as "the work of a redactor" and 10:19, 11:54 and 18:20,21 be set aside as "neutral"[81]. But when we ignore the prejudicial distinction between "hostile" and "neutral" refer-

---

[77] Von Wahlde (n. 25) e. g. 36−7, 52−3.

[78] See particularly H. Thyen, "Das Heil kommt von den Juden", *Kirche. Festschrift für G. Bornkamm*, hrsg. D. Lührmann & G. Strecker (Tübingen: Mohr, 1980) 185−204.

[79] Cf. Ashton (n. 28) 49.

[80] Von Wahlde (n. 25) 54.

[81] *Ibid.* 50−3.

ences and simply read the text noting likely references to "the Jews" = the Jewish/common people, a much stronger motif emerges – 6:41,52; 7:11(?); 7:15; 7:35(?); 8:22,31; 10:19,24(?); 11:19,31,33,36,45,54; 12:9,11; 13:33(?); 18:20; 19:20–21.

More important is the fact that von Wahlde has ignored a major Johannine theme – one which C. H. Dodd brought to attention[82], and which links most of these references – the theme of κρίσις (3:19; 5:22,24,27,29,30; 7:24; 8:16; 12:31) and σχίσμα (7:43; 9:16; 10:19). The point is, as Dodd noted, that the Book of Signs (ch. 3–12) is constructed in order to bring out the divisive effect of Christ (1:11–13), the escalating process of separation (κρίσις) and division (σχίσμα) which was the inevitable effect of the light shining (3:19–21)[83]. Throughout the Book of Signs there is a sifting going on. Some are attracted and follow, like the disciples and the Samaritans. Others are repelled ("the Jews" = the authorities). But in the middle are the ambivalent crowd (also "the Jews") who cannot make up their mind. They also "follow" him (6:2) but remain confused throughout the bread of life discourse, and in the end "many of his disciples drew back and no longer went about with him" (6:66). Throughout ch. 7 "the Jews"/"the crowd"[84] debate back and forth the significance of Jesus, with many believing (7:31) or reaching a positive though inadequate verdict (7:40), but with others sceptical (7:35), and the end result "a division among the people" (7:43). In ch. 8 the process of sifting continues, the process occasioned by the shining of "the light of the world" (8:12), with continued debate among "the Jews", some believing (8:31) and others rejecting (8:48); and in ch. 9 the episode of the blind man receiving his sight becomes a further illustration and occasion for further division (9:16). In ch. 10 the process is maintained, with further "division among the Jews" (10:19–21)[85], with some rejecting (10:31–9)[86] and others (many) believing (10:41–2). In ch. 11 the references to "the Jews" are unusually positive (11:19,31,33,36,45), with the note of division clearly enunciated in 11:45–6: "many of the Jews . . . believed

---

[82] C. H. Dodd, *The Interpretation of the Fourth Gospel* (Cambridge University, 1960) particularly 352–3. Von Wahlde is not the only one open to this criticism. So also, e. g., C. J. A. Hickling, "Attitudes to Judaism in the Fourth Gospel", *L'Évangile de Jean. Sources, rédaction, theologie*, par M. de Jonge (BETL 44; Leuven University, 1977) 347–54; S. Freyne, "Vilifying the Other and Defining the Self: Matthew's and John's Anti-Jewish Polemic in Focus", *"To See Ourselves as Others See Us". Christians, Jews, "Others" in Late Antiquity*. ed. J. Neusner & E. Frerichs (Chico: Scholars, 1985) 117–43, here 117, 131.

[83] Cf. Culpepper (n. 72), who qualifies von Wahlde's argument by finding an escalation of conflict between Jesus and "the Jews", particularly from ch. 5 to ch. 12 (276–80).

[84] "The Jews" – 7:11,15,35; "the crowd" – 7:12,20,31–2,40,43.

[85] The weakness of von Wahlde's (n. 25) analysis is highlighted by his comment on 10:19: "The hostile Jews are nowhere divided in the FG" (51). On von Wahlde's definiton, the comment is tautologous.

[86] The fact that "the Jews" here and in 8:48–59 are part of the sifting/division motif raises the question as to whether these references also should not be referred to the crowd.

in him; but some of them went to the Pharisees . . .". Ch. 12 forms an effective climax, with "the crowd" again prominent (12:9,12,17,18,29,34), and once again a division between those Jews who believe (12:11) and bear witness to him (12:17−19) and those who refuse (12:37−40), and with the κρίσις process occasioned by the light continuing to the end (21:31−43).

All this is not to deny that many of the Johannine references to "the Jews" are best taken as indicating "the Jewish authorities", as most agree − 5:10,15,16,18; 7:1,13; 8:48,52,57(?); 9:18,22; 10:31,33 and 11:8(?), not to mention 18:12,14,31,36,38; 19:7,12,14,31,38; 20:19. But even in the passion narrative, where the hostile references are most intense, John preserves the memory that Jewish responsibility for Jesus' execution was largely confined to the high priestly party, as distinct from the Pharisees (the main representatives of the Jewish authorities of his own day)[87], and at the crucifixion the absence of any taunting by the crowd/people (such as we find in Matthew and Mark) actually softens and narrows the polemic against the Jews[88]. All in all, then, the motif focusing on "the Jews" is a good deal more complex than some have allowed, and the references to the hostile Jewish authorities have to be seen as only part of a larger plot[89].

c) The complexity of the motif is best explained by the historical situation confronting the Fourth Evangelist. There is a large scale consensus that John was writing at around the end of the first century, during the period when the rabbinic council at Yavneh, under the leadership first of Yohanan ben Zakkai and then Gamaliel II, began the process of rebuilding the nation round the Torah and of defining Judaism more carefully in face of other claimants to the heritage of second temple Judaism, including Christianity[90]. In these circumstances it is very likely that John's use of οἱ Ἰουδαῖοι = the Jewish authorities reflects the claim beginning to be made at that time by the Yavnean authorities

---

[87] After ch. 12 Pharisees are mentioned only at 18:3; contrast the prominence given to the high priests (particularly 18:3,35; 19:6,15,21).

[88] D. Granskou, "Anti-Judaism in the Passion Accounts of the Fourth Gospel", *Anti-Judaism Vol. 1* (n. 16) 201−16, here 214−5.

[89] On the striking absence of οἱ Ἰουδαῖοι from ch. 13−17 (13:33 hardly constitutes an exception), note Ashton's (n. 28) comment: "If after scrutinizing the role of the Jews in the Gospel you conclude that the evangelist intends to portray them not just as the adversaries of Jesus but as a continuing threat to the wellbeing of the community, then you are left with the task of explaining why all direct reference to the Jews is dropped as soon as the situation of the community becomes the specific focus of interest" (67). The answer may be that the Johannine community's self-identity was not dependent on its confrontation with "the Jews" (as 1. John certainly seems to imply), but that that confrontation was nevertheless part of its then and continuing history (as ch. 9 in particular implies).

[90] On Yavneh see particularly G. Alon, *The Jews in their Land in the Talmudic Age* Vol. 1 (Jerusalem: Magnes, 1980); P. Schäfer, "Die Sogenannte Synode von Jabne. Zur Trennung von Juden und Christen im ersten/zweiten Jh. n. Chr.", *Studien zur Geschichte und Theologie des rabbinischen Judentums* (Leiden: Brill, 1978) 45−64; J. Neusner, "The Formation of Rabbinic Judaism: Yavneh (Jamnia) from AD 70 to 100", *ANRW* II.19.2 (1979) 3−42.

to be the only legitimate heirs to pre-70 Judaism, to be, in fact "the Jews"[91]. At the same time, there were other (ethnic) Jews who must have been "caught in the middle", the heirs of the much more diverse forms of late second temple Judaism caught between the competing claims of Yavnean rabbis and others (already designated by Yavneh as *Minim*, heretics), including the believers in Jesus Messiah[92]. These will be "the Jews" = the ambivalent crowd, uncertain which competing claim to accept. As Martyn perceived, ch. 9 seems clearly to reflect the sort of pressures and uncertainties and hard decisions which confronted many ethnic Jews of that time[93].

If there is anything in this we can also say that John's usage indicates not so much a clear distancing of the Johannine congregation from "the Jews" (§ 3.2) as an acknowledgment of a dispute over the heritage of pre-70 Jewish religion – a dispute in which the believers in Messiah Jesus were in part involved and in part distant: in part involved as "the Jews" = the crowd indicates; in part distant, as indicated by the sharp antithesis between Jesus and "the Jews" = the religious authorities. Furthermore, since the process of κρίσις in John in the end results in the crowd eventually siding against Jesus (12:37–40)[94], we could say that John assumes that Christians are losing the battle, that "the Jews" = the crowd will side with "the Jews" = the authorities (the dominant usage in ch. 18–19) – that is, that the Yavnean authorities will succeed in imposing their definition of Judaism on the more diverse patterns (Judaisms) of the second temple period. To that extent John would be ceding the claim to the title 'Ιουδαῖος to the rabbis, and with it something of the claim to the heritage of post-exilic Judaism. But only something of that claim, if our earlier observations on the distinction between 'Ισραηλ(ίτης) and 'Ιουδαῖος (§ 3.4) are sound. In other words, John may be willing to cede the self-understanding of Judaism which largely comes to expression in the distinction of "Jew" from "Gentile", while continuing to claim that the true Israelite recognizes Jesus to be "king of Israel" (1:47,49). Moreover, John's handling of the passion narrative, noted above in (b), suggests a polemic more carefully directed against the Jewish authorities, with some hope still entertained regarding the crowd, not to mention those symbolized by Nicodemus (19:39)[95].

---

[91] Particularly influential has been J. L. Martyn, *History and Theology in the Fourth Gospel* (Nashville: Abingdon, 1968; revised 1979). See e.g. Meeks (n. 21) 183; Hickling (n. 82) 347; Freyne (n. 82) 125; D. M. Smith, "The Contribution of J. Louis Martyn to the Understanding of the Gospel of John", *The Conversation Continues. Studies in Paul and John. In Honor of J. L. Martyn*. ed. R. T. Fortna & B. R. Gaventa (Nashville: Abingdon, 1990), 275–94.

[92] For discussion of the *birkat-ha-minim* see particularly W. Horbury, "The Benediction of the *Minim* and Early Jewish-Christian Controversy", *JTS* 33 (1982) 19–61.

[93] Cf. Freyne (n. 82): "... the Pharisaic element is the one singled out as constituting the real opposition" (135; referring to 1:24; 3:1; 7:32,45,48; 9:16,40; 11:47,57; 18:3).

[94] The use of Isa 6:10 in 12:40 is thus closely parallel to that in Acts 28:26–7.

[95] On the ambivalent role and significance of Nicodemus see e.g. M. de Jonge, "Nicodemus and Jesus", *Jesus: Stranger from Heaven and Son of God* (Missoula: Scholars, 1977) 29–47; R.

This would also help explain why christology is such a make or break issue in the Fourth Gospel. For it was precisely the development of John's Wisdom/ Logos christology to the expression of Jesus as the incarnation of God which seems to have been the decisive last straw for the Yavnean authorities (reflected particularly in 5:18 and 10:33), Christian *minim* being adjudged in effect as guilty of the "two powers heresy" and of abandoning the unity of God[96]. In which case we may fairly deduce that it was the sharpness of rebuttal by the Yavnean authorities which lies behind the Fourth Evangelist's polemic against "the Jews". In the Fourth Gospel we overhear only one side of what was evidently a very acrimonious debate, a debate in which the two major strands emerging from second temple Judaism fought vigorously for the commitment and loyalty of the (other) Jews caught in the middle (20:31). For John the debate may have been lost at one level, but was still a debate within the bounds of pre-70 Judaism, and even though those boundaries were at that very time being redrawn more tightly by the Yavnean authorities to exclude John's understanding of "the way, the truth and the life", for John himself the issue was still in dispute[97]. In other words, although the parting of the ways is close at hand, John, in his own perspective at least, is still fighting a factional battle within Judaism rather than launching his arrows from without, still a Jew who believed that Jesus was Messiah, Son of God, rather than an anti-semite.

d) This suggests in turn that the dualism of John's polemic is a matter more of rhetoric than of calculated prejudice. It is true that κόσμος in John represents the world of humanity in its otherness from God and in its hostility to his Son (particularly 1:10c; 3:17b; 8:23; 12:31; 14:17,30; 15:18−19; 16:8,11,33; 17:6,9,14,16,25; 18:36), so that the implicit identification of "the Jews" with "the world" in ch. 8 intensifies the anti-Jewish polemic[98]. But this is all part of John's rhetorical schema devised to focus attention on Jesus. So, for example, he alone is "from above" (3:31; 8:23), they are "from below", "of this world" (8:23). But so also is Pilate's authority (19:11). And so also are Nicodemus, the secret believer (3:3,7,13), and John the Baptist, the model witness (3:31). By intensifying the focus on Jesus in this way, *any* or *all* other claimants to final or definitive revelation from God, not just "the Jews", are set in the shadow[99]. And since this christological claim is contested at this point chiefly by "the

E. Brown, *The Community of the Beloved Disciple* (London: Chapman, 1979) 72 n. 128; Freyne (n. 81) 127, 140; D. Rensberger, *Johannine Faith and Liberating Community* (Philadelphia: Westminster, 1988) ch. 2−3.

[96] See particularly J. D. G. Dunn, "Let John be John − A Gospel for its Time", *Das Evangelium und die Evangelien*, hrsg. P. Stuhlmacher (WUNT 28; Tübingen: J. C. B. Mohr, 1983) 309−39.

[97] *Pace* Townsend (n. 73) 81, 88.

[98] Cf. Granskou (n. 88) 204. Note however that the identification is only implicit. There is no formal identification of 'Ιουδαῖοι and κόσμος anywhere in the Gospel (Ashton [n. 28] 66).

[99] Granskou (n. 88) 209.

Jews" (the Yavnean authorities), it is they who bear the brunt of John's dualistic polemic. But it is not an ontological dualism, far less a dualism dividing Jews from others (they are all "from below", "of the flesh" – 1:13; 3:6; 8:15), rather a rhetorical dualism which intensifies the alternative in order to precipitate a decision (3:19–21; etc, again)[100].

More important, the dualism is a central part of John's salvation schema[101]. The dualism is deepened precisely in order to emphasize the scope of God's saving purpose through his Son. "The Word became flesh" (1:14), his flesh is given for the life of the world (6:51), and it is precisely by eating this flesh that life is received (6:53–6). God loves the world and gave his Son for it; the number of positive references to "the world" in this vein is striking (1:29; 3:16–17; 4:42; 6:33,51; 8:12; 9:5; 12:19), and the theme is particularly prominent in the conclusion to the Book of Signs (12:46–7). Although "his own" reject him (1:11), he also loves "his own" (13:1). And the fact that Jesus dies for "the people", as a necessity recognized by the High Priest, is given emphasis by being repeated (11:50; 18:14). Here again we can hardly speak of anti-semitism or even anti-Jewish polemic[102]. What lies behind these themes, as behind the whole treatment of "the Jews" is evidently a contest for the minds and hearts of the Jewish people, a contest which "the Jews" = the Yavnean authorities seem to be winning, but a contest which the Fourth Evangelist has not yet given up as lost[103].

5.3. All this suggests that there is a grave danger of misreading John's treatment of "the Jews". The danger is (1) of failing to appreciate the complexity of that treatment even when abstracted from the rest of the Gospel, (2) of failing to give enough attention to the historical context within which John was

---

[100] See e. g. J. H. Charlesworth, "A Critical Comparison of the Dualism in 1QS 3.13–4.26 and the 'Dualism' Contained in the Gospel of John", *John and Qumran*, ed. J. H. Charlesworth (London: Chapman, 1972) 76–106; and the brief review in R. Kysar, *The Fourth Evangelist and His Gospel. An Examination of Contemporary Scholarship* (Minneapolis: Augsburg, 1975) 215–21.

[101] Cf. Grässer (n. 73), who links the dualism to the κρίσις theme (85, 88–9) and sees the whole as put in service not to anti-semitism but to the practical concern of warning the Christian community itself against worldliness (Verweltlichung) (90).

[102] The point can be applied even to the fierce language of ch. 8 cited at the beginning. Cf. T. Dan. 5.6: "your prince is Satan" – "not an antisemitic but inner-Jewish invective" (Thoma [n. 10] 157).

[103] Cf. C. K. Barrett, *The Gospel of John and Judaism* (London: SPCK, 1975) 65–9: "the fact is that there was a continuing relation between Christianity and Judaism which involved both attraction and repulsion" (69); Ashton (n. 28) 74; Beck (n. 16) 249–51; Freyne (n. 82) 128. I therefore have some reservation about speaking of "Johannine sectarianism" (as in W. Meeks, "The Man from Heaven in Johannine Sectarianism", *JBL* 91 [1972] 44–72; and F. F. Segovia, "The Love and Hatred of Jesus and Johannine Sectarianism", *CBQ* 43 [1981] 258–72), which may not make enough allowance for the rhetoric of John's symbolism and may assume lines more sharply drawn than the setting of the Gospel within its historical context indicates.

writing and enough weight to the pressures under which he was writing, and (3) of failing to integrate that treatment into the Gospel as a whole, to appreciate the overall positive purpose of his portrayal, and to take account of the rhetoric he used to achieve that purpose. The problem of definition indicated at the beginning (§ 2) cannot be escaped even in John. The Fourth Evangelist is still operating within a context of intra-Jewish factional dispute, although the boundaries and definitions are themselves part of that dispute. It is clear beyond doubt that once the Fourth Gospel is removed from that context, and the constraints of that context, it was all too easily read as an anti-Jewish polemic and became a tool of anti-semitism. But it is highly questionable whether the Fourth Evangelist himself can fairly be indicted for either anti-Judaism or anti-semitism.

6. Is Matthew "anti-semitic"?

6.1. Matt 27:25 was one of the two texts cited at the beginning as having provided one of the most active roots of anti-semitism. And it has probably been used more than any other NT text to legitimate anti-semitism[104]. That text apart, however, Matthew appears to be much more virulently anti-Pharisaic (as we shall see in a moment) than anti-Jewish, far less anti-semitic. The polemic against the Pharisees in Matt 23, for example, becomes much more understandable within a context similar to that already indicated for John – that is, in a post-70 context when the most direct heirs of the Pharisees were attempting to define Judaism in their own terms, as most agree[105].

The issue, however, is more complex. In terms of the discussion as reviewed by Graham Stanton[106], the question needs to be posed thus: is Matthew a Jewish Christian writing (or the final redaction being completed) still *within* Judaism; or is his community *extra muros*, yet still defining itself over against Judaism; or is he a Gentile no longer arguing with contemporary Judaism? If the first of the three is the case, then anti-Judaism is an inappropriate description for the Gospel. But if either of the latter is true, then a verdict of anti-Judaism may be necessary. Among recent contributions, for example, Hare finds "strong evidence of gentilizing anti-Judaism" in Matthew[107]; Erwin Buck

---

[104] B. Przybylski, "The Setting of Matthean Anti-Judaism", *Anti-Judaism Vol. 1* (n. 16) 181–200, here 182, referring to C. Y. Glock & R. Stark, *Christian Beliefs and Anti-Semitism* (New York: Harper & Row, 1966) 197; also above n. 13.

[105] See e. g. G. D. Kilpatrick, *The Origins of the Gospel According to St Matthew* (Oxford: Clarendon, 1946) particularly 108–111; Meeks (n. 32) 109; W. D. Davies & D. C. Allison, *Matthew* (ICC; Edinburgh: T. & T. Clark; Vol. 1, 1988) 136–8.

[106] G. N. Stanton, "The Origin and Purpose of Matthew's Gospel. Matthean Scholarship from 1945 to 1980", *ANRW* II.25.3 (1985) 1890–1951, here 1910–21.

[107] Hare, *Anti-Semitism* (n. 17) 38, using the therefold distinction referred to in § 2 above.

speaks of "the pronounced anti-Judaism of Matthew"[108]; and Stanton continues to maintain the second of the three options outlined above, "Matthew's community has recently parted company with Judaism after a period of prolonged hostility"[109], although he thereby presupposes that "Judaism" was a sufficiently clearly defined entity and uncontested concept at that time, a presupposition we have been calling into question throughout the present essay. In contrast, Benno Przybylski finds that the evidence points to a "limited internal Jewish dispute" and that Matthew "has no anti-Semitic overtones"[110]. And Freyne sees Matthew, like John, engaging in vilification of Jewish opponents, but nevertheless operating with community concerns to define "an independent and exclusive place within Judaism"[111]. In such a case, where the debate is becoming narrowed to fine distinctions and disputed nuances, can anything more usefully be said or greater clarity achieved?

6.2. Przybylski covers most of the key matters and has made several of the main points which had occurred to me before I read his able study. It will probably suffice if I simply review briefly the main areas of discussion and add a few points of my own.

a) One important test case is provided by Matthew's references to the Pharisees and Sadducees. Georg Strecker in particular has argued that Matthew's portrayal of the Pharisees and Sadducees does not reflect his own situation in relation to Judaism but represents rather his own (unhistorical) view of the situation confronting Jesus during his ministry[112]. The implication is that this is not actual polemic against the Judaism of Matthew's time. On the contrary, Matthew writes as a Gentile Christian, within the context of a church already distinct from the synagogue[113]. But as Przybylski points out[114], the combination "Pharisees and Sadducees" appears in only two passages (Matt 3:7 and 16:1–12), albeit four (or five) times in the latter; and "Sadducees" appears on only one other occasion, and that on their own (22:23), the question about the resurrection, which certainly came to Matthew in the tradition (Mark 12:18). In contrast, the real objects of Matthew's attack are the Pharisees, or perhaps more accurately, the scribes and Pharisees. More to the point, several of the references to both are redactional or belong to Matthew's special material.

---

[108] E. Buck, "Anti-Judaic Sentiments in the Passion Narrative According to Matthew", *Anti-Judaism Vol. 1* (n. 16) 165–80, here 179.

[109] G. N. Stanton, "The Gospel of Matthew and Judaism", *BJRL* 66 (1984) 264–84, here 273.

[110] Przybylski (n. 104) 198–9.

[111] Freyne (n. 82) 140.

[112] G. Strecker, *Der Weg der Gerechtigkeit* (Göttingen: Vandenhoeck, ³1971) 140–1; see also J. P. Meier, *The Vision of Matthew. Christ, Church and Morality in the First Gospel* (New York: Paulist, 1979) 17–23.

[113] For others who hold variations of this view see Stanton (n. 106) 1916–20.

[114] Przybylski (n. 104) 187–90.

Occurrences of "Pharisee" in Matthew

	Matthew		Mark	Luke
Q	3:7*	(+ Sad*)		3:7
M	5:20	(+ Scr)		
Mk	9:11		= 2:16	5:30
Mk	9:14		= 2:18	5:33
M	9:34			
Mk	12:2		= 2:24	6:2
Mk	12:14		= 3:6	
Mk	12:24*		3:22	11:15
Q	12:38*	(+ Scr*)		11:29
Mk	15:1	(+ Scr)	7:1	
M	15:12			
Mk	16:1	(+ Sad*)	8:11	
Mk	16:6	(+ Sad*)	8:15	12:1
M	16:11	(+ Sad)		
M	16:12	(+ Sad)		
Mk	19:3		10:2	
M	21:45	(+ HP)		
Mk	22:15		12:13	
Mk	22:34*		12:28	
Mk	22:41*		12:35	
M	23:2	(+ Scr)		
Q	23:13*	(+ Scr)		11:52
M	23:15	(+ Scr)		
Q	23:23	(+ Scr*)		11:42
Q	23:25	(+ Scr*)		11:39
Q	23:26*			11:40
Q	23:27*	(+ Scr*)		11:44
Q	23:29*	(+ Scr*)		11:47
M	27:62	(+ HP)		

* = redactional   M = Matthew's special material   Scr = Scribes
Sad = Sadducees   HP = High Priests

The significance, of course, lies in adding the M passages to the passages marked with an asterisk. Particularly striking are two features. First, the fierceness of the polemic in ch. 23, against "scribes and Pharisees", where in every case Matthew has edited that tradition which we know of in other forms. And second, the introduction of the Pharisees to an active part in the trial before Pilate, whereas the other Synoptics retain the historical awareness that it was primarily the high-priestly faction who were involved in the proceedings against Jesus (above n. 63). All this suggests, *pace* Strecker, that Matthew's polemic has been determined in some measure at least by the situation confronting him and his community, and that the "scribes and Pharisees" are real opponents whom his readers would have no difficulty in recognizing. That is, most likely, the Yavnean authorities, who were the immediate heirs of the pre-70 Pharisees. Matthew's references to the Sadducees, on the other hand, are probably sufficiently explained if we say simply that they reflect part historical tradition (22:23) and part an attempted (albeit inaccurate)[115] historicizing of the tradition (3:7; 16:1−12) by Matthew. Such artificiality, however, need not signify complete ignorance on the part of Matthew (or that he therefore was a Gentile); simply an attempt by him to show that other pre-70 factions had also been a threat to Jesus and his teaching and not just the contemporary opponents (the Pharisees = rabbinic authorities).

b) Another possible indication of Gentile authorship, or at least of a Jewish Christian looking at Judaism "from outside", and who can therefore be categorized in terms of "anti-Judaism", is the appearance of the phrase "*their* synagogue(s)" (4:23; 9:35*; 10:17(M); 12:9*; 13:54*) in five of Matthew's nine references to "synagogues", four of them unique to Matthew (also 23:34* − "your synagogues"). Yet there is a danger of exaggerating the case here too. For "their" can be a quite natural adjective to describe something belonging to others, without necessarily implying a great distance between "theirs" and "ours". In other words, "their synagogues" may simply mean the synagogues of the people to whom Jesus was at that time ministering, as in Mark 1:23 and 1:39 (= Matt 4:23). And even where a more negative note enters (as in 10:17 and 23:34), "their synagogue" may denote simply *their* synagogue and not *ours*, rather than their (the Jews') *synagogues*[116]. This possibility is given support by several factors. (1) Matthew also speaks of "the synagogue" (6:2,5; 23:6), and precisely where he is comparing and contrasting the spirituality and behaviour of "the hypocrites" with the spirituality and conduct he seeks to inculcate within his own community[117]; note also 23:7−8 − the hypocrites "love to be called rabbis by others, but you are not to be called rabbi". This suggests not a set of completely antithetical values, but a set of shared practices, where antagonism is so fierce precisely because they are so close. (2) Matthew also speaks of "their scribes" (7:29); but in 8:19 and 23:34 scribes are portrayed in a positive

[115] Stanton (n. 106) 1919 quotes with approval the judgment of J. le Moyne, *Les Sadducéens* (EB; Paris: Gabalda, 1972): "c'est un assemblage artificiel qui ne représente pas la réalité historique" (123).

[116] Kilpatrick (n. 105) 110−1; R. Hummel, *Die Auseinandersetzung zwischen Kirche und Judentum im Matthäusevangelium* (München: Kaiser, 1966) 28−33; S. Brown, "The Matthean Community and the Gentile Mission", *NovT* 22 (1980) 193−221, here 216.

[117] Cf. Przybylski (n. 104) 193−5.

light, and the view has been long popular which sees in 13:52 Matthew's own description of *himself* and of the task he set himself in compiling his Gospel, or at least a reference to scribes in his own community[118]. This is a clear reminder that the redactional hostility to scribes indicated in the previous table is not a hostility to scribes as such, nor, therefore to Judaism as such. On the contrary, it is the conflict of two groups who share the same heritage (particularly the Torah – 5:17–20; 23:2–3) and style of teaching ("binding and loosing" – 16:19 and 18:18; the rabbinic-style treatment of 19:3–9); and *that* is why their mutual hostility is so fierce[119]. (3) It is also important to recall that Matthew alone of the Evangelists uses ἐκκλησία (16:18; 18:17), and that behind it lies the familiar OT concept of the קהל ישראל, "the congregation of Israel". In other words, we see a claim that the Matthean community represents the eschatological people of God (cf. also Matt 19:28). This is certainly a claim from within the heritage of second temple Judaism (cf. § 3.4), not from "outside". And though that claim would no doubt have been contested by "their scribes" (and Pharisees), and though his claim invites an antithesis between "church" and "synagogue", the implication of the self-definition of Matthew's own community is clear enough.

c) A good deal can be made of the passages which seem to indicate that the Jewish people as a whole have been rejected by God – particularly 8:11–12, 21:43, 22:7–8 and 23:37–9[120]. But is their message so clear? (1) The last two references are more readily understandable as allusions to the catastrophe of AD 70 than as a rejection of the people as such. (2) In the first (8:11–12), the reference to "the sons of the kingdom" is reminiscent of the factional claims by earlier groups within Judaism to be the true heirs of God's covenant ("the righteous" as "God's son" – WisSol 2:18; "sons of the covenant" – PssSol 17:15 and 1QM 17.8); and the warning itself is reminiscent of that given by Amos 9:7–8 and John the Baptist (Matt 3:9) – in other words, of a piece with intra-Jewish factionalism and prophetic foreboding. Here also to be noted is the fact that the denunciations in Matt 23 directed against the scribes and Pharisees are elsewhere in Matthew directed against the disciples themselves[121], indicating that this is the style of minatory exhortation aimed at those who probably share

---

[118] Cf. now Przybylski (n. 104) 190–1.

[119] See further Freyne (n. 82) 119–23, 132–4.

[120] So particularly Hare (n. 17) 38–40; and earlier, D. R. A. Hare, *The Theme of Jewish Persecution of Christians in the Gospel according to St. Matthew* (SNTSMS 6; Cambridge University, 1976) 152–6. "More than any other Gospel, Matthew emphasizes the utter rejection of Israel" – L. Gaston, "The Messiah of Israel as Teacher of the Gentiles. The Setting of Matthew's Christology", *Interpreting the Gospels*, ed. J. L. Mays (Philadelphia: Fortress, 1981) 78–96, here 87.

[121] S. Légasse, "L'antijudaisme dans l'Évangile selon Matthieu", *L'Évangile selon Matthieu. Rédaction et Théologie*, par M. Didier (BETL 29; Leuven University, 1972) 417–28, here 426; E. Schweizer, *The Good News according to Matthew* (London: SPCK, 1976) 464; D. Garland, *The Intention of Matthew 23* (NovTSup; Leiden: Brill, 1979) particularly 121–3; Freyne (n. 82) 137–9, table on 143.

both the heritage of the Pharisees and its dangers. (3) The use of the singular in the second passage (21:43 – "the kingdom of God will be taken away from you and given to a nation producing the fruits of it"), rather than "nations" = Gentiles (Matthew's regular use elsewhere), makes the point less than clear cut. Had a complete rejection of the Jewish people been intended we would have expected the normal antithesis (Gentiles = non-Jews as a whole, or as a category), but the reference of ἔθνος (singular) in 21:43 is at best uncertain[122]. Perhaps then it is significant that Matthew retains Mark's note that the audience recognized that the parable was spoken against them (Mark 12:12) and identifies the audience on this occasion as "the chief priests and the Pharisees" (Matt 21:45). In other words, Matthew intends the warning of 21:43 primarily for the leaders of the people. Which suggests in turn that there is something in the view that Matthew wanted to portray the crowds as much more sympathetic to Jesus than their leaders[123].

d) This brings us finally to the infamous Matt 27:25, where we started. But even here Matthew's "anti-Judaism" needs much more careful statement than it usually receives. (1) Matthew's use of λαός. The negative force of 27:25 ("all the people") is unsurpassed in Matthew. However it is paralleled at least in some measure by 13:15 and 15:8, both of them in quotations from Isa (13:15 = Isa 6:10; 15:8 = Isa 29:13). In other words, the other negative references to "the people" in Matthew belong, once again, to the category of prophetic polemic and warning. They also have to be set alongside the more positive references: 1:21 – Jesus "will save his people from their sins"; 4:23 – Jesus "was healing every disease and every malady within the people"; and 26:5 – the chief priests decided to arrest Jesus "not during the feast, lest there be a tumult among the people". In many ways the most striking of all is 27:64: the chief priests and (NB) the Pharisees ask Pilate to secure Jesus' tomb lest his disciples steal the body and "tell the people, 'He has risen from the dead', and the last fraud will be worse than the first". Here the distinction between leaders (including Pharisees) and people is clear. And, more notable still, "the chief priests and the Pharisees" fear lest the gospel of Jesus' resurrection will find favour with "the people". That is to say, even after 27:25, "the people" may still be won to the gospel, and are an object of competition between the Pharisees and the bearers of the resurrection message. (2) Related to this is one use of "Jews"

[122] J. P. Meier, "Nations or Gentiles in Matthew 28:19", *CBQ* 39 (1977) 94–102, argues that in 21:43 ἔθνος must mean "the new people of God . . . made up of both Jews and Gentiles" (97); cf. Stanton (n. 109) 269, 275.

[123] S. van Tilborg, *The Jewish Leaders in Matthew* (Leiden: Brill, 1972) 142–65. Matt 10:23 fits quite readily within this scenario, especially when set within the whole discourse, including 10:11–13 and 40–2; as does Matt 23:34, addressed to "scribes and Pharisees" (*pace* E. Schweizer, *Matthäus und seine Gemeinde* [SBS 71; Stuttgart: KBW, 1974] 11–12, 36–7).

which seems to parallel John's more extensive negative usage – Matt 28:15[124]. But even that is an overstatement. Ἰουδαῖοι here is anarthrous: the story (of Jesus' body being stolen while the guard slept) has been spread among Jews in general (not "the Jews"). The reference, in other words, is purely descriptive, and hardly different, for example, from the typical usage of Josephus described in §3 above. One who was himself a Jew and who still hoped to counter that story among his own people would hardly have spoken otherwise. (3) It should not be assumed that the self-indictment of 27:25, "His blood be on us and on our children", was so sweeping and comprehensive as has often been inferred (all Jews then and thereafter). The most closely related of Matthew's other uses of τέκνα imply a more limited scope (2:18; 3:9; 15:26; 23:37). And no Jewish reader could fail to recall the much tougher and more far-reaching terms laid down in one of the central statements of the covenant – "visiting the iniquity of the fathers upon the children and the children's children, to the third and fourth generation" (Ex 20:5; 34:7; Num 14:18; Deut 5:9)[125]. In other words, even Matt 27:25 can be ranked as an intra-covenant statement, milder in its force than the classical warnings of the covenant contract, and so also holding out (by implication) the classical, covenant hope of restoration for those who experienced the curses of the covenant but who returned to the Lord their God, they and their children (Deut 30:1 ff.)[126].

6.3. In the debate as to whether Matthew is writing *intra muros* or *extra muros*, therefore, the evidence on the whole seems to favour the former. The parting of the ways has not yet taken place. No doubt Matthew's opponents and the opponents of Matthew's community (the Pharisees and "their scribes") regarded them as "outsiders", meaning outside the walls of (Yavnean) Judaism. But Matthew still speaks as an "insider" and is attempting to portray a Jesus who would be attractive to others who also considered themselves "insiders". In other words, once again we seem to find ourselves confronted with the situation where the narrowing channels of rabbinic Judaism and Christianity respectively were still in competition for the head waters flowing from the broader channels of second temple Judaism[127]. In which case, once again, the

---

[124] Stanton (n. 106) 1914 – "a thoroughly Johannine way" which "seems to indicate that the Matthean community saw itself as a separate and quite distinct entity over against Judaism".

[125] D. Senior, *The Passion Narrative according to Matthew. A Redactional Study* (BETL 39; Leuven University, 1975), notes the absence of a "forever" clause, in contrast e.g. to 1. Kings 2:33 (260). He also points out, however, how difficult it is to read ὁ λαός as a reference simply to the crowd as distinct from the Jewish nation (258–9).

[126] T. B. Cargal, "'His Blood be Upon Us and Upon our Children': A Matthean Double Entendre?", *NTS* 37 (1991) 101–12, suggests the possibility that Matthew intended a play on the only other reference to "blood" in the Gospel (26.28), implying the hope of forgiveness for "the people", echoing Deut 21.8 (110–12).

[127] J. A. Overman, *Matthew's Gospel and Formative Judaism. The Social World of the Matthean Community* (Minneapolis: Fortress, 1990), reaches the same conclusion; see particularly 141–61.

charge of anti-semitism or anti-Judaism against Matthew has either to be dismissed or to be so redefined within its historical context as to lose most of its potential as justification for the anti-semitism of later centuries.

7. Conclusions

7.1. The main effect of the present study has been to reinforce the impression that each of the writings examined above was composed within a period when the character of what we have to call "Judaism" (or Judaisms) was under dispute and its boundaries in process of being redrawn. All three certainly reflect the fact that the bulk of the Jewish people had (so far) rejected the message of Jesus the Christ. All three reflect the puzzlement, hurt, and, yes, anger which that rejection provoked. But they still write as those for whom the issue is not closed. The case may already have been lost so far as the rabbinic authorities of Yavneh were concerned; and lost in historical fact, as we can see with the benefit of hindsight, since the rabbinic sages in the event were able to extend their authority over the rest of the Jews. But at the period under discussion (AD 70-135) they were by no means the only Jews. And they did not succeed in establishing their authority over the other Jews as quickly as is often assumed[128]. For Luke, John and Matthew, the match was not over; all was still to play for. Judaism was not yet solely rabbinic Judaism. Christian Judaism was not yet simply Christianity. Others may be building the walls in a tighter circle round the Torah. But Matthew, John and even Luke still see themselves as within the older walls of the Judaism of Jesus' time[129].

7.2. Most, if not all of the polemic in these three writings has the character and the intensity of sibling rivalry – able to be so hurtful, because the weak points are so well known; having to be so dismissive, in order to establish their own identity in distinction from the other. But there is at least something also of prophetic critique in the polemic. For example, Matthew's rebuke of "an evil and adulterous generation" (12:39; 16:4) has strong echoes of Ezek 23 and Hos 3:1, not to mention James 4:4. And the fact that Stephen's denunciation in Acts 7:51–3 deliberately draws on OT language is well known (Ex 33:3,5; Lev 26:41; Num 27:14; Isa 63:10; Jer 6:10; 9:26). There is a robustness in all this which Englightenment liberalism finds profoundly disturbing. In the more sensitive, sophisticated and mild-mannered present, not only an Inquisition's treatments

---

[128] See particularly the caution of Alon and Schäfer on this point (n. 90), and Alexander above.

[129] Meeks (n. 32) makes the interesting observation that whereas Christianity seems to have expanded chiefly in the cities of the ancient world, "the living Judaism that survived . . . seems rather to have been a rural and small-town phenomenon. Thus the massive, confrontation between 'apostolic Christianity' and 'normative Judaism', which even now haunts the imagination of students of Christian origins, never happened" (115).

of heretics, or a Calvin's burning of Servetus disturbs and offends. But also the bluntness of a prophet's denunciation of unfaithfulness, or Jesus' rebuke of Peter as "Satan", or Paul's similar denunciation of other "apostles of Christ" in 2. Cor 11. We should beware of reading such language with pedantic literalism, not least because we hear only one side of the several arguments involved. We should certainly be slow to let our own sensitivities dictate a verdict of anti-Judaism or anti-semitism on those whose world of discourse was so very different from our own.

7.3. We have not looked closely at the issue raised by Ruether as to whether Christian claims for Christ carried with them an inevitable anti-Jewish corollary (§ 1). Certainly the issue in the case of Matthew and John at least is christologically determined. But in neither is it a straightforward case of christocentrism opposed to Torah-centrism. It is not Christ against "Judaism". But Christ within (second temple) Judaism, as the climax of the heritage enshrined in the Jewish scriptures; and it is by no means clear in any of the three cases that in order to be a Christian, a Jew has to cease being a Jew or to abandon the Torah. Indeed, to focus the issue on christology may be to misconceive the debate of that period and to force it too quickly into the later exclusivism of the fourth century. In the late first century and early second century the question was much more *theo*logical, as the issue of how the one God had most clearly revealed his will and effected his saving purpose. And that was still a debate about relativities (Christ more than Torah) than of complete and mutually exclusive opposites[130].

7.4. The question still remains: what to do with scriptures which, whatever their original context and interest, have fed and provoked anti-semitism down through the centuries. Some advocate radical surgery, to remove the most offensive passages, by "sensitive interpretative translation", or by putting them into footnotes, or by excising them from church lectionaries[131]. But this is no answer and quickly becomes as manipulative as the abuses it seeks to avoid, obscuring the historical reality embodied in these texts just as much as those who read them too literally. The answer is not to run away from our historical roots and the hurt of the earliest "parting of the ways", but to enter more fully into it, to understand it afresh "from inside" so far as that is possible, and to re-evaluate the whole period and its outworkings in company with those who also regret that parting.

---

[130] See now my *The Partings of the Ways* (London: SCM/Philadelphia: TPI, 1991) chs. 9–11.

[131] Particularly Beck (n. 16); but also Gaston (n. 120) 95; Hare (n. 17) 43 in the same connection mentions D. D. Runes, *The Gospel According to St John* (New York: Philosophical Library, 1967) v–vi.

The Parting of the Ways: the Evidence of Jewish and Christian Apocalyptic and Mystical Material

by

CHRISTOPHER ROWLAND

There is now a widespread recognition that apocalypticism played an important part in the emergence and maintenance of the earliest Christian communities[1] and that it may well have been a more influential force in nascent rabbinic Judaism than has often been allowed. What I shall attempt in this paper is a descriptive analysis of some of the main witnesses to the apocaplytic tradition and a summary statement of the evidence for a mystical tradition in rabbinic Judaism. While my concern by and large will be the apocalypses, I have included for reasons of comparison some account of eschatological material from the synoptic gospels and a brief survey of the indebtedness of the Fourth Gospel to this world of thought. I have confined myself to apocalyptic material mainly (by which I refer to those works which purport to offer visions and revelations of the world beyond or from agents who come from that world). Although my prime interest is with visionary material, I have not included all the eschatological material from the period, except, where, as I have already indicated, there are reasons for so doing in order to illustrate how similar concerns emerge in the way in which eschatological discourse functions within early Christian paraenesis. I accept Martin Hengel's summary of apocalyptic as 'higher wisdom through revelation'[2] and consider that eschatology can frequently be part of the *content* of that revelation but does not define its character. With the possible exception of Revelation we have no certain way of knowing who wrote these texts nor can we be sure whether claims of visions played as significant role in determining attitudes within late first century Judaism. If the evidence of the New Testament is anything to go by, however, it probably did[3]. As such it is likely that attention should be devoted to the way in which such claims could butress or undermine established practices. Certainly

---

[1] See C. Rowland, *The Open Heaven,* London 1982, W. Meeks in D. Hellholm, *Apocalypticism in the Mediterranean World,* Tübingen 1983 and J. Collins, *The Apocalyptic Imagination,* New York 198.

[2] M. Hengel, *Judaism and Hellenism,* London 1974 vol. i, p. 210.

[3] Rowland op. cit. pp. 358 ff.

when we get to the second century the appearance of the apocalyptic genre among the gnostic texts suggests that it provided a literary support for special interests[4] which may well have conflicted substantially with emerging orthodoxy. As such claim to visionary authority could play an important role in determining the shape of a movement and justifying its assumptions.

The concerns of this essay are as follows:

(i) What form were Christians and Jews giving to their apocalyptic tradition at the end of the first century?

(ii) Was apocalyptic material marginal or central in the parting of the ways between Church and Synagogue[5]?

(iii) What developments in form and content can one note in comparison with earlier examples of the apocalyptic tradition (e. g. 1. Enoch)?

iv) Apocalyptic was a vehicle of hope and offers an important witness to the shape of that hope in the non-rabbinic writings of Judaism. That being the case, where does the apocalyptic enthisiasm (in the form of visions, prophecy) fit into the process of routinisation and in emerging rabbinic Judaism with its tighter boundaries? Did apocalyptic offer a means of challenging or supporting established conventions? Did it offer a vehicle to indulge in speculative interest or was its concern for the future in the main determinative of present responsibilities?

This paper starts with an examination of Revelation and contemporary apocalypses, 4. Ezra, the Syriac Apocalypse of Baruch and the Apocalypse of Abraham and then moves on to a consideration of evidence for mystical ideas within late first century tannaitic Judaism, the Fourth Gospel and the Apocalyptic and Mystical Tradition; a comparative study of the synoptic eschatological discourses; and apocalyptic as a recource for dealing with the lack of eschatological fulfilment.

The Apocalypse

The Apocalypse[6] sets out to reveal things as they really are in both the life of the Christian communities and the world at large. For the powerful and the complacent it has a message of judgement and doom, whereas for the powerless and oppressed it offers hope and vindication. The critique of the present is effected by the use of a contrast between the glories of the future and the inadequacies of the present. The process of unveiling the true nature of things involves an

---

[4] See I. Gruenwald in J. Dan and F. Talmage, *Studies in Jewish Mysticism*, Cambridge Mass. 1982.

[5] See P. R. Davies, 'The social world of the apocalyptic writings' in R. E. Clements *The World of Ancient Israel*, Cambridge 1989.

[6] C. Rowland, *Radical Christianity*, Oxford 1988, pp. 66ff.

attempt to delineate the real character of contemporary society and the super-human forces at work in the opposition to God's righteousness in the world. Revelation seeks to persuade its readers that the present moment is a time of critical importance. The outline of future history is offered as the basis for a change of heart to engage the whole of life which will have drastic consequences for the one who reads it. Acceptance or rejection of its message is nothing less than the difference between alignment with the reign of God which is to come or sharing the extinction of all that is opposed to God.

The Apocalypse can remind readers of early Christian literature that the hope for a reign of God on earth, when injustice and oppression will be swept away and the structures of an evil society broken down, is an important component of the Christian gospel. Rev. offers canonical justification for the cosmic and historical context[7] of divine activity. The Book of Revelation has provided encouragement for all those who look for the fulfilment of God's righteousness in human history. It would have been easy for the early Christians to have capitulated to their feelings of political powerlessness by concentration on individual holiness only. The Apocalypse does not easily allow a retreat into the religious world, for it persuades the saints to prophesy before the world about the righteousness of God and the dreadful consequences of ignoring its implementation.

The central theological theme of the book is the overcoming of opposition between God and earth[8]. In this respect the contrast between the vision of the new Jerusalem in ch. 21 with the initial vision of the heavenly court in ch. 4 also should be noted. In Rev 4 the seer is granted a glimpse into the environs of God. Here God the Creator and Libertor is acknowledged, and, as we notice from the following chapter, it is from the God of the universe that the historical process begins which leads to the establishment of a new aeon after the manifestation of divine judgement. In Rev 4 ff. God is still in heaven, and it is there that the heavenly host sing his praise and magnify his name. There is a contrast with Rev 21 where God's dwelling is on earth; it is no longer in heaven. This contrast between heaven and earth disappears in the new creation. Now the tabernacling of God is with humanity, and they shall be God's people. It is only in the new Age that there will be the conditions fo God and humanity to dwell in that harmony which was impossible while there was rejection of the

---

[7] On the widespread use of chiliastic ideas in early Christian theology see J. Daniélou, *The Theology of Jewish Christianity*, London 1964 and on their mutation G. Bonner 'Augustine and Millenarianism' in ed. R. D. Williams *The Making of Orthodoxy*, Cambridge 1989. It is interesting to compare Rev with 4. Ezra where the eschatological hope hardly alters the extreme pessimism of the dialogues. Rev offers a more coherent eschatological message in which Rev 21 is more intimately related to the earlier chapters than 4. Ezra 13 is to what precedes it.

[8] See also P. Minear, 'The Cosmology of the Apocalypse' in W. Klassen and G. Snyder *Current Issues in New Testament Interpretation*, New York 1962, pp. 23 ff.

divine righteousness in human affairs. In the apocalyptic vision, therefore, the contradictions of a fractured existence are resolved in the harmony offered by the apocalyptic text. What seems impossible in the real world of social contradictions is overcome in literary form. In the chapters following 4—5 we find the picture of a world afflicted but unrepentant, indeed, manifesting precisely the kind of misguided devotion to evil which has to be rooted out before God's kingdom can finally come.

Apocalyptic writers were convinced that this divine immanence was reserved solely for the New Age, however. The glory which the apocalyptic seer enjoyed in his revelation was a matter of living experience here and now for those who confessed Jesus as messiah and participated in the eschatological spirit. Already those who possessed the spirit of God were sons and daugthers of God; already those in Christ were a new creation and a Temple of the divine spirit (cf. 1. Cor 6.13). That hope for the final resolution of the contrast between heaven and earth was already perceived by those who had eyes to see and know it.

The role of the follower of the messiah is not quiet resignation, therefore. In the unfolding eschatological drama in the main body of the apocalypse the involvement of the seer in chapter 10 when he is instructed to eat the scroll and commanded to prophesy is a direct call to participate actively as a prophet rather than merely be a passive spectator of it. Revelation is insistent that the role of the martyr or witness is of central importance. That will involve suffering in the great tribulation, but those who join the messianic throng are those 'who have washed their robes and made them white in the blood of the Lamb'. In ch. 11 the church is offered a paradigm of the true prophetic witness as it sets out to fulfil its vocation to prophesy before the world. Utilising the figures of Moses and Elijah that prophetic witness takes place in a social scene opposed to God where that witness must take place even though it ends up with martyrdom.

The readers of the letters to the seven churches are not allowed to indulge their curiosity about future bliss. They are brought face to face with the obstacles which stand in the way of its fulfilment and the costly part to be played by them in that process. Revelation differs from utopian programmes in the absence in it of any detailed acount of the construction of the ideal, eschatological world. Such accounts of ideal worlds can distract from the demands of the present by distracting the reader's attention on the here and now (though, of course, that need not be the case). So utopianism can lead to an escape from reality however much its attempts betoken that yearning for something better[9]. Writers who resort to utopianism often do so as a compensation for the inability to do anything about the world as it is[10]. The demands for present obedience are

---

[9] On utopianism see the survey in B. Goodwin and K. Taylor, *The Politics of Utopia*, London 1982.

[10] See Rowland, *Radical Christianity*, pp. 112—114 and V. Geoghegan *Marxism and Utopianism*, London 1987.

evident in the letters to the churches which introduce the vision of hope and in the concluding admonitions which stress the authority of the text. The book of Revelation offers a timely reminder in its own form about supposing that its preoccupation with eschatological matters offers an opportunity to avoid the more challenging preoccupations of the present. Thus, the vision of hope inaugurated by the exaltation of the Lamb is set within the framework of the Letters of the Seven Churches. The promise of a part in the New Jerusalem is linked with present behaviour.

There are features which suggest that we have a text here which is resisting compromise and accommodation[11] and advocating keeping alive the spirit of Jesus and the apostles in faith and practice by an advocacy of a critical distance from contemporary culture in the character of social relations and the language of its religious discourse. Let me offer some examples.

Firstly, the invective against complacency in the Letters to the Churches has been interpreted as an indication of growing laxity and lack of rigour. The concern for holiness in Jewish culture was tied up with the maintenance of an alternative culture over against the nations. This can be seen in the repudiation of idolatry, the food laws, circumcision and sabbath observance. Likewise the call to martyrdom indicates the need for resistance, even if that means non-participation in the Roman economic system. One of the prime issues in the letters to the seven churches is 'eating food sacrificed to idols', and 'immorality', almost certainly a reference to idolatry (2.14 and 2.20). The strictures against those who recommend eating food sacrificed to idols indicates the need to create some distance between the conduct of Christians and the typical behaviour of society[12]. The references to idolatry and immorality in these passage are to be understood as in the tradition of the concern for holiness, that distinctive pattern of life over against the nations: 'it shall not be so with you ... (Mk 10.43)'[13]. There is a challenge to the assumption that the disciple is going to be able to take part without too much comfort in the social intercourse of the contemporary world.

Secondly, for Rev. the spirit and prophecy have a central role as they were to have in the Montanist movement[14] a century later. By the prophecy was viewed with suspicion, so much so that Rev's place as part of the canon was challenged. Ambivalence with regard to prophecy has always characterised religion[15]. Rev stands out against those who would quench the spirit and despise prophecy.

[11] See K. Wengst, *Pax Romana and the Peace of Jesus Christ*, London 1987, p. 133f.

[12] A. Y. Collins, 'The Political Perspective of the Revelation to John', *Journal of Biblical Literature* 96 (1977) pp. 44ff.

[13] On holiness see J. H. Yoder, *The Priestly Kingdom*, Notre Dame 1984.

[14] On Montanism see Rowland *Open Heaven*, pp. 392ff.

[15] On the phenomenon of prophecy in the ancient world and early Christianity see D. Aune, *Prophecy in Early Christianity and the Ancient Mediterranean World*, Grand Rapids 1983.

Indeed, it is arguable that one of the most distinctive features of its theology over against, say, 4. Ezra, where the eschatological spirit is not active in the communty of the elect, is its pneumatology. As with the messianic/chiliastic/ apocalyptic tradition, prophecy was too deeply-rooted in the Christian memory to be allowed to be anathematized, so that other ways had to be found to domesticate it. So the book of Revelation, written either in the 60's or 90's, keeps alive apocalyptic ideas in circumstances where we might expect something more sober. It is a testimony to the pervasiveness of apocalyptic in early christianity that at a time when stability seemed to be required its voice speaks in a different tone from the religion of convention and consolidation.

A question might be raised about the extent to which the form apocalyptic took in this early christian example contributed to tension between emerging Judaism and Christianity. The presentation of God's throne *is* different from other examples: Rev 5 and 7 have the Lamb sharing it with God. Whether passages like Rev 5.12 and 7.10 would have been impossible theologically for nascent rabbinic Judaism is unclear[16].

Finally, the apocalyptic imagery and cosmology itself betokens a view of the world where protest and resistance to compromise are the order of the day. The dualistic cosmology encouraged a separatist mentality. Even the language and syntax of Rev refuse to conform to established convention. It demands of the reader that s/he is open to the darker side of the world. The eschatological horizon with its alternative to the present order show up the discredited social processes of the present in the starkest possible relief. It was not just a case of relativising the world order in the light of the glory of the City of God, for it also involved revealing that the power behind the structures was diabolical and exposing its concerns as oppressive. There is little room for accommodation with the Beast and Babylon. Now all this not to suggest that the apocalyptic outlook could not be 'appropriated and neutralised' by its incorporation into the dominant ideology[17]. Clearly that did happen to some extent, not least by its incorporation into the canon. But it was a difficult process, for such subversive ideas could never be completely tamed.

---

[16] See R. Bauckham, 'The Worship of Jesus in Apocalyptic Christianity', *New Testament Studies*, L. Hurtado, *One God One Lord*, Philadelphia 1987, A. Segal, *Two Powers in Heaven*, Leiden 1978. It always strikes me as significant that Christ is symbolized in Rev generally as a Lamb in Rev and only in 1.13 ff. is there a description in angelomorphic terms. It is thus possible that the use of the symbol of the Lamb as the way of expressing God's messianic activity is a way of *reducing* the threat to monotheism implicit in a human figure sharing God's throne and sovereignty.

[17] See Frederic Jameson, *The Political Unconscious*, London 1981.

4 Ezra, Syriac Baruch and the Apocalypse of Abraham[18]

These apocalypses which are usually dated to round about the end of the first century CE offer contrasting attitudes in their form and content. There is similarity of outlook in the first two which have led some to suppose some kind of literary relationship between them. The Apocalypse of Abraham stands apart from the other two in its use of a traditional heavenly ascent pattern which includes a vision of God as well as the usual eschatological concerns. The only area in which it overlaps to any significant extent with the other two is in its preoccupation with issues of theodicy[19]: why does God allow Israel to suffer, a matter which is covered with varying degrees of sophistication in the other two.

In 4. Ezra eschatological beliefs make their appearance (e. g. 4.37 ff.; 6.18 ff.; 7.28 ff. and 13). What is interesting about the eschatology of 4. Ezra are the signs that there emerges here, possibly for the first time in such an explicit form, evidence for a hope for a new age which is transcendent. It appears, however, *alongside* the conventional hope for a thisworldly reign of God (7.28 f. cf. 5.45). In this it parallels Rev where the vision of the new heaven and new earth is preceded by the millenial mesianic reign. This juxtaposition has led some commentators to suppose that there is evidence of a later editorial addition. Much more likely is that this particular pattern represents a significant development of late first century eschatology when political despair may have contributed to the emergence of a transcendent eschatology alongside the hope for a messsianic kingdom on earth.

These concerns are eclipsed by the other concern: the evil of humanity, the wrestling with the apparent merciless character of the divine purposes and human fraility in the face of God's inscrutability. Throughout the book there is a consistent attempt at theodicy. Israel is oppressed and yet is the elect of God (3.30). Even biblical traditions are subjected to questioning and shown to be irrelevant to the eschatological concerns which should occupy the attention of the righteous (7.102 f.). There is a concern for the majority of humanity whose unrighteousness seems to be about to consign them to perdition (7.62 ff.). At times it appears that Ezra's concerns are more merciful than the divine reply. Such sentiments, however, are dealt with by urging the righteous to concentrate on the glory which awaits those who are obedient to God (8.52; 9.13). God's patience is not for the sake of humanity but because of faithfulness to the eternal plan which is laid down before creation (7.74). What the righteous need

---

[18] On 4. Ezra and Syr. Baruch see W. Harnisch, *Verhängnis und Verheißung der Geschichte*, Göttingen 1969. We need to recognise that we have these apocalypses extant only in translations. Certainty with regard to a late first century date must, therefore, be out of the question.

[19] On this theme see A. L. Thompson, *Responsibility for Evil in the Theodicy of 4. Ezra*, Missoula 1977.

to do is to view all things *sub specie aeternitatis* rather than concentrate exclusively on the apparent injustices of the present (7.16). Throughout, the ways of God are vindicated. God is the one who orders the times and the seasons and alone will bring the new age about (6.5). God is most high (a title occurring over sixty times throughout the work), and seemingly indifferent to the terrible fate awaiting most of humanity. Just as in the book of Job where the divine answer contrasts human and divine wisdom, so here too the impossibility of understanding the divine purposes in the midst of the old order is stressed (4.1ff.; 4.21; 5.36)[20].

Ezra longs for the righteousness of the holy to be taken into account when God judges Israel (8.27), but even here the sense of solidarity with the people disappear. Instead there emerges a pervasive individualism in which the righteous are urged to attend to their destiny and desist from understanding matters which are too hard for them even when they seem to contradict all the characteristics of justice and mercy. What is important is obedience to the law of God. The divine law must be vindicated whatever else happens (7.19; 9.37). Few will be saved (8.3), and it is necessary to choose now (7.129) so that the fate which awaits the bulk of humanity can be avoided (7.129).

The problem with humanity is that is has continued to sin even though God has endowed it with understanding (cf. Rev. 9.20). What emerges in the work is a perceptive understanding of the pervasiveness of evil which makes difficult the attempts of men and women to fulfil the divine command. There is free will (3.8; 8.50f.), but Adam's sin has had devastating effects (3.20; 4.30; 7.118). Even so, Ezra can justly wonder why God does not give any further assistance to enable that obedience which is required (3.20). Of course, for those who persevere the message is not gloomy. A blessed place is reserved for the fortunate few who endure to the end and are saved.

In Syriac Baruch there is a more obvious concern with the destruction of Jerusalem (the fictitious setting is of the eve of the fall of Solomon's temple). The reader is left in little doubt that this destruction is not only ordained by God but carried out with God's active participation (ch. 3 and 80). Israel is culpable and entirely deserves judgement at God's hand (ch. 6). Zion's destruction is not a total disaster. However, as it paves the way for God's eschatological act (ch. 20) which is near at hand (ch. 23) when the nations are to be judged (ch. 13; 82). As in 4 Ezra there is questioning of the way the world is: is there any profit in being righteous (ch. 14)? There is clear assurance that for those like Baruch and Ezra there is the promise of being 'taken up' (48.30 cf. 4. Ezra 14). In the present what is essential is obedience to the Law (ch. 32; 44; 46; 51.7; 77.13). Continual vigilance is necessary (88.8ff.) as there is nothing left but this one

---

[20] On the link with Job see M. Knibb, 'Apocalyptic and Wisdom in 4. Ezra', *Journal for the Study of Judaism* 13 (1982) pp. 56ff.

guide to God's purposes and humanity endowed as it is with understanding is without excuse and deserves to be punished. Attempts to pierce the mysteries of God's purposes are subject to the frailty of the human mind (23; 48). Once again eschatological material (which is much more extensive in this work: 25–30; 35–40; 53–76) serves to remind the reader of the imminent (23; 85.10) consummation of all things and the present need to use the limited time available which will enable achievement of Paradise.

In Apoc Abraham (an apocalypse which has many more affinities with the Enochic apocalypses) 20ff. there is also a discussion of human evil. Once again the freedom of God to act in any way that God chooses is enunciated but it is also linked with an explanation which sees the emergence of evil and the oppression of Israel. Because God foresees their attitude to Israel they are permitted to desire evil so that the nations can ultimately be punished for their deeds. Also Abraham is urged to take an eschatological perspective. It is only when Abraham sees the glorious eschatological future unfolding that he will be able to glimpse someting of the wisdom of the divine counsels.

The issues which are raised are what we would have expected Jews to have struggled with after the traumatic experience of 70CE. There would be an inevitable reappraisal of attitudes with needs for more precise definitions of what was required of the people of God and an emphasis on the centrality of the Law. What is also significant is the *continuing* pervasiveness of eschatological interest and the clear belief that the consummation of all things is near. Thus the debacle of 70 does not appear to have lessened the impact of these beliefs, and there is evidence to suppose that the years between the two revolts continued to be full of eschatological hope. Still the burning question in both 4 Ezra and Syr. Baruch is not so much: 'when will the End be?' but 'How can one make sense of the present and ensure participation in the eschatological paradise of God?' Eschatology forms a part of the divine answers to the seers' questions which usually concern pressing matters of present concern. It is part of the way in which the impoverished character of existence and the injustices of the world are given a different perspective.

One suspects that all these apocalyptists would have endorsed the sentiments of Theodor Adorno:

The only philosophy which can be responsibly practised in the face of despair is the attempt to contemplate all things as they would present themselves from the standpoint of redemption. Knowledge has not light but that shed on the world by redemption: all else is reconstruction, mere technique. Perspectives must be fashioned that displace and estrange the world, reveal it to be, with its rifts and crevices, as indigent and distorted as it will appear one day in the messianic light . . . it is also the utterly impossible thing, because it presupposes a standpoint removed, even though by a hair's breadth, from the scope of existence, whereas we all know that any possible knowledge must not only be first wrested from what is, if it shall hold good, but it is also marked for this very reason, by the same distortion and indigence which it seeks to escape[21].

Merkabah Mysticism and Rabbinic Judaism: the position in the late first century

In the Mishah (Hagigah 2.1) brief reference is made to exposition of the first chapters of Genesis and Ezekiel. The cryptic reference there indicates that it is a matter of some concern to the authors and is a hint of the central importance mystical and apocalyptic ideas played in the religion of rabbinic Judaism. Gershom Scholem's assertion that there was a connection between the apocalyptic tradition of early rabbinic Judaism and strands within Second Temple Judaism has been widely accepted[22]. Even if Scholem's position can be questioned and the early rabbis did not inherit the apocalyptic and mystical tradition immediately, emerging rabbinic Judaism would have been faced with the issue of controlling a lively apocalyptic tradition after AD 70.

There is evidence of controversy concerning the canonicity of the book of Ezekiel during the first half of the first century AD (bHag 13a, Shabb 14b, Men 45a). This controversy is said to have been resolved by Hanniah b. Hezekiah b. Gorion, a Shammaite teacher of the period. There may have been a connection with the 'danger story' of the child consumed by fire (or: whose teacher was consumed by fire) while studying Ez 1 in the Beth Midrash, which also mentions an attempt to conceal the book (bHag 13a). These two stories seem to indicate that the restrictions recorded by Origen concerning the study/teaching of Ez 1 have their origins in this period. Thus by 70 Ez 1 was already a restricted text.

This is confirmed by study of the lists of restricted targumin (MMeg 4.10, TosMeg 4(3).31ff.; bMeg 251−b). In his doctoral dissertation Dr. C. Morray-Jones has argued that the nucleus of the baraita is a list of passages whose

---

[21] T. Adorno, *Minima Moralia*, p. 247. The importance of Adorno's links with Gershom Scholem is a feature of twentieth century theology which cannot be overestimated (see D. Biale, *Kabbalah and Counter-History*, Cambridge 1979). Both were instrumental in publicising the work of Walter Benjamin (J. Roberts *Walter Benjamin*, London 1982, who in turn was influenced by Ernst Bloch (see W. Hudson, *The Marxist Philosophy of Ernst Bloch*, London 1982); Bloch himself influenced the theology of Jürgen Moltmann, see R. Bauckham *Messianic Theology in the Making*, Basingstoke 1987). All this is a reminder of the part played by this Jewish/Marxist tradition in the discussion of messianism in the twentieth century.

[22] E.g. in his *Major Trends in Jewish Mysticism*, London 1955 and also I. Gruenwald, *Apocalyptic and Merkavah Mysticism*, Leiden 1978), though it has been challenged by David Halperin in *The Merkabah in Rabbinic Literature*, New Haven 1980 (though his more nuanced treatment in *Faces of the Chariot*, Berlin 1987 should be welcomed). This section owes much to the work of Christopher Morray-Jones who has effectively rebutted the approach of Halperin (Dissertation Cambridge 1987).

liturgical use was resticted because they told of breaches of the prohibited relations of Lev 18. Other passages were added to this list from a number of different context. One such context is the restriction on *exegesis* of *'arayot, ma'aseh bereshit* and *hammerkabah*, recorded independently by MHag 2.1. MMeg 4.10 seems to record the process whereby items originally extraneus to the 'incest list' were added to it. Ez 1 does not figure in BT's list, while public reading of the chapter is emphatically permitted by Tos: here the formula employed is radically unlike that of the other items on the list. The indication is that the permissive ruling was formulated in a context of controversy. The Mishnah forbids the use of Ez 1 as a *haftarah* but records a minority opinion permitting this. This opinion is ascribed to R. Judah. Even the generally liberalising trend that seems to have influenced the development of these lists and given the fact that Ez 1 *did* become the *haftarah* for *sabuot*, it seems virtually certain that the restrictive opinion recorded in the Mishnah is the earlier. The Mishnah thus indicates that the early second century as the period in which public reading of Ez 1 in the synagogue began to be permitted by some authorities. Prior to this it seems to have been forbidden. Thus restrictions concerning the study and public reading of Ez 1 go back at least as far as the early first century and may well be much older. At the end of the first century there is every reason to believe that these restrictions were still in force, though it is possible to detect the beginnings of a more permissive attitude at or shortly after this period.

Turning to M. Hagigah 2.1 it seems virtually certain that the three items circulated independently of each other. The numerical sequence is derived from the *beyahid* of the *merkabah* restriction; this did not originally carry a strictly numerical significance but meant 'by an individual (on his own account)'. There are grounds for believing that the merkabah-restriction was originally expressed in the past tense. This pre-mishnaic form may be detectable in Eleazar ben Arak's lecture before Yohanan ben Zakkai. So, in the first century this was already believed to be an ancient tradition. Morray-Jones has argued that the *merkabah*-restriction originally meant that only a 'mantic' wise man who was able to understand the text on the basis of his esoteric knowledge was permitted to 'expound' (in the sense of giving teaching about) Ez 1. The restriction is derived from apocalyptic-wisdom tradition. Thus the background and context are an esoteric tradition concerned with divine secrets.

It thus seems probable that esoteric traditions associated with Ez 1 and similar passages were inherited by *some* of the early tannaim from this apocalyptic milieu. Doubtless these traditions (as in apocalyptic) had both an exegetical and a 'practical' (i.e. visionary-mystical) aspect. *Ma'aseh merkabah* indicates a systematization of such traditions within the context of rabbinic Judaism (though of course such traditions were also shared by extra rabbinic groups as well). A feature of the rabbinic development of these traditions was their association with and subordination to the Sinai revelation[23]. In the earliest strata of tradition, as in the apocalyptic texts, this connection is not always evident, and it seems likely that this association was developed in order both to legitimize and control the development within a rabbinic context, a process which probably began during the first century.

Analysis of the story of Eleazar ben Arak's *merkabah* lecture and the associated traditions linking Yohanan ben Zakkai with *ma'aseh merkabah* suggest that the talmudic perspective which makes Yohanan the authoritative source of *ma'aseh merkabah* tradition is inaccurate. The import of the original story seems to have been that Eleazar, Yohanan's student, 'performed' what his master could not. This included the production of the phenomenon of fire and other charismatic/ecstatic effects associated with Ezekiel's vision. The tradition concerning the eighty disciples of Hillel the Elder, of whom Yohanan was the least, also indicates that Yohanan did not have access to this tradition, or lacked charismatic power. Analysis of Yohanan's relations with charismatic figures (Haninah ben Dosa and especially Eliezer ben Hyrcanus) also suggests that Yohanan did not have access to the ecstatic-esoteric tradition. In the case of both Eliezer ben Hyrcanus and Eleazar ben Arak the later redactors of the tradition altered it so as to present Yohanan as the authoritative source. These considerations suggest that an esoteric, visionary-mystical tradition, probably with a strong magical or thaumaturgical aspect, were inherited by some tannaim but not by Yohanan. The stories about the exposition were probably developed in circles associated with their heroes and seem to have undergone a development in three stages: (i) stories telling how various figures performed what Yohanan could not; (ii) the same stories re-shaped so as to indicate that Yohanan recognised and approved of such things – a necessary development if the tradition was to gain acceptance, and (iii) the talmudic redactional tradition which makes Yohanan the source.

This reconstruction is confirmed by the Hekalot texts which nowhere cite Yohanan as the source of their tradition (quite an astonishing phenomenon, if their intention was to claim fictitious talmudic authority for their traditions). These texts consistently cite Akiba and Ishmael as the sources of their tradition, who received them from Eliezer ben Hyrcanus and Nehuniah ben HaQannah respectively. Nehuniah is an obscure figure in talmudic literature, and it seems unlikely that he would be invoked in order to give talmudic authority to these traditions. Eliezer's charismatic and magical powers are well documented. Indeed, he is paired with Eleazar ben Arak as the best student of Yohanan be Zakkai (M. Aboth 2.8 cf. ARN (B) 13, PRE 1,2 where there is a clear reference to charismatic or ecstatic speech). Moreover, both Eliezer and Eleazer ended their lives in disgrace and exile from the mainstream rabbinic community.

---

[23] Cf. Rowland, *The Open Heaven* p. 293.

Ecstatic-mystical and esoteric exegetical traditions were being developed in circles associated with some rabbinic teachers during the first century CE. Eleazar ben Arak, Nehunyah b. Ha Qannah and Eliezer ben Hyrcanus can be identified with far more certainty as focal points of this tradition. Perhaps in the light of evidence from 2. Cor 12.2 we might surmise that Gamaliel, Paul's teacher, was familiar with these traditions. The tradition was universally recognised and widely accepted, though some authorities (possibly including Yohanan) seem to have disapproved of it. This hostility probably never died out and certainly extended down to the time of the redaction of the Mishnah (it seems likely that Rabbi disapproved of the tradition – j. Hagigah 2.1). By the early second century the esoteric tradition was known to and practised by leading rabbis such as Akiba. Thus some controversy concerning the status and legitimacy of the tradition is likely to have occurred during the first century, probably because of the way in which such traditions were developed in extra-rabbinic circles, not least Christianity. We know Paul was influenced by apocalyptic ascent ideas (2. Cor 12.2 ff.) and emphasises the importance of this visionary element as the basis of his practice (Gal 1.12 and 1.16 cf. Acts 22.17). Perhaps he should be linked with those other significant figures who became marginal to rabbinic Judaism or a focus of hostility: Eliezer ben Hyrcanus, Eleazar ben Arak and Elisha ben Abuyah. After all his apocalyptic outlook enabled him to act on his eschatological convictions, so that his apocalypse of Jesus Christ became the basis for his practice of admitting Gentiles to the messianic age without the Law of Moses. His relegation of Sinai below the new covenant in the Messiah contrasts with the firm subordination of the apocalyptic spirit of Ezekiel 1 to the Sinai theophany in the rabbinic mystical traditions. The threat posed by apocalyptic may be discerned elsewhere (and indeed could have contributed to the development of christology in early christianity). It may be that the controversy about two centres of divine power with roots deep within the apocalyptic tradition may lie behind the stories of Elisha ben Abuyah's confrontation with the archangel Metatron[24].

How far is it possible to reconstruct the content of *ma'aseh merkabah* tradition in the late first century? In the first place, of cource, there is a continuity between apocalyptic, *ma'aseh merkabah* and Hekalot mysticism. The earliest strata of the talmudic tradition do not talk of a heavenly ascent but simply of supernatural phenomena (pre-eminently fire) which accompanied *merkabah* exposition. Only in the time of Akiba do we find suggestions (in versions of the story of the four who entered *pardes*, b Hagigah 14b, jHag 77b, Tosefta Hagigah 2.3f. and Shir ha-Shirim Rabbah 1.4) of heavenly ascents being practised. The story of the 'four who entered *pardes*' is probably based on the Song of Songs not on Ez 1. A vision of the King (God) in glory may be

---

[24] See Segal op. cit. and Rowland, *The Open Heaven*, pp. 94 ff.

implied, however. What was later to become the Hekalot visionary tradition was a synthesis of a number of different traditions which employed a variety of texts, pre-eminently Ez 1, Is 6 and the Song (the latter being particularly important for the *shi'ur qomah*, as their basis. These aimed at the achievement of ecstatic trance experiences (such traditions were probably very old). *Ma'aseh merkabah* will have been the rabbinic development of the traditions associated with Ez 1 in apocalyptic. Heavenly ascents were probably associated with some traditions in some circles. At an early stage it may well have been the case that the content of the *merkabah* tradition was primarily (though not exclusively) exegetical. The focus of the tradition was the throne-chariot of Got and the glorious figure enthroned upon it. Probably highly emotionally-charged (perhaps even at this stage ritualized) visualization practices were also in some quarters associated with this exposition. If the 'Great Seance' of Hekalot Rabbati involving Nehuniah ben HaQannah has any basis in actual practice during the late first century then ascent traditions may have been practised in this period too (as some apocalypses seem to indicate)[25]. Paul's trance-vision in the Temple (Acts 22.17) is similar enough to suggest the tradition is this old[26]. The only question is: to what extent were such practices current and respectable in mainstream academies? Neusner[27] suggested that meditation on passages like Ezekiel 1, set as it is in Exile and in the aftermath of a previous destruction of the Temple, would have been particularly apposite as the rabbis sought to come to terms with the devastation of AD 70. Of course, if the practical methods were among the most closely guarded secrets of the tradition, and if some influential rabbis were hostile to them, we should expect the sources to be very reticent about them, escpecially when the practice was liable to cause theological and halakic deviance.

The Fourth Gospel, Revelation and the Apocalyptic tradition

The apocalyptic credentials of the book of Revelation require little support despite the occasional attempt to put distance between it and the Jewish apocalyptic tradition. The opening of the book says quite clearly where the text stands in relation to other literary genres of the period and the debt to books like Daniel and Ezekiel in particular are a telling pointer to the literary background from which the book comes. It may be more of a surprise to find that the Fourth Gospel should be classed with the apocalyptic and mystical writings of

---

[25] See Scholem, *Jewish Gnosticism, Merkabah Mysticism and Talmudic Tradition*, New York 1965.

[26] On this verse see O. Betz, 'Die Vision des Paulus im Tempel von Jerusalem' in Betz et al. *Abraham unser Vater*, Wuppertal 1970, pp. 113ff.

[27] See J. Neusner, *A Life of Rabban Johanan ben Zakkai*, Leiden 1970, p. 140.

the period. Without necessarily supposing common authorship there seem to be good reasons for supposing that we should class the Fourth Gospel in a broadly similar tradition. Despite significant differences in use it is that tradition which forms the basis of a counter-cultural position in both and in the Fourth Gospel is the foundation of its christology[28].

The goal of the apocalyptic seer and the visionary is the glimpse of God enthroned in glory (1. Enoch 14), the manifestation of God's secret purposes (Apocalypse of Abraham 20ff.) and in the case of the late first century CE apocalypses issues of theodicy (apparent in 4. Ezra, SyrBaruch and the ApocAbraham). Apart from the unique reference a the end of chapter 1 (1.51) where the characteristics of the apocalyptic tradition are manifested in the references to an open heaven, angelic mediators and a heavenly son of man, there is little in the Fourth Gospel which might suggest that this a text which is at all interested in apocalypticism. But if we accept that apocalyptic is constituted by 'higher wisdom through revelation' rather than the paraphernalia of eschatology, then there is a sense in which the Fourth Gospel can be seen as falling quite clearly within that world of discourse. That is not to say that the concern with the minutiae of hidden mysteries is a preoccupation of the evangelist. Quite the reverse in fact. Rather, he wants to stress that the vision of God is to be found in Jesus (1.18; 6.46; 12.41; 14.9) and, to borrow from the letter to the Colossians, 'in whom are hid all the treasures of wisdom and knowledge' (Col 2.3)[29]. Jesus is represented as the supreme revelation of God and God's character. Unlike Jesus the Jews have never seen God's form or heard his voice (5.37). All visions and ascents are invalid if they are understood without reference to Jesus the Son of Man who alone has ascended and descended (3.13). The Son of Man is the goal of the angels search for the divine mysteries (1.51), much as in 1. Peter 1.11−12.

We would expect in an apocalypse dualism[30] to be an important component of its epistemology[31]. It is an essential ingredient of its attempt to offer that alternative perspective on reality by positing another, divine dimension to human existence and thereby indicating that the form of the present order is

---

[28] H. Odeberg, *The Fourth Gospel*, Uppsala 1929, A. Segal op cit. and further literature cited in C. Rowland, 'John 1.51 and the Targumic Tradition', *New Testament Studies* 30 (1984) pp. 498ff. and T. Ashton *Understanding the Fourth Gospel* Oxford 1991.

[29] On Colossians and its connection with Jewish mysticism and apocalyptic see C. Rowland, 'Apocalyptic Visions and the Exaltation of Christ in the Letter to the Colossians', *JSNT* 19 (1983) pp. 73ff.

[30] On Johannine dualism see e. g. J. Charlesworth's essay in id. *John and Qumran*, London 1972 and O. Böcher, *Der johanneische Dualismus im Zusammenhang des nachbiblischen Judentums*, Gütersloh 1965.

[31] On apocalyptic epistemology see the suggestive comments in J. L. Martyn, 'Epistemology at the Turn of the Ages', in N. R. Farmer et al., *Christian History and Interpretation*, Cambridge 1967 and further M. Soards (ed.), *Apocalyptic in the New Testament*, Sheffield 1989.

only temporary. In Rev the present contrast between heaven where God is enthroned and acknowledged as creator on the one hand and earth in rebellion and the recipient of God's wrath on the other contrasts with the future when God will dwell with humanity. The contrast between appearance and reality with the latter laid bare by the revelation, the drawing back of the veil which hides God's mysteries, is one of the fundamental aspects of apocalyptic. That epistemology is fundamental to the Fourth Gospel also. Since the discovery of the Dead Sea Scrolls we have becomes used to finding the background to these ideas in such sectarian sources. The Apocalypse's concern to offer the truth of the situation, whether it be the spiritual condition of the churches or the reality of the unfolding of the divine purposes, is matched by the Fourth Gospel's dualistic contrasts which serve to throw into the sharpest possible relief the impoverished character of the world and the blindness of its inhabitants. Here as elsewhere both Revelation and the Fourth Gospel are indebted to the apocalyptic tradition.

Of course, there are differences between the Fourth Gospel and Revelation. However restrained the vision of the enthroned God might be in Rev 4.2ff. in comparison with Ez 1.26 John of Patmos still claims to have a vision of God. That is not on offer in the Fourth Gospel. Claims to see God must be regarded as claims to see Jesus. If they are not, they are to be rejected as spurious. Elsewhere, there is similarity of language between the description of the new age in Rev 21 and the prologue of the Fourth Gospel. In Rev 21.3 the tabernacling of God with humankind is fulfilled in the new creation. It is an eschatological hope which awaits the completion of that process of judgement on the unrighteous institutions which barred the way to God's reign. In contrast Jn 1.14 speaks of the tabernacling of the Divine Word in history not as an event in the future but as an event in the past, in the person of Jesus of Nazareth. While in Rev 21 the dwelling of God with humanity takes place in a world made holy and acceptable for this, in Jn the Incarnation takes place in an environment where the 'world knew him not' (Jn 1.10). The twin emphases on realised eschatology and lack of concern for the kind of cosmic redemption which marks the climax of eschatology are in stark contrast with Rev. The preoccupation is on the life of a group of disciples whose task is to overcome an alien world which hates them as it hated their master (15.18ff.)[32].

So whatever hope there may be for the future (and I am convinced that the Fourth Gospel has not moved entirely to a realised eschatology), the focus is on the first coming as the ultimate moment to which the witness of the community and the Spirit-Paraclete both point. Those who love Jesus and keep his commandments are those to whom the incarnate Son of God comes and with whom the Father and the Son make their abode (Jn 14.21 and 23). However we

---

[32] D. Rensberger, *Overcoming the World*, London 1989.

interpret the enigmatic reference to the Son of Man and Jacob's ladder in Gen 28.12 there is the idea of communion between heaven and earth in the past revelation of glory in Jesus (cf. 1. Jn 1.1). Also, the presence of the eschatological glory among the disciples who love him has about it a 'vertical' dimension in which the coming son of man is not primarily a figure who appears as a reproach to the nations. The disciple now looks forward to a time when s/he will be with Jesus to behold his glory (17.24)[33]. It is now not a question of 'they shall look upon him whom they pierced' (Rev 1.9) but 'the world will see me no more but you will see me' (Jn 14.19).

Both the Fourth Gospel and Revelation manifest concerns which are typical of the apocalyptic tradition as it is found at the end of the first century. We have noted already that the Fourth Gospel vigorously locates revelation in the person of Jesus and denies the significance of all other claims to divine knowledge without relation to him. There is a similar restraint in 4. Ezra. Heavenly ascents are not the means of revelation (4.20 and 8.21). Indeed, there is a vigorous denial of it (and there is no evidence of that tradition in SyrBaruch though it *does* emerge in the roughly contemporary ApocAbraham). 4. Ezra instead places great emphasis in a situation of crisis on the necessity of the elect to keep the Torah. That means avoiding unnecessary speculation about matters which are too difficult to understand (a constant theme of the divine reply to Ezra). Like the mishnaic restriction on speculative activity in MHagigah 2.1 and earlier in Sirach 3.22, 4. Ezra echoes Job's divine pronouncement about the inscrutability of God's purposes. There is necessity for a single-minded devotion to God's will in order to attain the eschatological bliss. That emphasis on ethical rectitude at the expense of satisfying eschatological and theosophic curiosity is echoed in several works of the period. At a time when the upheaval caused by the decimation of Jewish institutions had thrown the whole tradition into the melting-pot there is a remarkable convergence of opinion in Jewish and Christian apocalyptic and mystical sources on the primacy of ethical rectitude as the key to salvation. As we have seen, Rev sets the apocalyptic revelation about the age to come in the context of letters to the seven churches. The present is marked by costly struggle not leisurely dreams of the future. The latter's purpose is to reinforce the demand for righteousness and to assure those who are seeking to enter by the narrow gate that there is hope of vindication and fulfilment. Likewise in the Fourth Gospel acceptance of Jesus' messiahship is demonstrated by love of the brethren, something made even more explicit in 1. John where division over christological controversy is rooted in separatism and inability to relate to one's fellow believers in the way that God requires (1. John 3). Apocalyptic is a luxury which cannot be divorced by the pressing demands for practical righteousness. It serves to enhance the power of the demand by

---

[33] W. Pascal, *The Farewell Prayer of Jesus*, Dissertation Cambridge 1982.

rooting it in the direct voice of God. Any other pursuit of the divine mysteries appears indulgent and a distraction from the real task in hand.

Synoptic Eschatological Material: a Comparison of the Concerns of Other First Century Eschatological Discourses[34]

When viewed in the light of Rev the synoptic discourses show some remarkable omissions. It is true that they manifest the same kind of preoccupation with the messianic woes which are so characteristic of several eschatological passages from writings of this period of Judaism. While there my will be some kind of connection between the sort of focus of evil which is outlined so cryptically in Mk 13.14 and the hubris of the man of lawlessness mentioned in 2. Thess 2, nothing is said about the effects of the coming of the Son of Man on the forces of evil. Indeed, the description of the coming of the Son of Man in all three synoptic gospels is linked explicitly with the vindication of the elect, thus focussing on the final aspect of the messianic drama in the vision of the man from the sea in 4. Ezra 13. The certainty of vindication is there but the lot of the elect when they have been gathered from the four corners of the earth is not touched on at all in Mk. The element of judgement at the Parousia of the Son of Man is not entirely absent, however, from the synoptic discourses as the climax of the Matthean version is the account of the final assize with the Son of Man sitting on God's throne separating the 'sheep from the goats' (Matt 25.31ff.). But here as elsewhere in these discourses the focus of attention is on the present response of the elect. It is the recognition of the heavenly Son of Man in the brethren who are hungry, thirsty, strangers, naked, weak and imprisoned in the present age who will inherit the kingdom prepared by God from the foundation of the world.

In the Mk discourse the preoccupation of the bulk of the material is not so much the satisfaction of curiosity about the detail of the times and seasons so much as dire warnings of the threat of being led astray, of failing at the last and of the need to be ready and watchful to avoid the worst of the disasters which are to come. In the bleak moments of the last days in Jerusalem there is little attempt to dwell on the privileges of discipleship (though an eschatological promise is made to the disciples a little later in the lucan story in Lk 22.29f. in the context of the supper discourse). It is not a future without hope but the thoughts of the hearers are made to dwell on responsibilities in the short and medium term as the essential prerequisite of achieving their eschatological inheritance. In comparison with the more extended accounts of the coming of the new age to be found in other material both Christian and Jewish the

---

[34] See D. Wenham for a guide to the literature on the eschatological discourses.

synoptic discourses concentrate on the period of strife and tribulation leading up to the coming of the son of man. What happens therafter is not explored. In the Lucan account, however, there is the expectation that the arrival of the Son of Man is but the beginning of the process of liberation, for which the tribulations and destruction had been the prelude. This point is made very clearly in the climax of the discourse in Lk 21.26ff.: 'when these things come to pass, stand up right and hold your heads high, because your liberation draws near' (v. 28). It is only when what has been described in the series of predictions come to pass that the kingdom of God begins to draw near. The implication is that the kingdom does not arrive with the coming of the Son of Man; that is only part of the eschatological drama whose climax is still to come, when there will be a reversal of Jerusalem's fortunes (v. 24). There is in fact very little attempt made to sketch the character of the liberation which draws near. The sketch of the ideal society or the ideal world is lacking, a mark of either a lack of any political realism or of a merely utopian fixation (in the sense of merely dreaming about the form of the ideal society). Rather they prefer to hint at their conviction that one is coming without being too precise about what it will involve.

The eschatological discourse is set within the context of the narrative of Jesus' life, itself a paradigm of discipleship. The discourse material in the gospels must be seen within their narrative context. It is attention to the whole that is needed. The discourses must not be allowed to function as instructions which abstract the reader from the challenge of the messianic way as it intersects with an order which is passing away. But what happens when the discourse material does become abstracted from the narrative can be glimpsed in the Gospel of Thomas and the Apocalypse of Peter. In their different ways these works use teaching to effect an otherworldy preoccupation on the part of the readers. The former by its concentration on Jesus as a teacher of wisdom makes the understanding of the divine knowledge he brings the goal of salvation. Similarly, the knowledge of the delights of Paradise and the horrors of Hell in other parts of the apocalyptic tradition[35] and its derivatives can lead to a morbid curiosity with the world beyond and the believer's participation in it which can detract from the impact of that future age in the ruins of the age which is passing away.

---

[35] M. Himmelfarb, *Tours of Hell*, Cambridge Mass. 198.

The Resources of Apocalyptic as Compensation
for Eschatological Disappointment[36]

A question which always arises when the development of Christianity at the end of the first century CE is discussed is the issue of the problem caused of the non-fulfilment of the expectation of imminent fulfiment of the reign of God. This theory is one which has been extraordinarily influential within biblical exegesis over the last century or so. The classic theory which ascribes the emergence of orthodox Christian doctrine as part of the response to the problem caused by the delay has been subjected to critical scrutiny over the years. There is little doubt that the explicit evidence for the delay of the parousia being a problem within primitive Christianity is not as large as is often suggested, 2. Peter 3 is in fact a rather exceptional piece of evidence. Other passages which are often mentioned in Matt and Luke, for example, have to be set alongside other indications which point in the opposite direction. But while one would want to question the view that the delay of the parousia *must* have been a problem, it has raised issues which are of particular importance for understanding the development of the apocalyptic tradition.

The apocalyptic tradition in its various forms so pervades the early Christian thought world. The apostle Paul's theology and self-understanding cannot be properly understood without reference to it. This ranged from his conviction that God had revealed the mystery of salation to him and his part in it (Gal 1.12 and 16) to his expectation of the partial presence and imminent expectation of a new age. From Schweitzer to Sanders via Munck[37] it is the eschatological hope which is offered as the best way to understand Paul. The mission to the Gentiles and probably also the collection for the saints in Jerusalem[38] were intimately linked with the framework of an eschatological drama in which Paul is a crucial actor. Thus what had happened in the Christ event was linked with his own mission within the overall scheme of salvation history.

In many ways Paul's thought offers us one of the best examples of what Karl Mannheim has called, 'chiliastic mentality'[39]. One aspect of this type, he argues, is the way in which the present moment becomes the Kairos, the moment to take decisive action. The utopian then takes it upon himself:

to 'enable the absolute to interfere with the world and condition actual events' . . . the present becomes the breach through which what was previously inward bursts

---

[36] On the Parousia and its delay see Rowland, *Christian Origins*, pp. 285 ff. and below n. 41.

[37] A. Schweitzer, *The Mysticism of Paul the Apostle*, London 1931, E. P. Sanders, *Paul and Palestinian Judaism*, London 1977, J. Munck, *Paul and the Salvation of Mankind*, London 1959.

[38] On the collection D. Georgi, *Die Geschichte der Kollekte des Paulus für Jerusalem*, Hamburg 1965.

[39] K. Mannheim, *Ideology and Utopia*, London 1960.

out suddenly, takes hold of the outer world and transforms it . . . the chiliast is always on his toes awaiting the propitious moment . . . he is not actually concerned with the millennium to come; what is important for him is that it has happened here and now . . . the chiliastic mentality has no sense for the process of becoming; it was sensitive only to the abrupt moment, the present pregnant with meaning[40].

That sense of destiny which probably undergirded Paul's self understanding and his activity actually enabled his thinking to cohere as an expression of the outlook of one who believed himself called to be an agent in the dawn of the new age, the means by which the Gentiles became fellow heirs of the commonwealth of Israel (cf. Matt 19.28). Of course, that is most clearly expressed in Ephesians where not only the Apostle's but also the church's role as the bearers of the divine mysteries is stressed (3.5ff.). As Ephesians indicates, it was possible for a later generation to keep alive that framework of thought provided that there is a clear understanding of the soteriological role of apostle and community. Once that sense of being part of the 'propitious moment' disappears, however, the understanding of present activity as an integral part of that drama and its relationship with the future consummation of the divine purposes gradually disappears also. When that happens it does become more difficult to see that future consummation as anything other than an article of faith rather than a goal in which present activity forms an indispensable part in 'interfering with the world and conditioning actual events'.

Richard Bauckham has argued that already within the eschatological tradition there was an attempt to come to terms with the delay of the coming of God's reign, and he argues that 'there are traces of a positive theological understanding of the Delay in terms of God's long-suffering and his desire for his people's repentance'[41]. He is right to point to the apocalypses as important evidence of a resource for dealing with the non-fulfilment of God's reign on earth. Many have recognised that the apocalypses are as interested in the world above where God's reign is acknowledged by the heavenly host and where the apocalyptic seer can have access to the repository of those purposes of God for the future world. Thus the apocalyptic seer can glimpse either in the heavenly books about the mysteries of eschatology or by being offered a preview of what will happen in human history in the future. In most apocalypses that experience of a disclosure of the heavenly mysteries is reserved for the apocalyptic seer, but it was perfectly possible to extend that privilege to a wider group. It is that which we find in different forms in the Hodayoth (1QH) and the Odes of Solomon both of which offer the elect group a present participation in the lot of heaven and a foretaste of the glory which is to come. The identification of the ecclesia of the elect with Christ in the heavenly places is stressed in the letter to

---

40 Mannheim op. cit. p. 192–5.
41 R. Bauckham, 'The Delay of the Parousia', *Tyndale Bulletin* 31 (1980) pp. 3ff.

the Ephesians (1.21 cf. 3.5ff.), so that the present life of the church becomes a glimpse, a foretaste of the kingdom of God, just as the Spirit enables the believers to regard the present as a participation 'in the powers of the age to come' as the writer of the Letter to the Hebrews puts it (Heb 6.5)[42].

An important example of apocalyptic being used by a group which found itself alienated from the mainstream of life is to be found in the Jewish-Christian apocalypse the Ascension of Isaiah[43]. There is a clear reference to the promise of Christ's coming in 4.14ff. Elsewhere, particularly in the Vision of Isaiah in the last part of the work the concern is wholly with the descent and ascent of the Beloved with its promise of hope for the glorified elect with the patriarchs and prophets in the highest heavens. The coming relates to the descent of the Beloved and his Incarnation (unless the christology is entirely docetic). Like the Gospel of John the marginalised visionary group is the focus of attention. It has separated itself from society at large and joined with the prophet in the desert:

And many . . . who believed in the ascension to heaven withdrew and settled on the mountain. And they all put on sackcloth and they all were prophets; they had nothing with them, but were naked and bitterly lamented the apostasy of Israel (2.9).

In many respects the Ascension of Isaiah in its final form offers a interesting contrast to the book Revelation among the extant Jewish and Christian apocalypses. The second half of the work describes the ascent of Isaiah through the seven heavens to the presence of God and then proceeds to describe the descent of the Beloved to the world below. That process in which the keepers of the lower heavens are deceived during the ascent only to find themselves caught out by his triumphal ascent back to the Father offers a pattern of salvation which may be hinted at from time to time in the New Testament (e.g. 1. Cor 2.9ff. and 1. Peter 3.20). In the second half of the apocalypse there is lack of any historical dimension to eschatology, though this makes its appearance in the first part of the work.

We have in the Ascension of Isaiah an apocalypse which raises in the acutest possible form the question of the relationship between apocalypticism and gnosticism[44]. The guardians of the lower heavens, described as they are in terminology derived from the Jewish theophany tradition, echo the cry of the

---

[42] H. W. Kuhn, *Enderwartung und gegenwärtiges Heil*, Göttingen 1966, D. Aune, *The Cultic Aspect of Realised Eschatology in Early Christianity*, Leiden 1972.

[43] On the Ascension of Isaiah see the dissertation of J. M. Knight (forthcoming).

[44] On the connection between apocalyptic and gnosticism see the comments of R. M. Grant, *Gnosticism and Early Christianity*, London 1959. It is probable that gnosticism's dualism allowed the possibility of outward conformity with society at large while offering a view of the world which regarded human beings as entirely alien within it, see R. M. Grant in A. Logan and A. Wedderburn, *The New Testament and Gnosis*, Edinburgh 1983.

gnostic demiurge that there is no other divinity apart from them (10.13). Just as in the Hypostasis of the Archons and the Untitled Work from Nag Hammadi there is a debt to the merkabah tradition[45], so here too we find in them a question raised about the extent to which apocalyptic contributed to the development of certain forms of gnostic religion. Apocalyptic could lend itself to a radical form of otherworldliness in which the light of the heavenly throne-room of God offered a stark contrast to a benighted creation. In a political situation in which hope was at a premium apocalyptic may have offered a significant catalyst to the development of that distinctive and systematic denigration of this world which is at the heart of fully-fedged gnosticism. Any account of the parting of the ways between Judaism and Christianity has to take account of this trend.

The issue of the contrasting ways in which eschatological hope were handled in the gradually separating communities is a central part of the story of the parting of the ways. There is a sense in which early Christianity's muting of its realised/inaugurated eschatology, whether by routinisation in ritual expression or institutional control, represents a telling expression of Christian identity at this period. In this respect Christianity became more like the groupings from which it was parting than the eschatological sectarianism which is more likely to have characterised much of its early existence.

Conclusion

Apocalyptic has performed a variety of different functions within religion. Its interest in visions of a world beyond with its myriad of angels and preoccupation with the means of achieving communion with that world makes it a classic example of offering an opportunity of an opiate for those who wish to escape from a heartless world. And yet it has also frequently been a spur for those engaged in movements of change where visions of hope have fuelled powerful societal forces demanding change in the existing order. It is a matter of dispute whether apocalyptic functioned in this way in our period or at the time of the First Revolt[46], though in later Christian apocalyptic movements it did perform exactly that function. The Elect were offered conviction of their identity and certainty to engage in that struggle to actualise their visions of the eschatological reign of God. In the apocalyptic material we have been examining there is little sign that it was the motor of violent change. That should not necessarily surprise us. In its textual form we would expect it to have undergone a process

---

[45] See F. Fallon, *The Enthronement of Sanaoth*, Leiden 1978 and Gruenwald art. cit. (see n. 4).

[46] M. Goodman, *The Ruling Class of Judea*, Cambridge 1987 and T. Rajak, *Josephus*, London 1983.

of taming among those groups who had the sophistication and communitarian persistence to engage in writing and to ensure that their work was preserved. Those who used apocalyptic as part of their struggle for change did not leave any literary memorial which would have been preserved by more careful successors. Its role in the extant late first century AD apocalypses is to encourage obedience by stimulating the reader to recognise the temporary nature of present realities and the urgent need to persevere to receive the promise which is to come. One might say that in some of thes works, both Jewish and Christian, there is a 'stick and carrot' approach to religion: eschatological bliss is offered to those who take the difficult decision in the present to stay with the ancestral laws or their obedience to the messianic way. In all this material there is probably a secondary theme running through them: the need to maintain an identity as a religious community in circumstances of difficulty[47]. The apocalypse offers a demonstration of the divine undergirding of the religious community, its practices and beliefs in a situation where that identity might have been under threat because of the extreme disjunction between tradition and reality. So apocalyptic functions not so much as vehicle for change at this stage as a means of reaffirming what has been received and an incisive encouragement to endure (to borrow a favourite word from Revelation) and to build up the ancient ruins.

In the Jewish material it should not surprise us that a central focus is the Law. Syr. Baruch articulates the position most clearly in asserting that there is nothing left except obedience to it. The conclusion of 4. Ezra likewise makes a clear link between Ezra's visions and the Law of Sinai as being part of one continuing revelation from God. With those markers of Judaism, such as the Temple and the whole apparatus of the sacrifical system based on the centrality of Jerusalem, suddenly gone what was left became all the more important, to anchor the religious communities and prevent them being moved too far from their moorings. Apocalyptic in this situation was an essential way of increasing certainty in the validity of what was left. Likewise in the Christian texts the emerging emphasis on the centrality of Christ[48], particularly in the Fourth Gospel, guaranteed by the assertion of the ultimacy of the revelation in and through him, was the sole foundation for a Jewish-Christian group seeking to maintain its messianic convictions and their link with the biblical tradition. The indications are that there was little opportunity for diversity when the pressure was there to hang on to what was left, whether it be particular interpretations of the Law or the assertion that the same Law found its fulfilment in the life of the Messiah.

---

[47] Meeks art. cit (see above n. 1) and *The First Urban Christians*, New Haven 1983.

[48] On suggested developments of the apocalyptic tradition see W. Baumgarten, *Paulus und die Apokalyptik*, Neukirchen 1975 cf. J. C. Beker, *Paul the Apostle*, Edinburgh 1980.

For all these differences there is also a consistent theme running throughout much of the material that we have examined. Apocalyptic is not here offered as a means of satisfying curiosity. In most cases it is subordinated entirely to the demand for obedience and ethical rigour on the part of the reader. From the letters to the seven churches via the mishnaic regulations to the vision of 4. Ezra there is a consistent emphasis on the need for an ethical response, often, in the apocalypses at least, left unspecified in any detail. We are left with the clear impression that it is this which must provide the setting for the visions whose main aim is to admonish and encourage.

Apocalyptic literature by its very nature encourages a feeling of certainty in the reader by appearing to offer the authentic word of God on a variety of matters. There is something of this kind of tone in Revelation where the concluding verses seem to give the book an authoritative air quite without parallel in the rest of the New Testament (22.18f.). Yet apocalyptic symbolism made such certainty in the process of deriving meaning from its symbolism much more speculative and open to constant questioning. In this sense most apocalypses flatter to deceive. They appear to offer final answers by their revelatory form and yet frequently prove to be opaque in their interpretation. It is rather different in the Fourth Gospel. Here the emergence of an exclusive christology serves to demand an unequivocal response concerning the centre of divine revelation. So, despite the revelation from God about what is to come the apocalyptic genre in Rev allows for a considerable degree of ambiguity about the precise content of the revelation and the demands it makes upon the reader both doctinally and ethically. It is true that the text offers a resolution of the contradictions of the world in its vision of the future but alongside this it demands participation in present struggle. That is the immediate reality confronting the readers in their everyday life. The paradise of God is still future, and the precise way there is hardly clear. What is apparent is that there can be no compromise with the old order and every expectation that a price will have to be paid for the patient endurance of the saints. Similarly in 4. Ezra apocalyptic offers no clear answers to the heart-felt questions of the seer. By the end of the book we are left with a clear message of hope but little real insight about why it is that the glory which is to come is so exclusive in its scope. In the apocalypses the readers are asked to stay with the confusions and contradictions of the world as it is. Apocalypse is not a means of offering easy answers and certain remedies which will ensure participation in the Paradise of God. The apocalyptic genre demands of the people of God, whether in Judaism or Christianity, a response in action which will ensure the continuation of the divine righteousness not through fantastic speculation but patient endurance: 'Here is a call for the endurance of the saints, those who keep to commandments of God [and the faith of Jesus]' Rev 14.12).

The Parting of the Ways:
Eschatology and Messianic Hope

by

ANDREW CHESTER

1. Introduction

For the period 70–135 this is a potentially vast theme, although the evidence (both Jewish and Christian) is in some respects limited or difficult to evaluate. Some relevant texts will be touched on only briefly, since they are being dealt with elsewhere in this collection.[1] In this essay, I will first consider some main aspects of the Jewish evidence, starting with the potentially important but often neglected SibOr 4 and 5, and then come to the larger, rather disparate, range of Christian texts from the Apostolic Fathers and early Apologists. Throughout, the intention is to indicate some of the main points of agreement and difference, and to perceive some of the issues that loom large as Judaism and Christianity begin to grow increasingly apart in this period.

Jewish Texts

2. Sibylline Oracles

2.1. Sib 5

Sib 5 is the better-known and more discussed of the two texts[2]; it is also the more prolific in eschatological and messianic themes. The most striking passage at least for our purpose in the whole of Sib 5 is 414–427:

---

[1] See especially the essays by Rowland and Horbury.
[2] On Sibylline Oracle 5, see e.g. J. J. Collins 1974a; J. J. Collins 1983a; J. J. Collins 1984, 187–191; J. J. Collins 1987; Hengel 1983; Chester 1991a.

2.1.1. 5.414–427

For there came from the expanses of heaven a blessed man
having a sceptre in his hands which God had delivered to him,
and he gained control over all things well, and gave back,
to all the good, the wealth which men had formerly taken.
He removed every city from its foundation with a great fire
and burned nations of mortals who had formerly done evil.
And the city which God desired, this he made
more brilliant than stars and sun and moon,
and he adorned it and made a holy temple,
splendidly beautiful in its form, and he fashioned
a great and enormous tower over many stadia
touching the clouds and visible to all,
so that all faithful and all righteous people should see
the glory of eternal God, a form desired.

The main themes here are: (i) the advent of a *messianic* figure[3]; he is not specifically designated 'messiah', but the description and role given him set him firmly in this category. He is a heavenly figure who comes to earth for a specific messianic, eschatological purpose;
(ii) he restores the fortunes of the righteous Jews, and brings divine judgement and destruction on their enemies (the wicked);
(iii) this heavenly, messianic figure also restores specifically Jerusalem and, above all, the *temple*[4].

This last theme needs to be set in context of the immediately preceding and following sections, that is, 397–413 and 428–433. The former passage represents, negatively, a bitter attack against Rome for destroying the Jerusalem temple in 70, and, positively, an idealized portrayal of the temple and of the Jewish people who are sanctified by the temple and the fact that they worship there ('... the ever-flourishing, watchful temple of God made by holy people and hoped ... to be always imperishable. For among them no one carelessly praises a God of insignificant clay ... but they honoured the great God ... with holy sacrifices'). The latter passage depicts the messianic age, with the holy people and temple implicitly set in complete contrast to the vices of Imperial Rome that will no longer be found.

Thus, for the writer, in the messianic age the Jewish people need the temple, in order that they can exist in relation to God and fulfil their role as a holy, God-fearing people. That is, the restored temple is an integral and essential feature

---

[3] For brief discussion of the portrayal of a messianic figure here and in the other passages in Sib 5, cf. J. J. Collins 1974a; J. J. Collins 1983a; J. J. Collins 1984, 189f.; J. J. Collins 1987; Horbury 1985; Chester 1991a; Chester 1991b.

[4] For fuller discussion of the theme of messiah and temple in Sib 5, cf. Chester 1991a and the further references given there.

of eschatological restoration and the final, glorious messianic age that God is going to bring in. Hence also we can appreciate the force of a distinctive feature of our text (420–427), where a main positive function of the Messiah is the rebuilding of the Temple in a manner worthy of God and his chosen people[5]. Thus the central focus of the writer's vision of the messianic age is made very clear.

2.1.2. 5.256–259

There will again be one exceptional man from the sky
who streched out his hands on the fruitful wood
the best of the Hebrews, who will one day cause the sun to stand
speaking with fair speech and holy lips.

There are obvious similarities here with 414 ff.; again we have a messianic figure (as in Sib 5 otherwise, not specifically designated 'messiah') who comes from heaven. In view of the obvious reference to the crucifixion at 1.257, this whole section has not surprisingly been seen as a later Christian interpolation[6]. If that is the case, this passage cannot of course be used to build up our picture of messianism in Sib 5. But there is no compelling reason why the passage apart from 257 should not be understood as authentically Jewish and original to the oracle[7]. Thus, for example, the designation 'man' is attested elsewhere in first-century sources as a messianic designation.

It is also the case that 256–259, omitting 257, fits well into the context; indeed, the specific reference to a messianic figure should again be understood within the passage as a whole here (238–285). This larger section comprises mainly a eulogy of the Jewish people, with the sub-theme of polemic and judgement against the Jews' enemies and the unrighteous. But running right through it is the emphasis on the land of Israel, set in idealized, virtually utopian, terms, with reference both to the past and also to the eschatological consummation. This may be the case already in 238–239, but above all, with the messiah having come, the land (and especially Jerusalem) can be pictured in quasi-divine terms in relation to the final age that is thus set in motion ('. . . the

---

[5] Gaston 1970, 148 argues that it is God not the messiah who rebuilds the temple here; but it is much more probable that the messiah is the subject of the verbs in these lines, while the reference in 432–43 to God accomplishing these things means only that the messiah is acting as God's agent. See further on this Chester 1991a; cf. also Sanders 1985, 87.

[6] So e. g. Geffcken, 1902a, 29; Lanchester, in Charles 1913, vol. II 373 f., 402; Volz 1934, 57; Noack 1964; Schürer–Vermes–Millar(–Goodman) 1973–87, vol. III.I, 664.

[7] Thus Nikiprowetsky 1972, 58–65, argues that the whole passage refers to a Jewish messiah; for the more plausible view that only line 257 represents a Christian interpolation into an originally Jewish messianic passage, cf. Billerbeck 1922–26, vol. I, 12–13. This is also considered as a possibility, but no more than that, by e. g. J. J. Collins 1974a; J. J. Collins 1983a, 392, 399; Hengel 1983, 674. Cf. also Chester 1991a.

divine and heavenly race of the blessed Jews, who live around the city of God in
the middle of the earth . . . Blessed one . . . divinely born, wealthy, sole-desired
flower, good light, holy shoot, beloved plant, delightful Judaea, fair city,
inspired with hymns . . . the holy land of the pious will bear these things, a
honey-sweet stream from rock and spring, and heavenly milk will flow for all
the righteous. For with great piety and faith they put their hope in the one
begetter, God'). In this messianic age, they will observe Torah (264–265);
above all, the central focal point for the Jewish people will be the temple and
the cult (256–259). Indeed, not only are Jerusalem and the temple the focal
point for the (now perfect) Jewish people in the messianic age, but Jerusalem
(and implicitly the temple) will be the centre of gravity for the whole world as
well[8]. Many of these themes, especially the paradisal, perfect state of land and
people in the final (messianic) age, and the portrayal of the temple as the
central focus of the people's lives, are held in common with the (much earlier)
Sib 3[9]. But the emphasis on the city (or temple) as the centre of the world is
found only here within the Sibylline tradition, although it is familiar from
Jewish sources otherwise[10]. Thus here again we are given a vivid portrayal of
what the writer sees as the context and impact of the coming of a messianic
figure and the onset of the messianic age.

2.1.3. 5.108–109, 155–161

Then a certain king sent from God against him   (108–109)
will destroy all the great kings and noble men.

But when after the fourth year a great star shines,   (155–161)
which alone will destroy the whole earth, because of
the honour which they first gave to Poseidon of the sea,
a great star will come from heaven to the wondrous sea
and will burn the deep sea and Babylon itself
and the land of Italy, because of which many
holy faithful Hebrews and a true people perished.

These two passages from earlier in Sib 5 are also usually seen as messianic. Thus
108–109 portrays God sending a king as the instrument of his judgement and
retribution, specifically against Nero and the Roman oppression of the Jews
(93–110), but implicitly also against the oppressive rulers and people of Egypt

---

[8] For further discussion of this point, cf. Chester 1991a.

[9] See e.g. Sib 3.213–215,573–587,616–634,657–668,702–731,767–795; cf. further J. J.
Collings 1974a, 44–55; Sanders 1985, 85–88; Chester 1991a.

[10] The scriptural basis for this idea is found in e.g. Ezek 5.5; 38.12; the development of the
theme is especially obvious in Jub 8.19; cf. also 1. Enoch 26.1; Letter of Aristeas 83–84. For
discussion of the cosmic symbolism and significance of this developed tradition, see e.g.
Wensinck 1916, 11–36; Jeremias 1926, 40–45; Hayman 1986; Chester 1991a.

(52–92) and the East (111–136). In 155–161 we are given the picture, again as the climax of God's judgement against Rome, of a great star bringing destruction on the centre of the Empire.

It has to be said that neither of these passages is unambiguously messianic, and they both clearly differ considerably from 256ff. and 414ff. In fact they are much closer than are these two to the main passages seen as messianic in the earlier Sib 3. Thus 3.286f. speaks of God sending a king to execute his judgement, while 3.652f. portrays God sending a king 'from the sun' to bring judgement and prevent war from breaking out. In both cases it may be implied that God is sending a messianic figure from heaven (cf. 3.286 'the heavenly God will send . . .'), in which case the connection will be closer with 5.155–161 (158 'a great star will come from heaven') and of course 5.256 and 5.414, than with 5.108f. But both passages in Sib 3 may be much closer to 5.108f., if the reference is to human royal figures already on earth, in a quite general sense, and it is anyway disputed whether a Jewish messianic figure is intended at all in Sib 3[11]. In any case, we have to be careful in our interpretation of both passages in Sib 5; thus 155–161 could be seen as only generally cosmic and astral, not specifically messianic, in scope, although I find it much more plausible that the double reference to the great star from heaven is a deliberate allusion to the 'star from Jacob' of Num 24.17, which with the developed interpretations attached to it becomes one of the most important messianic proof-texts of post-biblical Judaism[12]. In that case there will be close links with the messianic figure of heavenly origin in the two later passages in Sib 5, but that can scarcely be the case with 108f. There are in any case obvious differences between 108f. and 155–161 on the one hand, and 256ff. and 414ff. on the other. The former are brief, enigmatic and negative in emphasis, while the latter are much fuller and clearer, containing not only the theme of judgement (as in 108f., 155–161) but also positive emphasis on the nature of the messianic age that is shortly to be brought in, and especially the place of the Jews, land, Jerusalem and temple centrally within this. These differences should, then, make us cautious about too readily producing a conflate 'messianism' for Sib 5 by merging these four passages together. All four come from separate oracles, and it is by no means

---

[11] For the view that Sib 3 in these two places refers to an Egyptian saviour-king, not a Jewish messiah, see especially J. J. Collins 1974a, 40–44, 52f.; 1983a, 68–70; 1984, 96–98; cf. also Bidez and Cumont 1938, vol II 372 note 3; Schürer–Vermes–Millar–(Goodman) 1973–87, vol. III.I, 636 note 211. The predominant understanding of these two passages, however, is still that they refer to a Jewish messianic figure, either exclusively so or else as consciously fused with the Egyptian saviour-king; for this view, cf. e. g. Lanchester, in Charles 1913, vol. II 384; Nikiprowetsky 1970, 133–137, 323; Hengel 1974, vol I 184–185, vol. II 124–125; Momigliano 1975; Kippenberg 1983, 433; Schwier 1989, 236–237, 242–243; Chester 1991a; Chester 1991b.

[12] This is evident from, for example, the renderings of Num 24.17 in the LXX and the Pentateuchal Targums, and the use made of the verse in the Qumran texts, as e. g. CD 15.7–21; 1QM 11.4–7; 4Q175 (4QTest); cf. further Chester 1991b.

certain that they derive from the same author[13]; the first two and last two passages are not mutually contradictory, but they may well represent different messianic hopes and concepts.

These are the four passages generally seen as messianic in Sib 5. But there is at least one further passage that is worth considering as contributing to a fuller picture of the messianic and eschatological emphasis of the book as a whole: 5.375—385.

And a wintry blast will blow throughout the land,
and the plain will be filled again with evil war.
For fire from the floors of heaven will rain on men,
fire and blood, water, lightning, darkness, heavenly night,
and destruction in war, and a mist over those who are slain
will destroy at once all kings and noble men.
Then pitiful destruction of war will thus cease
and no longer will anyone fight with swords or iron
or with weapons at all, which will no longer be lawful.
But a wise people which is left will have peace,
having experienced evil that it may later rejoice.

The striking feature of this text is not so much, again, the divine judgement brought upon Nero, but the vision of an age when war will cease and the Jews will live in perfect peace. It can thus be seen as representing a fulfilment of the eschatological prophecy of Isa 2.2—4 (= Mic 4.1—4). It belongs to the same overall outlook as 414ff., and it agrees with this passage in the central thrust of both its positive and negative themes. Clearly the eschatological vision in 375—385 corresponds, especially in its positive aspects, to the portrayal of the messianic age in 414ff., but what is thus to be understood implicitly as the messianic age in 381—385 is portrayed without any reference to a messiah. It is, apparently, God himself who brings about all these events directly (there could be an allusion to an eruption on the pattern of Vesuvius in 372f.[14], but whether the cosmic disasters are supposed to be general or specific, they clearly come about through divine agency). Thus both within particular sections or oracles, as well as between them, there are differences of portrayal and emphasis; in view of what we know of Jewish messianic and eschatological material otherwise, this should not surprise us.

At the very least, 375—385 also serve to confirm the main themes of the eschatological emphasis of Sib 5, within which the specifically messianic passages are set: negatively, prophecy of savage divine judgement and retribution on Israel's enemies (above all, Rome; also Egypt, Eastern kingdoms, the wicked generally), and positively, the prophecy of a glorious messianic age, in

---

[13] Cf. J. J. Collins 1974a, 57—64; Collins 1984, 187f.

[14] Cf. e.g. J. J. Collins 1974a; Chester 1991a.

which the righteous Jews, and their land, sacred city and temple, will all be characterized by perfection and divine favour. It is an idealized, indeed utopian, vision certainly, and it depends on direct divine intervention and (for the most part) the advent of a heavenly messianic figure; but it is in no sense otherworldly in emphasis. The scale of events is frequently cosmic, but there is no cosmic dualism implied; the new messianic age is centered on the present world, and above all on the Jews living in peace in Jerusalem, offering sacrifice to God in the temple.

Sib 5, and the oracles it contains, did not come into being in a vacuum. It belongs to a specific, concrete situation (political, social, economic and religious), and it addresses itself directly to that situation, as well as itself being directly a product of it. In general terms, it shows considerable similarity with Sib 3, but there are also striking differences between the two works, especially (for Sib 5) in the fierce denunciation of and invoking of judgement upon Romans, Egyptians and others, the much starker eschatological themes as a whole, and the much more developed messianic hope. The contexts within which the two works are set are correspondingly different. For Sib 5, in the late first or early second century AD, compared to the second-century BC setting of Sib 3, the foreign Empire (Rome) under which the Jews are set is experienced as much more oppressive and intolerable; the experience of Nero, the events of 66—70 and the destruction of the temple at Jerusalem (as also at Leontopolis), have probably marked a watershed in relationships and attitudes. At the same time, the Egyptians have been responsible for persecution and oppression of the Jews at a local level. The attacks found in Sib 5 on idol-worship on the part of non-Jews correspond to the attacks on pagan temples carried out in the 115—117 revolt[15]. It is at first sight a surprising feature, but it again relates to a very specific situation, of religious persecution and constraint by the Egyptians, as well as the destruction of the temples at Jerusalem and Leontopolis. It is also notable, especially in context of Leontopolis, that there is such strong attachment in diaspora Egypt to the Jerusalem temple; it may partly reflect (as may the revolt of 115—117) an influx into Egypt of Zealots and other refugees from the failure of the 66—70 revolt[16]. At any rate, these issues are joined, very specifically and bitterly, on religious grounds, which are themselves inextricably caught up in and influential upon the political, social and economic constraints and causes.

For the mass of ordinary Jews (as distinct from a privileged aristocracy in, for example, Alexandria), the social and economic conditions represented a situation of exploitation, and their political and religious freedom was clearly

---

[15] For discussion of the destruction of pagan temples during the revolt, see e. g. Fraser 1950; Applebaum 1951; Fuks 1961, 98—99; Smallwood 1976, 397—410; Applebaum 1979, 267 ff.; Hengel 1983, 660—662. On the relation between Sib 5 and this theme, cf. Hengel 1983, 672.

[16] Josephus, BJ 7.413—416; on this, cf. Hengel 1983, 666, 681.

circumscribed. As has been shown[17], Sib 5 represents part of the situation and radical political response of the Jews, that has its most obvious and dramatic expression in the revolt against Rome of 115–117. Too little is known of this revolt in detail; but it is clear that it was an extraordinarily bitter conflict, that Egypt was one of the main centres of the revolt, and that it was a primarily politically motivated revolt under messianic leadership (at least in Cyrene, and perhaps more widely). So the stark eschatological themes and developed messianic hope of Sib 5 belong to the context that gave rise to this revolt. It is a messianism that is related directly to the real lives and situation of ordinary Jews, and which echoes their hopes for the end of oppression and their yearning for religious freedom and the improvement of their material lot.

Thus already it appears that there are a number of aspects emerging that may be relevant to the theme of the 'Parting of the Ways': religious particularism, concentration on exclusive claims for Jews alone in the land or the eschatological age, temple and sacrifice as main focal points of the new age, and bitter hatred not only of overlords but also of neighbours and fellow-countrymen. The idea that we have here evidence for an important divisive development is of course strengthened by the fact that, as we have seen, Sib 5 shares many themes in common with Sib 3, but by comparison is much more bitter, stridently nationalistic and exclusive in emphasis. We seem to be well on the road to a ghetto-mentality. Again, however, it is necessary to be careful about jumping to conclusions. Sib 5 may turn out to have less to offer directly for our particular theme, at least on this level; relations with Christians are not an issue, again a reflection of the situation in Egypt at this period, and it would in any case be dangerous to generalize from material much of which is quite stereotyped.

2.1.4. Sibylline 4

Sib 4 (or at least 1–48, 102–172/192), dating from shortly after 80 AD, stands in considerable constrast to Sib 5, although roughly contemporary with it. Certainly it contains strong denunciation of Rome (especially Nero), but it has nothing of a messianic figure, and far from making Jerusalem and the temple the focal point of Jewish eschatological expectation, it appears in the earlier part of the oracle to disparage all temple and cultic activity[18]. Equally striking is the emphasis (162ff.) on undergoing baptism for repentance as the means of averting for oneself the divine judgement and destruction of the wicked. The

---

[17] Cf. above all here Hengel 1983; cf. also J. J. Collins 1974a, 94–95; Schwier 1989, 339–340.

[18] Thus 6–11, 27–30; for the view that the Jerusalem temple is included in this polemic, cf. especially J. J. Collins 1974b. For arguments to the contrary (that is, that only gentile temples are included in the attack) cf. e. g. Nikiprowetsky 1970, 233–235; Nikiprowetsky 1972, 34–35; Schürer–Vermes–Millar–(Goodman) 1973–87, vol. III.I, 642. For discussion of this issue, cf. also Chester 1991a.

final section (172–192) is also notable for the way in which it portrays, after cosmic destruction and conflagration, God bringing about a general bodily resurrection, followed by a final universal judgement, resulting in the condemnation of the wicked and the rewarding of the righteous, who are restored to paradisal life on earth[19].

There are then a few points of contact with Sib 5, for example, divine judgement on and destruction of Rome (or Israel's enemies generally); and the theme of reward for the righteous in their final blissful state on earth (187–192: 'But as many are pious, they will live on earth again when God gives spirit and life and favour to these pious ones. Then they will all see themselves looking on the delightful and pleasant light of the sun. O most blessed, whoever will live to that time') is reminiscent of the way the new messianic age is portrayed in Sib 5, even though the description is much briefer. But again it must be stressed that there is no hint of a messiah, and in other respects also, both positively and negatively, the two works stand far apart. This should not surprise us, not least because the conceptual disjunction probably corresponds to a geographical separation. It is generally, although not universally agreed, that Sib 4 emanates not from Egypt but from the region of the Jordan, and specifically from a Jewish group not otherwise known to us, but having some affinities for example with the Essenes or the Baptistic movement[20].

It may seem therefore that there is little point comparing Sib 4 and Sib 5, or drawing any conclusions from their similarities and dissimilarities. It can also be argued that the Sibylline Oracles as a whole comprise a rather strange and unrepresentative phenomenon emanating from a fairly isolated corner of Diaspora Judaism. But the juxtaposition of these two Sibyllines at least serves to show something of the divergence and pluriformity within Jewish eschatology and messianic hope and conceptualization. Thus we can find messianic belief set prominently at the centre of one work, with a vivid portrayal of an imminent, material messianic age as the focal point of Jewish hope on the one hand, and no messiah at all and only a brief glimpse of the new age on the other. And even within the same work there is an apparant divergence of messianic conception.

It can also be shown that the Sibylline literature generally is by no means unrepresentative of or isolated within Judaism, even if the form and some of the content of the oracles are not altogether typical. There is, certainly, a dearth of evidence from Egypt or the Diaspora more generally to provide us with an immediate point of connection with the eschatological and messianic emphases

---

[19] For further discussion of this theme, cf. e. g. J. J. Collins 1974b.
[20] For discussion of the setting of Sib 4, cf. Thomas, 1938, 46–52; Peretti 1962, 256–295; Nikiprowetsky 1972, 46–47; Collins 1974b.

of Sib 5[21]; but, as we have seen, what Sib 5 represents is closely bound up with popular Jewish experience and expectation, as evidenced in the disastrous revolt of 115–117. As far as Sib 4 is concerned, we have already noted close points of contact with other Jewish groups. And if we move from the Diaspora to Palestine, there are clear points of contact with these messianic and eschatological hopes.

3. 4 Ezra and 2 Baruch

The most obvious points of contact for the eschatological and messianic themes in Sib 5, within the period 70–135, are of course 4 Ezra and 2 (Syriac) Baruch. Both of these works are important for understanding the development of eschatology and messianism in Judaism in the post-70 period. In this essay, however, I will not treat these texts at all fully, but simply touch on a few relevant points. This is because I have already included brief reference to both 4 Ezra and 2 Baruch in my essay in the previous collection of papers for the Symposium, but more especially because discussion of both these texts is provided in Christopher Rowland's essay in the present volume.

3.1. 4 Ezra

In both 4 Ezra and 2 Baruch the appearances of messianic figures are simply part of a much larger eschatological scenario. Thus in 4 Ezra, there is a heavy concentration of material concerning the end; this is itself closely related to what Rowland shows to be the main concern of the book, that of theodicy[22]. Thus the emphasis is predominantly negative, and is dominated by the question it poses in 4.33: 'How long and when will these things be? Why are our years few and evil?', and it constantly repeats its lament for the judgement on the Jews, and its invocation for God's judgement on the Romans. The portrayal of the messiah is somewhat disparate, but is again closely bound up with these themes[23]. Thus 7.26–131 speaks of the signs of the end, the revealing of the messiah and the advent of the messianic kingdom, which will last for 400 years. There then follows the death of the messiah and the final judgement. This judgement is shown to be irrevocably final; no intercession is possible. It stands between the end of the present age and the beginning of the immortal age to

---

[21] As far as literary evidence is concerned, Philo and the LXX can be adduced as potentially relevant, but only in a limited and rather general way; cf. Chester 1991b.

[22] Cf. Rowland 1982, 128–135 (and on eschatology in 4 Ezra more generally, 167–170); cf. also the essay by Rowland in this volume. See also Harnisch 1969; Thompson 1977; Willett 1989, 65–75.

[23] Cf. Willett 1989, 71–74; on the portrayal of the messiah more generally in 4 Ezra, cf. especially Stone 1968; Stone 1987.

come. The righteous after death are given a vision of God and enter Paradise.

The portrayal of the messiah in the later chapters, 12–13, is notably different, as a heavenly transcendent figure with no hint of his death or vulnerability, but his role is essentially the same. Thus in the interpretation of the Eagle Vision in 12.31–39, the messiah is portrayed as appearing at the end of days, judging and destroying the wicked and delivering the faithful remnant of the Jews. In 13.21–58, the vision of the Man from the Sea is interpreted as 'my son' (32–33,51–52), that is the messiah. As part of this vision, all the nations of the earth are pictured as ceasing war against each other and coming together to Jerusalem. But this is not a vision of an idyllic messianic kingdom of peace, with the nations paying homage to the Jewish messiah and God. Instead, they are united only to attack the messiah, along with the capital and sanctuary. In face of this, the scene the vision presents us with (35–36) is of both messiah and temple as symbols of Jewish defiance of and divine judgement against their oppressors, but this remarkable vision does not result in the pagan enemies having any part in the events of the end, or of making any positive response. None of this negative emphasis should strike as at all surprising in the post-70 situation of 4 Ezra; so also, laments and prayers for the now-destroyed Zion and temple (10.7,19–24; 12.47) are precisely what we would expect. Yet the vision of the messiah taking his place on Zion, and the mount of the sanctuary miraculously appearing, introduce a positive note, while at 10.25–28 there is a remarkable vision of a new Jerusalem ('. . . there was an established city, and a place of huge foundations showed itself . . .').

Thus the near-despair and searching questioning of 4 Ezra allow at least a glimpse of hope for the future, centered on the messiah and temple, although it is not clear whether this is firmly rooted on earth, or is removed to a transcendent, heavenly realm.

3.2. 2 Baruch

2 Baruch also repeatedly laments the destruction of the temple (both in 587 and 70), and speaks of final tribulation, judgement and retribution, in context of its general eschatological emphasis[24] (10–11; 25–28; 32; 35; 54.13–22; 67). Here, however, there is much more emphasis than in 4 Ezra on the restoration of the temple and the coming of the longed-for messianic age. Reference to the messiah is comparatively rare, but he is nevertheless assigned an important

---

[24] On the significance of eschatology in 2 Baruch, cf. Rowland 1982, 131–135, 140ff., 171ff.; cf. also the essay by Rowland in this present volume. For discussion of the eschatology of 2 Baruch as specifically intended to be part of the theodicy of the work, see Willett 1989, 95–120.

role[25]. Thus in the remarkable passage 29.3—8, his coming inaugurates an age of extraordinary abundance on earth[26]:

And it will happen that when all that which should come to pass in these parts has been accomplished, the messiah will begin to be revealed. And Behemoth will reveal itself from its place, and Leviathan will come from the sea, the two great monsters which I created on the fifth day of creation and which I shall have kept until that time. And they will be nourishment for all that are left. The earth will also yield fruits ten thousandfold. And on one vine will be a thousand branches, and one branch will produce a thousand clusters, and one cluster will produce a thousand grapes, and one grape will produce a cor of wine. And those who are hungry will enjoy themselves, and they will, moreover, see marvels every day. For winds will go out in front of me every morning to bring the fragrance of aromatic fruits and clouds at the end of the day to distil the dew of health. And it will happen at that time that the treasury of manna will come down again from on high, and they will eat of it in those years because these are they who will have arrived at the consummation of time.

Nor is this an isolated vision of the transformation to be brought about in the messianic age, although it is alone in its emphasis on the great wealth of produce the land will bring forth. In 72, we are told the messiah will appear to judge and destroy Israel's oppressors. There then follows the description of the idyllic messianic kingdom in 73 (1—7):

And it will happen that after he has brought down everything that is in the world, and has sat down in eternal peace on the throne of the kingdom, then joy will be revealed and rest will appear. And then health will descend in dew, and illness will vanish, and fear and tribulation and lamentation will pass away from among men, and joy will encompass the earth. And nobody will again die in an untimely way, nor will any adversity take place suddenly. Judgement, condemnations, contentions, revenges, blood, passions, zeal, hate and all such things will come into damnation, for they will be uprooted. For these are the things that have filled this earth with evils, and because of them the life of men attained yet greater confusion. And the wild beasts will come from the wood and serve men, and the asps and dragons will come out of their holes to subject themselves to a child. And women will no longer

---

[25] For brief discussion of the messiah in 2 Baruch, see e.g. Rowland 1982, 171—174, 177; Willett 1989, 116—119.

[26] On 2 Baruch 29.3—8 in its Jewish (and wider) context, see Billerbeck 1922—26, vol. IV, 889, 951, and especially De Jonge 1979, 37—49. Cf. also e.g. Resch 1906, 166f.; Rowland 1982, 171f. The same basic tradition represented by this passage can also be seen (although in less developed form) in, for example, the earlier 1 Enoch 10.18—19: 'And in those days, the whole earth will be cultivated in righteousness; all of it will be planted with trees, and it will be filled with blessing, and all of it will be planted with pleasant trees, and they will plant on it vines; and the vine which is planted on it will produce fruit in abundance. And every seed that is sown on it, each measure will produce a thousand, and each measure of olives will produce ten baths of oil.' The saying attributed to Jesus by Papias, in the tradition as it is transmitted by Irenaeus, also stands in very close relationship to the main thrust of this passage in 2 Baruch; cf. Gry 1933—34; Gry 1946; Jeremias 1963, 38, and below, 5.2.

have pain when they bear, nor will they be tormented when they yield the fruits of their womb.

Here, then, what is envisaged is the fulfilment of the 'messianic' prophecy of Isa 11.6–9; the fulfilment of this prophecy is also anticipated in SibOr 3.787–795, in different terms. The striking fact, however, is that Sib 3 was written in a period of relative calm and peace for the Jews in Egypt (even allowing for the effects of the reign of Antiochus IV); in this situation, the golden age of the future might have seemed a realistic hope. In contrast, the desolation and despair of the post-70 period could hardly have seemed a promising basis for such expectation. Certainly there is no sign of such hope in Sib 5, or in 4 Ezra either. But 2 Baruch shows that a vivid, material vision of a new age soon to dawn could be sustained even in these circumstances; indeed, as we know from examples otherwise within Judaism and from other societies and religious traditions, it is precisely in such situations of oppression and deprivation that yearning and expectation of this kind, expressed in quite concrete terms, can flourish[27]. Again, not only is the vision of 2 Bar 73 found in other Jewish writings, such as Sib 3; so also is that of 2 Bar 29. The yearning for a messiah and messianic age survived not only the catastrophe of 70, but also that of 132–135, as for example the third-century Hebrew Apocalypse of Elijah shows us[28]:

On the 20th Adar the messiah comes, and with him 30000 righteous. As it says: righteousness is the girdle of your loins. When the nations of the world see this, then they will immediately be crushed, along with their horses, as it says: This will be the blow . . . At that time the Holy One will say to the nations of the world: Woe to you, you wicked! All of you, who are at the end of the four world kingdoms, you will all be driven out of the world! Then will a cor of wheat yield nine hundred cor; and so with wine and so with oil; all trees will be laden with wonderful fruits; as it says: You mountains of Israel, let your branches sprout . . .! And Israel will eat and rejoice for 40 years.

From the limited literary evidence available to us for Judaism for the period 70–135, and from this brief sampling of it, it is clear that messianic hope, and expectation of God's final intervention, still play an important role in at least some texts and circles within Judaism, despite the catastrophic events of 70; or, indeed, precisely as a response to these. Thus first there is clear evidence of hopes being centered on a messianic figure. This point should not be exagger-

---

[27] Cf. e. g. Thrupp 1962; Worsley 1968; Sharot 1982.

[28] The text I have used of the Hebrew Apocalypse of Elijah is that in Jellinek 1853, III.65–68 (the specific passage cited here, 66, lines 23–30). In context of the wider Jewish tradition, and some of the texts considered later in this paper (e. g. Revelation, Irenaeus, Hermas), it is worth noting that later in this Apocalypse (Jellinek 1853, III.67, lines 29–30) the seer has a vision of a great and beautiful city descending from heaven; that is, in the messianic age, the heavenly Jerusalem is brought down to earth and the fulfilment of Jewish hopes and of divine promise (already set with God in the heavenly world) is realized in material form.

ated, since it is evident that in Sib 5, 4 Ezra and 2 Baruch, reference to the messiah is relatively limited, and in Sib 4 there is no such reference at all. Nor is the portrayal consistent throughout, even within the same work, as we have seen in the case of 4 Ezra. Nevertheless, the messiah is variously assigned an important role, as in his rebuilding of the temple in Sib 5, and his inauguration of the messianic kingdom and exercise of judgement in 4 Ezra and 2 Baruch (54.13 ff., 67.4). Thus also, secondly, the inauguration of the messianic kingdom is an important theme in 4 Ezra and 2 Baruch. In 2 Baruch this is portrayed as something looked for in the immediate future (29; 72−73) in material terms, and thus presumably on earth; in 4 Ezra it is less clear whether it is conceived of as something that will come about on earth, or whether it has been removed to a transcendent, heavenly realm. Thus, thirdly, there is a lack of uniformity in the focus of future hope; it may be predominantly material, centered on the land, as we have seen with 2 Baruch, or it may be primarily spiritual, centered on the heavenly world. Where the emphasis is laid on the building of a new temple, as in Sib 5, the most obvious way of understanding this is as referring to a this-worldly, material sanctuary. But it is less easy in practice to be certain whether the new Jerusalem and temple are earthly or heavenly, material or spiritual. The point at issue, again, is whether the future hope, including messianic hope, is set in continuity with the present order (however much it may involve transformation of it), or whether this hope is shifted to a spiritualized, transcendent realm, deliberately removed from the present order[29]. Thus both 4 Ezra and 2 Baruch are caught up in the political and related conditions of the Palestine of their time; specifically, they represent a response to the catastrophe of 66−70. In the case of 4 Ezra, they come dangerously close to losing hope and removing themselves from the real world altogether.

4. Messianism and Eschatology: Popular Jewish Hope

Thus it has to be said that the texts and literary evidence that can be drawn on for the Judaism of this period give us a picture of only limited messianic and eschatological expectation; a picture which is indeed by no means consistent. At the same time, however, it needs to be emphasised that the literary evidence has obvious limitations in another sense as well; as I have noted in my earlier

---

[29] Again, however, the point needs to be made that these categories of earthly and material on the one hand, and heavenly and spiritual on the other, should not simply be set up as mutually alternative and incompatible; this is not least because especially in the Jewish apocalyptic tradition, the depiction of the heavenly world can be used to show what is, or soon will be, really the case on earth (as e.g. with the passage from the Apocaplypse of Elijah referred to in the previous note); cf. Hengel 1983, 676; and more generally Rowland 1982. Nevertheless, the basic distinction is worth making in many cases, as will become clear in some of the texts considered here.

essay[30], this literature derives, as in all peasant societies, from a very small and unrepresentative proportion of the population. Hence we need to go beyond this evidence as far as possible. So, then, it is clear that the yearning for God to intervene and bring about his kingdom on earth in the immediate future persisted among the ordinary Jewish people; and we have various indications, which should not surprise us, that concern for the restoration of Jerusalem and the Temple was often bound up with this. Fervent messianic and eschatological hopes survive the catastrophe of 66—70. Before the fall of Jerusalem and the destruction of the temple, at least some of the Pilgrim Festivals centered on the temple would have served as focal points for the expression of eschatology and messianic hopes[31]; thus, in the case of Passover, the re-enactment of the deliverance from Egypt would clearly be pregnant with significance for Jews living under Roman rule. The festivals were in no sense narrowly religious; they provided a meeting together of Jews from all over Palestine and much further afield, and were thus events with social, religious and political significance. The temple itself was an important political symbol of and focus for Jewish hopes, despite some ambivalence on the part of some of the people concerning its importance and demands. After 70, these gatherings, with their fervent expressions of eschatological hope and deliverance, no longer took place; but memories of them and traditions associated with them were of course carried through into the post-70 period.

4.1. Synagogue Prayers

These memories and traditions were sustained in part at least by the synagogue services and statutory prayers. Our knowledge of the exact nature and form of these for the period 70—135 is sadly much more deficient than we would like[32], but at any rate in general it can be said that they assumed central importance for Jewish life after the demise of the temple.

4.1.1. The Amidah

Thus the invocations to God in the Shemoneh Esreh reflect something of this deep-rooted hope, as for example in the following:

7 Look upon our afflictions and defend our cause,
   and redeem us for your name's sake.
   Blessed are you, O Lord, the Redeemer of Israel.
10 Blow a blast upon the great horn for our freedom.

---

[30] Chester 1991b.
[31] Cf. Rowland 1985, 41—42, and the further references given there.
[32] See especially Heinemann 1977; cf. also Zunz 1892; Elbogen 1931; Schürer—Vermes—Millar(—Goodman) 1973—87, vol. II, 447—463.

And raise up a banner for the gathering in of our exiles.
Blessed are you, O Lord, who gathers the dispersed of his people Israel.
11 Restore our judges as of old,
And our leaders as at the beginning,
And reign over us, you alone.
Blessed are you, O Lord, who loves justice.
14 Have compassion, O Lord our God, in your abundant mercy,
On Israel your people.
And on Jerusalem your city,
And on Zion,the abode of your glory,
And on the royal seed of David, your justly anointed.
Blessed are you, O Lord, God of David, Rebuilder of Jerusalem.
16 May it be your will, O Lord our God, to dwell in Zion,
And may your servants worship you in Jerusalem.
Blessed are you, O Lord our God, for it is you whom we worship in reverence.

It would be possible to cite other petitions from the 18 Benedictions as well, as pointing to a strong eschatological emphasis, or concerned with deliverance[33]. Thus at least a third, and perhaps nearer a half, of the 18 Benedictions reflect Jewish yearning for God's intervention and deliverance to effect the restoration of the temple or the messianic kingdom. Clearly caution is needed in assessing the question of how fixed and widespread the use of the Amidah was in the period 70–135. The different recensions and wording of the benedictions themselves remind us that we cannot know precisely what form the prayer took in this period[34]. Equally, it is not certain that the requirement that they should be said three times daily goes back to the period with which we are concerned. Nevertheless, there are good reasons for supposing that these prayers were central to the everyday lives of most Jews[35]. Hence despite the inevitable

---

[33] Thus especially the 15th Benediction in the Babylonian version: 'Cause the shoot of David to sprout forth quickly, and raise up his horn by your salvation. For we wait on your salvation all the day. Blessed are you, Lord, who causes the horn of salvation to shoot forth.' The version of the Benedictions given here is that of an old Palestinian text from the Cairo Genizah; for the text, see Schechter 1898, 656–657; cf. further Heinemann 1978, 26ff. The fact that this is an obviously ancient text-form should not, however, lead to the conclusion that it represents the original form of the text, or that it would have been the text known and used in the 70–135 period; cf. Heinemann 1978, 26–31, 45–48. For a different version of the Palestinian Amidah, and for a version of the text of the Babylonian Amidah, see Schürer–Vermes–Millar(–Goodman) 1973–87, II, 456–461. The fact that there are variations in the text and form of the Amidah does not mean that it cannot provide any useful evidence for the 70–135 period; the differences do not greatly affect the issues under consideration here.

[34] Cf. the previous note, and Heinemann 1978, 30–31, 40–69, who rightly insists that such variation and developments are inherent in the nature of liturgical usage, and that it is therefore fruitless to try to reconstruct a hypothetical 'original' text. But again the fact that we cannot know the exact form of the text in use does not mean we cannot appeal to the Amidah as evidence.

[35] Involved here is not only the question of whether legislation relating to statutory prayers at a later stage goes back to traditions current in this period, but also that of the precise nature

uncertainty about the precise wording and use of the Amidah, the importance of these benedictions as an expression and focus of hope for the majority of Jews in this period should not be underestimated. Indeed, since it is probable that the Amidah was still in a fluid state between 70–135, and open to creative development and innovation, it could readily serve as a means of responding and adjusting to changed circumstances, in their future hope as in other ways[36].

4.1.2. The Kaddish

Here, then, we have strong (if not certain) evidence of eschatological and messianic yearning being written into the lives of the mass of the Jewish people, reflecting at least something of the hopes that continued to be held and expressed at a popular level after 70. It may indeed be possible to find hints of these hopes, or at least expressions that would help sustain them, in other prayers and parts of the synagogue that would have been central to the experience of ordinary Jews in the period 70–135. Thus, for example, we find in the Kaddish[37]:

May his great name be magnified and sanctified in the world that is to be created anew, when he will bring the dead back to life and raise them up to life eternal, rebuild the city of Jerusalem, and establish his temple in its midst, and uproot all alien worship from the earth and restore the worship of the true God. May the Holy One, blessed be he, establish his kingdom and his glory during your life and during your days, and during the life of all the house of Israel, speedily and at a near time; and say Amen.

4.1.3. The Shema

Even the Shema could have been drawn on as a source of hope. The main emphasis of the Shema is, of course, on the oneness of God and on Israel's response and obedience to him, but the conclusion of the third passage that makes up the Shema in its full form (Num 15.37–41) speaks of God delivering his people from Egypt (thus the concluding words of this section and the whole Shema: 'I am the Lord your God, who brought you out of the land of Egypt, to be your God; I am the Lord your God'), while the second passage (Dt 11.13–21) contains promises of God bringing about increase in the produce of

---

of synagogue worship in the late first and early second centuries. It is, however, most plausible to see synagogue worship as of central importance for Judaism by this stage.

[36] This is the case with the 12th Benediction, the Birkat ha-Minim, in the period after 70, with its potentially great importance for the relations between Jewish and Christian communities, as well as, for example, reference in other Benedictions to the rebuilding of the temple and the coming of the Davidic messiah to establish God's reign on earth.

[37] On the nature and development of the Kaddish, cf. esp. Heinemann 1978, 266–268 (cf. also 24–25, 62–63).

the land. Along with the Shema itself, its surrounding benedictions again belong integrally within the synagogue service from an early stage, and again express the same basic themes of deliverance and restoration centered on the land of Israel and the Jewish people[38]. Thus within the first of the benedictions, preceding the Shema, we find:

There is none to be compared to you, Lord our God, in this world, and there is none beside you, our King, in the life of the world to come; there is none but you, our Redeemer, in the days of the Messiah; nor is there any like you, our Deliverer, in the resurrection of the dead.

Then in the second benediction, immediately preceding the Shema, it is said:

Because we have trusted in your holy, great and revered name, we shall rejoice and be glad in your salvation. O bring us in peace from the four corners of the earth, and make us go upright to our land; for you are a God who works salvation. You have chosen us from all peoples and tongues, and have brought us near to your great name for ever in faithfulness, that we might in love give thanks to you, and proclaim your unity. Blessed are you, Lord, who has chosen your people Israel in love.

4.1.4. Haftarah Benedictions

The strong yearning and supplication for the restoration of Jerusalem and the coming of the messianic kingdom on earth, which we have seen in the Amidah and to an extent in the Shema and its Benedictions, is evident also in the second and third petitions of the Benedictions after the Haftarah, which again is integrally part of the synagogue service and probably goes back to an early stage[39]:

Have mercy on Zion, for it is the home of our life, and save her who is grieved in spirit speedily, even in our days. Blessed are you, O Lord, who makes Zion joyful through her children.

Make us glad, O Lord our God, with Elijah the prophet, your servant, and with the kingdom of the house of David, your messiah. May he soon come and make our hearts rejoice. Let no stranger occupy his throne, and let others no longer possess themselves of his glory; for by your holy name you did swear to him, that his light would not be quenched for ever. Blessed are you, O Lord, the Shield of David.

---

[38] On the Shema and its Benedictions, cf. Heinemann 1978, 23, 29−31, 33−35, 171−172, 218ff.; cf. also Elbogen 1931, 16−26; Heinemann and Petuchowski 1978, 15−28; Schürer-−Vermes−Millar(−Goodman) 1973−87, vol. II, 454−455, 481−482.

[39] On the Haftarah Benedictions, cf. esp. Heinemann 1978, 227−229, 260−266.

4.1.5. Birkat ha-Mazon

Many other similar passages from Jewish synagogal, statutory and private prayers could be given; the one further example here is chosen at least partly because it served as the model for Didache 9–10, which will be considered further on in this paper. This is the first three petitions of the standard Grace after Meals, the Birkat ha-Mazon[40]:

1. Blessed are you, Lord our God, King of the universe, who sustains the whole world with goodness, grace and mercy. Blessed are you, Lord, who sustains all.
2. We thank you, Lord our God, for having caused us to inherit a good and pleasant land, for the covenant, Torah, life and sustenance. For all these things we thank you and praise your name for ever and ever. Blessed are you, O Lord, for the land and sustenance.
3. Have compassion, Lord our God, on Israel your people, on Jerusalem your city, on your temple and your dwelling-place, and on Zion your resting-place, and on the great and holy sanctuary over which your name was called, and may you restore the kingdom of the house of David to its place in our days, and speedily build Jerusalem. Blessed are you, O Lord, who builds Jerusalem.

The prayers cited in this section are only a small part of the potentially relevant evidence. Again, of course, it must be stressed that the argument here is not that these prayers necessarily originated or had this precise form in the 70–135 period, but rather that they (or else prayers of a very similar form) would have been integral to the synagogue service, or otherwise of fundamental importance for many Jews at this time. The significance of this is brought out very well by Heinemann[41]:

... It was customary from earliest times to insert brief petitions into prayers of praise and thanksgiving, especially petitions for the speedy coming of the final Redemption, which would naturally come to mind while mentioning the redemptions of the past. In fact, both the mention that is made in petitionary prayers of

---

[40] On the Birkat ha-Mazon, see esp. Finkelstein 1928–29, although his insistence on getting back to the original text is misconceived. A different, fuller version is provided in Heinemann-Petuchowski 1975, 91–93. In this version it is worth noting especially the clause of thanks for 'having brought us forth from the land of Egypt, and freed us from the house of slavery'.

[41] Heinemann 1978, 239; cf. also the whole discussion at 237–240, and in context of the main themes of the prayers at 33–36, e.g. 34–35: '... the central motif in the world-view of the prayers is unquestionably the belief in the Redemption, and the longing for its realization ... Granted that the messianic supplications inserted in these prayers do not occur in all of the rites, and that some of the G^eonim and the later codifiers of the law objected strenuously to them, nonetheless their persistence in many of the rites is an eloquent testimony to the impassioned yearning of generations of Jewish worshippers who were unable to restrain themselves from adding an urgent plea for the speedy coming of the future Deliverance whenever they were to recall, or to praise God for, the deliverances of the past ... the belief in the future Redemption was of paramount importance to the worshippers and to the composers of the prayers themselves.'

God's paradigmatic actions and the brief petitionary insertions into prayers of thanksgiving, referring to past miracles, are merely two sides of the same coin; and both very likely came into being spontaneously.

4.2. *Popular Jewish Messianic Movements*

Obviously the catastrophe of 70 dampened the messianic and eschatological fervour of many Jews in Palestine, at least in the form of militant expression and organized revolution against Rome. Yet the hopes for deliverance by God, or by his Messiah, from Roman oppression and (in the changed circumstances after 70) for the rebuilding of the temple certainly did not die out; they were constantly sustained and reinforced, not least by prayers and liturgical pieces of the kind I have noted above. Of course we know little or nothing specifically about the beliefs and expectations of ordinary Jews, individually or even collectively. Even if there were an abundance of Jewish texts from this period, it is unlikely that they would resolve the perennial problem of the lack of direct evidence of popular belief; but in any case there is a dearth of literary (and, to a large extent, epigraphic) evidence to help inform us of the precise nature and beliefs of Judaism at any level in this period. Nevertheless, we do at least know from Josephus that there were large popular movements in the first century prior to 70, attracted by a message (or symbolism) of eschatological deliverance or by a leader claiming messianic status[42]. The New Testament, and especially the Gospels, are further evidence for popular perceptions, and the widespread appeal, of a messianic and eschatological movement looking apparently to liberate the people. Thus the large-scale attraction of movements such as these is a further indication that messianic and eschatological hope would scarcely simply die out post-70, even if it was subdued or even suppressed. And there are, of course, more tangible signs of its continuation. I have already noted, for the Diaspora setting, the fact that the messianic hope of Sibylline 5 is entirely compatible with the little we know of the massive outbreak of messianic revolt amongst Jews in Egypt, Cyprus and Cilicia[43]. Again it is frustrating that there is so little detailed evidence available to us concerning this revolt, but we know that there was at least one self-styled messianic leader, and that there was huge popular support over a wide area.

---

[42] Cf. Hengel 1989a, 229–245, 290–302; Horsley 1984; Horsley and Hanson 1985.

[43] Cf. 2.1.3 and note 17 above; for further discussion of this revolt, see Applebaum 1951; Fuks 1961; Applebaum 1979; Schürer–Vermes–Millar 1973–87, vol. I, 529–534; Hengel 1983.

4.3. The Bar-Kochba Revolt

Within Palestine, the fervent messianic and eschatological hopes that were caught up in yet survived the catastrophe of 66−70 helped give rise to, and find their focal point in, the further revolt, again under a messianic leader, of 132−135. The bar Kochba coins and documents from Muraba'at, inter alia, leave us in no doubt about the hopes vested in this further revolt against Rome[44]. Thus some of the Muruba'at documents speak of the 'liberation of Israel', and are dated according to the particular year of the liberation (that is, the liberation is equated with the start of the revolt, and this becomes the first year of the dating); these clearly indicate the messianic and eschatological nature of bar Kochba's movement. Similarly, some of the Muruba'at coins are dated according to the particular year of the 'liberation of Israel' or 'liberation of Jerusalem' (the first year of this again being equivalent to the start of the revolt). Some coins also show that Simon ben Kosiba gave himself the title 'prince of Israel', while others have the representation of a star (set over that of a temple). The use of the star motif serves to confirm the designation of ben Kosiba as bar Kochba, 'Son of a Star', which is attributed to Rabbi Aqiba and denotes bar Kochba as fulfilling the messianic prophecy of Num 24.17. It is evident, then, that bar Kochba both claimed to be a messianic leader and was also acclaimed as such. It should also go without saying that this messianic uprising, with large popular support, could hardly have appeared in a vacuum; taken along with the revolt against Rome of 66−73 in Palestine, and that of 115−117 in the Diaspora, it bears further witness to the central place and strong potential force of messianic hope for many Jews in this period.

In view of the scale of Roman repression of the revolt and reprisals against the Jews, it would not be surprising if Rabbinic or other Jewish authorities should do as much as they could to discourage such hopes. Hence also it has been argued that it is precisely for this reason that the Mishnah, compiled around the end of the second-century AD, is silent about the messiah[45]. Yet at the same time, it is hard to imagine that these hopes did not persist, however latent, unreal and unrealised they had to remain. Indeed, with Jewish messianic, eschatologically-orientated, movements, as with millenarian and related movements more generally, the point that has been made in more recent studies, and which needs especially to be emphasized, is that there is considerable continuity in the ideology and ideals of such movements, even if their specific outbreaks seem sporadic and of very limited duration.

---

[44] Cf. further Reifenberg 1947; Benoit, Milik and De Vaux 1961; Yadin 1963; Meshorer 1967; Fitzmyer 1971, 305−354; Schürer−Vermes−Millar(−Goodman) 1973−87, vol. I, 543−549.

[45] So esp. Neusner 1987; caution however, is needed in drawing conclusions about the significance of this silence, and proper account needs to be taken of the kind of work the Mishnah is; cf. Sanders 1990, 309−331.

5. Josephus

Josephus is our main source of information concerning popular messianic movements within Palestine in the pre-70 period (see 4.2, above). But he is himself of course writing after 70, and occasionally touches on messianic and eschatological themes; one famous passage is where Josephus reflects on the cause of the catastrophe of the 66–70 revolt, in BJ VI.312–313:

> But more than anything else what drove them towards war was an ambiguous oracular pronouncement, which had also been found in the sacred scriptures, that one man from their country would at that time become ruler of the world. This they took to mean a member of their own people, and many wise men erred in their interpretation of it; but the oracle in fact signified the sovereignty of Vespasian, who was proclaimed Emperor on Jewish soil.

Here, then, Josephus discusses an 'ambiguous oracle' which he claims was misunderstood by the Jews, and in fact had its proper fulfilment in Vespasian becoming Emperor. This might seem to suggest that Josephus sees Vespasian as himself a messianic figure and the fulfilment of Jewish messianic hope (perhaps on the model of Cyrus, in Isa 45.1, or the interpretation sometimes offered for the messianic passage in SibOr 3.286–7, 652–6). But this is in fact improbable[46]. In the first place, Josephus nowhere otherwise uses the technical terminology of Jewish messianic or eschatological hope in connection with Vespasian. Secondly, the reference to this oracle, and the identification of the promised ruler with Vespasian, are not original to Josephus. The same tradition is also found in Tacitus and Suetonius, and they clearly all draw independently on a common source[47]. In fact it is not just in this brief passage, but also for the whole of 288–315 that Josephus is largely drawing on a source common at least to Tacitus as well. Certainly he adapts and adds to it, but this simply serves to confirm that, in the reference to the oracle and its application to Vespasian, Josephus is not using his own idea.

Again, it is plausible that Josephus intends the mention of the 'sacred scriptures' here to refer specifically to Num 24.17, which, as one of the most important messianic passages in Second Temple Judaism, was an important source for the Zealot and related revolutionary movement[48]. Hence it may be deliberately used here by Josephus to defuse this messianic hope and reinterpret it of Vespasian, over against the claims of a Jewish messianic, revolutionary leader. Thus also it is notable that within the section 288–315 as a whole, Josephus introduces, as one of the portents of the disaster, the account concerning the activity and death of Jesus b. Hananiah. This report may seem quite

---

[46] Cf. the discussion in U. Fischer 1978, 157–167; Hengel 1989, 237–240.

[47] Tacitus, Hist 5.13; Suetonius, Vesp 4.5. Cf. Hengel 1989, 237; U. Fischer 1978, 161–167.

[48] See esp. the argument in Hengel 1989, 237–240, 384; cf. also U. Fischer 1978, 158–161.

bizarre to us, but a striking aspect of it is that this is one of very few prophetic and related figures that Josephus does not simply condemn. The point seems to be that he is both a solitary figure, and also a prophet (although Josephus does not use that term of him) of doom and judgement against the Jewish people. That is, he is not the leader of a prophetic movement looking for deliverance or advocating revolt. For such figures and movements Josephus has nothing but contempt, holding them responsible for the revolt against Rome and the catastrophe that has overtaken the Jewish people. Thus in the section immediately preceding 6.288−315, and therefore of direct relevance for the passage we have been considering, we find Josephus explaining that 6000 people perished in one incident because they were led astray by a false prophet. Thus he says (6.286−7):

They owed their destruction to a false prophet, who had on that day proclaimed to the people in the city that God commanded them to go up to the temple court, to receive there the tokens of their deliverance. Numerous prophets, indeed, were suborned by the tyrants at that time to delude the people. They announced that they should await help from God, so that fewer would desert and so that those who lived in fear and mistrust would be encouraged by hope.

This passage is typical of Josephus. Thus he scorns popular movements and leaders, and in 6.312−313 he deliberately defuses popular messianic hope, shifting the emphasis away from final deliverance towards acceptance of Roman rule as God-given. This also helps explain another famous passage, BJ 3.350−354, 399−408, Josephus' account of his own prophecy, on surrendering to the Romans at Jotapata, of Vespasian's accession to the imperial throne[49]. In view of the similarity of the subject matter, and the fact that Josephus claims to interpret an ambiguous dream, it has often been held that we have here Josephus' sudden realization of Vespasian as the fulfilment of Jewish messianic hope, and the basis for 6.312−313[50]. But in fact this passage is almost certainly a contrived account by Josephus of his ploy to save his own skin. It is, then, a mistake to see Josephus himself as holding to popular Jewish messianic hope, with its yearning for national and earthly realization[51]. In fact he goes in precisely the opposite direction, deliberately defusing and de-eschatologizing it, and reinterpreting it to make it apply to the Roman Emperor, seeing him as a ruler, certainly, but equally certainly not of the end time. It is completely consistent with this that, as has been pointed out, Josephus fails to use any of the prophecies of salvation in Daniel, although he makes considerable reference to Daniel otherwise[52]. In short, Josephus has no collective, material

---

[49] Cf. U. Fischer 1978, 168−174; Schalit 1975, 208ff.; Hengel 1989, 235.

[50] So e.g. Weber 1921, 42−48; Lindner 1972, 70−71.

[51] This view is variously represented by e.g. Gerlach 1863, 81ff.; Bruce 1965, 160; Schlatter 1970, 34.

[52] Cf. esp. the argument of U. Fischer 1978, 174−181.

eschatological hope; where he indicates his own eschatological views, they turn out to be of a completely individualizing, philosophical character, very much the antithesis of the messianic traditions he touches on elsewhere[53].

Thus, clearly, there is considerable variety in messianic and eschatological hope within Judaism. Josephus is in many respects similar to Philo, above all in the defusing and de-eschatologizing of popular Jewish messianic hope[54]. Although Josephus, like Philo, is scarcely representative of a great many Jews, and goes against what we can detect (not least from Josephus' own account) to be the main popular tradition, he is probably not an isolated figure either. In face of the political and military consequences that fervent messianic hope might give rise to, it would obviously be tempting for some groups, especially the aristocracy to which Josephus (as, again, Philo) belonged, to attempt to defuse such hope and maintain the status quo. Thus Jewish messianic and eschatological hope was more of a battleground than an area of consensus both before and during the period when the nascent Christian movement was beginning to define itself distinctively.

Christian Texts

6. Revelation and the Early Christian Millenarian Tradition

6.1. Revelation

On the Christian side, the most obvious point of contact with the main Jewish texts discussed (especially Sib 5, 4 Ezra and 2 Baruch) is the Apocalypse of John; this again is not discussed properly here, since it is dealt with in Christopher Rowland's essay in this volume[55]. Here once more we find bitter denunciation of Rome and invoking of divine judgement and destruction on this evil Empire and, at the same time, a vision of a new Jerusalem on earth and paradisal conditions for those who receive this as a reward for their faithfulness. The Apocalypse is a work whose message is fundamentally caught up in the events and political issues of its time, and vice-versa[56]. Both its condemnation

---

[53] Cf. esp. U. Fischer 1978, 144–156. Thus, for example, at BJ III. 372ff., in context of the Jotapata incident already referred to, Josephus speaks of the body as mortal and perishable, but the soul as immortal, living for ever, the divine destiny of the body, and which at death is given a most holy, heavenly place.

[54] For discussion of Philo in this respect, cf. Hecht 1987; Chester 1991a. U. Fischer 1978, 157–213 brings out very well the similarities here between Philo and Josephus.

[55] For discussion of important themes in Revelation, see for example, in addition to Rowland's essay in the present volume, Rowland 1982, 403–441; Rowland 1988, 66–81; Fiorenza 1985.

[56] On the relation of Revelation to contemporary events and political issues, cf. especially

of Rome and its looking for the consummation of the messianic age in the near future are throughly political in scope and intent. There are, obviously, points of difference vis-à-vis the Jewish texts we have considered: the portrayal of the messiah, and (in contrast to Sib 5) the emphasis on there being no temple in the new Jerusalem. But the Apocalypse is itself also in most respects a thoroughly Jewish work, reflecting tensions in relationships with Jewish communities and synagogues in Asia Minor. Hence there may be significance in both its agreements and disagreements with the Jewish texts we have considered already.

6.2. Early Christian Millenarianism

Revelation is also of significance for the influence it has had in some parts of the developing Christian tradition, especially in its vision of the millenium and the new Jerusalem in 20–21[57]. The central importance of the 'millenial' or 'chiliastic' theme, with its emphasis on the earthly, material realization of the messianic kingdom, assumes prominence in a number of early Christian writers.

6.2.1. Papias

The earliest witness we know of to this millenial position is Papias (c. 130 AD). His views are probably most familiar from Eusebius' well-known report concerning him[58]:

(He) has quoted . . . certain strange parables of the Saviour and teachings of his, and some other things of a rather mythical character as coming to him from unwritten tradition. And among these is his statement that there will be a certain period of a thousand years after the resurrection from the dead, when the kingdom of Christ must be set up in material order on this earth.

The way in which Papias would have conceived of the nature of this messianic kingdom can be gauged from the report that Irenaeus gives of teaching that Papias handed on[59]:

The days will come in which vines shall grow, each having ten thousand branches, and on each branch ten thousand twigs, and on each true twig ten thousand shoots, and on every one of the shoots ten thousand clusters, and on every one of the

---

A. Y. Collins 1977; Wengst 1987, 118–135; Rowland 1988, 66–81, and above all Fiorenza 1985, 181–199.

[57] On Rev 20–21, cf. e. g. Bietenhard 1951, 192–204; Bietenhard 1955, 11–29; Rissi 1952; Rowland 1982, 434–439.

[58] Eusebius, Hist. Eccl. III.39.11–12; see Lawler and Oulton II, 112–116. Cf. also 4.3 above, and De Jonge 1979, 37–39, who notes the differences in wording in the editions of the text; cf. also Daniélou 1964, 380–383; Hill 1986.

[59] Irenaeus, Adv. Haer V. 33.3–4; cf. e.g. Jeremias 1963, 37–38; Daniélou 1964, 380–383; De Jonge 1979, 37–39; Hill 1986.

clusters ten thousand grapes, and every grape when pressed will give twenty-five measures of wine. And when any one of the saints takes hold of any one of their clusters, another will cry out, 'I am a better cluster, take me; bless the Lord through me'. In like manner, a grain of wheat would produce ten thousand ears, and every ear would have ten thousand grains, and every grain would yield ten pounds of clear, pure, fine flour; and apples and seeds and grass will produce in similar proportions; and all animals, feeding then only on all these products of the earth, will become peacable and friendly to each other, and be in perfect subjection to man.

According to Irenaeus, Papias had received this as Jesus' own teaching, via John the disciple of Jesus. It is certainly doubtful that this teaching derived from Jesus, although it is probable enough that the tradition goes back before Papias; but in any case, there is no reason to doubt that it represents Papias' own understanding of the kingdom[60]. Indeed, Irenaeus makes it clear that Papias transmits this tradition with approval, emphasizing positively that it is a word of the Lord that true believers accept and which specifically looks for the fulfilment of Isaiah 11[61]. It is also the case, of course, that the conclusion to this Papias' passage not only looks back to the prophecy of Isa 11.6−9, but is reminiscent of SibOr 3.787−795 and 2 Bar 73.6. In addition, there is a striking resemblance between the start of this passage and part of 2 Bar 29 (as also the Hebrew Apocalypse of Elijah), cited above. Thus what we have here is the early Christian tradition drawing on its Jewish heritage, as well as the tradition of Jesus' teaching and the Apocalypse of John, as an integral part of its portrayal of the glorious future to come.

It is a matter for great regret that we do not possess any of Papias' own writings in full, especially the five-volume *Exegesis of the Lord's Gospel*, only scraps of which have been preserved[62]. Papias' comments, and the tradition he was representing, on some gospel texts might have been extremely illuminating for his (or at least, a prominent early Christian) understanding of Jesus' proclamation of the kingdom and when and how it would be realized. The problem of lack of evidence applies, of course, not simply to Papias in this early period. Thus, for example, it is plausible that millenial beliefs and the specific expectation of the kingdom in material terms characterized the Ebionites;

---

[60] For discussion of Papias, cf. e. g. O'Hagan 1968, 36−44; cf. also Gry 1933−34; Gry 1946; Jeremias 1963, 37−38.

[61] Thus Irenaeus, Adv. Haer V. 33.4, specifically cites Isa 11.6−9 in full, along with Isa 65.25, as the prophecy that will be fulfilled by the miraculous increase of produce, in the saying Papias attributes to Jesus.

[62] Irenaeus, Adv. Haer V. 33.4, refers to five books composed by Papias, while Eusebius, Eccl. Hist. III.39.1, specifically notes that Papias was responsible for a five-volume work entitled *Exegesis of the Lord's Gospel*. For the text of the few fragments that have survived, see De Gebhardt 1878 Appendix, 87−104; Funk-Bihlmeyer 1924, 133−140; see also Rousseau 1969 for a rather different text of the fragment preserved by Irenaeus.

certainly they appear to have stressed material reward and blessing of the poor[63]. It may also be that other groups were millenarian in outlook and emphasis; but this is largely speculative conjecture, since we simply do not possess the evidence from which to form a judgement.

6.2.2. Justin and Irenaeus

Despite the paucity of evidence, it is nevertheless clear that millenarian beliefs continued to exercise considerable influence within early Christian communities and tradition. Indeed, it has been claimed that early Christianity was completely chiliastic. Thus, although apart from Revelation and the brief fragments of Papias there is little direct evidence for the period 70–135, millenarian attitudes can be found extensively in texts from the later second century onwards. Both Justin and Irenaeus are good instances of this, and although their writings come from the post-135 period of the second century, they clearly reflect the continuation of a tradition they have taken over and can be considered briefly here.

6.2.2.1. Irenaeus

The main evidence for Papias' millenarian views derives, as we have seen, from Irenaeus; it is appropriate to consider him first, although he is later than Justin, not only because he is our direct link with Papias but also because he provides the fullest second-century statement of the millenarian position. This is to be found in AdvHaer V. 32–36, at the end of his long anti-Gnostic work. The section as a whole is an extended treatment of the millenial kingdom that is to come about on earth. Irenaeus is concerned to argue throughout (against Gnostic heresy) that the kingdom must be understood as specifically material, not spiritual, and also that it represents the complete fulfilment, centered on Christ, of God's promises to Israel. Thus he sets out the position clearly at the start (32.1):

... It is appointed that the righteous first, in this creation which is being renewed, rising again at the appearance of God, should receive the promise of the inheritance which God promised to the fathers and reign in it, and that afterwards the judgement should take place.

---

[63] For discussion of aspects of millenarian emphasis in the Ebionite movement, cf. e.g. Schoeps 1949, 82–87; Daniélou 1964, 379–380. The main evidence (slender though it is) for this belief of the Ebionites is gained from Jerome's Commentary (LXVI.20), where he speaks of the Ebionites understanding 'all the delights of the thousand years in a literal sense', and also perhaps, implicitly, from the Clementine Recognitions (I.61), which emphasises the poor receiving material, earthly reward.

That is, the kingdom represents the renewal of creation on earth; those who reign there will do so where they have already suffered. This, Irenaeus argues, also represents the fulfilment of God's promise of the land to Abraham in material form, as the inheritance of the earth in the resurrection of the just and the fulfilment of Jesus' promises in the Beatitudes (32.2). It is also (33.1–2) in this kingdom that the fulfilment is to be found of Jesus' promises concerning drinking his cup anew, the banquet for the poor and the hundredfold recompense for what has been given up. Again Irenaeus says that Isaac's blessing of Jacob makes no sense unless it is realized in the kingdom (33.3):

Therefore the blessing mentioned relates unquestionably to the times of the kingdom, when the just shall reign, rising again from the dead; when also the creation, being renewed and delivered, shall bring forth plenty of all kind of nourishment, of the dew of heaven and of the fatness of the earth.

This leads directly into Irenaeus' citation of Papias and his tradition; this tradition is central to Irenaeus' case. Here, as we have seen, is to be found the fulfilment of the prophecy of Isa 11.6–9, which Irenaeus interprets in a very literal, material manner. He then cites (33.4) a number of Old Testament prophecies that he interprets as referring to bodily resurrection and the restoration of the people to the land; these and other promises are made not just to Israel but also to the church and the Gentiles. So also, the prophecies of a glorious future for Jerusalem are in fact to be interpreted concerning believers, or the church, in the final kingdom on earth (as he says, 35.1, in this resurrection the just will reign on earth). Thus he continues (35.2):

Now all these sayings, being of this kind, cannot be understood of things above the heavens . . . but of the times of the kingdom, when the earth is again summoned by Christ, and Jerusalem rebuilt, after the pattern of the Jerusalem that is above . . .

He then cites a succession of texts to show that the heavenly Jerusalem will be brought down on earth and, finally, argues that it is not a question of God destroying his creation, but rather of a new creation in continuity with the old; merely the 'fashion' of this world passes away, but the substance and essence remain. It is the new heaven and new earth that 'man made young again' (that is, the church) enters, and it will continue without end. So also it is important for Irenaeus that scripture and prophecy are consistent in looking for the material restoration on earth, and that God is consistent, in creating man in the first place and bringing about the new creation 'in the resurrection of the just'. There is further continuity in those who inherit the kingdom, and in the kingdom belonging to God's son, who is the image and likeness of God. Thus Irenaeus' eschatological vision is thoroughly bound up with his ecclesiology and christology; they are important and integral to it, even though they are not developed at all fully or deeply here.

It is very common to hold up Irenaeus' millenarian emphasis to ridicule, seeing it as a regrettable lapse (after a splendidly sustained attack on Gnosticism) into a crude, materialist Jewish eschatology[64]. But although Irenaeus of course has to be subjected to critical analysis here, this kind of rather superior (even arrogant) dismissal of him does less than justice to the force of the vision he presents, its place in his overall theological conception and his reason for giving the millenarian view such prominence at the end of his work, quite apart from the negative assessment of Jewish eschatology that it entails[65].

6.2.2.2. Justin

The classic statement of Justin's millenarian outlook is found in Dial 80–81, where Justin responds to a challenge from Trypho on the whole issue:

Trypho: . . . Tell me, do you really admit that this place, Jerusalem, will be rebuilt? And do you expect your people to be gathered together, and made joyful with Christ and the patriarchs, and the prophets, both the men of our nation and other proselytes who joined them before your Christ came?
Justin: . . . I admitted to you previously that I and many others are of this opinion, and really (believe) that this will take place. But on the other hand, I indicated to you that many who belong to the pure and pious faith, and are true Christians, think otherwise . . . But I and others, who are right-minded Christians on all points, are assured that there will be a resurrection of the dead, and a thousand years in Jerusalem, which will then be built, adorned and enlarged, as the prophets Ezekiel and Isaiah and others declare.

Justin then cites the whole of Isa 65.17–25 as referring to the millenium[66], and concludes the section thus:

And further, there was a certain man with us, whose name was John, one of the apostles of Christ, who prophesied by a revelation that was made to him that those who believed in our Christ would dwell for a thousand years in Jerusalem; and that after that, the general, and in short the eternal, resurrection and judgement of all men would similarly take place. Just as our Lord also said (text of Lk 20.35–36).

---

[64] Cf. e.g. Robertson 1901, 133–134; Cohn 1957, 33; for more muted criticism, cf. Lampe 1953, 25. It is still more common to pour scorn on Papias, picking up from Eusebius' characterization of him, in context of his millenial teaching (Eccl. Hist. III.39), as 'a man of very meagre intelligence'; cf. e.g. Lampe 1953, 25; Jeremias 1963, 38.

[65] For an attempt to give Irenaeus a fairer hearing on this point, see O'Rourke Boyle, 1969. For a useful presentation of Irenaeus' eschatological conception overall, cf. Kirchner 1863; the section dealing specifically with chiliasm is at 329–344.

[66] Justin argues that the 'days' in this passage should be understood according to Ps 90.4; this is a common point of reference in a millenarian or related framework, as e.g. at Ep Barnabas 15.4 (cf. 7.1 below).

Justin thus emphasises the material, earthly nature of the millenium, especially over against denials, by what he describes as heretical Christian groups, of bodily resurrection. He uses biblical (that is, Old Testament) texts profusely to convince Trypho that he stands fully in line with the Jewish tradition the latter represents here, and to offer a vision of the fulfilment of the messianic age and the kingdom, where the earth, and all human and social relationships, are transformed.

This, then, is the locus classicus for Justin's millenarian views; but it is not the only place where Justin sets out his eschatological vision. Thus he interprets Noah's blessings at 139.5:

... Christ has come according to the power given him from the Almighty Father, and summoning men to friendship, and blessing, and repentance and dwelling together, has promised, as has already been shown, that there will be a future possession for the saints in this same land. And hence all men everywhere, whether bond or free, who believe in Christ and recognise the truth in his own words and those of his prophets, know that they will be with him in that land, and inherit everlasting and incorruptible good.

Here again the emphasis is obviously material, portraying Christians reigning with Christ on this earth, and again it provides a vision of the transformation of the earth and of human relationships; there are also other, similar passages in the Dialogue[67]. Thus although this theme, and eschatology as a whole, is not proportionately prominent in Justin's work, it is nevertheless an important and integral part of his theology and apologetic.

This tradition is subsequently continued and developed, beyond Justin and Irenaeus, by Tertullian, Hippolytus, Methodius and Victorinus, amongst others, before it reaches its climax in Lactantius[68]. Its demise, at least as far as orthodox credal Christianity is concerned, soon follows, in the face of denunciation by Augustine[69] (himself following the example of Origen and others)[70], and it was officially declared a heresy at the Council of Ephesus in 431.

---

[67] Thus e.g. Dial 85: 'Jesus commanded us to love even our enemies, as was predicted by Isaiah in many passages, in which there is also contained the mystery of our own regeneration, as well in fact as the regeneration of all who expect that Christ will appear in Jerusalem, and by their works earnestly endeavour to please him'; Dial 113: '... and as (Joshua), not Moses, led the people into the holy land, and as he distributed it by lot to those who entered with him, so also Jesus the Christ will turn again the dispersion of the people, and will distribute the good land to each one, though not in the same manner. For the former gave them only a temporary inheritance, since he was neither Christ who is God, nor the Son of God; but the latter, after the resurrection of the saints, will give us the eternal possession'.

[68] For a brief outline, cf. e.g. Grant 1917; Bietenhard 1953; Hill 1986.

[69] De Civitate Dei XX.7; cf. Sermo CCLIX.2.

[70] Thus e.g. Origen, De Principiis II.11.2; Jerome, Comm. on Dan 7.17.

6.3. Non-Chiliastic Christianity

Millenialism or chiliasm were thus of central importance for the early Christian tradition. But this was not the only form the Christian tradition took, despite some of the claims that have been made. Thus from an early stage, there is a substantial part of the Christian tradition whose eschatology is not material in emphasis, and in some cases not particularly imminent either; indeed, in some texts, eschatology itself is not particularly prominent.

It is apparent, then, that a millenarian or chiliastic position is not the only option taken up as the new Christian messianic movement developed in the first and early second centuries. This point has been developed further in a interesting argument recently by Hill[71]. Thus he is concerned to show that chiliasm represents neither a homogeneous nor a dominant stance in the Christian tradition of the second to fourth centuries. He argues that from an early stage there is clearly a substantial movement that can be characterized as 'non-chiliastic orthodoxy', which has to be recognized by chiliastic writers both as differing decisively from their position yet also not able to be dismissed as heterodox. Hence Hill makes a great deal of Irenaeus' reference to non-chiliastic orthodoxy[72], and sees such a designation as representing a substantial concession on the part of this apologist. Hill also, not surprisingly, points to the apparent contradictions in Justin, drawing attention to the complete lack of reference in the Apology to the expected earthly kingdom of Christ[73]. He also argues for inconsistency within the Dialogue, as well as between the Dialogue and the Apology. Thus the Dialogue, just as the Apology, speaks in a number of places of general resurrection and final judgement; it also talks of an eternal kingdom on earth[74]. Dial 80–81 he describes as 'openly though not enthusiastically chiliastic', but argues that Justin is inconsistent more widely on the questions of eschatology, life after death and the state of the dead. That is, Justin either combines chiliasm with the belief in there being no immediate entry of the soul into God's presence at death, or else simply represents chiliasm on its own.

Hill then finds these themes combined in several other of what are usually seen as main representatives of the chiliastic tradition from the late second through to the fourth century. Thus, he argues, in Papias, Irenaeus, Justin, Tertullian, Commodianus, Victorianus and Lactantius, these two different eschatological teachings are held together; they represent on the one hand chiliasm, on the other the view that the souls of the righteous await the day of resurrection in a state of refreshment in a subterranean world. In the case of

---

[71] Hill 1986.
[72] Irenaeus, Adv. Haer V. 31.1–32.1; cf. Hill 1986.
[73] Hill 1986.
[74] Justin, Dial 45,113,139; Apol I.11; cf. Hill 1986.

Methodius, who says nothing of this intermediate state at all, Hill argues that he
scarcely represents anything that can be called chiliastic either; Novatian, on
the other hand, clearly portrays the intermediate state but again, despite claims
made to the contrary, has nothing at all of chiliasm. These two, however, are
not representative; the main position of 'chiliastic' writers is that they hold their
chiliastic belief along with that of the intermediate state; Hill argues that this
combination can be found in earlier Jewish sources, especially 4 Ezra and 2
Baruch, and this represents the composite, fundamentally illogical, tradition
which is drawn on by these Christian writers[75].

It is not clear, however, that Hill's argument disposes of chiliasm, or removes
it from its position of central importance in the early Christian tradition, in the
way that he implies. Thus it is not incongruous or logically inconsistent to hold
belief in a millenium along with that of an intermediate state. That is, if these
writers affirm the theme of the divine kingdom on earth for the righteous, then
it is clear that they will be faced with the problem of what happens to those
righteous who have died before the kingdom is ushered in. The idea of the
intermediate state, already available (as is that of the millenium) in Jewish
tradition, is one obvious way of resolving this. The question is much less
common and acute in Jewish writings, since in contrast to the developing
Christian tradition it is not held that the messiah has already come and that the
messianic kingdom should therefore follow soon. In 2 Baruch and 4 Ezra, the
issue is bound up with concern with theodicy; that is, the question of what has
become of righteous Jews who have perished in the revolt against Rome, as well
as the fate of the Jewish people as a whole[76]. Hence the vision of the coming
messianic kingdom is linked with that of the souls of the righteous being kept in
waiting for this under the earth. So also, for example, in the case of Justin, the
differences between the Dialogue and the Apology are explicable on the basis
of the different nature and purpose of the two works rather than a failure on
Justin's part to think consistently. That is, in the Dialogue he needs to show how
Christianity represents the fulfilment of Judaism, including the promises concerning the messianic age, and his full statement of the millenarian position
comes in context of this. In the Apology, by contrast, it would obviously be
tactically dangerous and misconceived in addressing the Roman authorities to
introduce the theme of a new kingdom to be ushered in in a newly rebuilt
Jerusalem. Hence he eschews mention of it, and the supposed inconsistencies
within Justin are thus considerably diminished[77]. All this may, however, be to
suggest too logical and considered a development. Perhaps the most that can be

---

[75] Hill 1986.

[76] Cf. 3.1 above; cf. also Rowland 1982, 128–135; Willett 1989, 65–72, 95–112. For a
brief, and somewhat superficial, discussion of the intermediate state in Judaism, cf. Bailey
1934.

[77] Cf. e.g. Bietenhard 1953, 15.

said is that in these Jewish texts it is clear, on one level at least, how these themes would have been understood, while this formulation is then available for the early Christian writers and easily adapted by them. The problem for the latter, put simply, is that of holding on to the hope of the divine kingdom on earth while being confronted increasingly with the delay of the Parousia. Again, however, this is not primarily an abstract or logical problem to be resolved; much more, it is the fact that the divine kingdom has not yet materialized while believers continue to pass away, so it becomes both necessary and urgent to make clear what has happened to these believers and how they will still be able to participate in the kingdom.

Hence Hill is right to stress the importance and widespread nature of the idea of the intermediate abode of the righteous dead in the Christian tradition of the early centuries, and to show that chiliasm is a less prevalent phenomenon than has sometimes been supposed. Yet it is equally necessary not to underestimate the importance of the millenarian tradition in early Christianity[78]. This is all the more so (paradoxical though it may sound) precisely in view of the fact that it is variously abandoned, compromised or made ambiguous in the ways that Hill indicates. It is a pity, not least in this respect, that Hill refuses so dismissively to take seriously the potential contribution that social theory (or more specifically, as he refers to it, sociological and anthropological analysis) would have to make for the understanding of the phenomena that he is examining. The study of millenarian and related movements in these disciplines is very wide-ranging[79]; not surprisingly, there is no unanimity concerning the theoretical framework to be used or conclusions to be reached in examining these movements, but they provide (in various ways) important insights for helping make sense of them. More recently, there has been sociologically informed analysis of specifically Jewish messianic, millenarian and related movements[80]. Amongst the issues dealt with in some of the studies in general are the structure and organization of the movements, their life-span, and the nature of their hope for or expectation of an imminent future utopian or materially abundant consummation[81]. It is precisely this kind of analysis that could be profitably applied to the early Christian movement, or at least various parts of it[82].

Thus it is both the Jewish tradition, which Hill takes account of, and also sociological and anthropological analysis, which he repudiates, that need to be considered together in relation to millenarianism in early Christianity. Indeed, if those strands of the Jewish tradition which he neglects were to be considered,

---

[78] For discussion, from various perspectives, of the nature and importance of millenarianism (or chiliasm) in early Christianity, cf. e. g. Gry 1904; Bietenhard 1953; Daniélou 1964.

[79] See e. g. Y. Talmon 1962; Lanternari 1965; Worsley 1968; Burridge 1969; Thrupp 1970; La Barre 1971; Adas 1979.

[80] Cf. e. g. Isenberg 1974; Sharot 1982; S. Talmon 1987.

[81] See e. g. Thrupp 1962.

[82] This has been undertaken, to a limited extent, by e. g. Isenberg 1974; Gager 1975.

more would need to be said about the importance of the land, and material and terrestrial hope more generally. It has been shown in recent studies[83] that this specific focus of hope is important in both Jewish and Christian traditions in this period, as for example the Bar Kochba and Muraba'at evidence shows us for the one side, and for example Papias, Justin and Irenaeus for the other. It is precisely the fact that the glorious transformation of the land has not taken place that makes the Christian messianic claim vulnerable to Jewish attack[84], while equally the Jewish and Christian sources clearly share the same tradition and scriptural passages, and are in many ways difficult to distinguish[85]. Hence it is the close conjunction between the Jewish and Christian positions that is subjected to polemic by Christian opponents of chiliasm, such as Origen, in order to establish the Christian position as distinctive and rid it of crude materialism. It should not surprise us, in view of what we know of millenarian and related movements otherwise, that the Christian messianic movement takes up these themes from Judaism, and that for both Jews and Christians there is a common interest in the material realization of the messianic age. Nor should it surprise us that for the early Christian tradition and communities the failure of these hopes to be realized presents problems, and elicits different modes of resolution. None of this, however, is considered by Hill.

This issue does indeed go deep. It is not, *pace* Origen, just a question of crude materialism. Instead it is matter of taking seriously, as the Jewish tradition does, the vision of the new age that God will bring in, and the restoration of the world (or creation) to its true and pure state. This does of course involve a utopian view, or myth of origin, in one sense at least, but it is important to note that this vision of future restoration is fully consistent with the understanding of God's creation of and deliverance for all people. This restoration can be seen both as transformation of and also as continuity with the present world, to be enjoyed by the righteous (or all people) as God's gift and new creation. In some respects, then, it comes close to the issues raised in contemporary interpretation (for example, in liberation and materialist exegesis)[86]; this may often appear one-sided, but the challenge to Origen and others (as also to the contemporary emphasis in Western scholarship on 'spirituality') is the refusal to acquiesce in a 'spiritual' or heavenly kingdom, or realization of the promise, and an insistence instead on the concrete manifestation of this kingdom.

---

[83] Cf. Wilcken 1986; Horbury 1988.
[84] Thus e. g. Justin, Dial 80–81; Origen DePrinc 4.2.1; cf. Wilcken 1986.
[85] Cf. Wilcken 1986.
[86] Cf. e. g. Miranda 1974; Pixley 1981; Belo 1981.

7. Barnabas and the Didache

Thus it is clear both that the contrast between chiliasm and non-chiliasm, or material and spiritual expectation, in early Christianity represents an over-simplification, and also that the specific nature of the messianic kingdom and Christian future hope looms large not least in those works that are caught up in debate or dispute with Jews (as for example Justin's Dialogue, in contrast to the Apology).

7.1. The Epistle of Barnabas

These factors are relevant to the Epistle of Barnabas, a work that is permeated by Jewish themes and motifs, and which is yet at the same time fervently and polemically anti-Jewish. In this respect, at least, it is reminiscent in general terms of the Gospel of Matthew and more specifically of the Epistle to the Hebrews, in the way that it disallows for the Jews the validity of the temple, sacrifice and covenant, and instead appropriates them for the Christian community. Barnabas is also run through with typically Jewish eschatological themes. Thus for example, it speaks of the end as imminent (4.3ff.), the present both as the last days (4.9; 6.13) and also as an evil time which the believers must withstand (2.1; 4.9), although it will involve suffering, before the final judgement that is to come (4.12) and the advent of the kingdom of Christ, whose reign the believers will share in (4.13; 8.13).

Hence, in view of this scenario that Barnabas presents, it is not surprising that it has often been seen as a chiliastic work, an integral part of the same tradition as that represented by Justin and Irenaeus. Yet although it speaks of the believers participating in Jesus' kingdom, it lacks features that other chiliastic texts have, and its chiliastic credentials have therefore been doubted. Daniélou, noting the lack of reference in Barnabas to fulfilment of messianic prophecies such as Isa 11, characterizes it as belonging not to the 'Asian' type of millenarianism or chiliasm (represented by, for example, Papias, Justin, Irenaeus and Montanism), but to the 'Syrian' (as, for example, Theophilus of Antioch and Hippolytus), which is much more restrained and less exuberant[87]. But this kind of distinction between different 'chiliasms' still begs obvious questions, and this categorization of Barnabas leaves open the issue of whether Barnabas is a fully millenarian work, and how it stands in relation to Jewish hope. A crucial passage here is 15, especially 4–8:

Notice, children, what he means by the words 'He completed them in six days', He means this: in six thousand years the Lord will make an end of all things; for in his reckoning the 'day' means 'a thousand years'. He is himself my witness when he

---

[87] See Daniélou 1964, 396–401.

says, 'Behold, a day of the Lord is a thousand years'. Therefore, children, in six days, in the course of six thousand years, all things will be brought to an end. 'And he rested on the seventh day.' This is the meaning: when his son returns, he will put an end to the era of the Lawless One, judge the wicked and change the sun, the moon and the stars. Then on the seventh day he will properly rest. Furthermore he says, 'You shall sanctify it, clean of hand and heart'. Therefore, if anyone is able at present to sanctify, clean of heart, the day on which God has sanctified it, then we are the victims of deception. Consider; we shall, as it seems, properly rest and sanctify it then only when we are able to do so after being ourselves justified and having received the promised blessing; when there is no more iniquity and all things have been made new by the Lord, then at last we shall be able to sanctify it, because we have first been sanctified ourselves. He further says to them, 'Your new moons and sabbaths I despise'. Consider what he means; not the sabbaths of the present era are acceptable to me, but that which I have appointed to mark the end of the world and to usher in the eighth day, that is, the dawn of another world.

An obvious reading of this passage is that at his Second Coming, or Parousia, Christ will bring an end to the present evil age, usher in the final judgement and inaugurate a kingdom of a thousand years. But there are some inherent ambiguities; thus it is not certain whether there are two distinct eschatological sabbaths (the seventh and eighth day, separately), or whether the kingdom that will be inaugurated is temporal and terrestrial or not. The question has also been raised whether the subject of the verbs in the latter part of v. 5 ('judged . . . reign') is 'the Son' or 'God'. Thus Hermans argues strongly that God, not Christ, is the subject of v. 5b, that the 'eighth day' (v. 8) follows the sixth directly, and that thus God brings an end to the present order and initiates the new age, without any temporary messianic reign of Christ with the believers on earth[88]. This, he claims, makes better sense of the usage and overall argument of the passage, as well as the Jewish traditions of the cosmic week and eschatological sabbath. Thus there is no millenium, or chiliastic concept overall; the point instead is to disallow the Jewish sabbath and to show how this is appropriated and properly fulfilled within the Christian tradition, which will soon reach its final consummation.

Throughout, Hermans provides detailed exegesis and argues the strongest conceivable case for this view. Indeed, much of his argument overall is convincing; but it remains at best a possibility that God is the subject of the verbs in 5b, while the straight identification of the seventh and eighth sabbaths is an ingenuous, but too simple, solution to the complexities of this passage[89]. The main problem, of course, is posed by the introduction of the eighth day and second sabbath; otherwise, the picture is reasonably clear. That is, the eschatological

---

[88] Cf. Hermans 1960.

[89] Cf. O'Hagan 1968, 63, who sees Hermans' argument as almost too neat to be really convincing.

scenario that Barnabas presents (using the cosmic week tradition) sets the final events at the end of the sixth day, or sixth millenium, when Christ's Parousia and final judgement take place, along (apparently) with some form of cosmic renewal. But then 15.8, which speaks of the eighth day marking the final end and the 'dawning of a new age', complicates the picture, since logically it would suggest a further stage and second set of final events (and re-creation). It is more likely, however, that Barnabas introduces it precisely in order to show that the Jewish sabbath is superseded and to justify the Christian observance of the first, not last, day of the week. Hence the seventh and eighth days, the first and second sabbaths, have to be merged into each other, marking the final end of the present order and the transition to the new, without positing a further eschatological denouement. This may seem to agree with Hermans, but differs in suggesting that Barnabas' picture is to an extent messy and inconsistent, since he is bringing different arguments and traditions together for different purposes, rather than presenting a coherent, unified case throughout[90].

Hence the question of whether Barnabas presents a fully millenarian picture is still, *pace* Hermans, left open. It is certainly plausible to understand Barnabas as working with a general millenarian view of history, along with other traditions. According to O'Hagan, the final judgement (cf. also 5.10; 21.3) and change of heavenly bodies at 15.5, belonging as they do to the general Jewish tradition of eschatological change and the renewal of the whole universe, denote both a moral and material re-creation. The 'rest' in 15.5 is then to be understood as parallel to that at 15.7, denoting the joyful repose of the spiritually renewed elect, the eschatological sabbath, in a material creation that has also been completely renewed. So also O'Hagan takes the reference to the 'promise' (ἐπαγγελία) in 15.7 to denote the Jewish tradition of the eschatological promise of the land to Israel (a promise deriving ultimately from the Abraham tradition)[91]. In fact O'Hagan's interpretation overall probably has to read too much into the reference to sun, moon and stars in 15.5, and in any case (as he himself notes) does not correspond to a millenarian belief proper. On the other hand, 15.8 is to be closely linked with 15.5−7, and in speaking of 'the dawn of another world', it very probably points to renewal or re-creation on this earth, and so could suggest a millenarian view.

Other passages in Barnabas, however, cast doubt on whether a terrestrial messianic kingdom can be intended in 15. Most striking of all here, 6.8−19 interprets the promise of the land to Abraham (6.8, drawing loosely on Old Testament passages) allegorically to mean the Christian community (6.9−16), and the 'milk and honey' that the land is flowing with as faith in the promised blessing and as the Word by which the community, like children, are sustained

---

[90] Cf. also O'Hagan 1968, 54−65. On the millenial (or cosmic) week theme more widely, cf. Daniélou 1948.

[91] Cf. O'Hagan 1968, 50−60.

and kept alive (6.17). Thus is appears that the promise of the land and its produce is spiritualized, while the renewal of creation, or second creation, is also taken to refer, narrowly, to the Christian community, which is also designated as a holy temple (6.15).

This passage also, however, O'Hagan claims to be centrally concerned with material re-creation[92]. He admits that the various allegories make the picture complex, but argues that the point of the allegorical interpretation of the Old Testament, and the refusal to take the Christ-land allegory to its logical conclusion, is to promote the doctrine of a new creation in a new order. He concedes that 6.8–10 presents a spiritual interpretation of 'land', but holds that the 'land' in 6.17 ('... once we possess life, we shall rule the land') is the land of the eschatological promise, as at 15.7. So also he argues that in the following verses, at the climax of the passage (18–19), Barnabas is very close to hope for a return to Paradise, in the tradition especially of Isaiah 11 and developed Jewish interpretation. Thus Barnabas looks for a situation where humanity is again the lord of all created things; this implies a material, and not simply spiritual, renewal. On this interpretation, the second creation and second possession of the promised land of Paradise have already begun in a spiritual sense, while the material fulfilment is still to be consummated at the end of the era, when Christians enter their inheritance, that is, the new kingdom of God. Just as the spiritual re-creation is based on Christ, so also is the material.

At least some of this argument, however, appears to be special pleading. Thus it is not clear that 6.17 denotes the 'land' of eschatological promise, or that 6.18–19 represents any kind of fulfilment of Isaiah 11[93]; these verses seem much closer to the Genesis 1 tradition of the human race's domination of the natural order, and it is misleading to suggest that Isa 11.6 ('the little child will lead ...') implies the same kind of mastery. So also the reference to the temple in 6.15 is taken up in 16, where it is again emphasised that the new temple is to be found not in any material form but in the Christian community (thus 16.8, and especially 16.10: 'This is a spiritual temple that is now being built for God')[94]. Thus 6.8–19 and 16.6–19, along with several passages in Barnabas, can plausibly be interpreted as spiritualizing. Further, given that Barnabas is concerned to deny to the Jews the true possession of all the central themes of Judaism and to appropriate these for the Christian community, an obvious ploy would be to disallow or deride these central tenets on a concrete material level, and to interpret them spiritually or figuratively instead[95]. So also, since the

---

[92] Cf. O'Hagan 1968, 45–50; on this passage, cf. also Dahl 1950.

[93] Wengst 1984, 157, also sees 6.19 as based on Isa 11, and as belonging as well to the same tradition as 2 Bar 73.6 and Papias.

[94] According to Vielhauer 1979, 153–154, followed by Wengst 1984, 201, in 16.6–10 Barnabas has also individualized the image of the temple, in contrast to Paul, who applies it to the community as a whole.

[95] The passage dealing with the temple in 16 raises further interesting issues. It has been

promise of the glorious messianic age had conspicuously failed to materialize, it would seem simplest to remove the millenium (as with the land) to a spiritual or heavenly sphere.

Even so, it is impossible to be certain that Barnabas is simply spiritualizing; the evidence is difficult to assess and tie down to one specific meaning. Thus in the case of ch. 15, the whole can be seen as portraying a millenium ushered in by God, which could plausibly have material, terrestrial form and be participated in by the believers. Yet, equally, it is simply not clear whether this is so for the new (or renewed) world here; the same is true of what is said of the inheritance in 4.3 and the kingdom in 4.13, 8.5−6, 21.1, although 8.5−6 may indicate that the kingdom is to be understood as having been inaugurated already on earth and to be identified to an extent with the church. That is, in none of these passages is there any compelling evidence that the millenium, or kingdom or new world is to be understood specifically as material, on the pattern of Jewish millenarian or Christian chiliastic formulations. Hence it has to be said, against O'Hagan, that the use of the terms themselves is not sufficient to prove that they belong to this tradition, and the fact that the writer does not take any of the obvious opportunities to spell out the material blessings that await believers, along with the spiritualizing interpretation in 6 and especially 16, may lead us to suspect that it is neither millenarian nor very material in concept. Hence I am inclined to see the writer's treatment of this material as analogous to what Paul

---

argued, on the basis also of other Jewish and Christian sources, that 16.2−4 refers to the fact that the Jews, after Hadrian's accession, were beginning on the rebuilding of the temple, with Roman approval (thus e. g. Barnard 1958, 102−103; Schlatter 1966, 63−67). But these sources are late or irrelevant, or both, and this understanding of the passage has been rejected on the grounds that it runs completely counter to Hadrian's policy concerning alien religions. Hence Barnabas is taken, by means of a small textual emendation, to agree with the report of Dio Cassius lxix 12.1−2 (cf. Historia Augusta Vit. Hadr 14,2) that the Romans under Hadrian were building a pagan temple in place of the ruined Jewish temple, in the Aelia Capitolina set up in Jerusalem (cf. e. g. Windisch 1920, 387−390; Schürer−Vermes−Millar(−Goodman) 1973−87, vol. I 535−541; Wengst 1984, 114−118). Clearly the Roman historians' version of events is to be believed, but that does not in itself settle the question of how this passage in Barnabas is to be understood. There is no manuscript evidence for the emendation, and the text as it stands would naturally be taken to mean that the Romans, who had destroyed the temple, were now rebuilding it. Even if Barnabas' account does not correspond to any historical reality it may still accurately reflect reports or rumours that had reached the writer, that the Romans were about to start with the Jews on the reconstruction of the temple. Thus Barnabas, written before the bar Kochba war and without the benefit of hindsight of that catastrophe, may have been prepared to believe that the Romans' policy towards the Jews was more conciliatory than it actually turned out to be. If so, Barnabas could be allegorizing and spiritualizing the temple to deal with the problem that the Jews really possess what they claim to possess, while the Christians have nothing. If, however, Barnabas here is in fact referring to the building of a pagan temple, the point in 16.6−10 would presumably be that this is all the Jews are left with in Jerusalem, thus visibly demonstrating that their claims about the temple have always been false, while the Christians fulfil in their own community of the end time what the true nature of the temple has always been.

says in, for example, Rom 8 and 1 Cor 15; thus the language and imagery of Jewish eschatological hope are used, but the vision of the new world or creation (especially in Rom 8) is probably deliberately vague and not tied to any realization in material or terrestrial terms. But the fact remains that in Barnabas the evidence is ambiguous, and a thoroughly materialist millenial hope cannot in fact be ruled out.

Despite these uncertainties of interpretation, it is at least clear that what Barnabas presents us with is a situation where the parting of the ways has already come about, and where the concern is to drive the wedge still more deeply between Christianity and Judaism[96]. The overriding concern is to show that none of the claims the Jews make for themselves have ever had any validity. There is thus a radical discontinuity; Christianity is in no sense to be seen as the fulfilment of Judaism. Hence there is an urgent need to show that all the Old Testament promises are fulfilled in the Christian community, and this community therefore also becomes a central focus of attention. It is in this context that the issue of the promise of the land and also of Jewish eschatological hope is raised. The impression Barnabas gives is that the essential point, here as throughout in dealing with Old Testament and Jewish material, is to stress that they are already completely fulfilled in the Christian community. Or at least, they are fulfilled in anticipation; the final fulfilment may still be awaited, and to this extent Barnabas looks ahead to the final age. But the nature of the final age is not the main concern; hence, partly, the problem in deciding precisely what Barnabas' position is on these issues.

7.2. The Didache

The Didache has a number of similarities with Barnabas[97]; amongst these is the fact that the eschatological expectation is very sharply presented, although here there is no hint of millenarian concepts. It draws heavily on traditional material, both Christian and Jewish[98]. While both very Jewish in character and also very close to Matthew in a number of respects, unlike Matthew it does not appear for the most part to reflect tensions or antagonism concerning a particular Jewish

---

[96] Thus Knoch 1980, 365, amongst others, sees Barnabas as reflecting an internal debate within the Christian community rather than a live debate with Judaism.

[97] The nature of the relation between Barnabas and the Didache (or literary interdependence) has been the subject of a great deal of discussion; see e.g. Muilenburg 1929; Burkitt 1932; Robinson 1934; Audet 1958, 122–163; Wengst 1984, 20–23.

[98] However, the discussion of this by Middleton 1935, arguing that the Didache is simply a collection of traditions, and therefore unoriginal and of no use, fails to do justice to the issue, while Butler 1960, although more sophisticated, too easily makes the Didache directly dependent on Matthew. More nuanced and helpful are Wengst 1984, 20–32; Niederwimmer 1989, 48–78.

community and its leaders[99]. Although the precise date and setting of the Didache are difficult to determine[100], its character as a 'primitive' teaching manual, largely unaffected by theological and ecclesiological developments, remains clear and is particularly interesting for consideration of the nascent Christian movement in relation to Judaism.

The main eschatological section in the Didache is represented by ch. 16, the conclusion to the whole work; but there is also interesting eschatological material elsewhere, especially in the section on the eucharist (9–10). Thus, first, it is necessary to consider 9.1–4:

1 Concerning the eucharist: give thanks in the following way.
2 First, as regards the cup:
   We give thanks to you, our Father,
   for the holy vine of David your servant,
   which you have made known to us through Jesus, your servant;
   to you be glory for ever.
3 Concerning the broken bread:
   We give thanks to you, our Father,
   for the life and knowledge,
   which you have made known to us through Jesus your servant;
   to you be glory for ever.
4 As this broken bread was scattered on the mountains,
   and when gathered became one piece,
   so may your Church be gathered together
   from the ends of the earth into your kingdom.
   For yours is the glory and the power
   through Jesus Christ for ever.

The whole of 9–10 represents an early liturgical form[101], drawing on Jewish prayers for before and after meals and adapting these to specifically Christian context and worship[102]. 9.2–3 offer thanks to God for the gifts he has provided through Jesus; as v. 4 shows, these are not simply food, but have eschatological significance. Thus, specifically, the reference to Jesus as servant (of God) and the linking of him closely to David (particularly the vine of David) suggest that thanks are offered to God for bringing about the final fulfilment of his promises to David through Jesus[103]. Thus implicitly here Jesus is given messianic designa-

---

[99] The main relevant text is 8.1–2, which urges avoiding praying and fasting in the same way as the 'heretics' (that is, clearly, Jews); cf. Knoch 1980, 356–359; Wengst 1984, 29–30; Niederwimmer 1989, 165–168.

[100] For a brief discussion of the main issues, cf. e.g. Audet 1958, 187–210; Wengst 1984, 61–63; Niederwimmer 1989, 78–80. Composition around the beginning of the second century in Syria or Palestine is usually favoured.

[101] Cf. e.g. Clerici 1966; Sandvik 1970, 37–40; Niederwimmer 1989, 173ff.

[102] Cf. e.g. Klein 1908; Finkelstein 1928–29; Peterson 1944; Clerici 1966; Wengst 1984, 48–57; Niederwimmer 1989, 175ff.

[103] Cf. Niederwimmer 1989, 183–185, who argues that the model the Didache uses here is

tion, as servant[104], and the messianic deliverance, promised for the Jews but not realized, is now fully revealed and fulfilled through Jesus, and experienced in anticipation in the eucharist[105].

The climax of this section, and the strikingly distinctive development, follow in 4. This goes beyond the model of prayers at meals, although it is still closely related to Jewish prayers more generally, especially those that are addressed as petitions to God for the bringing of the Jews from the Diaspora to Jerusalem and for deliverance and freedom from oppression[106]. The important point here is the symbolism; that is, as bread is made into a single whole (loaf) from the corn that is scattered over the hills, so this prayer asks God for the church to be brought together into a single unity from its scattered existence[107]. It is an obviously eschatological invocation; the church will find its final fulfilment and true purpose in God's kingdom. But it should therefore be noted that the kingdom of God is thus effectively defined in terms of the church, just as the church is oriented towards the kingdom, and there is no hint that the kingdom is more than or different to the basic nature of the unified church. O'Hagan, while accepting that the church here replaces the Jewish Diaspora, claims that this represents the true fulfilment of the promises to Israel, so that the kingdom is to be understood not only in an eschatological but also in an earthly sense, as in the Jewish national eschatological tradition of material restoration[108]. Thus Jewish converts in the community, praying prayers that express expectations of the eschatological kingdom, would substitute church for nation, but would still keep the earthly connotation, exactly as we find in Justin. In the Didache it would probably not be specifically millenarian, although it might be implied that Palestine or Jerusalem were still linked to the Christian eschatological hope. But O'Hagan's argument of course begs the question of whether the use of 'kingdom' here implies the whole Jewish tradition, in material form, or

---

one of promise and fulfilment; thus the use of 'vine' brings to mind for the community the gift of salvation, long promised but now finally realized, while the designation of Jesus as 'servant' implies that he is the eschatological mediator of salvation and end-time revealer. Cf. also Wengst 1984, 48−49.

[104] Cf. Wengst 1984, 48−49, who points to the 'messianic' use of servant in Lk 1.69; Acts 4.25, and argues that for the community of the Didache the Jewish messianic promise is seen as revealed and fulfilled.

[105] The dispute over whether the eucharist is referred to here, or follows only after 10.6 does not affect the issue here; for discussion and differing opinions, cf. e.g. Audet 1958, 372ff.; Wengst 1984, 43ff.; Niederwimmer 1989, 176−180.

[106] Cf. section 4.1 above; cf. further Clerici 1966, 67−92.

[107] Moule 1955 argues against this interpretation, pointing out that the vocabulary used here (e.g. κλάσμα = broken bread; scattered; mountains) is very strange if it is supposed to suggest the making of a loaf of bread from corn that has been sown; he suggests that it is more plausible to see this passage as alluding to Jn 6.3ff., where the setting is the hills, and the fragments of bread are gathered together. Cf. also Goodenough 1945; Cerfaux 1959. But against this, cf. Riesenfeld 1956; Clerici 1966, 92−94; Vööbus 1969.

[108] O'Hagan 1968, 18−22.

whether it has been qualified and redefined in terms of church, to give it a different sense[109]. The same basic issues and set of questions are also involved at 10.5.

Secondly, then, it is important to consider 10.2−6, the thanksgiving after the meal, which has close links with 9.1−4:

2 We give thanks to you, holy Father,
for your holy name,
which you have made to dwell in our hearts,
and for the knowledge and faith and immortality
which you have made known to us through Jesus, your servant;
to you be glory for ever.
3 You, Lord, Almighty,
have created all things for the sake of your name,
you have given food and drink to men to enjoy,
that they may give thanks to you;
but to us you have graciously given spiritual food and drink, and eternal life,
through [Jesus] your servant.
4 For everything we give thanks to you, because you are mighty;
to you be glory for ever.
5 Remember, Lord, your church,
to deliver her from all evil,
and to perfect her in your love,
and gather her, the sanctified one, from the four winds,
into your kingdom, which you have prepared for her;
for yours is the power and the glory for ever.
6 May grace come, and this world pass away!
Hosanna to the God of David!
If any one is holy, let him come;
if anyone is not, let him repent.
Maranatha! Amen.

Again, this whole passage draws very closely on Jewish meal-prayers, and again is clearly eschatological in emphasis, as the conclusion (6) shows vividly. Although in many respects it is closely parallel to 9.1−4, the specific Jewish model here is the Prayer after Meals, the Birkat ha-Mazon[110]; the Didache, however (or at any rate the tradition it draws on), makes quite free adaptation of this. Thus 2a is not properly parallel to the Birkat ha-Mazon, but is obviously closely parallel to 9.2−3. Again, the basic idea is that Jewish hopes and expectations are fulfilled through Jesus, as servant, the agent of God's deliverance and the revealer at the end-time of God's promises, that are now brought about. The gifts of the final age that come through Christ include immortality, but are described only in very general terms. 3−4 specifically take up the Birkat

---

[109] Cf. Clerici 1966, 61−64.
[110] Cf. above 4.1.5, and Finkelstein 1928−29.

ha-Mazon. The thanksgiving here, however, is not only for material provision (of food and drink), but also for the spiritual provision of the eucharist and eternal life. This is the distinctive development in the Didache, and it is therefore on the spiritual realization of God's promises within the Christian community that the emphasis now falls. Again, as in 9.2−3 and 10.2, these gifts and this final fulfilment of God's will are specifically attributed to Christ.

Clearly 10.5 is parallel to 9.4, but it represents a more developed form; it also draws on the third petition of the Birkat ha-Mazon. The Jewish prayer invokes the concept of God's remembering with specific reference to the covenant promises God has made with his people; the seventh petition of the Amidah has a similar theme. Thus in these Jewish prayers, appeal is made to God to intervene and deliver his people, implicitly at the end of time (and by means of the messiah), on the basis of the covenant made with them. Thus the use of 'remember' here has greater resonance than might appear at first sight, and is deeply rooted in this tradition[111]; at the same time, the precise significance of it here cannot simply be assumed and taken over from the Jewish model. Here the central focal point is the church, and the three petitions concerning it take on particular significance. The first two bring ethical and eschatological considerations closely together. Thus the eschatological orientation may be implied by the taking over of the first petition from the Lord's Prayer and the use of τελειῶσαι in the second petition[112]; it is clear in any case from the immediate context of the 'kingdom' in the third petition, and from the petitions in 6. But in the context of the Didache as a whole, and the specific way it adapts the Jewish prayer model, the ethical emphasis is obviously the more important, as is clear, for example, from the petition to perfect the church in love. It also therefore again raises (as at 9.4) the issue of the meaning of the third petition; again, the eschatological significance of the 'kingdom' is not in doubt, but it may be that what is implied here is the ethical 'perfection' of the church (a theme that is also detectable in Matthew), that is, the perfect harmony and conduct of the community as prerequsite for the fulfilment of God's promises concerning the kingdom. Thus again the eschatological kingdom is defined specifically in terms of the final goal and consummation of the church. Hence Jewish eschatological paradigms are adapted and interpreted; it is notable here that the kingdom is spoken of as being 'prepared for' the church, implicitly, that is, as the divine purpose from the beginning.

10.6 represents a distinctive development beyond the Birkat ha-Mazon, although again the basic theme and emphasis are clearly still rooted in Jewish tradition and eschatological hope. There are obvious links also with early

---

111 Cf. esp. Clerici 1966, 48−64; Dahl 1976, 23−24; Niederwimmer 1989, 199−200.

112 So Clerici 1966, 95 ff.; Niederwimmer 1989, 200. But it is very questionable to suggest, as Clerici does, that the Lord's Prayer itself has this ethical sense.

Christian tradition, above all 1 Cor 16.22[113]. The theme in both places appears to be above all the fervent expectation on the part of the Christian community of the Parousia of their Lord from heaven and the climax of the end of the ages. So 6a can be seen implicitly as a cry for messianic deliverance in the final age, looking for the passing away of the present world, and implicitly the coming of the new, although that is not specified. That is, there is a total lack of indication about how this hope is to be realized in any positive or material way.

Hence although to understand this utterance in a completely spiritual sense scarcely does justice to it, at the same time it is not clear whether there is a specifically material hope implied[114]. The cry of Hosanna had probably already taken on messianic significance within Judaism by the first century AD[115]. Certainly that is the obvious way of taking the phrase here, bound up as it is with the reference to David. One form of the text here, 'Hosanna to the *Son* of David', would make this sense quite explicit; but this is in fact the least likely original. Nevertheless, either of the alternative readings, 'God of David' or 'house of David', carries a messianic sense; it would be either ('God of David') a cry of praise to God in anticipation of his fulfilling his promises (messianically understood) to David, or else ('house of David') a shout of acclamation to the Davidic (that is, messianic) line, again exulting in the fulfilment of what has come about in Christ, and in anticipation of its imminent final consummation[116]. The implication is that the community experiences the Parousia of Christ in a very real way in the Eucharist or common meal, and therefore expresses fervently the vivid expectation of the final Parousia in the near future[117].

After the invitation to participate, with the conditions of entry spelt out, comes the further cry 'Maranatha!'. Although the precise form and meaning of this are disputed, it probably represents (both here and at 1 Cor 16.22) the Aramaic Maran (a)tha, 'Our Lord, come!', with the verb in the imperative rather than the perfect (Maran atha, 'Our Lord has come!')[118]. Even so, the

---

[113] Cf. e.g. Bornkamm 1952, 123ff.; Cullmann 1963, 208–212; Hahn 1969, 93–97, although they all assume rather than demonstrate a liturgical or eucharistic setting for 1 Cor 16.22.

[114] O'Hagan 1968, 24 allows the possibility that 'may this world pass away' should be understood in a spiritual sense, as at 1 Cor 7.31, but prefers to see it as a quasi-technical expression, implying the dissolution of the material earth. But even if this is accepted, it is not necessarily the case, as he wants to argue, that the implication is of a contrast between the present age and the age to come, when the messianic kingdom will come about on earth.

[115] Cf. Sandvik 1970, 37–38.

[116] Cf. Sandvik 1970, 38–40; cf. also Niederwimmer 1989, 201–203, who sees present and future eschatology flowing into each other here.

[117] It is, however, necessary to emphasise with Hahn 1969, 97, against Cullmann 1963, 208ff., that the reference is primarily future and eschatological, not to the coming of the Lord in the eucharist.

[118] It is not possible to do justice here to the issues and wide-ranging discussion; cf. e.g. Hahn 1969, 93–101; Fitzmyer 1981, 218–235.

precise sense intended here (as also at 1 Cor) is not thus finally resolved. So Niederwimmer argues strongly that the second half of 6 stands in sharp contrast to the first, and is to be understood not as a cry of jubilation but as an invitation and, especially, a warning[119]. The sense of Maranatha, on this view, emerges from the context, not of 6a, that is, but instead that of the call to repentance. Thus the invocation of Christ, expressed directly in Maranatha, has the character here essentially of a threat, since the reference is to the Lord coming as an eschatological judge; the same basic sense, Niederwimmer argues, is also intended at 1 Cor 16.22. This interpretation is possible, at least as far as the Didache is concerned, especially in view of 16.1−2, where reference to Christ's coming is linked with a strongly negative warning about the consequences of not being properly prepared; but it is by no means convincing. As Niederwimmer has to admit, indeed stress, this interpretation of Maranatha is contingent on the understanding of the preceding clause, and the 'contextual' meaning is limited to a very narrow context, going against the first half of the verse. It in fact makes more sense of Maranatha here to understand it in a fundamentally positive, joyful sense, denoting the urgent expectation on the part of the community of the return of their Lord. This does not of course preclude the theme of judgement; the coming of the Lord (that is, God) in Old Testament texts is usually double-edged. The need to be holy, to be fit for his coming and able to withstand it is consistent with this (cf. also 16.2). But the sense of Maranatha is overridingly positive, in parallel to Hosanna.

Thus in 9−10 as a whole, there is strong eschatological emphasis; specifically, the concrete themes of Jewish hope concerning the kingdom and God's deliverance of his people in the final, messianic age are interpreted essentially in terms of the church in context of the community's common meal. From this context, we come to the Didache's most sustained eschatological section, in 16.1−8:

(1) Watch over your life; your lamps must not go out, and your loins must not be ungirded. On the contrary, be ready; for you do not know the hour in which our Lord is coming. (2) Gather together frequently, and seek what is necessary for your souls; for the whole time of your faith will be of no use to you, if you do not attain perfection in the last time. (3) For in the last days the false prophets and corrupters will increase, and sheep will turn into wolves and love will turn into hate. (4) For when lawlessness is on the increase, they will hate and persecute and betray each other; and then the Deceiver of this world will appear as the Son of God and will perform signs and wonders, and the earth will be given over into his hands, and he will perpetrate lawless acts of a kind that have not happened since before the beginning of time. (5) Then humankind will come into the fire of testing, and many

---

[119] Niederwimmer 1989, 203−205; thus he claims εἴτις οὐκ ἔστιν (ἅγιος) clearly has the character of a warning, setting the specific conditions of entry to the eucharist. It uses a formula already found at 1 Cor 16.22, and the sense and implications are made clear from later liturgical formulations. So also Moule 1959−60 suggests that Maranatha should be understood as a curse or imprecation. But against this, cf. Fitzmyer 1981, 228.

will be led astray and perish; but those who endure in their faith will be saved by the Accursed One himself. (6) And then there will appear the signs of truth; first, a sign consisting of an opening in heaven; next, a sign consisting of the sounding of the trumpet; and the third sign consisting of the resurrection of the dead; (7) not, however, of all, but as it has been said: The Lord will come, and all the saints with him. (8) Then the world will see the Lord coming on the clouds of heaven.

This closing passage of the Didache is closely related in style and substance to early Christian tradition, above all the so-called Synoptic Apocalypse. Whatever the precise nature of the relationship of the Didache to this tradition[120], the fundamentally Jewish character of the material here is again evident throughout. 1–2 represent an exhortatory introduction, urging constant watching and readiness in face of the coming Parousia. The stark emphasis is on the fact that in the final time their lives are at risk; salvation depends on being perfect at the coming of the Lord.

The main eschatological section proper, in 3–8, consists primarily of material which belongs to the common stock of Jewish eschatology and, dependent on it, early Christian tradition, especially the Synoptics; there are, however, some interesting distinctive features. As in 1–2, the main emphasis here is negative. This in large part derives from the stereotyped theme of the eschatological woes, with trials and disasters on a cosmic scale, that immediately precede the final end. Yet it is probable that the warning against false prophets and internal strife in 3–4 reflects something of the specific situation of those the Didache addresses. Certainly the overall setting of the Didache is a situation, probably in Syria or Palestine, where wandering teachers and prophets still operate significantly, and form the main characteristic group continuing the tradition[121]. Along with this, there is clearly a real problem of false prophets and teachers; this is especially so since it threatens to divide and destroy the community from within. Those who are most to be feared, and who are likely to cause most damage, are not outsiders or those (whether Jews or Romans) threatening persecution, but former members of the community now turned against it, perverting their own faith and potentially that of others also. The following themes, in 4b–5, of the appearance of the Antichrist and the Great Apostasy, are much more stereotyped. The ultimate source, and main point of reference, for these themes is Dan 12[122]. But although this material is mainly stereotyped by the time of the Didache, the idea that those who stand firm will be saved by the accursed (one or thing) is especially striking. If this text is correct, the most plausible (although still difficult) exegesis of it is to take it to

---

[120] Butler 1960 sees the Didache as directly dependent on Matthew; against this, cf. Niederwimmer 1989, 247–256; Kloppenborg 1979. Cf. also Bammel 1961.

[121] Cf. Niederwimmer 1977; Wengst 1984, 32–34.

[122] For the lapse of faith, the tradition represented by Mt 24.10 is more immediately relevant.

imply the designation of Christ as the 'Accursed' (or 'one under a curse', as Paul calls Christ in Gal 3.13), taking up the stigma imputed by his enemies[123].

If this interpretation is right, it may link directly with the immediately following 6−7, and the more distinctive theme of the three signs of truth. The first of these, the σημεῖον ἐκπετάσεως ἐν οὐρανῷ, is also enigmatic, but it is most often taken to be a reference to the cross of Christ appearing in heaven immediately before his Parousia[124]. This may be right, although it seems to me that the rendering 'opening in heaven', denoting the opening of heaven as the immediate and necessary prelude to the coming of Christ from heaven to earth, and setting the passage clearly in the apocalyptic tradition of a vision of the heavenly world being opened, should be given more serious consideration than it often is. But if the reference is to the cross, then it is specifically the crucified (accursed) Christ who comes in glory to bring final victory and judgement. The other two signs are more straightforward: the eschatological trumpet, herald of the final age, and the resurrection of the dead, limited to the Christians. O'Hagan takes the reference in 7, indicating the resurrection of the just alone, to be an important element in the concept of material re-creation, connected in Jewish tradition with the idea of the restored kingdom on earth. This leads him to posit a millenarian view on the part of the Didache here[125]. The use (in 8) of the terminology of Dan 7.13, to portray the Parousia, is of course familiar from Jewish and early Christian sources. It is notable here, however, that the 'one like a son of man' of Dan 7 is now represented by the designation κύριος, the same exalted (or messianic) title, of course, that is contained in Marantha. It is generally agreed that the original end of this passage (and, therefore, of the Didache as a whole) is now missing, but that it would have included, as a main part, the theme of the judgement that Christ brings[126].

There is, however, no consensus on the overall significance of the eschatological material in the Didache. Thus Niederwimmer argues for the eschatological emphasis being of central significance for the Didache as a whole. So he claims that the Didachist has introduced and heightened the eschatological emphasis in his adaptation of the sources he draws on. He suggests, then, that the redactional section 1.3b−6 is deliberately introduced in order to make the Two Ways discourse more Christian, and thus, along with other additions, effectively move it away from a rigorous Jewish or Jewish-Christian moral catechism in the direction of the eschatological demand of Jesus[127]. The author, or redactor, has also then added the conclusion to the Two Ways section (6.2−3), specifically as a paraenetical epilogue with eschatological outlook. So, more

---

[123] So Wengst 1984, 99; Niederwimmer 1989, 264−265.
[124] So e. g. Niederwimmer 1989, 265−267.
[125] O'Hagan 1968, 29.
[126] Cf. e. g. Audet 1958, 73−74; Niederwimmer 1989, 268−269.
[127] Niederwimmer 1989, 67 ff.

generally, the way the Didache uses Synoptic traditions make the gospel take on the character of an eschatological command. The whole of 9−10 shows the eschatological fulfilment of God's promises through Jesus finding its consummation in the eschatological kingdom. Finally, in place of the original brief eschatological conclusion to the Two Ways section, the writer has set ch. 16 as an extended eschatological section, to be the climax to his work.

For O'Hagan, as we have seen, the Didache not only has strong eschatological emphasis, but specifically understands the eschatological consummation to be a restored material creation[128]. Clerici's position is less clear; in one place he stresses that the Didache has christianized the Jewish tradition in a spiritualizing way (that is, the eschatological hope is made ethical, and the concept of the kingdom supraterrestrial)[129]; in other words, he goes completely contrary here to O'Hagan, if not also Niederwimmer. But in a later discussion, he seems to leave open the question of whether the Didache is ethically spiritualizing, and whether specifically the kingdom is on earth or in heaven, and effectively to dismiss it as irrelevant[130].

The former position of Clerici, at least, comes close to that of Wengst, who argues that it is now ethics, not eschatology, that has become the controlling element in the Didache, in contrast to the New Testament and especially the Jesus tradition[131]. The concluding ch. 16 is set at the end by the writer not in order to make eschatology the climax of the book, but instead to strengthen the urgent warning given to the reader, and thus to orientate the reader to the instruction set out in the rest of the book. Thus at 16.2 (cf. also 10.5), perfection can be achieved through standing fast in the last time, when the decisive proving takes place. So eschatology has become a sub-aspect of ethics, and a mere section of teaching concerning the last things. Whereas in the proclamation of Jesus and the early Christian movement, the expectation of the end included hope for world-wide and fundamental change and for radical transformation, with ethics understood as conduct corresponding to and anticipating this hope, in the Didache the weight has shifted; now, that is, ethics is no longer set under the perspective of eschatology, but instead eschatology has become an appendix of ethics.

Wengst's judgement may seen one-sided in some respects, failing to do justice to the intense, urgent eschatological expressions in 9−10, where the eucharist, not ethics, is the main concern, and also perhaps ignoring the fact that the Didache as a whole is intended not as a proclamation of the gospel but instead as detailed teaching. Yet Wengst in fact shows himself fully aware of the issues involved here, and argues that it is precisely the nature of the Didache, as

---

128 O'Hagan 1968, 18−30.
129 Clerici 1966, 60 ff.
130 Clerici 1966, 95 ff.
131 Wengst 1984, 59−61.

a teaching manual, that indicates its particular purpose and the way it has developed the tradition. That is, its ethics are mainly traditional Jewish, and denote an attempt to push the primitive eschatological consciousness of the community, signifying above all opposition to the world and expectation of radical change, in the direction of giving in to the pressure to conform that the world applies, or indeed of conforming altogether[132]. He also argues, however, that whereas the Didache has shifted considerably in this direction, it has by no means succumbed completely to the pressure to conform, but has preserved something of its distinctive Christian identity. An important part of this identity is indicated by expressions such as 10.6 and 16.1−8, as well as the characterization of itinerant prophets and teachers in ch. 11. Indeed, to some extent Wengst's understanding of the Didache is not so far removed from that of Niederwimmer; the latter certainly sees 16 as introduced by eschatological paraenesis (as does O'Hagan), with the idea of 'standing fast' (16.5; cf. 10.5) guaranteeing a share in the eschatological rest. But Niederwimmer may not allow enough weight to the central importance of ethical emphasis in eschatological passages in the Didache. Thus at 10.5 he admits that τελειῶσαι αὐτὴν ἐν τῇ ἀγάπῃ σου could be taken ethically, that is, perfection in the sense of sanctification, but prefers to understand it as eschatological perfection, of the final unity of the church, as in the following clause[133].

In fact here, as also elsewhere in the Didache, it is probable that both ethical and eschatological themes are bound up together; but in any case, Wengst's argument must be considered seriously. That is, for all the isolated examples of fervent eschatological expectation, the Didache has no indication of the concrete realization of its hopes or the transformation of the world, in contrast to the earlier tradition, nor any indication of how its ethical perspective has effect specifically (or politically) on the world around. And if against this it is argued that the Didache is intended primarily as an internal teaching manual, that is of course precisely to beg the question; in what situation and in what changed perspective does this kind of work come onto the agenda? Nor does simply describing the work as a set of teachings provide sufficient explanation of what it does not say. So, for example, the letter of James also provides a great deal of teaching, and is also closely related to the Synoptic tradition (especially Matthew); but equally it is strongly eschatological in emphasis, and addresses itself to specific social situations and, implicitly, the transformation of the world around. So the Didache, like James, is thoroughly Jewish in form and content, and in its ethical and eschatological material it also belongs clearly enough

---

[132] In this context it is worth noting that O'Hagan 1968, 26−27, although stressing the theme of material re-creation in the Didache, sees ch. 16 as having above all moral emphasis (as e.g. with 'Watch' in the sense of 'be ready').

[133] Niederwimmer 1989, 200; on 16.1−2 as eschatological paraenesis, cf. 256−259.

within one strand of Jewish tradition. But, as distinct from James, it stands in notable contrast (as Wengst argues) to the primitive tradition of Jesus' proclamation.

8. The Shepherd of Hermas

This work presents many problems, including that of dating; but it is hardly later than the mid second-century, and much of the material probably goes back considerably earlier[134]. This question is bound up with the precise nature of Hermas. It purports to be prophetic and visionary in character, but it has often been held that this is simply a facade, and that the visions have merely a stereotyped form. Hence also it has sometimes been denied that Hermas is an apocalyptic work proper, on the grounds that the so-called visions are not really such, and also that it entirely lacks any eschatology. Yet although the visions may well have been modified and adapted, there is a genuinely visionary character evident within them[135]. Equally, while the insistence on eschatology being a central element in apocalyptic rests on a dubious view of apocalyptic itself, it has in fact been demonstrated that there is more eschatological material in Hermas than might at first appear[136].

The main section where eschatological emphasis is prominent in Hermas is the Fourth Vision, which is concerned with the final great tribulation ([ἡ]θλῖψις ἡ ἐρχουένη/μελλούσα ἡ μεγάλη) that is about to come. This theme is anticipated briefly in the Second Vision (6.7−8), but is not dealt with at length until the Fourth. It is obviously the case that this tribulation is a time of persecution and suffering that will be brought upon the church; it is equally clear, however, that it is not simply an allusion to persecution from the Roman Empire, but is a vision of the eschatological time of testing that the church (or some of it) must undergo and come through. The final and determinative nature of this 'great tribulation' is brought out very clearly at the end of the work, above all 24.2−5:

Listen, she said; the black is the world in which you dwell, but the colour of fire and blood shows that this world must perish through blood and fire. The golden part are you who have escaped from this world. For as gold is tested by fire, and thus becomes useful, so are you tested who dwell in the world. Those of you, therefore, who remain steadfast and are put through the fire, will be purified by means of it. For as gold casts off its dross, so also you will cast away all sorrow and straitness, and will be made pure so as to be useful for the building of the tower. And the white part is the age that is to come, in which the elect of God will dwell; for those who have been chosen by God for eternal life will be spotless and pure.

---

[134] Cf. e.g. Bauckham 1974, 28−29; Knoch 1980, 351.
[135] Cf. e.g. Bauckham 1974; Rowland 1982, 388−392.
[136] Cf. e.g. O'Hagan 1961; O'Hagan 1968, 113−132; Bauckham 1974.

The speaker who addresses the seer here is the virgin, who symbolises the church (23.1–2); the picture she presents is of the destruction of the world by 'blood and fire', but the survival of the 'elect', that is, those of the church who 'withstand' (or 'endure': οἱ μείναντες) and thus escape this conflagration. Their reward is life eternal in the world to come. The temporal dualism here is apparent; the end of the present age is at hand, and the beginning of the new world is already set in motion. This is the eschatological perspective of the Fourth Vision. Both the imagery used throughout, and the themes themselves, are largely familiar to us from Jewish (and early Christian) eschatological or apocalyptic material, above all, at least as the ultimate point of reference, the book of Daniel. Yet there are also aspects of Hermas here that set it apart from Jewish eschatology and apocalyptic, not least that the persecution, and tribulation as a whole, is seen as having a purifying effect on the Christian community[137].

The idea here of the elect 'dwelling (κατοικέω) in the world to come' can be understood to imply a vision on the part of Hermas of the messianic kingdom on earth[138]; although if this is so, it has to be said that there is very little indication of its precise nature. It is also possible to trace connections between this climax to the Fourth Vision and other themes of eschatological importance elsewhere in Hermas. Thus here the elect who are purified will be useful for the building of the tower; so the tower takes on an eschatological dimension as well, and indeed it can be argued that the tower has eschatological significance implicit in it in any case[139]. The tower also plays an important role in Hermas more widely, above all in the Third Vision[140]. Here it is specifically identified with the church (11.3), although the imagery is more fluid than any simple identification would suggest. The setting of the tower in the plain (9.2–4; 22.2; 90.1), resonant with themes from Isa 40 and developed Jewish tradition (3.4), has obvious eschatological implications[141]. In Sim IX, the tower set in the plain is portrayed as having a 'great white rock', higher than all the mountains, as the foundation for the tower itself. This has obvious links with the tradition of the 'mountain of the Lord', or the holy mountain of Zion, as a developed tradition of eschatological hope[142]. It is also of course the case that the use of the eschatological

---

[137] Cf. Bauckham 1974, who argues that the positive interpretation of suffering allows the great tribulation to become the means of transition from the present world to the next.

[138] Cf. Peterson 1959, 307; O'Hagan 1968, 127.

[139] Cf. Peterson 1959, 307; O'Hagan 1968, 114.

[140] O'Hagan 1968, 114 argues that in III.2 the fact that the building of the tower is nearly complete shows the end to be very near.

[141] Thus e. g. Zech 14; SibOr 3.777ff.; 1 Bar 5. Cf. also the argument of O'Hagan 1968, 116 that the reference to the Lord's coming to inspect the tower in Sim IX (87.1) indicates an eschatological visitation; cf. Peterson 1959, 291–292.

[142] So e. g. Isa 2.2–4/Micah 4.1–4; Ezek 40–48; Zech 14; 4 Ezra 13.36. The connection with the messianic age is clear in 4 Ezra, but it is in any case an easy development out of Isa 2/ Micah 4. Cf. further O'Hagan 1968, 120–121.

mountain or Zion theme in connection with the tower connects with traditions concerning the Jerusalem of the final age, as is suggested by other passages in Hermas which concern the tower (thus, for example, 50.1: 'the city in which you will dwell'), and which have the theme of the woman or virgin. Overall, then, these traditions relating to the tower and to the woman, both identified with the church in Hermas, and both closely connected with developed eschatological traditions in Isaiah, Ezekiel, the Sibylline Oracles, 4 Ezra, Revelation and other writings, can be interpreted as indicating that Hermas also has a vision of the final age on earth in the new Jerusalem, a paradise that is about to come[143].

Yet it is also important to stress the inherent limitations of the brief and tantalizing eschatological hints given in Hermas, and beware of making too much of them. Thus specifically it is worth emphasising the main purpose and nature of Hermas. It is essentially a prophetic work concerned with the present life and conduct of the church. Hence the point of the eschatological material, both in 24.2−5 and also in the other passages touched on, is to instil a sense of urgency into the Christian community regarding its conduct as the final age dawns. This point emerges throughout the work, as for example at 23.4b−6:

You have escaped from a great tribulation on account of your faith, and because you did not doubt in the presence of so great a beast. Go, therefore, and tell the elect of the Lord his mighty acts, and say to them that this beast is a figure of the great tribulation that is coming. If, therefore, you prepare yourselves, and repent with all your heart and turn to the Lord, it will be possible for you to escape it, if your heart is pure and spotless, and you spend all the rest of the days of your life serving the Lord blamelessly. Cast your cares upon the Lord, and he will direct them. Believe in the Lord, you doubleminded, for he is all-powerful, and can turn his anger away from you, and send plagues on those of you who are doubleminded. Woe to those who hear these words and despise them; it were better for them not to have been born.

The picture that emerges from this passage is consistent with the main theme of Hermas overall. Thus eschatology serves the ethical interests and orientation. It is the church that is central to Hermas; to the extent that it has any developed theology at all, it lies in the area not of eschatology (still less Christology), but rather of ecclesiology. Hence it is not surprising that Hermas can appear thoroughly Jewish in many respects; its eschatology in Vision IV, although it has distinctive features, is a good example of this. So also in its advocacy of moral conduct, good works and righteousness, it is thoroughly at home within the concept of the covenant people of God. This is also really where the concept of the church is rooted; it assumes an essential unity of revelation and continuity of dispensation. Yet of course at the same time, it is the specific community of the *church* that is now the concern of God's dealings and election; so, correspondingly, the eschatological themes here mark out the church as the sphere of

[143] This, effectively, is the argument of Peterson 1959, 307−308; O'Hagan 1968, 121−132.

God's saving activity, and allow the possibility of being brought through to the new world. But from the traditions concerning a messianic age or kingdom, nothing is taken up. Thus Hermas is clearly rooted within Jewish traditions, and within a particular Jewish and early Christian mode of interpreting and developing the eschatological tradition.

9. 1 & 2 Clement

9.1. 1 Clement

The main concentration of eschatological themes in 1 Clement (written at the very end of the first century) is to be found in 23–27. It is clearly the delay of the Parousia that constitutes one main problem that the writer has to deal with (23.2–5; thus e. g. 3: 'Far from us be the scripture where it says: Wretched are the doubters, those who are divided in their hearts, who say, These things we heard even in the time of our fathers, and behold, we have grown old and nothing of them has happened to us'). Hence over against the (obviously) commonly-held doubts that the promise of Christ's second coming will be fulfilled, the writer asserts both the certainty and also the sudden nature of the Second Coming (23.5: 'Truly, quickly and suddenly shall his will be fulfilled, as scripture also bears witness: Quickly he will come, and will not delay …'). There are obvious points of contact here with 2 Pet 3 and (as we shall see below) with 2 Clement as well. The emphasis on the certainty that God will fulfil his promises and bring about what he has planned is repeated in 27 (at the conclusion of this section), following the discussion of the resurrection of the body in 24–26. The striking aspect of 27 is the insistence that the fulfilment of God's promise will come about according to God's plan, as and when he pleases, and not according to any human expectation. 24–26 provide the main, central thrust of this section as a whole, arguing for the resurrection of the body as not in the least improbable, on the analogy of the seed dying in order to produce fruit and the phoenix rising from the ashes. Clearly the writer sees the doubts about the Parousia, and those about the resurrection of the believers, as closely bound up together. 26 forms the conclusion specifically to the question of bodily resurrection, while 27 applies to both. Thus in face of doubts on the part of the community that they have any assurance for the future, both as far as Christ's Second Coming and their own being alive to participate in the promised future, the writer asserts emphatically the certainty of God's promise and also his creative power. There is, then, here no sense of any fulfilment of the divine promise or final age in the present; hope is to be fixed fully in the future[144].

The same collocation of the Second Coming of Christ and the bodily resur-

---

[144] O'Hagan 1968, 94 notes that 1 Clem (e. g. 5.4,7; 45.8) sets the martyrs already in heaven

rection of the righteous (that is, members of the community) is found in 50.3–4 ('All the generations from Adam to the present day have passed away; but those who according to God's grace have been perfected in love possess the place of the godly. They will be made manifest at the appearance of the kingdom of Christ. For it is written: Enter into the chambers for just a little while until my anger and fury are past, and I will remember a good day, and I will raise you up out of your graves'). The theme of the appearing (literally here 'visitation') of the messianic kingdom and the participation of the righteous in it is familiar from parts of the apocalyptic tradition, and more widely within Judaism. The use of these motifs here is clearly linked to the writer's purpose, evident in 23–27, of reassuring his community about the future. Yet although 50 goes further in spelling out clearly the participation of the members of the community in the final messianic kingdom that Christ will usher in, nothing is said in any detail about the nature of this kingdom: whether it is conceived of as earthly and material or not. O'Hagan argues that if 'kingdom of Christ' here has the specific sense (at it would in Jewish usage) of 'messianic kingdom', then it clearly implies earthly renewal: he acknowledges that the term in itself cannot simply be assumed to have that meaning, but holds that this sense can be supported by what we find elsewhere in 1 Clement. Thus, especially, the reference to the judgement to come (27.4; cf. 23.5) probably implies a material view; still more, however, the idea of bringing 'rebirth to the world' (παλιγ-γενεσία κόσμῳ) points to cosmic renewal, while the theme of the promise in ch. 10, and especially at 31.3, with the technical terminology of Jewish messianic tradition would again indicate that what is involved is the eschatological promised land[145].

Yet none of these arguments, or passages, are convincing on closer examination for a fully material view[146], and it is more plausible to see the kingdom in 50 as set fully in the future, in non-specific terms. The only further reference to the kingdom comes in 42.3, in the summary account of the apostles' activity, as proclaiming the kingdom of God. Meanwhile, for the present, and in order to be acceptable at the time when the final promises are suddenly fulfilled, the writer advocates in detail the way of life to be followed: for example, repentance, sound ethical conduct, promoting unity in the community, dutiful obedience to elders or leaders of the community and to the state authorities[147].

In view of this, it is not surprising that Knoch, in his important work on 1 Clement, argues that Clement has made the kingdom no longer central, as it is in the early Christian proclamation, and has removed the element of burning

---

with Christ, but that otherwise it has an intermediate state for the righteous who are already dead, on the pattern of Jewish tradition and the theme of bodily resurrection.

[145] O'Hagan 1968, 96.
[146] Cf. further, specifically on 9.4, Knoch 1964, 268–272, 297–299.
[147] Cf. further esp. Wengst 1987, 105–118.

expectation[148]. Thus he claims that in the reference to the proclamation of the kingdom in 42, Clement has de-eschatologized Easter and Pentecost; the kingdom is no longer already breaking in through these. Thus for Clement, the kingdom has a purely future and transcendent dimension; it is not in any sense present, even in the church. Thus Clement fails properly to understand and preserve the tension between present and future that is an essential element of New Testament eschatology (especially Paul). Certainly Clement in many respects stands in clear continuity with early Christian eschatology; thus in 23 it represents the primitive expectation of the end, as a fixed element (cf. 42) of the Christian faith, belonging to the apostolic tradition. Clement equally is a witness to the experience of the delay of the Parousia, and the ensuing eschatological crisis of faith that has been instrumental in the troubles at Corinth especially. Against this, Clement uses already fixed and developed Christian apologetic (23.5), but shifts from the parousia being near to it being sudden[149]. Along with this, Clement moves to an individual eschatology, with the emphasis on future rewards and benefits, rather than the full establishment of the kingdom[150]. Thus while Clement's defence of the expectation of the end serves as a statement of the eschatological hope, it is now relativized, as an item of faith, decisive in its implications for the conduct of Christians, but no longer a vivid, threatening force, such that the Christ event can be seen as the decisive turning-point for world-history and salvation-history. Thus, Knoch argues, Clement has denuded the Christian tradition of its end-time universal signifi-cance, by individualizing and moralizing it; thus it is no longer general eschatol-ogy and the threat of judgement that are important, but stress on individual reward and punishment. More generally, then, Clement has consciously de-eschatologized the primitive Christian understanding of the world and the present age, and in very much the same manner as Luke-Acts has caused the basic thrust of the eschatological understanding to be reorientated in terms of the delay of the Parousia and the time of the church[151].

Knoch's argument is in many ways plausible. Thus it makes sense, in spite of arguments to the contrary, to see Clement as having lost the eschatological cutting-edge of the early Christian message and having largely emptied the kingdom of any real content and significance. It is also convincing, in general, to note the basic affinities with Luke-Acts, especially to the extent that 1 Clement engages in political apologetic and advocates quietism and confor-mity. It is certainly the case that in 1 Clement there is no vision of a messianic

---

[148] Thus Knoch 1964, e.g. 103–105; the attempt by Van Unnik 1951 to show that ch. 34, and 1 Clem more generally, has kept a sharp eschatological cutting-edge is not convincing.

[149] Knoch 1964, 126–136.

[150] Knoch 1964, 122–124, 136–141.

[151] Cf. Knoch 1964, e.g. 141–145, 154–161, 193–202, 214–215, 220; cf. also Wengst 1987, 117–118.

kingdom involving a challenge to the ruling Roman authorities or a transformation of society; instead there is a conformist, accepting attitude to the world,
constrained only by emphasis on the sudden end and individual reward or
punishment to come. So also Knoch is right to indicate close connection
between 27.5c and Acts 1.6. In fact the reference to the kingdom in 42 should
also be brought into the discussion here, since the central importance of the
kingdom is thus implicitly removed from being the dominant theme of Jesus'
message and is instead transferred to the preaching of the Apostles and the age
of the Church.

Yet at the same time Knoch begs a number of questions. Not least of these is
his characterization of the early Christian message, above all the assumption
that the understanding of Easter and Pentecost as anticipating the final age (and
thus helping both indicate and resolve the tension between now and not yet) is
an essential component part of this. Certainly the fact that there is some tension
between present and future in the proclamation of Jesus, particularly in the
message of the kingdom, is to be accepted, but the understanding of Easter and
Pentecost as representing the embodiment of the fulfilment of the kingdom is
very much more a secondary development in Paul or Acts, and in modern
scholarship in succession to both of them. I would wish to argue that to see
Easter and Pentecost in this way represents potentially much more a modification (or compromise) than a fulfilment of the basic Christian message; the
question, then, needs to be taken back much further than it is by Knoch. So
also, Knoch's argument that 1 Clement is de-eschatologizing or denuding the
basic Christian message is close in some respects to the argument I advanced in
my essay in the previous volume of this Colloquium in relation to *Paul*; that is,
that Paul has neutralized or defused the radical thrust of Jesus and the early
Christian message about the messianic kingdom and what it involves. Hence it
may be that 1 Clement is nearer to Paul than Knoch is prepared to allow; it may
also be that the need to shift to an emphasis that is almost purely future has been
brought about not simply by the delay of the Parousia or the concern of
individuals about their own resurrection, but also by the failure of the messianic
kingdom to materialize.

9.2. 2 Clement

In the case of 2 Clement, there is much less certainly about the exact dating of
the work, and whether indeed it is early enough to come within our period[152]. It
shares, as we have seen, some points in common with 1 Clement; not least of

---

[152] Donfried 1974, 1–15 argues that 2 Clem should be dated c. 98–100 A.D., that is,
immediately following 1 Clem, since 2 Clem is to be understood as a hortatory discourse
written by the presbyters for whose reinstatement 1 Clem pleads. But this reconstruction of the
situation, and consequent dating, is improbable and has not gained general acceptance; more

these is the problem of the delay of the Parousia. Thus, as 1 Clement and 2 Peter, it shows that this problem is central (11.2; 16.3), and stresses the suddenness of Christ's coming, in order to combat the fears of the community. Along with this, 2 Clement emphasizes above all the reality of the day of judgement; this is the absolute future point of reference for the writer and those whom he addresses. The threat of the final judgement, and the need to live in fear of this, are set out explicitly in 15.5–16.3; 17.4–18.2 and indeed implicitly throughout the work as a whole[153]. So also the correlative of this, that it is the community's (or, more precisely, individual members') conduct in the present that will be decisive for determining their fate in the future judgement, is set out in this eschatological section and reflected in the work overall. Indeed, a central theme of the work is that correct ethical behaviour in the present is the essential prerequisite for reward in the final judgement[154]. Thus also it is made clear (6.9: 'But if even righteous people such as these are not able by their own righteous acts to save the children, with what confidence will we enter the kingdom of God, if we do not keep baptism pure and untainted?') that being baptized into the community does not in itself guarantee acceptance at the final judgement or participation in the benefits of the final age. Final redemption will come only if they keep themselves (or their bodies, or flesh) pure[155]. It is consistent with this, and indeed helps set the theme for the work as a whole, that the Epistle starts by portraying Jesus as the judge of both the living and the dead (1.1–2). The final reward for proper conduct, and the benefits of the future age, are represented as rest and eternal life. The promise, set fully in the future, will be fulfilled in the coming age and in rest in the kingdom[156]. But little is said about the specific nature of the kingdom, either here (in 5–6), or in 12, where the kingdom is referred to, but again mainly as conditional upon present conduct for participation.

In his discussion of 2 Clement, Donfried argues (in connection with chapter 10) that the writer uses a twofold cosmological dualism, that is both vertical (between heaven and earth) but also horizontal (between this world and the world to come)[157]. That is, Donfried maintains, he uses this Jewish horizontal or temporal schema precisely in order to emphasize the *future* nature of the promises, and to counter (as he does throughout the book) a tendency to a libertine, over-realized eschatology, similar to that which 1 Clement has to combat and Paul has to contend with in 1 Corinthians. So Donfried also argues

---

usually 2 Clem is dated within the first half of the second century, c. 120–150 (cf. e. g. Wengst 1984, 213–214, 224–227).

[153] Cf. Donfried 1974, 85, 90–91, 99–104, 166–179, 180–181; cf. also O'Hagan 1968, 71–73.

[154] Cf. Donfried 1974, 99–104, 150–152, 166ff.

[155] Cf. Donfried 1974, 126–128.

[156] Cf. Donfried 1974, 99–104, 113, 120–124, 152–154; cf. also O'Hagan 1968, 78–80.

[157] Donfried 1974, 147–150.

that the writer in 9.1ff. specifically takes issue with the four main ways in which the Pauline view of the resurrection could be weakened or distorted; that is, by introducing or emphasizing the themes of the immortality of the soul, the delay of the Parousia, realized eschatology and docetic Christology[158]. Yet at the same time, Donfried says, the writer here manages to misrepresent Paul or at least fail to do justice to the subtlety of his argument, by not distinguishing the different senses of flesh (σάρξ) as Paul does. Thus 2 Clement, by emphasizing salvation in the flesh, effectively ignores the tension that is essential for Paul's view of the resurrection of the body. Hence Donfried criticizes 2 Clement for being 'simplistic, crude and one-dimensional' in equating the flesh of the future resurrection life with that of the present[159].

There are obvious similarities between Donfried's argument and that of Knoch concerning 1 Clement. This is not surprising in view of the similarities between 1 and 2 Clement, and the strengths and weaknesses of Donfried's position are correspondingly close to those we have already noted in the case of Knoch. Thus Donfried is right to point to the fact that the emphasis in 2 Clement is almost wholly on sound, ethical conduct as the main concern of the community, as prerequistite for enjoying the final rewards of salvation, and correspondingly the experience of and participation in the divine promise at present are pushed to the background. Correspondingly, Jesus is presented primarily, and almost exclusively, as an eschatological judge, not as the one who has brought about the turn of the ages and who therefore serves as the focal point for the tension between now and not yet. But it has to be said that Donfried is operating with an outmoded and untenable view of Jewish apocalyptic, with its supposed central focus on the dualism between this world and the world to come, and that this in turn is too crude and unsophisticated a mode of evaluating the significance of 2 Clement. Again, it may be the case that 2 Clement's understanding of the resurrection of the flesh, or body, is crude and simplistic compared with that of Paul, as Donfried claims (although he is careful to explain that Paul should not simply be made the standard for evaluating all other theological positions and developments)[160]; but it could of course be argued that 2 Clement has deliberately chosen to develop and explain this theme in this way, in order to make clear that the messianic kingdom and the final age are essentially physical and material, not simply spiritual (contrary to what Paul may be understood to be claiming in 1 Cor 15.42–50). If so, this position may certainly appear theologically less subtle and sophisticated than that of Paul, but that would not in itself affect the validity of the attempt to reassert the fact both that the

---

[158] Donfried 1974, 142–146.
[159] Donfried 1974, 146.
[160] Donfried 1974, 180.

messianic kingdom has in no sense already arrived, its fulfilment still being awaited in the future, and also that it cannot be spiritualized without detracting from its essential nature.

It is something close to this position that is advocated by O'Hagan, who draws attention to a number of features in 2 Clement that both individually and cumulatively imply (although not conclusively) a tradition of earthly re-creation[161]. The resurrection of the body, or flesh, is one main element in this, as for example at 12.5–6 (linked to the final age, but dependent on human conduct) and 14.3 (bound up with redemption). This is so especially in the denouement of the eschatological scene in 8–9 (e.g. 8.4; 9.1–6), where there are strong hints that the resurrection of the flesh implies that the kingdom of God is earthly (so especially 9.4; cf. 9.6). Secondly, the judgement of all creation marks the division between this world and the world to come, while 16.3 (cf. ch. 17) probably implies that this world will be destroyed by fire, but that this purifying will lead to earthly re-creation. Thirdly, 17.3–4 has the same basic tradition, of the gathering together of the elect, as Did 9–10, and, similarly, implies a renewed, recreated promised land; likewise, the reference to 're-demption' here (λυτρώσεται; cf. Lk 2.38; 24.21) uses the technical terms of Jewish messianism and political liberation, again denoting hope for the restoration of an earthly kingdom. This same section (17.5) cites the messianic passage from Isa 66 three times, and O'Hagan argues that the portrayal of Christ as king of the world should again be understood in an earthly sense[162]. In this connection, O'Hagan also wants to argue for 12.1–2 (cf. 12.6), denoting Christ as king of the world, as earthly in its reference as well. This is also how he interprets 5.5 ('the coming kingdom and eternal life'; cf. 6.3). So fifthly, he sees the same passage, 5.5, as denoting the promised repose (cf. 6.7; 11.5–7; 10.3–4) that is the essence of the future kingdom, and closely linked with bodily resurrection (14.5; cf. 1.7). Above all here, O'Hagan draws attention to the reference in 10.4 to the 'bliss' (τρυφή) of the coming kingdom, which he sees as very close to millenarian concepts, and in any case setting the eschatological doctrine of 2 Clement very close to earthly hopes within Jewish tradition.

This interpretation of 2 Clement seems to me on the whole to be more plausible than Donfried's position, although it indulges in some special pleading and has obvious weaknesses. One of these O'Hagan himself clearly indicates; that is, 19.4 ('he shall live . . .'), which he sees as indicating an individualizing eschatology in a superterrestial heaven, which is obviously then very difficult to make compatible with a view of earthly restoration. He explains

---

[161] O'Hagan 1968, 70–80.

[162] O'Hagan 1968, 75–76; in connection with the gathering together of the elect, he also argues (74) that the citation of Isa 66 should be understood as denoting earthly re-creation, and further that the final gathering together should be seen as parallel to Christian meetings for worship, themselves symbolic of the final eschaton to come.

this problem away by arguing that 19–20 are a later addition[163]. But although this view has been advanced by others, there are no strong grounds for it[164]. Hence it would be necessary to pursue further than O'Hagan does his further argument, that 19.4 does not necessarily denote immediate possession of the joy of heaven at death, but may rather be part of the overall moral exhortation ('suffering is short, but the future glory eternal'), and his explanation of the 'prince of immortality' and 'life of heaven' at 20.5 (a verse which he sees as original) as being concerned not with eschatology but with the life of grace, or heavenly life, established by Christ on earth. Here again, then, we have what amounts to special pleading by O'Hagan (as also, perhaps, with his explanation of 19.3; 20.2 as consistent with earthly renewal), for what constitutes a serious difficulty for his argument.

Otherwise, the case for 2 Clement having a messianic, materialist hope can be quite impressive; but to lay very much emphasis on this is probably to go beyond what 2 Clement intends. It says very little indeed to give us any idea of what it understands the future kingdom, and promised rest, to consist of. The main preoccupation, as with 1 Clement (and 2 Pet 3), is with the delay of the Parousia and the need to counter this problem by explaining the fact that Christ's return will be sudden and that life meanwhile must be lived in preparation for that. Indeed, as O'Hagan properly notes, the basic concern of 2 Clement is moral exhortation[165], and the eschatological material (as the other theological themes in 2 Clement) are merely to be found piecemeal in relation to this.

10. Ignatius and Polycarp

10.1. Polycarp

The main emphasis of Polycarp's Epistle to the Philippians is moral (he writes 'concerning righteousness', e.g. 3.1), and eschatological themes are found only scattered around, in relation to this. The most striking passage is 5.2–3:

If we please him in this present world, we will also receive the future world, just as he has promised us that he will raise us again from the dead, and that if we live as good citizens worthily of him, we will also reign together with him, provided only that we believe. Likewise, let the young men also be blameless in all things, being especially careful to preserve purity, and reigning themselves in, as with a bridle, from every kind of evil. For it is good that they should be cut off from the lusts that are in the

---

[163] O'Hagan 1968, 82–85.

[164] For a similar argument for the secondary nature of 19–20, cf. e.g. Di Pauli 1903; Schüssler 1907; but against this, see Wengst 1984, 209–210.

[165] O'Hagan 1968, 86.

world, since 'every lust wars against the spirit'; and 'neither adulterers, nor those
who are effeminate, nor those who abuse themselves with mankind will inherit the
kingdom of God', nor those who do things that are inconsistent and unbecoming.

The use of 'we shall reign with' here obviously indicates that what Polycarp
envisages is the Christians sharing in the coming kingdom with God (or Christ);
indeed, sharing not only in the possession but also in the rule of it. The fact that
the kingdom is an important theme for Polycarp is confirmed by the reference
to it at the end of this passage, when he quotes 1 Cor 6.9, and also from 2.2–3,
where he cites Mt 5.5. Taking these passages together, it is obviously tempting
to link 5.2 with Mt 19.28, and understand Polycarp to be giving the Christians
he addresses an even greater role than that assigned to the disciples in Matthew;
that is, to be ruling in the new kingdom on earth[166]. The fact remains, however,
that nothing is said either here in 5.2–3 or in 2.2–3 about the specific nature of
the kingdom, or whether it is set on earth or in heaven. What is apparent, as we
have already noted, is that the main concern lies elswhere; that is, with Polycarp's insistence that those he addresses live as good citizen (πολιτεύομαι) in
the present, in order to have any future reward at all[167]. So also in 2.2–3, the
main emphasis is on the way the Christian community should conduct itself
rather than the nature of the kingdom. Thus the main point is the social and
moral constraints set on the Christian community, and the correlation between
their moral behaviour and their reward; the same is true at 12.2 where what is
meant by the 'inheritance with the saints' is not specified at all, but the moral
standards required are clearly spelt out[168]. So also the clear, frequent reference
to God's final judgement are directed to the moral demands made on the
community, as also are the references to the resurrection. Thus the importance
of eschatological material in Polycarp's Epistle to the Philippians is evident; but
equally, it is difficult to be sure where it stands on a number of important issues,
since it is subordinate to the main interest in giving moral teaching and exhortation.

10.2. Ignatius

In the Letters of Ignatius, written on his way to martyrdom in Rome in 115, the
themes of the imminent end and the final judgement are certainly found (e. g.
Mag 5.1; Eph 16.2; and especially Eph 11.1; 'Therefore these are the last times;
let us show shame, let us fear the forbearance of God, lest we have wrong ideas
about the riches of God's generosity and clemency; for let us either fear the
coming wrath or love the grace that is already here in the present life. Only let

---

[166] Cf. O'Hagan 1968, 91–92.
[167] Cf. O'Hagan 1968, 90–91; cf. also J. A. Fischer 1956, 243.
[168] Cf. J. A. Fischer 1956, 242–244; O'Hagan 1968, 92–93.

us be found in Christ Jesus unto true life'). Nevertheless, although these eschatological themes are obviously held in common with other early Christian (and Jewish) writers, and clearly reflect this common heritage, they are in no sense a central or dominant aspect of his thought or letters. More specifically, in Ignatius there is no concept of the continuity, renewal or transformation of the present world or social order. Nor is there anything of the theme of the messianic kingdom on earth or the glorius fulfilment of the prophecy of Paradise restored. Instead, the hope that Ignatius holds out, as he goes to Rome and impending death, is set on being found in Christ (or with Christ) in the heavenly world[169]. The final age has already been inaugurated by Christ's first coming; its consummation will be realized individually, and not on a material level. So also the final eschatological gathering of the elect has already taken place (Mag 10.3), and is not still awaited in the future[170]. It is perhaps surprising, in view of the fate awaiting him, that Ignatius places so little emphasis on the future life and hope; but it appears that what has happened is that he has spiritualized the future hope in terms of life with Christ, and removed it from the earthly realm altogether. Ignatius does indeed lay stress on the resurrection of the body at the final Parousia, but this is only as a part of an overall thoroughly individualizing eschatology[171]. So also it is fully consonant with this that Ignatius sets up a polarization between Christians and the world and between the Church and the world[172]. Thus salvation for Ignatius is to be found in the Church, provisionally, in the present world, but only fully in heaven with Christ in the future.

It is again a consistent part of this theological stance that Ignatius has a negative stance towards the world in general; this is mainly directed, of course, to the non-Christian world and those outside the church, but Ignatius makes no attempt to suggest that there is any positive evaluation of the world, the material present setting or the creation, in view. Certainly Ignatius does have a vision (Eph 19.1−3) of a brilliant star (a tradition deriving from Num 24.7) in heaven, which affects events on earth, destroys the present evil kingdom and death, and brings in eternal life[173]. This has obvious affinities with the kind of vision we find in the Sibylline Oracles (SibOr 5.155−161)[174] and other Jewish texts. The striking fact with Ignatius, however, is that although there is obvious messianic reference, there is nothing at all of a messianic kingdom, in the way that this is provided for on the Jewish model. Instead, the emphasis again is on the future, heavenly, eternal life. Here, then, what we have essentially is a

---

[169] Cf. Corwin, 1960, 155, 174.

[170] Cf. O'Hagan 1968, 105−106.

[171] O'Hagan 1968, 107−108 wants to see more positive emphasis here on material re-creation than I am prepared to allow.

[172] Cf. O'Hagan 1968, 105, who stresses that the contrast is not between the present aeon and the aeon to come, but between the present aeon and the church.

[173] Cf. on this esp. Corwin 1960, 175−185.

[174] Cf. above 2. 1. 3.

Jewish messianic theme that is used christologically by Ignatius and bound up
directly with the future, heavenly sphere that is the ultimate aspiration and
reward of those who belong to Christ. So also Ignatius has a markedly
developed Christology otherwise; the essential features of this Christology are
shown not so much by the star reference as by the use of the Logos category and
the emphasis on the pre-existence of Christ. Along with this, and integrally
bound up with it, Ignatius also presents a developed ecclesiology, with the
concepts of the church, hierarchy of leadership and authority and obedience all
assuming importance. Clearly the specific context of Ignatius' letters, not only
his impending martyrdom but also the threat of Gnosticism that he is concerned
to oppose, is important in helping us understand the specific themes he
develops in his work.

11. The Epistle to Diognetus

It is very doubtful whether the Epistle to Diognetus belongs integrally to this
discussion, since although claims have been made for it to be early (even first-
century), it is probably considerably later[175]. At any rate, it serves as a good
example of a document where the eschatology is thoroughly 'otherworldly'.
This draws a sharp contrast between the present life on earth and the life (or
kingdom) in heaven, viewing the former negatively and the latter positively, as
at 5.9 ('They spend their days on earth, but have their citizenship in heaven.')
and 6.7−8:

The soul is locked up in the body, yet it is the very thing that holds the body
together; so too, Christians are shut up in the world as if in a prison, yet it is
precisely they who hold the world together. Although immortal, the soul is
lodged in a mortal tenement; so too, Christians, although residing as strangers
among corruptible things, look forward to the incorruptibility that awaits them
in heaven.'

The immediately preceding 6.3−6 are also relevant to this theme. Again,
although there is stress on the future, final judgement (7.6; 'Some day, of
course, he will send him as a judge, and who will then endure his coming?'), the
kingdom is equally set in the heavenly realm, and can have nothing to do with
the imperfect earthly world[176]. The present world, then, is something to be
escaped from, not to be renewed or transformed into the fulfilment of messianic
prophecy.

---

[175] For a brief and cogent survey of different datings and the arguments for them, cf.
Wengst 1984, 305−309; Wengst himself places the composition of Diognetus between the end
of the second century and the time of Constantine.

[176] For further discussion of these themes, cf. e. g. Wengst 1984, 294−304; O'Hagan 1968,
108−110.

12. Conclusion

Clearly messianism and eschatology are very important, potentially, for the nature and development of Judaism and Christianity in the 70–135 period, and for what is at issue between them. Thus as we have seen, there is evidence, both for Palestine and the Diaspora, of hope for final deliverance from oppressors and also for a messianic figure and kingdom as centrally significant for many Jews and the focus of messianic movements and uprisings. This is so before 70, and continues well beyond 70. So also, eschatological hope is of primary importance for the early Christian movement, centered on Jesus' proclamation of the kingdom. But one question obviously raised, then, is whether what begins as an essentially Jewish, messianic movement, looking for the realization of the messianic kingdom, continues in close association with and continuity of Jewish tradition and community or moves away from them.

The argument I have presented in this paper may seem deliberately to have blurred the distinctions between Judaism and Christianity, to have set up an over-simple dichotomy between material and spiritual hope and to have passed a negative judgement on the latter and a positive judgement on the former too readily. But in fact the theological, historical, social, economic and political issues involved here are much more complex than that would suggest; hence I am dubious about setting up so simple a contrast and critical of attempts to do so. Thus, for example, O'Hagan is too prone to make the material and spiritual contrast normative and determinative in all cases, and to find material re-creation everywhere[177]. The further problem is that he too easily assumes that the use in Christian texts of the 'technical terminology' of Jewish national restoration hope implies a full commitment in these texts to that tradition. This, however, is precisely the question that has to be discussed each time, more rigorously than it is by O'Hagan, in order to determine if possible the extent to which continuity or discontinuity with Jewish tradition is involved, and whether the use of Jewish terminology involves adherence to that main tradition.

In fact, as we have seen (e. g. 4 Ezra; Barnabas; Didache), it can often be difficult to be sure whether a particular text represents an expression of material hope or of spiritualizing tendency. Thus also it can be hard to know in the case of Christian texts whether references to the kingdom are intended to point to its realization on earth or not. But the main point here is that the various divergent positions found in these Christian texts are already clearly present within Judaism. Hence, for example, while a spiritualizing, individualizing interpretation of the kingdom (and eschatology more widely) may seem to be a distinctive development in the Christian tradition, we need look no further than Josephus (or, of course, Philo) for a clear instance of this. Equally, of course, the

---

[177] O'Hagan 1968.

tradition of material or millenial hope is deeply rooted and widely attested within Judaism, not least in the case of popular movements and synagogal prayers. This is so not just for Palestine but for the Diaspora as well, as we have noted with Sibylline 5 and the closely related messianic uprising. Indeed, as Hengel argues, Sib 5 merely represents the tip of the iceberg in the Diaspora, and the whole developed tradition from Papias to Lactantius would be unintelligible without it[178]. It would obviously be easy to argue that the millenial, material hope is crude, and limited in appeal to the simpleminded, whereas for those having to adapt the tradition to a more sophisticated environment, spritualizing interpretation is inevitable[179]. But while it may indeed be the case that this kind of interpretation may arise in order to deal with problems of potentially dangerous political or military expression of messianic hope or the fact that the promised messianic age has not been realized[180], this argument fails to do justice to the powerful potential of the material tradition for helping effect the transformation of the world or conditions of oppression in which the people are set. Millenial and related hope can of course easily turn into a fantasy world, but that is by no means the only possibility. In any case, the point again is that the divisions and tensions involved here go deep within both Jewish and Christian traditions. The Christian texts certainly show evidence of distinctive developments, but they are also in essential continuity with Judaism throughout.

As far as the theme of the 'Parting of the Ways' is concerned, then, the evidence I have been dealing with appears somewhat ambivalent. The reasons why Christians separated from Jews, or whether they had really done so, is not clear in at least some cases. The 'Jewish' and 'Christian' traditions and texts may be divided as much within themselves as against each other. It may be, of course, that the issues look more confused than they should because I have not considered sufficient evidence; a considerable number of other texts, not least many within the New Testament, would have helped provide a fuller picture, while it would also have been worthwhile to extend the scope of this paper to consider distinctive christological formulations, rather than simply messianic expectation. But to do so would raise its own questions. To take the Fourth

---

[178] Hengel 1983, 657–658, 682. He criticizes the one-sided conclusion of U. Fischer 1978 that Hellenistic Diaspora Judaism had only the slightest trace of imminent eschatological expectation. The problem, as Hengel indicates, is that Fischer has based his discussion on too limited a selection of sources, and at least e.g. the Sibylline Oracles, the Testaments of the Twelve Patriarchs and the Apocalypse of Abraham should have been included in order to help redress the balance. It is also the case, of course, that Hengel's own penetrating discussion of the revolt of 115–117 has helped give a much clearer picture of main currents in Diaspora Judaism.

[179] Cf. Hengel 1983, 682; but note also his qualification of this view.

[180] Cf. e.g. the discussion in Hecht 1987; Chester 1991b (relating especially to Philo and Paul); the same argument could be advanced for e.g. Josephus.

Gospel: the most highly developed christology in the New Testament has lost touch almost completely with the concrete realization of Jesus' proclamation and the messianic hope, whereas in the Apocalypse the christology is hardly developed at all, but the vision of God's kingdom on earth is given its most superb expression. The lamb who conquers brings about a new heaven and a new earth, and heaven on earth in the form of the new Jerusalem. The Son of Man or Logos leaves the heavenly world only to return there, and shows that the gulf between heaven and earth remains as great as ever. It can of course be claimed that it is precisely the high christology of the Fourth Gospel, and the nature of the claims made about Jesus, that forces the division between Judaism and Christianity, and there is surely some truth in that; but we have also to ask to what extent the formulation of a christology of this kind was meant to work retrospectively, to justify the situation in which the Johannine community found itself[181].

The reasons for separation may in some cases, then, be more mundane and less purely theological than we are sometimes led to suppose. This may be so in other ways as well. We know that in the Bar Kochba revolt at least some Jewish Christians were put under great pressure to give allegiance to the messianic leader and revolt. It is likely enough that the same would have happened in the 66–70 revolt as well. Thus in Hebrews two of the problems that the writer has to deal with are the continuing attraction of the sacrificial cult, and how Jesus can be shown to be unique, and superior to anything to be found within Judaism. Perhaps, in context of 66–70, there was emotional pull and political pressure to change messianic allegiance, and this could have been a recurring problem, but also a cause of final separation between Jews and Christians, for at least some groups and individuals. Political events and constraints play an important role in the formation of at least some messianic concepts, and they may also turn out to be one of the decisive factors in driving a wedge between some Jewish and Christian groups.

What is involved in all this, of course, is the fact that the way the Christian texts take over and use Jewish eschatological and messianic traditions is bound up with their struggle to establish their own self-identity. Thus we have seen that in a number of texts the kingdom is more or less defined in terms of the church, and the fulfilment of the messianic age effectively takes the form of the community living in a pure and holy way in its present existence. Ethics and eschatology are of course bound up with each other in the Jewish tradition (as for example Qumran) as well as in the Christian movement from an early stage;

---

[181] It would also be worth raising similar questions about other New Testament texts from the post-70 period; thus e. g. Matthew, where we have a more developed Christology than elsewhere in the Synoptics, and also a spiritualizing of the kingdom (in the Beatitudes), and Luke-Acts, with its developed theme of the Spirit and diminished emphasis on eschatology.

but it is apparent, as Wengst indicates in the case of the Didache[182], that ethical concern can easily blunt the eschatological cutting-edge of the Christian proclamation and shift the fulfilment of these hopes and their impact on the world around towards preoccupation with the conduct and organisation of the Christian community internally. The concentration on the community is itself a thoroughly Jewish theme, but the particular expression of it obviously serves to enhance the differences. So also, of course, even a vision of the end expressed in apparently universal and inclusive terms can become centered on limiting and exclusive aspects (thus, for example, nation, land, Jerusalem and temple in the case of Judaism; church, baptism, Christ and Spirit in the case of the Christian texts). Thus as far as the themes of this paper are concerned, in the period 70–135 the Christian texts show considerable evidence of continuity with their Jewish heritage. But although there is still a great deal of common ground, the way the eschatological hopes and messianic promises are in many cases given their fulfilment in the Christian community serves to deepen and harden the division.

Bibliography

Adas, M. 1979: *Prophets of Rebellion. Millenarian Protests against the European Colonial Order*, North Carolina 1979.

Applebaum, S. 1951: "The Jewish Revolt in Cyrene in 115–117 and the subsequent recolonization", in: *JJS* 2 (1951) 177–186.

– 1979: Jews and Greeks in Ancient Cyrene (SJLA 28), Leiden 1979.

Audet, J.-P. 1958: *La Didachè. Instructions des apôtres*, Paris 1958.

Bailey, J. 1934: "The Temporary Messianic Reign in the Literature of Early Judaism", in: *JBL* 53 (1934) 170–187.

Bammel, E. 1961: "Schema und Vorlage von *Didache* 16", in: F. L. Cross (ed.) *Studia Patristica* vol IV. II, Berlin 1961, 253–262.

Barnard, L. W. 1958: "The Date of the Epistle of Barnabas – A Document of Early Egyptian Christianity", in: *JEA* 44 (1958) 101–107.

– 1961: "A Note on *Barnabas* 6.8–17", in: F. L. Cross (ed.) *Studia Patristica* vol. IV. II, Berlin 1961, 263–267.

Bauckham, R. J. 1974: "The Great Tribulation in the Shepherd of Hermas", in: *JTS* n.s. 25 (1974) 27–40.

Belo, F. 1981: *A Materialist Reading of the Gospel of Mark*, ET Maryknoll 1981.

Benoit, P., Milik, J. T. and De Vaux, R. 1961: *Les Grottes de Murabba'ât* (Discoveries in the Judaean Desert 2), Oxford 1961.

Bidez, J. and Cumont, F. 1938: *Les Mages Hellénisés. Zoroastre, Ostanés et Hystaspes d'après la Tradition Grecque*, vol. 1 (Introduction), vol. 2 (Les Textes), Paris 1938.

---

[182] Cf. Wengst 1984, 59–61.

Bietenhard, H. 1951: *Die himmlische Welt in Urchristentum und Spätjudentum* (WUNT 2) Tübingen 1951.

– 1953: "The Millenial Hope in the Early Church", in: *SJT* 6 (1953) 12–30.

– 1955: *Das tausendjährige Reich*, Zürich 1955.

Billerbeck, P. 1922–28: *Kommentar zum Neuen Testament aus Talmud und Midrasch*, vols. I–IV, Munich 1922–26.

Bornkamm, G. 1952: *Das Ende des Gesetzes*, Munich 1952.

Bruce, F. F. 1965: "Josephus and Daniel", in: ASTI 4 (1965) 148–162.

– 1973: "Eschatology in the Apostolic Fathers", in: D. Neiman and M. Schatkin (ed.) *The Heritage of the Early Church. Essays in honor of the Very Reverend G. V. Florovosky*, Rome 1973, 77–89.

Burkitt, F. C. 1932: "Barnabas and the Didache", in: *JTS* 33 (1932) 25–27.

Burridge, K. 1969: *New Heaven, New Earth. A Study of Millenarian Activities*, Oxford 1969.

Butler, B. C. 1960: "The Literary Relations of Didache, Ch. XVI", in: *JTS* n.s. 11 (1960) 265–283.

Causse, A. 1947: "De la Jérusalem terrestre à la Jérusalem céleste", in: *RHP* 27 (1947) 12–36.

Cerfaux, L. 1959: "La multiplication des pains dans la liturgie de la Didachè", in: *Biblica* 40 (1959) 943–958.

Charles, R. H. (ed.) 1913: *The Apocrypha and Pseudepigrapha of the Old Testament* 2 vols., Oxford 1913.

Charlesworth, J. H. 1983–85: *The Old Testament Pseudepigrapha*, London vol. 1 (Apocalyptic Literature and Testaments), 1983; vol. 2 (Expansions of the "Old Testament" and Legends, Wisdom and Philosophical Literature, Prayers, Psalms and Odes, Fragments of Lost Judeo-Hellenistic Works), 1985.

Chester, A. 1991a: "The Sibyl and the Temple", in: W. Horbury (ed.) *Templum Amicitiae. Essays on the Second Temple presented to Ernst Bammel* (JSNTSS 48), Sheffield 1991, 37–69.

– 1991b: "Jewish Messianic Expectations and Mediatorial Figures and Pauline Christology", in: M. Hengel and U. Heckel (ed.) *Paulus und das antike Judentum*, Tübingen 1991, 17–89.

Clerici, L. 1966: *Einsammlung der Zerstreuten. Liturgiegeschichtliche Untersuchung zur Vor- und Nachgeschichte der Fürbitte für die Kirche in Didache 9,4 und 10,5*, Münster 1966.

Cohn, N. 1957: *The Pursuit of the Millenium*, London 1957.

Collins, J. J. 1974a: *The Sibylline Oracles of Egyptian Judaism* (SBLDS 13), Missoula 1974.

– 1974b: "The Place of the Fourth Sibyl in the Development of the Jewish Sibyllina", in: *JJS* 25 (1974) 365–380.

– 1983a: *Between Athens and Jerusalem: Jewish Identity in the Hellenistic Diaspora*, New York 1983.

– 1983b: "The Sibylline Oracles", in: J. H. Charlesworth (ed.) *The Old Testament Pseudepigrapha*, vol. 1, London 1983, 317–472.

– 1984: *The Apocalyptic Imagination. An Introduction to the Jewish Matrix of Christianity*, New York 1984.

– 1987: "Messianism in the Maccabean Period", in: J. Neusner, W. S. Green and E. S. Frerichs (ed.) *Judaisms and their Messiahs at the Turn of the Christian Era*, Cambridge 1987.

Corwin, V. 1990: *St. Ignatius and Christianity in Antioch*, New Haven 1960.

Cullmann, O. 1963: *The Christology of the New Testament*, ET London ²1963.

Dahl, N. A. 1950: "La terre où coulent le lait et le miel selon Barnabé 6,8–19", in: *Mélanges M. Goguel*, Neuchâtel–Paris 1950.

– 1976: *Jesus in the Memory of the Early Church*, Minnesota 1976.

Daniélou, J. 1948: "La typologie millénariste de la semaine dans le christianisme primitif", in: *VC* 2 (1948) 1–16.

– *The Theology of Jewish Christianity*, ET London 1964.

De Gebhardt, O. and Harnack, A. 1878: *Barnabae Epistula*, Leipzig 1878.

De Jonge, H. J. 1979: "Βοτρυς Βοηςει. The Age of Kronos and the Millenium in Papias of Hierapolis", in: M. J. Vermaseren (ed.) *Studies in Hellenistic Religions*, Leiden 1979.

Dibelius, M. 1923: *Der Hirt des Hermas* (HNT), Tübingen 1923.

– 1938: "Die Mahl-Gebete der Didache", in: *ZNW* 37 (1938) 32–41.

Di Pauli, A. 1903: "Zum sog. 2. Korintherbrief des Clemens Romanus", in: *ZNW* 4 (1903) 321–329.

Donfried, K. P. 1974: *The Setting of Second Clement in Early Christianity*, Leiden 1974.

Elbogen, I. 1931: *Der jüdische Gottesdienst in seiner geschichtlichen Entwicklung*, Frankfurt 1931.

Finkelstein, L. 1928–29: "The Birkat Ha-Mazon", in: *JQR* n.s. 19 (1928–29) 211–262.

Fiorenza, E. S. 1985: *The Book of Revelation – Justice and Judgement*, Philadelphia 1985.

Fischer, J. A. 1956: *Die apostolischen Väter*, Darmstadt 1956.

Fischer, U. 1978: *Eschatologie und Jenseitserwartung im hellenistischen Diaspora-judentum*, Berlin–New York 1978.

Fitzmyer, J. A. 1971: *Essays on the Semitic Background of the New Testament*, London 1971.

– 1981: *To Advance the Gospel. New Testament Studies*, New York 1981.

Fraser, P. M. 1950: "Hadrian and Cyrene", in: *JRS* 40 (1950) 77–90.

Fuks, A. 1961: "Aspects of the Jewish Revolt in AD 115–117", in: *JRS* 51 (1961) 98–104.

Funk, F. X. and Bihlmeyer, K. 1924: *Die apostolischen Väter*, Tübingen 1924.

Gager, J. 1975: *Kingdom and Community. The Social World of Early Christianity*, Englewood Cliffs, N. J., 1975.

Gaston, L. 1970: *No Stone on Another: Studies in the Significance of the Fall of Jerusalem in the Synoptic Gospels* (SNT 23), Leiden 1970.

Geffcken, J. 1902a: *Komposition und Entstehungszeit der Oracula Sibyllina*, Leipzig 1902.

- 1902b: *Die Oracula Sibyllina* (GCS 8), Leipzig 1902.

Gerlach, E. 1863: *Die Weissagungen des Alten Testaments in den Schriften des Josephus und das angebliche Zeugniß von Christo*, Berlin 1863.

Goodenough, E. 1945: "John a Primitive Gospel", in: *JBL* 64 (1945) 145–182.

Grant, F. C. 1917: "The Eschatology of the Second Century", in: *American Journal of Theology* 21 (1917) 193–211.

Gry, L. 1904: *Le millénarisme dans ses origines et son développement*, Paris 1904.

- 1933–34: "Le Papias des belles promesses messianiques", in: *Vivre et Penser* 3 (1933–34) 113–124.

- 1946: "Hénoch 10,19 et les belles promesses de Papias", in: *RB* 53 (1946) 197–206.

Hahn, F. 1969: *The Titles of Jesus in Christology*, ET London 1969.

Harnack, A. 1893: *Geschichte der altchristlichen Literatur bis Eusebius*, 2 vols., Leipzig 1893.

Harnisch, W. 1969: *Verhängnis und Verheißung der Geschichte. Untersuchungen zum Zeit- und Geschichtsverständnis im 4. Buch Esra und in der syr. Baruchapokalypse*, Göttingen 1969.

Hayman, P. 1986: "Some Observations on Sefer Yeṣira: (2) The Temple at the Centre of the Universe", in: *JJS* (1986) 176–192.

Hecht, R. D. 1987: "Philo and Messiah", in: J. Neusner, W. S. Green and E S. Frerichs (ed.): *Judaisms and their Messiahs at the Turn of the Christian Era*, Cambridge 1987, 139–168.

Heinemann, J. 1977: *Prayer in the Talmud. Forms and Patterns* (Studia Judaica IX), Berlin–New York 1977.

Heinemann, J. and Petuchowski, J. J. 1975: *Literature of the Synagogue*, New York 1975.

Hengel, M. 1974: *Judaism and Hellenism. Studies in their Encounter in Palestine during the Early Hellenistic Period*, ET London 1974.

- 1983: "Messianische Hoffnung und politischer 'Radikalismus' in der 'jüdisch-hellenistischen Diaspora'", in: D. Hellholm (ed.): *Apocalypticism in the Mediterranean World and the Near East*, Tübingen 1983.

- 1989: *The Zealots. Investigations into the Jewish Freedom Movement in the Period from Herod I until 70 A.D.*, ET Edinburgh 1989.

Hermans, A. 1959: "Le Pseudo-Barnabé est–il millénariste?", in: *ETL* 35 (1959) 849–876.

Hill, C. E. 1986: *Regnum Caelorum. Chiliasm, Non-Chiliasm and the Intermediate State in the Early Church*, PhD thesis, Cambridge University 1986.

Horbury, W. 1985: "The Messianic Associations of the Son of Man", in: *JTS* 36 (1985) 34–55.

- 1988: "Messianism among Jews and Christians in the Second Century", in: *Augustinianum* 28 (1988) 71–88.

Horsley, R. A. 1984: "Popular Messianic Movements Around the Time of Jesus", in: *CBQ* 46 (1984) 471–495.

Horsley, R. A. and Hanson, J. S. 1985: *Bandits, Prophets and Messiahs. Popular Movements in the Time of Jesus*, Minneapolis 1985.

Isenberg, S. R. 1974: "Millenarism in Greco-Roman Palestine", in: *Religion* 4 (1974) 26–46.

Jellinek, A. 1853: *Bet ha-Midrasch*, 5 vols., Leipzig–Warsaw 1853.

Jeremias, J. 1926: *Golgotha* (ΑΓΓΕΛΟΣ: Archiv für Neutestamentliche Zeitgeschichte und Kulturkunde. Beihefte 1), Leipzig 1926.

– 1963: *Unbekannte Jesusworte*, Gütersloh [4]1963.

– 1966: *The Eucharistic Words of Jesus*, ET London 1966.

Joly, R. 1968: *Hermas le Pasteur*, Paris [2]1968.

Kippenberg, H. 1983: "'Dann wird der Orient herrschen und der Okzident dienen', Zur Begründung eines gesamtvorderasiatischen Standpunktes im Kampf gegen Rom", in: N. W. Bolz and W. Hubener (ed.): *Spiegel und Gleichnis*, FS J. Taubes, Würzburg 1983, 40–48.

Kirchner, M. 1863: "Die Eschatologie des Irenaeus", in: *Theologische Studien und Kritiken* 36 (1863) 315–358.

Klein, G. 1908: "Die Gebete in der Didache", in: *ZNW* 9 (1908) 132–146.

Kloppenborg, J. S. 1979: "Didache 16.6–8 and Special Matthaean Tradition", in: *ZNW* 70 (1979) 54–67.

Knoch, O. 1964: *Eigenart und Bedeutung der Eschatologie im theologischen Aufriß des ersten Clementsbriefes. Eine auslegungsgeschichtliche Untersuchung* (Theophaneia 17), Bonn 1964.

– 1980: "Die Stellung der Apostolischen Väter zu Israel und zum Judentum. Eine Übersicht", in: J. Zmijewski and E. Nellessen (ed.): *Begegnung mit dem Wort. Festschrift für H. Zimmermann* (BBB 53), Bonn 1980, 347–378.

La Barre, W. 1971: "Materials for the Study of Crisis Cults: A Bibliographic Essay", in: *Current Anthropology* 12 (1971) 3–44.

Lampe, G. W. H. 1953: "Early Patristic Eschatology", in: *Eschatology. Four Papers read to the Society for the Study of Theology*, Edinburgh 1953, 17–35.

Lanchester, H. C. O. 1913: "The Sibylline Oracles", in: R. H. Charles (ed.): *The Apocrypha and Pseudepigrapha of the Old Testament*, vol. 2: *Pseudepigrapha*, Oxford 1913, 368–406.

Lanternari, V. 1965: *Religions of the Oppressed*, New York 1965.

Lawlor, H. J. and Oulton, J. E. L. 1927–28: *Eusebius: The Ecclesiastical History and the Martyrs of Palestine*, 2 vols. London 1927–28.

Lightfoot, J. B. 1889: *The Apostolic Fathers*, London [2]1889.

Lindner, H. 1972: *Die Geschichtsauffassung des Flavius Josephus im Bellum Judaicum* (AGJU 12), Leiden 1972.

Meshorer, Y. 1967: *Jewish Coins of the Second Temple Period*, Jerusalem 1967.

Middleton, R. D. 1935: "The Eucharistic Prayers of the Didache", in: *JTS* 36 (1935) 259–267.

Miranda, J. P. 1974: *Marx and the Bible. A Critique of the Philosophy of Oppression* ET, New York 1974.

Momigliano, A. 1975: "La portata storica dei vaticini sul settimo re nel terzo libro degli Oracoli Sibillini", in: *Forma Futuri: Studie in Onore die Cardinale Michele Pellegrino*, Turin 1975, 1077–1084.

Moule, C. F. D. 1955: "A Note on *Didache* IX.4", in: *JTS* n.s. 6 (1955) 240–243.

- 1959–60: "A Reconsideration of the Context of *Maranatha*", in: *NTS* 6 (1959–60) 307–310.

Muilenburg, J. 1929: *The Literary Relations of the Epistle of Barnabas and the Teaching of the Twelve Apostles*, Marburg 1929.

Neusner, J. 1987: "Mishnah and Messiah", in: J. Neusner, W. S. Green and E. S. Frerichs (ed.): *Judaisms and their Messiahs at the Turn of the Christian Era*, Cambridge 1987, 265–282.

Niederwimmer, K. 1977: "Zur Entwicklungsgeschichte des Wanderradikalismus im Traditionsbereich der Didache", in: *WS* NF 11 (1977) 145–167.

- 1989: *Die Didache* (KAV 1), Göttingen 1989.

Nikiprowetsky, V. 1970: *La Troisième Sibylle* (Etudes Juives 9), Paris 1970.

- 1972: "Reflexions sur quelques problemes du quatrième et du cinquième livre des Oracles Sibyllins", in: *HUCA* 43 (1972) 29–76.

Noack, B. 1964: "Der hervorragende Mann und der beste der Hebräer (Bemerkungen zu OrSib v. 256–259)", in: *ASTI* 3 (1964) 122–146.

O'Hagan, A. P. 1966: *Material Re-Creation in the Apostolic Fathers* (TU 100), Berlin 1968.

O'Rourke Boyle, M. 1969: "Irenaeus Millenial Hope: A Polemical Weapon", in: *Recherches de Théologie Ancienne et Médiévale* 36 (1969) 5–16.

Peretti, A. 1962: "Echi di dottrine esseniche negli Oracoli Sibillini Giudaici" in: *La parole del passato* 17 (1962) 247–295.

Peterson, E. 1944: "Didachè cap. 9 e 10", in: *Ephemerides Liturgicae* 58 (1944) 3–13.

- 1959: *Frühkirche, Judentum und Gnosis*, Rome–Freiburg–Vienna 1959.

Pixley, G. 1981: God's Kingdom, ET New York 1981.

Reifenberg, A. 1947: *Ancient Jewish Coins*, Jerusalem ²1947.

Resch, A. 1906: *Agrapha*. Leipzig 1906.

Riesenfeld, H. 1956: "Das Brot von den Bergen. Zu Did 9,4", in: *Eranos Jahrbuch* 54 (1956) 142–150.

Rissi, M. 1952: *Zeit und Geschichte in der Offenbarung des Johannes*, Zürich 1952.

Robertson, A. 1901: *Regnum Dei: Eight Lectures on the Kingdom of God in the History of Christian thought*, London 1901.

Robinson, J. A. 1934: "The Epistle of Barnabas and the Didache", in: *JTS* 35 (1934) 113–146, 225–248.

Rousseau, A. 1969: *Irénée de Lyon. Contre les hérésies* (Sources chrétiennes), 2 vols. Paris 1969.

Rowland, C. 1982: *The Open Heaven. A Study of Apocalyptic in Early Judaism and Christianity*, London 1982.

- 1988: *Radical Christianity. A Reading of Recovery*, Cambridge 1988.

Sanders, E. P. 1985: *Jesus and Judaism*, London 1985.

- 1990: *Jewish Law from Jesus to the Mishnah. Five Studies*, London 1990.

Sandvik, B. 1970: *Das Kommen des Herrn beim Abendmahl im Neuen Testament* (ATANT 58), Zürich 1970.

Schäfer, P. 1981: *Der Bar Kochba-Aufstand: Studien zum zweiten jüdischen Krieg gegen Rom* (TSAJ 1), Tübingen 1981.

Schalit, A. 1975: "Die Erhebung Vespasians nach Flavius Josephus, Talmud und Midrasch. Zur Geschichte einer messianischen Prophetie", in: W. Haase and H. Temporini (ed.): *Aufstieg und Niedergang der römischen Welt* II.2, Berlin–New York, 208–327.

Schechter, S. 1898: "Genizah Specimens", in: *JQR* 10 (1898) 654–659.

Schlatter, A. 1966: *Synagoge und Kirche bis zum Barkochba-Aufstand. Vier Studien zur Geschichte des Rabbinats und der jüdischen Christenheit in den ersten zwei Jahrhunderten, Kleinere Schriften 3* (ed. T. Schlatter), Stuttgart 1966.

– 1970: *Kleine Schriften zu Flavius Josephus* (ed. T. Schlatter), Stuttgart 1970.

Schoeps, H.-J. 1949: *Theologie und Geschichte des Judenchristentums*, Tübingen 1949.

Schürer, E., Vermes, G., Millar, F. (and Goodman, M.) 1973–87: *The History of the Jewish People in the Age of Jesus Christ (175B.C.–A.D.135)*, A New English Version revised and edited by G. Vermes, F. Millar (and M. Goodman), Edinburgh, vol. I 1973, vol. II 1979, vol. III.I 1986, vol. III.2 1987.

Schüssler, W. 1907, "Ist der zweite Klemensbrief ein einheitliches Ganzes?", in: *ZKG* 28 (1907) 1–13.

Schwier, H. 1989: *Tempel und Tempelzerstörung: Untersuchungen zu den theologischen und ideologischen Faktoren im ersten jüdisch-römischen Krieg (66–74 n. Chr.)* (NTOA 11), Freiburg–Göttingen 1989.

Sharot, S. 1982: *Messianism, Mysticism and Magic: A Sociological Analysis of Jewish Religious Movements*, Chapel Hill 1982.

Smallwood, E. M. 1976: *The Jews under Roman Rule. From Pompey to Diocletian* (SJLA 20), Leiden 1976.

Stone, M. E. 1968: "The Concept of the Messiah in IV. Ezra", in: J. Neusner (ed.): *Religions in Antiquity: Essays in Memory of Erwin Ramsdell Goodenough* (Sup. Numen 14), Leiden 1968.

– 1987: "The Question of the Messiah in 4 Ezra", in: J. Neusner, W. S. Green and E. S. Frerichs (ed.): *Judaisms and their Messiahs at the Turn of the Christian Era*, Cambridge 1987.

Talmon, S. 1987: "Waiting for the Messiah: the Spiritual Universe of the Qumran Covenanters", in: J. Neusner, W. S. Green and E. S. Frerichs (ed.): *Judaisms and their Messiahs at the Turn of the Christian Era*, Cambridge 1987.

Talmon, Y. 1962: "Pursuit of the Millenium: the Relation between Religions and Social Change", in: *Archives européennes de Sociologie* 3 (1962) 125–148.

Thomas, J. 1938: *Le mouvement baptiste en Palestine et Syrie*, Gembloux 1938.

Thompson, A. L. 1977: *Responsibility for Evil in the Theodicy of IV Ezra* (SBLDS 29) Montana 1977.

Thrupp, S. L. (ed.) 1962: *Millenial Dreams in Action: Studies in Revolutionary Religious Movements* (Comparative Studies in Society and History, Suppl. II), The Hague 1962.

Van Unnik, W. C. 1951: "1 Clement and the 'Sanctus'", in: *VC* 5 (1951) 204–248.

Vielhauer, P. 1979: *Oikodome. Aufsätze zum Neuen Testament 2*, Munich 1979.

Volz, P. 1934: *Die Eschatologie der jüdischen Gemeinde im neutestamentlichen Zeitalter*, Tübingen ²1934.

Vööbus, A. 1969: "Regarding the Background of the Liturgical Traditions in the Didache. The Question of Literary Relation between Didache IX,4 and the Fourth Gospel", in: *VC* 23 (1969) 81–87.

Weber, W. 1921: *Josephus und Vespasian. Untersuchungen zu dem jüdischen Krieg des Flavius Josephus*, Stuttgart–Leipzig 1921.

Wengst, K. 1984: *Didache (Apostellehre), Barnabasbrief, Zweiter Klemensbrief, Schrift an Diognet*, Darmstadt 1984.

Wensinck, A. J. 1916: *The Ideas of the Western Semites concerning the Navel of the Earth*, Amsterdam 1916.

Wilcken, R. L. 1986: "Early Christian Chiliasm, Jewish Messianism, and the Idea of the Holy Land", in: *HTR* 79 (1986) 298–307.

Willett, T. W. 1989: *Eschatology in the Theodicies of 2 Baruch and 4 Ezra* (JSPSS 4), Sheffield 1989.

Windisch, H. 1920: *Der Barnabasbrief* (HNT), Tübingen 1920.

Worsley, P. 1968: *The Trumpet Shall Sound: A Study of 'Cargo' Cults in Melanesia*, London ²1968.

Yadin, Y. 1963: *Finds from the Bar-Kochba Period in the Cave of Letters*, Jerusalem 1963.

Zunz, L. 1892: *Die gottesdienstlichen Vorträge der Juden*, Leipzig 1892.

Jewish-Christian Relations in Barnabas and Justin Martyr

by

WILLIAM HORBURY

The ways have parted already, for the writers considered here. The author of the Epistle of Barnabas saw Christian and Jews as 'us' and 'them' (αὐτοί, ii 7, xiv 1, 4; the more adverse ἐκεῖνοι, iii 6, viii 7, x 12, xiii 1, xiv 5). Justin Martyr wrote that Christians who adopted Judaism had 'gone over' (μεταβάντας) to the polity of the law (*dial*. xlvii 4). For both authors, however, the ways still run close together.

To proceed from these writings to the relations of Jews and Christians in the second century is not, of course, straightforward. A. von Harnack, for example, allowed that Justin's *Dialogue* reflected genuine Jewish-Christian contact, and that it therefore formed one of the exceptions to his view that most writing *adversus Iudaeos* was really for internal consumption or *adversus gentes*; but he thought that the Judaism described in the Epistle of Barnabas was indeed abstract, standing for the influence of the scriptures inherited by Christians rather than the way of life of flesh-and-blood Jews[1]. His judgment remains influential in the study of patristic anti-Jewish writing in general and of Barnabas in particular, for instance in the commentaries by H. Windisch (1920) and K. Wengst (1984); but reasons for a different opinion in this instance have often been noted, perhaps especially fully and creatively in S. Lowy's reconstruction of a Jewish situation to which the Epistle responds[2]. Some of the arguments are reconsidered below, and it is urged here that Barnabas as well as Justin probably reflects the importance of the contemporary Jewish community for

---

[1] A. Harnack, *Die Altercatio Simonis et Theophili nebst Untersuchungen über die anti-jüdische Polemik in der alten Kirche* (TU iii 1, Leipzig, 1883), 73−4, 78 n. 59; Harnack, *Chronologie der altchristlichen Litteratur bis Eusebius* (2 vols., Leipzig, 1897, 1904), i, 415−6.
[2] H. Windisch, *Der Barnabasbrief* (1920), in W. Bauer, M. Dibelius, R. Knopf, H. Windisch, *Die apostolischen Väter* (Handbuch zum Neuen Testament, Ergänzungsband, Tübingen, 1920−23), 299−413 (322−3); K. Wengst, *Didache (Apostellehre), Barnabasbrief, Zweiter Klemensbrief, Schrift an Diognet* (Darmstadt, 1984), 112 (Wengst's view of the aims of the Epistle, as advanced in his earlier *Tradition und Theologie des Barnabasbriefes* (Berlin & New York, 1971), is criticized by Scorza Barcellona (as cited in n. 4, below), 166−170; S. Lowy, The Confutation of Judaism in the Epistle of Barnabas', *JJs* xi (1960), 1−33.

the early Christians; but Harnack's view serves to underline the truth that the writings in question are literature, not slices of life.

Barnabas and Justin as Christian Authorities

First, then, it may be noted that Barnabas and Justin have an importance for Jewish-Christian relations in antiquity, and in the second century in particular, simply by virtue of their places in the Christian *literary* inheritance. The Epistle of Barnabas went up to a very high place, being venerated as the work of an apostle or an apostolic man, and accordingly transmitted, as in Codex Sinaiticus and the biblical text followed in Jerome's *Hebrew Names*, at the end of the New Testament books; its wide circulation and high repute are confirmed by the early Latin version, and by remarks in Origen and Jerome[3]. Its striking judgment that the ritual and dietary laws were never meant to be kept literally was taken in a refined form through Origen into the Alexandrian stream of Christian assessment of the Old Testament, and it must be reckoned a considerable influence on early Christian views of Judaism and the Jewish scriptures[4]. Its specifically second-century éclat is marked by Clement of Alexandria's acceptance of the attribution to Barnabas (n. 3, above), and by the making of the Latin version in the early third century, or even before Tertullian[5]; moreover, its transmission with the New Testament books in the fourth century, despite the currency of criticism like that expressed by Eusebius, is most easily understood if its repute for apostolicity had been widespread since early times.

---

³ Eusebius, *H. E.* iii 24, 4 reckons it himself among the νόθοι, but when later writing on Clement of Alexandria (vi 13, 6; 14, 1) puts it higher, among the ἀντιλεγομέναι γραφαί – this is probably a tribute to the respectable company shared by Barnabas in Clement – in the course of recording how Clement of Alexandria cited some of these, including Barnabas, in his *Stromateis* (Wisdom, Ecclesiasticus, Hebrews, Barnabas, I Clement, Jude) and in his *Hypotyposes* (Jude, the other catholic epistles, Barnabas and the Revelation of Peter); apostolic authorship is affirmed by Clement of Alexandria, *strom.* ii 20 (116–7) and elsewhere; Origen, *contra Celsum* i 63, quotes 'the general epistle of Barnabas' without comment, as if it were undisputed, going directly on to cite Luke and I Timothy, and envisaging that Celsus might himself have known the Epistle of Barnabas; according to Jerome, *vir. ill.* vi, the epistle is read among the apocrypha, but the apostle Barnabas was the author – and when commenting on Ezek xliii 19 Jerome finds it natural to say that the bullock offered for us is mentioned in 'many places of the scriptures, and especially the Epistle of Barnabas, which is included among the apocryphal scriptures'.

⁴ The success of the Epistle in the early church was emphasized by J. Armitage Robinson (with Preface by R. H. Connolly), 'The Epistle of Barnabas and the Didache', *JTS* xxxv (1934), 113–46 (122–3).

⁵ J. M. Heer, *Die Versio Latina des Barnabasbriefes* (Freiburg i.B., 1908), 59 (before Cyprian, probably after Tertullian) (references to the Latin text below are to this edition); Wengst, *Didache …*, 105, n. 4 notes that Heer later (*RQ* xxiii (1909), 224) allowed with caution that the version might possibly be earlier than Tertullian; F. Scorza Barcellona, *Epistola di Barnaba* (Turin, 1975), ascribes the version to the second or third century.

Justin's lower place among the Christian authors was still the honourable position of a philosopher-martyr, and his works, including writings now lost, were current among 'many of the brethren' in the time of Eusebius (*H. E.* iv 18, 8–9). Tatian and Irenaeus had quoted Justin, and for the present purpose it is also notable that his biblical interpretation often overlaps with that of Irenaeus and Tertullian; there is a fair case for literary debt on the side of Tertullian, but in any case Justin is clearly representative of widespread second-century exegesis[6]. The writings here considered, therefore, all had a high repute among Christians in the second century; Barnabas was then widely accorded the lofty rank of an apostolic epistle, and Justin's work was both well-known and representative. These writings will have been correspondingly influential in forming second-century Christian attitudes to the Jews and Judaism.

Questions to be Considered

Secondly, however, it can be asked what pre-existing attitudes these writings reflect, and how far they illuminate Jewish-Christian relations in the earlier second century. These are the main questions considered below. Barnabas and Justin can reasonably be reviewed together, for although the Epistle of Barnabas is probably about fifty years earlier than Justin's writings (see below) they share so much in subject-matter and biblical testimonies that it is asked whether Justin used the Epistle[7]. (With different aims, but with a comparable linkage, Barnabas and Justin's Dialogue were translated and issued together in Switzerland towards the end of the Second World War as the two earliest post-biblical Christian statements on Christian as opposed to Jewish understanding of the scriptures[8].)

Justin is generally considered, as by Harnack, to reflect genuine contact with Jews, and so to promise some light not only on the Christian but also, with due allowance for his limited candle-power as an outsider, on the Jewish side of the

---

[6] A. Lukyn Williams, *Justin Martyr: The Dialogue with Trypho. Translation, Introduction and Notes* (London, 1930), p. xiv (overlaps with Tertullian and Irenaeus not amounting to clear evidence for literary dependence); T. D. Barnes, *Tertullian* (Oxford, 1971), 106–8 (Tertullian did not use Justin's *Dialogue* for his *Adversus Iudaeos*, but did use the *First Apology* in his own *Apology*).

[7] O. Skarsaune, *The Proof from Prophecy* (Supplements to *NT* lvi, Leiden, 1987), 110–113 (on shared Old Testament quotations), 307–11 (on similar treatments of the Day of Atonement) and 393–9, with n. 61 (on similar treatments of Amalek and the brazen serpent), concluding that Justin has never copied an Old Testament quotation from Barnabas, inclines to the view that for testimonies and other material too they had shared sources rather than direct contact.

[8] K. Thieme, *Kirche und Synagoge. Die ersten nachbiblischen Zeugnisse ihres Gegensatzes im Offenbarungsverständnis: Der Barnabasbrief und der Dialog Justins des Märtyrers, neu bearbeitet und erläutert* (Olten, 1945).

relationship. On the Epistle of Barnabas opinions diverge, as already noted. It is not a defence of Christianity 'against the Jews', although such defence forms a large part of its content, but a scriptural instruction which is also an earnest exhortation to a moral life, appropriately concluded by a version of the Two Ways. Despite the clear internal direction of its teaching and exhortation, the series of lively and embittered references to 'us' and 'them' cited from it above form one of the main grounds for thinking it a source for Christian attitudes not just to the scriptures and morality, but also and especially to the flesh-and-blood Jewish community.

With regard to Christian attitudes, it will be urged here that all these writings evince an outlook which, despite anti-Judaism, is formed by Jewish culture and influenced by Jewish public opinion. The Jews are in the majority as compared with the Christians: unlike the Christians, they are recognized as as an ancient nation loyal to their ancestral laws and customs: and despite their revolts (themselves no small proof of Jewish strength and numbers) they enjoy a public prestige symbolized by the general knowledge of their assemblies for the reading of the law ('palam lectitant . . . vulgo aditur sabbatis omnibus', Tertullian, *Apology* xviii 8).

In the Epistle of Barnabas, after the suppression of the first Jewish revolt against Rome, and probably before those which broke out under Trajan, the writer thinks that Christians are in danger of going over to the Jewish community, and for Justin too this is a live possibility. Christians accordingly share in prevailing moods of Jewish communal feeling, notably in excitement at the prospect of a rebuilt temple and in the related patriotic hopes for the redemption of Israel current during this epoch of Jewish upheavals (66−70, 115−8, 132−5). It seems likely that differences in attitude among Christians on these subjects correspond to contemporary differences in the Jewish community.

The less-documented Jewish side of the relationship with the Christians has left some traces in Barnabas, but is much more fully documented in Justin. His writings, like the Epistle of Barnabas, evince a marked share in Jewish public opinion. A brief reassessment of his knowledge of the Jewish community leads to consideration of his report of Jewish reaction to Christianity. The Jewish measures against Christian dissent which he describes (measures thought by Justin to be of long standing) resemble those suggested by some New Testament passages. They will have derived their effectiveness, it is suggested, from a communal solidarity which was no doubt enhanced by the strong patriotic feeling already noted, but in any case involves intercommunal communication and cohesion.

Dating

The works of Justin considered here, the Apologies and the Dialogue with Trypho, were written between 151 and Justin's death, which occurred when Junius Rusticus was prefect of Rome (162−8)[9]. The Dialogue was probably composed after the First Apology, and has many links with it, escpecially in proof-texts. Both these works refer to the 'war in Judaea', Bar Cocheba's revolt of 132−5; in the First Apology (xxxi) it is spoken of as recent, and the Dialogue is envisaged as taking place not long after it had broken out (i 3, cf. ix 3; xvi 2 seems to presuppose the suppression of the revolt). These evocations of the wartime and post-war situation underline the significance of the works, despite their later date, for the period (ending in 135) primarily considered in this volume. Jewish questions are important in the First Apology, but become the main subject of the Dialogue, which according to Eusebius (*H. E.* iv 18, 6) was set in Ephesus. The interchanges of the speakers are marked by a striking and lifelike contrast between the personal courtesy for the most part maintained by Justin (and especially by Trypho), and the bitterly harsh remarks of Justin (and occasionally of Trypho too) when they are speaking as representative of their communities. The Dialogue is an artistically contrived literary work, and one which has not survived in its entirety; but behind it there are genuine Jewish-Christian communal contacts, and the author had his own experience of them[10].

The date of the Epistle of Barnabas cannot be treated so rapidly. The *genius loci* honoured at the Durham symposium, J. B. Lightfoot, statet that 'it was certainly written after the first destruction of Jerusalem under Titus to which it alludes, and it was almost as certainly written before the war under Hadrian ending in the second devastation, about which it is silent, but to which it could hardly have failed to refer, if written after or during the conflict[11]. Attempts at greater precision in dating turn mainly on two pairs of passages. First, there are possible but not certain allusions at xi 9, to the Syriac Apocalypse of Baruch lxi 7 (this passage from Barnabas is taken over without reference to a source by Clement of Alexandria, *strom.* iii 12 (86)); and at xii 1, to II Esdras iv 33 and v 5, but with a clause not in our II Esdras v 5. Literary contact between Barnabas

---

[9] Harnack, *Chronologie*, i, 274−84; H. Chadwick, 'Justin Martyr's Defence of Christianity', *BJRL* xlvii (1965), 275−97 (277−8); G. Visonà, *S. Giustino, Dialogo con Trifone* (Milan, 1988), 18−19 (with discussion of recent literature).

[10] For dicussion see Williams, *Dialogue*, xi−xix (on the text and its sources); Chadwick, 'Defence', 281−2 (testimony-collections probably used in both Barnabas and Justin); G. N. Stanton, 'Aspects of Early Christian-Jewish Polemic and Apologetic', *NTS* xxxi (1985), 377−92 (378), P. R. Trebilco, *Jewish Communities in Asia Minor* (Cambridge, 1991), 29−30, and especially Visonà, 46−57 (the Dialogue includes genuine reflection of Jewish-Christian contacts in general and in Justin's own experience).

[11] J. B. Lightfoot, *The Apostolic Fathers, Part I. S. Clement of Rome* (end edn, 2 vols., London, 1890), ii, 505.

and these two apocalypses is indeed far from certain; at xi 9 there is a fair argument for allusion, rather, to Ezek xx 6, 15, for a later chapter in Ezekiel is clearly in view in verse 10, and at xii 1 an apocryphal Jeremiah may be the source[12]. Even if the two allusions were certain, however, the dates of the Syriac Apocalypse of Baruch and II Esdras iii−xiv could only be said to be soon enough after A.D. 70 for the destruction of Jerusalem to be acutely resented, with a strong argument for placing the eagle vision of II Esdras xi−xii in the reign of Domitian (81−96)[13]. More important than the limited significance of these passages for dating is their manifestation of some kinship in the choice of material between Barnabas and Jewish apocalypses from the years after 70.

Secondly, another pair of passages in Barnabas probably refer to contemporary events. At iv 3−5 the epistle gives a prophecy, veiled in the language of Dan vii 7f., 24, and recalling the oracle based on this passage in Sib iii 396−400, that three horns out of ten horns will be humbled under one 'little horn'. The 'little horn' in Daniel is illomened, and strong candidates for identification with it are therefore Vespasian, destroyer of Jerusalem and humbler of the three emperors who preceded him in quick succession, or Nero redivivus, awaited as humbler of the triad of Flavian emperors; but the passage cannot be confidently assigned to a particular reign. The second of the two passages offers more hope in this respect. In xvi 3−4 the writer holds that the prophecy 'they who destroyed this temple shall themselves rebuild it' (an adaptation of Isa xlix 17 LXX) is now being fulfilled; 'because they [the Jews] went to war, it was destroyed by the enemy; now they themselves, the servant of the enemy, will build it up again'. The reference (further discussed in section II, below) is probably to the temple of the Jews at Jerusalem. If so, the passage can be associated with the reign of Nerva (18.ix.96−27.i.98), who favoured the Jews by removing the 'calumny of the Jewish exchequer', and was well remembered by Christians too (Eusebius, H. E. iii 20, 8−9); a belief that the temple would be rebuilt can readily be envisaged in his reign[14]. The early years of Hadrian are often suggested (especially on the basis of the praises of Hadrian at the beginning of the fifth Sibylline), and they are certainly likely to have revived Jewish hopes; but Nerva's reign seems preferable, not only because his CALVMNIA

---

[12] The evidence is set out and discussed by Heer 67−8, Scorza Barcellona, 151−2, and Wengst, Didache ..., 171 n. 185, 200 n. 189; the suggestion of Ezek xx 6 at xi 9 goes back at least to the early eighteenth-century W. Lowth, cited by J. Potter, ed., Clementis Alexandrini Opera (2 vols., Oxford, 1715), ii, 550, n. 2. That no literary dependence on the two apocalypses can be established was the conclusion of J. A. T. Robinson, Redating the New Testament (London, 1976), 318, n. 34.

[13] On the date of II Esdras, E. Schürer, G. Vermes, F. Millar, M. Black, M. D. Goodman & P. Vermes, A History of the Jewish People in the Age of Jesus Christ, iii. 1 (Edinburgh, 1986), 297−300.

[14] For the importance of Nerva's action to the Jews, see M. D. Goodman, 'Nerva, the fiscus Judaicus and Jewish Identity', JRS lxxix (1989), 40−44.

SVBLATA coinage was a particularly clear public sign of favour to the Jews, but also because the growth of the great reputation of the epistle as apostolic is easier to understand if its date is earlier than the time of Hadrian[15]. If this is right, the interpretation of Daniel in iv 3−5 will have been re−applied from Vespasian to Nerva, who does not suit the bad character of the little horn, but is as well qualified as Vespasian (for neither could claim to rule by right of descent) to be called an offshoot 'on the side'[16]. The epistle could then be assigned, with fair probability, to the very end of the first century.

Barnabas

(i) The Epistle and the Sources

The Christian outlook on Judaism represented in Barnabas and Justin can now be considered further. An attempt to reconstruct something of this outlook from Barnabas will be made through attention, first, to the fear of assimilation manifest, it will be argued, especially in a controverted passage, iii 6; then to the radical theory of the Jewish scriptures developed throughout chapters ii−xvi; and finally to the dependence of the writer on Jewish culture and opinion.

The wide differences in estimate of Barnabas have been noted already. Rabbinic students have repeatedly suggested a Jewish background for its exegesis, and have also noted rabbinic responses to the polemical positions it represents; notable predecessors of S. Lowy (n. 2, above) include M. Güdemann, K. Kohler, A. Marmorstein and G. Al(l)on, and at least one New Testament student with strong rabbinic interests, Adolf Schlatter[17]. This posi-

---

[15] Theories of dating are reviewed, with preference (following Lightfoot) for Vespasian's reign, by J. A. T. Robinson, *Redating*, 313−9, and with preference (following A. Hilgenfeld) for Nerva's reign, by P. Richardson & M. B. Shukster, 'Barnabas, Nerva, and the Yavnean Rabbis', *JTS* NS xxxiv (1983), 31−55; the argument for the early years of Hadrian (following W. Volkmar and J. G. Müller, with L. W. Barnard and others noted by Wengst, *Tradition*, 107−8, nn. 25−6) is put by G. Al(l)on, *The Jews in their Land in the Talmudic Age* (edited and translated by G. Levi, repr. Cambridge, Mass., 1989), 448−52. M. Hengel, 'Hadrians Politik gegenüber Juden und Christen', in *Ancient Studies in Memory of Elias Bickerman* [= *JANES* xvi−xvii (1984−5)] (1987), 153−82 (160 & n. 36), gives no special discussion of the date of Barnabas and regards xvi 4 as obscure ('dunkel'), but accepts it as one of the indications that Jews between 117 and 130 possibly hoped for the rebuilding of Jerusalem and the temple.

[16] The argument is more fully presented by the present writer (arguing that Ber.R. lxiv 10, an anecdote also implying belief that the temple would be rebuilt by Roman permission, more probably reflects conditions under Nerva than under Hadrian) in 'The Jewish Revolts under Trajan and Hadrian', forthcoming in *The Cambridge History of Judaism*, iv.

[17] M. Güdemann, *Religionsgeschichtliche Studien* (Leipzig, 1876), 99−131, known to me only as reported by K. Kohler, 'Barnabas', *JE* i (1902), 537−8 and J. Muilenburg, *The Literary Relations of the Epistle of Barnabas and the Teaching of the Twelve Apostles* (Marburg, 1929), 98−100; A. Marmorstein, 'L'Épître de Barnabé et la polémique juive, *REJ* lx (1910), 213−20 [rabbinic polemic attacks positions which are represented in Barnabas]; G. Allon, 'The

tion is reflected in H. Veil's introduction (in E. Hennecke's handbook to the
New Testament apocrypha), G. Hoennicke's book on Jewish Christianity, B.
Reicke's study of early Christian 'zeal'[18], and, in fuller treatments of the
Epistle, in the work of J. Muilenburg (n. 15, above) and F. Scorza Barcellona
(n. 4, above). On the other hand, Harnack's position was developed in Germany not only in the commentaries by Windisch and Wengst (n. 2, above), but
also in the church history of Hans Lietzmann (who saw the writer of the Epistle
as a 'learned manikin', unable to resist composing a pamphlet); it has also
influenced the French commentary by R. A. Kraft and P. Prigent[19]. In England, however, the importance of the Jewish community for the author found
greater recognitition; W. J. Ferrar summed up the setting of the Epistle in the
words 'Its bitterness and contempt for the Jewish polity must have been stirred
by real danger of a relapse to Judaism among Christians', and Armitage
Robinson, although he found no bitterness or animosity in the severe things
said about the Jews as a people, agreed that the writer's situation was one in
which Judaism might be perceived as 'after all a nobler and more sustaining
creed than the Christianity which, since it had broken away from its original
stock, was already shewing signs of decay' in moral decadence[20].

The literary basis for this disagreement over the setting of Barnabas lies
especially in the possibility of distinguishing between the framework of the
Epistle, with its emphasis on the right understanding of the scriptures by the
writer's spiritual 'sons and daughters' and on godly living (for example at i
1,5−8; iv 9−14; xviii−xxi), and the more polemical contents of chapters ii−xvi,
the anti-Judaism of which may then be assigned to the past setting of the sources
employed (especially the testimonies) rather than to the present situation of the
author (the argument is concisely stated by Windisch, 322−3 and Wengst,
112−3).

The author as well as his source seems to be involved in anti-Judaism,
however, for example at iii 6 (considered in the following paragraph), iv 6, xv

---

Halakhah in the Epistle of Barnabas' [in Hebrew], *Tarbiz* xi (1939), 23−8; A. Schlatter, *Die Tage Trajans und Hadrians* (1897), reprinted in id., *Synagoge und Kirche bis zum Barkochba-Aufstand* (Stuttgart, 1966), 9−97 (63f.).

[18] H. Veil, 'Barnabasbrief', in E. Hennecke (ed.), *Neutestamentliche Apokryphen* (2nd edn., Tübingen, 1924), 503−18 (503−4, with a brief criticism of Windisch); G. Hoennicke, *Das Judenchristentum im ersten und zweiten Jahrhundert* (Berlin, 1908), 95−7, 284−6 (inclining to the view that the author of Barnabas was Jewish); B. Reicke, *Diakonie, Festfreude und Zelos in Verbindung mit der christlichen Agapenfeier* (Uppsala Universitets Årsskrift 1951:5, Uppsala, 1951), 378−82.

[19] H. Lietzmann, *The Beginnings of the Christian Church* (E. T., 2nd edn, London, 1949), repr. 1961), 217; P. Prigent & R. A. Kraft, *L'Épître de Barnabé* (Paris, 1971), 29 & n. 1.

[20] W. J. Ferrar, *The Early Christian Books* (London, 1919), 38−9; Armitage Robinson, 'Barnabas', 121, 125−6, 145−6 (his stress on the writer's moral concern coheres with his view that the author of Barnabas originally composed the treatise on the Two Ways; the present writer would view the treatise as a pre-Christian Jewish work taken over in the Epistle).

8–9, xvi 1, and, although he certainly presents his teaching as 'knowledge' in general, it often involves rebuttal of the Jews in particular, and his own attitude cannot readily be distinguished from that which emerges from the whole series of passages on 'us' and 'them' noted already. It is perhaps unlikely, in any case, that so much lively polemic should have been gathered together in circumstances to which it did not speak. Accordingly, the repeated assertion in Barnabas of the Christian claim to the Jewish scriptures should not be too confidently assessed as an academic exercise, for this assertion was fundamental *adversus Iudaeos*, as Justin shows (Dialogue xxix 2). In general, it is worth noting that the view represented by Harnack, Windisch and Wengst originated when an early and decisive separation of the Christians from the social influence of the large Jewish population in the eastern Roman provinces was more widely accepted than would now be the case[21]. Lastly, as Armitage Robinson stressed, the author's concern with moral exhortation coheres with his anxiety about Judaism, for it presupposes a precarious state of Christian morals which might well have made the Jewish community appear more honourable in life-style as well as prestige.

(ii) Fear of Christian Assimilation to the Jews

A striking characteristic of the outlook on Judaism in the Epistle, then, can provisionally be identified as a combination of evident fear of Christian assimilation to the Jews with the radical view of the ritual laws noted already. Fear of assimilation, the first point to be considered, emerges when the initial argument of the Epistle that sacrifices were never needed and are done away (chapter ii) culminates in a section on fasting (chapter iii). Here the declaration of the fast which the Lord has chosen (consisting of charitable works) in Isa lvii 6–10 is taken as a manifestation of God's will beforehand 'to us' (the Christians), ἵνα μὴ προσρησσώμεθα ὡς ἐπήλυτοι τῷ ἐκείνων νόμῳ, 'lest we be shipwrecked as (if) proselytes to their law' or 'lest we be dashed against their law as (if) proselytes' (iii 6). (Compare the Latin 'ut non incurramus tamquam proselyti ad illorum legem', 'that we may not rush in as (if) proselytes to their law' or 'that we may not run up against their law (if) proselytes'.) The clause is sometimes understood, as by Windisch and Wengst in their comments ad loc., as a warning against Judaistic Christianity rather than lapse into Judaism. It is certainly likely that Judaizers within the Christian fold are among envisaged here, for in the next chapter (iv 6) there is a condemnation of those who say that 'the

---

[21] Thus, in a repristination of Harnack's general view of the *adversus Iudaeos* texts, live Jewish-Christian polemic is allowed for up to the middle of the second century by D. Rokeah, *Jews, Pagans and Christians* (Jerusalem & Leiden, 1982), 9–10, 61–5; there is of course a strong case for important contacts throughout the patristic period, as J. Juster, Marcel Simon, B. Blumenkranz and others have shown.

covenant is theirs and ours' (not 'ours' only, as the author would maintain). In this instance, however, as is shown by the context of 'us' and 'them' (iii 1, 3, 6; iv 6−8), any Judaistic Christianity known to the writer would clearly be not simply a response to the literal sense of the ritual and dietary laws, but a response made in awareness of 'them', the Jewish community, and in the knowledge that this is the way in which the Jews observe 'their law'.

This observation is underlined by the consideration that fasting, the matter in view, was much more prominent in ancient Jewish custom than it is in the Pentateuchal laws. Fasting is not a main subject of the Pentateuch, apart from the fast of the Day of Atonement, Lev xvi 29, xxiii 26−32 and elsewhere, and the recognition that women's private vows may involve fasting, Num xxx 13. Although the Day of Atonement is not mentioned in Barn iii (a point emphasized by Lowy [n. 25, below]), it is indeed likely that fasting owes its original connection with the sacrifices here in Barnabas to that Day, with which an underlying testimony-chain will have linked the sacrifices, newmoons and sabbath condemned in Isa i 11−13 (Barn ii 4−6); this is suggested not only by the inclusion of the Day of Atonement in Isa i 13 LXX (the quotation in Barn ii 5 stops just before the relevant words)[22], but also by the use made of Isa lviii in comparable sections of Justin's Dialogue (xl 4, and in the scheme underlying xii 3−xv) and of Irenaeus (*Haer* iv 17, 3)[23]. Nevertheless the choice of this text from Isa lviii on fasting as the final link in the underlying chain implies a view of the Day of Atonement as 'the Fast' par excellence (the name of the Day as found for example in Philo, *SpecLeg* ii 193, 200; Acts xxvii 9) which itself reflects the great importance of fasting in general in current Jewish practice[24]. Moreover, this chapter of Barnabas as it now stands is on fasting in general rather than on the unmentioned Day of Atonement in particular, although the Day will become the main subject, with emphasis again on the fast, in chapter vii; and the space given to fasting in chapter iii is accordingly best understood, as Lowy showed, against the background of other regular (probably weekly) communal fasting by Jews, such that the fasts, of which the unmentioned Day of

---

[22] I. L. Seeligmann, *The Septuagint Version of Isaiah* (Leiden, 1948), 102−3, on ἡμέραν μεγάλην and νηστείαν.

[23] Skarsaune, 168−9, 179.

[24] Compare, for instance, Philo's statement that sacrifices are offered 'some daily, some on the seventh day, some on new moons and holy days, some at fast-days (νηστείαις), some at the three seasonal festivals' (*SpecLeg* i 168); Philo apparently is thinking principally of 'the Fast', the Day of Atonement (ibid 186), but his language recalls the association of sacrifices, festivals and fasting in Barnabas ii−iii, and suggests the general importance of fasts, on which see also the following footnote. Similarly, the spiritual interpretation of fasting and its association with the Day-of-Atonement laws as a Pentateuchal focus is illustrated by Philo, *Post. Caini* 48, taking the commandment 'to humble the souls on the tenth of the month' (Lev xxiii 27) in an inward and moral sense.

Atonement would simply form the supreme example, could seem to belong to the staple of 'their law'[25].

Lastly, the importance of Jewish custom in the setting of Barn iii is further suggested by Jewish use of the prophetic passage which forms the Christian proof-text. The prophecy in Isa lviii, quoted at length in Barnabas iii and Justin, Dialogue xv, and forming the standard proof-text here and elsewhere in Barnabas and Justin for the Christian interpretation of fasting, was used, according to the Tosefta, in a form of the admonition to be addressed by the elders to a community beginning a fast (TosTaanith i 8); it was also read, as is still the case, on the Day of Atonement (baraitha in Meg 31a, designating the passage beginning Isa lvii 15). These passages probably represent usage well established in the early third century, and likely to go back at least to the second. The liberal second-century Christian recourse to Isa lviii on fasting therefore corresponded to contemporary and later Jewish association of this passage with communal fasts, an association which, when the second-century and earlier Christian material is viewed in conjunction with the rabbinic texts, seems not unlikely to be pre-Christian[26].

Rebuttal of Christian Judaizing in respect of fasts, which was probably one object of the warning in Barnabas here, would therefore necessarily have been at the same time an attempt to neutralize the overshadowing presence of the Jewish community. To summarize, Christian awareness of the Jews is already plain in the contextual references to 'us' and 'them' (iii 1, 3, 6); further, the remarkable prominence of fasting in Barnabas iii corresponds not to its relatively modest place in the Pentateuchal laws, but to its high importance in contemporary Jewish custom; lastly, the prophetic text used in Barnabas to justify Christian deviation from this custom was one associated in Jewish usage with communal fasts. These points together confirm that the Jews themselves, not simply Christian Judaizers, concern the author. It is therefore reasonable to take iii 6 in the sense which its vigorous language most naturally suggests:

---

[25] Among the material considered by Lowy, 2–10 note Josephus, *Ap* ii 282 (Jewish pious observances widely adopted in Greek and barbarian cities are specified as the sabbath rest, fasts, lighting of lamps and many of the dietary customs); the inclusion of material under the healing 'fasting' (Taanith, Taaniyoth) in the Mishnah and Tosefta, and the assumption therein that Monday and Thursday are appropriate days for a fast (M. Taanith i 6, TosTaanith ii 4); and Didache viii 1 (fast on Wednesdays and Fridays, for 'the hypocrites' fast on Mondays and Thursdays). Lowy well suggests, following and adapting G. Al(l)on, that the Jewish custom of Monday and Thursday fasting reflected in the Didache is attested in a baraitha in Shabb. 24a, and is also in view in Barnabas; he adds that it is likely to have had special significance as the accompaniment of urgent prayer for messianic redemption. Compare Luke xviii 12 (the devout Pharisee thought to fast twice weekly), Matt vi 16–18 (Christian fasting).

[26] The association of Isa lviii with the Day of Atonement explains the incorporation of Isa lviii 6 into the quotation of Isa lxi 1–2 (linked with Atonement as the beginning of Jubilee) at Luke iv 18, according to C. Perrot, 'Luc 4, 16–30 et la lecture biblique de l'ancienne synagogue', in J.-E. Ménard (ed.), *Exégèse biblique et judaisme* (Strasbourg, 1973), 170–86 (178–9).

namely that, although the writer would certainly condemn Judaizing practices, one of his main purposes was to ward off the danger of Christian lapse to the Jewish community; the Greek, followed in this by the Latin, neatly combines the thoughts of violent and disastrous motion to, and of becoming a proselyte to, 'their law'.

Finally, there is a good case for supposing that the assimilation feared in iii 6 was encouraged not just by the attraction of the old paths and the more honcured society, but also by active propaganda. Reicke, noting that the ethical interpretation of the unclean beasts, fishes and birds in chapter x of the Epistle recalls vices often attributed to political intriguers, finds that internal agitation and propaganda by Christian Zealots is being countered in chapters vi, xv and xvi[27]. His view is supported by the clear indication of internal strife at iv 6. It is by no means inconsistent with Lowy's suggestion of propaganda by Jews themselves; for Lowy, the lawlessness leading to the final stumbling-block (iv 1−3) is constituted by Jewish movements towards national messianic redemption, accompanied by propaganda which is the πλάνη to be resisted at all costs (ii 10, iv 1, cf. iv 10−13), and was very possibly voiced by Jewish prophets in oracles like those preserved in the apocalypses and the Jewish Sibyllines[28]. This view is supported by the association of πλάνη and its cognates elsewhere, from the LXX Pentateuch onwards, with false prophecy and mutual Jewish and Christian charges of false teaching, notably in the strong sense of seduction to apostasy[29]. Lowy's interpretation would cohere closely, also, with G. W. H. Lampe's later suggestion that Jewish anti-Christian propaganda, including prophecy, is to be discerned behind I Clement, Ignatius, the Johannine Epistles, and many of the later New Testament writings (Lampe does not discuss Barnabas)[30]. The content of the propaganda denounced in Barnabas could be envisaged partly as argument for the law, the land and the temple-service (central points in the author's own apologetic), and partly, perhaps, as criticism of the teaching of Christ and the disciples, such as is attested in Justin and Celsus (the references in Barnabas to Christ's expected advent (vii 9, xii 9, xv 5−7) and his love for Israel (v 8) on the one hand, and to the lawless character of his disciples (v 9) on the other, might then represent, respectively, response and concession to such polemic). However the content is to be envisaged, propaganda from Jews and from Christians close to their position is likely to have strengthened the tendency towards assimilation to the Jews evident at iii 6.

---

[27] Reicke, 378−82.

[28] Lowy, 9−10, 13−17, 26, 31.

[29] W. Horbury, 'I Thessalonians ii.3 as Rebutting the Charge of False Prophecy', *JTS* NS xxxiii (1982), 492−508 (497−9, on seduction to apostasy); Stanton, 'Aspects' [n. 10, above], 379−82 (on Jewish anti-Christian polemic).

[30] G. W. H. Lampe, '"Grievous Wolves" (Acts 20:29)', in B. Lindars & S. S. Smalley (edd.), *Christ and Spirit in the New Testament: Studies in Honour of C. F. D. Moule* (Cambridge, 1973), 253−68.

The Epistle therefore reflects a Jewish encouragement of proselytes which is often ruefully attested from the early Christian standpoint. Justin in the Dialogue represents Trypho as exhorting him to join the Jews (viii 3–4); Justin himself exhorts Trypho 'and those who wish to be proselytes' (to the Jews, probably, rather than the Christians)[31] to come over (xxiii 3, xxviii 2), and complains that proselytes blaspheme the name of Christ twice as much as born Jews (cxxii 2); proselytes, says Tertullian gloomily, usually hope not in Christ's name, but in Moses's ordinance, and the 'large people' ('populus amplus') to be confuted by the new law in Christ going forth from Zion (Isa ii 3–4) is 'first of all that of the Jews and their proselytes' (*AdvMarc* iii 21, 3); comparably, Tertullian envisages in his *Adversus Iudaeos* that the Jewish case is being argued with a Christian by a proselyte.

Such early Christian evidence supplies part of a fuller picture of Jewish-Christian missionary rivalry, in competition for the same potential non-Jewish adherents, and not without hope for converts from the other side[32]. These attitudes emerge clearly from the passages just cited from Justin's Dialogue. In Barnabas, however, the stance is notably defensive. Hopes for fresh adhesion by Jews are not expressed. The overriding necessity is to justify the position of 'us' vis-à-vis 'their' law, and to ward off the peril of assimilation to and absorption in the Jewish community. The attack on the Jewish position represented by the Epistle's exclusive claim to the Jewish scriptures can be classified, in the context provided by the Epistle, as the best form of defence.

(iii) Theory of the Jewish Scriptures

The anxiety at the prestige and influence of the Jews among the Christians evident at iii 6 thus in turn helps to explain the second characteristic of the Epistle to be considered here, its radicalism on the Jewish scriptures. For this author, the seemingly literal sense of the ritual laws was never divinely intended, and within the law and the prophets this truth, now recognized by 'us', was continually indicated in vain to 'them'.

The covenant, indeed, according to this Epistle, belonged to the Jews only

---

[31] Arguments for this view of Dialogue xxiii 3 are set out by Skarsaune, 258–9; Jewish προσήλυσις to Christianity is envisaged at xxviiii 2, and the phrase 'Christ and his proselytes' occurs at cxxiii 5 in a deliberate contrast with the Jewish proselytes who are being discussed, but comparison of xxiii 3 with the opening of the Dialogue, and Justin's usage of 'proselyte' simply for Jewish proselytes (as in cxxii 1–cxxiii 2), suport the view that Jewish proselytes are intended at xxiii 3.

[32] See Simon, *Versus Israel*, 271–305, 390–5, with special reference to rivalry at 135, 284; B. Blumenkranz, 'Die christlich-jüdische Missionskonkurrenz (3. bis 6. Jahrhundert)', reprinted from *Klio* xxxix (1961), 227–233 in id., *Juifs et Chrétiens: Patristique et Moyen Age* (London, 1977); W. H. C. Frend, *Martyrdom and Persecution in the Early Church* (Oxford, 1965), 186–93.

for the brief time until they worshipped the golden calf and Moses broke the
tables (Exod xxxii 7, Deut ix 12 as interpreted in Barn iv 4—6, 14 and xiv 3—6);
the Christian inheritance of the covenant was prophesied in what the scripture
says concerning Isaac and Rebekah, Ephraim and Manasseh, and Abraham
himself (xiii). The ceremonies, biblical and post-biblical, of the Day of Atonement were simply intended to foretell the Lord's passion and kingdom (vii); the
same applies to the related rite of the Red Heifer (viii)[33]; an evil angel misled
the Jews to understand circumcision carnally, despite biblical injunctions on the
circumcision of the heart (ix 4—5; does this view depend on an unmentioned
interpretation of the giving of 'statutes that were not good' in Ezek xx 25, on the
lines of that given by Origen, *Contra Celsum* vii 20[34]?); the dietary laws were
never meant to be literally observed, as again the biblical text itself indicates
(Deut iv 1, 5 and perhaps 14 interpreted in Barn x 2 as 'I will make a covenant of
my ordinances with *this* people', cf. Barn i 2); on the other hand, the scriptures
(here mainly in the prophets and the Pentateuch) clearly foretell the Christian
rite of baptism in its accociation with the cross (Barn xi—xii); the sabbath
commandment in the Decalogue cannot be observed now, during 'the era of the
lawless one', because (as Gen ii 2 shows) it refers forward to the time of the
Lord's Advent, and Christians can accordingly meanwhile observe their own
'eighth day' (xv, cf. vi 19).

This series of radically spiritual and ecclesiastical interpretations suggests
that already in chapter ii the testimony-chain is probably understood in a
particularly negative way when, after a typical Christian application of Isa i
11—14, it is added that the Jews always erred in offering sacrifices rather than
the oblation of a godly life (Jer vii 22—3 taken, no doubt in the light of Amos v
25, as a *question* whether the forefathers who came out of Egypt were commanded to offer sacrifices, and interpreted in Barn ii 7—9 as a divine declaration 'to them'). The linked testimonies from Isa i and Jer vii would be later used
elsewhere to show that the sacrificial laws, literally intended, were a concession
to the Jews' weakness (Justin, *dial.* xxii 1—6; Irenaeus, *haer.* iv 17, 1—3)[35]; but
in Barnabas it seems likely that the true meaning of the sacrificial laws is
thought to have been, from the beginning, their moral significance (compare x
27). A contrast with Justin comparable with that which has been suggested

---

[33] For illustrations (including Mishnah, Parah iii 1) of the association between the Red
Heifer and the Day of Atonement assumed at Heb ix 13 see W. Horbury, 'The Aaronic
Priesthood in the Epistle to the Hebrews', *JSNT* xix (1983), 43—71 (51—2).

[34] Christian exegesis of this verse in Ezekiel as signifying a divine punishment of the Jews is
reviewed by F. Dreyfus, 'La condescendance divine *(synkatabasis)* comme principe her-
méneutique de l'Ancien Testament dans la tradition juive et dans la tradition chrétienne', in J.
A. Emerton (ed.), *Congress Volume, Salamanca 1983* (SVT xxxvi, Leiden 1985), 96—107
(98—9); this chapter of Ezekiel was probably used at Barn xi 9 (n. 12, above). On Barn ix 5 see
n. 44, below.

[35] Dreyfus, 97—9, 102—3.

regarding Barn ii 7−9 comes out more plainly at Barn ix 6. An objection to the interpretation of circumcision noted above is there envisaged as: 'the people received circumcision as a seal' (the mystical description of circumcision also attested at Rom iv 11, and applied to baptism in Christian tradition). The objector's view of circumcision is in fact a view accepted by Justin in the Dialogue (xvi 2, xix 2), with the harsh polemical twist that it was meant to permit the Jews to be singled out for their present sufferings (in the aftermath of the Bar Cocheba revolt). In Barnabas, however, the possibility that circumcision was a divine mark of distinction is wholly and contemptuously dismissed (ix 6) with the argument that, if so, even Syrians, Arabs and Egyptians, circumcised as they are, should all be regarded as heirs of the covenant. In this remark, perhaps a sign of the Egyptian setting of the Epistle[36], there is a hostility which recalls the scorn for Jewish 'bragging about circumcision' in the Epistle to Diognetus (iv 1, 4). Comparably, the author can adopt the adverse phrase '*their law*' in iii 6, considered above; here it will mean the law as understood and observed by Jews, but in the anger of the moment this qualification is left unspoken.

How then is the theory of the Jewish law in Barnabas to be classified? Its exceptional character has probably sometimes been over-emphasized. P. Prigent assessed it as much more moderate than the attitude taken in the Epistle to Diognetus[37], and it certainly allows to the ritual laws an abiding value – but only as encoded moral commandments and prophecies, the meaning of which was declared in vain to the Jews in the law and the prophets, but is now understood by the Christians. Herein Barnabas takes up a primitive Christian theme classically expressed in II Cor iii 12−16[38], and becomes the forerunner of the harmony of the Old and New Testaments as it was achieved by Origen and his successors in Alexandria and the west; for them the hidden spiritual sense of the law was that primarily envisaged by Moses, its true *raison d'être*, and in this truest sense the law was fulfilled by Christ[39]. The Epistle of Barnabas can

---

[36] Syrians, named first in ix 6, were disliked by the Greeks in Egypt (E. J. Bickermann, *The Jews in the Grek Age* (Cambridge, Mass. & London, 1988), 184; compare the mockery of Agrippa I by the Alexandrians as a Syrian king, Philo, *Flacc* 39); 'all the priests of the idols', mentioned without reference to nationality after Syrians and Arabs, can well be understood as Egyptian priests; and the crowning absurdity of pride in circumcision here is the fact that 'even Egyptians' – particularly despised by Greeks and Jews in Egypt – are circumcised.

[37] Prigent & Kraft, *Barnabé*, 158−9, nn. 4 & 5 (also contrasting the comparably scornful Tertullian, *AdvMarc* v 5).

[38] In its context in II Corinthians this passage subserves Paul's self-defence, as shown by E. Bammel, 'Paulus, der Moses des Neuen Bundes', *Theologia* liv (Athens, 1983), 399−408 (401−2), but its reference of testimony-linked commonplaces on Jewish hardening (and blinding, iv 4, which may still refer to Jews, cf. Rom xv 31) to Jewish (mis-)understanding of the law is paralleled at Acts vii 51−3, and is likely to be pre-Pauline; II Cor iii and Acts vii 1−53 are both Moses-centred passages (Bammel, 399; M. Simon, *St Stephen and the Hellenists in the Primitive Church* (London, 1958), 44−5).

[39] Among passages from Origen, Didymus the Blind, Cyril of Alexandria, the Ambrosias-

perhaps be detected in the background of the passages in Origen (cited in the previous footnote) in which it is recalled that the giving of the Mosaic law was followed by the sin of the calf, but Jesus gave the second law and covenant, or in which it is stressed that Moses himself intended the spiritual sense when he spoke of circumcision, Passover, new moons and sabbaths, and when he broke the tables of the *written* law. However that may be, the continuity between the Epistle and later Alexandrian and western exegesis in attitude to the law might seem to lend support to the view that its theory is relatively moderate, because of its great respect for the scriptures; although the strongly anti-Jewish aspect of this later exgesis would itself suggest that in the Epistle too this theory could subserve anti-Jewish polemic. At any rate, Barnabas can be seen to offer an early example of the allegorical and timeless harmonization of the testaments, as opposed to the more historical harmonization (adumbrated in Justin and developed by Irenaeus and others, following Gal iii−iv) which divides the legislation into moral and ceremonial laws, and allows that the latter were valid in their literal sense for a limited time[40].

Important though it is to notice how Barnabas's view suited the later Christian mainstream, these observations so far do less than justice to the anti-Jewish aspects of the theory, as the contrasts with Justin sketched above may already have suggested. First, the theories such as this, which have contributed towards resolution of the inner-Christian problem of the harmony of the testaments, all betray in their early history a considerable tension over the law as understood by the Jews; thus, in the 'historical' solutions just noticed, the ceremonial laws can be harshly designated, as in Irenaeus, as bonds of servitude imposed on the Jews as a punishment[41]. A similar tension is likely to have affected Barnabas, and it seems to appear especially in the historical element of the Epistle's theory, the contention that the breaking of the tables of the law cancelled the covenant with Israel (iv 7−8, xiv 1−4), but the Beloved gave the covenant to 'us' (iv 8, xiv 4). This second making of the tables of the commandments and the

---

ter and Marius Victorinus gathered by M. F. Wiles, *The Divine Apostle* (Cambridge, 1967), 64−6, note Origen, *Hom. in Num* v 1 (PG xiii 603 'Moyses intelligebat sine dubio quae esset vera circumcisio', etc.) and *Comm. in Rom* ii 14 (PG xiv 917 'Moyses et sprevit, et abiecit, et contrivit litteras legis, hoc sine dubio iam tunc designans, quod honor et virtus legis non esset in litteris, sed in spiritu'). On the sin of the Calf as response to the law-giving, and the second law and covenant given by Christ, see also Origen, *Contra Celsum* ii 74−5. Origen's treatment of the law is discussed with reference to predecessors, including Barnabas, by C. P. Bammel, 'Law and Temple in Origen', in *Templum Amicitiae: Essays on the Second Temple presented to Ernst Bammel* (Sheffield, 1991), 464−76 (469, n. 22 gives a more negative interpretation of 'their law' in Barn iii 6 than that ventured in the text above).

[40] An attempt to sketch these two approaches to the harmony of the testaments is made by the present writer, 'Old Testament Interpretation in the Writings of the Church Fathers', in M. J. Mulder & H. Sysling (edd.), *Mikra* (Assen & Philadelphia, 1988), 727−87 (746, 759−61).

[41] Irenaeus, for example at *haer* iv 16, 5; see Horbury, 'Interpretation', 760−1, Dreyfus, 'Condescendance', 99, and, for surveys of the development of theories of the ritual law in the context of anti-Jewish polemic, M. Simon, *Verus Israel* (E. T. Oxford, 1986), 85−91, 163−9.

associated covenant, including festival and sabbath laws (Exod xxxiv 1–28, cf. Deut x 1–5) is not expressly mentioned in Barnabas, as Simon emphasizes[42]; but it seems likely that, as Simon also argued[43], it is assumed to be the covenant given by the Beloved, which was at the same time the ritual law misunderstood by the Jews. This assumption could arise naturally from Exod xxxiv 27–8 (linking the renewed covenant with the Decalogue rewritten by God and with mainly ritual laws written by Moses).

On such an interpretation, Barnabas would be familiar with the concept of a 'second law', but would differ from the treatment of it in the Didascalia, and the closely allied views of the ritual law in Justin and Irenaeus; it was widely held, following biblical hints like that in Deut iv 14 noted above in connection with Barn x 2, that the second law-giving by Moses himself after the incident of the Golden Calf, a legislation marked especially by the ritual and dietary laws, was punitive, disciplinary or educative (so Irenaeus, *haer.* iv 15, 1 & 5, appealing to the interpretation of the Calf incident in Stephen's speech, Acts vii 38–43).

In Barnabas, then, it may be suggested, the familiar concept of this second law, which according to Exod xxxiv 10–28 was given together with the renewed covenant, is unmentioned but assumed; and it is identified with the legislation constantly misunderstood by the Jews, but really ab initio meant for the Christians and accompanying the covenant given to *them*. Consequently, although the Epistle seeks the inward meaning of the ritual law and refrains from scoffing at its superstition, this respect for scripture takes the form of a Christian claim to this law and its associated covenant, which is also an exclusion of any Jewish claims whatever to the covenant and the law.

Secondly, the Epistle is concerned not only with the scriptures inherited by the church, but also with the customs currently observed by the Jews, and in line with Jewish practice it treats the scriptures and the customs as a unity, as already noted in connection with the fasts, the Day of Atonement and the Red Heifer. (There is a striking contrast here with such New Testament passages as Mark vii 3–15, Matt xv 1–9.) This way of thinking is back-handedly exemplified, the present writer would suggest, in the angry reference at iii 6 to 'their law' – 'the law as they keep it'. It is accepted that, for those who think differently from the author, the standard interpretation of the law is summed up by the contemporary Jewish polity. The theory of the law sketched in the Epistle, therefore, is not just a theory of the Christian Old Testament, but a theory of the whole Jewish constitution and way of life, of what Justin would

---

[42] Simon, *Verus Israel*, 88 treats failure to mention the second law-giving as the main weakness of the Epistle's argument, but his stricture seems to be implicitly modified by his suggestion that the remaking of the tables is perhaps envisaged in references to the testament of the Beloved (see the following footnote).

[43] This view was briefly put forward by Simon, *Verus Israel*, n. 125 to p. 88, and p. 149 (Barnabas seems to find in Exod xxxiv 1–10 a symbolic prefiguration of Christianity; it is the testament of the Beloved), and stated more fully by Simon, *Stephen*, 106.

later call 'the polity of the law' (ἡ ἔννομος πολιτεία, *dial.* xlvii 4). Thus defined, however, the Epistle's theory seems more strongly anti-Jewish as well as Jewish; if accepted, it exposes the Jewish way of life as a demonic illusion (see Barn ix 5), and validates the Christian polity[44].

Thirdly, in accord with this conclusion, the theory is accompanied by hostile comments on 'them'; in accord with their regular failure to understand, *they* smote the shepherd of Zech xiii 7 (v. 12, adapting the second person plural imperative of LXX; contrast with Barnabas the first person singular divine subject given to the verb (now in the indicative) when the text is quoted in the New Testament, and Justin's second person *singular* imperative[45]). Similarly, they bound the righteous man of Wisd ii 12 (vi 8), their circumcision is no seal of election (ix 6), and their temple was heathenish (xvi 2). Correspondingly, the radical and influential theory of the scriptures in Barnabas can be seen to have anticipated the golden age of patristic exegesis in securing a significance, albeit a Christian one, for the whole Mosaic code as currently interpreted by Jews; but at the same time it excludes the Jews from the covenant and law they think to be theirs, and can be seen to have arisen form the Christian need for justification vis-á-vis the Jews, and to present a sharply anti-Jewish cutting edge.

(iv) Dependence on Jewish Culture and Opinion

The anxiety about assimilation to the Jews which is one aspect of this theory of the scriptures is consistent with the last characteristic of the Epistle to be reviewed, its marked dependence on Jewish culture and public opinion. Some signs of literary dependence on ultimately Jewish material have already appeared, notably in the use of the Two Ways (Barn xviii–xxi)[46] and of descriptions of the rites of the scapegoat[47] and the Red Heifer (vii–viii). A sharing in contemporary Jewish opinion is also evident, as the passages considered above for guidance on dating show. It was clear that Barnabas xi 9 and xii 1 have material in common with Jewish apocalypses of the end of the first century A.D., and a

---

[44] A paper on ix 5 by Mr J. N. B. Carleton Paget of Queens' College, Cambridge, with whom I have hat the benefit of discussing the Epistle, is forthcoming in *Vigiliae Christianae*.

[45] Skarsaune, 121; for the likely origin of the New Testament wording in emphasis on a divine plan when the text was quoted in isolation, see B. Lindars, *New Testament Apologetic* (London, 1961), 131.

[46] See S. P. Brock, 'The Two Ways and the Palestinian Targum', in P. R. Davies & R. T. White (edd.), *A Tribute to Geza Vermes* (JSOT Supplement Series, 100, Sheffield, 1990), 139–52 (distinguishing the form of the treatise used in Barnabas as presupposing not only a link between Jer xxi 8 and Deut xxx 15, 19 to give the concept of two ways, as found in the Didache, but also a description of the ways in dualistic terms of light and dark, as found in 1QS).

[47] Barn vii 6, Justin, *Dial* xl 4, and Tertullian, *AdvIudaeos* xiv 9–10 = *AdvMarc* iii 7, 7–8 state without express biblical warrant that the two goats must resemble one another; this practice is recommended in M. Yoma vi 1.

similar bond emerges from the passage on the Roman emperors in iv 3—5, interpreting Dan vii; here the Epistle, like the book of Revelation, expects the imminent fall of Rome, to be followed by the messianic reign of the saints, when the Beloved comes to his inheritance (iv 3); and it therefore shares the outlook of Jewish apocalypses such as II Esdras xi—xii, xiii and Sib v 403—33.

Future expectations which the writer shares with the Jews and assumes that his readers also share reappear elsewhere in the Epistle. Thus, the Son of God will tear up Amalek by the roots at the end (Exod xvii 14 as interpreted in Barn xii 9). This passage in Exodus received comment in the name of rabbis of the turn of the first an second centuries; Elizer ben Hyrcanus and Joshua ben Hananiah both ascribe the cutting-off of Amalek to the time when the kingdom of God is established (Mekhilta, Beshallah, Amalek, ii, on Exod xvii 14 & 16, respectively)[48]. Amalek can stand in rabbinic thought for Rome or for the power of evil, and a similar range of meaning seems possible in Barnabas, in the light of Justin's association of Amalek both with the demons and with the earthly authorities whom they influence[49]. Similarly, when Barnabas looks forward to the true sabbath-rest of the messianic millennium (xv 5—8), sabbath observance is indeed being rebutted, but the expectation of a thousand-year sabbath to come is shared with the Jews[50].

The extent of the dependence in Barnabas on Jewish culture and opinion goes far to explain the vigour of the Epistle's argument for divergence from the Jews on points thought vital for the continuance of the Christian community. One strand of this argument suggests strong Christian attraction to the patriotic Jewish outlook glimpsed in the shared expectations just discussed, in a development described by Reicke as an 'anti-Roman Zionism'[51]. In vi 8—19 the command to enter the 'good land, flowing with milk and honey' (Exod xxxiii 1, 3) leads to the thought of the Christians as a new creation, so that 'the

---

[48] J. Z. Lauterbach, *Mekilta de-Rabbi Ishmael*, ii (Philadelphia, 1933), 158—60; that the exegesis ascribed in the text (Lauterbach, ii, p. 158, line 155) to Eleazar (of Modin) should be in the name of Eliezer (ben Hyrcanus), for Eleazar's exegesis is given immediately before, is shown by W. Bacher, *Die Agada der Tannaiten*, i (2nd edn, Straßburg, 1903, repr. Berlin, 1965), 142, n. 1.

[49] L. Ginzberg, *The Legends of the Jews*, vi (1928, repr. Philadelphia, 1968), 24—5, nn. 141, 147; Justin, *dial* xlix 8, cxxxi 4—5 with Williams, 99, n. 3.

[50] For example, in the interpretations of the title of Ps xcii 'for the sabbath day', in S. Buber (ed.), *Midrash Tehillim* (Wilna, 1891, repr. Jerusalem, 1977), 402 foot (ii 22, the seventh age is all sabbath and rest), 405 (v, the day when Isa xxxii 15 is fulfilled, and wars cease), cited among other passages including Barn xv 4 by Ginzberg, *Legends*, v (1925, repr. Philadelphia, 1968), n. 140. A. Hermans, 'Le Pseudo-Barnabé est-il Millénariste?' (*Analecta Lovaniensia Biblica et Orientalia* iii 15), *ETL* xxxv (1959), 849—76 gives the answer No, but 7—8 can be read without difficulty as envisaging a millennial sabbath leading to a new world beginning, like the old, on the first (eighth) day.

[51] Reicke, *Diakonie*, 381—2; this aspect of early Christian thought is further studied by R. L. Wilken, 'Early Christian Chiliasm, Jewish Messianism, and the Idea of the Holy Land', *HTR* lxxxix (1986), 298—307.

habitation of our heart is a holy temple to the Lord' (vi 15); this passage probably counters Jewish emphasis on the duties of possessing the land and building the temple, such as is seen, close to the probable date of Barnabas, at the beginning of the summary of the law in Josephus's *Antiquities*[52]. In xvi 4−10, also discussed in section I, above, the writer takes pains to show that opinions of this kind on the Jerusalem temple should not be shared. The presupposition here is that Jews are rebuilding the temple, with Roman sanction, and therefore as 'servants of the enemy' (xvi 4). The Romans are 'the enemy', as in chapter iv. The author of Barnabas insists that the true temple is inward and spiritual, as at vi 15, probably attempting, in line with the interpretation of iii 6 advanced above, to check Christians who are attracted to the Jewish community when its hopes appear to be fulfilled by the prospective revival of the temple-service[53]. Jewish hopes centred on the land and the temple are rejected, therefore, but assumptions about Rome as 'the enemy' are still unquestioningly shared, as in iv 3.

(v) The Christian and Jewish Settings of Barnabas's Outlook

These impressions of fear of assimilation to the Jews, of an anti-Jewish theory of the Jewish polity, and of a dependence on Jewish culture and public opinion in Barnabas together suggest a reasonably coherent outline of the defensive outlook on the Jewish community manifest in the Epistle. Admittedly, it represents only one section of Christian opinion. The Christians form a divided minority over against the Jews; some Christians admit that the Jews are the people chosen to receive the covenant, and simply claim for the Christians a share in it (iv 6); some, perhaps an overlapping group, are strongly attracted to go over to the Jewish community (iii 6; Christians in this position are probably also envisaged in xvi). This division of the Christian community into Judaizers, non-Judaizers and potential Jewish proselytes is reflected again in Justin's Dialogue (xlvii 1−4); the author of the Epistle was not far from the opinion of those mentioned by Justin who thought that Judaizing Christians could not be saved, and those attracted to Judaism in Barnabas may be compared with those in Justin who have gone over to the polity of the law. Christian Judaizers reappear in Celsus and Origen (Origen, *Contra Celsum* v 61, cf. ii 1), and the

---

[52] Josephus, *ant* iv 199−201 (when you have conquered the land, found one city chosen by God, with one temple and one altar); similar emphasis is later exemplified in the developments of Exod xv 16−17 into different versions of a saying 'Let Israel come into the land and built the temple', in Mekhilta, Beshallah, Shirata, ix & x (Lauterbach, ii, 75−6, 78).

[53] The present writer has argued this more fully in 'Messianism among Jews and Christians in the Second Century', *Augustinianum* xxviii (1988), 71−88 (82−3); the widely-held view that the reference is to Hadrian's construction of a temple of Zeus, mentioned by Cassius Dio lxix 12, 1 (so Wengst, *Didache* . . ., 114−5), makes the text in Barnabas so harshly paradoxical that one would have expected a phrase of elucidation.

various positions emerging in Barnabas doubtless long continued to be represented among the Christians, although the proportion of Christians who took the Judaistic view was probably declining, like the (not identical) proportion of Christians who were of Jewish birth, during the second century[54].

At the time of the Epistle, however, these divisions are likely to have involved considerable proportions of the small Christian population. The Epistle can give some guidance to the outlook on the Jews even among Christians whose view the author rejects, for these Christian divisions are all determined by the attitude taken to the Jewish polity. They will have contributed accordingly to a sense that the Christians were weak and upstart by comparison with the large, ancient and determinative Jewish body. This sense, in conjunction with the cultural dependence of the Christians on the Jews and the experience of propaganda by Jews and Judaizers, explains the fear of assimilation to the larger body evident in Barnabas.

Correspondingly, the Epistle's theory of the Jewish law is a justification of the non-Judaizing practice which rapidly became the Christian norm, denying the Jews' claim to their ancestral covenant and law in a vigorous attack by the smaller body on the greater. Its thoroughgoing adoption of the law made it a particularly useful key to scripture in later Alexandrian exegesis, and a particularly powerful instance of the widespread ante-Nicene assertion that the Christians have replaced the Jews as the elect people of God[55]. As in some other polemic of this period, the name 'Israel' is conceded without hesitation to the Jews, as at v 8 (one more example of the Epistle's indebtedness to Jewish usage)[56]; but the Christian claim to the Jewish heritage is nonetheless total and exclusive, and (by contrast with a good deal of anti-Jewish writing, including Justin's work) there is no explicit reference to a return of Israel, whether in the near future by baptism or in the last days; it is particularly notable that this theme is not mentioned in chapter xi, on baptism, where the refusal of Israel to accept baptism is the point of departure. The setting of this lively contention is a

---

[54] The variety of Christian attitudes is emphasized by B. L. Visotzky, 'Prolegomenon to the Study of Jewish-Christianities in Rabbinic Literature', *AJS Review* xiv (1989), 47–70 (49–63), and (with special reference to the Nazoraeans) by W. Kinzig, '"Non-Separation": Closeness and Co-operation between Jews and Christians in the Fourth Century', *VC* xlv (1991), 27–53 (35).

[55] The argument is important in Justin's Dialogue (xii 4–5 and elsewhere); in Tertullian, Cyprian, the pseudo-Cyprianic *adversus Iudaeos* and *de montibus Sina et Sion* (see W. Horbury, 'The Purpose of Pseudo-Cyprian, *Adversus Iudaeos*', *Studia Patristica* xviii.3 (1989), 291–317 (302–3, 305); and in Aphrahat and Ephrem Syrus (R. Murray, *Symbols of Church and Kingdom* (Cambridge, 1975, corrected repr. 1977), 56–60, 67).

[56] This usage recurs in Melito's Paschal Homily, in the later second century, and the pseudo-Cyprianic *adversus Iudaeos*, probably of the early third century. Lowy, 29 urges that 'Israel' in Barnabas is always linked with scripture rather than contemporary life, and is on the way to being appropriated as a Christian title, but this may be too much to conclude from a text in which it is never easy to find anything unconnected with scripture; as occurrences bearing on the present, note especially v 2 ('Israel' contrasted with 'us'), xvi 5.

dependence on Jewish culture such that, when there is no reason to differ, Jewish opinion remains the norm, as has emerged from passages on the fall of Rome and the hope for redemption. Hence, although with regard to Justin it seems appropriate to speak of Jewish-Christian missionary rivalry, Barnabas seems primarily a work of defence.

The success of the Epistle in the later church should not obscure the connections between its outlook on the Jews and its contemporary setting. These appeared especially in the writer's need to counter excitement at the prospect of a rebuilt temple. If the Epistle was written for a readership in Egypt, as suggested by its early attestation and perhaps also by internal evidence (ix 6 and n. 36, above), it would have formed a suitable response to currents of Jewish opinion in Egypt towards the end of the first century. The temple of Onias at Leontopolis formed such a focus of Jewish unrest that it was closed by imperial order in 73 (Josephus, *B. J.* vii 420–35), and comparable zeal for national redemption would have been stirred again among Egyptian Jews by hope for the rebuilding of the Jerusalem temple twenty-five years later; in Sib v 403–33, cited above, and probably reflecting Egyptian Jewish thought before the revolt under Trajan, the messiah is to rebuild Jerusalem and the temple. It is likely that the inner-Christian divisions apparent in Barnabas are themselves related to differences of opinion in the Jewish body; and on this view of the setting, the writer's check on excitement over the temple could be compared up to a point with attempts by the Alexandrian Jewish communal leadership to quell enthusiastic Jewish reception of refugee Sicarii and their message in 72–3 (Josephus, *B. J.* vii 409–19). Similarly, the treatment of the laws in Barnabas is to some extent comparable with an attitude deplored by Philo, allegorical interpretation treated as justifying neglect in observance (*Migr. Abr.* 89–93). The Judaizing Christians, again, will reflect within the Christian community the zeal of the Jewish multitude who, according to Philo (ibid., 93), would censure such neglect.

These possible links between the Epistle's outlook and various currents of opinion among Jews in Egypt would not lose all their force if the setting were in fact to be sought elsewhere, for they relate to trends which can be envisaged as widespread in the Jewish community. A similar consideration applies to Lowy's suggestion, followed here in many respects, that the Jewish messianic movement which looked for national restoration forms the background of the Epistle; the view would suit an Egyptian setting, given the Egyptian manifestations of this way of thinking noted above, but the Jewish hopes concerned were very widespread, as is confirmed by the far-flung Jewish revolts under Trajan, and the centrality of redemption in the Eighteen Benedictions[57].

---

[57] On prayer for redemption in the Amidah, W. Horbury, 'The Benediction of the *Minim* and Jewish-Christian Controversy', *JTS* NS xxxiii (1982), 19–61 (38–9, 47, 49–50).

Justin Martyr

(i) Overlap with Jewish Opinion

Justin evinces a similar cultural debt and a similar overlap with Jewish public opinion. His cultural dependence is most obvious when he has to come to terms with Jewish revision of the LXX in the First Apology (xli) and the Dialogue (lxvi–lxviii, lxxi–lxxiii, lxxxiv, cxx), and when in the Dialogue (vii–viii) he presents his conversion as a learning to know the prophets. In both cases, however, he makes an independent Christian contention from within his indebtedness. He argues for Jewish doctrinal alteration and mutilation of the LXX, and himself quotes the text together with Christian interpolation, notably in Ps xcvi[58]; and he says that he was possessed by love of the prophets 'and of those men who are the friends of Christ' (Dialogue viii 1).

His overlap with Jewish opinion can be traced, as in the case of Barnabas, with regard to future hopes and with special reference to the fate of Rome. Here again there are distinctive Christian touches. So Amalek is fought 'with hidden hand' (Exod xvii 16 LXX), and Justin assumes that Trypho will agree that this will take place at the war of the glorious Advent, for Christians the second Advent; but in the cause of Christianity Justin goes on to ask how this interpretation can satisfy the expression 'with *hidden* hand', especially as the text describes a victory over Amalek in the past. He therefore applies it, rather, to the hidden power of God which was at work in the crucified Christ, before whom demons and all powers and authorities tremble (Dialogue xlix 8, resumed in cxxxi 5).

This Christian exegesis as presented by Justin includes phrases recalling the New Testament, but seems ultimately to depend on the all-important interpolated text of Ps xcvi (xcv), in which Christ reigns from the tree (verse 10), terrible over all demons (verses 4–5) and worshipped by the nations of the whole earth (verses 7–9)[59]. Two aspects of the interpretation are notable here. First, with the Epistle of Barnabas (notes 48–9, above), but independently of it (n. 7, above), Justin here treats a Pentateuchal narrative on which comparable vestiges of early rabbinic commentary survive[60]; both Barnabas and Justin draw on very early Christian comment of the Amalek episode, and their interpretations suggest, as noted already, that Christian and Jewish comments were

---

[58] R. Petraglio, 'Le interpolazioni cristiane del salterio greco', *Augustinianum* xxviii (1988), 89–109 (101–5 on Ps xcvi).

[59] This suggestion, supported by the association elsewhere in the Dialogue (lxxxiii 4) of Ps xcvi 5 with Ps cx as a prophecy of the power of Christ, may perhaps be added to the discussion of the Jewish background of this exegesis by Skarsaune, 394–5.

[60] Bacher, *Tannaiten*, i, 141 (Exod xvii 16 interpreted of the messianic age, in the name of Joshua b. Hananiah; cf. n. 48, above); 196–7 (remains of early rabbinic commentary preserved).

closely similar, Christians and Jews alike in this case setting the overthrow of
Amalek in the messianic age. Secondly, Justin's alternative and preferred
exegesis keeps the thought of divine victory over the powers, implicitly including the present Roman order, which belongs to his first exegesis and to Jewish
interpretation of Amalek.

Dan vii, once more, is quoted at length in the Dialogue (xxxi—xxxii) to
include the downfall of the Fourth Beast[61]; and the event symbolized by this
downfall is in mind in the First Apology (xii 7), when the Word – in scripture
and in Christ's sayings – is said to foretell that Rome cannot stop the Christian
movement. Correspondingly, the Romans are told a little later in the First
Apology (xlv) that Ps cx foretells the apostolic preaching of the powerful word;
but if they want to read these words (that is, the prophecy of David, as the
context suggests, rather than Justin's own words) from a hostile viewpoint, they
may – presumably then taking the psalm as a militant prophecy of the kingdom
of Christ. When Justin uses this boldness of speech, he has just mentioned
Roman suppression of prophecies, specifying the books of Hystaspes, the Sibyl
and the biblical prophets as prohibited on pain of death by the agency of the
demons (First Apology xliv, cf. xx). We read them none the less, he says, and
submit them for inspection by the Romans; and he evidently takes the prophets
of Israel to have the downfall of Rome as a main subject, in the manner of
Hystaspes and the Sibyl[62]. The downfall is no doubt implied in the many
references in the Dialogue to the millennial reign of Christ in Jerusalem
(notably at xl 4, lxxx—lxxxi, lxxxiii 3, lxxxv 7, cxxxviii 3, cxxxix 4—5)[63]. Their
political aspect is indicated by Justin's Christian reapplication of a nationalist
Jewish exegesis of Micah iv 1—7, on future restoration and reign in Jerusalem;
the text is said in the Dialogue (cix—cx) to apply to the Christians' persecution
and glorious millennium rather than to Jewish suffering, with a view to divinely
aided messianic restoration, after the war of Bar Cocheba.

Justin shares with Barnabas, therefore, a general dependence on Jewish
culture and a particular accord with Jewish hopes for redemption, evident
especially in expectations of the fall of Rome and of a millennial reign in
Jerusalem (the latter theme is present but not so strongly emphasized in
Barnabas (n. 50, above)). Justin is nearer to the Jews than Barnabas in one
important respect: he allows the legitimacy of Christian observance of the ritual

---

[61] This explanation of the long quotation is accepted, and linked with the alternations
between discretion and *parrhesia* on Rome in the First Apology, by E. dal Covolo, "Regno di
Dio" nel Dialogo di Giustino con Trifone Giudeo', *Augustinianum* xxviiii (1988), 111—23
(117—19, with n. 34), following and discussing E. Bodenmann, *Naissance d'une Exégèse*
(Tübingen, 1986), 227—31, on Dan vii in Justin.

[62] A brief conspectus of these works as 'resistance literature' is given by G. E. M. de Ste.
Croix, *The Class Struggle in the Ancient Greek World* (London, 1981), 442—3, with nn. 7—8.

[63] Justin's millenarianism is considered (not with special reference to this aspect) by
Skarsaune, 401—9 (cf. 338—44).

law (Dialogue xlvii 1–1). What is striking is the extent to which both authors, amid their engagement with Christian modification of Jewish tenets and customs, unquestioningly accept a Christian form of Jewish 'zeal', a messianism in contact with the anti-Roman feeling behind contemporary Jewish upheaval. It is striking less perhaps in its contrast with the emphasis also placed by Justin on the complementary biblically-derived commonplaces on obedience to rulers, for the contrasting emphases are equally held together in the scriptures, than in its reflection of characteristics which seem to have marked the Jews more clearly than other subjects of the Roman empire: a consistently sustained mood of opposition to Rome and readiness for revolt, and a self-awareness resembling nationalism in the modern sense[64].

The attutude shared by Barnabas and Justin may shed light on the fate of Christians under Bar Cocheba, as the writer has tried on the basis of this evidence to argue elsewhere[65]. Justin says in the First Apology (xxxi) that the Jewish leader punished Christians, if they would not deny Christ and 'blaspheme'. In view of the Christian share in Jewish hopes and Jewish hostility to Rome considered here, it would not have been unreasonable for participants in the revolt to expect that some Christians in Judaea would come over to the Jewish community at the time of its apparent success. The view expressed in Eusebius's Chronicle, Hadrian xvii, that Bar Cocheba killed 'Christians who were unwilling to help him against the Roman army' perhaps therefore conveys less of the inwardness of the transaction than Justin's report in the First Apology. In the Dialogue, as already noted, Justin condemns Christians who go over to the Jews (xlvii 4); and in Judaea under Bar Cocheba, a situation in many ways comparable with that addressed in Barn xvi, some are likely to have done so, whereas others refused to 'blaspheme' by uttering the curse-formula which will have been the effective sign of the transition from the first century onwards (as suggested by Acts xxvi 11, on compulsion 'to blaspheme' in the purging of Christians from the synagogues, viewed in conjunction with the formula ἀνάθεμα ᾽Ιησοῦς, I Cor xii 3)[66].

(ii) Jewish Reaction to Christianity

The report in the First Apology on Christians under Bar Cocheba introduces the second main topic in Justin to be considered, his notices of Jewish reaction to Christianity; but it also raises the frequently-considered question of his sources for Jewish and Palestinian matters, and his personal knowledge of the

---

[64] The Jews were unique in combining a common culture with traditions of political unity, and in mounting a general revolt in 66 after prolonged acquiescence in Roman rule, according to P. A. Brunt, *Roman Imperial Themes* (Oxford, 1990), 517–9 (cf. 126–8).

[65] Horbury, 'Messianism', 83–4.

[66] Horbury, 'Benediction', 53–4.

Jews and Palestine[67]. O. Skarsaune thinks it likely that existing Jewish-Christian material was used for his passages on the cursing of Christ by Jews and on the revolt under Hadrian, and suggests that it could have come to Justin through his Christian education; this might well have included teaching from Palestinian gentile Christians who had themselves made Jewish-Christian exegetical traditions their own[68]. Similarly, Justin would have used possibly Palestinian gentile traditions for his emphasis on the exclusion of Jews from Jerusalem when the revolt was suppressed, although these traditions are also in touch with Jewish exegesis, and it is hard to distinguish between gentile material and Justin's own contribution[69]. A strength of Skarsaune's proposals lies in their allowance for Justin's personal involvement in these subjects as well as his indebtedness to earlier teaching. Justin certainly used sources, especially the testimony traditions illuminatingly reconstructed by Skarsaune, but on some of these topics his personal contribution is also likely to have been important. The Bar Cocheba war, for instance, figures in his own narrative framework in the Dialogue (i 3, ix 3), and as a Palestinian he could have had his own information about it. Again, the subject of cursing crops up so many times, in varied ways but always with vehemence of expression, that it is natural to think that Justin himself, as well as his source, knew something of it.

To recall his background, he says at the beginning of the First Apology that his father and grandfather were 'from Flavia Neapolis, a city of Palestinian Syria', present-day Nablus. He could associate himself in the Dialogue with the Samaritans (cxx 6), and he names in the First Apology (xxvi 3−4) the villages from which the Samaritans Simon and Menander came; he himself, however, was an uncircumcised gentile (Dialogue xxviii 2, xli 3). He mentions various Palestinian localities, including the cave of Bethlehem (Dialogue lxxviii 5). He gives the name of Bar Cocheba (in the report discussed above); this becomes a notable point when one considers that Cassius Dio, to judge by the account of fair length and detail surviving in epitome (lxix 12−14), described the whole Jewish revolt under Hadrian without mentioning the name of the Jewish leader. Justin's specifically Jewish knowledge ranges in the Dialogue from the description of a phylactery (the lettering of which 'we [the Christians] assuredly consider holy', xlvi 5) to what sounds like an early form of the mystical reckoning of the divine stature later known as Shi'ur Qomah (cxiv 3, denouncing Jewish anthropomorphism in connection with Ps viii 3)[70]. It seems likely

---

[67] Studies of Justin's contacts with Judaism, including A. Harnack, *Judentum und Judenchristentum in Justins Dialog mit Trypho* (TU 39, Leipzig, 1913), are listed by Visonà, 72−3; on the haggadah, see also Ginzberg, *Legends*, vii (*Index* by B. Cohen, 1938), 594−5 (index of passages in Justin).

[68] Skarsaune, 290−5, 371−4.

[69] Skasaune, 372−3, 428−9.

[70] Second-century figures discussed in connection with the origins of the Shi'ur Qomah include Elchasai and the Gnostic teacher Marcus. Origen's comments on anthropomorphism,

that he learned even his Platonism in a school which was sympathetic to Jewish teaching[71]. His Palestinian and Jewish knowledge should not be exaggerated, but it is not negligible, and it is aided by Justin's own considerable overlap with Jewish ways of thinking[72]. If compared with the knowledge exhibited by a slightly later Palestinian gentile Christian, Julius Africanus of Aelia, in his letters on biblical subjects preserved by Origen and Eusebius, it can perhaps be said to show less classical and historical erudition bearing on the Jews, but a fuller acquaintance with Jewish exegesis and ethos[73].

Justin's notices of Jewish reaction to Christianity can therefore be approached in the expectation that, although defective reporting is inevitable in the circumstances, he will have had some good sources and some personal knowledge. Special interest attaches to his indignant remarks on specific communal measures. In the present context two aspects of them only can be considered: first, their witness to the great importance of corporate Jewish reaction for the Christians; secondly, the contact between Justin and other sources in the allegations of particular measures[74].

First, there are traces of a probably testimony-linked tradition on an organized Jewish rebuttal of the apostolic preaching; the passages are comparable and sometimes co-ordinated with the prominent tradition of the apostolic mission, already noticed in connection with Ps cx in the First Apology (xlv), and have a similar air of legendary development. Twice in the Dialogue (xvii 1–2, cviii 2, recalled at cxvii 3) Justin asserts that, after the crucifixion, the Jews sent chosen men throughout the world to denounce the appearance of the godless sect of the Christians, whose teaching is deception. Justin links the apostolic mission which they rebutted not only with Ps cx, but also with Isa ii 3 'out of Zion shall go forth the law', a text appearing as a quotation in the First Apology (xxxix) but only as an allusion in the Dialogue (xxiv 1, cf. xi 2), although the

---

Jewish and Christian, at one point seem to echo this passage in Justin (N. R. M. de Lange, *Origen and the Jews* (Cambridge, 1976), 44); but they are circumstantial enough to make it possible that they preserve authentic information on a Jewish mystical practice (M. S. Cohen, *The Shi'ur Qomah* (Lanham & London, 1983), 40, n. 65, on Origen, *in Gen hom* i 13). The same can be said of Justin here.

[71] M. J. Edwards, 'On the Platonic Schooling of Justin Martyr', *JTS* NS xlii (1991), 17–34, argues that Justin's Platonism belongs to the school represented by his contemporary Numenius of Apamea in Phrygia, cited by Clement of Alexandria, Origen and Eusebius as a philosopher who honoured Jewish beliefs and writings (e.g. Clem Alex, *Stromateis*, i 22, 150 (Numenius calls Plato 'Moses Atticizing'); Origen, *Contra Celsum* i 15, iv 51).

[72] Justin's inherited material shows that he was strongly influenced by Christianity evincing close gentile-Christian contact with Jewish exegesis (Skarsaune, e.g. 326, 429), and he continued to breathe this atmosphere.

[73] On Africanus's letter to Origen, see M. Harl & N. R. M. de Lange, *Origène, Philocalie 1–20, sur les Écritures, et la Lettre à Africanus sur l'Histoire de Suzanne* (SC 302, Paris, 1983); on his letter to Aristides (in Eusebius, *H. E.* i 7), R. Bauckham, *Jude and the Relatives of Jesus in the Early Church* (Edinburgh, 1990), 355–63.

[74] For further discussion see Horbury, 'Benediction' and Stanton, 'Aspects'.

parallel Micah iv 2 is quoted in this connection at cix 2, shortly after the passage on Jewish criticism in cviii. The counter-mission is linked at xvii 2 with the texts Isa iii 9−11 and v 18−20, used in connection with the death of Christ and Jewish criticisms of Christianity in the First Apology (xlviii−xlix)[75], but it seems likely that it also became attached to Isa xviii 1−2, which in the LXX becomes a woe on those responsible for the despatch of papyrus letters overseas. In Eusebius's commentary on Isa xviii 1−2, and in an exegesis of this passage in the tract on Antichrist in the name of Hippolytus (58), the counter-mission envisaged by Justin is conducted by Jewish emissaries sent overseas with letters. One may suspect a testimony-registration of the story of the anti-Christian emissaries, using texts from Isaiah, a book widely read as a prophecy of Jewish-Christian relations.

The connection of an imagined scene of organized Jewish response with the testimony tradition suggested here may be compared with early Christian treatment of the complementary theme of the repentance of the Jews and their acceptance of Christianity by baptism. This theme complements the denuncia-tion of their hostility in Justin's Dialogue, as in other Christian writings, often on the pattern of the testimony Isa i 14−16 (e. g. xii 3−xiii 1, xiv 1 (based on Isa i 14−16); cviii 3, immediately after the story of the counter-mission, cf. cxviii 3); and the elaboration of an imagined testimony-based scene in which Jews in fact seek Christian baptism can be traced in Cyprian[76]. It seems likely, then, that the story of organized Jewish denunciation twice told by Justin had similarly gained incorporation into the testimony traditions, and thereby into catechesis as well as apologetic. If so, the weight attached by the Christians to Jewish response makes itself most plainly felt.

Secondly, however, these passages are among a number of references to organized and corporate Jewish reaction which have some contact with other sources[77]. The story of official denunciation immediately after the crucifixion is told in the context of complaints about contemporary Jewish criticisms, which the Christians think to be disseminated among the gentiles by the community as a body (Dialogue xvii 1−2, cviii 2, cf. First Apology xlix). Despite the legendary character of this story, it corresponds to the currency of Jewish anti-Christian statements from a early period, as suggested by Matt xxviii 15; items of propaganda listed at cviii 2 recur elsewhere, and overlap with the rabbinic tradition according to which Jesus was executed because he practised sorcery and deceived and led astray Israel (Babylonian Talmud, Sanhedrin 43a)[78].

---

[75] On their possibly Jewish-Christian background see Skarsaune, 290−1; Jerome compar-ably refers to Jewish cursing of Christians in his comment on Isa v 18.

[76] Horbury, 'Pseudo-Cyprian', 304−5.

[77] They are surveyed by Harnack, *Trypho*, 78−81 and Horbury, 'Benediction', 19−23, 48−59.

[78] For the details see Horbury, 'Benediction', 54−8.

Comparably, other references to communal measures in Justin find external correspondence. The curses on *Christians* in the synagogues often mentioned in the Dialogue (especially xvi 4, xcvi 2) can be compared either with the Birkath ha-Minim or with cursing such as that associated with the cursing of Haman at Purim[79]. The blasphemy or anathematization of *Christ* in the synagogues (xxxv 8, xlvii 4) can be connected, as noted already, with a long-established purgation formula indirectly attested in Acts xxvi 11 and I Corinthians xii 3; what appears to be a related practice is described in the Dialogue as reviling of the Son of God and mockery of the king of Israel, 'such things as your rulers of synagogue (ἀρχισυνάγωγοι) teach, after the prayer' (cxxxvii 2). This too many be compared, following T. C. G. Thornton, with Purim cursing[80]; but Justin alleges a frequently-followed practice, and it is therefore also worth noting, despite its late date, a midrashic reference to curses uttered with scroll in hand at the end of the Eighteen Benedictions[81]. The prohibition of converse with Christians decreed by Jewish teachers (διδάσκαλοι, xxxviii 1, cxii 4) is comparable with the prohibition of dealings with *minim* attested at Tos Hullin ii 20–21.

From Justin, therefore, it emerges that corporate Jewish rejection of Christianity had so deeply impressed itself on Christians as to find a place in the testimony tradition, and that it was possible in his time to point to specific Jewish measures which expressed this corporate attitude. Further, his statements on these matters find some support in other sources, Jewish as well as Christian. It can be added that some kind of corporate Jewish antagonism to the Christians would accord with two features of the Jewish situation which, as noted already, were strikingly reflected and reproduced in the Christian subgroup itself: the zeal and national solidarity of the period of the Jewish revolts, and the welcome being extended to proselytes. These features reappear in the Eighteen Benedictions, in which prayer for national redemption (especially in

---

[79] T. C. G. Thornton, 'Christian Understanding of the *Birkath ha-Minim* in the Eastern Roman Empire', *JTS* NS xxxviii (1987), 419–31 (429 and n. 5) prefers the second possibility, and envisages spasmodic and informal cursing on the lines of the cursing of Christ later attested in probable connection with Purim; he stresses the lack of evidence, apart from Jerome, for later Christian understanding of the Benediction of the Minim as including a curse on the Christian body in general. The intensity of the Christian reaction reflected in Justin speaks, however, for a regularly-encountered Jewish response, and Justin and inner-Jewish evidence on the Benediction point to the same setting, the synagogues of the second century. I would therefore still incline to find the Benediction reflected in the Dialogue, and to associate later Christian silence on it with silence on the synagogue service in general, but the main point asserted in the text above – the correspondence of Justin's evidence with other sources – is not affected if Thornton's explanation is preferred.

[80] T. C. G. Thornton, 'The Crucifixion of Haman and the Scandal of the Cross', *JTS* NS xxxvii (1986), 419–26 (425).

[81] Midrash Panim Aherim on Est iii 8, quoted in Yalkut Shimeoni ad loc; one of the midrashic versions of Haman's anti-Jewish charges, discussed by S. Krauss in connection with the Benediction of the Minim, but of interest here as presupposing curses 'after the prayer' (Horbury, 'Benediction', 29–30).

the Tenth Benediction and onwards) includes a blessing on proselytes and a curse on apostates, oppressors, and heretics (*minim*) (the Eleventh and Twelfth Benedictions). Is it possible, however, to go beyond this appeal to the general atmosphere, and to attempt, on the basis of the specific allegations in Justin, more precise suggestions on organized Jewish reaction?

A start could perhaps be made with the suggestion that Justin's references to 'ruler of synagogue' and 'teachers' point to two related but distinct inter-communal networks of communication. *Archisynagogi* held an office which could involve supervision of the synagogue service (including a kind of teaching in the synagogue, according to Justin here), but was distinguished enough to be suitable for leading members of the community. So, to take one famous example, the Theodotus inscription shows a priest and *archisynagogus* wealthy enough to build a synagogue with appurtenances, and proud enough of his title to record that it was held by his father and grandfather before him[82]. Holders of this office would often be among the group of principal persons in the community, those πρῶτοι who are envisaged in the case of the Roman Jews in Acts as being in a position to receive 'letters from Judaea' or messengers concerning Jewish visitors (Acts xxviii 21). Such diaspora contacts with the Holy Land did not necessarily come to an end in 70, and it would be speculative but not unreasonable to envisage communication by way of Caesarea between western diaspora notables and the patriarchate emerging in Galilee[83].

'Teachers', on the other hand, are said to have decreed the prohibition of converse. The authority ascribed to them recalls that claimed in Justin's time by members of the nascent rabbinic movement. In the Fourth Gospel, διδάσκαλος is given as the rendering of the title Rabbi (John i 38, cf. xx 16); and the Greek title also occurs in Jewish inscriptions, while the respect it engendered is strongly suggested by the Aphrodisias inscription recording members of a Jewish group of φιλομαθεῖς[84]. It is likely that diaspora teachers would have had some direct or indirect contact with the rabbinic schools of Galilee and Judaea; Trypho is represented in Justin's Dialogue, presumably not implausibly, as a refugee from Judaea in Greece and Corinth (i 3), Aquila is depicted in the haggadah as a proselyte of Pontus who travels to the Holy Land to get instruction, and a practice of making journeys to the diaspora will underly the legends of rabbinic travel[85].

---

[82] E. L. Sukenik, *Ancient Synagogues in Palestine and Greece* (London, 1934), 69–70 and Plate XVIa.

[83] For the probably third- or fouth-century Beth She'arim epitaph of a 'Caesarean *archisynagogos*, [a native] of Pamphylia' see M. Schwabe & B. Lifschitz, *Beth She'arim* (Jerusalem, 1967), 91, no. 203.

[84] J. Reynolds & R. Tannenbaum, *Jews and Godfearers at Aphrodisias* (Cambridge, 1987), 30–34.

[85] A. E. Silverstone, *Aquila and Onkelos* (Manchester, 1931), 24–6, 30–31, quoting Tanhuma Buber on Exod xxi 1 and Sifra Lev xxv 7; the anecdotes of Akiba's journeys are

The Jewish communal recognition of such measures will have depended not only on these networks of inter-communal contact, but also on the constituency of the more zealous in each place. Their importance as watchdogs on law-breaking is chillingly evoked by Philo; with *Migr. Abr.* 93, cited above, compare *Spec Leg ii 253,* on the thousands of watchful 'zealots of the law, most exact guardians of the ancestral traditions'. In Acts xxi 20–21 a comparable group among the Christian Jews of Jerusalem is mentioned in order to induce Paul to demonstrate his own observance, although it is Jews from Asia who then accuse him (verse 27). The continuation of this mood of zeal after the First Revolt is both reflected and reproduced in Barnabas and Justin, as noted above.

Groups of synagogues and communities are likely, therefore, to have put these measures into action, partly by the authority of office-holders and teachers, partly through the solidarity of the more zealous. Cursing and prohibition of converse will have built on and reinforced earlier measures against the Christians, notably the exclusion from synagogue complained of the New Testament (Luke vi 22; John ix 22, xii 42, xvi 2). Although the ancient constitutional rule of high priest and king was lost, except for a brief revival under Bar Cocheba, it is likely that Diaspora contact with the Holy Land continued, and that office-holders and teachers in the communities began to form links with the nascent patriarchate and rabbinic movement.

Justin therefore witnesses not only to the profound significance of the Jewish reaction in Christian eyes, but also to continuity and cohesion in the second-century Jewish community. At the same time he presents a Christianity which is as much determined by Jewish culture and thought as that of Barnabas, but which breathes a less strictly defensive atmosphere, despite the context of missionary rivalry with the Jews. Justin can allow the validity of varied positions in the Christian camp, thereby drawing nearer than Barnabas to observant Jewish attitudes, and he can express hopes for Jewish conversion where Barnabas is preoccupied with resisting the strength of Jewish influence. The Christian future was with Barnabas's claim to the entire Jewish scriptures in their spiritual sense, but there would be an important place too for the more historical approach of Justin. Yet, for all their contribution to the Christian inheritance, the Epistle of Barnabas and Justin's works in their second-century setting are Jewish as much as Christian documents. Despite and partly because of their anti-Judaism, they attest the overshadowing spiritual power of the Jewish polity, and could properly be assigned to a Christian sub-section of Jewish literature.

---

examined by P. Schäfer, 'Rabbi Aqiva and Bar Kokhba', in W. S. Green, ed., *Approaches to Ancient Judaism*, ii (Chico, 1980), 113–130 (114–7).

Problems of the Clementine Literature

by

J. Neville Birdsall

The literary critic C. S. Lewis in his work on "The Allegory of Love" quotes an adage; "Let no one try to tell you what is in Kant's Critique of Pure Reason", which he applies to the medieval French poem, "Le Romaunt de la Rose". With equal aptness it could be applied to the two early Christian recognition romances which form the main body of the pseudo-Clementine literature. The framework of a story of a separated family, at length reunited, of a type known in the Latin comedian Plautus and in Shakespeare (under his influence), has become the repository of a bewildering variety of didactic and dramatic material, no doubt brought together for the purpose of edification.

It lies before us in two main forms[1]. The Homilies, so called because of the predominance of addresses and debates of the apostle Peter, are known in a Greek form, of which the earliest ms. is of the eleventh or twelfth century. Its early date however is assured by the Syriac version of several of its books, which is known from a dated ms. of AD 411. Both this and the Greek lie before us in a form which has been edited in the interest of the Arian theology, in its pre-Nicene form. Two Greek epitomes of wide circulation are also of importance. The Recognitions, as the second form is called, have not survived in Greek. This is probably due to the adulteration of the work in the interests of the Eunomian heresy. We have it in a Latin translation by Rufinus, transmitted in a great number of mss. dating from the fifth to the fifteenth centuries. A Syriac version of the early books is preserved in the same ms. as the Syriac version of the Homilies. Eusebius, in a reference to a pseudo-Clementine writing in h. e. III. 38.5, is in all probability alluding to the Homilies. This datum, together with the early Arianism revealed in the Homilies, places these as existing in the early years of the fourth century. Most scholars in the field consider that the Recognitions are based on the same ancestral document as the Homilies (Grundschrift): Some hold that the Homilies were also utilized by the author of

---

[1] Works in the bibliography of Georg Strecker, Das Judenchristentum in den Pseudo-klementinen 2., bearbeitete und erweiterte Auflage, Berlin 1981, are not given in the footnotes.

the Recognitions. The Grundschrift is dated as post AD 220 by its use of a work of Bardaisan, On Fate.

When we come however to the precise definition of the extent of the Grundschrift, and even more, to the course of its composition, we enter an area of debate. This has continued since the days of the Tübingen school and the resultant controversies. There are still occasionally some extreme positions occupied, but two main views may be discerned within the mass of books and articles which bear upon the Clementines, directly or indirectly, whose flood shows no signs of slackening its spate. The view of Rehm, editor of the posthumously published editions of both Homilies and Recognitions for the Berlin corpus, is repeated by Irmscher in the third edition of the handbook of Hennecke-Schneemelcher. The Grundschrift is the ultimate stage of the development of the Clementines to which we can attain. It is a document reflecting the outlook of the period of the Apologists. In Rehm's words, when we abstract its teaching, there is scarcely anything belonging to that, which a third century Catholic christian could not accept. (The major exception is the identification of Adam and Christ). Sources are not to be found. The Ebionite strain does not belong to any source: it is the result of the adoption of the first form of the Homilies by Ebionites, who found a number of sympathetic beliefs in it.

In contradistinction to this view, we have that most recently represented by Strecker, going back to Waitz, although with modifications and developments. Strecker considers that we may identify sources, of which he enumerates ten. Of these the major is the Kerygmata Petrou, a name taken from the Epistle of Clement which the compiler of the Grundschrift has prefaced to the Homilies. Another of importance he names the Anabathmoi Jakobou II (indicating its relation to but distinction from a document to which Epiphanius gives this name). However, although he says that the figure of Simon Magus must have been derived from a source, he is unwilling to give this the title of Praxeis Petrou, as Waitz had done. In fact, these two named sources apart, the rest are without title, except the known work of Bardaisan.

Strecker's work is of complex structure, primarily because of its argumentative method. He is arguing a case, based on Waitz (1904) and directed against Rehm (1939). He praises Rehm as a methodological model, and in his arguments against him, modifies a number of the points made by Waitz. It is almost impossible to use Strecker without having the work of the older scholars open by one's side. Moreover, so frequent are the textual references to both Homilies and Recognitions, often with several passages from each given as the basis for a particular point, that the editions of these (and translations and summaries too) must also be arrayed. This complexity arises from Strecker's considered conclusion that the sources of the Grundschrift may be identified by content but generally, are not fully to be reconstructed because of the their rehandling in both Grundschrift, and in the use of that by Homilist and Recognitionist.

This is especially the case with the Kerygmata Petrou, which is the source most germane to our interests in the Symposium. In spite of describing it in terms such as are just paraphrased, he nevertheless (in his discussion of Jewish Christianity in the second edition of Bauer's Rechtgläubigkeit und Ketzerei)[2] declares it to be a direct witness for Greek speaking Syrian Jewish Christianity, which alone enables him to make the conclusion he has just reached about the Didascalia Apostolorum. He dates it as a document either contemporary with the Didascalia or a few decades earlier, the first half of the third century or the latter half of the second century. In attempting to investigate some points at which the Clementines may cast light upon Jewish Christianity, I have largely followed Strecker, while attempting to trace and check as many of his multiplicity of references in works ancient and modern as was feasible in a relatively short time.

In one matter, however, I have been able to pursue a little original research, namely in looking at a sampling of instances which bear on the scriptural citations in the Clementines. These have been studied by scholars since the heyday of the Tübingen school, a number of whom have believed that they could discern the use of non-canonical gospel material in the Clementines, *ex hypothesi* derived from Jewish Christian gospels. I took two samples: the first was the citations which might be classified as from the Gospel of Luke, the second was the instances from which Gilles Quispel[3] considered that a link between the Clementines and the Nag Hammadi Gospel of Thomas might be proven in the matter of the derivation of "Synoptic" material. I chose the Lucan material for a simple reason, namely that we can now have recourse to the textual apparatus put together by the International Greek New Testament Project, and published in two volumes in 1984 and 1987[4]. There were always many problems attendant upon its production and a number of years as its executive editor affected my health. I was saddened but not surprized to discover that most of the faults I strove to eliminate are still present in it: and some unfavourable reviews have drawn attention to them. I mention this to make an emphatic assertion that, in spite of these grave blemishes, the work is of great value, in at least two respects. It gives a complete coverage word by word of all the materials upon which it draws, Greek manuscripts, the majority of ancient versions, and Greek, Latin, and Syriac Fathers. And in respect of

---

[2] Walter Bauer, Rechtgläubigkeit und Ketzerei im ältesten Christentum. Zweite Auflage mit einem Nachtrag von Georg Strecker (BHTh 10, Tübingen) 1964, pp. 260–274.

[3] L'Évangile selon Thomas et les Clémentines. VigChr 12 (1958) 181–196 (repr. 1975 in Gnostic Studies II, Istambul, pp. 17–29).

[4] The New Testament in Greek. The Gospel according to St. Luke. edited by the American and British Committees of the International Greek New Testament Project, 2 volumes, Oxford 1984 & 1987.

those fathers, it gives a wealth of information about their quotation of this gospel, which cannot be found elsewhere in this updated form (much of it was known to Tischendorf and used by him with preternatural accuracy and acumen: but needless to say, our patristic texts are considerably improved in the intervening years.) When I have attempted, in the confines of the available time, to extend my work to Matthew, the paucity of available textual evidence[5], both in extent and in simple cataloguing, has been the more striking because of what is at hand for Luke.

Collated against those materials, we see that the citations of the gospels in the Clementines partake of many characteristics frequently encountered in patristic citations of many distinct periods. Side by side with close agreements with the text transmitted in manuscripts, there will be found many small divergences. Some of these may appear as variant readings of isolated manuscripts, or in the renderings within the versions: they fit in with certain tendencies of variation such as substitution of synonyms, echoes of parallel passages, intrusion of Old Testament parallels without New Testament ms. support. Again, many citations will present mixed texts, sometimes of harmonization, especially within the gospel corpus, sometimes of passages of similar theme, where phrases will be transposed in combinations which the manuscript tradition does not attest. Then there are found instances where the sense or gist of a passage in the gospels will appear in a paraphrase sharing little in vocabulary or construction with the original. Lastly, sayings of scriptural tone, unknown in the manuscript tradition, will be found, sometimes attributed to gospels, or to Jesus, sayings of the type of the so-called *agrapha*. To find this somewhat bewildering variety is no uncommon experience even in the study of the quotations of such late authors as John of Damascus or Photius. It says nothing of the use of written traditions other than the gospels of the canon.

When we study the pseudo-Clementine citations, we find that they are frequently shared by second and third century writers, occasionally almost word for word, more often in salient readings. Justin Martyr figures largely in the attestation, but Marcion's text, when ascertainable, gives support, some apostolic fathers, and Clement of Alexandria. In other words, just as Rehm categorizes the outlook of the Clementines as that of the age of the Apologists, so we find that the kind of citation of gospel material is frequently akin to what we find in the same period. This not only renders uncertain, or even invalid, attempts such as that of Waitz to relate the identification of sources to the type of variation shown in scriptural links, but also the arguments of Quispel. Both

---

[5] This is in part due to the incidence of variation, and not to inadequacies of edited apparatus. Texts without apparatus give the ratio of Matthean extent to Lucan as 11:11, while the full text and apparatus of von Soden gives the ratio as 10:14, and Tischendorf Editio Octava Maior (in which there is considerable discursive discussion) yields 10:15.4.

A. F. J. Klijn[6] and Haenchen[7] have made powerful criticisms of the detail of his various papers in which he sought to find a non-canonical tradition represented in the Clementines, Thomas, the Diatessaron in its various avatars, in the work of pseudo-Macarius and so on. Klijn particularly lays stress on the many instances such as those here summarized where both a wide variety of patristic citation produces similar or even identical variation to that on which the sayings of Thomas seem to rest, and also where manuscript text-traditions show parallel variant readings.

In my view the erroneous interpretation of the data of the citations in the pseudo-Clementines especially as exemplified in Quispel's work (and extending there, as it does, to interpretation of many other sources of information such as "Thomas", pseudo-Macarius, and so on) is a symptom of a problem of interpretation still affecting text-critical discussion. We are still dominated unconsciously by the categories of a century ago, when all data tended to be interpreted by a literary model. Textual data were seen as the evidence of quite specific written entities, clearly diffentiated each from other, and perhaps even due to the deliberate literary activity of recension. We should not blame the scholars of the period of Hort and his successors for such a view. They had to account for several centuries for which they possessed no documentary evidence. But we have no excuse, for we have gospel papyri of the second century, and third century evidence for much of the rest of the New Testament. From this evidence it appears that we should see the state of the text in the second century in the model, say, of a spectrum where although distinct colours may be said to dominate different sectors, there is no rigid point of demarcation between them, but one shades into another as the eye follows the arc. The work of taxonomists of textual types, such as Griffith and Duplacy, has helped us to see this very clearly.

Interpreted against this background, the common ground shared by the Clementines and their allies in textual variation helps to define their place within the use of the text, but does not provide any grounds for arguing that a form of the gospel material was known to the author of the Grundschrift or of his sources, so distinct that we must postulate a gospel other than those of the canon. It may be that Leslie L. Kline[8] is right that a gospel harmony was known to Justin and to the author of the Grundschrift: but such a harmony presupposes the canonical synoptic gospels.

Subsequent to my own investigations, I have perused the work of Strecker on

---

[6] A. F. J. Klijn, A Survey of the Researches into the Western Text of the Gospels and Acts, Part Two 1949–1969 (NT. S XXI) Leiden 1969, pp. 5–28.

[7] Inaccessible to me, but noted by Klijn op. cit. (in fn. 6), pp. 19.21,23.

[8] Leslie L. Kline, The Sayings of Jesus in the Pseudo-Clementine Homilies (SBL Dissertation Series 14) Missoula, Montana 1975.

this point[9]: in a number of cases he clarifies variations of text by his observation of interpretative tendencies derived from the theology of the author. These remove a great deal of perplexity, and would enable a convincing detailed exposition.

There can be no doubt thant the fortunes of transmission of this literature were related to its content of heterodox teaching: in the East the Homilies had an increasingly slight circulation, as their manuscript tradition shows, and their place was taken by the two epitomes, which are emphatically trinitarian and Chalcedonian in phraseology. In the West, the Recognitions had a wide circulation, but this was due to the degausing activities of Rufinus in his work of translation. It is in the Kerygmata Petrou, as defined by Strecker, that the teaching, increasingly deemed unorthodox, is to be found, to a brief survey and comment upon which we now turn.

Basic is the teaching about the True Prophet, and his nature and work. The true prophet is a being who manifests himself in different forms in a succession from Adam to the Lord Jesus. Noah, Abraham, Jacob, and Moses are amongst the other members of the succession. In his discussion Strecker states that the details of these manifestations and their relation one to another remain unclear. A close examination shows that this is certainly the case. The term Incarnation is used by Strecker: but this is not a term used in the Clementines themselves. One of the clearest statements (and ascribed by Strecker to the oldest stratum of the Clementines) is in Hom III.20,2 "from the beginning of the world, he passes through the world, changing forms at the same time as names, until coming to his own times through labours, anointed by the mercy of God, he will have rest (anapausin) for ever". But the method of these changes is never specified. Certain passages may be interpreted as indications of the identity of the various patriarchal figures, with the True Prophet perceived as Jesus the Teacher: but in others (Hom. XVIII.13,6: Rec. II.48,2) Noah, Moses, Jacob, are distinguished from the True Prophet and said to have known him. Strecker resolves the problem by postulating that the latter passages are later interpretations. May the resolution however be found in a concept such as we find in Philo's understanding of Moses, who by affinity and obedience to the divine Logos, becomes himself the *Logos empsykos*? Nearer to the Jewish Christian background, we may recall the quotation found in Jerome (on Isaiah, Bk 4, ch. 11, vs. 2) and ascribed to the Gospel of the Hebrews. At the Baptism of Jesus, the spirit declares that she had sought him in all the prophets, and having now found him, finds rest in him. Affinity leads at length to identification and embodiment.

Other than these links, research has been hard put to it to find parallels to the thought of the Clementines, in this matter. Mani and the Mandaean literature

---

[9] Op. cit. pp. 117–136.

have a concept of forerunners of the final messenger of the Truth, who in some sense are that messenger in an earlier manifestation. The teaching of the Elkesaites, as described by Hippolytus (Ref. IX.14,1), comes very close to the views of Hom III.20,2 quoted before. Christ was not born for the first time from a virgin but, having been previously born and being reborn, he thus appeared and exists, undergoing alterations of body at each birth, and moving from body to body.

The manifestation of the true prophet takes place within a dualistic system. Each manifestation is preceded by an adversarial counterpart, σύζυγος, thus, Abel by Cain, Moses by Aaron, Jesus, son of Man, by John, greatest of those born of woman, the apostle Peter by Simon Magus, and so on. Up to the creation of Man, the bad follows the good, thus heaven and earth, and so on, culminating in Adam followed by Eve. The feminine principle is evil, the masculine good: there is a constant strife between the two, and the teaching of the truth, which the manifestations of the true prophet proclaim according to needs of particular generations, is always adulterated and falsified by the feminine prophecy which the evil *syzygoi* promulgate. Here we encounter another characteristic of the teaching of the Clementines, the doctrine of the false pericopae. This denotes the teaching that both the law and the prophets uttered a true doctrine, but in its written form it was adulterated, especially in ways derogatory to the figures in whom the True Prophet was manifest. Thus, Adam was depicted as sinning and fallen, Noah as drunken, Moses a murderer. This is the answer here given to the age-old problems of the unworthy and the contradictory in scripture. But not only are these dealt with, but a number of aspects of Old Testament teaching are rejected as no part of the Truth. In keeping with a tendency which may be perceived in the Targumim, passages where God's responses are described in terms of human emotion are ascribed to adulteration and removed. References to gods other than the Ruler and Creator are likewise treated, again in parallel with Targumic practice. Linked with this is a tendency to play down the significance of the Prophets of the Old Testament. In contrast with the Pentateuchal writings, the prophets are little cited in this literature. In citing Matt 5.17, the words "and the prophets" are left out, the passage Lk 10.24//Matt 13.17 is used to underline the inadequacy of prophetic foreknowledge, while the introductory Epistle of Peter, refers to the ambiguity of the prophetic writings. This runs parallel to the subordination of Prophets to Torah in Rabbinic material and synagogue practice and to the slender use of the prophets by Philo. The quotation from the gospel of the Nazareans (Jerome, adv. Pelagium III 2) may be based on a similar mistrust, with its words Even in the prophets after they had been anointed by the Holy spirit there was found *sermo peccati* (sinful statement *or* matter of sin). Blood offerings, temple cultus and the institution of kingship are all relegated in the Clementines to the rank of falsifications of the divine will.

Anti-Pauline teaching is the hallmark of the Clementines, even though the figure of Paul is hidden, generally under the figure of Simon, sometimes as "echthros anthropos". In Strecker's view, the figure of Simon is introduced by the composer of the Grundschrift from another source, but the anti-Paulinism is a trait of the Kerygmata. Paul is viewed within the setting of the "counter-parts" or *syzygoi:* he is the antithesis of Peter. The Pauline claim to a vision of the risen Christ is countered by an exegesis of vision and their recipients: visions are a means of Divine communication with an enemy of God, and show anger, not approbation. The polemic, here and elsewhere, engages with the canonical text, here with the Acts accounts of Paul's conversion, and draws too upon the confession of Caesarea Philippi and the account in Galatians of the confronta-tion of Peter and Paul at Antioch.

Baptism, too, is seen within the dualistic scheme. The present age is the age dominated by the feminine principle, and to it belongs the first *genesis*, which takes its origin from desire. To be capable of receiving the teaching of the True Prophet, and by obedience to his revealed interpretation of the Law, to inherit the kingdom of heaven, there is need for baptism. Even if one's life has been in accordance with the Law, baptism is necessary: if it has not been so, baptism brings forgiveness. The basic justification for baptism is that it is commanded by the true prophet. But secondly, it is intimated that, just as the spirit in the beginning moved on the face of the waters, so there is in the waters of baptism, a certain (power of) mercy[10]. This enables the good works which must charac-terize the baptized, for whom the terminology of "begotten by the Father from the water" is used. In addition, however, to the initial baptism there are also enjoined ritual purifications of the body to match the inner purity, especially after sexual intercourse within marriage. Entry into the kingdom is no sinecure for the baptized disciple of the True Prophet. Over his activity there broods the anticipation of the day of judgement.

In the Recognitions (I 33−44,53−71) a sketch of Old Testament history and an account of disputations between the apostles, and the Jews led by Caiaphas is to be found. This Strecker identifies as a Jewish Christian document, and wishes to ascribe to it the name of the Anabathmoi Iakobou, of which Epiphanius gives a summary account (Panarion 30.25.1ff.). He believes the document here discernible and that summarized by Epiphanius to be two forms based on a common original. A number of common features of doctrine are shared with the Kerygmata Petrou, but there are glaring differences. In com-mon are the notions that sacrifice was contrary to the revealed divine will, that the kings of Israel sought their own glory, that Paul was the enemy of Christian-ity. But, on the other hand, the True Prophet (only twice named here and thus perhaps introduced by the composer of the Grundschrift) appears *to* Abraham

---

[10] Homilies XI,26,3 (GCS 42.167); Recognitions VI,9,3 (GCS 51.192).

(not *in* him), and Jesus is not identified with Moses but is greater than Moses, namely the prophet foretold by him. In the K. P., there is no mention of the death of Jesus: here we find a number of references. The Gnostic features of the Feminine element in the world, and of the Syzygiai, are absent from the Anabathmoi. Allusions to the destruction of Jerusalem and to the Edict of Hadrian, make a mid-second century date necessary, but it would appear that a period of time has elapsed since the edict exiling the Jewish nation from their land.

To derive from this complex mass of material what is strictly relevant to the rift between Judaism and Christianity in the period between the Jewish revolts of AD 66 and AD 135 is at best an exercize in hypothesis. Whether we take the view of Rehm and see the Grundschrift as a gnosticizing document later adopted and revised by an "Ebionite", or that of Strecker, in which an early Jewish Christian document has been gnosticized before its incorporation in the Grundschrift, we are dealing at the earliest with a second century document in a revised form dating from the third century. The Anabathmoi Iakobou, however, are considered to have been adapted without too much redaction, although the Homilist has seen fit to omit them entirely, and the Recognitionist to modify them by large insertions. In themselves, in Strecker's view, they may be dated about AD 150, by calculation from their allusion to the Edict of Hadrian banishing the Jews.

In neither source is there much that can contribute material of historical worth. The destruction of Jerusalem is alluded to in Hom 3.15.2f., but although Waitz wished to make of this a clear allusion to the recent destruction of the city after Bar Kochba's revolt, the passage is so obscure that other constructions are equally tenable. In Rec 1.39.3, within the Anabathmoi, is a reference both to destruction and to exile, which must be placed accordingly after AD 135. The destruction is also referred to in the earlier chapter 37 of the same book. In an adaptation of Mark 13.14, and 9–10, chapter 64 shows its interpretation of history, but sets it within a fictional debate with Caiaphas, with appropriate future tenses.

A striking feature of both sources is the rarity with which events of the life of Jesus are alluded to, although much is made of the teaching (This, as has been indicated, is, even at this level, based largely upon the canonical gospels, with a few paraphrases and agrapha). There is no reference to the birth of Jesus, in either source. The death of Jesus finds allusion in the Homilies only in the suspect phrase *idiou aimatos ēmelei* of 3.19.1, in a passage which Strecker considers to have been worked over by a redactor. There are several allusions however in the Anabathmoi: yet they are of the barest, concentrating on the aspect of rejection after the bestowal of many benefits. For any reference to traditions of the resurrection of Jesus, we again must turn to the Anabathmoi, for no trace is found in the Homilies nor in any stratum of Recognitions identified as Kerygmata Petrou. A single reference is made in the Anabathmoi (Rec 1.42.4) in the context of allusion to the darkness from the sixth to the ninth hour, with a number of reminiscences of Matthew 27 and 28, or the tradition there to be found. But no theological weight is placed on any of these aspects. These features show similarity to the rarity or absence of references to Jesus' life in many of the apologists. A similar silence is to be noted in the Rabbinic materials about Jesus, in any case very sparse. It seems to be a mark of the second century in general, and presumably extended to Jewish Christianity.

The complex structure of the pseudo-Clementines makes it difficult to attempt any definition of the relationship which its account may bear to debates between Jew and Christian, or between Christians of Jewish and Gentile background in the latter years of the first Christian century and the early years of the second. Accounts such as the debates between representatives of the Jewish sects and a succession of apostles in the Anabathmoi, Rec. I.54−60 prove upon examination to be literary constructions whose themes need no other source than the New Testament to explain them. Strecker's analyses of the distinctive doctrines of the Kerygmata Petrou show that there is little which may explained from one source only: there are Rabbinical parallels, Qumranic parallels, parallels in Hellenistic Judaism, and in all the documents which have been the arena for the hunters of the "questing beast" of Gnosticism. This multiplicity also involves us in the problem of the origin and nature of Gnosticism. Did it arise out of heterodox Judaism or, coming from outside, influence its rise, is it a Christian exercize in demythologizing apocalyptic or an independent world religion? Our explanations and exegeses depend upon our decisions on these matters. Some echoes of debate by early Christians against Judaism may be perceived in the presence of testimonia, which both figure in the Rabbinic treatment of the question of "Two powers in heaven" and are found also in early Christian writing, from the New Testament and into the literature typified in Cyprian, pseudo-Gregory of Nyssa, and the fictitious debates of the various dialogues between Christian and Jew.

In the enigmatic figure of the true prophet, Adam-Christ, we see the blending of a concept which must owe something to Aggada about Adam, perhaps influenced by a dialectic with Pauline concepts, rejected or modified, but then developed under Gnosticizing influences and provided with the dualistic framework of the male-female antinomy and the two aions. It seems most probable that this would be a development taking place in the second century.

Koester remarks[11] that Strecker's work is only a beginning in that tracing of West Syrian Christianity which he thinks an important necessary task. In his essay on Jewish Christianity in the second edition of Bauer's Rechtgläubigkeit

---

[11] James M. Robinson, Helmut Koester, Trajectories through Early Christianity, Philadelphia 1971, p. 125 fn. 21.

und Ketzerei for which he was responsible, Strecker has taken the product of his literary and conceptual analysis further forward. There he emphases both that Jewish Christianity in the Clementines meets us in a developed form and that Jewish Christianity was no unity but was divided within itself and in its relationship with the "great church". As the concordance to the Clementines appears, and helped by other tools such as the index of the scriptural allusions and quotations which *Biblia Patristica* provides, we shall be able to make advances in the analysis of the Clementines and in the provision of a commentary upon them, which seems to me one of the most urgent tasks. But we shall not expect to find the Clementines bearing in any simple fashion upon the questions which are the focus of this symposium[12].

To attempt to give a reasoned account of the historical background in Syria of the basic materials of the Pseudo-Clementines is necessarily tentative. There are so many unknowns that it is practically impossible to devise a calculus to solve the problems or even to set up the proper equations for resolution. A review of the available data gives a strong impression of continuity from the early second century at least through to the dateable manuscript tradition; but it would demand more speculative reconstruction of schemes of ideas than the present writer considers justified in historical research to compose a consecutive account. What follows is more a collection of vignettes.

Prior to the early second century, we have the evidence of the Acts and the Paulines that Antioch figured in the first expansion of Christianity beyond its Jewish matrix. However we resolve the problems of the date and sources of Acts or the evidential value of Paul's assertions, it will remain a fixed point that controversy arose in that city over questions of praxis affecting the possibility of intimate fellowship between Christians of Jewish extraction and those from the non-Jewish Gentilic world. The majority of references to Antioch lie in the chapters of Acts referring to this controversy and its ostensible resolution by the "Apostolic Decree"; the only other in Acts is the laconic reference (in a series of such) in Acts 18.22. After that (dateable in the early fifties, whatever our chronology), the city and its church affairs find no more mention. Of the references in the Paulines, Gal 2.11 belongs with the events of the early chapters of Acts. II Tim 3.11 presumably belongs to Pisidian Antioch.

The problems of Antioch then submerge so far as the record goes, but we have no reason to think that they disappeared in fact. The letters of Ignatius written towards the end of his life (his episcopate however began, according to Jerome, in AD 68, although other considerations make it more likely that it was in fact a decade or more later) reveal a bishop convinced of the distinctiveness of Christianity struggling against "Judaizing" and "Sabbatizing" both in his own

---

[12] In the discussion of the preceding paragraphs, the original paper given to the symposium, the lecturer was asked to attempt to place the Clementine material in the historical setting of Syrian Christianity. The paragraphs which follow are the response to this request.

jurisdiction and within the Asian churches with whom his martyr journey
brought him into contact. At the same time, he is fighting a battle against
tendencies toward docetic accounts of Christ. Interpreters disagree whether
these tendencies coexisted in the teaching and practice of one faction or were
representative of two wings of the church: some weighty opinions see them as
two sides of the characteristics of one group.

Already, according to the heresiologists amongst the fathers, gnostic teaching had been promulgated in Antioch by Menander[13], a disciple of Simon
Magus (*ca.* AD 80) and later, in the mid-second century, by Satornilos (or
Saturninus)[14] in the same succession. For knowledge of their teaching we have
in the main only Irenaeus to rely upon, whose picture of Simonian gnosis may
probably have been coloured by its imitation of some Christian features in a
century of competition: yet it may be significant that in what is said about both
Helen and Simon[15], we have the notion that a heavenly messenger may assume
different human persons in different periods. This may give some hint of the
type of thinking which lay behind the perplexing aspects of the figure of the
"true prophet".

Theophilus[16] is the next Christian leader and bishop known to us after
Ignatius: we have few details of his life however, but an apology addressed to
the emperor survives. This is marked in its exegesis of the Old Testament by
features shared with Jewish exposition[17]. Its ethical teaching is largely Pentateuchal in its derivation, but the ceremonial law is not dwelt upon; its
institution by the will of God is, however, acknowledged. R. M. Grant, who has
devoted much attention to Theophilus, seeks in a recent exposition to show that
underlying the Old Testament exegesis there may be perceived guiding hermeneutical principles derived from the teaching and example of Jesus. These
show themselves in a very restrained way: but one is striking. He omits from his
statement about the Decalogue commandments about God's Name, and
observance of the Sabbath. In the interpretation of Grant, we may see here the
functioning of a principle plainly stated in the Clementine Homilies (3.49.2)
that, relying on the teaching of Jesus, we may differentiate true elements from
false in the Old Testament. The omissions in Theophilus's rehearsal of the
commandments may be seen as arising from Jesus's "blasphemous" assumption
of Divine status (e. g. Jn 10.30,33) and Sabbath breaking (e. g. Jn 5.18; 9.16)[18].

---

[13] Irenaeus *AH* 1.23.4; Gnosticism. An Anthology. Edited by Robert M. Grant, London
1961, p. 30.

[14] Irenaeus ibid. 24.1; Grant op. cit. pp. 31 f.

[15] Irenaeus ibid. 23.1 & 2; Grant op. cit. pp. 23 f.

[16] Theophilus of Antioch. *Ad Autolycum.* Text and Translation by Robert M. Grant,
Oxford 1970.

[17] Robert M. Grant, Greek Apologists if the Second Century, London 1988, Chapter 18
"Theophilus and the Bible".

[18] Ibid, p. 162.

Yet the Christology of Theophilus is so reticent in expression that Grant finds himself uncertain whether an Incarnation of the Logos is in fact envisaged. While we may perceive allusions to "incarnational" passages in Luke 2 and John 1 (Ad Autolycum 2.10 & 22), no more specific statement is made than that the Logos is "sent by God and is present in a place"[19]. It is the same with his arguments concerning Resurrection: it is the general notion and reasoning by analogy that occupies him, not the discussion of the Resurrection of Jesus. Nevertheless, there are allusions to the Johannine story of the apostle Thomas, and to the climax of the parable of the rich man and Lazarus[20].

Was Theophilus simply "letting down lightly" those whom he sought to convince, and thus underplayed – as we should perhaps see it – the stumbling-blocks of specific Christian belief? or do we see hints of the supremacy of the more Jewish side of Antiochene Christianity, and of an uncertainty about the singularity of God's revelation in Jesus, in the ancestry of which may lie the docetism of the age of Ignatius? Grant summarizes thus: "there is a sharp break between the incarnational Christology of Ignatius and the reticent monotheism of Theophilus. Who was to say that one was orthodox and the other not? These problems, arising in very early times, were to plague the church at Antioch for centuries[21]." Grant goes on to characterize the views of Paul of Samosata as "sharing the ideas of Theophilus". The circles from with sprang the "dynamic modalism" which he characterizes appear to have been motivated by apologetic[22].

We have anticipated in this reference to Paul of Samosata. Between him and Theophilus comes Serapion[23] amongst those Antiochene bishops about whom we have more information than their mere name. He wrote to ban the use of the Gospel of Peter, on the grounds of its docetic tendencies, in a letter preserved in part by Eusebius, and to an apostate to Judaism, in a letter not so preserved. It is at least clear that the problems of the Ignatian time are still present, and that here we have a bishop whose theological inclinations are in the same sense as those of Ignatius. Two decades later, Origen is a visitor to Antioch, albeit at the invitation of the mother of the emperor, expounding Christianity to her. But thirty years on, Paul of Samosata is elected bishop. Is it reading too much into these general lines of succession and the theological emphasis of the bishops about whom we know a little to suggest that the Antiochene church was haunted by these vigorous debates and that first one faction and then another gained the ascendancy?

---

[19] Ibid. Chapter 19 "The Theology of Theophilus".

[20] Ibid. pp. 173f.

[21] Ibid. p. 173.

[22] J. N. D. Kelly, Early Christian Doctrines, Fifth Edition, London 1977, pp. 116–119; 158–160.

[23] Eusebius of Caesarea. *h. e.* 5.19 & 22; 6.12.

The Didascalia[24], which all its investigators place in Syria and in the third century, probably in its earlier half, must next be treated. We find here a document which is very emphatically written to promulgate Catholic Christianity, so that it is, in the intention of its writer, a document of the mainstream. But like the *Grundschrift* of the Clementines, or the *Kerygmata Petrou* utilized in that (if we follow Strecker) there is much which later Catholic teaching or practice would have eschewed, although there is little overlap. This is mainly because the Clementines transmit, by intention or by the accident of the literary motives at work in their composition, very specific theological teaching, whereas the Didascalia is much more concerned with practice. Simon Magus is for both the beginning of heresy, and is opposed by Peter. Each is concerned to eliminate parts of the Old Testament as an influence upon the recipients, but different means are used, the notion of false pericopae in the Clementines, that of the *deuterosis* in the Didascalia. Extra-canonical traditions are still influential in both, the Didascalia showing a strong colouring from the Gospel of Peter, and also maintaining the tradition that the night of Jesus's arrest was the third day of the week[25].

Over against the Jews, there prevails an ambiguous attitude. Many close contacts with Judaism are shown by the writer's detailed knowledge, and the Jewish people are described as "brethren". The Christians' celebration of the Lord's passion is to be dated by the calculations of the Jews. Yet the observance of Jewish lustrations or food laws are to be forbidden. The fasts of the week of the Passion are interpreted as mourning for the unbelief of their brethren and the destruction of Jerusalem. We are dealing with a centre where there is a community of Christians of Jewish extraction and self-identification within the Church, and where the attitude towards the Jewish people is irenical, but where nevertheless, there is concern at the continuation of some aspects of Jewish religious practice. This is in marked contrast to the generally strident antagonism to the Jews and Judaism which increasingly prevails in Christianity as the centuries pass. Afrahat has been praised in the study by Neusner for his reasonable attitudes in argument with and against the Jews: but he is unusual. In the Greek and Latin speaking worlds, bitterness and anger were there from the second century onwards, with roots in the New Testament. When, a century and a half beyond the date of the Didascalia, when we come to John Chrysos-

---

[24] The most recent editions of the Syriac text and of the Latin fragments are: The Didascalia Apostolorum in Syriac, edited and translated by Arthur Vööbus (CSCO 401,402,407,408: Scriptores Syri 175,176,179,180) Louvain 1979: & Didascalia apostolorum Canonum ecclesiasticorum Traditionis apostolicae versiones latinae recensuit Erik Tidner (TU 75) Berlin 1963.

[25] Didascalia ch. XXI (Vööbus CSCO 407, pg. 206 lines 15f., id. 408, pg. 189 lines 9f.); cp. A. Jaubert La Date de la Cène (Paris 1957), pp. 79–87. (Latin text of Didascalia not extant at this point).

tom's orations against the Jews[26], which like the Didascalia warn against adoption of Jewish practices and the celebration of Jewish feasts, we are wholly in the world of polemic, in the atmosphere of anti-Semitism which has marred Christianity ever since.

The Didascalia appears to show a part of the Church where there are still distinctively Jewish Christians, known as such and even in some respects to be followed; the writer, whom many students of the work believe on internal grounds to have been a bishop, is clearly in something of a quandary in his dealing with them and the problems which they cause him as a pastor of non-Jews. The emphasis is upon praxis. One question coincides with an aspect of the community of the pseudo-Clementines, namely immersion after connubial intercourse. The Clementines' interests are however much more theological. It is possible that the community of Jewish Christians from which they arose was identical with that in the view of the author of the Didascalia: but it would be an attempt at a *tour de force* to try to demonstrate that. The community of the Clementines is, in its beliefs, eccentric; we have discussed the main details of this problem. The attempt at an historical survey in these last paragraphs may have shown that there was a continuity with certain strands in earlier Syrian Christianity. By the time of the composition of the Grundschrift it would seem that this type of theology was losing the specific quality which distinguishes it so markedly; there is almost a "last-ditch" note about the rehearsal of the details of belief and argument. The Didascalia may show how such a community as the Clementines presuppose was swallowed up in the great church.

It would be another task, and equally subject to speculative methods, to test the suggestion that in Arianism we have the descendant of a Jewish Christian Theology akin to the Clementines. The line of descent Paul of Samosata – Lucian – Arius is sometimes hypothesised. We may note that the Didascalia was adapted to be part of the Apostolic Constitutions by a writer who is generally identified with the Arian reviser of Ignatius: but to link either of these opinions with the main theme would take us far beyond our remit, and would call for further investigations of the nature and thought of both the Constitutions and of the pseudo-Ignatian corpus.

---

[26] Marcel Simon, Versus Israel (2 ème édition) Paris 1964, pp. 368 f.

Concluding Summary

by

JAMES D. G. DUNN

Introduction

The following summary focuses exclusively on the "parting of the ways" theme. It draws as much, and in some cases more on the discussion occasioned by the original papers than on the papers themselves, which, of course, have in turn been revised subsequently. The value of the Symposium is thus represented in three different ways: (a) in bringing together several scholars of related fields and interests and asking them to focus their diverse specialisms and previous research on a particular issue in the original papers which formed the raw material for the symposium; (b) in the thorough discussion of these contributions during the course of the symposium, which involved a wider circle of scholars and research students than the paper-givers, which tested and helped refine the insights and hypotheses of the original papers, and which is now summarized in what follows; and (c) in the revised form of the papers themselves, in some cases considerably reworked in the light of the symposium and the discussion it generated. Since the total sum of knowledge is now so vast even in a relatively small area of historical inquiry, it is only by such pooling of specialist interests and by such genuine dialogue and joint inquiry that we can entertain any real hope of gaining fresh clarity on issues and events whose outcome still shapes our perception of ourselves and of others.

Philip Alexander, 'The Parting of the Ways' from the Perspective of Rabbibic Judaism

The main point to emerge from PA's paper is that we may have to date "the parting of the ways" much later than the period under study, because of the evidence in rabbinic tradition of continuing interaction between rabbis and *Jewish* Christian *minim*. From the perspective of the rabbinic sources, we cannot really talk of a parting of the ways within the Jewish community until the triumph of rabbinism within the Jewish community. In an important sense, the rest of the symposium consisted of a progressive clarification and qualifying of PA's claim at this point.

Martin Goodman, *Diaspora Reactions to the Destruction of the Temple*

MG underlined Philip Alexander's point that the rabbis took much longer to
establish their authority than is often stated; the Yavnean assembly was only
the beginning of a much longer process than many NT scholars and historians of
Christian beginnings allow. At the same time MG noted some evidence of a
parting of the ways in the late 1st and early 2nd centuries. (a) Judeo-Greek
writings from before about 100 were preserved only by Christians, but those (if
any) written after that time were preserved by neither rabbis nor Christians.
(b) The implication of the *fiscus Judaicus*, as providing a means of distinguishing Jew from non-Jew: it may have enabled a Jewish Christian to continue
affirming his Jewishness (by paying the tax), and was perhaps therefore a factor
in the evolution of the *birkat-ha-minim* as a means of categorizing Jewish
Christianity as unacceptable; the definition of a Jew by Romans primarily in
religious terms after 96 ties in with the fact that a clear distinction between Jew
and Christian appears regularly in Roman texts after about the same date (96).

Martin Hengel, *Die Septuaginta als von den Christen beanspruchte Schriftensammlung bei Justin und den Vätern vor Origines*

The fact that the LXX functioned to such an extent as Christian scripture has
obvious implications for the parting of the ways, particularly when married to
the further fact that the synagogue kept reading the scriptures in Hebrew.
Particularly interesting is the possibility that Aquila was intended as a riposte
from the Jewish side – something like a targum for Greek-speaking Jews.
Indeed, it may be that Aquila should be seen as part of the rabbis' campaign to
rabbinize Greek-speaking Jews. If so, this would again point to the early second
century as a crucial period for the parting of the ways.

Hermann Lichtenberger, *Synkretische Züge in jüdischen und judenchristlichen Taufbewegungen*

The degree to which baptismal movements show overlap or similarity across the
boundaries between Jew and Christian, as demonstrated by HL, sheds further
light on the whole area of continuing Jewish-*Christian*ity. So far as the parting
of the ways is concerned, the implication may well be both that the middle
ground retained vigorous life for some time, and that Jewish-Christian baptismal movements functioned more as retarding factors.

Graham Stanton, *Matthew's Christology and the Parting of the Ways*

This was the first paper to focus on christology; here on the double charge against Jesus – (a) that he practised sorcery, and (b) that he was a deceiver. The evidence reviewed in Matthew (1) tended to confirm other evidence that these were important elements in the criticism (not just Jewish criticism) of Christianity, and (2) implied that the parting of the ways was well advanced by the time of Matthew, but (3) also that these charges go back in at least some form to the time of Jesus.

John McHugh, *In Him was Life: John's Gospel and the Parting of the Ways*

JMcH highlighted the dramatic character of the Fourth Gospel, the schematic and formulaic character of its christology suggesting issues more intellectual than pressingly personal, with the further implication that the debate with Judaism was past, and that what was at stake now was more a matter of self-definition. This occasioned a lively debate, with 9:22, 16:2 and 19:15 in particular suggesting to others something much more pressing and urgent. C. K. Barrett recalled his own previous observation that the anti-Judaism of John is essentially a *theological* phenomenon; whereas by the time of Ignatius it has become more of a *social* phenomenon.

Peter Stuhlmacher, *Das Christusbild der Paulus-Schule – eine Skizze*

PS reminded us (a) of the centrality of the christological issue and (b) of how deeply rooted and developed it was already in Paul and the Pauline tradition. On the one hand, this points us back to the passion and resurrection of Jesus itself and to the christology grounded there as the basic cause of the split. On the other, passages like Col 1:15–20, especially when linked with Eph 2, show that already we must talk of a new concept of the community of God's people.

James Dunn, *The Question of Amti-semitism in the New Testament Writings of the Period*

JD's main point was that the so-called "anti-Judaism" material of Acts, John and Matthew does *not* imply that the parting of the ways has already happened, since "Judaism" was in process of redefinition at that time and the reference of the term "Judaism" was itself part of the larger debate in which these writers were involved. In the resulting discussion there was some dispute as to how much we know and can say about Yavneh and the *birkat-ha-minim*, which highlighted (1) the importance of the argument from convergence (that is, of a number of disparate factors which point to the late first and early second centuries as critical for the parting of the ways), and (2) the importance of distinguishing *self*-definition from phenomenological definition (that is, early Christians might claim that they are still within the parameters of their Jewish heritage = Jews, when it was already obvious from a spectator's perspective that they had become something different).

Christopher Rowland, *The Parting of the Ways: the Evidence of Jewish and Christian Apocalyptic and Mystical Material*

The importance of this range of material is ambiguous and its significance is rather like that of the material reviewed by Hermann Lichtenberger or of the gnostic question; that is, since it is a common factor on both sides, it does not help us greatly in defining the parting of the ways. The discussion focused on christology and particularly on the contentious issue of how significant (in parting-of-the-ways terms) is the language used of Christ in Revelation. On the one hand, the fact that close parallels are to be found in the Metatron speculation of *3 Enoch* suggests an issue still alive within Judaism, and strengthens the likelihood that the Christian affirmation of Jesus was bound up with the same complex of material which can be summarily referred to as "the two powers heresy". Here the crucial factor would have been the identification of *Jesus* with the awesome heavenly figure common to such (Jewish) speculation. On the other hand, Peter Stuhlmacher insisted on the characteristic and distinctively Christian features which run through all earliest christology, Revelation included – the crucified Messiah, who makes atonement, the "first-born from the dead". So Revelation's christology cannot simply be subsumed within Jewish catagories.

Andrew Chester, *The Parting of the Ways: Eschatology and Messianic Hope*

AC pointed up two significant features: (1) The difficulty of speaking of a parting of the ways when dealing with Jewish-Christian writings pretending to be pagan. Also important is his observation that "The 'Jewish' and 'Christian' traditions and texts may be divided as much within themselves as against each other". (2) The importance of messianic nationalism, not as a constant factor, but as a constantly recurring factor – in the 18 Benedictions, the 66–70 revolt and the 132–5 revolt.

William Horbury, *Jewish-Christian Relations in Barnabas and Justin Martyr*

Both Barnabas and Justin seem to assume that the parting of the ways is past but that the ways are still close together. The outlook is one of anti-Judaism, but formed by Jewish culture and influenced by Jewish public opinion. In particular, the bitterness of Barnabas implies a danger of relapse into Judaism and hence also that the ways are still close. A number of points emerged from one of the most profitable of the discussions: (1) The reference in Barnabas to the temple (16:3–4) ties in with the likelihood of a heightened Jewish expectation of the rebuilding of the temple at the end of the Flavian dynasty (Martin Goodman). (2) On the relation between Justin's reference to cursing and Jewish reaction to Christians, two observations are of particular relevance: (a) we can surely speak of some sort of trajectory stretching from Paul's persecution of the church, through Acts 26:11, Gal 4.29 and John 9:22, to the situation envisaged by Justin; and (b) the rise of Jewish nationalism was bound to result in Jewish attempts to marginalize Christians. (3) Was Jewish reaction to Christians in different areas spontaneous or organized from some centre? WH thought something of both. (4) WH also raised the question of whether Jewish Christians had their own form of Jewish nationalism, with Rome as the enemy, and noted that the Christian hope of the Christ's second coming shared the militaristic categories of the more popular Jewish messianic hope.

Neville Birdsall, *Problems of the Clementine Literature*

NB brought out the importance of the Pseudo-Clementines as reflecting a later phase in the parting of the ways, that is, what happened to one strand of Jewish Christianity. They seem to indicate a form of Jewish Christianity, probably in Syria, with a Gnostic tinge, in symbiotic relation with Catholic Christianity – the end of a trajectory stretching from opponents of Paul – a twilight picture of a Jewish Christian group hanging on to their anti-Paulinism, but on the point of being swallowed up by Catholic Christianity.

Conclusions

1. "The parting of the ways", properly speaking, was very "bitty", long drawn out and influenced by a range of social, geographical, and political as well as theological factors. On the one hand, we must beware of thinking of a clear or single "trajectory" for either Christianity or Judaism; and we should also avoid using imagery which necessarily implies an ever widening gap between Christianity and Judaism. On the other hand, "Christianity" *did* emerge from

a Jewish matrix, and "Christianity" and "Judaism" *did* become separate and distinct, so that the basic image, "the parting of the ways", is appropriate.

2. The period under review, 70—135, does seem to have been one of particular importance for "the parting of the ways".

(a) This is indicated by the growing political and social distinctiveness of the two movements during this period, climaxing in the 132—5 revolt; but always with a broad Jewish-Christian middle ground, whose dimensions we can no longer chart with any certainty, but which certainly retained vitality long beyond this period.

(b) The period saw the beginning of the process of self-definition on the rabbinic side and the *beginning* of the attempt made by the Yavneans and their successors to extend their authority over other Jews and to rabbinize Judaism.

3. The Symposium remained divided regarding christology, not on the fact that Christian claims regarding Jesus were the crucial factor in "the parting of the ways", but on how and when these christological claims made the breach inevitable. For some, the period under review was marked by a heightening of the christological claims by Christians, which, though rooted in Jesus' ministry and earliest Christian perception of Jesus, and though using Jewish categories, were nevertheless during this period posed in such terms (Christ's deity, Christ as the incarnation of God) as to prove increasingly unacceptable to emerging rabbinic Judaism at least, unacceptable to a degree which had not been true of the earlier claims. For others, the breach was already inevitable in Paul's day and even earlier: it was not the apotheosis of Jesus which made the breach, but the emphasis already on the *crucified* Jesus as exalted to God's right hand; the most decisive developments in christology took place between 30 and 45 (Martin Hengel).

4. A crucial question thus raised is the extent to which our judgments on these issues are formed more by hindsight than by the historical data. With the benefit of hindsight we see that certain developments and corollaries were inevitable; but were they so at the time? and would these outcomes have appeared inevitable to those *in via*? (a) So, with regard to the preceding issue (3): at what stage did it become impossible to contain the explicit Christian claims regarding Jesus within the Judaism of the time? (b) And with regard to Judaism: certainly, rabbinic Judaism claimed to be normative, and in the event become so – that is why rabbinic Judaism forms the "Jewish" side in talk of "the parting of the ways"; but during the period under review (and beyond) it was still by no means clear that rabbinism was going to triumph and so also that Christianity was going to be excluded from "the Jewish community" (Philip Alexander).

List of Contributors

PHILIP S. ALEXANDER, Department of Middle Eastern Studies, University of Manchester

J. NEVILLE BIRDSALL, formerly Department of Theology, University of Birmingham

ANDREW CHESTER, Faculty of Divinity, University of Cambridge

JAMES D. G. DUNN, Department of Theology, University of Durham

MARTIN GOODMANN, Oxford Centre for Postgraduate Hebrew Studies

MARTIN HENGEL, Institut für antikes Judentum und hellenistische Religionsgeschichte, University of Tübingen

WILLIAM HORBURY, Corpus Christi College, University of Cambridge

HERMANN LICHTENBERGER, Institutum Judaicum Delitzschianum, University of Münster

JOHN McHUGH, formerly Department of Theology, University of Durham

CHRISTOPHER ROWLAND, Queen's College, University of Oxford

GRAHAM N. STANTON, Department of Theology and Religious Studies, King's College, University of London

PETER STUHLMACHER, University of Tübingen

Index of Sources

Author Index

Subject Index

Abraham, 131, 142, 143-46, 170, 221, 265, 275, 328, 352, 354

Adam, 48, 145, 220, 292, 348, 352, 353

Aenon, 130

Agrippa II, 27

Akiba, 224, 225, 259

Alcibiades, 93, 94, 95

Alexandria, 27, 30, 36, 39, 40, 44, 67, 184, 245, 329

Amidah, 253-54, 281, 336

Anti-Christian polemic, 18-19, 115, 326, 342

anti-Judaism/semitism, 1, 24, 30, 177-83, 187, 191, 193, 195, 196, 202, 203, 204, 206, 208, 209, 211, 318, 322, 332, 335, 345, 360, 367

anti-Jewish polemic, 61-63, 99, 157, 179, 193, 201, 202, 203, 273, 315, 322-23, 330, 360

Antichrist, 285, 342

Antioch, 27, 30, 159, 161, 162, 164, 168, 171, 184, 190, 191, 354, 357, 358, 359

Apocalypse
— of Abraham, 219, 221, 229
— of Peter, 231

Apocalyptic, 93-94, 213, 214, 215, 218, 219, 222, 223, 224, 225, 227, 228, 229, 231, 232, 233, 234, 235, 236, 237, 252, 286, 289, 290, 293, 297

Apostolic council, 161, 357

Aqedah, 19

Aquila, 49, 50, 52, 67, 68, 69, 70, 74, 77, 344, 364

Ascension of Isaiah, 234

Atonement, 86, 166, 169-70, 171, 172, 173, 366

Augustine, 268

Baptism, 85, 86, 87, 89-96, 125, 127, 128, 130, 136, 147, 246, 296, 305, 328, 329, 335, 342, 352, 354, 364

Bar Kochba revolt, 22, 35, 36, 42, 102, 160f., 196, 258-59, 271, 305, 319, 329, 338, 339, 340, 345, 355

Baraita, 7, 222, 325

Barnabas, 161, 316
—, Epistle of, 48, 181, 273-78, 315, 316, 317, 318, 319, 320, 321-36, 345

Beelzebul, 105f., 107, 111, 118

Ben Sira, 13, 14

Birkat ha-minim, 7, 8, 9, 10, 11, 254, 343, 364, 365

Birkatha-Mazon, 256-57, 281, 282

Caiaphas, 155, 354, 355

Canon, 46, 47, 48, 61, 66, 67, 68, 69, 76, 80, 81

Cestius Gallus, 27

Chiliasm (see Kingdom, messianic)

Christ, Jesus, 17, 18, 42, 43, 44, 50, 51-56, 57-62, 63, 65, 68, 77, 81, 86, 87, 89, 90, 91, 99-115, 123-58, 160, 161, 164, 165, 166, 167, 168, 169, 170, 171, 172, 173, 174, 178, 182, 186, 190, 193, 194, 195, 197, 198, 200, 201, 202, 205, 206, 208, 210, 211, 216, 227, 228, 229, 231, 234, 236, 263, 264, 266, 268, 273-74, 276, 279, 280-81, 283, 284, 285, 286, 287, 292, 293, 295, 296, 297, 298, 299, 300, 301, 305, 326, 329, 330, 337, 340, 342, 343, 348, 352, 354, 355, 359

Christology, 50, 54, 91, 99, 100, 108, 109, 115, 160, 165, 166, 167, 168, 169, 170, 172, 173, 174, 195, 196, 200, 201, 211, 225, 227, 229, 234, 237, 266, 291, 301, 304, 358, 359, 365, 366, 368
— adoptionist, 167, 168

— docetic, 296, 357, 359
— logos, 201, 228, 301, 304, 358
— wisdom, 173, 200-201
Chrysostom, John, 360
Church, 125, 128, 130, 172, 173, 174, 175, 207, 214, 215, 228, 233, 234, 277, 278, 279, 280, 282, 288, 289, 290, 291, 292, 293, 294, 295, 300, 301, 305, 331, 336, 360
— early, 43, 48, 50, 65, 66, 76, 78, 83, 87, 96, 119, 139, 160-62, 165, 166, 169, 193, 195
Circumcision, 4, 23, 89, 91, 94, 217, 328, 329, 330, 332
City of God (see Jerusalem, New)
1 Clement, 292-95
2 Clement, 295-99
Clement of Alexandria, 47, 67, 74, 75, 76, 78, 79, 82, 87, 96, 316, 319, 350
Clement of Rome, 47, 55
Corinth, 163, 165, 189, 190, 344
Cornelius, 134, 189
Covenant, 5, 6, 44, 47, 83, 126, 142, 151, 186, 207, 209, 257, 273, 281, 291, 324, 327, 328, 329, 330, 331, 332, 334, 335
Covenantal nomism, 2
Creation, 172, 173, 235, 298, 301, 353
— new, 172, 173, 215, 216, 220, 228, 255, 265, 266, 272, 274, 275, 276, 277, 286, 293, 297, 298, 303, 333
Creator, 55, 215, 228, 281, 353
Crucifixion, 56, 58, 165-73, 174, 199, 241, 286, 337, 341, 342, 366, 368

Damascus, 161, 162, 168, 184
David, 53, 58, 62, 279, 281, 283
Day of Atonement, 324, 325, 328, 331
Diaspora Judaism, 19, 21, 22, 27-31, 32f., 34, 35f., 37, 49, 65-66, 69, 140, 160, 183, 245, 247, 259, 280, 302, 303, 344, 345
Didache, 278-88
Didascalia, 331, 349, 359-61
Diognetus, Epistle to, 302, 329
Domitian, 29, 32, 33, 320

Ebionites, 52, 69, 74, 85, 88-91, 94, 95, 96, 144, 264, 348

Eighteen Benedictions, 6-11, 254, 336, 343, 366
Eleazar b. Arak, 223, 224, 225
Elect, election, 186, 218, 219, 229, 230, 234, 235, 275, 289, 290, 291, 298, 301, 332, 335
Eliezer ben Hyrcanus, 16, 25, 224, 225, 333
Elijah, 216
Elisha b. Abuyah, 225
Enoch, 48
Ephesus, 49, 74, 163, 190, 319
Ephraem the Syrian, 118, 120
Epiphanius, 72, 73, 75, 85, 88, 89, 90, 91, 93, 94
Eschatology, 43, 112-14, 123-25, 165-66, 207, 213, 214, 215, 216, 217, 218, 219, 220, 221, 225, 227, 228, 229, 230, 231, 233, 234, 236, 239, 240, 241, 243, 244, 245, 246, 247, 248, 249, 254, 258, 259, 261, 266, 267, 268, 269, 273, 274, 275, 278f., 280, 281, 282, 283, 294, 285, 286, 287, 288, 289, 290, 291, 292, 293, 294, 296, 297, 298, 299, 300, 301, 302, 303, 304, 305
Essenism, 29, 247
Ethics, 286-88, 291, 297, 298, 299, 300, 305, 318, 323, 328, 330
4 Ezra, 219-20, 221, 229, 236, 237, 247-49

Faith, 77, 127, 140, 144, 147, 148, 153-54, 156, 160, 161, 163, 166, 170, 171, 173, 174, 175, 198, 217, 233, 267, 275, 284, 291, 294, 299
Fasting, 323, 324, 325, 331
Feast of the Dedication, 151
Feast of Passover, 56, 156, 165f., 252
Feast of Tabernacles, 141, 150
fiscus Judaicus, 31-32, 33, 364
Flavian, 367
Flesh, 201, 202
Forgiveness, 86, 88, 96, 166, 354

Gamaliel II, 7, 199, 225
Genesis Rabba, 19
Gentile, 24, 32, 35, 60, 109, 126, 134, 142, 151, 155, 157, 162, 180-81, 190, 191, 192, 195, 200, 203, 204, 206, 208, 225, 233, 340, 342, 357

Greek and Hebrew Words and Phrases

GREEK WORDS AND PHRASES

HEBREW WORDS AND PHRASES